1998 Edit

Questionable Doctors

Sidney Wolfe, M.D.
Kathryn M. Franklin, Ph.D.
Phyllis McCarthy
Alana Bame
Benita Marcus Adler

Disciplined by State and Federal Governments

Alaska, Idaho, Montana, Oregon, Washington, Wyoming

Public Citizen is a nonprofit membership organization in Washington, D.C., dedicated to advancing consumer rights through lobbying, litigation, research, publications, and information services.

Since its founding by Ralph Nader in 1971, Public Citizen has fought for consumer rights in the marketplace, for safe and secure health care, for fair trade, for clean and safe energy sources, and for corporate and government accountability.

© 1998 Public Citizen's Health Research Group

First printing

All rights reserved. No part of this book may be reproduced or utilized in any form or by any means electronic or mechanical, including photocopying, recording or by any information storage and retrieval system, without written permission from the authors.

ISBN 0-937188-69-7

Acknowledgments

The authors would like to acknowledge the important efforts of many people and institutions which made this study possible.

First, we are grateful to the state licensing or disciplinary boards which cooperated with our requests for doctor-specific information by sending us lists which, in many cases, required them to reorganize data in a form which would be more useful to us. Similarly, the Inspector General's Office of the Department of Health and Human Services (HHS) has been extremely cooperative with our requests for information on those physicians who were sanctioned by the Peer Review Organizations and those who were the subject of other HHS sanctions. The Drug Enforcement Administration (DEA), belatedly, incompletely and only in the face of a lawsuit from Public Citizen, gave us the data on doctors with uncontested restrictions or revocations of their narcotics licenses. Several consumer groups, including the New York Public Interest Research Group (NYPIRG) have also provided us with valuable information.

Special thanks to Elizabeth Schramm who designed the cover and assisted in all stages of production.

But the lion's share of time spent on this report was in the time-consuming process of data entry, checking, rechecking and *rechecking* for accuracy and editing of information. A group of Public Citizen employees and former Public Citizen employees assisted in this enormous task including Elizabeth Hanson, Edith T. Burpee, Christine E. Dehlendorf, and Lauren Dame.

Toufic Rahman, Public Citizen's computer consultant, spent many long hours refining our programs and providing computer assistance. Dr. Lynn Soffer provided us with critical advice on the computer formatting of these data and with a detailed system for ensuring that the data in the report accurately reflect those which we obtained from the states and the federal government. David Vladeck, an attorney with and Director of the Public Citizen Litigation Group, spent many long hours going over our summaries of the legal actions taken by state boards to ensure that they correctly interpreted the lengthier statements we received from the states.

Previous authors of the first four editions were Nicole Simmons, Ingrid VanTuinen, Durrie McKnew and Mary Gabay. Other Public Citizen employees who worked on earlier editions include Dana Hull, Joan Stieber, Joanne Mott, Stephen Moore, Beverly Wellman, Kate Moore, Lauren Kanee and Kathy Cashel.

Table of Contents

Executive Summary VII
    Recommendations..X
How To Use This Report 1
    If you are selecting a doctor 1
    If your current doctor is on this list 2
    If you have a complaint about a doctor 2
    If you want to improve medical quality assurance in the state or nation 3
Introduction 4
    The U.S. "System" of Medical Quality Control 6
    The Magnitude of the Problem of Inadequate Doctor Discipline 8
    The Impact of Substance Abuse 11
    Sexual Abuse or Misconduct 11
Findings 13
    National Comparison of State Disciplinary Actions 13
    Table A: Ranking of Serious Doctor Disciplinary Actions
              by State Medical Licensing Boards 1996 14
    Table B: Ranking of States 1991-1996: Serious
              Disciplinary Actions 16
    Disciplinary Actions from Public Citizen's Database 18
    Table C: Disciplinary Actions by State and
              Federal Agencies 19
    Types of Disciplinary Actions and Offenses 20
    Table D: Disciplinary Actions Reported to Public Citizen: A
              Breakdown of the Types of Disciplinary Actions
              Contained in This Report 21
    Table E: Offenses for which Disciplinary Action was Taken...................23
    Table F: Disciplinary Actions Taken Against Doctors
              Cited for Sexual Abuse of or Sexual Misconduct
              with a Patient 24
    Table G: Disciplinary Actions Taken Against Doctors
              Cited for Substandard Care, Incompetence
              or Negligence 25

	Table H:	Disciplinary Actions Taken Against Doctors Cited for Criminal Convictions	26
	Table I:	Disciplinary Actions Taken Against Doctors Cited for Misprescribing or Overprescribing Drugs	27
	Table J:	Disciplinary Actions Taken Against Doctors Cited for Substance Abuse	28

Conclusions 29
Recommendations for Action 31
    Recommendations for the Federal Government 31
    Recommendations for States 32
Appendix 1: Glossary 36
Appendix 2: How We Compiled This Report 40
    Sources of Information 40
    Generating the Database 41
    Counting Physicians and Actions 46
    Generation of the State-by-State Lists 47
    Appeals, Reinstatements 48
    Charts, Tables, Statistics 49
Appendix 3: Addresses of Federal Agencies 50
References 53

Executive Summary

A license to practice medicine is a hard-won privilege. It is a privilege to hear our innermost thoughts, to see us naked, to cut us open, and to provide us with potentially dangerous drugs. Yet for too long the state and federal government agencies chartered to protect us from those no longer fit to hold that privilege have fallen down on the job. Many state medical boards and other regulatory agencies have either entirely failed to catch doctors guilty of incompetence, drunkenness, or patient abuse, or have let them get away with slaps on the wrist such as fines or reprimands.

For just as long, doctors and their ostensible gate-keepers have failed to realize that consumers need to protect themselves. They have either refused to provide information on those shoddy doctors they have spotted, or they have made it awfully hard to get.

Information in the one federal repository of disciplinary actions by State medical boards and federal agencies--the National Practitioner Data Bank--is kept secret from both patients and from almost all physicians. It is partially in protest to this congressionally-mandated secrecy that Public Citizen's Health Research Group has established our own publicly-available data bank of doctors who have been disciplined. What follows are just a few of the main findings from our study of the data as reported in the national version of *16,638 Questionable Doctors* and in the regional versions:

- 16,638 doctors disciplined by either state medical boards or federal agencies are listed in the national books. This represents an increase of 4,652 new physicians since the last time we analyzed the data in early 1996.

- These 16,638 doctors had a total of 34,049 disciplinary actions taken against them, the most common of which were probation (6,802 times), license suspension (3,197 times), fine (3,141 times), and license revocation (2,889 times). (See other types of disciplinary actions in Table D, Findings, pg. 21.)

- For those doctors with disciplinary actions for which the states or federal agencies supplied specific information on the offenses they had committed (about ⅔ of the doctors in the book), the following numbers of doctors committed the five most serious offenses (see other types of offenses in Table E, Findings, pg. 23):

    1. Sexual abuse of or sexual misconduct with a patient: 393 doctors

2. Substandard care, incompetence or negligence: 2,391 doctors
3. Criminal Conviction (includes plea of guilty or no contest): 1,861 doctors
4. Misprescribing or overprescribing of drugs: 1,521 doctors
5. Substance abuse: 1,309 doctors

An analysis of the 1,883 doctors who were the subject of DEA disciplinary actions revealed that 477 or 25% were not the subject of any state disciplinary action even though their federal narcotics license had been revoked or restricted.

Similarly, of the 2,174 Medicare doctors who were the subjects of the 2,214 Medicare disciplinary actions, 601 or 27% were not disciplined by their state boards even though most (99.5% of actions) had involved exclusion from Medicare.

Thus, many states are not acting promptly, if at all, against physicians about whom a federal agency has already compiled sufficient information to discipline them for very serious offenses. Even for those states which do discipline doctors, for most of the serious offenses, some states frequently do little more than slap physicians on the wrist, leaving the majority free to practice with few if any restrictions.

Overall, the majority of physicians who were disciplined for the five most serious offenses-- sexual abuse or sexual misconduct, substandard care, incompetence, or negligence, criminal conviction, misprescribing or overprescribing of drugs, or substance abuse were not required to stop practicing even temporarily. The most common disciplinary action for each of these five offenses was probation, the severity of which varies widely from state to state. Following are the percentages and numbers of physicians for each offense who did not have to stop practicing despite the offenses which they had committed:

- Sexual abuse of or sexual misconduct with a patient: 393 doctors.

Only 66% of these physicians had to stop practicing, even temporarily. 34% or 133 doctors were not required to stop. (See Table F, Findings, pg. 24).

- Substandard care, incompetence or negligence: 2,391 doctors.

Only 32% of these physicians had to stop practicing, even temporarily. 68% or 1,626 were not required to stop. (See Table G, Findings, pg. 25)

- Criminal conviction (includes plea of guilty or no contest): 1,861 doctors.

Only 60% of these doctors had to stop practicing, even temporarily. 40% or 744 were not required to stop. (See Table H, Findings, pg. 26)

- Misprescribing or overprescribing of drugs: 1,521 doctors.

Only 31% of these physicians had to stop practicing, even temporarily. 69% or 1,049 were not required to stop. (See Table I, Findings, p. 27)

- Substance abuse: 1,309 doctors.

Only 41% of these doctors had to stop practicing, even temporarily. 59% or 772 were not required to stop. (See Table J, Findings, pg. 28)

Thus, it is likely that most of the doctors in these above very serious offenses are currently practicing medicine, with few if any of their patients aware of these offenses.

Precisely because regulators provide so many protections for these health care practitioners, in 1988 the Congressional Office of Technology Assessment concluded that a formal disciplinary action against a doctor provides a good reason to question his or her care.

Our study of the nation's medical quality control system led us to conclude that:

- Too little discipline is still being done. The rate of serious disciplinary actions was only 3.96 per 1,000 doctors or 2,731 serious actions in 1996. Therefore only an extremely small fraction of the nation's doctors face any serious state sanctions each year despite the fact that an estimated 80,000 patients are killed and 234,000 injured as a result of negligence in hospitals, most cases involving doctors.

- Far too few state medical board disciplinary actions are for medical negligence or incompetence. Of the 14,053 instances in which we knew the basis (the offense) for which a disciplinary action was taken and for which the basis of the action was not an action by another state, only 2,531 of those cases (18.0%) were for substandard care, incompetence or negligence.

This country's system for ensuring medical quality needs to be made much stronger. We suggest several avenues towards improvement. Most states need to strengthen their medical practice statutes, restructure their medical boards, and dramatically increase both funding and staffing. Most states should also establish programs to audit and weed out bad doctors so that patient injuries can be prevented rather than simply reacted to. The few states we are aware of that already have some kind of proactive program in place include Georgia, Mississippi, Missouri, Oregon, Utah, Virginia, and West Virginia.

The total number of serious state disciplinary actions against physicians decreased from 2,803 reported for 1995 to 2,731 in 1996 for a nationwide rate of 3.96 serious actions per 1,000 physicians. A difference greater than 6-fold exists between Mississippi, the state with the highest rate (10.83 per 1,000), and New Hampshire, with the lowest rate, (1.76).

It is clear that state-by-state performance is spotty. Only one of the nation's 15 largest states, Ohio, is represented among those 15 states with the highest disciplinary rates. In fact, as seen in Table A, Findings, pg. 14, all of the top 10 states had rates at least 1.5 times higher (5.42 serious actions per 1,000 physicians or higher) than those of large states such as Texas (3.47 per 1,000), Pennsylvania (3.58), Illinois (2.43), Massachusetts (2.87), North Carolina (2.24), and Virginia (2.20).

It is not unreasonable to estimate that a nationwide average rate of at least 10 serious disciplinary actions per 1,000 doctors can be attained (the number was 3.96 in 1996) since, each year, one or more states (Mississippi, in 1996) actually takes this many actions. This would amount to 6,891 serious disciplinary actions a year, far in excess of the 2,731 serious disciplinary actions in 1996. If this had occurred, there would have been 4,160 more serious disciplinary actions that year.

Recommendations

Congress should require cooperation and routine data-sharing between state medical boards, Medicare Peer Review Organizations, state Medicaid agencies, and the Drug Enforcement Administration in catching and sanctioning malfeasant physicians.

The National Practitioner Data Bank, which began collecting information on questionable doctors in September 1990, should be opened to the public. This change will require legislation.

The Drug Enforcement Administration should routinely tell the public and pharmacists which doctors' controlled substances prescription licenses it has pulled or restricted.

State medical boards should be required to promptly make public all their disciplinary actions and the offenses for which their actions were taken, and to regularly distribute lists of actions to consumers, the press, and other health care consumer organizations. In addition, boards should publicly disclose information they have concerning final hospital disciplinary actions and malpractice payouts against doctors.

How to Use This Report

Questionable Doctors was designed to assist consumers in making better informed health care choices. The individual doctor listings aid patients in understanding the quality of care they would potentially receive or have already received from a particular practitioner. The general discussion of disciplinary actions and offenses within a state and the nation help to interpret the information we received.

Please Note...

Names sound alike. Just because a doctor whose name resembles your doctor's is listed in this report doesn't mean your doctor has been sanctioned. Some states failed to give us much identifying information on each doctor, and of the half a million doctors in this country, at least two are bound to have the same name.

Many things change with time. While your doctor's license may be listed as having been revoked, suspended or restricted in this edition of the report, this doesn't necessarily mean those restrictions are still in effect. The information contained in this edition is information we received from the state medical boards by January 31, 1997. We also included information received through December 15, 1997 regarding previous actions which were either overturned or terminated, leaving the physician with an unrestricted license. However, the state may have fully reinstated a doctor's license or lifted their probation or other restrictions in materials received after our deadlines.

Boards don't always have the final say. Your doctor may have appealed his or her disciplinary action and had it overturned by a court. Although we strive to provide the most current information, we are unable to obtain information on many appeals.

If you are selecting a doctor...

- Call the medical board in the state where the doctor practices or used to practice. The board can frequently provide information on the physician's educational and specialty background, and whether the doctor has been disciplined or formally charged with misconduct. (Contact information for each state board is listed at the end of each state's introductory section in this book.)

- Check to see if your local consumer group has published a guide to local doctors.
- Look your doctor up in the American Medical Association's American Medical Directory or the Directory of Medical Specialists, which can be found in all medical libraries and many large public libraries. These directories list the physician's educational background and whether or not he or she is board-certified in a specialty. You should not select a self-designated specialist who has not been trained in the specialty field.
- Ask the doctor for the names of hospitals where he or she has admitting privileges. Your local university teaching hospital will probably be the most selective about the physicians it admits to its staff. Also, should you need to be hospitalized, you will want a doctor who can admit you to the best hospital.

If your current doctor is on this list...

- Check which state(s) or federal agency has disciplined him or her.
- Request a copy of the doctor's disciplinary file from the state or federal agency. State agency addresses are listed in the "Addresses" section of each state section. Federal addresses are in Appendix 3, pg. 50.
- Read the file before making a decision about whether to switch doctors. Some of the information contained in our report is sketchy and may not include a full explanation of the reason for the disciplinary action because states may not have sent these details to us. Some of the actions taken involve offenses that were administrative in nature and do not necessarily reflect on the physician's ability to practice.
- Ask your doctor why he or she was disciplined. If your doctor can convince you that any problem that resulted in the disciplinary action has been resolved or is irrelevant to your future care, fine. Otherwise, you should consider switching.

If you have a complaint about a doctor...

Some examples of reportable actions are:
- if a doctor over-charged you or charged for treatment that was not delivered;
- if a physician failed to order or properly administer appropriate tests or treatment;

- if you suspect that a doctor may be abusing drugs or alcohol;
- if a physician inappropriately touched you in a sexual manner or conducted a sexual relationship with you while you were a patient;
- if you suspect a physician is unable to function mentally or physically.

- Find out what degree your doctor has, whether a medical doctor (M.D.), osteopathic physician (D.O.), chiropractor (D.C.), podiatrist (D.P.M.), or dentist (D.D.S. or D.M.D.). Different state agencies often regulate these different professionals.

- File your complaint with the state medical disciplinary agency. This agency is the only one that can remove dangerous or incompetent doctors from practice, impose limitations on a physician's license to practice, and truly protect other patients from being harmed. Your complaint could lead to the suspension or revocation of a doctor's license directly, or it could aid the medical board in detecting a pattern of poor medical care.

- File the complaint in the state where the doctor is licensed--i.e., where his or her office is located. Turn to that state's section under our "State by State Listings." Find the "Address" heading. Look for the address of the agency that regulates that type of doctor.

- If your care was within a hospital, you should also file a complaint with the hospital's peer review committee, which has the power to revoke or limit a doctor's privileges to practice there.

- You may also want to file a complaint with Medicare (Addresses, Appendix 3, pg. 50).

- Call the agency you have found to inquire about how to file a formal complaint. Some agencies have toll-free hotlines for complaints. Others require complaints to be filed on a specific form.

- Ask whether your complaint will remain confidential. State laws vary. If the agency intends to reveal your name to your doctor, you may want to consider switching to another physician before pursuing any action.

- File a written complaint containing as much information as possible. Make sure to include the doctor's full name, correctly spelled, office address, and the exact date when the conduct you are complaining of occurred. The state may also ask you to release your medical records for review.

- Ask the agency to notify you of the outcome of your complaint.

If you want to improve medical quality assurance in the state or the nation...

- Write your state representatives, your congressional representative, and your senators. Ask them to pass the legislation we recommend on pg. 31.

Introduction

For more than a quarter of a century, Public Citizen's Health Research Group has been striving to provide consumers with information they can use to make educated choices about their doctors. It has not been an easy road. Doctors generally don't like comparative information on quality to be released.

In the nation's first consumer's directory of local physicians, which we published in 1974 for Prince Georges County, Maryland, we wrote, "Most people can find out more about a car they plan to buy than they can about a doctor who may hold their life in his or her hands."[1] Unfortunately, that statement is still largely true today. In the process of collecting information from doctors for that directory, the Maryland State Medical Association threatened doctors who cooperated with loss of their license, arguing that "information that would point out differences between doctors" is illegal.

Another example of the barriers to public access to information on specific doctors: the federal government began collecting information on state disciplinary actions, malpractice payments, and revocations and restrictions of hospital privileges for its National Practitioner Data Bank (NPDB) in September 1990. The problem is that consumers (and even doctors--except for information on themselves) are forbidden by law to have access to the data. This information is available primarily to hospitals, Health Maintenance Organizations, and state and federal government agencies that regulate the quality of medical care. [2,3,4]

In the wake of efforts to pass legislation to open up the NPDB, the American Medical Association, whose earlier efforts had succeeded in a prohibition against public disclosure when the law creating the NPDB was passed in 1986, passed a resolution at its 1993 annual convention stating: "Resolved, that the American Medical Association...call for the dissolution of the National Practitioner Data Bank." Now, as then, the AMA seems to want to protect the minority of American physicians about whom there is data in the NPDB from the scrutiny of their own patients and other physicians.

It should be noted that a number of states have been increasingly using their disciplinary power to address administrative issues. Illinois and Medicare are sanctioning many physicians for defaulting on student loans; the District of Columbia targets physicians who failed to renew their license before the expiration date; and Pennsylvania suspends doctors for not paying a liability insurance surcharge. Although we do not advocate physicians shirking financial responsibilities, we feel that the public would be better served if boards focused more of their resources on exposing and preventing more serious patient abuses. We include such actions in our book because the agencies supplying this information have labeled them "disciplinary;" consumers, however, can and should differentiate between physicians sanctioned for true quality of care issues and administrative violations. These administrative actions, however, make up only a small fraction of cases listed in *16,638 Questionable Doctors*.

There has been some progress in the area of informing the public about poorly practicing physicians. Much information on state and federal government discipline of physicians is now public, although often difficult to obtain, and we have used that data to compile this report. State medical boards, licensing bureaus, and medical societies have increased public access to physician sanctions and license status via toll-free numbers and Internet postings; South Dakota for the first time has provided information to be included in this book; New York and California have made concerted efforts to enhance the exchange of information with other medical boards.

The United States has approximately 689,000 medical doctors, most of them competent and dedicated. *16,638 Questionable Doctors* includes only that 2.4% of physicians whose care or conduct was substandard enough to be cited by a state medical disciplinary board, Medicare, or the federal Drug Enforcement Administration, or whose eligibility to participate in Food and Drug Administration (FDA) experiments was rescinded.

In a 1988 study on medical care quality assessment, the Congressional Office of Technology Assessment concluded that "a sanction imposed on a physician by a state or a Medicare Peer Review Organization is good reason to question the quality of his or her care. [5] The rigorous due process followed by state medical boards lends credibility to the validity of their formal disciplinary actions against physicians," stated the report. "State boards are reluctant to censure physicians and accord accused physicians extensive opportunities for appeal."

But until the day that consumers can have access to as much information about their health care providers as they can about buying a car Public Citizen will continue to battle the shroud of secrecy in which the medical community envelops itself.

The U.S. "System" of Medical Quality Control

The United States has a patchwork system for protecting the public from poor quality health care that is still largely uncoordinated and ineffective.

The first lines of defense are the state medical boards, the state government agencies charged with licensing physicians who meet certain standards. These boards are also responsible for catching already-licensed doctors who fall below standards of conduct or competence in any of a number of areas. They are legally empowered to discipline these doctors: to reprimand them, require them to take course work, impose fines, place them on probation, and, in the worst cases, to suspend them from practice or revoke their licenses altogether.

These licensing and disciplinary systems vary from state to state. In some states the medical board is an independent state agency. In others, it is contained within the state department of licensing, of health, or of consumer affairs. In some states there is one board or agency for medical licensing and another for medical discipline. In a few states, one board or agency regulates all the health care professions--doctors, nurses, dentists, and so forth. In others, there are separate licensing and disciplinary boards for medical (allopathic) physicians, for osteopathic physicians, for dentists, and so on.[6]

In all states, the licensing boards are required to provide consumers with some disciplinary information about a specific doctor. The state agencies' addresses, including their website address if applicable, and phone numbers are listed in the "Addresses" section of each state's listing in this report.

The U.S. Department of Health and Human Services, through its Medicare and Medicaid programs, also disciplines health practitioners. It excludes doctors from participation in Medicare or Medicaid for specified periods of time, and may fine them for violations as well.

The Department's Inspector General must exclude a doctor for at least five years for a criminal conviction related to the Medicare or Medicaid programs and for patient abuse or neglect.[7] It may also impose sanctions based on other types of convictions, on license revocation or suspension by a state agency, or on a sanction by any state Medicaid program. The Inspector General may also sanction a doctor for fraud, for accepting kickbacks, for failing to cooperate with investigators, for failing to pay loans, and, based on a recommendation by the Medicare Peer Review Organizations for each state, for providing substandard or unnecessary care. The Inspector General's office accepts consumer complaints at the phone numbers and addresses listed in Appendix 3, pg. 50.

The Drug Enforcement Administration (DEA), which is part of the U.S. Department of Justice, tracks down doctors who overprescribe or abuse the so-called "scheduled drugs"--drugs such as narcotics, tranquilizers, and amphetamines that may be addictive or otherwise abused. The DEA issues licenses to doctors and dentists that allow them to prescribe these "controlled dangerous substances." No doctor may legally prescribe drugs listed as controlled substances without a valid DEA license. Some states require a separate state controlled substance license as well.

The DEA may deny a license to prescribe these drugs, restrict a doctor's prescription privileges, or revoke his or her privileges to prescribe controlled substances. It publishes notices of such disciplinary actions in the *Federal Register* when the actions have been contested. The address to direct complaints to the DEA is listed in Appendix 3, pg. 50.

The Food and Drug Administration (FDA) sanctions physicians who violated FDA laws, regulations, or policies regarding clinical research on patients.

State medical societies and specialty societies, both of which are unofficial trade associations for doctors, not government agencies, have peer review committees and have a role to play in medical discipline. However, they cannot prevent a doctor from continuing to practice, and their vested interest, in most cases, is in protecting their members, not the public.

Hospitals are required to have peer review committees to review the quality of medical care in their institutions. Consumers who have complaints about the quality of care in a hospital should file them with these committees. The committees may throw doctors off their staffs or restrict doctors' privileges to practice there. Unfortunately, most hospitals regard their peer review activities and disciplinary actions as confidential and will not inform patients about them. The National Practitioner Data Bank (NPDB), as of December 31, 1997, contained information on 6,793 clinical privilege actions against doctors [8] but, as mentioned above, these data are kept secret. There is also serious concern that hospitals are not reporting all of the hospital disciplinary actions against doctors as required by law. During the first three years and four months of operation of the NPDB, 75 percent of U.S. hospitals had not reported even one physician to the NPDB [9] By 1996, according to NPDB staff, the situation had improved and "only" two-thirds of hospitals had not reported a single physician to the NPDB.

Malpractice insurers can also play a role in quality control: they can cancel the policy of a physician who presents a bad risk, raise his or her rates, or offer coverage only if his or her practice is restricted.[10] Unfortunately, many states guarantee every doctor access to malpractice insurance, no matter how poor his or her record. Without an insurance policy, few doctors could afford to continue practicing and, in many states, would not be legally allowed to. Some state medical boards are informed when a doctor has had malpractice insurance canceled and will tell consumers.

The Magnitude of the Problem of Inadequate Doctor Discipline

Though it has improved during the past 15 years, the nation's system for protecting the public from medical incompetence and malfeasance is still far from adequate.

Gaps and breakdowns in communication still exist, although the National Practitioner Data Bank is helping to prevent doctors from being able to indiscriminately cross state lines to evade disciplinary boards. Those dangerous doctors who do fall through the cracks continue to kill, maim, defraud, and otherwise injure their unknowing patients.

Too many state medical boards, despite a clear duty to protect the public,[11] still believe their first responsibility is to rehabilitate "impaired physicians" and to protect them from the public's prying eyes. And the definition of "impaired" has expanded: it now covers doctors who may be drunk on the job, strung out on drugs, mentally ill, or habitual sex offenders.

Arizona, unlike any of the other state medical boards, states in its orders about doctors that it interprets the Americans with Disabilities Act as a reason for not "disciplining" physicians for substance abuse simply because they are already in or will be required to be in a rehabilitation program. Therefore, these actions are viewed as a "voluntary agreement" between the Board and the doctors, not as a disciplinary action.

While it is important for doctors who suffer from emotional problems or drug or alcohol addiction to receive appropriate treatment, this must be balanced with the state's responsibility to protect the public from doctors who are not able to deliver good medical care. Some states show a dangerous pattern of letting chemically dependent doctors return to practice after numerous failed attempts at rehabilitation. And while behavior that is sexually abusive may result from a mental illness, it is also a crime and is never acceptable in the context of patient care.

Although medical boards are now able to communicate with each other, at least indirectly, about doctors they have disciplined, the boards are often far too slow to act on what they have learned. And many state medical boards seldom communicate with the other agencies that guard against medical incompetence, fraud, and abuse--the federal Department of Health and

Human Services, the Medicare Peer Review Organizations, the federal Drug Enforcement Administration, and the agencies that run state Medicaid programs.[12] Many of our recommendations to the states and federal government call for improved and regular communication between these groups.

Only a few of the country's better medical boards, for example those in Utah, West Virginia, Georgia, Oregon, and a few others attempt to proactively sleuth out highly questionable physicians before receiving complaints, in order to prevent misconduct and poor care.

The College of Physicians and Surgeons in the Canadian province of Ontario, by contrast, visits physicians' offices and performs random audits of their care in order to "be assured that licensed physicians meet minimal requirements for safe practice."[13,14] Physicians who fail to meet those standards, as many as 12% of family doctors and 2% of specialists, must undergo intensive educational retraining and in rare cases face disciplinary action. To our knowledge, no American state has yet attempted such a far-reaching quality control program.

Most importantly, most state medical boards have not refined the art of speaking to their primary constituency: the public.

Because of a commendable increase in requirements to report malpractice information to them, states are now repositories of masses of information on the quality of individual doctors, but they have few effective ways of disseminating it.

Many consumers when selecting a doctor still feel that they are floundering in the dark. They are unfamiliar with the role or the existence of medical boards. They are unaware that they can request disciplinary information, or that they can file complaints. Unwarned, too many of these people are treated by doctors guilty of previous acts of malpractice. And unwarned, too many of them are harmed.

Too little discipline is still being done. Fewer than one-half of 1% of the nation's doctors face any serious state sanctions each year. 2,731 total serious disciplinary actions a year, the number state medical boards took in 1996,[15] (see Table A, pg. 14) is a pittance compared to the volume of injury and death of patients caused by negligence of doctors. It has been estimated that between 150,000 and 300,000 Americans are injured or killed each year in hospitals alone as a result of doctors' negligence based on the results of three studies.

- Harvard researchers found that 1% of a representative sample of patients treated in New York state hospitals in 1984 were injured, and one-quarter of those died, because of medical negligence.[16] Nationwide, that would have translated into 234,000 injuries and 80,000 deaths in 1988 from negligence in American hospitals. Most of this involves physicians. There is no clear evidence that there has been significant improvement since then.

- A similar study conducted in California in 1974 found that 0.8% of hospital patients had either been injured by negligence in the hospital or had been hospitalized because of negligent care.[17] Extrapolation of those findings would have yielded an estimate of 249,000 injuries and deaths from negligent medical practice in 1988.
- In 1976 the HEW Malpractice Commission estimated similarly that one-half of 1% of all patients entering hospitals are injured there due to negligence. That estimate would have indicated 156,000 injuries and deaths resulting from doctor negligence in 1988.[18]

Expanding these estimates to include general medical practice outside of a hospital, the potential abuse by physicians is even greater. An in-depth interview with 53 family physicians revealed that 47% of the doctors recalled a case in which the patient died due to physician error. Only four of the total reported errors led to malpractice suits, and none of these errors resulted in an action by a peer review organization.[19]

Medical students at SUNY-Buffalo were asked to recall incidents during their clinical training that raised ethical concerns. More than 200 students responded (40% of total sample); the majority of instances they reported (60%) did not in the researchers' opinions threaten the patient's life, health or welfare. This, however, implies that potentially 40% did.[20]

Systemic changes over time may also suggest a rise in physician malpractice. In a journal commentary, Dr. Alvan R. Feinstein reflects that in his 40 years of experience the manner in which medicine is now conducted may be sufficiently more complex as to contribute to an "epidemic of negligent medical errors."[21] A review of 43 malpractice insurance claims also indicates that systemic causes significantly contribute to pediatrician error; 91% of these claims, however, were also attributed to alleged errors of physician judgment involving diagnosis and treatment.[22] Even medical students and residents are now being held legally accountable for their mistakes,[23] thus broadening the pool of recognized physician error.

Given that many state medical boards now have the same information on claims and payments, they should be able to discipline at least as many doctors as malpractice carriers do. A 1989 Tufts University study found that physician-owned malpractice insurers sanctioned 13.6 of every 1,000 doctors they covered. The insurers terminated policies of 6.6 of every 1,000 policyholders in 1985 because of negligence-prone behavior, and they restricted the practice or imposed other sanctions on another 7 of every 1,000 doctors whose care was found to be substandard.[24] In an estimated population of 689,121 nonfederal doctors, this would translate to 9,372 doctors being disciplined a year.

The Impact of Substance Abuse

Specific physician attributes also contribute to this rate. Two studies surveyed residents to determine the incidence of substance use. Recent alcohol use was extremely high in both groups (87% within the last year for emergency medicine residents; 74% within the past 30 days for surgery residents).[25,26] Additional findings proved extremely disturbing; although the emergency medicine program directors accurately determined the incidence of alcohol use amongst residents, they dramatically underestimated the percent who were actually impaired by the substance as indicated by diagnostic tests (1% estimate impaired vs. 13% diagnosed.)[27] This does not bode well for creating a medical system that prevents mishaps before they occur. And although the surgery residents reported negligible recent cocaine use, when employed, the drug was typically obtained from the hospital supply,[28] indicating a greater ease of access than for the general population.

Hughes reported that approximately 1-3% of physicians are disciplined or treated for substance abuse with an AMA estimated lifetime prevalence of 6-8% for alcoholism and 1-2% for drug dependency.[29] In 1985, Smith proposed that 17,000 doctors suffered from substance abuse.[30] Six percent of physicians indicated lifetime alcohol abuse and 1.6% reported either alcohol dependency or abuse within the last year alone.[31] If only 1% of physicians needed disciplining for chemical dependency, that alone would translate to 6,891 doctors.

Sexual Abuse or Misconduct

Sexual abuse of or sexual misconduct with a patient is also a serious issue. Six to ten percent of psychiatrists surveyed confessed to having engaged in sexual contact with a patient [32,33] and in a longitudinal study, Garfinkel at al. noted that of the original 70 psychiatrists they tracked, 2 (2.9%) had lost their medical licenses due to repeated violations of sexual boundaries with patients.[34] In reviewing their own rate of disciplinary actions for the years 1991-1995, the Oregon Board of Medical Examiners determined that of 100 open complaints investigated against 80 doctors during this time period, 5.9% were alleged to be sexual misconduct. More than one-third (39%) of these were classified as sexual impropriety, 31% were categorized as sexual transgression and 30% sexual violation. Disciplinary action was reported in 5%, 27%, and 54% of the instances, respectively. Twenty-five percent of the closed complaints also resulted in reportable disciplinary action.[35]

In light of these findings, it is not unreasonable to estimate that at least 1 percent of doctors in this country deserve some serious disciplinary action each year. This would amount to 6,891 physicians being disciplined each year, a number that, unfortunately far exceeds the actual number of physicians disciplined.

Findings

National Comparison of State Disciplinary Actions

Based on the Federation of State Medical Boards' (FSMB) data released annually on the number of disciplinary actions taken against doctors, Public Citizen calculated the rate of serious disciplinary actions per 1,000 doctors in each state and compiled a national report ranking state boards by the extent to which they are taking serious disciplinary actions against doctors (See Table A, Findings, pg. 14).

Public Citizen has had and continues to have, two disputes with the FSMB over these data. First, we choose to look only at the most serious actions taken by state medical boards as a way of evaluating them, whereas the FSMB looks at "prejudicial" actions, a broader category which includes relative slaps on the wrist such as fines and reprimands as well as what we deem "serious" disciplinary actions. This category, in our view, should include only license revocations, suspensions or surrenders, plus probations, restrictions or other limitations on license (categories A & B in the FSMB data).

Second, the Federation states "it is virtually impossible to make sound comparisons of one medical board to another," and thereby avoids doing a ranking of state boards. We strongly disagree, and the Federation admits that the structure and funding of medical boards may have a direct impact on their effectiveness. Public Citizen believes that a valid uniform measure of board effectiveness is the rate of serious disciplinary actions per 1,000 doctors per year--a belief shared by Richard Kusserow, formerly Inspector General of the federal Department of Health and Human Services.

According to James R. Winn, M.D., the Federation's executive vice-president, "Boards that are independent or semi-autonomous, adopting their own budgets and allocating revenues to their operations, appear to perform their role of public protectors more effectively than those boards that are classified as subordinate or advisory." So, although the FSMB disagrees with the idea of our rankings based on their data, it admits to differences between boards.

Table A — Ranking of Serious Doctor Disciplinary Actions by State Medical Licensing Boards 1996

1996 Rank	State	Number Of Serious Actions 1996	Total Number of Nonfederal Doctors 1995	Serious Actions Per 1,000 Doctors
1	Mississippi	45	4157	10.83
2	North Dakota	13	1419	9.16
3	Iowa	46	5368	8.57
4	Colorado	79	9526	8.29
5	Arizona	82	10019	8.18
6	Alaska	7	955	7.33
7	Oklahoma	41	5745	7.14
8	Ohio	161	26974	5.97
9	Nevada	16	2702	5.92
10	Vermont	10	1846	5.42
11	West Virginia	21	3948	5.32
12	Kansas	28	5665	4.94
13	Montana	9	1849	4.87
14	Kentucky	38	8091	4.70
15	Arkansas	22	4768	4.61
16	Utah	19	4209	4.51
17	Maine	13	2903	4.48
18	New York	313	70751	4.42
19	Georgia	67	15268	4.39
20	New Jersey	105	23970	4.38
21	Idaho	8	1878	4.26
22	Florida	160	37964	4.21
23	New Mexico	16	3819	4.19
24	Nebraska	15	3589	4.18
25	Rhode Island	13	3231	4.02
26	Delaware	7	1753	3.99
27	California	339	86317	3.93
28	Michigan	83	22149	3.75
29	Oregon	29	7834	3.70
30	Missouri	46	12525	3.67
31	Wyoming	3	836	3.59
32	Pennsylvania	130	36266	3.58
33	Indiana	41	11608	3.53
34	Wisconsin	43	12241	3.51
35	Texas	133	38352	3.47
36	District of Columbia	13	3911	3.32
37	Connecticut	40	12134	3.30
38	Alabama	28	8563	3.27
39	Hawaii	10	3215	3.11
40	Washington	43	13931	3.09
41	Maryland	59	19215	3.07
42	South Dakota	4	1358	2.95
43	Massachusetts	73	25467	2.87
44	Louisiana	28	10396	2.69
45	South Carolina	19	7708	2.46
46	Illinois	76	31304	2.43
47	Minnesota	29	12298	2.36
48	North Carolina	38	16966	2.24
49	Tennessee	29	12949	2.24
50	Virginia	36	16362	2.20
51	New Hampshire	5	2849	1.76
	TOTAL	2731	689121	3.96

Our calculation of rates of serious disciplinary actions per 1,000 doctors by state is created by taking the number of such actions (as defined above) and dividing it by the American Medical Association data on non-federal M.D.s, and then multiplying the result by 1,000 to get state disciplinary rates. Nationwide, there were 2,731 serious disciplinary actions in 1996 out of 689,121 nonfederal M.D.s, which is a rate of 3.96 serious disciplinary actions per 1,000 physicians. State rates ranged from 10.83 (Mississippi) to 1.76 (New Hampshire).

Best States. Those with the highest rates of serious disciplines. Table A lists each state's ranking in descending order. The top 10 states, or those with the highest rate of serious disciplinary actions per 1,000 physicians are (in order): Mississippi, North Dakota, Iowa, Colorado, Arizona, Alaska, Oklahoma, Ohio, Nevada, and Vermont. Seven of these 10 states (all but Nevada, North Dakota, and Oklahoma) were also in the top 10 in 1995, and three, (Mississippi, Iowa, and Alaska) have been leaders for six straight years. Georgia, 19th this year and West Virginia, 11th this year, were both in the top 10 for the previous five years (1991-1995). Oklahoma (7th this year) has been a top 10 state for five of the last six years. Colorado (4th this year) and North Dakota (2nd), have been top 10 states for four of the last six years. (See Table B, Findings, pg. 16)

It is clear that state-by-state performance is spotty. Only one of the nation's 15 largest states, Ohio, is represented among those 15 states with the highest disciplinary rates. In fact, as seen in Table A, pg. 14, all of the top 10 states had rates at least 1.5 times as high (5.42 serious actions per 1,000 physicians or higher) as those of large states such as Texas (3.47 per 1,000), Pennsylvania (3.58), Illinois (2.43), Massachusetts (2.87), North Carolina (2.24), and Virginia (2.20).

Worst States. Those with the lowest rate of serious disciplines. The bottom 10 states, those with the lowest serious disciplinary rates in 1996, were, starting with the lowest: New Hampshire, Virginia, Tennessee, North Carolina, Minnesota, Illinois, South Carolina, Louisiana, Massachusetts and South Dakota. Four of the bottom 10, New Hampshire, Illinois, South Carolina and Virginia, were also in the cellar in 1995. In 1996, the bottom 21 states all had rates of serious disciplinary action that were less than one-third of Mississippi's 10.83, and the lowest (New Hampshire) had a rate only one-sixth that of the leader.

States with significant change from 1991 through 1996. By observing the actual rates of serious disciplinary actions for the years 1991 through 1996, we did a statistical analysis to see in which states the rate had significantly increased or decreased during that time. This was done using regression analyses.

Table B   Ranking of States 1991-1996: Serious Disciplinary Actions

Rank 1996	Rank 1995	Rank 1994	Rank 1993	Rank 1992	Rank 1991	State
1	1	9	9	6	6	Mississippi
2	34	10	3	5	13	North Dakota
3	2	7	5	2	3	Iowa
4	5	12	6	8	17	Colorado
5	10	17	16	22	22	Arizona
6	8	2	8	7	1	Alaska
7	12	5	2	1	2	Oklahoma
8	9	24	22/23	19	23	Ohio
9	11	31	20	25	26	Nevada
10	6	39	17	15	10	Vermont
11	7	6	1	3	8	West Virginia
12	46	22	37/38	20	25	Kansas
13	18	3	14	10	19	Montana
14	14	4	4	16	5	Kentucky
15	23	28	26	18	29	Arkansas
16	38	46	39	43	18	Utah
17	32	33	41	44	46	Maine
18	17	29	34	39	49	New York
19	4	8	10	9	4	Georgia
20	25	19	18	28	20	New Jersey
21	36	30	37/38	23	34/35	Idaho
22	22	25	25	21	27	Florida
23	15	43/44	49	33	33	New Mexico
24	41/42	15	50	38	39	Nebraska
25	26	26	42	41	50/51	Rhode Island
26	48	48	43	51	16	Delaware
27	20	34/35	32	42	37	California
28	21	34/35	35	40	40	Michigan
29	16	20	22/23	24	14	Oregon
30	37	13	12	13	12	Missouri
31	3	1	21	4	9	Wyoming
32	43	47	48	48	47	Pennsylvania
33	28	16	7	14	15	Indiana
34	47	41	27	26	34/35	Wisconsin
35	19	23	28	29	21	Texas
36	50	51	51	45	45	Dist. of Columbia
37	27	42	36	35	30	Connecticut
38	30	43/44	29	30	31	Alabama
39	51	50	46	50	41	Hawaii
40	24	27	24	17	24	Washington
41	29	21	19	27	42/43	Maryland
42	33	11	13	32	50/51	South Dakota
43	40	37	45	46	48	Massachusetts
44	13	18	11	12	7	Louisiana
45	44	14	15	11	11	South Carolina
46	45	40	31	36	36	Illinois
47	39	45	33	31	28	Minnesota
48/49	35	36	40	34	42/43	North Carolina
48/49	31	38	44	49	38	Tennessee
50	41/42	32	30	37	32	Virginia
51	49	49	47	47	44	New Hampshire

In 15 states, there was a significant change during that period. For 11 states, the change was in a positive direction. Arizona (5th in 1996), California (27th), Colorado (4th), Massachusetts (43rd), Maine (17th), Michigan (28th), Nevada (9th), New York (18th), Ohio (8th), Pennsylvania (32nd), and Rhode Island (25th). In other words, in those states there was a significantly improved trend in the rate of serious disciplinary actions from 1991 to 1996 even though some of them are still not among the best boards in the country.

In four states, however, the change was in a negative direction, meaning that there was a significant decrease in the rate of serious disciplinary actions over the 1991-1996 interval. These states were South Carolina (45th in 1996), Louisiana (44th), Minnesota (47th), and Oklahoma (7th). It should be pointed out that many other boards which steadily maintained high or low rates of serious disciplinary actions did not have significant changes during those years but still can be judged on the merits (or lack thereof) of their steady rates.

This analysis raises serious questions about the extent to which patients in many states with poorer records of serious doctor discipline are being protected from physicians who might well be barred from practice in states with boards that are doing a better job of disciplining physicians. It is likely that patients are being injured or killed more often in states with poor doctor disciplinary records than in states with consistent top 10 performances. It is not unreasonable to estimate that at least 1 percent of doctors in this country deserve some serious disciplinary action each year, a number comparable to Mississippi's rate of 10.83 actions per 1,000 doctors or 1.083 percent. In fact, each year one or more states achieves a rate of serious disciplinary actions of approximately 10 per 10,000 doctors. This would amount to 6,891 (1% of 689,121 non-federal doctors) serious actions a year, which cover only a small fraction of the 80,000 patient deaths thought to occur each year in American hospitals as a result of negligence, almost all of it involving physicians.[36] The current overall national rate of serious disciplinary actions, 3.96 per 1,000 or .396 percent is far short of the rate of 1.083 percent in Mississippi. If rate of serious disciplinary actions had been 10 per 1,000 (1 percent), the national total would have been 6,891 actions or 4,160 more actions in 1996 than the 2,731 that actually occurred in 1996.

Considering what is known about substandard doctoring, not even Mississippi's disciplinary rate seems adequate. Most states have a long way to go before they even begin to offer serious protection for citizens from doctors who are incompetent, who sexually abuse patients or who otherwise have serious problems that interfere with delivery of high-quality medical care in a compassionate way. Given that national projections from the Harvard University study referred to above estimate 80,000 deaths a year caused by negligence, mainly by physicians, the 2,731 serious disciplinary actions in 1996 is a dangerously small drop in the bucket of adequate consumer-protective doctor discipline. All states, even those with best records, need to strengthen the structure and functions of their licensing boards. The statement by the Federation that you cannot compare the disciplinary rates of boards with each other because they are set-up, structured and funded differently is preposterous.

Disciplinary Actions from Public Citizen's Database

As shown in Table C, pg. 19 of the 34,049 disciplinary actions reported by state boards or the federal government to Public Citizen (representing actions against 16,638 doctors), the majority (29,812 or 87.6%) of these were imposed by state medical boards. A description and statistical breakdown of the actions provided to Public Citizen by each state is provided in the "State by State Listings" section. These counts represent the two most serious disciplinary actions for each sanction reported. Some sanctions included more than two actions against the doctors. These less serious actions are not included in these counts. (For a more detailed discussion of how disciplinary actions are reported, refer to "How We Compiled This Report," Appendix 2, pg. 40.)

Please note that the period of years covered in the database varies from state to state--e.g. we may have received disciplinary materials covering six years for one state but only three years for another state. Therefore, our statistics should not be viewed as nationally representative for any specific time period.

The federal agencies account for the remaining 4,237 disciplinary actions imposed; 5.9% (2,006) were DEA sanctions in contested and uncontested cases, 6.5% (2,214) were fines and exclusions from the Medicare program, and 17 were restrictions placed on a physician's eligibility to participate as investigators in FDA experiments.

An analysis of the 1,883 doctors who were the subject of DEA disciplinary actions revealed that 477 or 25% were not the subject of any state disciplinary action even though their federal narcotics license had been revoked, surrendered, or restricted.

Similarly, of the 2,174 Medicare doctors who were the subjects of the 2,214 Medicare disciplinary actions, 601 or 27% were not disciplined by their state boards even though most (99.5% of actions) had involved exclusion from Medicare.

Table C Disciplinary Actions by State and Federal Agencies			
State/Federal Agency	**Number of Actions**	**State/Federal Agency**	**Number of Actions**
Alabama	198	Mississippi	255
Alaska	101	Missouri	597
Arizona	971	Montana	80
Arkansas	82	Nebraska	107
California	2021	Nevada	136
Colorado	644	New Hampshire	60
Connecticut	365	New Jersey	1534
Delaware	39	New Mexico	123
District of Columbia	242	New York	2358
DEA	*2006*	North Carolina	524
Florida	3080	North Dakota	122
FDA	*17*	Ohio	1211
Georgia	937	Oklahoma	532
Hawaii	130	Oregon	309
Idaho	41	Pennsylvania	949
Illinois	1313	Rhode Island	153
Indiana	557	South Carolina	404
Iowa	510	South Dakota	51
Kansas	289	Tennessee	530
Kentucky	614	Texas	1693
Louisiana	452	Utah	219
Maine	112	Vermont	118
Maryland	645	Virginia	575
Massachusetts	718	Washington	559
Medicare	*2214*	West Virginia	450
Michigan	901	Wisconsin	501
Minnesota	660	Wyoming	40
		TOTAL	**34049**

Thus, many states are not acting promptly, if at all, against physicians about whom a federal agency has already compiled sufficient information to discipline them for very serious offenses.

Types of Disciplinary Actions and Offenses

The following tables provide a statistical national look at the types of disciplinary actions and the offenses for which they were taken.

Table D, Types of Disciplinary Actions Reported to Public Citizen (pg. 21) shows that the most common type of state disciplinary action of those submitted to us was probation. States imposed probation 20.0% of the times (6,802 times) when practitioners were disciplined. They revoked licenses 8.5% of the time (2,889 times), suspended licenses 12.4% of the time (4,205 times), and accepted a doctor's surrender of his or her license 7.3% of the time (2,489 times). Cumulatively, only 9,583 or 28.2% of the actions against doctors listed in this report were ones which resulted in at least a temporary loss of ability to practice medicine (revocation, suspension and surrender). Most of the doctors who are listed in this book never had to stop practicing medicine and many more who had suspensions may once again be practicing. It is not likely that many of their patients are aware of these actions. **A total of 16,638 different physicians were the subject of the 34,049 disciplinary actions taken by state and federal agencies.**

Table D	Disciplinary Actions Reported to Public Citizen: A Breakdown of the Types of Disciplinary Actions Contained in This Report		
Disciplinary Action		**Number**	**Percent**
Probation		6802	20.0%
Suspension		3197	9.4%
Revocation		2889	8.5%
Fine		3141	9.2%
Surrender		2489	7.3%
Reprimand		2445	7.2%
Exclusion from the Medicare Program		2189	6.4%
Practice Restriction		1812	5.3%
Revocation, Surrender, Suspension of Controlled Substance License		1850	5.4%
Restriction of Controlled Substance License		1264	3.7%
Emergency Suspension		1008	3.0%
Education		1069	3.1%
Physician Monitoring		967	2.8%
License Denial		440	1.3%
Required to Enter an Impaired Physicians Program or Drug or Alcohol Treatment		449	1.3%
Other Actions		2038	6.0%
Total Actions		**34049**	**100.0%**

Table E, Offenses for which Disciplinary Action was Taken (pg. 23). The reason an action was taken--the offense--was provided by state and federal authorities for 19,424 of the records in our database. For a number of offenses, more than one action was taken. In 5,371 cases, the stated reason for the action was action taken by another state. Among those 14,053 actions for which specific reasons other than discipline by another state or agency were reported, the five most serious offenses were as follows.

Criminal conviction: The most common single reason for which states disciplined doctors was a criminal conviction (plea of guilty or nolo contendere--no contest) which accounted for 18.1% of all the 14,053 actions for which a specific offense was stated. A total of 1,861 different doctors were disciplined for this offense.

Substandard care, incompetence or negligence, the second largest category, accounted for 18% of known offenses other than those listed as disciplinary action by another state. A total of 2,391 different doctors were disciplined for these offenses involving substandard care, incompetence or negligence.

Disciplinary actions taken because of *misprescribing or overprescribing drugs* accounted for an additional 11.6% of known offenses. A total of 1,521 different doctors were disciplined for these offenses.

Substance abuse accounted for an additional 11.1% of known offenses for which doctors were disciplined. A total of 1,309 different doctors were disciplined for these offenses.

Sexual abuse of or sexual misconduct with a patient accounted for 3.0% of the total known offenses for which doctors were disciplined. A total of 393 different doctors were disciplined for these offenses.

The five offenses listed above, all extremely serious, accounted for 62% or almost two-thirds of all of those disciplinary actions in which a specific offense other than discipline by another state or agency was listed.

Table E	Offenses for which Disciplinary Action was Taken*	
Offense	**Number**	**Percent**
Criminal Conviction	2545	18.1%
Substandard Care, Incompetence, or Negligence	2531	18.0%
Misprescribing or Overprescribing Drugs	1632	11.6%
Substance Abuse	1566	11.1%
Professional Misconduct	1576	11.2%
Noncompliance with a Board Order	953	6.8%
Noncompliance with a Professional Rule	1233	8.8%
Practicing without a License	477	3.4%
Practicing without a Controlled Substance License	55	0.4%
Providing False Information to Medical Board	384	2.7%
Sexual Abuse of or Sexual Misconduct with a Patient	425	3.0%
Physical or Mental Impairment	365	2.6%
Hospital Privilege Loss or Restriction	162	1.2%
Insurance or Medicare/Medicaid Fraud	75	0.5%
Falsifying/Altering Medical Records	34	0.2%
Overcharging	32	0.2%
Exceeding Professional Limitations	8	0.1%
Total Records With Offense Cited	**14053**	**100.0%**

* Frequencies and types of violations cited by states or federal government for disciplinary actions. Includes only those actions for which an offense was reported and for which we had a corresponding term in our database. This table does not include the 5,371 cases in which the stated reason was action by another state.

Table F, Disciplinary Actions Taken Against Doctors Cited for Sexual Abuse of or Sexual Misconduct with a Patient, below, shows that of the 393 different doctors who were disciplined for sexual abuse of or misconduct with a patient, there were 260 actions (81 revocations, 39 surrenders, 99 suspensions plus 41 emergency suspensions) which required those doctors, at least temporarily, to stop practicing medicine. Thus, assuming that there is usually only one such serious action per doctor, because these four actions are mutually exclusive, and most of the subsequent multiple state actions have the offense listed as action by another state rather than the sexual offense and are therefore counted only once per doctor, dividing these 260 actions by the 393 doctors shows that at the most, 66% of doctors disciplined for this offense had to stop practicing medicine at least temporarily. But this means that at least 34% of doctors (133 doctors) were allowed to continue practicing, their behavior probably unknown to most if not all of their patients. It is likely that other doctors, especially those whose licenses were only suspended temporarily, are once again practicing medicine.

Table F	Disciplinary Actions Taken Against Doctors Cited for Sexual Abuse of or Sexual Misconduct with a Patient	
Action	**Number**	**Percent**
Revocation	81	13.1%
Surrender	39	6.3%
Suspension	99	16.0%
Emergency Suspension	41	6.6%
Probation	146	23.5%
Fine	65	10.5%
Other Actions	149	24.0%
Total Actions	**620**	**100.0%**

Table G, Disciplinary Actions Taken Against Doctors Cited for Substandard Care, Incompetence or Negligence, below, shows that of the 2,391 different doctors who were disciplined for substandard care, incompetence or negligence, there were 776 actions (238 revocations, 188 surrenders, 282 suspensions plus 68 emergency suspensions) which required those doctors, at least temporarily, to stop practicing medicine. Thus, assuming that there is usually only one such serious action per doctor, because these four actions are mutually exclusive, and most of the subsequent multiple state actions have the offense listed as action by another state rather than the substandard offense and are therefore counted only once per doctor, dividing these 776 actions by the 2,391 doctors shows that at the most, 32% of doctors disciplined for this offense had to stop practicing medicine at least temporarily. But this means that at least 68% of doctors (1,626 doctors) were allowed to continue practicing, their behavior probably unknown to most if not all of their patients. It is likely that other doctors, especially those whose licenses were only suspended temporarily, are once again practicing medicine.

Table G	Disciplinary Actions Taken Against Doctors Cited for Substandard Care, Incompetence or Negligence	
Action	**Number**	**Percent**
Revocation	238	6.4%
Surrender	188	5.1%
Suspension	282	7.6%
Emergency Suspension	68	1.8%
Probation	917	24.8%
Practice Restriction	281	7.6%
Fine	668	18.0%
Reprimand	341	9.2%
Other Actions	719	19.4%
Total Actions	**3702**	**100.0%**

Table H, Disciplinary Actions Taken Against Doctors Cited for Criminal Convictions, below, shows that of the 1,861 different doctors who were disciplined because of a criminal conviction, there were 1,120 actions (477 revocations, 115 surrenders, 431 suspensions plus 97 emergency suspensions) which required those doctors, at least temporarily, to stop practicing medicine. Thus, assuming that there is usually only one such serious action per doctor because these four actions are mutually exclusive, and most of the subsequent multiple state actions have the offense listed as action by another state rather than the conviction offense and are therefore counted only once per doctor, dividing these 1,120 actions by the 1,861 doctors shows that at the most, 60% of doctors disciplined for this offense had to stop practicing medicine at least temporarily. But this means that at least 40% of doctors (744 doctors) were allowed to continue practicing, their behavior probably unknown to most if not all of their patients. It is likely that other doctors, especially those whose licenses were only suspended temporarily, are once again practicing medicine.

Table H	Disciplinary Actions Taken Against Doctors Cited for Criminal Convictions	
Action	**Number**	**Percent**
Revocation	477	15.6%
Surrender	115	3.8%
Suspension	431	14.1%
Emergency Suspension	97	3.2%
Probation	524	17.1%
Fine	173	5.7%
Other Actions	1240	40.6%
Total Actions	**3057**	**100.0%**

Table I, Disciplinary Actions Taken Against Doctors Cited for Misprescribing or Overprescribing Drugs, below, shows that of the 1,521 different doctors who were disciplined because of misprescribing or overprescribing drugs, there were 476 actions (111 revocations, 110 surrenders, 200 suspensions plus 55 emergency suspensions) which required those doctors, at least temporarily, to stop practicing medicine. Thus, assuming that there is usually only one such serious action per doctor, because these four actions are mutually exclusive, and most of the subsequent multiple state actions have the offense listed as action by another state rather than the misprescribing/overprescribing offense and are therefore counted only once per doctor, dividing these 476 actions by the 1,521 doctors shows that at the most, 31% of doctors disciplined for this offense had to stop practicing medicine at least temporarily. But this means that at least 69% of doctors (1,049 doctors) were allowed to continue practicing, their behavior probably unknown to most if not all of their patients. It is likely that other doctors, especially those whose licenses were only suspended temporarily, are once again practicing medicine.

Table I	Disciplinary Actions Taken Against Doctors Cited for Misprescribing or Overprescribing Drugs	
Action	**Number**	**Percent**
Revocation	111	4.7%
Surrender	110	4.6%
Revocation, Surrender, or Suspension of Controlled Substance License	266	11.2%
Suspension	200	8.4%
Emergency Suspension	55	2.3%
Probation	580	24.4%
Restriction of Controlled Substance License	321	13.5%
Fine	269	11.3%
Education	145	6.1%
Other Actions	324	13.6%
Total Actions	**2381**	**100.0%**

Table J, Disciplinary Actions Taken Against Doctors Cited for Substance Abuse, below, shows that of the 1,309 different doctors who were disciplined because of substance abuse, there were 538 actions (73 revocations, 90 surrenders, 237 suspensions plus 138 emergency suspensions) which required those doctors, at least temporarily, to stop practicing medicine. Thus, assuming that there is usually only one such serious action per doctor, because these four actions are mutually exclusive and most of the subsequent multiple state actions have the offense listed as action by another state rather than the substance abuse offense and are therefore counted only once per doctor, dividing these 538 actions by the 1,309 doctors shows that at the most, 41% of doctors disciplined for this offense had to stop practicing medicine at least temporarily. But this means that at least 59% of doctors (772 doctors) were allowed to continue practicing, their behavior probably unknown to most if not all of their patients. It is likely that other doctors, especially those whose licenses were only suspended temporarily, are once again practicing medicine.

Table J	Disciplinary Actions Taken Against Doctors Cited for Substance Abuse	
Action	**Number**	**Percent**
Revocation	73	3.1%
Surrender	90	3.9%
Revocation, Surrender, or Suspension of Controlled Substance License	99	4.3%
Suspension	237	10.2%
Emergency Suspension	138	5.9%
Probation	716	30.8%
Restriction of Controlled Substance License	134	5.8%
Fine	41	1.8%
Required to Enter an Impaired Physician Program or Drug or Alcohol Treatment	222	9.6%
Other Actions	572	24.6%
Total Actions	**2322**	**100.0%**

Conclusions

1. The current rate of serious disciplinary actions is a dangerously small drop in the bucket of adequate, consumer-protective doctor discipline.
2. All states, especially those with the worst records, need to strengthen the structure and functions of their licensing boards.
3. The increase in the total number of disciplinary actions may not indicate that more doctors are being caught. Much of the disciplinary activity involves insuring that doctors, once caught by one state, are disciplined when they move to another. There has also been a noticeable increase in sanctioning doctors for administrative purposes.
4. Questionable doctors can still cross state borders, though with less impunity than before. The extent to which one board shares information with another still varies widely by state.

    - In many instances discipline is still too slow although the case backlogs in some states have been greatly reduced. Wisconsin sanctioned a number of doctors only after they had already retired from practice.
    - The vast majority of states continue to require reporting of hospital disciplinary actions and malpractice claims or payments to the medical board, but few check whether the required reports have actually been filed. And some still fail to act on the information they receive.
    - Medical boards are much too forgiving. Many still see their priority as "rehabilitation," and their disciplinary actions are too light. Probation is the most common sanction against doctors for all of the five most serious offenses: sexual abuse or misconduct; substandard care; conviction; prescription violations, or substance abuse. Arizona, unlike any other state board, interprets the Americans with Disabilities Act to indicate that action for substance abuse is a "voluntary agreement" between the physician and the Board, not a disciplinary action.
    - Far too few board actions, only 18% of the 14,053 identified offenses, were for medical negligence or incompetence. Instead boards focus on more easily documentable offenses such as prescription violations and fraud convictions or disciplinary action in another state as potential indicators of substandard care. Other instances of incompetence may be overlooked because the investigations soak up

resources like a sponge.

To date, legislation--mainly at the state level--on medical malpractice, the injury and death of patients caused by doctor negligence, has been to punish the victim instead of disciplining the perpetrator. Legislative attention must be given to requiring states to significantly improve the discipline of physicians in order to prevent future death and injury.

Recommendations for Action

Complain. As discussed in *How To Use This Report*, pg. 1, file your complaints about poor medical care or medical misconduct with your state medical board and with the federal Department of Health and Human Services. If the offense occurred in a hospital, also file a complaint with the hospital peer review committee. Your complaints are needed to protect others!

Organize. Form citizens' action or victims' rights groups to improve medical quality assurance in your area. The American Association of Retired Persons publishes a guide that can help you mobilize a group for reform.[37] Try to get a representative of your group appointed to the state medical board or the Medicare Peer Review Organization for your state.

Write to your Congresspersons, at both state and federal levels urging actions as listed below.

Recommendations for the Federal Government

Create grants and standards. Congress should create a small program of grants-in-aid to state medical boards. The grants should be tied to the boards' agreements to meet certain performance standards, which should be developed by the Public Health Service, as the Department of Health and Human Services Office of Inspector General recommended in 1990.[38]

In developing these standards, the Public Health Service should work with the Federation of State Medical Boards' Assessment Task Force. In September 1990 the FSMB received a federal contract for $200,000 to undertake the development of a self-assessment instrument for state medical boards. The goal of the task force was to produce a sound and objective means by which boards could assess their performance over time and in comparison with other boards.[39] In April 1992 the Federation released its "Self-Assessment Instrument for State Medical Boards" and the accompanying handbook. The Instrument is a survey that each board can fill out regarding its own activities, enabling boards to eventually share information with each other and compare resources and performance. The standards should include (but not be limited to) the following: processing complaints within a certain limited period of time; maintaining a certain level of staffing and having staff meet certain qualifications; disseminating disciplinary information to the public; having at least 30% of board members be consumer members; regularly publishing a newsletter that includes names of disciplined physicians and descriptions of the disciplinary actions taken against them; issuing an annual report that includes meaningful disciplinary statistics; and other standards.

The Medicare Peer Review Organizations (PRO), which have been practically moribund in disciplining physicians for substandard care, should become more aggressive. The PROs should hire investigators and advisers trained in law enforcement so that fewer of their sanctions will be overturned.

As a 1990 Institute of Medicine report noted, the PROs are not evaluated on their ability to detect and correct poor quality care.[40] The Department of Health and Human Services should change its evaluation procedures to place more emphasis on quality.

Open the National Practitioner Data Bank. In 1986 Congress passed the Health Care Quality Improvement Act. This act mandated the establishment of a data bank containing information on adverse professional review actions taken against doctors, and on doctors who had been sued for malpractice and on whose behalf settlement or adjudicated payments had been made. Unfortunately, the law establishing the data bank also required that it be closed to the general public. Congress should pass legislation opening the data bank to consumers and loudly rebuke the American Medical Association's resolution to destroy the data bank.

The Drug Enforcement Administration should release a monthly list of all practitioners whose controlled substance prescription licenses have been revoked, surrendered, restricted, or denied. The list should be widely distributed to pharmacies, state pharmacy and medical boards, and the general public. Far too many doctors continue to prescribe controlled substances after their DEA licenses have expired or have been revoked. The DEA should consider requiring pharmacies to subscribe to an on-line service with which they could check the validity of these DEA license numbers.

Require doctor recertification. Congress should consider legislation proposed by Rep. Pete Stark, D-California, to require physicians who accept Medicare patients to be periodically recertified for competency.

Recommendations for States

Strengthen the statutes. States that have not already done so should adopt a version of the Model Medical Practice Act developed by the Federation of State Medical Boards,[41] or, preferably, stronger laws.

Restructure the boards. States should sever any remaining formal links between state licensing boards and state medical societies. Members of medical boards (and separate disciplinary boards, where present) should be appointed by the governor, and the governor's choice of appointees should not be limited to a medical society's nominees. At least 50% of the members of each state medical board and disciplinary board should be well-informed and well-trained public members who have no ties to health care providers. The governor should appoint members to the Medical Board whose top priority is protecting the public's health, not providing assistance to physicians who are trying to evade disciplinary actions.

Inform the public. Each state's Open Records Law and its Medical Practice Act should state that all formal disciplinary actions against licensed professionals are fully public records. Each legislature should require widespread dissemination of final disciplinary orders. Lists of those disciplined and full disciplinary orders should be promptly available by mail to all requesting them.

Notices of disciplinary actions should be sent to the local news media and to all hospitals, health maintenance organizations (HMOs), and other health care providers in the state, as well as to other state agencies, the federal Department of Health and Human Services, and the federal Drug Enforcement Administration. Federal law already requires that such information be reported to the National Practitioner Data Bank, which began operating on September 1, 1990.

Strengthen board authority. Every medical board should have the authority to impose emergency suspensions pending formal hearing in cases where a doctor poses a potential danger to the public health. Boards should aggressively use this authority when they learn of a potentially dangerous doctor.

Medical boards should have the authority to rapidly, after confirmation, accept the findings of other state boards and of the federal Department of Health and Human Services and the Drug Enforcement Administration. If a physician has been disciplined by another state, any subsequent state's medical board should be required to impose sanctions at least as stringent as those imposed by the first state. Each state should require physicians who have been licensed in other states and who seek licensure in a new state to submit affidavits that they are not under investigation elsewhere before being granted a new license. Physicians who are under investigation should not be permitted to practice until the board has heard the details of their case and can evaluate their competency. Each legislature should grant its state medical licensing board the authority to examine physicians for physical, mental and professional competence and to test them for alcohol and drug use upon reason to believe that a problem exists in one of these areas.

Encourage complaints. Each legislature should provide for the protection of confidentiality and immunity to those who report violations of the Medical Practice Act to a board. Such protections should also be extended to board members, their staff, and consultants.

Each legislature should require all licensed health care practitioners to report Medical Practice Act violations by other practitioners to the medical board, with large civil penalties for failure to do so. Boards should aggressively use their authority to enforce the requirement that all health care providers report such violations. Each legislature should also require hospitals to report all revocations, restrictions, or voluntary surrenders of privileges.

Courts should be required to report all indictments and convictions of physicians to the medical disciplinary board. In addition, each legislature should require liability insurers to report all claims, payments, and policy cancellations to state medical disciplinary boards. It should request reports from other state agencies, Medicare, the DEA and other federal agencies. It should also require impaired physicians' programs to report the names of doctors who fail to successfully complete their programs. Medical boards should conduct random audits of institutions to check compliance with these reporting requirements, and should fine those who fail to comply. After a doctor is disciplined, a board should fine any other practitioners who knew of that doctor's offense, but failed to report it.

Keep the courts in check. Each legislature should pass laws that make clear their intent that the judgements of the medical board be given extreme deference, and that, barring extraordinary circumstances, disciplinary actions should take immediate effect pending appeal.

Each legislature should adopt the 'preponderance of the evidence' standard of proof in medical disciplinary cases, replacing the tougher-to-meet 'clear and convincing evidence' standard now in effect in most states. According to the August 1990 report on state medical boards issued by the Office of the Inspector General, "The 'clear and convincing evidence' standard of proof is more rigorous than the 'preponderance of evidence' standard that is typically required to justify tort damages for negligence in civil cases. The more rigorous standard provides greater protection for physicians, but adds complexity to the investigative process and appears to make it less likely that a board will persevere on a case through a full evidentiary hearing."[42]

Furthermore, the Project Work Panel of the Federation of State Medical Boards, in its

August 1989 report "Elements of a Modern State Medical Board: A Proposal," recommended that each state medical board "use preponderance of evidence as the standard of proof" and that they each have the power "to issue final decisions when acting as trier of fact in the performance of [their] adjudicatory duties."[43]

Beef up funding and staffing. Each legislature should permit the medical board to spend all the revenue from medical licensing fees, rather than being forced to give part to the state Treasury. The medical boards should raise their fees to $500 a year. All boards could benefit from hiring new investigators and legal staff. Boards should employ adequate staff to process and investigate all complaints within 30 days, to review all malpractice claims filed with the board, to monitor and regularly visit doctors who have been disciplined to ensure their compliance with the sanctions imposed, and to ensure compliance with reporting requirements. They should hire investigators to seek out errant doctors, through review of pharmacy records, consultation with medical examiners, and targeted office audits of those doctors practicing alone and suspected of poor care.

Require risk prevention. States should adopt a law, similar to one in Massachusetts, that requires all hospitals and other health care providers to have a meaningful, functioning risk prevention program designed to prevent injury to patients. Massachusetts also requires all adverse incidents occurring in hospitals or in doctors' offices to be reported to the medical board.

Require periodic recertification of doctors based on a written exam and audit of their patients' medical care records.

Appendix I
Glossary

Controlled substances, controlled dangerous substances: drugs which are regulated under the federal Controlled Substances Act because of their potential for addiction or abuse.

D.O.: the academic degree awarded to osteopathic physicians.

DEA: the federal Drug Enforcement Administration, an agency of the U.S. Justice Department. Its mission is to enforce controlled substances laws.

DEA license, DEA registration, or DEA certificate: every person who handles or prescribes controlled substances, including physicians and dentists, must legally have a registration number issued by the Drug Enforcement Administration.

Disciplinary action: any of a number of ways a regulatory agency can limit or forbid a doctor's practice or formally indicate its displeasure. Includes license revocations, suspensions, and probations, consent agreements placing conditions on a doctor's continuing practice, monetary fines, and letters of reprimand.

Disciplinary action rate: total state disciplinary actions per 1,000 M.D.s practicing in a state.

Emergency suspension: a disciplinary action in which a medical board may remove a doctor from practice temporarily, without a formal disciplinary hearing, if it finds the doctor's continued practice could endanger the public health. Generally, boards are required to then hold a formal hearing on the case within a specified time period.

Impaired physicians program: a program to rehabilitate physicians suffering from an illness. Impaired physicians programs generally serve alcohol and drug abusers, but they have also been used to aid the mentally or physically ill, as well as habitual sex offenders.

Liability insurer: a company that insures doctors against malpractice lawsuits.

M.D.: the academic degree awarded to U.S. medical doctors, or allopathic physicians.

Medical Board: used generically, any state regulatory agency that licenses and/or disciplines M.D.s. Medical boards may also license other practitioners and health care paraprofessionals.

Osteopath: a physician who graduated from a school of osteopathic medicine. Osteopaths have training in skeletal manipulation in addition to their medical training.

Peer Review Committee: a hospital committee that reviews the quality of care in the institution. The committee may admit physicians to the hospital staff or revoke or limit their privileges.

Peer Review Organization: a state-based group under contract to the federal Medicare program to audit the necessity and quality of Medicare patients' care.

Probation: a disciplinary action or agreement wherein a doctor must abide by certain conditions for a definite or indefinite period of time, or face a more severe penalty. Probationary conditions are generally tailored to the individual.

Reinstatement: issuance of a new medical license to a doctor who previously surrendered his or her license or had it revoked.

Reprimand: a formal letter to a doctor criticizing a particular episode of misconduct or poor care. Sometimes called an admonition or letter of censure.

Restriction: a disciplinary action which limits the type of medicine a doctor may practice. For instance, a doctor's license may be restricted to prevent him or her from practicing surgery, or to limit practice to a certain clinic.

Revocation: the cancellation of a doctor's state or DEA license. State laws regarding revocations vary. In some states, revocations are permanent; in others, doctors may reapply for a new license immediately; in others, doctors must wait for a certain time period before reapplying.

Sanction: a formal disciplinary action.

Schedule I: controlled substances such as marijuana and heroin, which are usually held to have no approved medical purpose.

Schedule II: controlled substances with approved medical uses, but with high potential for addiction or abuse. This category includes raw opium, codeine, amphetamines, and some barbiturates.

Schedule III: controlled substances whose use may lead to low-moderate physical dependence or high psychological dependence and are therefore considered to have some potential for abuse. This category includes many barbiturates and other depressant drugs, and narcotics which include moderate amounts of codeine.

Schedule IV: controlled substances whose use may lead to limited physical and psychological dependence. This category includes Valium, Xanax, and other benzodiazepine tranquilizers, sleeping pills such as Halcion and anorectic stimulants, which are frequently used for weight loss.

Schedule V: controlled substances whose abuse potential is low. This category includes many non-prescription narcotic antidiarrheal drugs and cough suppressants.

Scheduled drugs: see Controlled Substances.

Serious disciplinary actions: Public Citizen's term for revocations, suspensions, surrenders, and probations, as they are reported by the Federation of State Medical Boards.

Serious disciplinary action rate: the number of revocations, suspensions, surrenders and probations per 1,000 M.D.s practicing in a state.

Summary suspension: see emergency suspension.

Surrender: a voluntary agreement by a doctor to give up his or her license to practice. Some surrender agreements permit a doctor to reapply for a new license; others are permanent.

State medical society: a local trade association of physicians. It serves no governmental function.

Stay: a stayed disciplinary action is like a suspended sentence: it does not take effect unless the doctor who has been disciplined disobeys the board or commits some further offense.

Suspension: the temporary removal of a doctor from practice. Some suspensions run for a definite period of time; others are indefinite, and a doctor must apply for the suspension to be lifted.

Triplicate prescription program: a program, now in effect in nine states, that requires copies of prescriptions for certain scheduled drugs to be sent to the state regulatory authority. Intended to prevent drug dealing and overprescribing of drugs that can easily be abused.

Appendix 2
How We Compiled This Report

Sources of Information

In the fall of 1989, using a list published by the Federation of State Medical Boards, Public Citizen contacted all the medical boards from the 50 states and the District of Columbia and requested the name of every physician the boards had disciplined since the beginning of 1985. We also asked at that time to be placed on the boards' mailing lists to receive notification of future disciplinary orders. Since that initial request, Public Citizen has periodically contacted these boards to obtain additional information on disciplinary actions. Most recently, we sent a letter to each state in October 1997 requesting updated information for this edition of *Questionable Doctors*.

For the first time, this edition reflects disciplinary actions taken against doctors from all 50 states, the District of Columbia, the U.S. Department of Health and Human Services, the Drug Enforcement Administration, and the Food and Drug Administration. South Dakota, the previous sole holdout, finally relented after Public Citizen sent a personal representative to retrieve the requested materials. The extent of information each medical board provides regarding disciplinary actions varies by state; some boards enclose a detailed synopsis of the case history and findings, whereas others simply supply the physician's name and resulting action within a quarterly newsletter. A description of the information we received from each state is included in the "State by State Listing" section of this report

The time period reflected in this edition of *Questionable Doctors* spans from 1987 through 1996. Public Citizen made every effort to include information from every state for each of these years, but due to either periodic board inactivity or inoperation, data was not always available. The cutoff date for receipt of disciplinary materials in this report was January 31, 1997. Although the earliest editions of *Questionable Doctors* included disciplinary actions against dentists, chiropractors, and podiatrists if the state Board provided that information, because we did not consistently receive information on such health care providers from all medical boards, we decided to eliminate these entries on such professionals from our database.

Public Citizen obtained from the Inspector General's office of the U.S. Department of

Health and Human Services a list of all health care providers excluded from the Medicare program for disciplinary purposes through December 1996. The list is called the Medicare/Medicaid Sanction--Reinstatement Report. It includes the doctor's name, degree and/or specialty, address, date of the sanction notice, period of exclusion from the program, and section of the Social Security Act violated. We included all physicians (both M.D.s and D.O.s) listed in these reports in our database. Previously, from January 1987 through October 1990, the Inspector General's office also provided Public Citizen with copies of the notices of all sanctions, both fines and exclusions, imposed by the Department of Health and Human Services as a result of recommendations from Medicare Peer Review Organizations (PROs), which may sanction doctors for substandard or unnecessary care. The sanction notices included the physician's name, address, the PRO that recommended disciplinary action, the number of cases of substandard or unnecessary care for which the doctor was cited, sometimes the Department's findings about that care, the type of disciplinary action being taken, the length of an exclusion or the amount of a fine, and any information on appeals then available.

Public Citizen obtained from the *Federal Register* notices about doctors whose Drug Enforcement Administration registrations to prescribe controlled substances were revoked, restricted or denied following contested cases dated from 1988 through December 1996. The *Federal Register* notices include the doctor's name, address, and DEA certificate number, a description of the conduct that led to the agency's action, the type of action taken, and the effective date. *16,638 Questionable Doctors* also includes most of the physicians who did not contest the DEA's decision and agreed to surrender or restrict their prescribing privileges.

From the Food and Drug Administration, Public Citizen obtained information on physicians who were sanctioned because they had violated FDA laws, regulations, or policies regarding clinical research on patients. These physicians are ineligible to receive investigational products for research purposes. Our database includes actions taken through December 1996.

Generating the Database

From the information received from the states, the Drug Enforcement Administration, the Food and Drug Administration, and the Department of Health and Human Services, we created database entries on individual practitioners. Each entry included (when available) the doctor's full name, degree, license number, date of birth, and location (street address, city and state), the disciplinary state or agency, and the date of the disciplinary action. When it was unclear whether a physician was an M.D. or D.O., we listed the physician's degree as "DR".

We included up to two types of disciplinary actions taken on a given action date, and one violation or offense that served as the basis for that action (see below). Any additional actions were described in the "Notes" heading of items on individual doctors. Details and information on appeals, when available, are also included in this section. Information regarding appeals was not generally available, and hence it is possible that some doctors have had their sanctions stayed or overturned on appeal. Public Citizen made a special effort to obtain information on court actions/decisions that overrule or change previous disciplinary actions taken by state boards. In October of 1997, we sent a letter to all boards requesting this information. Not all boards were able to fulfill this request, but of the information received, any actions that were overturned by the courts on appeal or for which litigation in the matter had ended in the physician's favor were deleted from the database.

Each disciplinary action was classified into one of 25 categories. For each disciplinary order, we chose what we viewed as the two most "severe" actions. These were included under the heading "Disciplinary Action:" on the individual doctor listings.

Following is a listing of our categories of disciplinary actions, in order of "severity."

- license revocation
- surrender of license
- nonrenewal of license
- revocation of license to prescribe controlled substances
- surrender of license to prescribe controlled substances
- nonrenewal of license to prescribe controlled substances
- denial of new license
- denial of license reinstatement (following surrender or revocation)
- license reinstatement (following surrender or revocation)
- license suspension
- suspension of authority to prescribe controlled substances
- emergency suspension (pending a formal disciplinary hearing)
- probation
- controlled substance license placed on probation
- fine
- restriction placed on license to practice
- restriction placed on license to prescribe controlled substances

- public reprimand
- required to take additional medical education
- required to enter an impaired physician program or drug or alcohol treatment
- cease and desist order
- monitoring of physician performance
- community service

Medicare program sanctions and actions taken against physicians by the Food and Drug Administration were classified in the following two categories respectively:

- exclusion from the Medicare program
- investigator ineligible to receive investigational new drugs for experimental purposes

We placed any further details about disciplinary actions under the heading "Notes." Any disciplinary actions that do not fall into the above categories are detailed in the notes sections and classified as "Other Actions" in our charts and statistical summaries.

When a state provided information on the legal violation or offense that led them to discipline a doctor, we classified that violation into one of 18 categories. If several violations were listed by the Board, we chose the one that appeared to contribute the most to the disciplinary decision. If that choice was unclear, we selected the offense that ranked highest on our hierarchy of offenses as listed below. We included the violation under the heading "Offense" in the listings of individual doctors.

Following are the lists of our categories of offenses, and definitions as needed, in order of presumed importance:

- disciplinary action by another state or agency
- criminal conviction or plea of guilty, nolo contendere, or no contest to a crime
- practicing without a valid license
- practicing without a valid controlled substance license
- loss or restriction of hospital privileges
- failure to comply with a previous board order
- providing false information to the medical board
- substandard care, incompetence or negligence
- sexual abuse of or sexual misconduct with a patient
- substance abuse
- overprescribing or misprescribing drugs

- physical or mental illness inhibiting the ability to practice with skill and safety
- insurance, Medicare or Medicaid fraud
- falsifying or altering patient records or medical reports
- overcharging
- exceeding professional limitations
- professional misconduct (see below)
- failure to comply with a professional rule (see below)

The category "professional misconduct" includes a variety of offenses that are more serious than the violation of a professional rule but do not fit into any of the other categories listed above. Some examples of offenses classified as professional misconduct are:

- "unprofessional conduct"
- a criminal offense of which the physician has not been actually convicted
- ordering or performing unnecessary or inappropriate procedures for a patient deliberately, rather than because of incompetence
- failing to supervise a physician's assistant, or other non-medical personnel
- permitting an unlicensed person to practice medicine
- tax violations
- intimidating a patient in an attempt to convince them not to seek a second opinion
- terminating a patient's medical care without transferring the patient to another's care
- abandonment of a patient
- making fraudulent representations in medical practice
- assuring a cure for an incurable disease
- offering to treat by a "secret method"
- accepting payments from laboratories for sending them patients' tests
- procuring a criminal abortion
- performing medical services that the board has declared to be of no value (frequently chelation therapy)
- soliciting patients in a deceitful manner
- disruption of residency program
- improperly transferring a patient from a treatment center to a hospital
- engaging in lewd conduct
- clearly excessive use of diagnostic procedures

- unlawful possession of a controlled substance outside the practice of medicine
- fraud in medical research
- operating an illegal drug lab
- unspecified perjury
- diversion of drugs (not specifically prescription drugs) or drug use
- presigning blank prescription pads so that an unlicensed person may practice medicine
- breaching physician-patient confidentiality
- charging for services as supervising physician even though not present during the course of treatment
- selling drugs and devices for financial gain
- sending out letters to request payment using an attorney's name without the attorney's knowledge or consent
- use of disposable syringes on multiple patients
- rendering a psychiatric evaluation without properly examining and treating the subject of said evaluation
- sexual abuse of a person other than a patient, or of an unspecified person
- not getting a consent form signed
- failing to provide information on license applications, renewals, etc., rather than actually giving false information
- unspecified malpractice settlement
- patient abuse

Examples of the types of violations included in the category "Failure to comply with a professional rule" are:

- violation of restrictions on advertising
- failure to respond to the board
- failure to maintain sanitary practice conditions
- violation of medical records laws (except for falsifying records) including failure to provide copies of records when requested or excessive charges for providing records
- requiring patients to purchase drugs or devices from physician
- failure to keep required documents on file
- employing an agent to solicit patients
- making excessive claims of expertise

- violating AMA ethics standards
- failure to report a disciplinary action in another state
- failure to report child abuse
- failure to pay fees
- failure to display a valid license
- endorsing a product
- keeping outdated or misbranded drugs
- failure to keep proper controlled substance records
- failure to report other medical personnel who are violating the Medical Practice Act to the medical board
- fee-splitting
- failure to report a suspicious death to the police
- failure to meet continuing medical education requirements
- allowing someone not in the doctor's employ and not under direct supervision to demonstrate a medical device to patients
- two-tiered billing
- failure to have liability insurance
- practicing under a name other than the one on his or her physician's license
- violating patient dumping regulations
- nonpayment of student loan

Counting Physicians and Actions

Counting physicians: It is impossible for us to know exactly how many physicians are in our database. There are two main reasons for this:

Many states are not consistent in how they list the names of physicians who have been disciplined, i.e. they may have reported only a first and last name in one newsletter, but included a middle initial and suffix (such as Jr. or Sr.) in another. We made numerous phone calls to try and resolve questions about multiple actions taken against what appeared to be a single physician by a single state and in some cases made calls regarding multiple actions taken against what appeared to be the same person by different states. These attempts were not always successful.

Many states do not include license numbers or birth dates in their listings of disciplined doctors, which can quickly clarify situations in which names appear similar but are not exactly alike.

After entering the corrected information obtained through phone calls, we counted all the physicians in the database. This is done by using a computer program that compared physician identifying information. The program used six database fields to "match" entries: last name, first name, middle name, the suffix (Jr., Sr., etc.), license number, and birth date. It compared two entries with the same first and last name and "matched" them if one or more of the following was true:

- they had the same birth date;
- they were sanctioned by the same state and had the same license number;
- a middle name in one matched the middle name in the other;
- a middle name in one matched the middle initial in the other;
- a suffix in one matched the suffix in the other; or,
- first and last names matched; no other information was given to indicate a non-match.

Entries within the same state with the same first and last name were not matched if they had differing birth dates or license numbers. When one record included a middle name and the other did not, the records were not considered a match unless the birth dates or license numbers matched. The same is true if one record had a suffix (Jr., Sr., etc.) and another did not.

Counting actions: Although each sanction may consist of several disciplinary actions, we entered only the two most serious disciplinary actions in each case. Both of these disciplinary actions were included when generating counts of actions taken by the state boards or federal agencies. Because we calculated only the two most serious actions, the counts of the less serious actions (such as fines, restrictions, education, and monitoring) will not reveal the frequency with which these less serious actions were imposed. Rather, they will only demonstrate how often these actions were among the two most serious actions levied.

Generation of the State-by-State Lists

In the "Disciplinary Actions" sections of each state listing, we attempted to include all doctors who had any connection with the state. For example, the New York "Disciplinary Actions" section includes:

- All disciplinary actions taken by the New York State Board of Regents;
- All disciplinary actions by other states, the Drug Enforcement Administration, the Food

and Drug Administration or Medicare/Medicaid against doctors for whom a New York state address is given;

- All other disciplinary actions against doctors with names like those included above, i.e., actions taken by another state or agency that the computer program described above "matched" to doctors disciplined by New York or located in New York.

Any time a doctor's license number is listed in an action, it is the license number of the state that is sanctioning the doctor.

> Some state listings may include doctors with similar names who are not, in fact, the same doctor.

When we were informed by state medical boards or other sources that a physician listed in the book had died, we deleted all records for the deceased doctor from the database. Using the matching program we ensured that all records that matched to the physician's identifying information were also deleted.

> Although we have made every effort to match physicians' names correctly, some materials we received did not include complete information on middle names, license numbers, or birth dates. Therefore, consumers should remember that non-disciplined physicians and physicians with different disciplinary actions may have similar names to those physicians listed in the state listing of disciplinary actions. Consumers should also remember that if they want the most current information on the status of a physician's license, they should contact the medical board of the state in which the physician practices or has practiced in the past.

Appeals, Reinstatements

While we attempted to acquire as much up-to-date information as possible on doctors whose disciplinary actions have been appealed to and/or overturned by the courts, we do not have information on all appellate actions. Therefore, we cannot guarantee that a doctor listed here as being disciplined has not had that action overturned or stayed by a court. We entered into our database all disciplinary actions we received by January 31, 1997 and all reinstatements to an unrestricted license and court appeals we received by December 15, 1997. Again, the medical board should be contacted for more detailed and up-to-date information.

> Some states did not supply us with information on license reinstatements or the lifting of license restrictions. We cannot guarantee that a physician listed as being suspended or restricted has not had that suspension or restriction lifted, or that a physician whose license was revoked has not obtained a new license.

Charts, Tables, Statistics

This report uses data on disciplinary actions from two general sources: Public Citizen's analysis of information on disciplinary actions provided by each state; and, the 1996 statistical summaries of state serious disciplinary actions released by the Federation of State Medical Boards. This latter source is only used to generate Tables A and B (pgs.14 and 16) in the national and regional reports.

These two data sources are not always comparable. States may not have published or sent Public Citizen all the disciplinary actions they counted in their statistical summaries or reported to the Federation of State Medical Boards. Furthermore, our categorization of disciplinary actions may differ from the Federation's.

In our rankings of the numbers of serious state disciplinary actions, we use the Federation statistics because they are the only statistics that are relatively uniform from state to state. However, the Federation is dependent on the states to supply it with disciplinary information, and the types of actions reported may be different from state to state. This may lead to inconsistencies in the rankings. In this report we have ranked states based on the total number of serious disciplinary actions reported to the Federation in 1996 (see Table A, pg. 14) and, in Table B, pg. 16, show the rankings of states for the past six years as far as the rate of serious disciplinary actions per 1,000 physicians.

For the tables summarizing the disciplinary actions taken by a state over a period of several years, we used our own method of counting only those actions in our database. Therefore, the numbers in these tables may look different from the numbers the Federation has released.

Appendix 3
Addresses of Federal Agencies

Drug Enforcement Administration (DEA)
Drug Enforcement Administration
U.S. Department of Justice
1405 I Street, NW
Washington, D.C. 20005

U.S. Department of Health and Human Services
Use these addresses and phone numbers for information on the Medicare/Medicaid sanctions program:

June Gibbs Brown
Inspector General
Department of Health and Human Services
330 Independence Ave. SW
Room 5250 Cohen Bldg.
Washington, DC 20201
(202) 619-3148

Judy Holtz
Public Affairs Office
Office of Inspector General
Department of Health and Human Services
330 Independence Ave. SW
Room 5551 Cohen Building
Washington DC 20201
(202) 619-1343

To get a current list of those sanctioned, contact:

William M. Libercci
Deputy Director
Health Care Administrative Sanctions
Office of Investigations
Office of Inspector General
Department of Health and Human Services
Room 1-D-13 Oak Meadows Building
6325 Security Boulevard
Baltimore MD 21207
(410) 786-9603

Use these numbers and addresses to file complaints about health care providers with the Medicare sanctions program:

Nationwide, 24-hour complaints hotline
Toll free 1-800-447-8477

Region I - Boston
(Connecticut, Maine, Massachusetts, New Hampshire, Rhode Island, Vermont,)
Regional Inspector General
Room 2425, JFK Federal Bldg.
Boston, MA 02203
(617) 565-2689

Region II - New York
(New York, New Jersey, Puerto Rico, Virgin Islands)
Regional Inspector General
Room 3900B, Federal Bldg.
26 Federal Plaza
New York, NY 10278
(212) 264-1691

Region III - Philadelphia
(Pennsylvania, Delaware, Maryland, Virginia, West Virginia, District of Columbia)
Regional Inspector General
P.O. Box 13716
Mailstop #9
Philadelphia, PA 19101
(215) 596-6743

Region IV - Atlanta
(Alabama, Florida, Georgia, Kentucky, Mississippi, North Carolina, South Carolina, Tennessee)
Regional Inspector General
Atlanta Federal Center
61 Forsyth Street, SW
Suite ST18
Atlanta, GA 30303-8909
(404) 562-7603

Region V - Chicago
(Illinois, Indiana, Michigan, Minnesota, Ohio, Wisconsin)
Regional Inspector General
23rd Floor 105 West Adams
Chicago, IL 60603
(312) 353-2740

Region VI - Dallas
(Arkansas, Louisiana, Montana, New Mexico, Oklahoma, Texas)
Regional Inspector General
Room 4E9, Federal Bldg.
1100 Commerce Street
Dallas, TX 75242
(214) 767-8406

Region VII - Kansas City
(Kansas, Nebraska, Missouri, Iowa)
Regional Inspector General
Room 284B Federal Bldg.
601 E. 12th Street
Kansas City, MO 64106
(816) 426-5959

Region VIII - Denver
(Colorado, Montana, North Dakota, South Dakota, Utah, Wyoming)
Division of Health Standards and Quality
Federal Building 1961 Stout Street
Denver, CO 80294
(303) 844-2121

Region IX - San Francisco
(Arizona, California, Hawaii, Nevada, Guam, American Samoa)
Regional Inspector General
DHHS, OIG, OI
Room 174, Federal Office Bldg.
50 United Nations Plaza
San Francisco, CA 94102
(415) 437-7961

Region X - Seattle
Regional Inspector General
(Alaska, Washington, Oregon, Idaho)
2201 Sixth Avenue, MS/RX-40
Seattle, WA 98121-2500
(206) 615-2306

References

1. Public Citizen's Health Research Group. A Consumer's Directory of Prince George's County Doctors 1974.

2. Public Health Service, Department of Health and Human Services. National Practitioner Data Bank for Adverse Information on Physicians and Other Health Care Providers. 45 CFR Part 60, *Federal Register*, October 17, 1989.

3. The Health Care Quality Improvement Act of 1986. *New Jersey Medicine* June 1987;84 (6): 401-403.

4. Iglehart John K. Congress Moves to Bolster Peer Review: The Health Care Quality Improvement Act of 1986. *New England Journal of Medicine* 1987;316 (15):960-964.

5. Office of Technology Assessment. The Quality of Medical Care: Information for Consumers. OTA-H-386. Washington, DC: U.S. Government Printing Office June 1988.

6. Federation of State Medical Boards. Exchange. Section 3: Physician Licensing Boards and Physician Discipline 1989/1990 edition.

Federation of State Medical Boards. Exchange. Section 3: Physician Licensing Boards and Physician Discipline 1988 edition.

7. Title II of the Social Security Act in Compilation of Social Security Laws including Social Security Act as amended and related enactments through January 1, 1989, Vol. 1, U.S. Government Printing Office 1989.

8. Health Resources and Services Administration. National Practitioner Data Bank Statistical Summary, As of Month Ending December 31, 1997.

9. Office of the Inspector General, Department of Health and Human Services. Hospital Reporting to the National Practitioner Data Bank. OEI-01-94-00050 February 1995.

10. Quality-of-Care Data Bank for Patients Coming Soon. *Internal Medicine News* April 15-30, 1989; 22 (8):9.

11. *Dent v. West Virginia*, 127 U.S. 114 (1889); see also *Klafter v. State Board of Examiners of Architects*, 259 Ill. 15, 102 N.E. 193 (1913); *In re Polk License Revocation*, 90 N.J. 550, 449 A.2nd 7 (1982).

12. Office of Evaluation and Inspections, Office of the Inspector General, U.S. Department of Health and Human Services. State Medical Boards and Medical Discipline, draft report April 1990.

13. McAuley R.G. Letter to the Editor, *New England Journal of Medicine* August 8, 1985.

14. Kusserow Richard, Inspector General, U.S. Department of Health and Human Services. Testimony before the U.S. House of Representatives Committee on Small Business, Subcommittee on Regulation, Business Opportunities and Energy June 8, 1990.

15. Federation of State Medical Boards. 1996 Summary of Board Actions Reported by State Licensing and Disciplinary Boards March 1997.

16. Harvard Medical Practice Study Group. Patients, Doctors and Lawyers: Medical Injury, Malpractice Litigation and Patient Compensation in New York 1990.

17. Mills, D.H. ed. California Medical Association and California Hospital Association Report on the Medical Insurance Feasibility Study. San Francisco: Sutter Publications 1977.

18. *Journal of Legal Medicine* February 1976.

19. Ely John W, Levinson Wendy, Elder Nancy C, Mainous Arch G III, Vinson Daniel C. Perceived Causes of Family Physicians' Errors. *The Journal of Family Practice* 1995;40(4):337-344.

20. Bissonette Raymond, O'Shea Robert M, Horwitz Mary, Route Cynde F. A Data-Generated Basis for Medical Ethics Education: Categorizing Issues Experienced by Students During Clinical Training. *Academic Medicine* 1995;70(11):1035-1037.

21. Feinstein Alvan R. System, Supervision, Standards, and the 'Epidemic' of Negligent Medical Errors. *Archives of Internal Medicine* 1997;157:1285-1289.

22. Pichert James W, Hickson Gerald B, Bledsoe Sandy, Trotter Tinsla, Quinn Doris. Understanding the Etiology of Serious Medical Events Involving Children: Implications for Pediatricians and Their Risk Managers. *Pediatric Annal* 1997;26(3):160-172.

23. Butters Janice M, Strope John L. Legal Standards of Conduct for Students and Residents: Implications for Health Profession Educators. *Academic Medicine* 1996;1(6):583-590.

24. Schwartz William B, Mendelson Daniel N. The Role of Physician-Owned Insurance Companies in the Detection and Deterrence of Negligence. *Journal of the American Medical Association* 1989;260(10):1342-1346.

25. McNamara Robert M, Margulies Jeffrey L. Chemical Dependency in Emergency Medicine Residency Programs: Perspective of the Program Directors. *Annals of Emergency Medicine* 1994;23(5):1072-1076.

26. Hyde Gordon L, Wolfe James. Alcohol and Drug Use by Surgery Residents. *Journal of the American College of Surgeons* 1995;181(1):1-5.

27. McNamara, op. cit.

28. Hyde, op. cit.

29. Hughes Patrick H, Brandenburg Nancy, Baldwin DeWitt C Jr, Storr Carla L, Williams Kristine M, Anthony James C, Sheehan David V. Prevalence of Substance Use Among US Physicians. *Journal of the American Medical Association* 1992;267(17):2333-2339.

30. Smith DE, Seymour R. A Clinical Approach to the Impaired Health Professional. *The International Journal of the Addictions* 1985;20(5):713-722, as cited in Centrella Michael. Physician Addiction and Impairment--Current Thinking: A Review. *Journal of Addictive Diseases* 1994;13:91-105.

31. Hughes, op. cit.

32. Gartrell N, Herman J, Olarte S, Feldsteing M, Localio R. Prevalence of Psychiatrist-Patient Sexual Contact. Sexual Exploitation in Professional Relationships. Washington, DC: American Psychiatric Press 1989:3-13, as cited in Garfinkel Paul E, Bagby RM, Waring EM, and Dorian Barbara. Boundary Violations and Personality Traits among Psychiatrists. *Canadian Journal of Psychiatry* 1997;42:758-763.

33. Kardener SH, Fuller M, Mensh IN. A Survey of Physician's Attitudes and Practices Regarding Erotic and Nonerotic Contact with Patients. *American Journal of Psychiatry* 1973;139:1077-81, as cited in Garfinkel, op. cit.

34. Garfinkel, op. cit.

35. Enbom John A, Thomas Claire D. Evaluation of Sexual Misconduct Complaints: The Oregon Board of Medical Examiners, 1991 to 1995. *American Journal of Obstetrics and Gynecology* 1997;176(6):1340-1348.

36. Harvard Medical Practice Study Group, op. cit.

37. American Association of Retired Persons. Effective Physician Oversight: Prescription for Medical Licensing Board Reform 1987.

38. Lohr Kathleen N, Schroeder Steven A, Institute of Medicine. A Strategy for Quality Assurance in Medicare. *New England Journal of Medicine* 1990;322(10):707-712.

39. Federation Receives Federal Contract to Develop Self-Assessment Instrument for State Medical Boards. *FSMB Newsletter* September 1990;36.

40. Lohr, op. cit.

41. Federation of State Medical Boards. Elements of a Modern State Medical Board: A Proposal August 1989.

42. Office of Evaluation and Inspections, Office of the Inspector General, U.S. Department of Health and Human Services. State Medical Boards and Medical Discipline August 1990:9.

43. Federation of State Medical Boards August 1989, op. cit.

ALASKA
1996 serious action rate: 7.33/1000
1996 ranking: 6th

The Alaska State Medical Board sent disciplinary reports covering actions taken from January 1987 through October 1996. Only for January 1991 through October 1992 did they send us the same forms as are sent to the Federation of State Medical Boards for reporting purposes. These include the physician's name, degree, license number, date of birth, address, date and type of action taken and the reason for the action. These reports include the physician's name, degree, the date and type of action taken, and the reason for the action. The reports also contain information on modifications and terminations of board actions but not on court decisions affecting board actions.

The information provided covers disciplinary actions taken against allopathic physicians (MDs) and osteopathic physicians (DOs).

Besides disciplinary actions taken by the State Medical Board, this listing also includes actions taken by the Medicare/Medicaid programs, the FDA, and the DEA against physicians located in this state. Disciplinary actions taken by other states against physicians located in Alaska or that match a physician disciplined by Alaska (see Appendix 2 for an explanation of the matching protocol) are also included.

> Although we have made every effort to match physicians' names correctly, some materials we received did not include complete information on middle names, license numbers, birth dates or addresses. Therefore, consumers should remember that non-disciplined physicians and physicians with different disciplinary actions may have similar names to those disciplined physicians listed in this state. Consumers should also remember that if they want the most current information on the status on a physician's license, they should contact the medical board of the state in which the physician practices or had practiced.

According to the Federation of State Medical Boards, Alaska took 7 serious disciplinary actions against MDs and DOs in 1996. Compared to the 955 MDs practicing in the state,

Alaska had a serious disciplinary action rate of 7.33 actions per 1,000 MDs, ranking 6th on that list (see Table A, Findings, pg. 14).

The tables below summarize the data Public Citizen received from Alaska.

Table 1.	Disciplinary Actions Against MDs and DOs January 1987 through October 1996*	
Action	**Number**	**Percent****
Revocation	2	2.0%
Surrender	5	5.0%
Suspension	4	4.0%
Probation	24	23.8%
Practice Restriction	15	14.9%
Action Taken Against Controlled Substance License	2	2.0%
Other Actions	49	48.5%
Total Actions	**101**	**100.0%**

* This table lists only the two most serious disciplinary actions taken against a physician.
** Percentages may not total 100% due to rounding.

Table 2.	Offenses for which MDs and DOs were Disciplined January 1987 through October 1996*	
Offense	**Number**	**Percent**
Criminal Conviction	1	1.8%
Sexual Abuse of or Sexual Misconduct with a Patient	2	3.6%
Substandard Care, Incompetence or Negligence	1	1.8%
Misprescribing or Overprescribing Drugs	5	9.1%
Substance Abuse	18	32.7%
Disciplinary Action Taken Against License by Another State or Agency	9	16.4%
Other Offenses	19	34.5%
Total Records With Offense Listed	**55**	**100.0%**

* Includes only those actions for which an offense was listed and for which we had a corresponding term in our database.

Table 3. Disciplinary Actions Taken for Substance Abuse		
Action	**Number**	**Percent**
Surrender	1	3.2%
Revocation, Surrender, or Suspension of Controlled Substance License	1	3.2%
Probation	12	38.7%
Required to Enter an Impaired Physician Program or Drug or Alcohol Treatment	4	12.9%
Other Actions	13	41.9%
Total Actions	**31**	**100.0%**

If you feel that your doctor has not given you proper medical care or has mistreated you in any way--whether or not he or she is listed in this report--it is important that you let your state medical board know. Even if they do not immediately act on your complaint, it is important that the information be recorded in their files because it is possible that other people may have filed or will file complaints about the same doctor. Send a brief written description of what occurred to the addresses below or call the phone numbers listed for more information on how to file a complaint.

Address
Alaska State Medical Board
Leslie G. Abel, Executive Secretary
3601 C St., Suite 722
Anchorage, AK 99503-5986
(907) 269-8160

Listing of Doctors Sanctioned by Offense

Sexual Abuse of or Sexual Misconduct with a Patient
MCGUIRE, JAMES R
THORNQUIST, ROBERT K

Substandard Care, Incompetence, or Negligence
COON, DUANE A

Criminal Conviction or Plea of Guilty, Nolo Contendere, or No Contest to a Crime
AKE, BURTON KENNETH

Misprescribing or Overprescribing Drugs
BEHYMER, KENNETH
CAMMACK, DAVID M
GRAUMAN, DAVID S
HALTER, LOREN
MUES, JOHN

Substance Abuse
BEIRNE, MARK JOSEPH
BENWARD, ROY E
BIGELOW, LOY FORSYTHE
CASTLEBERRY, JESSE WENDELL
DAVENPORT, WAYNE
DIBALA, ANNE C
ERICKSON, VINCENT J
GRAY, SCHARAZARD L
KILLEBREW, DAVID SCOTT
KINANE, THOMAS
KIRK, JACK T
LIEBERMAN, JON F
SAVIKKO, DOUGLAS M
TARASZKA, STEVEN R
THREET, RICHARD W

Caution: This list is designed to be used only in conjunction with the rest of this book which includes additional information on each physician such as license number, date of action and more complete descriptions of the offenses.

DISCIPLINARY ACTIONS

AARON, JOHN MD WAS DISCIPLINED BY IOWA ON DECEMBER 17, 1987.
DISCIPLINARY ACTION: DENIAL OF NEW LICENSE

AARON, JOHN MD, DATE OF BIRTH MAY 11, 1954, OF 5401 SHIRE COURT, FAIR OAKS, CA, WAS DISCIPLINED BY MONTANA ON JANUARY 13, 1989.
DISCIPLINARY ACTION: DENIAL OF NEW LICENSE
OFFENSE: PROVIDING FALSE INFORMATION TO THE BOARD
NOTES: FALSIFIED APPLICATION

AARON, JOHN MD WAS DISCIPLINED BY ALASKA ON JULY 13, 1990.
DISCIPLINARY ACTION: DENIAL OF NEW LICENSE
OFFENSE: DISCIPLINARY ACTION BY ANOTHER STATE OR AGENCY
NOTES: FALSIFIED APPLICATION; DISCIPLINARY ACTION IN NEVADA.

AARON, JOHN MD WAS DISCIPLINED BY WYOMING ON JULY 5, 1991.
DISCIPLINARY ACTION: DENIAL OF NEW LICENSE

AARON, JOHN MD, LICENSE NUMBER 045839L, OF 11618 FAIR OAKS BLVD, FAIR OAKS, CA, WAS DISCIPLINED BY PENNSYLVANIA ON OCTOBER 23, 1991.
DISCIPLINARY ACTION: FINE; REPRIMAND
OFFENSE: PROVIDING FALSE INFORMATION TO THE BOARD
NOTES: ON HIS LICENSE APPLICATION FOR PENNSYLVANIA, FAILED TO PROVIDE A COMPLETE DISCLOSURE OF MEDICAL SCHOOLS HE ATTENDED; FAILED TO INDICATE HE HAD A MEDICAL LICENSE IN NEVADA AND THAT DISCIPLINARY ACTION AGAINST HIS MEDICAL LICENSE HAD BEEN TAKEN BY NEVADA; SUBMITTED A NOTARIZED COPY OF HIS STANDARD ECFMG CERTIFICATE WHICH HAD BEEN REVOKED IN 11/85; ON 7/13/90 THE ALASKA MEDICAL BOARD DENIED HIS APPLICATION FOR LICENSURE FOR NOT PROVIDING FULL DISCLOSURE OF INFORMATION ON THE APPLICATION. ISSUED UNRESTRICTED LICENSE TO PRACTICE; MUST PAY $700 CIVIL PENALTY.

AKE, BURTON KENNETH MD, DATE OF BIRTH JUNE 17, 1948, LICENSE NUMBER 0001862, OF PO BOX 660, EAGLE RIVER, AK, WAS DISCIPLINED BY ALASKA ON JANUARY 18, 1991.
DISCIPLINARY ACTION: EMERGENCY SUSPENSION
OFFENSE: PROFESSIONAL MISCONDUCT
NOTES: SEXUAL MISCONDUCT.

AKE, BURTON KENNETH MD, LICENSE NUMBER 0044771, OF 9451 SPRING HILL DRIVE, ANCHORAGE, AK, WAS DISCIPLINED BY OHIO ON FEBRUARY 14, 1992.
DISCIPLINARY ACTION: LICENSE REVOCATION
OFFENSE: CRIMINAL CONVICTION OR PLEA OF GUILTY, NOLO CONTENDERE, OR NO CONTEST TO A CRIME
NOTES: GUILTY PLEA TO TWO FELONY COUNTS OF SEXUAL ASSAULT UPON PATIENTS WHILE PRACTICING IN ALASKA. PERMANENT REVOCATION.

AKE, BURTON KENNETH MD, DATE OF BIRTH JUNE 17, 1948, LICENSE NUMBER 0001862, WAS DISCIPLINED BY ALASKA ON MARCH 26, 1993.
DISCIPLINARY ACTION: LICENSE REVOCATION
OFFENSE: CRIMINAL CONVICTION OR PLEA OF GUILTY, NOLO CONTENDERE, OR NO CONTEST TO A CRIME
NOTES: CONVICTED OF RAPE.

AKE, BURTON KENNETH MD, DATE OF BIRTH JUNE 17, 1948, OF P.O. BOX 600, EAGLE RIVER, AK, WAS DISCIPLINED BY MEDICARE ON NOVEMBER 3, 1994.
DISCIPLINARY ACTION: 180-MONTH EXCLUSION FROM THE MEDICARE AND/OR MEDICAID PROGRAMS
OFFENSE: CRIMINAL CONVICTION OR PLEA OF GUILTY, NOLO CONTENDERE, OR NO CONTEST TO A CRIME
NOTES: CONVICTED OF A CRIME RELATED TO PATIENT ABUSE OR NEGLECT.

BEGUN, JEROME H MD WAS DISCIPLINED BY MARYLAND ON MARCH 14, 1990.
DISCIPLINARY ACTION: DENIAL OF NEW LICENSE
OFFENSE: DISCIPLINARY ACTION BY ANOTHER STATE OR AGENCY
NOTES: APPLIED FOR LICENSE 7/21/88; DENIAL ON BASIS THAT APPLICANT LACKED GOOD MORAL CHARACTER; LICENSE WAS REVOKED IN CALIFORNIA ON DECEMBER 24, 1971, INDIANA ON JANUARY 30, 1980 AND OHIO ON MAY 21, 1980. IN U.S. DISTRICT COURT FOR THE NORTHERN DISTRICT OF CALIFORNIA HE WAS CONVICTED OF 7 NARCOTICS COUNTS INVOLVING THE ILLEGAL SALES OF DRUGS AND 5 COUNTS OF ILLEGAL POSSESSION OF UNREGISTERED FIREARMS ON SEPTEMBER 3, 1970; SENTENCED TO SEVEN YEARS IMPRISONMENT; ALSO CONVICTED ON SEPTEMBER 10, 1981 IN U.S. DISTRICT COURT FOR THE EASTERN DISTRICT OF CALIFORNIA FOR FRAUD IN CLAIMS WITH THE CIVILIAN HEALTH AND MEDICAL PROGRAM OF UNIFORM SERVICES; SENTENCED TO TWO YEARS IMPRISONMENT WITH ALL BUT SIX MONTHS SUSPENDED AND 5 YEARS PROBATION

BEGUN, JEROME H MD, DATE OF BIRTH FEBRUARY 1, 1926, OF PO BOX 355, CAMBRIDGE, OH, WAS DISCIPLINED BY ALASKA ON MARCH 11, 1992.
DISCIPLINARY ACTION: DENIAL OF NEW LICENSE
OFFENSE: DISCIPLINARY ACTION BY ANOTHER STATE OR AGENCY
NOTES: LICENSE DENIED BASED ON REVOCATION IN INDIANA.

BEGUN, JEROME H MD WAS DISCIPLINED BY ALASKA ON OCTOBER 8, 1992.
DISCIPLINARY ACTION: DENIAL OF NEW LICENSE

BEHYMER, KENNETH MD, DATE OF BIRTH NOVEMBER 3, 1936, OF 9500 INDEPENDENCE DR, ANCHORAGE, AK, WAS DISCIPLINED BY MEDICARE ON MAY 18, 1989.
DISCIPLINARY ACTION: 18-MONTH EXCLUSION FROM THE MEDICARE AND/OR MEDICAID PROGRAMS
OFFENSE: CRIMINAL CONVICTION OR PLEA OF GUILTY, NOLO CONTENDERE, OR NO CONTEST TO A CRIME
NOTES: CONVICTION RELATING TO CONTROLLED SUBSTANCES. NO LONGER LISTED AS EXCLUDED.

BEHYMER, KENNETH MD, LICENSE NUMBER 0000838, WAS DISCIPLINED BY ALASKA ON MAY 23, 1989.
DISCIPLINARY ACTION: 2-MONTH LICENSE SUSPENSION; 36-MONTH PROBATION
OFFENSE: OVERPRESCRIBING OR MISPRESCRIBING DRUGS
NOTES: CRIMINAL NARCOTIC/PRESCRIPTION VIOLATIONS. CONDITIONS OF PROBATION: PERMANENTLY RESTRICTED FROM PRESCRIBING SCHEDULE II AND III SUBSTANCES; PARTICIPATION IN IMPAIRED PHYSICIANS PROGRAM. LICENSED AS OF 8/19/91.

BEIRNE, MARK J MD WAS DISCIPLINED BY ALASKA ON MARCH 10, 1995.
DISCIPLINARY ACTION: SURRENDER OF LICENSE
OFFENSE: FAILURE TO COMPLY WITH A PREVIOUS BOARD ORDER
NOTES: PROBATION VIOLATIONS INVOLVING ALCOHOLIC BEVERAGES.

BEIRNE, MARK J MD OF 800 E. DIAMOND BLVD SUITE 535, ANCHORAGE, AK, WAS DISCIPLINED BY DEA ON SEPTEMBER 26, 1995.
DISCIPLINARY ACTION: SURRENDER OF CONTROLLED SUBSTANCE LICENSE
OFFENSE: DISCIPLINARY ACTION BY ANOTHER STATE OR AGENCY

- ALASKA -

NOTES: STATE BOARD.

BEIRNE, MARK JOSEPH MD, DATE OF BIRTH SEPTEMBER 30, 1959, LICENSE NUMBER 0AA2477, OF PO BOX 14843, BATON ROUGE, LA, WAS DISCIPLINED BY ALASKA ON JUNE 6, 1991.
DISCIPLINARY ACTION: 60-MONTH PROBATION; REQUIRED TO ENTER AN IMPAIRED PHYSICIAN PROGRAM OR DRUG OR ALCOHOL TREATMENT
OFFENSE: SUBSTANCE ABUSE
NOTES: CHEMICAL DEPENDENCY (ALCOHOLISM). CONDITIONS OF PROBATION: MUST ATTEND INPATIENT SUBSTANCE ABUSE PROGRAM; MUST CONSUME NO CONTROLLED DRUGS OR ALCOHOL; MUST PARTICIPATE IN MONITORING PROGRAM APPROVED BY BOARD; MAY BE REQUIRED TO UNDERGO PSYCHIATRIC CARE; RANDOM DRUG SCREENS; NOTIFY HOSPITALS OF ORDER; ADVISE BOARD OF CHANGE IN PERSONAL PHYSICIAN; PERIODIC BOARD INTERVIEW; REPORTS TO BOARD.

BEIRNE, MARK JOSEPH MD WAS DISCIPLINED BY ALASKA ON FEBRUARY 2, 1995.
OFFENSE: FAILURE TO COMPLY WITH A PREVIOUS BOARD ORDER
NOTES: PROBATION VIOLATIONS. MEDICATIONS AND COUNSELING AS REQUIRED.

BENWARD, ROY MD WAS DISCIPLINED BY ALASKA ON FEBRUARY 23, 1990.
DISCIPLINARY ACTION: EMERGENCY SUSPENSION
OFFENSE: FAILURE TO COMPLY WITH A PREVIOUS BOARD ORDER
NOTES: VIOLATED PROBATION; CHEMICAL DEPENDENCY. LICENSE REMAINS SUSPENDED PENDING REVISED MEMORANDUM OF AGREEMENT AND POTENTIAL REINSTATEMENT BY BOARD.

BENWARD, ROY E MD, LICENSE NUMBER 0001095, WAS DISCIPLINED BY ALASKA ON MAY 4, 1987.
DISCIPLINARY ACTION: 48-MONTH PROBATION; REQUIRED TO ENTER AN IMPAIRED PHYSICIAN PROGRAM OR DRUG OR ALCOHOL TREATMENT
OFFENSE: SUBSTANCE ABUSE
NOTES: CHEMICAL DEPENDENCY. CONDITIONS OF PROBATION: INPATIENT CHEMICAL DEPENDENCY TREATMENT; CANNOT CONSUME CONTROLLED DRUGS OR ALCOHOL; MANDATORY AA ATTENDANCE; RANDOM DRUG SCREENS; REPORTS FROM PHYSICIAN, COUNSELOR AND HOSPITAL REQUIRED; MUST NOTIFY THE BOARD OF ABSENCES FROM STATE; PERIODIC REVIEW; RESTRICTIONS ON REMOTE EMPLOYMENT.

BENWARD, ROY E MD, LICENSE NUMBER 0001095, WAS DISCIPLINED BY ALASKA ON JULY 31, 1990.
DISCIPLINARY ACTION: 60-MONTH PROBATION; RESTRICTION PLACED ON LICENSE
OFFENSE: SUBSTANCE ABUSE
NOTES: CHEMICAL DEPENDENCY. CONDITIONS OF PROBATION: RESIDENTIAL TREATMENT; MUST CONSUME NO CONTROLLED DRUGS OR ALCOHOL; AFTERCARE PROGRAM; MANDATORY DRUG/ALCOHOL SCREENS; RESTRICTION ON REMOTE EMPLOYMENT; COUNSELING; REPORTS TO BOARD; PERMANENT TOTAL ABSTINENCE. LICENSED AS OF 8/19/91.

BIGELOW, LOY MD WAS DISCIPLINED BY ALASKA ON FEBRUARY 7, 1994.
DISCIPLINARY ACTION: SURRENDER OF LICENSE

BIGELOW, LOY F DO, LICENSE NUMBER 20A5362, OF HILLSIDE, NJ, WAS DISCIPLINED BY CALIFORNIA ON SEPTEMBER 9, 1992.
DISCIPLINARY ACTION: LICENSE REVOCATION
OFFENSE: DISCIPLINARY ACTION BY ANOTHER STATE OR AGENCY
NOTES: ACTION TAKEN BY ANOTHER STATE.

BIGELOW, LOY FORSYTHE DO OF 3212 DORIS STREET, ANCHORAGE, AK, WAS DISCIPLINED BY DEA ON MAY 8, 1990.
DISCIPLINARY ACTION: SURRENDER OF CONTROLLED SUBSTANCE LICENSE
NOTES: MEDICAL LICENSE PLACED ON FOUR YEARS PROBATION BEGINNING 05/27/92. NO UPDATE WITHOUT APPROVAL PLACED ON REGISTRATION 8/26/92.

BIGELOW, LOY FORSYTHE DO, DATE OF BIRTH MAY 14, 1957, LICENSE NUMBER 0002478, WAS DISCIPLINED BY ALASKA ON NOVEMBER 8, 1990.
DISCIPLINARY ACTION: 60-MONTH PROBATION; RESTRICTION PLACED ON LICENSE
OFFENSE: SUBSTANCE ABUSE
NOTES: CHEMICAL DEPENDENCY. CONDITIONS OF PROBATION: MUST CONSUME NO DRUGS/ALCOHOL; PRESCRIPTIVE AUTHORITY RESTRICTED; RESTRICTION ON REMOTE EMPLOYMENT; COUNSELING; REPORTS TO THE BOARD; PERMANENT TOTAL ABSTINENCE; MANDATORY DRUG SCREENS. LICENSED AS OF 8/19/91.

BIGELOW, LOY FORSYTHE DO, DATE OF BIRTH MAY 14, 1957, LICENSE NUMBER 0050536, OF 3212 DORIS STREET, ANCHORAGE, AK, WAS DISCIPLINED BY NEW JERSEY ON SEPTEMBER 5, 1991.
DISCIPLINARY ACTION: 60-MONTH LICENSE SUSPENSION
OFFENSE: DISCIPLINARY ACTION BY ANOTHER STATE OR AGENCY
NOTES: BASED ON DISCIPLINARY ACTION IN ALASKA RELATIVE TO IMPAIRMENT.

BIGELOW, LOY FORSYTHE DO, DATE OF BIRTH MAY 14, 1957, LICENSE NUMBER 0002478, OF 936 NORMAN STREET, ANCHORAGE, AK, WAS DISCIPLINED BY ALASKA ON MAY 28, 1992.
DISCIPLINARY ACTION: 48-MONTH PROBATION; RESTRICTION PLACED ON LICENSE
OFFENSE: FAILURE TO COMPLY WITH A PREVIOUS BOARD ORDER
NOTES: AMENDED PROBATION ORDER DUE TO RELAPSE. SUBSTANCE ABUSE. MUST PARTICIPATE IN PHYSICAL AND PSYCHIATRIC EXAMINATIONS, INPATIENT TREATMENT IF RECOMMENDED, ONE YEAR OUTPATIENT TREATMENT, PSYCHIATRIC REPORTS; SHALL CONSUME NO ALCOHOL OR DRUG UNLESS PRESCRIBED BY PHYSICIAN; 3 AA OR NARCOTICS ANONYMOUS MEETINGS PER WEEK; RANDOM TEST OF BODILY FLUIDS; REPORTS FROM PHYSICIAN; RESTRICTION ON REMOTE EMPLOYMENT; LIMITS ON ACCESS TO CONTROLLED MEDICATIONS WHILE WORKING INCLUDING NOT ORDERING DRUGS WITHOUT APPROVAL; EMPLOYMENT UNDER SUPERVISION WITH REPORTS; PERIODIC BOARD INTERVIEWS; SHALL NOTIFY ANY HOSPITAL WHERE SHE HAS PRIVILEGES OF THIS AGREEMENT; RESTRICTED PRESCRIPTIVE AUTHORITY.

BIGELOW, LOY FORSYTHE DO, DATE OF BIRTH MAY 14, 1957, LICENSE NUMBER 0002478, WAS DISCIPLINED BY ALASKA ON FEBRUARY 8, 1993.
DISCIPLINARY ACTION: EMERGENCY SUSPENSION

BOAS, EDWARD MD, LICENSE NUMBER 0003049, WAS DISCIPLINED BY ALASKA ON JANUARY 30, 1987.
DISCIPLINARY ACTION: 1-MONTH LICENSE SUSPENSION; REPRIMAND
NOTES: NARCOTIC VIOLATION. NOT PRESENTLY LICENSED; LICENSE LAPSED 12/31/88.

BOYD, ARTHUR MD WAS DISCIPLINED BY ALASKA ON FEBRUARY 2, 1988.
DISCIPLINARY ACTION: DENIAL OF NEW LICENSE
OFFENSE: PROVIDING FALSE INFORMATION TO THE BOARD
NOTES: FALSIFIED APPLICATION.

CAMMACK, DAVID M MD, LICENSE NUMBER 0000965, WAS DISCIPLINED BY ALASKA ON NOVEMBER 17, 1989.

- ALASKA -

DISCIPLINARY ACTION: 24-MONTH PROBATION; RESTRICTION PLACED ON CONTROLLED SUBSTANCE LICENSE
OFFENSE: OVERPRESCRIBING OR MISPRESCRIBING DRUGS
NOTES: EXCESSIVE PRESCRIBING. SURRENDERED AUTHORITY TO PRESCRIBE SCHEDULE II AND III SUBSTANCES; TRIPLICATE PRESCRIPTION SYSTEM; CONTINUING MEDICAL EDUCATION DONE. LICENSED AS OF 8/19/91.

CASTLEBERRY, JESSE W MD OF 12404 SUMMERPORT, WINDERMERE, FL, WAS DISCIPLINED BY NORTH DAKOTA ON JULY 19, 1991.
DISCIPLINARY ACTION: REQUIRED TO ENTER AN IMPAIRED PHYSICIAN PROGRAM OR DRUG OR ALCOHOL TREATMENT; MONITORING OF PHYSICIAN
NOTES: ISSUED LICENSE SUBJECT TO CERTAIN CONDITIONS: MUST PARTICIPATE IN A RANDOM BLOOD OR URINE SCREEN PROGRAM; MUST PARTICIPATE IN A SELF-HELP GROUP DAILY AND A SPECIFIED PROGRAM FOR RECOVERING PROFESSIONALS. ON 11/12/93 RESTRICTIONS WERE ORDERED RESCINDED; ISSUED UNRESTRICTED LICENSE.

CASTLEBERRY, JESSE WENDELL MD, DATE OF BIRTH OCTOBER 17, 1924, LICENSE NUMBER 0058083, OF 12404 SUMMERPORT LANE, WINDERMERE, FL, WAS DISCIPLINED BY MICHIGAN ON MAY 15, 1991.
DISCIPLINARY ACTION: 12-MONTH PROBATION

CASTLEBERRY, JESSE WENDELL MD, DATE OF BIRTH OCTOBER 17, 1924, LICENSE NUMBER 0AA2653, OF 12404 SUMMERPORT LANE, WINDERMERE, FL, WAS DISCIPLINED BY ALASKA ON JUNE 6, 1991.
DISCIPLINARY ACTION: 60-MONTH PROBATION; MONITORING OF PHYSICIAN
OFFENSE: SUBSTANCE ABUSE
NOTES: ADMITTED HISTORY OF ABUSE OF ALCOHOL. CONDITIONS OF PROBATION: CONSUME NO CONTROLLED DRUGS OR ALCOHOL; MONITORING BY BOARD APPROVED PROGRAM; MUST NOTIFY HOSPITALS OR EMPLOYERS OF ORDER; PERIODIC REPORTS TO BOARD; NOTIFICATION OF CHANGE IN PERSONAL PHYSICIAN OR WORK SITES.

CHUO, LI YUN MD WAS DISCIPLINED BY ALASKA ON OCTOBER 11, 1996.
DISCIPLINARY ACTION: REPRIMAND
OFFENSE: PROVIDING FALSE INFORMATION TO THE BOARD
NOTES: PROVIDED UNTRUTHFUL ANSWER ON APPLICATION.

COLESCOTT, PAULA MD WAS DISCIPLINED BY ALASKA ON MAY 2, 1996.
DISCIPLINARY ACTION: 60-MONTH PROBATION; FINE
OFFENSE: PROFESSIONAL MISCONDUCT
NOTES: MISCONDUCT WITH A PATIENT. SHALL UNDERGO PSYCHIATRIC CARE; PRACTICE LIMITED TO ER/URGENT CARE; DOCTOR/PATIENT RELATIONSHIP RESTRICTIONS; REMOTE EMPLOYMENT LIMITS; EMPLOYER/HOSPITAL REPORTS; INTERVIEWS WITH THE BOARD; SHALL SUBMIT QUARTERLY REPORTS TO THE BOARD. $10,000 CIVIL FINE.

COON, DUANE A MD, DATE OF BIRTH AUGUST 29, 1926, LICENSE NUMBER 00AA368, OF BOX 369, PETERSBURG, AK, WAS DISCIPLINED BY ALASKA ON DECEMBER 6, 1991.
DISCIPLINARY ACTION: PROBATION; RESTRICTION PLACED ON LICENSE
OFFENSE: SUBSTANDARD CARE, INCOMPETENCE, OR NEGLIGENCE
NOTES: INCOMPETENCE IN EMERGENCY SITUATIONS, POOR RECORD KEEPING. LICENSE PROBATION UNTIL HE SUCCESSFULLY COMPLETES A MEDICAL RECORDS KEEPING COURSE. RESTRICTED FROM PRACTICE IN ANY EMERGENCY ROOM EXCEPT FOR ASSISTANCE TO OR CONSULTATION WITH ANOTHER PHYSICIAN.

DANIELS, JOHN P MD, LICENSE NUMBER 0000799, WAS DISCIPLINED BY ALASKA ON NOVEMBER 5, 1987.
DISCIPLINARY ACTION: LICENSE REVOCATION
OFFENSE: PROFESSIONAL MISCONDUCT
NOTES: CRIMINAL SALE OF DANGEROUS DRUGS.

DAVENPORT, WAYNE MD, LICENSE NUMBER 0001178, WAS DISCIPLINED BY ALASKA ON FEBRUARY 22, 1988.
DISCIPLINARY ACTION: 60-MONTH PROBATION; RESTRICTION PLACED ON LICENSE
OFFENSE: SUBSTANCE ABUSE
NOTES: CHEMICAL DEPENDENCY. CONDITIONS OF PROBATION: MUST NOT CONSUME ALCOHOL OR CONTROLLED DRUGS; MANDATORY DRUG SCREENS; STATEMENT OF PHYSICAL AND MENTAL ABILITY TO PRACTICE; RESTRICTION ON REMOTE EMPLOYMENT; HOSPITAL AND COUNSELING REPORTS TO BOARD; PERIODIC INTERVIEW WITH THE BOARD. LICENSED AS OF 8/19/91.

DENTON, SANDRA M MD, DATE OF BIRTH JANUARY 20, 1946, LICENSE NUMBER 0030084, OF ANCHORAGE, AK, WAS DISCIPLINED BY COLORADO ON DECEMBER 13, 1993.
DISCIPLINARY ACTION: SURRENDER OF LICENSE
NOTES: NO UNPROFESSIONAL CONDUCT IDENTIFIED.

DIBALA, ANNE C MD WAS DISCIPLINED BY ALASKA ON OCTOBER 11, 1996.
DISCIPLINARY ACTION: RESTRICTION PLACED ON LICENSE; REQUIRED TO ENTER AN IMPAIRED PHYSICIAN PROGRAM OR DRUG OR ALCOHOL TREATMENT
OFFENSE: SUBSTANCE ABUSE
NOTES: HISTORY OF SUBSTANCE ABUSE AND DIAGNOSED MEDICAL CONDITION. RESTRICTION ON EMPLOYMENT; SHALL PROVE ABILITY TO PRACTICE; PSYCHIATRIC/PSYCHOLOGICAL CARE/COUNSELING; SHALL ABSTAIN FROM DRUGS AND ALCOHOL; HEALTH CARE PROVIDER SUPPORT GROUP; SHALL SUBMIT QUARTERLY SELF EVALUATION REPORTS; URINANALYSIS, BLOOD, AND HAIR TESTING; HER EMPLOYER SHALL REPORT TO THE BOARD; SHALL REPORT ABSENCE FROM HER AREA OF RESIDENCE; PERIODIC INTERVIEWS WITH THE BOARD; AND PERMANENT THERAPY REQUIREMENT; MUST COMPLY WITH SIGN AUTHORIZATIONS AND INSURE QUARTERLY REPORTS ARE SENT.

DOELL, WILLIAM EDWARD DO, DATE OF BIRTH MAY 26, 1933, LICENSE NUMBER 0015643, OF WHEAT RIDGE, CO, WAS DISCIPLINED BY COLORADO ON AUGUST 17, 1990.
DISCIPLINARY ACTION: LICENSE REVOCATION
OFFENSE: SUBSTANDARD CARE, INCOMPETENCE, OR NEGLIGENCE
NOTES: FAILED TO MEET GENERALLY ACCEPTED STANDARDS OF MEDICAL PRACTICE AND PRESCRIBED OTHER THAN IN THE COURSE OF LEGITIMATE PROFESSIONAL PRACTICE. APPEAL FILED 8/28/90; STAY DENIED BY MEDICAL BOARD AND COURT OF APPEALS. ON 12/12/91, COLORADO COURT OF APPEALS UPHELD FINDINGS OF SUBSTANDARD CARE, PRESCRIBING OTHER THAN IN THE COURSE OF LEGITIMATE PROFESSIONAL PRACTICE, AND REVOCATION OF MEDICAL LICENSE.

DOELL, WILLIAM EDWARD DO, DATE OF BIRTH MAY 26, 1933, OF 13040 WEST 80TH AVE, ARVADA, CO, WAS DISCIPLINED BY MEDICARE ON MAY 10, 1991.
DISCIPLINARY ACTION: EXCLUSION FROM THE MEDICARE AND/OR MEDICAID PROGRAMS
OFFENSE: DISCIPLINARY ACTION BY ANOTHER STATE OR AGENCY
NOTES: LICENSE REVOCATION OR SUSPENSION.

DOELL, WILLIAM EDWARD DO, DATE OF BIRTH MAY 26, 1933, OF 13040 WEST 80TH AVE, ARVADA, CO, WAS DISCIPLINED BY ALASKA ON JUNE 19, 1991.

- ALASKA -

DISCIPLINARY ACTION: DENIAL OF NEW LICENSE
OFFENSE: DISCIPLINARY ACTION BY ANOTHER STATE OR AGENCY
NOTES: LICENSE DENIED BASED ON REVOCATION OF COLORADO LICENSE.

DOELL, WILLIAM EDWARD DO WAS DISCIPLINED BY ALASKA ON DECEMBER 5, 1991.
DISCIPLINARY ACTION: DENIAL OF NEW LICENSE
OFFENSE: DISCIPLINARY ACTION BY ANOTHER STATE OR AGENCY
NOTES: BASED ON REVOCATION OF COLORADO LICENSE.

DOELL, WILLIAM EDWARD DO, DATE OF BIRTH MAY 26, 1933, OF 7777 W. 38TH AVENUE #124, WHEAT RIDGE, CO, WAS DISCIPLINED BY DEA ON JULY 12, 1993.
DISCIPLINARY ACTION: REVOCATION OF CONTROLLED SUBSTANCE LICENSE
OFFENSE: DISCIPLINARY ACTION BY ANOTHER STATE OR AGENCY
NOTES: COLORADO MEDICAL LICENSE REVOKED ON 8/17/90 DUE TO NUMEROUS INSTANCES OF SUBSTANDARD CARE, IN CONNECTION WITH SEVENTEEN PATIENTS, INCLUDING EXCESSIVE PRESCRIBING OF DILAUDID TO A PATIENT.

ERICKSON, VINCENT J MD WAS DISCIPLINED BY ALASKA ON JANUARY 29, 1993.
DISCIPLINARY ACTION: PROBATION; RESTRICTION PLACED ON LICENSE
OFFENSE: SUBSTANCE ABUSE
NOTES: SUBSTANCE ABUSE. PROBATION ONE WEEK. CONDITIONS OF PROBATION: MUST CONSUME NO ALCOHOL OR DRUG UNLESS ON PHYSICIAN ORDER; MUST HAVE DAILY URINE ANALYSIS OR BLOOD TEST; MUST HAVE PERSONAL PHYSICIAN; NO REMOTE EMPLOYMENT ALLOWED; MUST TELL CHIEF OF STAFF OF HOSPITAL IN WHICH HE HAS PRIVILEGES OF MEMO OF AGREEMENT AND PROVIDE COPY; MUST NOTIFY ADMINISTRATOR OF ANY ANESTHESIOLOGY GROUP EMPLOYING HIM OF MEMO OF AGREEMENT AND PROVIDE COPY.

ERICKSON, VINCENT J MD WAS DISCIPLINED BY ALASKA ON FEBRUARY 28, 1994.
DISCIPLINARY ACTION: RESTRICTION PLACED ON LICENSE
OFFENSE: SUBSTANCE ABUSE
NOTES: SUBSTANCE ABUSE. MEMORANDUM OF AGREEMENT. CONDITIONS: EMPLOYMENT RESTRICTION; PARTICIPATE IN COUNSELING; REPORTS TO THE BOARD; CONSUME NO ALCOHOL OR DRUG UNLESS PRESCRIBED BY HIS PHYSICIAN OR DENTIST; PARTICIPATE IN HEALTH CARE PROVIDER SUPPORT GROUP; URINE AND BLOOD TESTING AS REQUIRED BY BOARD; PERSONAL HEALTH CARE PROVIDER IDENTIFIED TO THE BOARD; EMPLOYER REPORTS; PERIODIC BOARD INTERVIEW. RESTRICTION FOR THREE YEARS FROM DATE HIS ALASKA LICENSE WAS ISSUED.

EUFEMIO, JOHN J MD, LICENSE NUMBER 0083563, OF KODIAK, AK, WAS DISCIPLINED BY NEW YORK ON DECEMBER 28, 1987.
DISCIPLINARY ACTION: REPRIMAND

FETTES, RICHARD C MD WAS DISCIPLINED BY ALASKA ON DECEMBER 10, 1993.
DISCIPLINARY ACTION: EMERGENCY SUSPENSION
NOTES: HE POSED DANGER TO PUBLIC AND/OR PATIENTS.

FETTES, RICHARD C MD WAS DISCIPLINED BY ALASKA ON JANUARY 31, 1994.
NOTES: DIAGNOSIS OF BIPOLAR DISORDER. CONDITIONAL LICENSE ISSUED FOR ONE YEAR. COUNSELING AND REPORTS TO THE BOARD. RESTRICTION ON SELF PRESCRIBING OF PSYCHOTROPIC MEDICATIONS. BOARD INTERVIEWS.

FETTES, RICHARD C MD, LICENSE NUMBER 0165974, OF 4308 E 8TH AVENUE, ANCHORAGE, AK, WAS DISCIPLINED BY NEW YORK ON JANUARY 30, 1995.
DISCIPLINARY ACTION: 12-MONTH PROBATION
OFFENSE: DISCIPLINARY ACTION BY ANOTHER STATE OR AGENCY
NOTES: ACTION IN ALASKA. AFFLICTED WITH A MEDICAL CONDITION WHICH IF LEFT UNTREATED IS CAPABLE OF AFFECTING HIS PRACTICE OF MEDICINE. ONE YEAR SUSPENSION STAYED.

GOODWIN, GEORGE MD WAS DISCIPLINED BY ALASKA ON AUGUST 1, 1990.
DISCIPLINARY ACTION: DENIAL OF NEW LICENSE
OFFENSE: DISCIPLINARY ACTION BY ANOTHER STATE OR AGENCY
NOTES: FALSIFIED APPLICATION; DISCIPLINARY ACTION IN ARIZONA.

GRAUMAN, DAVID S MD, DATE OF BIRTH JANUARY 29, 1945, LICENSE NUMBER 0AA1058, OF 1919 LATHROP ST #25, FAIRBANKS, AK, WAS DISCIPLINED BY ALASKA ON OCTOBER 9, 1991.
DISCIPLINARY ACTION: REPRIMAND; REQUIRED TO TAKE ADDITIONAL MEDICAL EDUCATION
OFFENSE: OVERPRESCRIBING OR MISPRESCRIBING DRUGS
NOTES: INAPPROPRIATE PRESCRIBING. APPROPRIATE PRESCRIBING EDUCATION; RESTRICTED FROM PRESCRIBING TO FAMILY MEMBERS.

GRAY, SCHARAZARD L MD WAS DISCIPLINED BY ALASKA ON JULY 10, 1995.
DISCIPLINARY ACTION: SURRENDER OF LICENSE
OFFENSE: SUBSTANCE ABUSE
NOTES: HAS ADMITTED REPEATED USE OF ILLICIT COCAINE. WAS IN ASMA PAC VOLUNTARY PROGRAM WHICH HE FAILED.

HALEY, THEODORE MD WAS DISCIPLINED BY ALASKA ON FEBRUARY 8, 1990.
DISCIPLINARY ACTION: DENIAL OF NEW LICENSE
OFFENSE: DISCIPLINARY ACTION BY ANOTHER STATE OR AGENCY
NOTES: FALSIFIED APPLICATION; DISCIPLINARY ACTION IN WASHINGTON.

HALTER, LOREN DO WAS DISCIPLINED BY ALASKA ON SEPTEMBER 23, 1994.
OFFENSE: OVERPRESCRIBING OR MISPRESCRIBING DRUGS
NOTES: PRESCRIBING VIOLATIONS. A $3,000 FINE WAS ISSUED. THE BOARD STAYED THE FINE FOR A PERIOD OF TWO YEARS.

HANNA, FAYEZ A MD WAS DISCIPLINED BY ALASKA ON JUNE 10, 1992.
DISCIPLINARY ACTION: DENIAL OF NEW LICENSE
OFFENSE: DISCIPLINARY ACTION BY ANOTHER STATE OR AGENCY

HAYWARD, ROBERT MERTON MD OF PO BOX 1125, EAGLE RIVER, AK, WAS DISCIPLINED BY DEA ON DECEMBER 20, 1989.
DISCIPLINARY ACTION: SURRENDER OF CONTROLLED SUBSTANCE LICENSE
OFFENSE: OVERPRESCRIBING OR MISPRESCRIBING DRUGS
NOTES: PRESCRIBED DIDREX FOR LONG PERIOD OF TIME FOR WEIGHT CONTROL.

ISAAK, PAUL G MD, DATE OF BIRTH JULY 10, 1921, LICENSE NUMBER 00II316, OF PO BOX 219, SOLDOTNA, AK, WAS DISCIPLINED BY ALASKA ON APRIL 30, 1992.
DISCIPLINARY ACTION: SURRENDER OF LICENSE; FINE
OFFENSE: PRACTICING WITHOUT A VALID LICENSE
NOTES: UNLICENSED PRACTICE FOR ABOUT FIVE YEARS WHICH INCLUDED WRITING PRESCRIPTIONS FOR SEVERAL CONTROLLED SUBSTANCES. HE ALSO FRAUDULENTLY RENEWED HIS DEA NUMBER. $5,000 FINE.

JENSEN, DAG MD WAS DISCIPLINED BY ALASKA ON OCTOBER 11,

- ALASKA -

1996.
DISCIPLINARY ACTION: FINE
OFFENSE: PRACTICING WITHOUT A VALID LICENSE
NOTES: UNLICENSED PRACTICE IN ALASKA. $1,000 FINE.

KILLEBREW, DAVID SCOTT MD WAS DISCIPLINED BY ALASKA ON DECEMBER 10, 1991.
DISCIPLINARY ACTION: 60-MONTH PROBATION; REQUIRED TO ENTER AN IMPAIRED PHYSICIAN PROGRAM OR DRUG OR ALCOHOL TREATMENT
OFFENSE: SUBSTANCE ABUSE
NOTES: CHEMICAL DEPENDENCY DUE TO ALCOHOL ABUSE. CONDITIONS OF PROBATION INCLUDE: INPATIENT TREATMENT; NO ALCOHOL OR CONTROLLED DRUGS; MONITORING THROUGH IMPAIRED PHYSICIAN PROGRAM; PSYCHIATRIC COUNSELING AND CARE; URINALYSIS AND BLOOD TESTING; NOTIFY HOSPITALS OF ORDER; NOTIFY BOARD OF ANY EXPECTED ABSENCES FROM THE STATE OF MORE THAN 7 DAYS; MAINTAIN A RELATIONSHIP WITH A PHYSICIAN TO SERVE AS HIS PRIMARY MEDICAL PROVIDER; AND INTERVIEWS WITH THE BOARD. ON 9/23/94 BOARD DENIED HIS REQUEST TO CHANGE THE PERIOD OF THIS PROBATION AND DETERMINED THAT HE MUST REMAIN ON IT FOR THE FULL PERIOD.

KINANE, THOMAS MD WAS DISCIPLINED BY ALASKA ON APRIL 9, 1990.
DISCIPLINARY ACTION: DENIAL OF NEW LICENSE
OFFENSE: SUBSTANCE ABUSE
NOTES: REFUSAL TO SEEK TREATMENT FOR ADMITTED CHEMICAL DEPENDENCY.

KIRK, JACK T MD WAS DISCIPLINED BY ALASKA ON APRIL 10, 1990.
DISCIPLINARY ACTION: DENIAL OF NEW LICENSE
OFFENSE: SUBSTANCE ABUSE
NOTES: HISTORY OF CHEMICAL DEPENDENCY; HE WAS NOT ABLE TO PROVIDE EVIDENCE OF RECOVERY.

LANGHAM, MARY L DO, DATE OF BIRTH JULY 27, 1954, OF PO BOX 671036, CHUGIAK, AK, WAS DISCIPLINED BY MEDICARE ON SEPTEMBER 12, 1993.
DISCIPLINARY ACTION: EXCLUSION FROM THE MEDICARE AND/OR MEDICAID PROGRAMS
OFFENSE: FAILURE TO COMPLY WITH A PROFESSIONAL RULE
NOTES: DEFAULTED ON HEALTH EDUCATION ASSISTANCE LOAN. REINSTATED ON 9/29/93.

LEWIS, CLEMENT J MD OF SALT LAKE CITY, UT, WAS DISCIPLINED BY NORTH DAKOTA ON JULY 31, 1987.
NOTES: LICENSE ISSUED UPON SPECIFIED CONDITIONS

LEWIS, CLEMENT JOHN MD, LICENSE NUMBER 0002405, WAS DISCIPLINED BY ALASKA ON FEBRUARY 3, 1989.
DISCIPLINARY ACTION: 24-MONTH RESTRICTION PLACED ON LICENSE; MONITORING OF PHYSICIAN
OFFENSE: PROFESSIONAL MISCONDUCT
NOTES: PRIOR SEXUAL MISCONDUCT IN ARIZONA. MUST HAVE ONGOING PSYCHIATRIC CARE; QUARTERLY REPORTS FROM PSYCHIATRIST. ON 11/1/90 UNCONDITIONAL LICENSE ISSUED, SATISFIED REQUIREMENTS IMPOSED ON INITIAL LICENSE. LICENSED AS OF 8/19/91.

LEWIS, JIM EARL DO, DATE OF BIRTH JUNE 12, 1954, LICENSE NUMBER 0006123, OF 711 MAIN STREET SW, RONAN, MT, WAS DISCIPLINED BY MONTANA ON MAY 20, 1991.
NOTES: UNSPECIFIED AGREEMENT AND ORDER.

LEWIS, JIM EARL DO, DATE OF BIRTH JUNE 12, 1954, LICENSE NUMBER 0AA1903, OF PO BOX 82931, FAIRBANKS, AK, WAS DISCIPLINED BY ALASKA ON JUNE 6, 1991.
DISCIPLINARY ACTION: 60-MONTH PROBATION; MONITORING OF PHYSICIAN

NOTES: PRIOR PSYCHIATRIC TREATMENT AND CHEMICAL DEPENDENCY EVALUATION. CONDITIONS OF PROBATION: MUST CONSUME NO CONTROLLED DRUGS OR ALCOHOL; MUST PARTICIPATE IN BOARD APPROVED MONITORING PROGRAM; MUST RECEIVE PSYCHIATRIC CARE; MUST NOTIFY EMPLOYER/HOSPITALS OF ORDER; REPORTS TO BOARD; MUST NOTIFY BOARD OF CHANGE IN PERSONAL PHYSICIAN AND ABSENCES FROM STATE. ON 9/23/94 ORDER AMENDED TO DE-EMPHASIZE SUBSTANCE ABUSE AS IT RELATES TO HIS UNDERLYING MENTAL CONDITION.

LIEBERMAN, JON F MD WAS DISCIPLINED BY TENNESSEE ON NOVEMBER 30, 1988.
DISCIPLINARY ACTION: REQUIRED TO ENTER AN IMPAIRED PHYSICIAN PROGRAM OR DRUG OR ALCOHOL TREATMENT
NOTES: LICENSE GRANTED WITH STIPULATION THAT HE MAINTAIN CONTRACT WITH IMPAIRED PHYSICIANS PROGRAM

LIEBERMAN, JON F MD, DATE OF BIRTH MAY 12, 1951, LICENSE NUMBER 0002658, OF PO BOX 81697, FAIRBANKS, AK, WAS DISCIPLINED BY ALASKA ON DECEMBER 6, 1991.
DISCIPLINARY ACTION: 36-MONTH PROBATION; MONITORING OF PHYSICIAN
OFFENSE: SUBSTANCE ABUSE
NOTES: CHEMICAL DEPENDENCY -- ALCOHOL. CONDITIONS OF PROBATION INCLUDE: MONITORING PROGRAM; PSYCHIATRIC COUNSELING/CARE; BLOOD AND URINE TESTING; NOTIFY HOSPITALS WHERE EMPLOYED; NOTIFY BOARD OF ABSENCES MORE THAN 7 DAYS; MAINTAIN RELATIONSHIP WITH A PHYSICIAN TO BE HIS PRIMARY MEDICAL PROVIDER; AND BOARD APPEARANCES. ON 5/29/92, PROBATION TERMINATED AND UNCONDITIONED LICENSE ISSUED.

MCGUIRE, JAMES R MD WAS DISCIPLINED BY ALASKA ON FEBRUARY 10, 1994.
DISCIPLINARY ACTION: LICENSE SUSPENSION; RESTRICTION PLACED ON LICENSE
OFFENSE: SEXUAL ABUSE OF OR SEXUAL MISCONDUCT WITH A PATIENT
NOTES: SEXUAL MISCONDUCT WITH A FEMALE PATIENT. BECAUSE OF SEXUAL MISCONDUCT WITH FEMALE PATIENT OVER ABOUT A FIVE AND A HALF YEAR PERIOD, BOARD ISSUED HIS LICENSE SUSPENDED UNTIL BOARD RECEIVES PROOF THAT HE IS ABLE TO PRACTICE SAFELY.

MCGUIRE, JAMES R MD, LICENSE NUMBER 0015236, OF STEILACOOM, WA, WAS DISCIPLINED BY WASHINGTON ON JULY 10, 1995.
DISCIPLINARY ACTION: FINE; RESTRICTION PLACED ON LICENSE
OFFENSE: DISCIPLINARY ACTION BY ANOTHER STATE OR AGENCY
NOTES: ACTION IN ALASKA WHERE HIS LICENSE WAS SUSPENDED. SHALL RESTRICT HIS PRACTICE TO THE TREATMENT OF ADULT MALES AT MCNEIL ISLAND CORRECTIONS CENTER; SHALL PRACTICE UNDER SUPERVISION; SHALL CONTINUE THERAPY AND HAVE A PHYSICAL EXAMINATION; SHALL REFRAIN FROM ALCOHOL AND MOOD-ALTERING SUBSTANCES; SHALL APPEAR BEFORE THE BOARD FOR A COMPLIANCE REVIEW IN SIX MONTHS. $1,000 FINE.

MONTAGUE, JOHN F MD, DATE OF BIRTH NOVEMBER 6, 1924, LICENSE NUMBER 0013052, OF LITTLETON, CO, WAS DISCIPLINED BY COLORADO ON SEPTEMBER 11, 1992.
OFFENSE: PHYSICAL OR MENTAL ILLNESS INHIBITING THE ABILITY TO PRACTICE WITH SKILL AND SAFETY
NOTES: PHYSICAL OR MENTAL DISABILITY. CONDITIONS TO BE MET FOR LICENSE RENEWAL. IF RENEWED, THEN INDEFINITE PROBATION. AGREES NOT TO PRACTICE

- ALASKA -

MEDICINE IN COLORADO WITHOUT PRIOR BOARD APPROVAL, AND COMPLIANCE WITH BOARD REQUIREMENTS AS MAY BE NECESSARY TO PROTECT PUBLIC SAFETY.

MONTAGUE, JOHN FRANCIS MD, LICENSE NUMBER 0AA2603, WAS DISCIPLINED BY ALASKA ON MARCH 18, 1991.
DISCIPLINARY ACTION: EMERGENCY SUSPENSION
NOTES: QUESTION ABOUT ABILITY TO SAFELY PRACTICE MEDICINE.

MONTAGUE, JOHN FRANCIS MD, LICENSE NUMBER 0002603, WAS DISCIPLINED BY ALASKA ON JANUARY 7, 1993.
DISCIPLINARY ACTION: RESTRICTION PLACED ON LICENSE
NOTES: SUBMIT RENEWAL WITH ALL FEES AND CONTINUING MEDICAL EDUCATION; EXAM BY PSYCHIATRIST; BE UNDER ONGOING CARE FOR BIPOLAR DISORDER; MAY NOT PRACTICE ALONE AND WILL BE SUPERVISED BY ANOTHER PHYSICIAN; RANDOM REVIEW OF CHARTS.

MOSELEY, CHARLES MD, LICENSE NUMBER 0000947, WAS DISCIPLINED BY ALASKA ON SEPTEMBER 2, 1987.
DISCIPLINARY ACTION: LICENSE SUSPENSION; 36-MONTH PROBATION
NOTES: NARCOTICS VIOLATIONS. SUSPENSION FOR 15 DAYS RETROACTIVE TO 02/09/87. CONDITIONS OF PROBATION: SHALL ATTEND CONTINUING MEDICAL EDUCATION; SEMIANNUAL PHYSICAL AND PSYCHIATRIC REPORTS; RESTRICTED FROM TREATING ONE PATIENT; DUPLICATE PRESCRIPTION SYSTEM FOR 12 MONTHS; CANNOT PRESCRIBE FOR FAMILY MEMBERS; RANDOM URINALYSIS. RETIRED FROM PRACTICE; LICENSE IS NOW INACTIVE.

MOSELEY, CHARLES H MD, LICENSE NUMBER 0006688, OF 3650 LAKE OTIS PARKWAY #110, ANCHORAGE, AK, WAS DISCIPLINED BY GEORGIA ON DECEMBER 7, 1988.
DISCIPLINARY ACTION: LICENSE REVOCATION
OFFENSE: DISCIPLINARY ACTION BY ANOTHER STATE OR AGENCY
NOTES: REVOKED BY PROCESS OF LAW FOR FAILURE TO RENEW; REPORTED BECAUSE OF PENDING DISCIPLINARY ACTION IN ANOTHER STATE.

MOSELEY, CHARLES HERBERT MD OF ANCHORAGE, AK, WAS DISCIPLINED BY NORTH CAROLINA ON APRIL 27, 1988.
NOTES: CONSENT ORDER, UNSPECIFIED.

MUES, JOHN MD, LICENSE NUMBER 0001555, WAS DISCIPLINED BY ALASKA ON MARCH 1, 1988.
DISCIPLINARY ACTION: REPRIMAND; REQUIRED TO TAKE ADDITIONAL MEDICAL EDUCATION
OFFENSE: OVERPRESCRIBING OR MISPRESCRIBING DRUGS
NOTES: INAPPROPRIATE PRESCRIPTION OF CONTROLLED SUBSTANCES. REPRIMAND TO BE REMOVED FROM FILE AFTER FIVE YEARS; MUST ATTEND CONTINUING MEDICAL EDUCATION ON PRESCRIBING CONTROLLED SUBSTANCES. AS OF 8/19/91 LICENSED WITHOUT RESTRICTIONS.

NARAMORE, LLOYD S MD WAS DISCIPLINED BY ALASKA ON DECEMBER 9, 1994.
DISCIPLINARY ACTION: DENIAL OF NEW LICENSE
OFFENSE: DISCIPLINARY ACTION BY ANOTHER STATE OR AGENCY
NOTES: ACTION IN ANOTHER STATE.

NARAMORE, LLOYD S JR DO, DATE OF BIRTH MARCH 2, 1945, LICENSE NUMBER 1006969, OF 225 N COURT AVE, COLBY, KS, WAS DISCIPLINED BY MICHIGAN ON DECEMBER 1, 1995.
DISCIPLINARY ACTION: LICENSE REVOCATION
OFFENSE: DISCIPLINARY ACTION BY ANOTHER STATE OR AGENCY
NOTES: FAILURE TO REPORT/COMPLY.

NARAMORE, LLOYD S DO, DATE OF BIRTH MARCH 2, 1945, LICENSE NUMBER 0002235, OF COLBY, KS, WAS DISCIPLINED BY KENTUCKY ON MAY 28, 1996.
DISCIPLINARY ACTION: LICENSE REVOCATION
OFFENSE: DISCIPLINARY ACTION BY ANOTHER STATE OR AGENCY
NOTES: DISCIPLINARY ACTION TAKEN BY OTHER STATE BOARDS.

NARAMORE, LLOYD STAN DO WAS DISCIPLINED BY WYOMING ON FEBRUARY 18, 1995.
DISCIPLINARY ACTION: SURRENDER OF LICENSE
NOTES: VOLUNTARY SURRENDER.

NARAMORE, LLOYD STAN DO, LICENSE NUMBER 2001095, WAS DISCIPLINED BY INDIANA ON DECEMBER 7, 1995.
DISCIPLINARY ACTION: SURRENDER OF LICENSE
OFFENSE: DISCIPLINARY ACTION BY ANOTHER STATE OR AGENCY
NOTES: SURRENDER IN LIEU OF FURTHER DISCIPLINARY PROCEEDINGS. PENDING MURDER AND ATTEMPTED MURDER CHARGES. ON 5/2/95 KANSAS REVOKED HIS LICENSE. ON 2/18/95 VOLUNTARILY RELINQUISHED LICENSE TO WISCONSIN FOR NOT ANSWERING TRUTHFULLY THAT HE WAS UNDER INVESTIGATION BY ANOTHER LICENSING BOARD. SHALL PAY COSTS OF $318.52.

NARAMORE, LLOYD STANLEY DO, DATE OF BIRTH MARCH 2, 1945, LICENSE NUMBER 0030724, WAS DISCIPLINED BY COLORADO ON JUNE 15, 1995.
DISCIPLINARY ACTION: SURRENDER OF LICENSE

NARAMORE, LLOYD STANLEY JR DO, LICENSE NUMBER 0002518, OF LOVELL, WY, WAS DISCIPLINED BY OHIO ON JANUARY 26, 1996.
DISCIPLINARY ACTION: EMERGENCY SUSPENSION
OFFENSE: CRIMINAL CONVICTION OR PLEA OF GUILTY, NOLO CONTENDERE, OR NO CONTEST TO A CRIME
NOTES: FOUND GUILTY IN DISTRICT COURT OF CHEYENNE COUNTY, KANSAS, OF SECOND DEGREE MURDER, A FELONY. OTHER ADDRESS: TOPEKA, KANSAS.

O'HEARN, CHARLES J MD WAS DISCIPLINED BY ALASKA ON FEBRUARY 21, 1991.
DISCIPLINARY ACTION: DENIAL OF NEW LICENSE
OFFENSE: PROVIDING FALSE INFORMATION TO THE BOARD
NOTES: PROVIDED FALSE INFORMATION ON INITIAL APPLICATION FOR ALASKA LICENSE. CANNOT PRACTICE MEDICINE IN ALASKA UNLESS ON A U.S. MILITARY BASE. ON 12/6/91 STIPULATION AND ORDER ISSUED.

OLMSTED, LEONARD JR MD WAS DISCIPLINED BY ALASKA ON FEBRUARY 3, 1995.
NOTES: APPLICATION QUESTIONS. NOT PRESENTLY LICENSED IN ALASKA.

RAMOS, VICTOR L MD, LICENSE NUMBER 0030484, OF CHESTERLAND, OH, WAS DISCIPLINED BY OHIO ON JUNE 14, 1989.
DISCIPLINARY ACTION: LICENSE SUSPENSION
NOTES: INDEFINITE SUSPENSION. ON 01/11/90 REINSTATED.

RAMOS, VICTOR L MD, DATE OF BIRTH DECEMBER 23, 1923, OF 14245 SWEEBRIAR LANE, NOVELTY, OH, WAS DISCIPLINED BY ALASKA ON MARCH 12, 1991.
DISCIPLINARY ACTION: DENIAL OF NEW LICENSE
OFFENSE: DISCIPLINARY ACTION BY ANOTHER STATE OR AGENCY
NOTES: BASED ON SANCTIONS BY OHIO IN REGARD TO FRAUD.

RAMOS, VICTOR L MD, LICENSE NUMBER 0030484, OF NOVELTY, OH, WAS DISCIPLINED BY OHIO ON SEPTEMBER 26, 1996.
DISCIPLINARY ACTION: 90-MONTH LICENSE SUSPENSION; PROBATION
OFFENSE: FAILURE TO COMPLY WITH A PREVIOUS BOARD ORDER
NOTES: FAILURE TO PROVIDE ACCEPTABLE DOCUMENTATION OF SATISFACTORY COMPLETION OF CONTINUING MEDICAL

- ALASKA -

EDUCATION AS REQUIRED BY 6/89 ORDER, DESPITE HAVING CERTIFIED ON HIS LICENSE RENEWAL APPLICATION THAT REQUISITE HOURS HAD BEEN COMPLETED. PROBATION FOR AT LEAST SIX YEARS.

ROUTH, LISA C MD WAS DISCIPLINED BY ALASKA ON MAY 5, 1995.
DISCIPLINARY ACTION: 6-MONTH PROBATION; FINE
NOTES: INFORMATION PROVIDED IN RELATION TO APPLICATION FOR ALASKA MEDICAL LICENSE. CONDITIONS OF PROBATION: PRACTICE MONITOR; CONSULTING PHYSICIAN MUST MEET WITH AND REVIEW SPECIFIC NUMBER OF CHARTS TO DISCUSS HANDLING AND MANAGEMENT OF PATIENTS AND PROVIDE REPORTS TO THE BOARD; MUST INFORM BOARD IF FORMAL CHARGES ARE FILED BY TEXAS STATE BOARD; $2500 FINE; A COPY OF THIS STIPULATION MUST GO TO MONITOR; MUST NOTIFY BOARD OF CURRENT ADDRESSES, EMPLOYER AND ALASKA HOSPITALS WHERE SHE IS ON STAFF.

RUSSELL, ALEXANDER B MD OF RT 2 BOX 29, WINDER, GA, WAS DISCIPLINED BY DEA ON OCTOBER 19, 1990.
DISCIPLINARY ACTION: SURRENDER OF CONTROLLED SUBSTANCE LICENSE
OFFENSE: OVERPRESCRIBING OR MISPRESCRIBING DRUGS
NOTES: GAVE PRESCRIPTION FOR CONTROLLED SUBSTANCE WITHOUT MEDICAL EXAMINATION.

RUSSELL, ALEXANDER B MD, DATE OF BIRTH MARCH 16, 1938, OF PO BOX 3302, SOLDOTNA, AK, WAS DISCIPLINED BY MEDICARE ON AUGUST 29, 1995.
DISCIPLINARY ACTION: 60-MONTH EXCLUSION FROM THE MEDICARE AND/OR MEDICAID PROGRAMS
OFFENSE: CRIMINAL CONVICTION OR PLEA OF GUILTY, NOLO CONTENDERE, OR NO CONTEST TO A CRIME
NOTES: CONVICTED OF A CRIME INVOLVING THE MEDICARE, MEDICAID, MATERNAL AND CHILD HEALTH SERVICES BLOCK GRANT OR BLOCK GRANTS TO STATES FOR SOCIAL SERVICES PROGRAMS.

SAVIKKO, DOUGLAS M DO, DATE OF BIRTH JUNE 7, 1951, LICENSE NUMBER 0001667, WAS DISCIPLINED BY ALASKA ON DECEMBER 16, 1988.
DISCIPLINARY ACTION: 60-MONTH PROBATION; MONITORING OF PHYSICIAN
OFFENSE: SUBSTANCE ABUSE
NOTES: CHEMICAL DEPENDENCY. HOSPITAL PRIVILEGES WERE DENIED; AFTER A REVIEW BY A THREE PHYSICIAN PANEL HE WAS FOUND SAFE TO PRACTICE AS HE WAS UNDER PSYCHIATRIC CARE. CONDITIONS OF PROBATION: MUST CONSUME NO ALCOHOL OR OTHER DRUGS; RANDOM DRUG SCREENS; MANDATORY AA; PRIOR DRUG TREATMENT ACCEPTED; PSYCHIATRIC CARE; PEER REVIEW; REPORTS TO THE BOARD FROM PSYCHIATRIC AND PEER REVIEW. LICENSED AS OF 8/19/91.

SAVIKKO, DOUGLAS M DO, DATE OF BIRTH JUNE 7, 1951, LICENSE NUMBER 0001667, OF 10928 EAGLE RIVER RD #130, EAGLE RIVER, AK, WAS DISCIPLINED BY ALASKA ON DECEMBER 18, 1989.
DISCIPLINARY ACTION: SURRENDER OF CONTROLLED SUBSTANCE LICENSE; 60-MONTH PROBATION
OFFENSE: SUBSTANCE ABUSE
NOTES: CHEMICAL DEPENDENCY. CONDITIONS OF PROBATION: MUST CONSUME NO DRUGS OR ALCOHOL; MANDATORY PARTICIPATION IN IMPAIRED PHYSICIAN PROGRAM; PSYCHIATRIC CARE; PEER REVIEW; GRADUAL RETURN TO WORK; REPORTS TO THE BOARD; PERMANENT TOTAL ABSTINENCE. LICENSED AS OF 8/19/91. ON 6/2/92 PRESCRIPTIVE RESTRICTIONS MODIFIED DUE TO HIS PROGRESSING IN HIS TERM OF PROBATION.

SAVIKKO, DOUGLAS M DO, DATE OF BIRTH JUNE 7, 1951, LICENSE NUMBER 0001667, OF 10928 EAGLE RIVER RD #130, EAGLE RIVER, AK, WAS DISCIPLINED BY ALASKA ON OCTOBER 9, 1992.
DISCIPLINARY ACTION: EMERGENCY SUSPENSION
OFFENSE: FAILURE TO COMPLY WITH A PREVIOUS BOARD ORDER
NOTES: VIOLATION OF PROBATION BY CONSUMPTION OF CONTROLLED AND NON-CONTROLLED DRUGS WITHOUT WRITTEN PRESCRIPTION, POSITIVE AND MISSED URINALYSIS.

SAVIKKO, DOUGLAS M DO, DATE OF BIRTH JUNE 7, 1951, LICENSE NUMBER 0001667, WAS DISCIPLINED BY ALASKA ON APRIL 27, 1993.
DISCIPLINARY ACTION: 60-MONTH PROBATION; RESTRICTION PLACED ON LICENSE
OFFENSE: FAILURE TO COMPLY WITH A PREVIOUS BOARD ORDER
NOTES: SUBSTANCE ABUSE AND FAILURE TO COMPLY WITH PREVIOUS MEMO OF AGREEMENT. CONDITIONS OF PROBATION: DEA REGISTRATION LIMITED TO SCHEDULES III, IV, V AND CANNOT ORDER OR POSSESS ANY CONTROLLED SUBSTANCES; NO PRESCRIPTIONS FOR SELF OR FAMILY; MUST NOT CONSUME ALCOHOL OR CONTROLLED SUBSTANCES; AA/NARCOTICS ANONYMOUS MEETINGS; PEER REVIEW; PSYCHIATRIC CARE; WORK LIMITED TO 40 HOURS A WEEK; URINE/BLOOD TESTING; REPORTS TO THE BOARD.

SAVIKKO, DOUGLAS M DO, DATE OF BIRTH JUNE 7, 1951, OF 10928 EAGLE RIVER ROAD #105, EAGLE RIVER, AK, WAS DISCIPLINED BY DEA ON OCTOBER 1, 1993.
DISCIPLINARY ACTION: RESTRICTION PLACED ON CONTROLLED SUBSTANCE LICENSE
OFFENSE: DISCIPLINARY ACTION BY ANOTHER STATE OR AGENCY
NOTES: VOLUNTARY SURRENDER OF SCHEDULE II AND IIN BASED UPON STATE ACTION. MEMORANDUM OF AGREEMENT WITH STATE MEDICAL BOARD SEVERELY RESTRICTS LICENSE.

SAVIKKO, DOUGLAS M DO OF 10928 EAGLE RIVER ROAD #105, EAGLE RIVER, AK, WAS DISCIPLINED BY DEA ON MAY 7, 1995.
DISCIPLINARY ACTION: RESTRICTION PLACED ON CONTROLLED SUBSTANCE LICENSE
OFFENSE: DISCIPLINARY ACTION BY ANOTHER STATE OR AGENCY
NOTES: STATE BOARD.

SKILLE, BOYD A MD, LICENSE NUMBER 0000441, WAS DISCIPLINED BY ALASKA ON MAY 24, 1989.
DISCIPLINARY ACTION: PROBATION; FINE
OFFENSE: PROFESSIONAL MISCONDUCT
NOTES: UNPROFESSIONAL CONDUCT INVOLVING FEMALE PATIENTS. LICENSED AS OF 8/19/91.

SKILLE, BOYD A MD, LICENSE NUMBER 0000441, WAS DISCIPLINED BY ALASKA ON JANUARY 23, 1991.
DISCIPLINARY ACTION: PROBATION; FINE
OFFENSE: PROFESSIONAL MISCONDUCT
NOTES: UNPROFESSIONAL CONDUCT. CONDITIONS OF PROBATION: MUST REFRAIN FROM INAPPROPRIATE VERBAL OR PHYSICAL CONTACT WITH PATIENTS; MAINTAIN OPEN ENTRYWAY TO EXAMINATION ROOM; $5000 FINE.

SKILLE, BOYD A DR, LICENSE NUMBER 0016003, WAS DISCIPLINED BY MINNESOTA ON MAY 8, 1993.
DISCIPLINARY ACTION: RESTRICTION PLACED ON LICENSE

SKILLE, BOYD A MD, LICENSE NUMBER 0094205, OF 3744 LAKE OTIS PARKWAY, ANCHORAGE, AK, WAS DISCIPLINED BY NEW YORK ON AUGUST 9, 1993.
DISCIPLINARY ACTION: SURRENDER OF LICENSE
OFFENSE: DISCIPLINARY ACTION BY ANOTHER STATE OR AGENCY
NOTES: DID NOT CONTEST CHARGES THAT HE HAD BEEN FOUND GUILTY OF IMPROPER PRACTICE OR PROFESSIONAL MISCONDUCT AND HAD BEEN DISCIPLINED BY THE ALASKA BOARD.

- ALASKA -

SNYDER, JACOB D MD WAS DISCIPLINED BY ALASKA ON FEBRUARY 2, 1995.
DISCIPLINARY ACTION: RESTRICTION PLACED ON LICENSE
NOTES: LICENSE APPLICATION QUESTIONS. RESTRICTED FROM EMERGENCY ROOM PRACTICE; MUST PROVIDE HOSPITALS WITH COPY OF THIS STIPULATION; MUST REPORT HIS CURRENT MAILING, PHYSICAL ADDRESS, PHONE NUMBERS AT BOTH HOME AND WORK; CANNOT WORK MORE THAN 50 HOURS A WEEK OR 10 HOURS PER DAY.

SPENCER, JOHN V MD OF ANCHORAGE, AK, WAS DISCIPLINED BY MISSOURI ON DECEMBER 13, 1993.
DISCIPLINARY ACTION: PROBATION
OFFENSE: DISCIPLINARY ACTION BY ANOTHER STATE OR AGENCY
NOTES: LIMITATIONS ON LICENSE IN ANOTHER STATE; LOSS OR RESTRICTION OF HOSPITAL PRIVILEGES.

SPENCER, RICHARD A MD WAS DISCIPLINED BY ALASKA ON MARCH 12, 1996.
DISCIPLINARY ACTION: DENIAL OF NEW LICENSE
OFFENSE: PROVIDING FALSE INFORMATION TO THE BOARD
NOTES: PROVIDED UNTRUTHFUL ANSWER ON APPLICATION.

SPENCER, RICHARD A MD WAS DISCIPLINED BY ALASKA ON AUGUST 2, 1996.
DISCIPLINARY ACTION: REPRIMAND
NOTES: MEMORANDUM OF AGREEMENT. ISSUED LICENSE WITHOUT RESTRICTIONS.

STEPHEN, PETER MD WAS DISCIPLINED BY ALASKA ON MARCH 12, 1996.
DISCIPLINARY ACTION: DENIAL OF NEW LICENSE
OFFENSE: PROVIDING FALSE INFORMATION TO THE BOARD
NOTES: PROVIDED UNTRUTHFUL INFORMATION ON LICENSE APPLICATION.

STEVENS, GEORGE V MD, LICENSE NUMBER G004703, OF ANCHORAGE, AK, WAS DISCIPLINED BY CALIFORNIA ON JANUARY 11, 1990.
DISCIPLINARY ACTION: 120-MONTH PROBATION
OFFENSE: SUBSTANDARD CARE, INCOMPETENCE, OR NEGLIGENCE
NOTES: DETERIORATING SKILLS IN CONTROLLING EXCESSIVE LOSS OF BLOOD IN NUMEROUS TONSILLECTOMIES CONSTITUTES INCOMPETENCE. REVOCATION STAYED.

STEVENS, GEORGE V MD, LICENSE NUMBER 0077149, OF ANCHORAGE, AL, WAS DISCIPLINED BY NEW YORK ON DECEMBER 24, 1991.
DISCIPLINARY ACTION: SURRENDER OF LICENSE

TALBOT, MARION L MD, DATE OF BIRTH MAY 15, 1939, LICENSE NUMBER 0001962, OF 10650 LONE TREE DRIVE, ANCHORAGE, AK, WAS DISCIPLINED BY ALASKA ON MAY 28, 1992.
DISCIPLINARY ACTION: SURRENDER OF LICENSE
NOTES: SURRENDERED LICENSE DUE TO PERSONAL HEALTH PROBLEMS.

TARASZKA, STEVEN R MD, LICENSE NUMBER 0009157, OF ATLANTA, GA, WAS DISCIPLINED BY VERMONT ON FEBRUARY 8, 1996.
DISCIPLINARY ACTION: SURRENDER OF LICENSE
NOTES: VOLUNTARY SURRENDER IN LIEU OF SUMMARY SUSPENSION HEARING.

TARASZKA, STEVEN R MD, LICENSE NUMBER 00AAAA2, WAS DISCIPLINED BY RHODE ISLAND ON MARCH 13, 1996.
DISCIPLINARY ACTION: DENIAL OF NEW LICENSE
OFFENSE: DISCIPLINARY ACTION BY ANOTHER STATE OR AGENCY
NOTES: ACTS IN ANOTHER JURISDICTION WHICH ARE GROUNDS FOR DISCIPLINE IN RHODE ISLAND.

TARASZKA, STEVEN R MD WAS DISCIPLINED BY ALASKA ON MAY 2, 1996.
OFFENSE: SUBSTANCE ABUSE
NOTES: SUBSTANCE ABUSE. CANNOT PRACTICE IN ALASKA UNTIL HE CAN PROVE HE CAN DO SO SAFELY. MUST COMPLY WITH RECOMMENDATIONS OF THE TREATMENT FACILITY AND BOARD PRIOR TO RESUMING HIS MEDICAL PRACTICE.

TARASZKA, STEVEN R MD WAS DISCIPLINED BY KANSAS ON JULY 1, 1996.
DISCIPLINARY ACTION: DENIAL OF NEW LICENSE
OFFENSE: DISCIPLINARY ACTION BY ANOTHER STATE OR AGENCY
NOTES: SURRENDERED HIS LICENSE IN VERMONT ON 2/8/96 BASED IN PART ON AN ADMISSION OF CHEMICAL ADDICTION.

TARASZKA, STEVEN R MD WAS DISCIPLINED BY NEW MEXICO ON SEPTEMBER 1, 1996.
NOTES: BOARD ACCEPTED WITHDRAWAL OF APPLICATION WITH AGREEMENT TO NEVER REAPPLY IN NEW MEXICO.

TARASZKA, STEVEN R MD, DATE OF BIRTH APRIL 22, 1965, LICENSE NUMBER 0063345, OF 4060 PEACHTREE RD NE SUITE D-252, ATLANTA, GA, WAS DISCIPLINED BY NEW JERSEY ON OCTOBER 21, 1996.
DISCIPLINARY ACTION: 3-MONTH SURRENDER OF LICENSE
OFFENSE: DISCIPLINARY ACTION BY ANOTHER STATE OR AGENCY
NOTES: ACTION IN VERMONT FOR SUBSTANCE ABUSE. MINIMUM THREE MONTH SURRENDER. SHALL APPEAR BEFORE THE BOARD TO DISCUSS HIS COMPLIANCE AND DEMONSTRATE HIS FITNESS TO REENTER ACTIVE PRACTICE PRIOR TO RESTORATION OF LICENSE.

TARASZKA, STEVEN R MD WAS DISCIPLINED BY ALABAMA ON OCTOBER 30, 1996.
DISCIPLINARY ACTION: LICENSE REVOCATION
OFFENSE: DISCIPLINARY ACTION BY ANOTHER STATE OR AGENCY
NOTES: VOLUNTARY SURRENDER OF HIS LICENSE IN VERMONT; AGREEMENT TO NEVER SEEK RELICENSURE THERE AND HIS ADMISSION THAT HE SUFFERS FROM THE DISEASE OF CHEMICAL ADDICTION.

TARASZKA, STEVEN R MD, DATE OF BIRTH APRIL 22, 1963, LICENSE NUMBER 0036885, OF 4060 PEACHTREE ROAD, SUITE D-252, ATLANTA, GA, WAS DISCIPLINED BY GEORGIA ON NOVEMBER 8, 1996.
DISCIPLINARY ACTION: LICENSE SUSPENSION
NOTES: SHALL NOT PRACTICE AS A PHYSICIAN IN GEORGIA UNTIL FURTHER ORDER OF THE BOARD. INDEFINITE SUSPENSION.

TARASZKA, STEVEN ROBERT MD, LICENSE NUMBER 0069664, OF ATLANTA, GA, WAS DISCIPLINED BY FLORIDA ON FEBRUARY 16, 1996.
DISCIPLINARY ACTION: EMERGENCY SUSPENSION
OFFENSE: DISCIPLINARY ACTION BY ANOTHER STATE OR AGENCY
NOTES: BEING UNABLE TO PRACTICE MEDICINE WITH REASONABLE SKILL AND SAFETY TO PATIENTS BY REASON OF ILLNESS OR USE OF ALCOHOL, DRUGS, NARCOTICS, CHEMICALS, OR ANY OTHER TYPE OF MATERIAL OR AS A RESULT OF ANY MENTAL OR PHYSICAL CONDITION.

TARASZKA, STEVEN ROBERT MD, LICENSE NUMBER 0069664, OF ATLANTA, GA, WAS DISCIPLINED BY FLORIDA ON JULY 15, 1996.
DISCIPLINARY ACTION: LICENSE SUSPENSION
OFFENSE: DISCIPLINARY ACTION BY ANOTHER STATE OR AGENCY
NOTES: CHARGED WITH HAVING LICENSE ACTED UPON BY ANOTHER JURISDICTION. BEING UNABLE TO PRACTICE MEDICINE WITH REASONABLE SKILL AND SAFETY TO PATIENTS BY REASON OF ILLNESS OR USE OF ALCOHOL, DRUGS, NARCOTICS, CHEMICALS OR ANY OTHER TYPE

- ALASKA -

OF MATERIAL, OR AS A RESULT OF ANY MENTAL OR PHYSICAL CONDITION. SUSPENSION UNTIL HE APPEARS AND DEMONSTRATES TO THE BOARD THAT HE CAN PRACTICE MEDICINE WITH REASONABLE SKILL AND SAFETY.

TARASZKA, STEVEN ROBERT MD, DATE OF BIRTH APRIL 22, 1965, LICENSE NUMBER 0014396, OF 4060 PEACHTREE ROAD, SUITE D252, ATLANTA, GA, WAS DISCIPLINED BY MISSISSIPPI ON JULY 18, 1996.
DISCIPLINARY ACTION: LICENSE REVOCATION

TARASZKA, STEVEN ROBERT MD OF ATLANTA, GA, WAS DISCIPLINED BY UTAH ON OCTOBER 4, 1996.
DISCIPLINARY ACTION: LICENSE REVOCATION
OFFENSE: DISCIPLINARY ACTION BY ANOTHER STATE OR AGENCY
NOTES: ACTION IN VERMONT.

TARASZKA, STEVEN ROBERT MD, DATE OF BIRTH APRIL 22, 1965, LICENSE NUMBER 9600070, OF ATLANTA, GA, WAS DISCIPLINED BY NORTH CAROLINA ON OCTOBER 17, 1996.
DISCIPLINARY ACTION: EMERGENCY SUSPENSION
OFFENSE: DISCIPLINARY ACTION BY ANOTHER STATE OR AGENCY
NOTES: SURRENDERED HIS LICENSE IN VERMONT DUE TO ALLEGATIONS OF NARCOTIC ADDICTION. MAY BE UNABLE TO PRACTICE MEDICINE WITH REASONABLE SKILL AND SAFETY BY REASON OF DRUNKENNESS, EXCESSIVE USE OF ALCOHOL, DRUGS, CHEMICALS, OR ANY OTHER TYPE OF MATERIAL.

THORNQUIST, ROBERT K MD WAS DISCIPLINED BY ALASKA ON JULY 20, 1994.
DISCIPLINARY ACTION: 60-MONTH PROBATION; RESTRICTION PLACED ON LICENSE
OFFENSE: SEXUAL ABUSE OF OR SEXUAL MISCONDUCT WITH A PATIENT
NOTES: SEXUAL MISCONDUCT WITH A FEMALE PATIENT. MUST PARTICIPATE IN THERAPY TO DETERMINE WHY HE VIOLATED PROFESSIONAL BOUNDARIES; MEET WITH PSYCHIATRIST AT LEAST EVERY 30 DAYS; TAKE PART IN MARITAL COUNSELING AND SUBMIT TO COMPLIANCE POLYGRAPH EXAMINATIONS; CHAPERONE WHEN TREATING FEMALE PATIENTS; OBTAIN CATEGORY I CONTINUING MEDICAL EDUCATION ON MAINTAINING PROFESSIONAL BOUNDARIES. EVALUATION IN NO MORE THAN 18 MONTHS; EMPLOYER REPORTS; NOTIFY HOSPITALS OF AGREEMENT; NOTIFY BOARD OF ABSENCES FROM COMMUNITY, BOARD APPEARANCES AS DIRECTED, AND COMPLY WITH LAWS AS THEY RELATE TO PRACTICE OF MEDICINE.

THREET, RICHARD W MD WAS DISCIPLINED BY ALASKA ON SEPTEMBER 21, 1995.
DISCIPLINARY ACTION: 60-MONTH PROBATION; RESTRICTION PLACED ON LICENSE
OFFENSE: SUBSTANCE ABUSE
NOTES: HISTORY OF SUBSTANCE ABUSE. EMPLOYMENT LOCATION IS RESTRICTED; REHABILITATIVE COUNSELING; PSYCHIATRIC COUNSELING/MONITORING; SHALL CONSUME NO DRUGS/ALCOHOL UNLESS ORDERED BY DOCTOR OR DENTIST; CANNOT SELF PRESCRIBE MEDICATIONS; AA/NARCOTICS ANONYMOUS MEETINGS; MUST HAVE AT LEAST FOUR URINE ANALYSIS/BLOOD TESTS PER MONTH AS ORDERED; MUST IDENTIFY PERSONAL HEALTH CARE PROVIDER; EMPLOYER REPORTS; MUST NOTIFY HOSPITALS OF THIS AGREEMENT; MUST HAVE PERIODIC BOARD INTERVIEW.

IDAHO
1996 serious action rate: 4.26/1000
1996 ranking: 21st

The Idaho State Board of Medicine provided a newsletter that contained only one name of a disciplined physician in 1991. In 1992, the Board sent one newsletter covering actions through December 1991 which listed the physician's name, degree, city and state of residence, date and type of action taken and reason for the action. Copies of board orders for actions taken from 1993 through 1996 which list the physician's name, degree, license number, the date and type of action taken and the reason for the action were also received. These orders contain information on modifications and terminations of board orders. There is minimal information on court decisions affecting board actions.

The information provided covers disciplinary actions taken against allopathic physicians (MDs) only.

Besides disciplinary actions taken by the State Medical Board, this listing also includes actions taken by the Medicare/Medicaid programs, the FDA, and the DEA against physicians located in this state. Disciplinary actions taken by other states against physicians located in Idaho or that match a physician disciplined by Idaho (see Appendix 2 for an explanation of the matching protocol) are also included.

> Although we have made every effort to match physicians' names correctly, some materials we received did not include complete information on middle names, license numbers, birth dates or addresses. Therefore, consumers should remember that non-disciplined physicians and physicians with different disciplinary actions may have similar names to those disciplined physicians listed in this state. Consumers should also remember that if they want the most current information on the status on a physician's license, they should contact the medical board of the state in which the physician practices or had practiced.

According to the Federation of State Medical Boards, Idaho took 8 serious disciplinary actions against MDs in 1996. Compared to the 1,878 MDs licensed in the state, Idaho had a serious disciplinary action rate of 4.26 serious actions per 1,000 MDs and a ranking of 21st on that list of states (see Table A, Findings, pg. 14).

The tables below summarize the data Public Citizen received from Idaho.

Table 1.	Disciplinary Actions Against MDs 1991 through 1996*		
Action		**Number**	**Percent****
Revocation		5	12.2%
Surrender		5	12.2%
Suspension		2	4.9%
Probation		3	7.3%
Practice Restriction		2	4.9%
Action Taken Against Controlled Substance License		4	9.8%
Other Actions		20	48.8%
Total Actions		**41**	**100.0%**

* This table lists only the two most serious disciplinary actions taken against a physician.
** Percentages may not total 100% due to rounding.

Table 2.	Offenses for which MDs were Disciplined 1991 through 1996*		
Offense		**Number**	**Percent**
Criminal Conviction		1	3.4%
Sexual Abuse of or Sexual Misconduct with a Patient		1	3.4%
Substandard Care, Incompetence or Negligence		4	13.8%
Misprescribing or Overprescribing Drugs		4	13.8%
Substance Abuse		1	3.4%
Disciplinary Action Taken Against License by Another State or Agency		16	55.2%
Other Offenses		2	6.9%
Total Records With Offense Listed		**29**	**100.0%**

* Includes only those actions for which an offense was listed and for which we had a corresponding term in our database.

If you feel that your doctor has not given you proper medical care or has mistreated you in any way--whether or not he or she is listed in this report--it is important that you let your state medical board know. Even if they do not immediately act on your complaint, it is important that the information be recorded in their files because it is possible that other people may have filed or will file complaints about the same doctor. Send a brief written description of what occurred to the addresses below or call the phone numbers listed for more information on how to file a complaint.

Address
Idaho State Board of Medicine
Darleene Thorsted, Executive Director
PO Box 83720, Statehouse Mail
Boise, ID 83720-0058
(208) 334-2822

Listing of Doctors Sanctioned by Offense

Sexual Abuse of or Sexual Misconduct with a Patient
LEGGETT, JOSEPH EDWARD

Substandard Care, Incompetence, or Negligence
DAVIS, GARY D
SPAULDING, BRADLEY B
WOODFIELD, BRENT E
YOUNG, LEONARD

Criminal Conviction or Plea of Guilty, Nolo Contendere, or No Contest to a Crime
APPLEBAUM, MICHAEL J

Misprescribing or Overprescribing Drugs
BOXALL, JOHN
GIBBONS, DE LAMAR J
GIBBONS, DELAMAR
GREENWOOD, WILLIAM H

Substance Abuse
FOX, FRANCIS H

Caution: This list is designed to be used only in conjunction with the rest of this book which includes additional information on each physician such as license number, date of action and more complete descriptions of the offenses.

DISCIPLINARY ACTIONS

APPLEBAUM, MICHAEL J MD OF SALT LAKE CITY, UT, WAS DISCIPLINED BY UTAH ON MAY 13, 1987.
DISCIPLINARY ACTION: 24-MONTH PROBATION; RESTRICTION PLACED ON CONTROLLED SUBSTANCE LICENSE
OFFENSE: SUBSTANCE ABUSE
NOTES: SCHEDULE II-IV CONTROLLED SUBSTANCE LICENSE SUSPENDED IMMEDIATELY; SCHEDULE V LICENSE ON PROBATION ALONG WITH MEDICAL LICENSE. ON 7/13/87 PROBATION TERMINATED AND LICENSES TO PRACTICE AND PRESCRIBE CONTROLLED SUBSTANCES WERE REINSTATED IN FAVOR OF A DIVERSIONARY PROGRAM TO BE COMPLETED BY APPLEBAUM.

APPLEBAUM, MICHAEL J MD, LICENSE NUMBER 00M5597, WAS DISCIPLINED BY IDAHO ON OCTOBER 13, 1989.
DISCIPLINARY ACTION: MONITORING OF PHYSICIAN
NOTES: CONDITIONAL LICENSE ISSUED: SHALL CONTINUE TO ATTEND AA ON A REGULAR WEEKLY BASIS AND WILL HAVE HIS AA SPONSOR SUBMIT QUARTERLY REPORTS TO THE BOARD; SHALL ABSTAIN FROM THE USE OF ALL MIND ALTERING CHEMICALS AND DRUGS, EXCEPT THOSE PRESCRIBED BY ANOTHER PHYSICIAN; SHALL IMMEDIATELY REPORT TO THE BOARD BY TELEPHONE ALL "SLIPS" FROM TOTAL ABSTINENCE; SHALL SUBMIT BIOLOGICAL FLUID SAMPLES ON A RANDOM BASIS TO THE BOARD; SHALL APPEAR FOR INTERVIEWS WITH THE BOARD WITH REASONABLE NOTICE; AND AGREES TO SUPERVISION TO ASSURE HIS COMPLIANCE WITH THESE TERMS AND CONDITIONS. CONDITIONS TERMINATED ON 3/18/94.

APPLEBAUM, MICHAEL J MD, LICENSE NUMBER 00M5597, WAS DISCIPLINED BY IDAHO ON AUGUST 14, 1996.
DISCIPLINARY ACTION: RESTRICTION PLACED ON CONTROLLED SUBSTANCE LICENSE; MONITORING OF PHYSICIAN
OFFENSE: CRIMINAL CONVICTION OR PLEA OF GUILTY, NOLO CONTENDERE, OR NO CONTEST TO A CRIME
NOTES: PLED GUILTY TO A FELONY COUNT OF ILLEGAL POSSESSION OF A CONTROLLED SUBSTANCE AND RECEIVED A WITHHELD JUDGEMENT FOR FELONY; USED FALSE AND FRAUDULENT STATEMENTS IN CONNECTION WITH LICENSING IN THAT IN REQUESTING BOARD TO TERMINATE PREVIOUS STIPULATION, FALSELY STATED HE WAS IN FULL COMPLIANCE WITH THE ORDER; PRESCRIBED OR FURNISHED NARCOTIC OR HALLUCINOGENIC DRUGS TO HIMSELF, AN ADDICTED PERSON, TO MAINTAIN HIS ADDICTION AND LEVEL OF USAGE WITHOUT ATTEMPTING TO TREAT THE PRIMARY CONDITION REQUIRING THE USE OF NARCOTICS AND FOR OTHER THAN TREATMENT OF ANY DISEASE, INJURY OR MEDICAL CONDITION; LICENSE REVOCATION, STAYED UNDER THE FOLLOWING TERMS AND CONDITIONS FOR A MINIMUM OF EIGHT YEARS: SHALL EXECUTE A CONTRACT WITH THE IDAHO MEDICAL ASSOCIATION PHYSICIAN HEALTH PROGRAM AND SHALL COMPLY WITH THE TERMS AND CONDITIONS OF THAT CONTRACT WITH REGULAR STATUS REPORTS ON COMPLIANCE; SHALL BE INELIGIBLE TO HOLD, AND SHALL NOT APPLY FOR, REGISTRATION WITH DEA OR THE IDAHO STATE BOARD OF PHARMACY TO PRESCRIBE, DISPENSE, OR ADMINISTER CONTROLLED SUBSTANCES, EXCEPT PSYCHOTROPICS AND ANTI-DEPRESSANTS; SHALL NOT PRESCRIBE, ADMINISTER, DISPENSE, ORDER, WRITE ORDERS FOR, GIVE VERBAL ORDERS FOR, OR POSSESS ANY CONTROLLED SUBSTANCES, EXCEPT PSYCHOTROPICS AND ANTI-DEPRESSANTS; SHALL ABSTAIN COMPLETELY FROM THE PERSONAL USE OR POSSESSION OF DRUGS, EXCEPT THOSE PRESCRIBED, ADMINISTERED, OR DISPENSED TO HIM BY ANOTHER PHYSICIAN; SHALL ABSTAIN COMPLETELY FROM THE USE OF ALCOHOL; SHALL SUBMIT TO RANDOM URINE SCREENINGS FOR DRUGS OF A WEEKLY BASIS OR AS OTHERWISE DIRECTED BY THE IMA PHYSICIAN HEALTH PROGRAM OR UPON BOARD REQUEST WITHOUT PRIOR NOTICE AND WITH REPORTS MONTHLY; SHALL HAVE A BOARD APPROVED MONITORING PHYSICIAN WHO SHALL PROVIDE REPORTS ON A QUARTERLY BASIS; SHALL GIVE A COPY OF THIS ORDER TO ANY HEALTH CARE ENTITY WHERE HE HAS PRIVILEGES; SHALL SUBMIT QUARTERLY DECLARATIONS UNDER PENALTY OF PERJURY STATING WHETHER THERE HAS BEEN COMPLIANCE WITH ALL THE CONDITIONS OF THIS ORDER; SHALL APPEAR FOR INTERVIEWS BEFORE THE BOARD AT THREE MONTH INTERVALS OR AS OTHERWISE DIRECTED; IF HE LEAVES IDAHO FOR THREE CONTINUOUS MONTHS HE MUST NOTIFY THE BOARD IN WRITING; AND PERIODS OF TIME OUTSIDE IDAHO WILL NOT APPLY TO THE REDUCTION OF THIS PERIOD.

BALDECK, EUGENE M MD, LICENSE NUMBER 00M2629, WAS DISCIPLINED BY IDAHO ON APRIL 25, 1996.
DISCIPLINARY ACTION: RESTRICTION PLACED ON LICENSE
OFFENSE: LOSS OR RESTRICTION OF HOSPITAL PRIVILEGES
NOTES: HIS SURGICAL PHACOEMULSIFICATION PRIVILEGES HAVE BEEN RESTRICTED BY ST. JOSEPH REGIONAL MEDICAL CENTER, IN LEWISTON, IDAHO. SHALL NOT PERFORM ANY SURGICAL PHACOEMULSIFICATION PROCEDURES FOR AT LEAST FIVE YEARS.

BEYMER, CHARLES H MD OF BOISE, ID, WAS DISCIPLINED BY WASHINGTON ON JANUARY 13, 1992.
DISCIPLINARY ACTION: RESTRICTION PLACED ON LICENSE
NOTES: CONDITIONAL LICENSE ISSUED WITH SPECIFIC CONDITIONS.

BLAISDELL, GLENN D MD, LICENSE NUMBER 00C5606, OF COLLEGE STATION, TX, WAS DISCIPLINED BY TEXAS ON OCTOBER 9, 1992.
DISCIPLINARY ACTION: SURRENDER OF LICENSE
NOTES: IN LIEU OF FURTHER DISCIPLINARY ACTION.

BLAISDELL, GLENN D MD OF MOSCOW, ID, WAS DISCIPLINED BY MISSOURI ON MARCH 24, 1994.
DISCIPLINARY ACTION: LICENSE REVOCATION
OFFENSE: DISCIPLINARY ACTION BY ANOTHER STATE OR AGENCY
NOTES: TEXAS LICENSE WAS FINALLY AND UNCONDITIONALLY REVOKED FOR FELONY CONVICTION OF POSSESSION OF A FIREARM, TERMINAL MISCHIEF AND INTEMPERATE USE OF ALCOHOL OR DRUGS. NO REAPPLICATION FOR LICENSE FOR SEVEN YEARS.

BOXALL, JOHN MD OF NAMPA, ID, WAS DISCIPLINED BY IDAHO ON AUGUST 1, 1992.
DISCIPLINARY ACTION: SURRENDER OF LICENSE
OFFENSE: OVERPRESCRIBING OR MISPRESCRIBING DRUGS
NOTES: PRESCRIBING CONTROLLED SUBSTANCES WITHOUT SUFFICIENT MEDICAL REASON. AGREED IN STIPULATION TO LIMIT PRESCRIPTION AUTHORITY, AND TO RETIRE FROM PRACTICE IN 1992.

BURKETT, ROX CHARLES MD, LICENSE NUMBER 0G29053, OF MODESTO, CA, WAS DISCIPLINED BY CALIFORNIA ON DECEMBER 6, 1992.
DISCIPLINARY ACTION: 1-MONTH LICENSE SUSPENSION; 60-MONTH PROBATION
NOTES: REVOCATION STAYED.

BURKETT, ROX CHARLES MD, LICENSE NUMBER 00M5976, OF 10378 FAIRVIEW AVENUE, BOISE, ID, WAS DISCIPLINED BY IDAHO ON AUGUST 22, 1994.
NOTES: SHALL NOT PRACTICE MEDICINE IN IDAHO PENDING HEARING.

BURKETT, ROX CHARLES MD, LICENSE NUMBER 0G29053, OF TIBURON, CA, WAS DISCIPLINED BY CALIFORNIA ON JANUARY 12,

- IDAHO -

1995.
DISCIPLINARY ACTION: 2-MONTH LICENSE SUSPENSION; 58-MONTH PROBATION
OFFENSE: FAILURE TO COMPLY WITH A PREVIOUS BOARD ORDER
NOTES: VIOLATED PROBATION OF PRIOR DISCIPLINE; LEFT CALIFORNIA TO PRACTICE IN IDAHO WITHOUT NOTIFYING THE BOARD. REVOCATION STAYED.

BURKETT, ROX CHARLES MD OF KETCHUM, ID, WAS DISCIPLINED BY UTAH ON AUGUST 22, 1995.
DISCIPLINARY ACTION: 15-MONTH PROBATION
OFFENSE: DISCIPLINARY ACTION BY ANOTHER STATE OR AGENCY
NOTES: DISCIPLINARY ACTION BY ANOTHER STATE FOR GROSS AND REPEATED NEGLIGENCE. REVOCATION STAYED.

BURKETT, ROX CHARLES MD, LICENSE NUMBER 00M5976, OF 10378 FAIRVIEW AVENUE, BOISE, ID, WAS DISCIPLINED BY IDAHO ON MAY 31, 1996.
OFFENSE: DISCIPLINARY ACTION BY ANOTHER STATE OR AGENCY
NOTES: ON 4/91 LICENSE APPLICATION HE STATED HE HAD NOT BEEN SUBJECT TO PROCEEDINGS BY A BOARD OR CONVICTED OF A FELONY OR MISDEMEANOR WHEN IN FACT IN 9/92 HE SIGNED A STIPULATION WITH THE CALIFORNIA BOARD AND HE WAS CONVICTED OF DRIVING UNDER THE INFLUENCE OFFENSES IN 1985 AND 1991. LICENSE LAPSED AND HE SHALL NOT APPLY FOR A LICENSE TO PRACTICE MEDICINE IN IDAHO FOR A MINIMUM OF FIVE YEARS. SHALL SUBMIT QUARTERLY DECLARATIONS UNDER THE PENALTY OF PERJURY STATING WHETHER THERE HAS BEEN COMPLIANCE WITH ALL THE CONDITIONS OF THIS ORDER; SHALL REPORT TO THE BOARD, AT THREE MONTH INTERVALS; AND SHALL EXECUTE A RELEASE AUTHORIZING ANY PERSON OR ENTITY HAVING INFORMATION RELEVANT TO HIS COMPLIANCE WITH THE PROVISIONS OF THIS ORDER TO GIVE THE INFORMATION TO THE BOARD.

BURTON, ROBERT C MD WAS DISCIPLINED BY NEVADA ON JANUARY 9, 1995.
DISCIPLINARY ACTION: FINE; REPRIMAND
OFFENSE: DISCIPLINARY ACTION BY ANOTHER STATE OR AGENCY
NOTES: IN 2/92 IDAHO LICENSE SUSPENDED FOR 30 DAYS AND HE PAID A FINE AS A RESULT OF PATIENT COMPLAINTS OF FAILURE TO COMMUNICATE. THIS ACTION RESULTED IN 8/94 REVOCATION OF HIS LICENSE IN CALIFORNIA AND HE FAILED TO REPORT THIS REVOCATION WITHIN 30 DAYS TO NEVADA. $1,000 FINE.

BURTON, ROBERT CALVIN MD, LICENSE NUMBER 0A29533, OF BOISE, ID, WAS DISCIPLINED BY CALIFORNIA ON MARCH 7, 1994.
DISCIPLINARY ACTION: LICENSE REVOCATION
OFFENSE: DISCIPLINARY ACTION BY ANOTHER STATE OR AGENCY
NOTES: BASED UPON DISCIPLINE BY IDAHO BOARD OF MEDICINE. DEFAULT DECISION.

CATELLI, WILLIAM FRANK MD OF WEST 620 NORTH 2ND, GRANGEVILLE, ID, WAS DISCIPLINED BY DEA ON AUGUST 28, 1993.
DISCIPLINARY ACTION: RESTRICTION PLACED ON CONTROLLED SUBSTANCE LICENSE
NOTES: VOLUNTARY SURRENDER OF CURRENT REGISTRATION; ISSUED RESTRICTED REGISTRATION.

DAVIS, GARY D MD OF COLUMBUS, GA, WAS DISCIPLINED BY IDAHO ON OCTOBER 19, 1989.
DISCIPLINARY ACTION: LICENSE REVOCATION
OFFENSE: SUBSTANDARD CARE, INCOMPETENCE, OR NEGLIGENCE
NOTES: BOARD ACTED TWICE IN 1990 TO DENY REINSTATEMENT.

DAVIS, GARY D MD, DATE OF BIRTH OCTOBER 17, 1945, OF MARTIN ARMY HOSP, #9200, FORT BENNING, GA, WAS DISCIPLINED BY MEDICARE ON JULY 19, 1990.
DISCIPLINARY ACTION: 24-MONTH EXCLUSION FROM THE MEDICARE AND/OR MEDICAID PROGRAMS
OFFENSE: DISCIPLINARY ACTION BY ANOTHER STATE OR AGENCY
NOTES: LICENSE REVOCATION OR SUSPENSION. REINSTATED ON 8/13/92.

DAVIS, GARY D MD, LICENSE NUMBER 0007202, OF FORT BENNING, GA, WAS DISCIPLINED BY ALABAMA ON SEPTEMBER 14, 1990.
DISCIPLINARY ACTION: 18-MONTH LICENSE SUSPENSION
OFFENSE: DISCIPLINARY ACTION BY ANOTHER STATE OR AGENCY
NOTES: ACTION BASED ON IDAHO BOARD'S REVOCATION OF LICENSE FOR PRACTICES INVOLVING THE RENDERING OF SUBSTANDARD MEDICAL CARE TO PATIENTS. ALABAMA FURTHER ORDERED THAT, SHOULD HIS IDAHO LICENSE BE REINSTATED PRIOR TO THE EXPIRATION OF THE 18-MONTH SUSPENSION PERIOD, THEN THE SUSPENSION WOULD BE SET ASIDE AND HIS LICENSE TO PRACTICE REINSTATED. IF HIS IDAHO LICENSE IS NOT REINSTATED WITHIN THE 18-MONTH SUSPENSION PERIOD, THEN HIS LICENSE WILL BE REVOKED AT THE EXPIRATION OF THE SUSPENSION PERIOD.

FOX, FRANCIS MD, LICENSE NUMBER 0143911, OF 11197 SANDHURST, BOISE, ID, WAS DISCIPLINED BY NEW YORK ON AUGUST 5, 1994.
DISCIPLINARY ACTION: SURRENDER OF LICENSE
OFFENSE: DISCIPLINARY ACTION BY ANOTHER STATE OR AGENCY
NOTES: DISCIPLINED BY IDAHO BOARD.

FOX, FRANCIS H MD, LICENSE NUMBER 00M5277, WAS DISCIPLINED BY IDAHO ON OCTOBER 8, 1993.
DISCIPLINARY ACTION: 6-MONTH SURRENDER OF CONTROLLED SUBSTANCE LICENSE; REQUIRED TO ENTER AN IMPAIRED PHYSICIAN PROGRAM OR DRUG OR ALCOHOL TREATMENT
OFFENSE: SUBSTANCE ABUSE
NOTES: IN THE PAST HE HAS ENGAGED IN EXCESSIVE USE OF CONTROLLED SUBSTANCES AND HAS DIVERTED CONTROLLED SUBSTANCES FOR HIS OWN USE; PRACTICED MEDICINE WHILE USING ADDICTIVE DRUGS; HAS PRESCRIBED OR FURNISHED DANGEROUS DRUGS FOR OTHER THAN THE TREATMENT OF DISEASE; HAS COMMITTED A FELONY. DURING THE SIX MONTH PERIOD OF SURRENDER HE SHALL BE INELIGIBLE TO HOLD AND SHALL NOT APPLY FOR REGISTRATION WITH DEA OR THE IDAHO STATE BOARD OF PHARMACY; SHALL NOT PRESCRIBE, ADMINISTER, ORDER, WRITE ORDERS FOR, GIVE VERBAL ORDERS FOR, OR POSSESS ANY CONTROLLED SUBSTANCES FOR A SIX MONTH PERIOD; SHALL IMMEDIATELY ENTER AN INPATIENT DRUG REHABILITATION HOSPITAL OR PROGRAM APPROVED BY THE BOARD AND SUCCESSFULLY COMPLETE THAT PROGRAM; SHALL ABSTAIN COMPLETELY FROM THE PERSONAL USE OR POSSESSION OF DRUGS EXCEPT WHEN DISPENSED TO HIM BY ANOTHER WHO IS AUTHORIZED TO DO SO; SHALL ABSTAIN COMPLETELY FROM THE USE OF ALCOHOL; SHALL SUBMIT TO RANDOM URINE SCREENINGS FOR DRUGS ON A WEEKLY BASIS; WITHIN 30 DAYS HE SHALL UNDERTAKE AND MAINTAIN PARTICIPATION IN AN ALCOHOL AND DRUG REHABILITATION PROGRAM, SUCH AS AA OR NARCOTICS ANONYMOUS AT LEAST FIVE TIMES A WEEK; SHALL HAVE A BOARD APPROVED MONITORING PHYSICIAN WHO SHALL PROVIDE QUARTERLY REPORTS ON HIS PROGRESS AND STATUS; SHALL PROVIDE ALL EMPLOYERS WHERE HE HAS PRIVILEGES WITH A COPY OF THIS ORDER; IF HE SHOULD LEAVE IDAHO FOR THREE CONTINUOUS MONTHS OR RESIDE OR PRACTICE OUTSIDE THE STATE, HE MUST NOTIFY THE BOARD OF HIS DATES OF DEPARTURE AND RETURN; PERIODS OF TIME SPENT OUTSIDE IDAHO WILL NOT APPLY TO THE REDUCTION OF THIS PERIOD; SHALL NOT REQUEST TERMINATION OF THIS ORDER FOR FIVE YEARS.

GIBBONS, DE LAMAR J MD, LICENSE NUMBER 00M5298, OF 204 OREGON STREET, KELLOGG, ID, WAS DISCIPLINED BY IDAHO ON DECEMBER 3, 1993.
DISCIPLINARY ACTION: LICENSE REVOCATION

- IDAHO -

OFFENSE: OVERPRESCRIBING OR MISPRESCRIBING DRUGS
NOTES: PRESCRIBED OR FURNISHED NARCOTICS TO ADDICTED PERSONS TO MAINTAIN THEIR ADDICTIONS AND LEVEL OF USAGE WITHOUT ATTEMPTING TO TREAT THE PRIMARY CONDITION REQUIRING USE OF NARCOTICS IN 18 CASES; THIS PRACTICE OF EXCESSIVE, UNWARRANTED AND INAPPROPRIATE PRESCRIBING IS A PATTERN OF INTENTIONAL AND DELIBERATE MEDICAL PRACTICE THAT ENDANGERS THE HEALTH AND SAFETY OF HIS PATIENTS. ON 12/22/93 A REQUEST FOR RECONSIDERATION WAS DENIED.

GIBBONS, DELAMAR MD OF KELLOGG, ID, WAS DISCIPLINED BY IDAHO ON SEPTEMBER 30, 1991.
DISCIPLINARY ACTION: REQUIRED TO TAKE ADDITIONAL MEDICAL EDUCATION
OFFENSE: OVERPRESCRIBING OR MISPRESCRIBING DRUGS
NOTES: INAPPROPRIATE PRESCRIBING OF CONTROLLED SUBSTANCES. AGREED TO CONTINUING MEDICAL EDUCATION STUDY AND EXAMINATION. STIPULATION EXPIRED ON 10/15/92.

GIBBONS, DELAMAR JOHNSON MD OF 204 OREGON STREET, KELLOGG, ID, WAS DISCIPLINED BY DEA ON DECEMBER 28, 1993.
DISCIPLINARY ACTION: SURRENDER OF CONTROLLED SUBSTANCE LICENSE
OFFENSE: DISCIPLINARY ACTION BY ANOTHER STATE OR AGENCY
NOTES: IDAHO MEDICAL LICENSE REVOKED. LOST FEDERAL CONTROLLED SUBSTANCE PRIVILEGES.

GREENWOOD, WILLIAM H MD, LICENSE NUMBER 00M2545, WAS DISCIPLINED BY IDAHO ON NOVEMBER 11, 1993.
DISCIPLINARY ACTION: 6-MONTH RESTRICTION PLACED ON CONTROLLED SUBSTANCE LICENSE
OFFENSE: OVERPRESCRIBING OR MISPRESCRIBING DRUGS
NOTES: ALLEGATIONS THAT HE HAS PRESCRIBED AND CONTINUES TO PRESCRIBE EXCESSIVE AMOUNTS OF CONTROLLED SUBSTANCES TO AT LEAST TWO PATIENTS; DOES NOT ADMIT THE ALLEGATIONS. CONDITIONS OF AGREED ORDER: SHALL NOT WRITE PRESCRIPTIONS OR HOSPITAL ORDERS FOR ANY CONTROLLED SUBSTANCES; HAS ATTENDED A SEMINAR ON PAIN MANAGEMENT AND WILL SUBMIT A REPORT WITHIN SIX MONTHS ON HOW HE WILL MODIFY FUTURE MANAGEMENT OF THE TWO SPECIFIED PATIENTS; SHALL SUBMIT QUARTERLY DECLARATIONS THAT HE IS IN COMPLIANCE; SHALL APPEAR FOR BOARD INTERVIEWS UPON REQUEST; SHALL NOTIFY THE BOARD IF HE LEAVES THE STATE FOR THREE MONTHS; TIME SPENT OUTSIDE THE STATE DOES NOT COUNT TOWARD TIME OF RESTRICTIONS; SHALL SUPPLY A COPY OF THIS ORDER ANYWHERE HE HAS PRIVILEGES. ON 6/8/94 THIS ORDER WAS TERMINATED AS HE HAD COMPLIED WITH ALL TERMS.

GREGORY, NANCY J MD, LICENSE NUMBER 0055095, OF 13 ADAMS COURT, AMESBURY, MA, WAS DISCIPLINED BY MASSACHUSETTS ON JUNE 23, 1993.
NOTES: VOLUNTARY SUSPENSION OF PRACTICE. ON 4/13/94 REQUEST TO RETURN TO PRACTICE ALLOWED.

GREGORY, NANCY JANE MD OF KETCHUM, ID, WAS DISCIPLINED BY ILLINOIS ON OCTOBER 1, 1994.
DISCIPLINARY ACTION: LICENSE SUSPENSION
OFFENSE: DISCIPLINARY ACTION BY ANOTHER STATE OR AGENCY
NOTES: AGREED TO VOLUNTARILY SUSPEND RIGHT TO PRACTICE IN MASSACHUSETTS. INDEFINITE SUSPENSION.

GWINNER, ROBERT A MD, LICENSE NUMBER 0018797, OF SUN VALLEY, ID, WAS DISCIPLINED BY OHIO ON MAY 13, 1992.
DISCIPLINARY ACTION: SURRENDER OF LICENSE
NOTES: PERMANENT VOLUNTARY RETIREMENT IN LIEU OF FORMAL DISCIPLINARY PROCEEDINGS ON ALLEGATIONS ISSUED BY BOARD ON 3/11/92.

HALE, BOYD J MD OF PRESTON, ID, WAS DISCIPLINED BY UTAH ON MAY 31, 1989.
DISCIPLINARY ACTION: PROBATION
OFFENSE: DISCIPLINARY ACTION BY ANOTHER STATE OR AGENCY
NOTES: DISCIPLINARY ACTION BY IDAHO; PROBATION IN ACCORDANCE WITH IDAHO TERMS. ON 10/4/90 PROBATION TERMINATED AND LICENSE REINSTATED WITH FULL PRIVILEGES.

HALLER, FREDERICK R MD OF SILVERTON, ID, WAS DISCIPLINED BY LOUISIANA ON JULY 5, 1991.
DISCIPLINARY ACTION: FINE
OFFENSE: DISCIPLINARY ACTION BY ANOTHER STATE OR AGENCY
NOTES: CHARGED WITH FRAUD, DECEIT OR PERJURY IN OBTAINING A LICENSE OR PERMIT AND ACTION AGAINST HIM BY THE LICENSING AUTHORITY OF ANOTHER STATE. SUSPENSION OF ONE YEAR STAYED; MUST PAY A $1,000 FINE AND GIVE PRIOR NOTICE TO BOARD OF INTENT TO RELOCATE TO PRACTICE IN LOUISIANA.

HART, BURTON B DO WAS DISCIPLINED BY WASHINGTON ON APRIL 28, 1995.
DISCIPLINARY ACTION: 24-MONTH PROBATION; FINE
OFFENSE: PROFESSIONAL MISCONDUCT
NOTES: ADVERTISING WHICH IS FALSE, FRAUDULENT OR MISLEADING. SHALL IMMEDIATELY CEASE AND REFRAIN FROM USING, ADVISING, PRESCRIBING, OR TREATING PATIENTS WITH INTRAVENOUS OR ORAL USE OF HYDROGEN PEROXIDE AND SHALL NOT ALLOW ANY AUXILIARY STAFF TO PERFORM OR CONSULT WITH OR TREAT PATIENTS WITH HYDROGEN PEROXIDE; SHALL MAKE HIS OFFICE AND OFFICE RECORDS AVAILABLE FOR PERIODIC BOARD INSPECTION; SHALL COMPLY WITH THE BOARD'S COMPLIANCE SURVEILLANCE PROGRAM INCLUDING SUBMITTING QUARTERLY DECLARATIONS WITH ALL THE CONDITIONS OF PROBATION AND APPEARING IN PERSON FOR COMPLIANCE INTERVIEWS; SHALL PROVIDE THE BOARD CURRENT HOME AND BUSINESS ADDRESSES AND ANY CHANGES IN ADDRESS; AND TIME NOT SPENT PRACTICING SHALL BE TOLLED. $1,500 FINE.

HART, BURTON B DO WAS DISCIPLINED BY IDAHO ON DECEMBER 11, 1995.
DISCIPLINARY ACTION: DENIAL OF NEW LICENSE
OFFENSE: DISCIPLINARY ACTION BY ANOTHER STATE OR AGENCY
NOTES: PRACTICE INCLUDES THE USE OF UNACCEPTED AND UNCONVENTIONAL MEDICAL PRACTICES INCLUDING SCLERA, EDTA, AND CHELATION THERAPIES; DISCIPLINED BY WASHINGTON BOARD FOR UNCONVENTIONAL AND UNACCEPTED USE OF HYDROGEN PEROXIDE; LIED ON IDAHO APPLICATION WHEN HE SAID HIS LICENSE WAS NOT RESTRICTED IN ANOTHER STATE; ADMITTED TO WASHINGTON BOARD THAT HE ENGAGED IN FALSE, FRAUDULENT OR MISLEADING ADVERTISING AND PROMOTING UNNECESSARY OR INEFFICACIOUS DRUGS, DEVICES, TREATMENTS, PROCEDURES AND SERVICES FOR PERSONAL GAIN.

HATFIELD, KENNETH B MD, LICENSE NUMBER 0022800, OF 3218 SPRUCEWOOD, WILMETTE, IL, WAS DISCIPLINED BY WISCONSIN ON MARCH 24, 1994.
DISCIPLINARY ACTION: LICENSE SUSPENSION
OFFENSE: DISCIPLINARY ACTION BY ANOTHER STATE OR AGENCY
NOTES: ON 5/14/92 THE ILLINOIS BOARD SUSPENDED HIS LICENSE AND REVOKED HIS CONTROLLED SUBSTANCES LICENSE FOR A MINIMUM OF FIVE YEARS BASED UPON A FINDING OF UNPROFESSIONAL CONDUCT. HE APPEALED THIS DECISION TO THE CIRCUIT COURT OF COOK COUNTY, ILLINOIS. IN 5/18/94 THE ILLINOIS COURT REVERSED THE ILLINOIS BOARD'S DECISION FINDING THE CONCLUSIONS WERE NOT SUPPORTED BY THE MANIFEST WEIGHT OF

- IDAHO -

THE EVIDENCE IN THE RECORD. ON 9/9/94 DR. HATFIELD SIGNED A SETTLEMENT AGREEMENT WITH THE ILLINOIS BOARD WHEREBY HIS LICENSE WAS RESTORED SUBJECT TO TERMS. HE FULLY COMPLIED WITH THESE TERMS AND HIS LICENSE TO PRACTICE IN ILLINOIS WAS RESTORED IN FULL ON 9/9/95. THIS ORDER WAS TERMINATED ON 5/22/96 IN RECOGNITION OF HIS SUCCESSFUL COMPLETION OF THE TERMS OF THE ILLINOIS ORDER.

HATFIELD, KENNETH B MD, LICENSE NUMBER 00M3768, WAS DISCIPLINED BY IDAHO ON MAY 16, 1995.
DISCIPLINARY ACTION: 12-MONTH CONTROLLED SUBSTANCE LICENSE PLACED ON PROBATION
OFFENSE: DISCIPLINARY ACTION BY ANOTHER STATE OR AGENCY
NOTES: ON 9/9/94 ILLINOIS BOARD PLACED CONTROLLED SUBSTANCES LICENSE ON PROBATION FOR ONE YEAR. THE IDAHO BOARD FOR THE PURPOSE OF RECIPROCAL DISCIPLINE INCORPORATES THE TERMS AND CONDITIONS OF THIS ORDER AND ORDERS HIM TO FULLY COMPLY WITH THEM. INACTIVE LICENSE.

HATFIELD, KENNETH B MD, LICENSE NUMBER 0092695, OF 3218 SPRUCEWOOD ROAD, WILMETTE, IL, WAS DISCIPLINED BY NEW YORK ON FEBRUARY 28, 1996.
DISCIPLINARY ACTION: 12-MONTH PROBATION
OFFENSE: DISCIPLINARY ACTION BY ANOTHER STATE OR AGENCY
NOTES: ACTION IN ILLINOIS FOR FAILING TO MAINTAIN ACCURATE PATIENT RECORDS. ONE YEAR SUSPENSION, STAYED WITH PROBATION UPON THE COMMENCEMENT OF PRACTICE IN NEW YORK.

HATFIELD, KENNETH B MD, DATE OF BIRTH NOVEMBER 7, 1933, LICENSE NUMBER 0022800, OF 3218 SPRUCEWOOD ROAD, WILMETTE, IL, WAS DISCIPLINED BY WISCONSIN ON MAY 22, 1996.
DISCIPLINARY ACTION: REPRIMAND
OFFENSE: DISCIPLINARY ACTION BY ANOTHER STATE OR AGENCY
NOTES: ACTION IN ILLINOIS. ON 5/14/92 INDEFINITELY SUSPENDED HIS LICENSE TO PRACTICE MEDICINE IN ILLINOIS AND REVOKED HIS CONTROLLED DANGEROUS SUBSTANCE LICENSE FOR A MINIMUM OF FIVE YEARS BASED ON A FINDING OF UNPROFESSIONAL CONDUCT. UPON RECEIPT OF THIS INFORMATION THE WISCONSIN DEPARTMENT OF REGULATION AND LICENSING FILED A FORMAL COMPLAINT ON 2/14/94. ON 03/24/94 WISCONSIN INDEFINITELY SUSPENDED HIS LICENCE TO PRACTICE MEDICINE AND SURGERY PENDING HIS APPEAL OF THE ILLINOIS ORDER. ON 9/09/94 HE AND THE ILLINOIS DEPARTMENT OF PROFESSIONAL REGULATION ENTERED INTO A SETTLEMENT AGREEMENT WHEREBY ALL APPEALS WERE DISMISSED AND HIS LICENSE TO PRACTICE MEDICINE AND SURGERY IN ILLINOIS WAS RESTORED SUBJECT TO TERMS AND CONDITIONS. HE HAS COMPLIED WITH ALL THE TERMS OF THE REVISED ILLINOIS ORDER OF 9/09/94 AND HIS LICENSE TO PRACTICE MEDICINE IN ILLINOIS WAS RESTORED IN FULL ON 9/09/95. THE INTERIM ORDER ENTERED BY THE BOARD ON 3/24/94 IS TERMINATED; HIS LICENSE TO PRACTICE MEDICINE AND SURGERY IN WISCONSIN IS SUSPENDED FOR A PERIOD TO COINCIDE WITH THE PERIOD OF SUSPENSION SERVED UNDER THE TERMS OF THE 3/24/94 INTERIM ORDER AND TO TERMINATE ON THE DATE THIS ORDER IS ADOPTED.

HOLLINGSWORTH, JAMES E DR OF 1661 SHORELINE DRIVE, BOISE, ID, WAS DISCIPLINED BY ILLINOIS ON DECEMBER 1, 1989.
DISCIPLINARY ACTION: SURRENDER OF LICENSE
OFFENSE: DISCIPLINARY ACTION BY ANOTHER STATE OR AGENCY
NOTES: ENTERED INTO STIPULATION WITH IDAHO BOARD WHICH HE AGREED TO SUBMIT A LIMITED FORMULARY OF DRUGS WHICH HE CAN DISPENSE; AGREED TO AVOID DISPENSING DRUGS NOT ON THIS LIST OUT OF HIS OFFICE BUT WILL WRITE PRESCRIPTIONS TO BE FILLED BY A PHARMACY; MAINTAIN COMPLETE AND ACCURATE INVENTORY OF ALL DRUGS ORDERED AND DISPENSED; WILL MAINTAIN MORE DETAILED WRITTEN RECORDS OF PATIENT VISITS

HOPKIN, JEFFREY MD, LICENSE NUMBER 0016117, WAS DISCIPLINED BY ARIZONA ON JULY 19, 1995.
DISCIPLINARY ACTION: MONITORING OF PHYSICIAN
OFFENSE: PROFESSIONAL MISCONDUCT
NOTES: ALLEGATIONS THAT HE EXHIBITED DISRUPTIVE BEHAVIOR AT HOSPITAL. WITHIN 45 DAYS, SHALL BEGIN COUNSELING WITH A BOARD-APPROVED COUNSELOR REGARDING THE ISSUE OF INTERPERSONAL RELATIONSHIPS. COUNSELOR SHALL SUBMIT QUARTERLY REPORTS TO THE BOARD. 1/1/96 ORDER TERMINATED.

HOPKIN, JEFFREY MD WAS DISCIPLINED BY IDAHO ON DECEMBER 20, 1995.
DISCIPLINARY ACTION: MONITORING OF PHYSICIAN
OFFENSE: DISCIPLINARY ACTION BY ANOTHER STATE OR AGENCY
NOTES: ON 9/18/95 THERE WAS A STIPULATION AND ORDER ISSUED BY THE ARIZONA BOARD. IDAHO BOARD ISSUED HIM A LICENSE ON THE CONDITION THAT WITHIN 45 DAYS HE SHALL BEGIN COUNSELING WITH A BOARD APPROVED THERAPIST REGARDING THE ISSUE OF INTERPERSONAL RELATIONSHIPS; THERAPIST SHALL SUBMIT QUARTERLY REPORTS TO THE BOARD; SHALL INFORM ANY HOSPITAL WHERE HE PRACTICES OF THE TERMS OF THIS STIPULATION. ON 12/18/96 ORDER TERMINATED.

JOHNSTON, JAMES C MD, LICENSE NUMBER 0022573, WAS DISCIPLINED BY ARIZONA ON OCTOBER 18, 1995.
NOTES: SHALL NOT PRACTICE MEDICINE IN ARIZONA PRIOR TO MEETING WITH THE BOARD.

JOHNSTON, JAMES CHRISTOPHER MD, DATE OF BIRTH NOVEMBER 20, 1959, LICENSE NUMBER 00G8880, OF NACOGDOCHES, TX, WAS DISCIPLINED BY TEXAS ON JUNE 22, 1994.
DISCIPLINARY ACTION: RESTRICTION PLACED ON LICENSE
OFFENSE: SEXUAL ABUSE OF OR SEXUAL MISCONDUCT WITH A PATIENT
NOTES: AS RECENTLY AS 6/8/94 CRIMINAL COMPLAINTS WERE FILED AGAINST HIM ALLEGING HE ENGAGED IN BEHAVIOR CONSTITUTING ATTEMPTED SEXUAL ASSAULT AGAINST INDIVIDUALS WHO WERE PATIENTS; DENIES ALLEGATIONS; BECAUSE HE DESIRES TO FOCUS RESOURCES AND TIME ON DEFENSE OF THE CRIMINAL CASE. AGREES TO THIS ORDER WITH THE BOARD. LICENSE IS RESTRICTED AS FOLLOWS: SHALL NOT EXAMINE OR TREAT PATIENTS AFTER THE ORDER DATE; WITHIN 30 DAYS SHALL SUBMIT HIMSELF FOR ASSESSMENT THROUGH THE BEHAVIOR CARE NETWORK PROGRAM OR OTHER BOARD-APPROVED PROGRAM WHICH WILL FOCUS ON THE DISPARITY BETWEEN THE COMPLAINTS AGAINST HIM AND HIS OWN VERSION OF EVENTS AND ATTEMPT TO DETERMINE THE DEGREE OF RISK TO THE PUBLIC INVOLVED IN HIS CONTINUED PRACTICE; SHOULD THIS EVALUATION INDICATE HIS PRACTICE CONSTITUTES NO THREAT TO THE PUBLIC HEALTH HE SHALL BE PERMITTED TO RESUME PRACTICE PENDING FURTHER ORDER OF THE BOARD PROVIDED HE SEES PATIENTS ONLY WHEN ACCOMPANIED BY A CHAPERONE APPROVED IN ADVANCE WHO WILL SIGN ALL CHARTS TO INDICATE PRESENCE; SHALL COOPERATE WITH THE BOARD IN VERIFYING COMPLIANCE; SHALL INFORM BOARD OF CHANGE OF ADDRESS WITHIN 10 DAYS.

JOHNSTON, JAMES CHRISTOPHER MD, LICENSE NUMBER 00M5411, WAS DISCIPLINED BY IDAHO ON DECEMBER 14, 1994.
DISCIPLINARY ACTION: RESTRICTION PLACED ON LICENSE; MONITORING OF PHYSICIAN
OFFENSE: DISCIPLINARY ACTION BY ANOTHER STATE OR AGENCY

- IDAHO -

NOTES: ON 9/30/94 TEXAS RESTRICTED HIS LICENSE BASED ON CRIMINAL ALLEGATIONS THAT HE HAD ENGAGED IN BEHAVIOR CONSTITUTING ATTEMPTED SEXUAL ASSAULT AGAINST PATIENTS. IDAHO BOARD ADOPTS AND INCORPORATES ALL TERMS AND CONDITIONS OF THE TEXAS ORDER WHICH INCLUDE: SHALL NOT EXAMINE OR TREAT ANY PATIENTS WITHOUT BEING ACCOMPANIED AT ALL TIMES BY A PROCTOR OR CHAPERONE APPROVED BY THE BOARD; SHALL OBTAIN AN EXAM TABLE THAT IS SPECIFICALLY DESIGNED FOR THE PERFORMANCE OF ELECTROMYOGRAPHY WITH A STANDARD ARM BOARD AND THE ABILITY TO ELEVATE THE HEAD OF THE PATIENT; SHALL REPOSITION HIS EXAMINATION TABLE SO THAT HE MAY WALK BEHIND PATIENTS TO EXAMINE THE SHOULDER AND PROXIMAL AREAS; SHALL NOT PLACE A PAGER OR INSTRUMENTS IN HIS POCKETS DURING EXAMINATION OF PATIENTS; PATIENTS SHALL BE REPOSITIONED DURING EVALUATIONS ONLY BY A NURSE OR TECHNICIAN; SHALL EXPLAIN TO ALL PATIENTS THOSE PROCEDURES WHICH INVOLVE CONTACT WITH HIM PRIOR TO SUCH CONTACT; SHALL ASK PATIENTS IN DETAIL REGARDING ANY PROBLEMS OR CONCERNS WHICH THEY MIGHT HAVE CONCERNING HIS EXAMINATIONS OR ANY PROCEDURES PERFORMED; SHALL UNDERGO ADDITIONAL PHALLOMETRIC TESTING WITHIN 60 DAYS.

JOHNSTON, JAMES CHRISTOPHER MD, LICENSE NUMBER 0A44527, OF NACOGDOCHES, TX, WAS DISCIPLINED BY CALIFORNIA ON DECEMBER 30, 1995.
DISCIPLINARY ACTION: SURRENDER OF LICENSE
NOTES: WHILE CHARGES PENDING.

JOHNSTON, JAMES CHRISTOPHER MD, LICENSE NUMBER 0018716, OF SAN ANTONIO, TX, WAS DISCIPLINED BY OREGON ON NOVEMBER 4, 1996.
DISCIPLINARY ACTION: SURRENDER OF LICENSE
NOTES: VOLUNTARY SURRENDER.

KRUEGER, PHILIP MICHAEL MD, LICENSE NUMBER 00D4187, OF BOISE, ID, WAS DISCIPLINED BY TEXAS ON APRIL 20, 1991.
DISCIPLINARY ACTION: PROBATION
OFFENSE: DISCIPLINARY ACTION BY ANOTHER STATE OR AGENCY
NOTES: MUST INFORM BOARD IN WRITING OF INTENT TO RESUME PRACTICING MEDICINE IN TEXAS.

LAMBERT, PAUL W MD, LICENSE NUMBER 0014916, OF CLARKSTON, WA, WAS DISCIPLINED BY WASHINGTON ON SEPTEMBER 8, 1994.
DISCIPLINARY ACTION: 60-MONTH PROBATION; FINE
NOTES: PROBATION HAS FOLLOWING TERMS AND CONDITIONS: SHALL UTILIZE A "SOAP" CHARTING FORMAT FOR ALL PATIENT FILES, SHALL WRITE ALL PRESCRIPTIONS FOR CONTROLLED SUBSTANCES FOR OUT-PATIENT USAGE ON SERIALLY NUMBERED TRIPLICATE PRESCRIPTION PADS, SHALL COMPLETE 25 HOURS OF CATEGORY I CONTINUING MEDICAL EDUCATION IN THE AREAS OF PRESCRIBING CONTROLLED SUBSTANCES, ADDICTION OR SUBSTANCE ABUSE AND SHALL PAY A $500 FINE. ON 5/11/95 HIS REQUEST WAS GRANTED TO HAVE A COMMISSION REPRESENTATIVE MAKE ANNUAL RATHER THAN SEMI-ANNUAL VISITS TO HIS PRACTICE. ON 9/11/97 BOARD GRANTED HIS REQUEST TO TERMINATE THIS ORDER.

LAMBERT, PAUL W MD, LICENSE NUMBER 00M4794, WAS DISCIPLINED BY IDAHO ON NOVEMBER 21, 1994.
DISCIPLINARY ACTION: PROBATION; REQUIRED TO TAKE ADDITIONAL MEDICAL EDUCATION
OFFENSE: DISCIPLINARY ACTION BY ANOTHER STATE OR AGENCY
NOTES: ON 9/8/94 WASHINGTON BOARD ACTION ISSUED FIVE YEAR SUSPENSION WHICH WAS STAYED WITH TERMS AND CONDITIONS BASED ON HIS PRESCRIBING EXCESSIVE AMOUNTS OF DANGEROUS DRUGS AND FAILING TO RECORD PRESCRIPTIONS FOR SIX PATIENTS BETWEEN 5/91 AND 2/93. THE IDAHO BOARD ADOPTS THIS RECIPROCAL DISCIPLINE, INCORPORATING THE TERMS AND CONDITIONS OF THE WASHINGTON ORDER WHICH INCLUDE PROBATION WITH THE FOLLOWING CONDITIONS: SHALL UTILIZE A SOAP CHARTING FORMAT FOR ALL PATIENT FILES; SHALL WRITE ALL PRESCRIPTIONS FOR CONTROLLED SUBSTANCES OF OUTPATIENT USAGE ON SERIALLY NUMBERED TRIPLICATE PRESCRIPTION PADS; SHALL NOT PRESCRIBE SCHEDULED DRUGS FOR MORE THAN TWO WEEKS FOR ANY SINGLE DIAGNOSIS OR COMPLAINT OR TO ANY PATIENT WITH AN ADDICTION HISTORY OR SUSPECTED ADDITION PROBLEM; SHALL COMPLETE 25 HOURS OF CATEGORY I CONTINUING MEDICAL EDUCATION IN THE AREAS OF PRESCRIBING CONTROLLED SUBSTANCES AND ADDICTION OR SUBSTANCE ABUSE; 13 OF THE HOURS MUST BE COMPLETED WITHIN ONE YEAR OF THE EFFECTIVE DATE OF THIS ORDER; THE REMAINING 12 HOURS SHALL BE COMPLETED WITHIN 24 MONTHS OF THE EFFECTIVE DATE OF THIS ORDER; SHALL APPEAR BEFORE THE COMMISSION SIX MONTHS FROM EFFECTIVE DATE; A REPRESENTATIVE OF THE COMMISSION MAY MAKE ANNOUNCED VISITS SEMI-ANNUALLY TO HIS PRACTICE TO REVIEW RECORDS AND OTHER ASPECTS OF HIS PRACTICE; SHALL INFORM THE BOARD OF ANY CHANGES IN HIS PRACTICE OR RESIDENCE ADDRESS. $500 FINE.

LAMBERT, PAUL W MD, LICENSE NUMBER 0C16439, OF CLARKSTON, WA, WAS DISCIPLINED BY CALIFORNIA ON SEPTEMBER 7, 1995.
DISCIPLINARY ACTION: SURRENDER OF LICENSE
NOTES: WHILE CHARGES PENDING.

LAUGHLIN, PATRICK A DO OF P.O. BOX 151 402 OLD STATE HWY., CASCADE, ID, WAS DISCIPLINED BY DEA ON OCTOBER 24, 1995.
DISCIPLINARY ACTION: SURRENDER OF CONTROLLED SUBSTANCE LICENSE
NOTES: IN LIEU OF ORDER TO SHOW CAUSE.

LAWYER, JAMES T MD OF 3248 NORTH MOUNTAIN LANE, BOISE, ID, WAS DISCIPLINED BY NEW MEXICO ON DECEMBER 21, 1994.
OFFENSE: DISCIPLINARY ACTION BY ANOTHER STATE OR AGENCY
NOTES: LICENSE PLACED UNDER UNSPECIFIED CONDITIONS.

LEGGETT, JOSEPH E MD OF 815 11TH STREET, HUNTSVILLE, TX, WAS DISCIPLINED BY DEA ON NOVEMBER 18, 1994.
DISCIPLINARY ACTION: SURRENDER OF CONTROLLED SUBSTANCE LICENSE
NOTES: IN LIEU OF PUBLIC INTEREST REVOCATION.

LEGGETT, JOSEPH EDWARD MD, DATE OF BIRTH JULY 10, 1943, LICENSE NUMBER 00E2676, OF 575 ELKINS LANE, HUNTSVILLE, TX, WAS DISCIPLINED BY TEXAS ON JUNE 17, 1992.
DISCIPLINARY ACTION: RESTRICTION PLACED ON LICENSE
NOTES: RESTRICTED TO THE TREATMENT OF MALE PATIENTS WITHIN THE DEPARTMENT OF CORRECTIONS UNTIL SUCH TIME THAT THE IDAHO BOARD'S ACTION IS RESOLVED.

LEGGETT, JOSEPH EDWARD MD, DATE OF BIRTH JULY 10, 1943, LICENSE NUMBER 00M5108, OF COEUR D'ALENE, ID, WAS DISCIPLINED BY IDAHO ON SEPTEMBER 11, 1992.
DISCIPLINARY ACTION: SURRENDER OF LICENSE
OFFENSE: SEXUAL ABUSE OF OR SEXUAL MISCONDUCT WITH A PATIENT
NOTES: CHARGED WITH HAVING SEX WITH TWO PATIENTS. HAS APPEALED A 9/28/89 ORDER OF THE BOARD REVOKING HIS LICENSE TO THE IDAHO SUPREME COURT. IN 11/91 DISTRICT COURT REJECTED AN APPEAL TO THE COURT. THE EARLIER APPEAL RESULTED IN A STAY OF THE REVOCATION ORDER. JUDGE CALLED FOR ADDITIONAL CONSIDERATION BY BOARD. A SECOND HEARING WAS CONDUCTED MAY 8-9 1990. ON 1/15/91 THE BOARD AFFIRMED THE 9/29/89 REVOCATION. ON 9/11/92, HE

- IDAHO -

AGREED TO VOLUNTARILY SURRENDER HIS LICENSE AND NEVER AGAIN APPLY FOR REINSTATEMENT; THE REVOCATION WAS WITHDRAWN.

LEGGETT, JOSEPH EDWARD MD, DATE OF BIRTH JULY 10, 1943, LICENSE NUMBER 00E2676, OF 575 ELKINS LAKE, HUNTSVILLE, TX, WAS DISCIPLINED BY TEXAS ON NOVEMBER 19, 1993.
DISCIPLINARY ACTION: 120-MONTH PROBATION; RESTRICTION PLACED ON LICENSE
OFFENSE: DISCIPLINARY ACTION BY ANOTHER STATE OR AGENCY
NOTES: ON 9/29/89 IDAHO BOARD REVOKED HIS MEDICAL LICENSE AFTER FINDING HE HAD ENGAGED IN IMPROPER SEXUAL CONDUCT WITH TWO PATIENTS; HE DENIED THESE CHARGES AND APPEALED THE RULING; THE DISTRICT COURT AFFIRMED THE BOARD'S RULING ON 11/22/91; HE APPEALED TO THE IDAHO SUPREME COURT; PRIOR TO A RULING BY THE COURT HE AND THE IDAHO BOARD ENTERED INTO A STIPULATION FOR DISMISSAL WITH PREJUDICE WHEREBY THE APPEAL WAS DISMISSED AND HE WAS ALLOWED TO SURRENDER HIS LICENSE IN LIEU OF REVOCATION; WAS ALSO INDICTED IN WYOMING FOR ALLEGED SEXUAL MISCONDUCT INVOLVING FEMALE PATIENTS; IS CONTESTING THESE ALLEGATIONS AND A TRIAL WAS PENDING AS OF THE ORDER DATE; HIS EMPLOYER IN TEXAS HAS PLACED HIM IN A PURELY ADMINISTRATIVE ROLE. TEXAS LICENSE SUSPENDED. SUSPENSION STAYED. CONDITIONS OF PROBATION: RESTRICTED FROM THE TREATMENT OF ANY PATIENT PENDING THE OUTCOME OF THE CRIMINAL MATTERS IN WYOMING; IF THIS DOES NOT RESULT IN A FINDING OF GUILT OR A CONVICTION MAY RETURN TO THE PRACTICE OF MEDICINE BUT MAY ONLY TREAT MALE PRISONERS. OTHER CONDITIONS INCLUDE: SHALL APPEAR BEFORE THE BOARD ONCE A YEAR; SHALL ATTEND AT LEAST 50 HOURS OF CONTINUING MEDICAL EDUCATION PER YEAR; SHALL GIVE A COPY OF THIS ORDER TO ANY HEALTH CARE ENTITY WHERE HE HAS PRIVILEGES; SHALL COOPERATE WITH THE BOARD IN VERIFYING COMPLIANCE; SHALL INFORM BOARD OF CHANGE OF ADDRESS WITHIN 10 DAYS OR IF HE LEAVES THE STATE; TIME SPENT OUT OF TEXAS DOES NOT COUNT TOWARD PROBATION. IF HE IS FOUND GUILTY OF THE PENDING CHARGES IN WYOMING, TEXAS LICENSE WILL BE REVOKED. SHALL NOT SEEK MODIFICATION FOR ONE YEAR.

LEGGETT, JOSEPH EDWARD MD, DATE OF BIRTH JULY 10, 1943, LICENSE NUMBER 00E2676, OF 575 ELKINS LAKE, HUNTSVILLE, TX, WAS DISCIPLINED BY TEXAS ON SEPTEMBER 20, 1994.
DISCIPLINARY ACTION: LICENSE REVOCATION
OFFENSE: CRIMINAL CONVICTION OR PLEA OF GUILTY, NOLO CONTENDERE, OR NO CONTEST TO A CRIME
NOTES: ON 9/14/94 IN WYOMING HE ENTERED PLEAS OF NOLO CONTENDERE TO CHARGES OF SECOND DEGREE SEXUAL ASSAULT; THE COURT ORDERED HIM PLACED ON FIVE YEARS OF SUPERVISED PROBATION UNDER CONDITIONS.

LEGGETT, JOSEPH EDWARD MD, DATE OF BIRTH JULY 10, 1943, OF 575 ELKINS LAKE, HUNTSVILLE, TX, WAS DISCIPLINED BY MEDICARE ON MAY 4, 1995.
DISCIPLINARY ACTION: 60-MONTH EXCLUSION FROM THE MEDICARE AND/OR MEDICAID PROGRAMS
OFFENSE: CRIMINAL CONVICTION OR PLEA OF GUILTY, NOLO CONTENDERE, OR NO CONTEST TO A CRIME
NOTES: CONVICTED OF A CRIME RELATED TO PATIENT ABUSE OR NEGLECT.

MCDONNELL, THOMAS R MD WAS DISCIPLINED BY WASHINGTON ON AUGUST 16, 1989.
DISCIPLINARY ACTION: 120-MONTH PROBATION; RESTRICTION PLACED ON CONTROLLED SUBSTANCE LICENSE
OFFENSE: SUBSTANCE ABUSE
NOTES: SUFFERS FROM THE DISEASE OF CHEMICAL DEPENDENCY AS A RESULT OF WHICH, ON A REGULAR AND FREQUENT BASIS, PERSONALLY USED CONTROLLED SUBSTANCES FOR NONTHERAPEUTIC PURPOSES DURING AND AFTER HIS OFFICE HOURS WHILE ENGAGED IN THE PRACTICE OF MEDICINE; PRESCRIBED CONTROLLED SUBSTANCES IN A NONTHERAPEUTIC MANNER; AND USED HIS POSITION AS A PHYSICIAN TO OBTAIN LARGE QUANTITIES OF CONTROLLED SUBSTANCES BY FRAUD. SUMMARY SUSPENSION DATED 6/2/86 IS STAYED TO 10 YEAR PROBATION UNDER THE FOLLOWING TERMS AND CONDITIONS: SHALL HAVE A BOARD APPROVED SUPERVISORY PHYSICIAN WHO SHALL SUBMIT REPORTS TO THE BOARD QUARTERLY FOR TWO YEARS AND EVERY SIX MONTHS THEREAFTER; SHALL BE MONITORED BY THE WASHINGTON MONITORED TREATMENT PROGRAM (WMTP) AND SHALL COMPLY WITH ALL CONDITIONS IN THE CONTRACT WHICH SHALL INCLUDE RANDOM URINE TESTING WITH QUARTERLY REPORTS FOR TWO YEARS AND EVERY SIX MONTHS THEREAFTER; SHALL APPEAR BEFORE THE BOARD EACH YEAR OR UPON BOARD REQUEST; SHALL REQUEST IN WRITING APPROVAL FROM THE BOARD PRIOR TO ENGAGING IN ANY MEDICAL PRACTICE; SHALL PERMIT THE BOARD TO MAKE UNANNOUNCED VISITS TO INSPECT RECORDS INCLUDING MEDICAL RECORDS, INTERVIEW STAFF AND SUPERVISORS, AND OTHERWISE REVIEW HIS PRACTICE TO MONITOR FOR COMPLIANCE WITH THIS ORDER; SHALL PRESCRIBE CONTROLLED SUBSTANCES TO HOSPITALIZED PATIENTS ONLY; MAY REQUEST A CHANGE IN ANY OF THE ABOVE CONDITIONS OF PROBATION IN NO SOONER THAN TWO YEARS; MUST NOTIFY THE BOARD IN WRITING IF HE LEAVES WASHINGTON; MAY REQUEST THE BOARD IN FIVE YEARS TO TERMINATE ITS PROBATION AND END JURISDICTION IN THIS CASE. ON 5/26/93 LICENSE FULLY REINSTATED.

MCDONNELL, THOMAS R MD, LICENSE NUMBER 0010443, OF SPANAWAY, WA, WAS DISCIPLINED BY WASHINGTON ON APRIL 8, 1996.
DISCIPLINARY ACTION: EMERGENCY SUSPENSION
OFFENSE: SUBSTANDARD CARE, INCOMPETENCE, OR NEGLIGENCE
NOTES: ALLEGED NEGLIGENCE. SUMMARILY SUSPENDED.

MCDONNELL, THOMAS R MD, LICENSE NUMBER 00M4828, WAS DISCIPLINED BY IDAHO ON AUGUST 13, 1996.
DISCIPLINARY ACTION: EMERGENCY SUSPENSION
OFFENSE: DISCIPLINARY ACTION BY ANOTHER STATE OR AGENCY
NOTES: EMERGENCY SUSPENSION IN WASHINGTON 4/08/96 FOR FAILING TO ADEQUATELY SUPERVISE NURSING STAFF AND MID-LEVEL HEALTH CARE PROVIDERS UNDER HIS SUPERVISION TO SUCH A DEGREE THAT CERTAIN PATIENTS AND EMPLOYEES HAVE BEEN EXPOSED TO AN UNREASONABLE RISK OF HARM; AND FELL BELOW THE STANDARD OF CARE OF A REASONABLY PRUDENT PHYSICIAN, THEREBY EXPOSING CERTAIN PATIENTS AND EMPLOYEES TO AN UNREASONABLE RISK OF HARM. THE IDAHO BOARD ADOPTS AND INCORPORATES THE TERMS AND CONDITIONS THE WASHINGTON ORDER.

MILLER, JOHN J MD WAS DISCIPLINED BY NEVADA ON OCTOBER 17, 1995.
DISCIPLINARY ACTION: LICENSE REVOCATION
OFFENSE: DISCIPLINARY ACTION BY ANOTHER STATE OR AGENCY
NOTES: CONVICTION OF A FELONY; CHARGED WITH BEING FOUND GUILTY OF TWO FELONIES IN MONTANA; DISCIPLINARY ACTION AGAINST HIS LICENSE IN MONTANA; SUSPENSION OF LICENSE BY ANY OTHER JURISDICTION; FAILURE TO REPORT, WITHIN 30 DAYS, THE SUSPENSION OF HIS LICENSE TO PRACTICE MEDICINE IN ANOTHER JURISDICTION.

MILLER, JOHN J MD OF JACKSONVILLE, FL, WAS DISCIPLINED BY

- IDAHO -

UTAH ON OCTOBER 28, 1995.
DISCIPLINARY ACTION: LICENSE REVOCATION; REVOCATION OF CONTROLLED SUBSTANCE LICENSE
OFFENSE: PHYSICAL OR MENTAL ILLNESS INHIBITING THE ABILITY TO PRACTICE WITH SKILL AND SAFETY
NOTES: ADMISSION OF INABILITY TO SAFELY ENGAGE IN THE PRACTICE OF MEDICINE BECAUSE OF A MENTAL OR PHYSICAL CONDITION.

MILLER, JOHN J MD, LICENSE NUMBER 0D27191, OF HIDDEN LAKE DRIVE, JACKSONVILLE, FL, WAS DISCIPLINED BY MARYLAND ON NOVEMBER 7, 1995.
DISCIPLINARY ACTION: PROBATION
OFFENSE: DISCIPLINARY ACTION BY ANOTHER STATE OR AGENCY
NOTES: ACTION BY MONTANA. REVOCATION STAYED.

MILLER, JOHN J MD, LICENSE NUMBER 0039841, OF DEER LODGE, MT, WAS DISCIPLINED BY FLORIDA ON MARCH 6, 1996.
DISCIPLINARY ACTION: LICENSE REVOCATION
OFFENSE: DISCIPLINARY ACTION BY ANOTHER STATE OR AGENCY
NOTES: CONVICTED OF A CRIME DIRECTLY RELATING TO THE PRACTICE OF MEDICINE.

MILLER, JOHN JOSEPH MD, DATE OF BIRTH FEBRUARY 14, 1942, LICENSE NUMBER 0003980, OF 310 SUNNYVIEW LANE, KALISPELL, MT, WAS DISCIPLINED BY MONTANA ON AUGUST 23, 1994.
DISCIPLINARY ACTION: EMERGENCY SUSPENSION
OFFENSE: SUBSTANCE ABUSE
NOTES: UNTREATED CHEMICAL DEPENDENCY. STIPULATION NOT TO SEEK REINSTATEMENT OF LICENSE UNTIL AFTER COMPLETION OF EVALUATION AND TREATMENT FOR ILLNESSES ON 8/31/94.

MILLER, JOHN JOSEPH MD, DATE OF BIRTH FEBRUARY 14, 1942, LICENSE NUMBER 00M5606, WAS DISCIPLINED BY IDAHO ON NOVEMBER 18, 1994.
DISCIPLINARY ACTION: LICENSE SUSPENSION
OFFENSE: DISCIPLINARY ACTION BY ANOTHER STATE OR AGENCY
NOTES: ON 8/24/94 MONTANA ORDERED THAT LICENSE BE PLACED ON EMERGENCY SUSPENSION; ALSO REQUIRED HIM TO HAVE A COMPLETE MENTAL AND PHYSICAL EXAMINATION. THE IDAHO BOARD FOR THE PURPOSE OF THIS RECIPROCAL DISCIPLINE INCORPORATES THE TERMS AND CONDITIONS OF THIS ORDER AND ORDERS HIM TO FULLY COMPLY WITH THEM.

MILLER, JOHN JOSEPH MD, DATE OF BIRTH FEBRUARY 14, 1942, LICENSE NUMBER 0021472, OF JACKSONVILLE, FL, WAS DISCIPLINED BY TENNESSEE ON FEBRUARY 23, 1995.
DISCIPLINARY ACTION: LICENSE REVOCATION
OFFENSE: DISCIPLINARY ACTION BY ANOTHER STATE OR AGENCY
NOTES: DISCIPLINARY ACTION TAKEN BY MONTANA BOARD. SUBSTANCE ABUSE. MUST APPEAR BEFORE BOARD IF REINSTATEMENT SOUGHT.

MILLER, JOHN JOSEPH MD, DATE OF BIRTH FEBRUARY 14, 1942, LICENSE NUMBER 00M5606, WAS DISCIPLINED BY IDAHO ON MAY 1, 1995.
DISCIPLINARY ACTION: LICENSE REVOCATION
OFFENSE: DISCIPLINARY ACTION BY ANOTHER STATE OR AGENCY
NOTES: IN 8/94 ENGAGED IN THE EXCESSIVE USE OF ALCOHOL OR OTHER SUBSTANCES TO THE EXTENT THAT THE USE IMPAIRED HIM PHYSICALLY OR MENTALLY; AS A RESULT HE WAS IN AN AUTO ACCIDENT WHICH CAUSED THE DEATH OF TWO PERSONS; LICENSE IN TENNESSEE WAS REVOKED ON 2/23/95. THE IDAHO BOARD ADOPTS THE FINDING OF THE TENNESSEE ORDER AND INCORPORATES ALL OF THE TERMS AND CONDITIONS OF THE TENNESSEE ORDER.

MILLER, JOHN JOSEPH MD, DATE OF BIRTH FEBRUARY 14, 1942, OF 215 SUNNYVIEW LANE #7, KALISPELL, MT, WAS DISCIPLINED BY MEDICARE ON MAY 4, 1995.
DISCIPLINARY ACTION: EXCLUSION FROM THE MEDICARE AND/OR MEDICAID PROGRAMS
OFFENSE: DISCIPLINARY ACTION BY ANOTHER STATE OR AGENCY
NOTES: LICENSE SUSPENDED FOR REASONS BEARING ON PROFESSIONAL PERFORMANCE.

MILLER, JOHN JOSEPH MD, DATE OF BIRTH FEBRUARY 14, 1942, LICENSE NUMBER 0003980, OF 3459 HIDDEN LAKE DRIVE WEST, JACKSONVILLE, FL, WAS DISCIPLINED BY MONTANA ON MAY 19, 1995.
DISCIPLINARY ACTION: PROBATION
OFFENSE: CRIMINAL CONVICTION OR PLEA OF GUILTY, NOLO CONTENDERE, OR NO CONTEST TO A CRIME
NOTES: CONVICTION OF FELONY; CHEMICAL DEPENDENCY. REVOCATION STAYED.

MILLER, JOHN JOSEPH MD, LICENSE NUMBER 0049431, OF JACKSONVILLE, FL, WAS DISCIPLINED BY VIRGINIA ON JUNE 13, 1995.
DISCIPLINARY ACTION: LICENSE SUSPENSION
OFFENSE: DISCIPLINARY ACTION BY ANOTHER STATE OR AGENCY
NOTES: REVOCATION BY TENNESSEE AND SUSPENSION BY MONTANA AFTER HE ENGAGED IN THE EXCESSIVE USE OF ALCOHOL OR OTHER SUBSTANCES.

MILLER, JOHN JOSEPH MD, DATE OF BIRTH FEBRUARY 14, 1942, LICENSE NUMBER 0031991, OF 3459 HIDDEN LAKE DR W, JACKSONVILLE, FL, WAS DISCIPLINED BY GEORGIA ON AUGUST 3, 1995.
DISCIPLINARY ACTION: LICENSE SUSPENSION
OFFENSE: CRIMINAL CONVICTION OR PLEA OF GUILTY, NOLO CONTENDERE, OR NO CONTEST TO A CRIME
NOTES: CONVICTION OF A CRIME. SUSPENDED INDEFINITELY.

MILLER, JOHN JOSEPH MD, DATE OF BIRTH FEBRUARY 14, 1942, LICENSE NUMBER 0009752, OF 3459 HIDDEN LAKE DRIVE WEST, JACKSONVILLE, FL, WAS DISCIPLINED BY WEST VIRGINIA ON NOVEMBER 20, 1995.
DISCIPLINARY ACTION: LICENSE REVOCATION
OFFENSE: DISCIPLINARY ACTION BY ANOTHER STATE OR AGENCY
NOTES: FOUND GUILTY OF TWO FELONY COUNTS OF NEGLIGENT HOMICIDE IN 2/95 IN MONTANA; HIS EXCESSIVE USE OF ALCOHOL CAUSED HIM TO BE IMPAIRED AND TO CAUSE THE DEATHS OF TWO PERSONS IN A MOTOR VEHICLE ACCIDENT. IN 2/95 THE TENNESSEE BOARD REVOKED HIS LICENSE. IN 11/94 THE IDAHO BOARD SUSPENDED HIS LICENSE AND IN 5/95 REVOKED HIS LICENSE. IN 8/94 MONTANA SUSPENDED HIS LICENSE AND IN 4/95 REVOKED HIS LICENSE AND THEN STAYED THE REVOCATION AS PROBATION UNDER SEVERAL TERMS AND CONDITIONS.

MILLER, JOHN JOSEPH MD, DATE OF BIRTH FEBRUARY 14, 1942, LICENSE NUMBER 0030589, WAS DISCIPLINED BY COLORADO ON JANUARY 11, 1996.
OFFENSE: CRIMINAL CONVICTION OR PLEA OF GUILTY, NOLO CONTENDERE, OR NO CONTEST TO A CRIME
NOTES: PLED GUILTY TO TWO FELONY CHARGES (NEGLIGENT HOMICIDE AS A RESULT OF A MOTOR VEHICLE ACCIDENT). ORDERED TO PERMANENTLY RELINQUISH HIS LICENSE TO PRACTICE MEDICINE IN COLORADO.

MILLER, JOHN JOSEPH MD, LICENSE NUMBER 0060453, OF DEER LODGE, MT, WAS DISCIPLINED BY OHIO ON FEBRUARY 14, 1996.
DISCIPLINARY ACTION: LICENSE REVOCATION
OFFENSE: DISCIPLINARY ACTION BY ANOTHER STATE OR AGENCY
NOTES: PRIOR ACTION BY MONTANA MEDICAL BOARD WHICH WAS BASED ON HIS ADMISSIONS THAT HE HAD ENGAGED IN EXCESSIVE USE OF ALCOHOL SO THAT HE WAS MENTALLY AND PHYSICALLY IMPAIRED AND THAT WHILE HE WAS IMPAIRED, HE WAS INVOLVED IN A MOTOR VEHICLE ACCIDENT THAT CAUSED THE DEATH OF TWO PEOPLE. CONVICTION OF TWO FELONY COUNTS OF NEGLIGENT HOMICIDE. PERMANENT REVOCATION.

- IDAHO -

MOORE, WILLIAM D MD, LICENSE NUMBER 0A16032, OF BOISE, ID, WAS DISCIPLINED BY CALIFORNIA ON FEBRUARY 3, 1995.
DISCIPLINARY ACTION: LICENSE REVOCATION
OFFENSE: CRIMINAL CONVICTION OR PLEA OF GUILTY, NOLO CONTENDERE, OR NO CONTEST TO A CRIME
NOTES: CONVICTION IN IDAHO FOR MURDER OF WIFE BY STRANGULATION. DEFAULT DECISION.

NAIL, GREGORY C MD, LICENSE NUMBER 00M3514, WAS DISCIPLINED BY IDAHO ON OCTOBER 7, 1996.
DISCIPLINARY ACTION: SURRENDER OF LICENSE
NOTES: PERMANENT SURRENDER.

NORMAN, CINDY RAE MD, LICENSE NUMBER 0025479, OF SPOKANE, WA, WAS DISCIPLINED BY WASHINGTON ON FEBRUARY 14, 1991.
DISCIPLINARY ACTION: EMERGENCY SUSPENSION
OFFENSE: SUBSTANCE ABUSE
NOTES: ALLEGATIONS OF PERSONAL USE OF CONTROLLED SUBSTANCES IN 1989 AND 1990, AND FAILED ATTEMPT AT TREATMENT FOR HER ADDICTION.

NORMAN, CINDY RAE MD, LICENSE NUMBER 0025479, OF SPOKANE, WA, WAS DISCIPLINED BY WASHINGTON ON SEPTEMBER 13, 1991.
DISCIPLINARY ACTION: PROBATION; FINE
OFFENSE: SUBSTANCE ABUSE
NOTES: USED HER POSITION AS A PHYSICIAN TO OBTAIN SUBSTANTIAL QUANTITIES OF CONTROLLED SUBSTANCES FOR HER OWN USE BY ISSUING PRESCRIPTIONS WRITTEN FOR FICTITIOUS PERSON; DURING 1989 AND 1990 PERSONALLY USED CONTROLLED SUBSTANCES FOR NON-THERAPEUTIC PURPOSES, INCLUDING THE USE OF MIND-ALTERING CONTROLLED SUBSTANCES; TREATED FOR CHEMICAL DEPENDENCY IN OREGON IN 1990 AND SUBSEQUENTLY SIGNED A FIVE-YEAR CONTRACT WITH THE WASHINGTON MONITORED TREATMENT PROGRAM ON 6/22/90; URINE SPECIMEN PROVIDED BY HER ON 12/7/90 TESTED POSITIVE FOR CODEINE; RETURNED TO OREGON ON 12/19/90 FOR EXTENDED CARE; WAS DISMISSED FROM A RESIDENCY PROGRAM OF INTERNAL MEDICINE AT DEACONESS/SACRED HEART MEDICAL CENTERS IN SPOKANE, WASHINGTON, BECAUSE OF THE POSITIVE URINALYSIS, EFFECTIVE 12/20/90. REVOCATION STAYED; PROBATION GRANTED UNDER FOLLOWING CONDITIONS: SHALL NOT CONSUME ANY ALCOHOL, CONTROLLED SUBSTANCES, OR LEGEND DRUGS, EXCEPT WHEN PRESCRIBED BY A LICENSED PHYSICIAN; SHALL CONTINUE TO UNDERGO ONGOING MONITORING OF HER PSYCHIATRIC MEDICATION AND THERAPY BY HER PSYCHIATRIST; SHALL HAVE HER URINE MONITORED ON A RANDOM BASIS FOR DRUGS AND ALCOHOL AT LEAST FOUR TIMES PER MONTH; MUST ATTEND A MINIMUM OF TWO AA MEETINGS PER WEEK; SHALL NOT PRACTICE MEDICINE MORE THAN 24 HOURS PER WEEK UNLESS APPROVED IN WRITING BY THE WASHINGTON MONITORED TREATMENT PROGRAM; SHALL PROVIDE A COPY OF A LETTER STATING SHE IS CURRENTLY INVOLVED IN RECOVERY FROM ALCOHOL AND SUBSTANCE DEPENDENCE TO ANY EMPLOYER; SHALL MEET WITH THE BOARD EVERY SIX MONTHS AND ANNUALLY THEREAFTER TO PROVE HER COMPLIANCE WITH ORDER; MUST HAVE HER PSYCHIATRIST AND EMPLOYER SUBMIT REPORTS TO THE BOARD; SHALL INFORM THE BOARD IF SHE CHANGES HER ADDRESS OR LEAVES THE STATE; DURATION OF PROBATION NOT COUNTED IF SHE IS OUT OF STATE; MUST PAY A $500 FINE; MAY NOT REQUEST TERMINATION OF THESE RESTRICTIONS FOR FIVE YEARS. ON 4/15/93 ORDER MODIFIED TO REMOVE LIMITATION UPON THE NUMBER OF HOURS SHE MAY PRACTICE MEDICINE AND SHALL APPEAR BEFORE THE BOARD FOR A COMPLIANCE APPEARANCE IN 3/94. ON 6/20/94 HER REQUEST GRANTED TO ALLOW SEMI-ANNUAL RATHER THAN QUARTERLY THERAPIST'S REPORTS; SHALL CONTINUE TO COMPLY WITH THIS ORDER AS MODIFIED.

NORMAN, CINDY RAE MD, LICENSE NUMBER 00M5498, WAS DISCIPLINED BY IDAHO ON JUNE 10, 1994.
DISCIPLINARY ACTION: EMERGENCY SUSPENSION
OFFENSE: DISCIPLINARY ACTION BY ANOTHER STATE OR AGENCY
NOTES: ON 6/10/94 WASHINGTON PLACED HER LICENSE ON EMERGENCY SUSPENSION. THE IDAHO BOARD ADOPTS THIS RECIPROCAL DISCIPLINE INCORPORATING THE TERMS AND CONDITIONS OF THE WASHINGTON ORDER AND ORDERING HER TO FULLY COMPLY WITH THESE.

NORMAN, CINDY RAE MD, LICENSE NUMBER 0025479, OF SPOKANE, WA, WAS DISCIPLINED BY WASHINGTON ON JUNE 10, 1994.
DISCIPLINARY ACTION: EMERGENCY SUSPENSION
OFFENSE: FAILURE TO COMPLY WITH A PREVIOUS BOARD ORDER
NOTES: FAILED TO COMPLY WITH 09/13/91 ORDER BY USING CONTROLLED SUBSTANCES DURING THE FIRST PART OF JUNE 1994.

NORMAN, CINDY RAE MD, LICENSE NUMBER 0025479, OF SPOKANE, WA, WAS DISCIPLINED BY WASHINGTON ON NOVEMBER 4, 1994.
DISCIPLINARY ACTION: LICENSE SUSPENSION; FINE
OFFENSE: PHYSICAL OR MENTAL ILLNESS INHIBITING THE ABILITY TO PRACTICE WITH SKILL AND SAFETY
NOTES: SHALL PAY A $500 FINE.

NORMAN, CINDY RAE MD, LICENSE NUMBER 00M5498, WAS DISCIPLINED BY IDAHO ON FEBRUARY 13, 1995.
DISCIPLINARY ACTION: LICENSE SUSPENSION; FINE
OFFENSE: DISCIPLINARY ACTION BY ANOTHER STATE OR AGENCY
NOTES: IN 11/94 WASHINGTON SUSPENDED HER LICENSE BASED ON DRUG USE AND NONCOMPLIANCE WITH A PREVIOUS ORDER. THE IDAHO BOARD FOR THE PURPOSE OF RECIPROCAL DISCIPLINE INCORPORATES THE TERMS AND CONDITIONS OF THIS ORDER AND ORDERS HER TO FULLY COMPLY WITH THEM.

RHODES, MICHAEL P DR, LICENSE NUMBER 0049411, WAS DISCIPLINED BY MASSACHUSETTS ON NOVEMBER 2, 1988.
DISCIPLINARY ACTION: LICENSE REVOCATION
OFFENSE: PROVIDING FALSE INFORMATION TO THE BOARD
NOTES: FRAUD ON APPLICATION

RHODES, MICHAEL P MD, DATE OF BIRTH JANUARY 13, 1947, LICENSE NUMBER 0023726, OF BOISE, ID, WAS DISCIPLINED BY IOWA ON JUNE 28, 1990.
DISCIPLINARY ACTION: FINE
NOTES: $750 FINE

RHODES, MICHAEL P MD, LICENSE NUMBER 0005010, WAS DISCIPLINED BY HAWAII ON MAY 19, 1993.
DISCIPLINARY ACTION: FINE
NOTES: CIVIL PENALTY OF $500.

RHODES, MICHAEL PATRICK MD, LICENSE NUMBER 0041067, OF BOISE, ID, WAS DISCIPLINED BY FLORIDA ON DECEMBER 19, 1990.
DISCIPLINARY ACTION: LICENSE REVOCATION
OFFENSE: DISCIPLINARY ACTION BY ANOTHER STATE OR AGENCY
NOTES: LICENSE REVOKED IN ANOTHER STATE.

RIDDLE, BRIAN T MD OF 175 NORTH 100 WEST #103, VERNAL, UT, WAS DISCIPLINED BY IDAHO ON APRIL 29, 1996.
DISCIPLINARY ACTION: DENIAL OF NEW LICENSE
OFFENSE: DISCIPLINARY ACTION BY ANOTHER STATE OR AGENCY
NOTES: CONVICTED OF THREE CRIMES INVOLVING MORAL TURPITUDE, INCLUDING PETIT THEFT IN APRIL 1980; SOLICITING SEX ACTS ON OR AROUND JUNE 21, 1985, AND SOLICITING PROSTITUTION ON OR AROUND 4/10/86; PROVIDED INCORRECT INFORMATION ON HIS APPLICATION IN SAYING HE HAD NEVER BEEN SUBJECT TO PROCEEDINGS WHEN IN FACT THE ARMY FOUND PROBLEMS WITH HIS STANDARD OF CARE, AND REQUIRED 100% SUPERVISION FOR THREE MONTHS; DID

- IDAHO -

NOT DISCLOSE THAT HALSTEAD HOSPITAL, KANSAS, DENIED HIS APPLICATION FOR PRIVILEGES; BASED ON THE PEER REVIEW PROCEEDINGS BY THE ARMY, HIS APPLICATION IS INCOMPLETE AND DOES NOT PROVIDE THE BOARD WITH SUFFICIENT INFORMATION TO ESTABLISH QUALIFICATION; FAILED TO APPEAR BEFORE THE BOARD ON THREE SEPARATE OCCASIONS.

ROBINSON, WENDELL E MD, LICENSE NUMBER 00M2970, WAS DISCIPLINED BY IDAHO ON JANUARY 24, 1993.
DISCIPLINARY ACTION: 60-MONTH PROBATION; FINE
OFFENSE: DISCIPLINARY ACTION BY ANOTHER STATE OR AGENCY
NOTES: ON 10/16/92 HE ENTERED INTO A CONSENT AGREEMENT WITH WASHINGTON BOARD WHICH WAS INVESTIGATING ALLEGATIONS THAT HE HAD SEXUALLY HARASSED A NURSE AND INTERFERED WITH AN INVESTIGATION OF THESE ALLEGATIONS. CONDITIONS OF WASHINGTON ORDER WHICH IDAHO HAS ADOPTED: SHALL OBTAIN COUNSELING FROM A BOARD-APPROVED THERAPIST WHO SHALL SUBMIT REPORTS TO THE BOARD; SHALL PROVIDE A COPY OF THE ORDER ANY WHERE THAT HE HAS PRIVILEGES; SHALL COMPLETE 10 HOURS OF CONTINUING MEDICAL EDUCATION IN MEDICAL ETHICS; SHALL APPEAR BEFORE THE BOARD IN ONE YEAR TO VERIFY COMPLIANCE; REPRESENTATIVE OF BOARD MAY MAKE UNANNOUNCED VISITS TO HIS PRACTICE; SHALL INFORM THE BOARD OF CHANGE OF ADDRESS OR IF HE LEAVES THE STATE; SHALL PAY A $1,000 FINE WITHIN 90 DAYS.

ROBINSON, WENDELL E MD, LICENSE NUMBER 0011542, OF RICHLAND, WA, WAS DISCIPLINED BY WASHINGTON ON MAY 3, 1994.
DISCIPLINARY ACTION: 36-MONTH PROBATION; FINE
NOTES: SHALL COMPLY WITH ALL CONDITIONS AND RESTRICTIONS PERTAINING TO CORONARY ANGIOGRAPHICS AND CONDITIONS CONCERNING CONTINUING MEDICAL EDUCATION. MUST PAY A $1000 FINE WITHIN 90 DAYS AND APPEAR BEFORE BOARD WHEN DIRECTED.

ROBINSON, WENDELL E MD, LICENSE NUMBER 00M2970, WAS DISCIPLINED BY IDAHO ON JULY 11, 1994.
DISCIPLINARY ACTION: 36-MONTH PROBATION; FINE
OFFENSE: DISCIPLINARY ACTION BY ANOTHER STATE OR AGENCY
NOTES: ON 5/22/94 WASHINGTON PLACED LICENSE ON PROBATION BASED ON ALLEGATIONS OF UNPROFESSIONAL CONDUCT WITH REGARD TO PERFORMING A CAROTID ANGIOGRAPHY ON A PATIENT THAT WAS OTHERWISE IN STABLE CONDITION. CONDITIONS OF WASHINGTON PROBATION WHICH IDAHO HAS ADOPTED ARE AS FOLLOWS: SHALL ONLY PERFORM CORONARY ANGIOGRAPHY STUDIES CONSISTENT WITH SPECIFIED CRITERIA; HE MUST CONSULT WITH A CARDIOLOGIST-MONITOR APPROVED BY THE BOARD OR ITS DESIGNEE PRIOR TO EVERY NON-EMERGENT CORONARY ANGIOGRAPHY; ON A QUARTERLY BASIS, HE SHALL FORWARD TO THE BOARD A COPY OF ALL OFFICE PATIENT CHARTS AND HIS WRITTEN REQUEST TO HAVE ALL HOSPITAL RECORDS FORWARDED FOR THOSE PATIENTS HE HAS PERFORMED ON OR PROPOSED ANGIOGRAPHY STUDIES; SHALL COMPLETE 24 HOURS OF CONTINUING MEDICAL EDUCATION IN CARDIOLOGY WITHIN 18 MONTHS; HIS COMPLIANCE WITH THE ABOVE WILL BE MONITORED QUARTERLY FOR THE FIRST YEAR AND SEMI-ANNUALLY EVERY YEAR THEREAFTER; SHALL PAY A $1,000 FINE WITHIN 90 DAYS.

ROBINSON, WENDELL E MD, LICENSE NUMBER 0A24617, OF RICHLAND, WA, WAS DISCIPLINED BY CALIFORNIA ON APRIL 23, 1995.
DISCIPLINARY ACTION: 60-MONTH PROBATION
OFFENSE: DISCIPLINARY ACTION BY ANOTHER STATE OR AGENCY

NOTES: DISCIPLINE BY WASHINGTON STATE MEDICAL BOARD AS A RESULT OF CHARGES OF SEXUAL HARASSMENT AT KADLEC HOSPITAL. REVOCATION STAYED.

RUCKS, ANDREW C MD, LICENSE NUMBER 0095375, WAS DISCIPLINED BY MASSACHUSETTS ON SEPTEMBER 5, 1990.
DISCIPLINARY ACTION: LICENSE REVOCATION

RUCKS, ANDREW C MD, DATE OF BIRTH JULY 27, 1953, OF 125 SHERMAN STREET, SPRINGFIELD, MA, WAS DISCIPLINED BY MEDICARE ON DECEMBER 20, 1990.
DISCIPLINARY ACTION: EXCLUSION FROM THE MEDICARE AND/OR MEDICAID PROGRAMS
OFFENSE: DISCIPLINARY ACTION BY ANOTHER STATE OR AGENCY
NOTES: LICENSE REVOCATION OR SUSPENSION.

RUCKS, ANDREW C MD, DATE OF BIRTH JULY 27, 1953, OF 125 SHERMAN STREET, SPRINGFIELD, MA, WAS DISCIPLINED BY IDAHO ON APRIL 29, 1996.
DISCIPLINARY ACTION: DENIAL OF NEW LICENSE
OFFENSE: DISCIPLINARY ACTION BY ANOTHER STATE OR AGENCY
NOTES: EXPELLED FROM THE RESIDENCY PROGRAM AT BOSTON HOSPITAL AND DID NOT COMPLETE THE PROGRAM AT MEHARRY HOSPITAL; FAILED TO SUCCESSFULLY COMPLETE A POST-GRADUATE PROGRAM; MASSACHUSETTS LICENSE REVOCATION IN 1990; IN FEBRUARY 1995 PAID $250,000 ON A MALPRACTICE CLAIM; SUBJECT TO MEDICAID PROVIDER SANCTIONS IN DECEMBER 1990; AND DOES NOT POSSESS THE REQUISITE QUALIFICATIONS TO PROVIDE THE SAME STANDARD OF CARE AS PROVIDED BY OTHER LICENSED PHYSICIANS IN IDAHO.

SCHROEDER, WALTER G MD WAS DISCIPLINED BY ARIZONA ON MARCH 26, 1990.
DISCIPLINARY ACTION: REQUIRED TO TAKE ADDITIONAL MEDICAL EDUCATION
OFFENSE: OVERPRESCRIBING OR MISPRESCRIBING DRUGS
NOTES: ACTION BASED ON PRESCRIBING PRACTICES. MATTER FILED WITH LETTER OF CONCERN FOR HIS PRESCRIBING AS RELATES TO PATIENTS OUTLINED IN STAFF SURVEY; HE MUST OBTAIN WITHIN SIX MONTHS 20 HOURS OF CATEGORY I CONTINUING MEDICAL EDUCATION IN CHRONIC PAIN MANAGEMENT; STAFF CONDUCT A FOLLOW-UP PHARMACY SURVEY IN SIX MONTHS TO ENSURE THAT HE HAS MADE APPROPRIATE MODIFICATIONS IN HIS PRESCRIBING PRACTICES. ON 1/23/92 BOARD ACCEPTED THE CONTINUING MEDICAL EDUCATION SUBMITTED BY DR. SCHROEDER AS FULFILLMENT OF THE BOARD ORDER AND TERMINATED THE STIPULATION AND ORDER. STAFF WILL CONDUCT A PHARMACY SURVEY IN SIX MONTHS TO DETERMINE IF HE IS APPROPRIATELY PRESCRIBING PAIN MEDICATIONS.

SCHROEDER, WALTER G MD, LICENSE NUMBER 0013043, OF PRESCOTT, AZ, WAS DISCIPLINED BY ARIZONA ON JANUARY 25, 1994.
DISCIPLINARY ACTION: RESTRICTION PLACED ON LICENSE
NOTES: ON 7/12/93 BOARD ORDERED THAT HE TAKE AND PASS THE SPEX EXAM BY 12/31/93. HE DID NOT TAKE THE EXAM AS ORDERED. TERMS OF ORDER: SHALL NOT USE HERBVEIL 8 CREAM ON SKIN LESIONS; SHALL TAKE PASS THE SPEX EXAM ON 3/17/94; AND SHALL APPEAR BEFORE THE BOARD AT ITS 7/94 MEETING. HE PASSED THE EXAM AND ON 7/13/94 HE ENTERED INTO AN ORDER WITH THE BOARD WHICH REQUIRED THAT HE NOT USE HERBVEIL 8 CREAM ON SKIN LESIONS NOR VITAMIN B-12 OR COLCHIZINE FOR OTHER THAN ACCEPTED THERAPEUTIC PURPOSES.

SCHROEDER, WALTER GENE MD OF 3012 CHEYENNE CIRCLE, PRESCOTT, AZ, WAS DISCIPLINED BY IDAHO ON JUNE 14, 1995.
DISCIPLINARY ACTION: DENIAL OF NEW LICENSE
OFFENSE: PROVIDING FALSE INFORMATION TO THE BOARD

- IDAHO -

NOTES: LIED IN RESPONSE TO A QUESTION ON HIS APPLICATION BY FAILING TO REPORT ACTIONS BY THE ARIZONA BOARD AND A HOSPITAL IN ARIZONA; HAD NUMEROUS LAWSUITS WITHIN A SHORT PERIOD OF TIME.

SPAULDING, BRADLEY B MD, LICENSE NUMBER 00M4664, WAS DISCIPLINED BY IDAHO ON FEBRUARY 18, 1994.
DISCIPLINARY ACTION: SURRENDER OF LICENSE
OFFENSE: SUBSTANDARD CARE, INCOMPETENCE, OR NEGLIGENCE
NOTES: ALLEGATIONS THAT HE PROVIDED HEALTH CARE WHICH FAILS TO MEET COMMUNITY STANDARDS OF CARE WHICH HE DENIES. ON TWO SEPARATE OCCASIONS IN 1992 AND 1993, WAS APPARENTLY UNDER THE INFLUENCE OF DRUGS, ALCOHOL, OR OTHER SUBSTANCES WHILE TREATING THREE PATIENTS. HE SHALL NOT REAPPLY FOR AN IDAHO LICENSE FOR THREE YEARS FROM 6/25/93.

SPAULDING, BRADLEY B MD OF MILFORD, UT, WAS DISCIPLINED BY UTAH ON OCTOBER 18, 1994.
DISCIPLINARY ACTION: 60-MONTH PROBATION; 60-MONTH CONTROLLED SUBSTANCE LICENSE PLACED ON PROBATION
OFFENSE: PROFESSIONAL MISCONDUCT
NOTES: UNLAWFULLY OBTAINING AND SELF-ADMINISTERING A SCHEDULE II CONTROLLED SUBSTANCE. REVOCATION STAYED TO PROBATION WITH CONDITIONS.

SPAULDING, BRADLEY B MD OF MILFORD, UT, WAS DISCIPLINED BY UTAH ON OCTOBER 21, 1995.
DISCIPLINARY ACTION: 1-MONTH RESTRICTION PLACED ON CONTROLLED SUBSTANCE LICENSE; CONTROLLED SUBSTANCE LICENSE PLACED ON PROBATION
OFFENSE: FAILURE TO COMPLY WITH A PREVIOUS BOARD ORDER
NOTES: FAILURE TO COMPLY WITH RESTRICTIONS IMPOSED ON HIS CONTROLLED SUBSTANCE LICENSE. REVOCATION STAYED SUBJECT TO RESTRICTIONS AND CONDITIONS. SCHEDULES II-V SUSPENDED FOR 30 DAYS. CAN ONLY PRESCRIBE AND ADMINISTER IN A HOSPITAL SETTING FOR INPATIENT OR EMERGENCY CARE PATIENTS DURING SUSPENSION. NO OUTPATIENT CARE PRESCRIPTIONS DURING SUSPENSION. FOLLOWING THE SUSPENSION PERIOD, HIS CONTROLLED SUBSTANCE LICENSE WILL REVERT TO ITS PRIOR PROBATIONARY STATUS. ON 11/30/95 SUSPENSION TERMINATED AND LICENSE PUT ON PROBATION CONSISTENT WITH PRIOR TERMS AND CONDITIONS.

STEVENS, SHERIDAN S MD, DATE OF BIRTH JUNE 8, 1939, LICENSE NUMBER 0016983, WAS DISCIPLINED BY MINNESOTA ON MARCH 9, 1996.
DISCIPLINARY ACTION: RESTRICTION PLACED ON LICENSE

STEVENS, SHERIDAN S MD, DATE OF BIRTH JUNE 8, 1939, LICENSE NUMBER 00M6194, OF 29 PARK LANE, MINNEAPOLIS, MN, WAS DISCIPLINED BY IDAHO ON JUNE 10, 1996.
DISCIPLINARY ACTION: REQUIRED TO TAKE ADDITIONAL MEDICAL EDUCATION; MONITORING OF PHYSICIAN
OFFENSE: DISCIPLINARY ACTION BY ANOTHER STATE OR AGENCY
NOTES: ACTION IN MINNESOTA ON 3/9/96 FOR FAILING TO ADEQUATELY EVALUATE AND TREAT A PATIENT POST-OPERATIVELY WHO HAD COMPLICATIONS AFTER HE PERFORMED RHINOPLASTY AND REMOVED A SEBACEOUS CYST ON THE RIGHT SIDE OF HER NOSE; KEPT INADEQUATE RECORDS IN THE CASES AND BY FAILING TO RESPOND TO PATIENT'S LETTER GAVE THE IMPRESSION OF INTENTIONALLY IGNORING THE PATIENT. THE IDAHO BOARD ADOPTS AND INCORPORATES THE TERMS AND CONDITIONS OF THE MINNESOTA ORDER INCLUDING: SHALL ATTEND A RHINOPLASTY SYMPOSIUM; SHALL SUCCESSFULLY COMPLETE A BOARD APPROVED COURSE IN RECORD KEEPING; AND IF HE RETURNS TO MINNESOTA TO PRACTICE MEDICINE AND SURGERY, SHALL COMPLETE AT LEAST THREE RHINOPLASTY PROCEDURES IN THE PRESENCE OF A BOARD APPROVED CERTIFIED PLASTIC SURGEON. $1500 FINE.

TILBY, BORNEY B MD, LICENSE NUMBER C029779, OF POTLATCH, ID, WAS DISCIPLINED BY CALIFORNIA ON MAY 18, 1987.
DISCIPLINARY ACTION: LICENSE REVOCATION
OFFENSE: DISCIPLINARY ACTION BY ANOTHER STATE OR AGENCY
NOTES: DEFAULT DECISION. DISCIPLINED BY THE IDAHO MEDICAL BOARD

TILBY, BORNEY BRIAN MD OF POTLATCH, ID, WAS DISCIPLINED BY UTAH ON JANUARY 7, 1987.
DISCIPLINARY ACTION: LICENSE SUSPENSION
OFFENSE: SUBSTANCE ABUSE
NOTES: INDEFINITE SUSPENSION, DRUG ABUSE

TILBY, BORNEY BRIAN MD, LICENSE NUMBER 0031491, WAS DISCIPLINED BY MINNESOTA ON DECEMBER 1, 1987.
DISCIPLINARY ACTION: REQUIRED TO ENTER AN IMPAIRED PHYSICIAN PROGRAM OR DRUG OR ALCOHOL TREATMENT; MONITORING OF PHYSICIAN
OFFENSE: DISCIPLINARY ACTION BY ANOTHER STATE OR AGENCY
NOTES: AS A RESULT OF FENTANYL ABUSE IDAHO BOARD PLACED HIM ON PROBATION 5 YEARS; UTAH SUSPENDED LICENSE 1/1/87; CALIFORNIA REVOKED LICENSE; RECEIVED INPATIENT CHEMICAL DEPENDENCY TREATMENT IN 1985. HAS BEEN CHEMICALLY FREE SINCE MARCH 1985. SHALL NOT PRESCRIBE ANY CONTROLLED SUBSTANCES FOR HIS OWN USE; SHALL ABSTAIN FROM MOOD-ALTERING CHEMICALS; SHALL ATTEND PHYSICIANS SERVING PHYSICIANS ON A MONTHLY BASIS WITH QUARTERLY REPORTS TO BOARD; SHALL ATTEND AA BIWEEKLY WITH QUARTERLY REPORT TO THE BOARD; RANDOM URINE SAMPLES; WILL MEET WITH SUPERVISING PHYSICIAN MONTHLY; ANY CHANGE IN PRACTICE SETTING SHALL BE APPROVED BY THE BOARD

TILBY, BORNEY BRIAN MD, LICENSE NUMBER 0031491, WAS DISCIPLINED BY MINNESOTA ON FEBRUARY 11, 1989.
DISCIPLINARY ACTION: LICENSE SUSPENSION
OFFENSE: FAILURE TO COMPLY WITH A PREVIOUS BOARD ORDER
NOTES: CONSUMED ALCOHOL IN VIOLATION OF PREVIOUS BOARD ORDER; FAILED TO ATTEND CONFERENCE WITH BOARD. SUSPENSION LIFTED AND LICENSE UNCONDITIONALLY REINSTATED 7/31/89 AFTER SHOWN NOT TO BE CHEMICALLY DEPENDENT.

TILBY, BORNEY BRIAN MD, LICENSE NUMBER 0031491, WAS DISCIPLINED BY MINNESOTA ON JANUARY 24, 1991.
DISCIPLINARY ACTION: RESTRICTION PLACED ON LICENSE
NOTES: UNCONDITIONAL LICENSE GRANTED ON 11/23/96.

TILBY, BORNEY BRIAN MD, LICENSE NUMBER 0031491, WAS DISCIPLINED BY MINNESOTA ON NOVEMBER 19, 1994.
DISCIPLINARY ACTION: RESTRICTION PLACED ON LICENSE
NOTES: AMENDED ORDER 11/18/95. UNCONDITIONAL LICENSE GRANTED ON 11/23/96.

WELLS, RONALD DAVID MD, LICENSE NUMBER G061284, OF TWIN FALLS, ID, WAS DISCIPLINED BY CALIFORNIA ON DECEMBER 28, 1989.
DISCIPLINARY ACTION: LICENSE REVOCATION
OFFENSE: DISCIPLINARY ACTION BY ANOTHER STATE OR AGENCY
NOTES: DISCIPLINED BY IDAHO FOR UNLAWFUL POSSESSION OF MARIJUANA. DEFAULT DECISION.

WITHERS, LAVAR M MD WAS DISCIPLINED BY IDAHO ON JULY 31, 1995.
DISCIPLINARY ACTION: SURRENDER OF LICENSE
NOTES: PERMANENT SURRENDER.

WOODFIELD, BRENT E MD, LICENSE NUMBER 00M4578, OF 79 WEST SUNSET ST, REXBURG, ID, WAS DISCIPLINED BY IDAHO ON JULY 16, 1993.
DISCIPLINARY ACTION: LICENSE REVOCATION

- IDAHO -

OFFENSE: SUBSTANDARD CARE, INCOMPETENCE, OR NEGLIGENCE
NOTES: BETWEEN 11/91 AND 7/92 PROVIDED SUBSTANDARD CARE TO A NUMBER OF PATIENTS INCLUDING PERFORMING UNNECESSARY SURGERY IN THREE CASES AND FAILING TO DO AN APPROPRIATE WORKUP IN ONE; FAILING TO INSURE THAT THERE WERE ADEQUATE BLOOD PRODUCTS AVAILABLE OR ORDERED PRIOR TO A SURGERY OF A PATIENT; SENDING A PATIENT HOME RATHER THAN TO THE HOSPITAL AFTER HE DIAGNOSED AN ECTOPIC PREGNANCY; SHOWED POOR SURGICAL TECHNIQUE IN THREE CASES; ENGAGED IN SEXUAL IMPROPRIETIES WITH A PATIENT. ON 4/28/94 ORDER REVERSED BY THE DISTRICT COURT OF IDAHO AND COURT OF APPEALS AND REMANDED TO THE BOARD FOR FURTHER CONSIDERATION. HIS TREATMENT DID NOT MEET COMMUNITY STANDARDS OF CARE WITH REGARDS TO SEVEN SURGICAL CASES INCLUDING: PERFORMED UNNECESSARY AND UNWARRANTED SURGERY IN TWO CASES, ONE A LAPAROTOMY AND ONE A D&C AND CONIZATION AND HIS FAILURE TO DO AN APPROPRIATE WORKUP OF THE SECOND SURGICAL CASE DEMONSTRATED A LACK OF UNDERSTANDING OF THE BASIC PRINCIPLES OF THE PRACTICE OF MEDICINE AND TO TAKE A BIOPSY WHEN A COLPOSCOPY WAS DONE; EXHIBITED CONFUSION IN RECOGNIZING A SACRAL PROMONTORY DURING SURGERY WHICH REPRESENTS AN INABILITY TO RECOGNIZE NORMAL ANATOMIC STRUCTURES; FAILED TO DEMONSTRATE AN AWARENESS OF A PATIENT'S BLOOD STATUS AND THE NEED FOR BLOOD PRODUCTS AT THE TIME HE PROCEEDED WITH SURGERY, PLACING A PATIENT AT JEOPARDY; HIS SURGICAL TECHNIQUE IN PERFORMING A HYSTERECTOMY WAS AWKWARD AND INDECISIVE AND REPRESENTED POOR SURGICAL TECHNIQUE; ENGAGED IN IMPROPER SEXUAL CONDUCT WITH ONE PATIENT WHICH CONSTITUTES A GROSS ETHICAL VIOLATION AND AN ABUSE OR EXPLOITATION OF THE PATIENT ARISING OUT OF THE TRUST AND CONFIDENCE PLACED IN THE PHYSICIAN BY THE PATIENT; BOARD DENIED HIS MOTION FOR RECONSIDERATION ON 4/25/96; THE IDAHO DISTRICT COURT HAS RULED THAT THIS ORDER SHALL BE STAYED PENDING APPEAL. CONSEQUENTLY HE HOLDS AN ACTIVE LICENSE.

YOUNG, LEONARD MD OF BOISE, ID, WAS DISCIPLINED BY ILLINOIS ON DECEMBER 1, 1990.
DISCIPLINARY ACTION: 36-MONTH PROBATION
OFFENSE: DISCIPLINARY ACTION BY ANOTHER STATE OR AGENCY
NOTES: LICENSE PUT ON INDEFINITE PROBATION BY IDAHO.

YOUNG, LEONARD MD, LICENSE NUMBER C022658, OF BOISE, ID, WAS DISCIPLINED BY CALIFORNIA ON FEBRUARY 4, 1991.
DISCIPLINARY ACTION: LICENSE REVOCATION
OFFENSE: DISCIPLINARY ACTION BY ANOTHER STATE OR AGENCY
NOTES: DISCIPLINED BY IDAHO BOARD BASED ON ACTIONS BY TWO HOSPITALS.

YOUNG, LEONARD MD OF BOISE, ID, WAS DISCIPLINED BY IDAHO ON DECEMBER 9, 1991.
DISCIPLINARY ACTION: LICENSE REVOCATION
OFFENSE: SUBSTANDARD CARE, INCOMPETENCE, OR NEGLIGENCE
NOTES: ACTION BASED ON FAILURE TO MEET COMMUNITY STANDARDS OF CARE. APPEALED BOARD ACTION TO DISTRICT COURT. THE APPEAL WAS DENIED. BOARD AGREED TO CONSIDER REINSTATEMENT IF HE RECEIVES A PASSING SCORE IN AN ACCEPTABLE EXAMINATION.

MONTANA
1996 serious action rate: 4.87/1000
1996 ranking: 13th

The Montana Board of Medical Examiners sent copies of reports submitted to the Federation of State Medical Boards from December 1988 through December 1996. The reports contain the physician's name, degree, license number, address, the date and type of action taken, and a brief summary of the reason for the action. In some cases copies of orders were sent. The reports contain some information on modifications and terminations of board orders but not on court decisions affecting board actions.

The information provided covers disciplinary actions taken against allopathic physicians (MDs) and osteopathic physicians (DOs).

Besides disciplinary actions taken by the State Medical Board, this listing also includes actions taken by the Medicare/Medicaid programs, the FDA, and the DEA against physicians located in this state. Disciplinary actions taken by other states against physicians located in Montana or that match a physician disciplined by Montana (see Appendix 2 for an explanation of the matching protocol) are also included.

> Although we have made every effort to match physicians' names correctly, some materials we received did not include complete information on middle names, license numbers, birth dates or addresses. Therefore, consumers should remember that non-disciplined physicians and physicians with different disciplinary actions may have similar names to those disciplined physicians listed in this state. Consumers should also remember that if they want the most current information on the status on a physician's license, they should contact the medical board of the state in which the physician practices or had practiced.

According to the Federation of State Medical Boards, Montana took 9 serious disciplinary actions against MDs and DOs in 1996. Compared to the 1,849 MDs in the state, Montana had a serious disciplinary action rate of 4.87 serious actions per 1,000 MDs and a ranking of 13th on that list (see Table A, Findings, pg. 14).

The tables below summarize the data Public Citizen received from Montana.

Table 1. Disciplinary Actions Against MDs and DOs December 1988 through December 1996*

Action	Number	Percent**
Revocation	9	11.3%
Surrender	6	7.5%
Suspension	2	2.5%
Probation	26	32.5%
Practice Restriction	9	11.3%
Action Taken Against Controlled Substance License	1	1.3%
Other Actions	27	33.8%
Total Actions	**80**	**100.0%**

* This table lists only the two most serious disciplinary actions taken against a physician.
** Percentages may not total 100% due to rounding.

Table 2. Offenses for which MDs and DOs were Disciplined December 1988 through December 1996*

Offense	Number	Percent
Criminal Conviction	5	8.8%
Sexual Abuse of or Sexual Misconduct with a Patient	1	1.8%
Substandard Care, Incompetence or Negligence	8	14.0%
Misprescribing or Overprescribing Drugs	2	3.5%
Substance Abuse	8	14.0%
Disciplinary Action Taken Against License by Another State or Agency	10	17.5%
Other Offenses	23	40.4%
Total Records With Offense Listed	**57**	**100.0%**

* Includes only those actions for which an offense was listed and for which we had a corresponding term in our database.

Table 3. Disciplinary Actions Taken for Substandard Care, Incompetence or Negligence

Action	Number	Percent
Revocation	2	20.0%
Surrender	1	10.0%
Probation	4	40.0%
Practice Restriction	2	20.0%
Other Actions	1	10.0%
Total Actions	**10**	**100.0%**

If you feel that your doctor has not given you proper medical care or has mistreated you in any way--whether or not he or she is listed in this report--it is important that you let your state medical board know. Even if they do not immediately act on your complaint, it is important that the information be recorded in their files because it is possible that other people may have filed or will file complaints about the same doctor. Send a brief written description of what occurred to the addresses below or call the phone numbers listed for more information on how to file a complaint.

Address

Montana Board of Medical Examiners
Patricia England, JD, Executive Secretary
PO Box 200513
Helena, MT 59620-0513
(406) 444-4284

Listing of Doctors Sanctioned by Offense

Sexual Abuse of or Sexual Misconduct with a Patient
VASQUEZ, NED FRANCIS

Substandard Care, Incompetence, or Negligence
BISCHOFF, JAMES STEPHEN
GALLUS, JOHN MACK
HOPKINS, GARY L
KRAFT, JEFFREY GALE
KURTZ, CURTIS G
LISTERUD, MARK BOYD
OBYE, JOHN ROGER
ZELMAN, RUSSELL HENRY

Criminal Conviction or Plea of Guilty, Nolo Contendere, or No Contest to a Crime
ERICKSON, BRUCE LELAND
KRAFT, JEFFREY GALE
MILLER, JOHN JOSEPH
MOTE, FREDERICK ANDREW
WINSTEAD, GLENN C

Misprescribing or Overprescribing Drugs
COWARD, HAROLD MARK
MOTE, FREDERICK ANDREW

Substance Abuse
BARGEN, RICHARD ALLAN
KENCK, RALPH JOSEPH
KRAUSE, ROBERT ALAN
KURTZ, GENE GAYLORD
MILLER, JOHN JOSEPH

Caution: This list is designed to be used only in conjunction with the rest of this book which includes additional information on each physician such as license number, date of action and more complete descriptions of the offenses.

DISCIPLINARY ACTIONS

AARON, JOHN MD WAS DISCIPLINED BY IOWA ON DECEMBER 17, 1987.
DISCIPLINARY ACTION: DENIAL OF NEW LICENSE

AARON, JOHN MD, DATE OF BIRTH MAY 11, 1954, OF 5401 SHIRE COURT, FAIR OAKS, CA, WAS DISCIPLINED BY MONTANA ON JANUARY 13, 1989.
DISCIPLINARY ACTION: DENIAL OF NEW LICENSE
OFFENSE: PROVIDING FALSE INFORMATION TO THE BOARD
NOTES: FALSIFIED APPLICATION

AARON, JOHN MD WAS DISCIPLINED BY ALASKA ON JULY 13, 1990.
DISCIPLINARY ACTION: DENIAL OF NEW LICENSE
OFFENSE: DISCIPLINARY ACTION BY ANOTHER STATE OR AGENCY
NOTES: FALSIFIED APPLICATION; DISCIPLINARY ACTION IN NEVADA.

AARON, JOHN MD WAS DISCIPLINED BY WYOMING ON JULY 5, 1991.
DISCIPLINARY ACTION: DENIAL OF NEW LICENSE

AARON, JOHN MD, LICENSE NUMBER 045839L, OF 11618 FAIR OAKS BLVD, FAIR OAKS, CA, WAS DISCIPLINED BY PENNSYLVANIA ON OCTOBER 23, 1991.
DISCIPLINARY ACTION: FINE; REPRIMAND
OFFENSE: PROVIDING FALSE INFORMATION TO THE BOARD
NOTES: ON HIS LICENSE APPLICATION FOR PENNSYLVANIA, FAILED TO PROVIDE A COMPLETE DISCLOSURE OF MEDICAL SCHOOLS HE ATTENDED; FAILED TO INDICATE HE HAD A MEDICAL LICENSE IN NEVADA AND THAT DISCIPLINARY ACTION AGAINST HIS MEDICAL LICENSE HAD BEEN TAKEN BY NEVADA; SUBMITTED A NOTARIZED COPY OF HIS STANDARD ECFMG CERTIFICATE WHICH HAD BEEN REVOKED IN 11/85; ON 7/13/90 THE ALASKA MEDICAL BOARD DENIED HIS APPLICATION FOR LICENSURE FOR NOT PROVIDING FULL DISCLOSURE OF INFORMATION ON THE APPLICATION. ISSUED UNRESTRICTED LICENSE TO PRACTICE; MUST PAY $700 CIVIL PENALTY.

ALLISON, ADOLPHUS R JR MD OF HILTON HEAD, SC, WAS DISCIPLINED BY SOUTH CAROLINA ON MAY 17, 1995.
DISCIPLINARY ACTION: FINE; REPRIMAND
OFFENSE: PROVIDING FALSE INFORMATION TO THE BOARD
NOTES: USED A FALSE STATEMENT ON APPLICATION FOR REACTIVATION. $1,000 FINE.

ALLISON, ADOLPHUS R JR MD, LICENSE NUMBER 0082455, OF 67 MOORING BUOY, HILTON HEAD, SC, WAS DISCIPLINED BY NEW YORK ON SEPTEMBER 3, 1996.
DISCIPLINARY ACTION: LICENSE REVOCATION
OFFENSE: DISCIPLINARY ACTION BY ANOTHER STATE OR AGENCY
NOTES: ACTION IN MONTANA AND SOUTH CAROLINA FOR FRAUDULENT STATEMENTS ON HIS LICENSURE APPLICATIONS.

ALLISON, ADOLPHUS REID JR MD, DATE OF BIRTH FEBRUARY 22, 1931, OF 67 MOORING BUOY, HILTON HEAD, SC, WAS DISCIPLINED BY MONTANA ON APRIL 3, 1995.
DISCIPLINARY ACTION: PROBATION
OFFENSE: PROVIDING FALSE INFORMATION TO THE BOARD
NOTES: FRAUD ON THE APPLICATION; PERMANENT LICENSE NOT GRANTED; TEMPORARY LICENSE GRANTED ON CONDITIONS RETROACTIVE TO 1/13/95.

BARGEN, RICHARD ALLAN MD, DATE OF BIRTH NOVEMBER 13, 1946, LICENSE NUMBER 0004366, OF SWEET MEDICAL CTR, PO BOX 1269, CHINOOK, MT, WAS DISCIPLINED BY MONTANA ON SEPTEMBER 28, 1993.
DISCIPLINARY ACTION: EMERGENCY SUSPENSION
OFFENSE: SUBSTANCE ABUSE
NOTES: PROCEEDINGS PENDING.

BARGEN, RICHARD ALLAN MD, DATE OF BIRTH NOVEMBER 13, 1946, LICENSE NUMBER 0004366, OF P.O. BOX 1320, YELLOWKNIFE NWT, CANADA, WAS DISCIPLINED BY MONTANA ON DECEMBER 6, 1993.
DISCIPLINARY ACTION: 60-MONTH PROBATION
OFFENSE: SUBSTANCE ABUSE
NOTES: IN RECOVERY FOR CHEMICAL DEPENDENCY. ORDER AMENDED ON 2/07/95 APPROVING PRACTICE SITE IN NORTH WEST TERRITORIES, CANADA.

BARGEN, RICHARD ALLAN MD, DATE OF BIRTH NOVEMBER 13, 1946, OF 708 INDIANA BOX 1269, CHINOOK, MT, WAS DISCIPLINED BY DEA ON JANUARY 24, 1994.
DISCIPLINARY ACTION: SURRENDER OF CONTROLLED SUBSTANCE LICENSE
OFFENSE: DISCIPLINARY ACTION BY ANOTHER STATE OR AGENCY

BISCHOFF, JAMES STEPHEN MD, DATE OF BIRTH JUNE 7, 1958, LICENSE NUMBER 0006567, OF P.O. BOX 1159, ENNIS, MT, WAS DISCIPLINED BY MONTANA ON MARCH 11, 1994.
DISCIPLINARY ACTION: 24-MONTH PROBATION
OFFENSE: SUBSTANDARD CARE, INCOMPETENCE, OR NEGLIGENCE
NOTES: MALPRACTICE OR NEGLIGENT PRACTICE.

BOOR, SAMUEL V MD OF ROUNDUP, MT, WAS DISCIPLINED BY UTAH ON MAY 12, 1994.
OFFENSE: DISCIPLINARY ACTION BY ANOTHER STATE OR AGENCY
NOTES: DISCIPLINARY ACTION IN ANOTHER STATE FOR ACTS AND PRACTICES WHICH ARE A BASIS FOR UTAH DISCIPLINE. LICENSE SUSPENDED FOR THREE YEARS WITH A STAY OF ENFORCEMENT ON THE SUSPENSION AS LONG AS HE REMAINS IN FULL COMPLIANCE WITH TERMS AND CONDITIONS OF HIS MONTANA PROBATION. ON 2/23/95 PROBATION TERMINATED AND LICENSE REINSTATED WITH FULL PRIVILEGES.

BOOR, SAMUEL VLADIMIR MD, DATE OF BIRTH OCTOBER 6, 1932, LICENSE NUMBER 0004717, OF P.O. BOX 97, ROUNDUP, MT, WAS DISCIPLINED BY MONTANA ON JANUARY 11, 1994.
DISCIPLINARY ACTION: EMERGENCY SUSPENSION
OFFENSE: PROFESSIONAL MISCONDUCT
NOTES: PENDING FURTHER INVESTIGATION OF ALLEGATIONS OF UNPROFESSIONAL CONDUCT.

BOOR, SAMUEL VLADIMIR MD, DATE OF BIRTH OCTOBER 6, 1932, LICENSE NUMBER 0004717, OF PO BOX 97, ROUNDUP, MT, WAS DISCIPLINED BY MONTANA ON FEBRUARY 16, 1994.
DISCIPLINARY ACTION: 36-MONTH PROBATION
NOTES: DIAGNOSED AS HAVING BIPOLAR DISORDER. HE CONTESTS THE DIAGNOSIS, HOWEVER, HE HAS FULLY COOPERATED WITH BOARD REQUIREMENTS FOR TREATMENT AND AFTERCARE. THE BOARD HAS NO CURRENT INFORMATION INDICATING THAT HE IS PRESENTLY UNABLE TO PRACTICE MEDICINE WITH REASONABLE SKILL AND SAFETY. ON 1/18/95 TERMINATION OF PROBATION; LACK OF CONTINUED NEED.

CABRERA, HERMINIO BAUZON MD, DATE OF BIRTH DECEMBER 23, 1922, LICENSE NUMBER 0003310, OF PO BOX 780336, ORLANDO, FL, WAS DISCIPLINED BY MONTANA ON MARCH 16, 1996.
DISCIPLINARY ACTION: LICENSE REVOCATION
OFFENSE: FAILURE TO COMPLY WITH A PROFESSIONAL RULE
NOTES: FAILURE TO COOPERATE WITH A BOARD INVESTIGATION.

CANNON, MAX K MD OF 400 15TH AVENUE SOUTH, GREAT FALLS, MT, WAS DISCIPLINED BY DEA ON DECEMBER 8, 1994.
DISCIPLINARY ACTION: SURRENDER OF CONTROLLED SUBSTANCE LICENSE

- MONTANA -

NOTES: IN LIEU OF PUBLIC INTEREST REVOCATION.

CANNON, MAX KENT MD, DATE OF BIRTH OCTOBER 28, 1958, LICENSE NUMBER 0007314, OF 400 15TH AVENUE, SUITE 105, GREAT FALLS, MT, WAS DISCIPLINED BY MONTANA ON MAY 24, 1994.
DISCIPLINARY ACTION: EMERGENCY SUSPENSION
OFFENSE: PROFESSIONAL MISCONDUCT
NOTES: ALLEGATIONS OF SEXUAL MISCONDUCT RELATED TO PRACTICE OF MEDICINE; SUSPICION THAT HE MAY BE SUFFERING FROM A MENTAL OR PHYSICAL CONDITION WHICH MAKES HIM UNABLE TO SAFELY PRACTICE MEDICINE. SHALL IMMEDIATELY SURRENDER LICENSE AND ALL CERTIFICATES. ORDERED TO SUBMIT TO A COMPLETE MENTAL AND PHYSICAL EVALUATION, INCLUDING BUT NOT LIMITED TO A FULL CHEMICAL DEPENDENCY EVALUATION; SHALL PROVIDE BOARD WITH COPIES OF ALL RECORDS RELATING TO THIS EVALUATION. ON 9/6/94, SUSPENSION LIFTED FOR THREE WEEKS FOR THE SOLE PURPOSE OF ALLOWING HIM TO COMPLETE AND SIGN HOSPITAL CHARTS PENDING AT THE TIME OF SUSPENSION.

CANNON, MAX KENT MD, DATE OF BIRTH OCTOBER 28, 1958, LICENSE NUMBER 0007314, OF 1108 E PATTERSON SUITE 2, KINKSVILLE, MO, WAS DISCIPLINED BY MONTANA ON MARCH 10, 1995.
DISCIPLINARY ACTION: PROBATION; RESTRICTION PLACED ON LICENSE
NOTES: FROM 3/8/94 THROUGH 5/21/94 HE WAS TAKING CORTICOSTEROIDS PRESCRIBED BY HIS TREATING PHYSICIANS FOR A CERVICAL DISC CONDITION; HAS BEEN DIAGNOSED BY THREE PSYCHIATRISTS, WHOSE OPINIONS ARE ACCEPTED BY THE BOARD, AS HAVING HAD A RECOGNIZED SIDE EFFECT OF STEROIDS, I.E. A SUBSTANCE-INDUCED MOOD DISORDER WITH MANIC FEATURES, WHICH, DURING THAT PERIOD, RESULTED IN OFFENDING BEHAVIOR. SUSPENSION LIFTED. CONDITIONS OF PROBATION: SHALL ESTABLISH A MENTOR RELATIONSHIP WITH A BOARD APPROVED PHYSICIAN WHO HE SHALL CONSULT WITH ON A REGULAR BASIS; SHALL NOT WORK ANY MORE THAN 55 HOURS PER SEVEN DAY WEEK WITHOUT OBTAINING BOARD APPROVAL; SHALL KEEP A LOG OF HOURS WORKED; SHALL GET BOARD APPROVAL FOR PRACTICE LOCATION; SHALL ESTABLISH A RELATIONSHIP WITH A PRIMARY CARE PHYSICIAN WHO WILL ASSUME RESPONSIBILITY FOR HIS ONGOING CARE; SHALL CONTINUE HIS ONGOING RELATIONSHIP WITH PSYCHIATRIST; SHALL ABSTAIN COMPLETELY FROM THE USE OF ANY AND ALL POTENTIALLY MOOD-ALTERING SUBSTANCES EXCEPT WHEN PRESCRIBED BY A LICENSED PHYSICIAN; SHALL REPORT ANY SUCH PRESCRIPTIONS TO THE BOARD; SHALL NOT WRITE, PHONE IN OR OTHERWISE ORDER PRESCRIPTIONS FOR HIMSELF OR ANY MEMBER OF HIS FAMILY; SHALL ENTER INTO AN AGREEMENT WITH THE MONTANA PROFESSIONAL ASSISTANCE PROGRAM; SHALL EXECUTE ANY RELEASES NECESSARY FOR BOARD TO VERIFY COMPLIANCE WITH THIS AGREEMENT; SHALL MEET ANNUALLY WITH THE BOARD. ON 8/11/95 ORDER MODIFIED SUCH THAT RESTRICTIONS ON THE NUMBER OF HOURS PER WEEK HE MAY WORK ARE LEFT TO THE DISCRETION OF HIS TREATING PSYCHIATRIST.

COAN, BRUCE J MD, DATE OF BIRTH AUGUST 14, 1942, OF 969 PRYOR CREEK RD, HUNTLEY, MT, WAS DISCIPLINED BY MEDICARE ON MARCH 22, 1988.
DISCIPLINARY ACTION: 24-MONTH EXCLUSION FROM THE MEDICARE AND/OR MEDICAID PROGRAMS; FINE
NOTES: NO LONGER LISTED AS EXCLUDED.

COOPER, DONALD ASHLEY MD, DATE OF BIRTH MAY 4, 1930, LICENSE NUMBER 0004371, OF 214 14TH AVENUE SW, SIDNEY, MT, WAS DISCIPLINED BY MONTANA ON MAY 3, 1991.
DISCIPLINARY ACTION: PROBATION
OFFENSE: FAILURE TO COMPLY WITH A PROFESSIONAL RULE
NOTES: QUESTIONABLE CONTROLLED SUBSTANCE PRESCRIBING AND MEDICAL CARE. VIOLATION OF MEDICAL PRACTICE ACT ADMITTED.

COOPER, DONALD ASHLEY MD, DATE OF BIRTH MAY 4, 1930, LICENSE NUMBER 0004371, OF 214 14TH AVENUE, SW, SIDNEY, MT, WAS DISCIPLINED BY MONTANA ON DECEMBER 18, 1995.
DISCIPLINARY ACTION: 12-MONTH PROBATION; REQUIRED TO TAKE ADDITIONAL MEDICAL EDUCATION
NOTES: UNDERTAKE FOCUSED CONTINUING MEDICAL EDUCATION AND IMPROVED CHARTING. PROBATION EXTENDED ONE ADDITIONAL YEAR.

COWARD, HAROLD MARK MD, DATE OF BIRTH JUNE 19, 1947, LICENSE NUMBER 0005149, OF 3700 SOUTH RUSSELL #115, MISSOULA, MT, WAS DISCIPLINED BY MONTANA ON OCTOBER 21, 1992.
DISCIPLINARY ACTION: 60-MONTH PROBATION
OFFENSE: OVERPRESCRIBING OR MISPRESCRIBING DRUGS
NOTES: OVERPRESCRIBING OF ADDICTIVE DRUGS, PSYCHOLOGICAL CONDITION. ON 7/24/95 PROBATION MODIFIED TO ADD CONTINUING MEDICAL EDUCATION AND CHARTING REQUIREMENTS.

COWARD, HAROLD MARK MD, DATE OF BIRTH JUNE 19, 1947, LICENSE NUMBER 0023667, OF 3700 SOUTH RUSSELL, #115, MISSOULA, MT, WAS DISCIPLINED BY IOWA ON MARCH 21, 1994.
DISCIPLINARY ACTION: PROBATION
OFFENSE: DISCIPLINARY ACTION BY ANOTHER STATE OR AGENCY
NOTES: PROBATION TO RUN CONCURRENTLY WITH MONTANA'S PROBATION

DAVIS, ROBERT C MD WAS DISCIPLINED BY IOWA ON DECEMBER 1, 1988.
DISCIPLINARY ACTION: 3-MONTH LICENSE SUSPENSION
OFFENSE: DISCIPLINARY ACTION BY ANOTHER STATE OR AGENCY

DAVIS, ROBERT C MD OF 1519 WEST 90TH SOUTH, WEST JORDAN, UT, WAS DISCIPLINED BY NEW MEXICO ON DECEMBER 15, 1993.
DISCIPLINARY ACTION: LICENSE REVOCATION
OFFENSE: CRIMINAL CONVICTION OR PLEA OF GUILTY, NOLO CONTENDERE, OR NO CONTEST TO A CRIME
NOTES: CRIMINAL CONVICTION IN ANOTHER STATE.

DAVIS, ROBERT CHARLES MD, DATE OF BIRTH OCTOBER 25, 1953, OF 1781 WEST 9000 SOUTH, WEST JORDAN, UT, WAS DISCIPLINED BY MEDICARE ON MAY 29, 1987.
DISCIPLINARY ACTION: 120-MONTH EXCLUSION FROM THE MEDICARE AND/OR MEDICAID PROGRAMS
OFFENSE: CRIMINAL CONVICTION OR PLEA OF GUILTY, NOLO CONTENDERE, OR NO CONTEST TO A CRIME
NOTES: PROGRAM-RELATED CONVICTION.

DAVIS, ROBERT CHARLES MD, DATE OF BIRTH OCTOBER 25, 1953, LICENSE NUMBER 0005035, OF 1781 WEST 90TH S, WEST JORDAN, UT, WAS DISCIPLINED BY MONTANA ON MARCH 30, 1989.
DISCIPLINARY ACTION: 12-MONTH LICENSE SUSPENSION; 48-MONTH PROBATION
OFFENSE: PROVIDING FALSE INFORMATION TO THE BOARD
NOTES: FAILURE TO DISCLOSE DISCIPLINARY ACTION IN OTHER STATE IN RENEWING LICENSE

DAVIS, ROBERT CHARLES MD, DATE OF BIRTH OCTOBER 25, 1953, LICENSE NUMBER 0005035, OF 1781 WEST 90TH S, WEST JORDAN, UT, WAS DISCIPLINED BY MONTANA ON JANUARY 24, 1991.
DISCIPLINARY ACTION: SURRENDER OF LICENSE
OFFENSE: FAILURE TO COMPLY WITH A PROFESSIONAL RULE
NOTES: FAILURE TO DISCLOSE UTAH DISCIPLINARY ACTION IN A

- MONTANA -

TIMELY MANNER.

DAVIS, ROBERT CHARLES MD OF SANDY, UT, WAS DISCIPLINED BY UTAH ON JULY 19, 1993.
DISCIPLINARY ACTION: LICENSE REVOCATION; REVOCATION OF CONTROLLED SUBSTANCE LICENSE
OFFENSE: CRIMINAL CONVICTION OR PLEA OF GUILTY, NOLO CONTENDERE, OR NO CONTEST TO A CRIME
NOTES: CONVICTION OF CRIMES OF MORAL TURPITUDE WHICH RELATE TO HIS PRACTICE OF MEDICINE AND DEMONSTRATE A THREAT TO THE PUBLIC HEALTH, SAFETY AND WELFARE. HE FILED A REQUEST FOR AGENCY REVIEW ON 07/08/93 AND THE REVOCATION WAS STAYED PENDING THE ISSUANCE OF AN ORDER ON THE REQUEST. ORDER WAS UPHELD IN ITS ENTIRETY.

DAVIS, ROBERT CHARLES MD, DATE OF BIRTH OCTOBER 25, 1953, LICENSE NUMBER 0023956, OF 1519 WEST 90TH STREET, WEST JORDAN, UT, WAS DISCIPLINED BY IOWA ON JUNE 6, 1994.
DISCIPLINARY ACTION: LICENSE REVOCATION
OFFENSE: DISCIPLINARY ACTION BY ANOTHER STATE OR AGENCY
NOTES: CHARGES THAT UTAH TOOK ACTION FOR FRAUD.

DAVIS, ROBERT CHARLES MD, DATE OF BIRTH OCTOBER 25, 1953, OF RR 2 BOX 9000, SAFFORD, AZ, WAS DISCIPLINED BY MEDICARE ON OCTOBER 10, 1994.
DISCIPLINARY ACTION: 300-MONTH EXCLUSION FROM THE MEDICARE AND/OR MEDICAID PROGRAMS
OFFENSE: CRIMINAL CONVICTION OR PLEA OF GUILTY, NOLO CONTENDERE, OR NO CONTEST TO A CRIME
NOTES: CONVICTED OF A CRIME INVOLVING THE MEDICARE, MEDICAID, MATERNAL AND CHILD HEALTH SERVICES BLOCK GRANT OR BLOCK GRANTS TO STATES FOR SOCIAL SERVICES PROGRAMS.

DE MATA, MARCELINO MD, DATE OF BIRTH DECEMBER 22, 1941, OF 158 EAST 47TH STREET, HIALEAH, FL, WAS DISCIPLINED BY MONTANA ON OCTOBER 14, 1994.
DISCIPLINARY ACTION: 36-MONTH PROBATION; FINE
OFFENSE: PROVIDING FALSE INFORMATION TO THE BOARD
NOTES: FRAUD ON APPLICATION AND RENEWAL. MUST PAY $500 FINE AND PASS USMLE.

DONDERO, JOHN A DR, LICENSE NUMBER 0014421, WAS DISCIPLINED BY MINNESOTA ON JANUARY 6, 1996.
NOTES: STAYED SUSPENSION.

DONDERO, JOHN A MD, DATE OF BIRTH FEBRUARY 29, 1928, LICENSE NUMBER 0018302, OF MENDON, MA, WAS DISCIPLINED BY KENTUCKY ON JUNE 17, 1996.
DISCIPLINARY ACTION: 60-MONTH PROBATION; MONITORING OF PHYSICIAN
NOTES: MUST ADVISE BOARD IF HE RESUMES PRACTICE IN KENTUCKY; MUST MAINTAIN LOG OF CONTROLLED SUBSTANCES; IS SUBJECT TO REVIEW OF PATIENT CHARTS.

DONDERO, JOHN ANTHONY MD, DATE OF BIRTH FEBRUARY 29, 1928, LICENSE NUMBER 0078686, OF 13 BLACKSTONE STREET PO BOX 86, MEDON, MA, WAS DISCIPLINED BY NEW YORK ON JUNE 23, 1995.
DISCIPLINARY ACTION: 24-MONTH PROBATION
OFFENSE: SUBSTANDARD CARE, INCOMPETENCE, OR NEGLIGENCE
NOTES: NEGLIGENCE ON MORE THAN ONE OCCASION AND FAILURE TO MAINTAIN ACCURATE PATIENT RECORDS. HE FAILED TO OBTAIN ADEQUATE MEDICAL HISTORIES, FAILED TO PERFORM ADEQUATE PHYSICAL EXAMINATIONS AND ORDERED TESTS OR RENDERED TREATMENT WITHOUT MEDICAL JUSTIFICATION. TWO YEAR SUSPENSION, STAYED WITH PROBATION UPON COMMENCING PRACTICE IN NEW YORK.

DONDERO, JOHN ANTHONY MD, DATE OF BIRTH FEBRUARY 29, 1928, LICENSE NUMBER 032316E, OF BLACKSTONE STREET, PO BOX 86, MENDON, MA, WAS DISCIPLINED BY PENNSYLVANIA ON FEBRUARY 14, 1996.
DISCIPLINARY ACTION: LICENSE SUSPENSION
OFFENSE: DISCIPLINARY ACTION BY ANOTHER STATE OR AGENCY
NOTES: RECIPROCAL ACTION FROM NEW YORK. LICENSE SUSPENDED UNTIL HE DEMONSTRATES SUCCESSFUL COMPLETION OF PROBATION IN NEW YORK.

DONDERO, JOHN ANTHONY JR MD, DATE OF BIRTH FEBRUARY 29, 1928, LICENSE NUMBER 0003608, OF 13 BLACKSTONE ST. P.O. BOX 86, MENDON, MA, WAS DISCIPLINED BY NORTH DAKOTA ON MARCH 22, 1996.
OFFENSE: DISCIPLINARY ACTION BY ANOTHER STATE OR AGENCY
NOTES: ACTION IN NEW YORK BASED ON QUALITY OF CARE AND RECORD KEEPING ISSUES. TWO YEAR SUSPENSION STAYED.

DONDERO, JOHN ANTHONY MD, DATE OF BIRTH FEBRUARY 29, 1928, LICENSE NUMBER 0003895, OF 13 BLACKSTONE ST. BOX 86, MENDON, MA, WAS DISCIPLINED BY MONTANA ON SEPTEMBER 20, 1996.
DISCIPLINARY ACTION: 24-MONTH PROBATION; MONITORING OF PHYSICIAN
OFFENSE: DISCIPLINARY ACTION BY ANOTHER STATE OR AGENCY
NOTES: PROBATION IN NEW YORK AS OF 6/14/95; RECORD KEEPING. CONDITIONS OF MONTANA PROBATION: SHALL COMPLY WITH THE NEW YORK PROBATION; SHALL GIVE THE MONTANA BOARD WRITTEN NOTICE OF ANY CHANGE IN EMPLOYMENT OR PRACTICE AND SHALL AT ALL TIMES KEEP THE BOARD ADVISED OF HIS RESIDENCE AND BUSINESS ADDRESSES AND TELEPHONE NUMBERS; SHALL MAINTAIN COMPLETE AND ACCURATE RECORDS OF HIS PURCHASE, ADMINISTRATION, DISPENSING OR PRESCRIBING OF CONTROLLED SUBSTANCES, AND SHALL MAKE SUCH RECORDS AVAILABLE TO THE BOARD; SHALL MAINTAIN LEGIBLE AND COMPLETE MEDICAL RECORDS WHICH ACCURATELY REFLECT EVALUATION AND TREATMENT OF HIS PATIENTS WHICH SHALL BE AVAILABLE TO THE BOARD; SHALL PROVIDE THE BOARD WITH ANY NOTES, REPORTS, MEMORANDA, OR OTHER RECORD OF ANY REVIEWS; AND SHALL GIVE THE BOARD 30 DAYS ADVANCE NOTICE PRIOR TO RESUMING ACTIVE PRACTICE IN MONTANA.

EICHELBERGER, DALE LEROY MD, DATE OF BIRTH MARCH 18, 1934, LICENSE NUMBER 0015302, WAS DISCIPLINED BY MINNESOTA ON MARCH 9, 1991.
DISCIPLINARY ACTION: RESTRICTION PLACED ON LICENSE

EICHELBERGER, DALE LEROY MD, DATE OF BIRTH MARCH 18, 1934, LICENSE NUMBER 0015302, OF 4410 165TH AVE, NE, NEW LONDON, MN, WAS DISCIPLINED BY MINNESOTA ON AUGUST 22, 1991.
DISCIPLINARY ACTION: LICENSE SUSPENSION
OFFENSE: FAILURE TO COMPLY WITH A PREVIOUS BOARD ORDER
NOTES: VIOLATION OF BOARD ORDER.

EICHELBERGER, DALE LEROY MD, DATE OF BIRTH MARCH 18, 1934, LICENSE NUMBER 0003691, OF 4410 165TH AVE NORTH, NEW LONDON, MN, WAS DISCIPLINED BY MONTANA ON MARCH 5, 1992.
DISCIPLINARY ACTION: LICENSE REVOCATION
OFFENSE: DISCIPLINARY ACTION BY ANOTHER STATE OR AGENCY
NOTES: ALCOHOL RELAPSE.

ELY, NEAL EUGENE MD, DATE OF BIRTH NOVEMBER 4, 1922, LICENSE NUMBER 0005115, OF 2112 FAIRVIEW PLACE, BILLINGS, MT, WAS DISCIPLINED BY MONTANA ON DECEMBER 9, 1988.
DISCIPLINARY ACTION: REPRIMAND
OFFENSE: PROVIDING FALSE INFORMATION TO THE BOARD
NOTES: FAILURE TO REPORT DISCIPLINARY ACTION IN ANOTHER

- MONTANA -

STATE IN RENEWING LICENSE

ERICKSON, BRUCE L DR, LICENSE NUMBER 0026117, WAS DISCIPLINED BY MINNESOTA ON NOVEMBER 23, 1996.
DISCIPLINARY ACTION: LICENSE SUSPENSION

ERICKSON, BRUCE LELAND MD, DATE OF BIRTH OCTOBER 15, 1951, OF 333 FOX DRIVE, GREAT FALLS, MT, WAS DISCIPLINED BY MEDICARE ON JULY 18, 1994.
DISCIPLINARY ACTION: 180-MONTH EXCLUSION FROM THE MEDICARE AND/OR MEDICAID PROGRAMS
OFFENSE: CRIMINAL CONVICTION OR PLEA OF GUILTY, NOLO CONTENDERE, OR NO CONTEST TO A CRIME
NOTES: CONVICTED OF A CRIME INVOLVING THE MEDICARE, MEDICAID, MATERNAL AND CHILD HEALTH SERVICES BLOCK GRANT OR BLOCK GRANTS TO STATES FOR SOCIAL SERVICES PROGRAMS.

ERICKSON, BRUCE LELAND MD, DATE OF BIRTH OCTOBER 15, 1951, LICENSE NUMBER 0004984, OF 1717 4TH STREET SOUTH, GREAT FALLS, MT, WAS DISCIPLINED BY MONTANA ON MAY 22, 1995.
DISCIPLINARY ACTION: LICENSE REVOCATION
OFFENSE: CRIMINAL CONVICTION OR PLEA OF GUILTY, NOLO CONTENDERE, OR NO CONTEST TO A CRIME
NOTES: FELONY CONVICTION OF FRAUD. REVOCATION FOR MINIMUM OF TWO YEARS. ON 6/8/95 DISTRICT COURT GRANTED A STAY DURING JUDICIAL REVIEW. ON 4/26/96 COURT AFFIRMED BOARD REVOCATION AND LIFTED COURT IMPOSED STAY.

GALLUS, JOHN MACK MD, DATE OF BIRTH APRIL 5, 1937, LICENSE NUMBER 0003483, OF 320 SOUTH CLARK, BUTTE, MT, WAS DISCIPLINED BY MONTANA ON DECEMBER 27, 1993.
DISCIPLINARY ACTION: 12-MONTH PROBATION
OFFENSE: SUBSTANDARD CARE, INCOMPETENCE, OR NEGLIGENCE
NOTES: NEGLIGENCE.

GALLUS, JOHN MACK MD, DATE OF BIRTH APRIL 5, 1937, LICENSE NUMBER 0003483, OF 320 SOUTH CLARK, BUTTE, MT, WAS DISCIPLINED BY MONTANA ON DECEMBER 30, 1994.
DISCIPLINARY ACTION: RESTRICTION PLACED ON LICENSE
OFFENSE: FAILURE TO COMPLY WITH A PREVIOUS BOARD ORDER
NOTES: INABILITY TO COMPLETE PROBATION REQUIREMENTS.

HARKNESS, JAMES EMERSON DO, DATE OF BIRTH DECEMBER 9, 1950, LICENSE NUMBER 0005134, OF 1220 CENTRAL AVENUE, GREAT FALLS, MT, WAS DISCIPLINED BY MONTANA ON FEBRUARY 3, 1993.
DISCIPLINARY ACTION: PROBATION
OFFENSE: PROFESSIONAL MISCONDUCT
NOTES: SEXUAL MISCONDUCT. HAS ENTERED TREATMENT WITH THE MONTANA PROFESSIONAL ASSISTANCE PROGRAM. LICENSE REACTIVATED UNTIL 7/31/93 ON INDEFINITE PROBATION; SHALL FULFILL ALL TERMS AND CONDITIONS OF HIS AGREEMENT WITH THE MONTANA PROFESSIONAL ASSISTANCE PROGRAM. ON 7/23/93 TEMPORARY REACTIVATION OF LICENSE EXTENDED TO 3/31/94. ON 3/11/94 LICENSE FULLY REACTIVATED. ALL OTHER TERMS AND CONDITIONS REMAIN IN FULL FORCE AND EFFECT. SATISFACTORY COMPLIANCE WITH PROBATION.

HARRISON, MURKE FRANKLIN IV DO, LICENSE NUMBER 0004058, OF BUTTE, MT, WAS DISCIPLINED BY OHIO ON APRIL 15, 1993.
DISCIPLINARY ACTION: PROBATION; RESTRICTION PLACED ON LICENSE
OFFENSE: DISCIPLINARY ACTION BY ANOTHER STATE OR AGENCY
NOTES: ACTION BY MONTANA BOARD AND TREATMENT FOR CHEMICAL DEPENDENCY.

HARRISON, MURKE FRANKLIN IV DO, DATE OF BIRTH JUNE 24, 1956, LICENSE NUMBER 0027091, OF BUTTE, MT, WAS DISCIPLINED BY COLORADO ON JUNE 11, 1993.
OFFENSE: SUBSTANDARD CARE, INCOMPETENCE, OR NEGLIGENCE
NOTES: SUBSTANDARD CARE; MENTAL DISABILITY. ORDER REQUIRES COMPLIANCE WITH TERMS OF AN AGREEMENT WITH THE MONTANA MEDICAL BOARD.

HARRISON, MURKE FRANKLIN IV DO, DATE OF BIRTH JUNE 24, 1956, LICENSE NUMBER 0009497, OF PO BOX 3052, BUTTE, MT, WAS DISCIPLINED BY MICHIGAN ON OCTOBER 15, 1993.
DISCIPLINARY ACTION: EMERGENCY SUSPENSION
OFFENSE: PHYSICAL OR MENTAL ILLNESS INHIBITING THE ABILITY TO PRACTICE WITH SKILL AND SAFETY

HARRISON, MURKE FRANKLIN IV DO, DATE OF BIRTH JUNE 24, 1956, LICENSE NUMBER 0006511, OF PO BOX 3052, BUTTE, MT, WAS DISCIPLINED BY MONTANA ON NOVEMBER 5, 1993.
DISCIPLINARY ACTION: SURRENDER OF LICENSE
OFFENSE: FAILURE TO COMPLY WITH A PREVIOUS BOARD ORDER
NOTES: VIOLATION OF CHEMICAL DEPENDENCY MONITORING AGREEMENT. INDEFINITE SURRENDER.

HARRISON, MURKE FRANKLIN IV DO, DATE OF BIRTH JUNE 24, 1956, LICENSE NUMBER 0009497, OF POST OFFICE BOX 3052, BUTTE, MT, WAS DISCIPLINED BY MICHIGAN ON APRIL 7, 1994.
DISCIPLINARY ACTION: 6-MONTH LICENSE SUSPENSION
OFFENSE: SUBSTANCE ABUSE
NOTES: MENTAL/PHYSICAL INABILITY TO PRACTICE-DRUG RELATED.

HARRISON, MURKE FRANKLIN IV DO, DATE OF BIRTH JUNE 24, 1956, LICENSE NUMBER 0027091, OF BUTTE, MT, WAS DISCIPLINED BY COLORADO ON MAY 13, 1994.
DISCIPLINARY ACTION: SURRENDER OF LICENSE
OFFENSE: FAILURE TO COMPLY WITH A PREVIOUS BOARD ORDER
NOTES: VIOLATION OF MONTANA AND COLORADO STIPULATIONS. HABITUAL INTEMPERANCE OR EXCESSIVE USE OF A CONTROLLED SUBSTANCE.

HARRISON, MURKE FRANKLIN IV DO, LICENSE NUMBER 0004058, OF BUTTE, MT, WAS DISCIPLINED BY OHIO ON JUNE 15, 1994.
DISCIPLINARY ACTION: LICENSE REVOCATION
OFFENSE: FAILURE TO COMPLY WITH A PREVIOUS BOARD ORDER
NOTES: VIOLATION OF CONDITIONS OF LIMITATION IMPOSED BY 4/15/93 CONSENT AGREEMENT DUE TO FAILURE TO COMPLY WITH TERMS OF PROBATION IMPOSED ON MONTANA MEDICAL LICENSE BY MONTANA BOARD; SUBMISSION OF FALSE STATEMENTS TO OHIO BOARD REGARDING PROBATIONARY COMPLIANCE. PERMANENT REVOCATION. NOTICE OF APPEAL FILED BY DOCTOR WITH FRANKLIN COUNTY COURT OF COMMON PLEAS ON 7/5/94. COMMON PLEAS SUSTAINED BOARD'S MOTION TO DISMISS HIS APPEAL. MOTION FOR RECONSIDERATION OF DISMISSAL OF APPEAL ORDER FILED BY HIM ON 5/19/95. DECISION FROM 10TH DISTRICT COURT OF APPEALS DENYING MOTION FOR RECONSIDERATION FILED ON 6/15/95. NOTICE OF APPEAL TO THE OHIO SUPREME COURT FILED BY HIM ON 6/23/95. ON 10/18/95 THE SUPREME COURT DECLINED TO ACCEPT JURISDICTION OF HIS APPEAL.

HOBBS, WILLIAM DOUGLAS MD, DATE OF BIRTH MARCH 30, 1944, LICENSE NUMBER 0005254, OF 410 S EARLING, P.O. BOX 1000, MILES CITY, MT, WAS DISCIPLINED BY MONTANA ON APRIL 21, 1994.
DISCIPLINARY ACTION: SURRENDER OF LICENSE
OFFENSE: FAILURE TO COMPLY WITH A PROFESSIONAL RULE
NOTES: UNABLE FOR PERSONAL REASONS TO COMPLY WITH ORDER FOR EVALUATION. ON 12/28/94, AFTER HE COMPLIED WITH BOARD'S ORDER FOR EVALUATION LICENSE FULLY REINSTATED ON ACTIVE STATUS; RETURN TO HEALTH.

HOBBS, WILLIAM DOUGLAS MD, DATE OF BIRTH MARCH 30, 1944, OF 410 S EARLING AVENUE, MILES CITY, MT, WAS DISCIPLINED BY

- MONTANA -

MEDICARE ON DECEMBER 5, 1994.
DISCIPLINARY ACTION: EXCLUSION FROM THE MEDICARE AND/OR MEDICAID PROGRAMS
OFFENSE: DISCIPLINARY ACTION BY ANOTHER STATE OR AGENCY
NOTES: LICENSE SURRENDERED FOR REASONS BEARING ON PROFESSIONAL COMPETENCE. REINSTATED ON 3/1/95.

HOPKINS, GARY L MD, DATE OF BIRTH APRIL 11, 1948, LICENSE NUMBER 0004596, OF 14 S MAIN STREET, STEVENSVILLE, MT, WAS DISCIPLINED BY MONTANA ON DECEMBER 13, 1990.
DISCIPLINARY ACTION: LICENSE REVOCATION
OFFENSE: SUBSTANDARD CARE, INCOMPETENCE, OR NEGLIGENCE
NOTES: THE ALLEGATIONS ON WHICH LICENSEE WAS FOUND GUILTY INCLUDE: NEGLIGENCE, INSURANCE FRAUD, IMPROPER PRESCRIBING OF SCHEDULED DRUGS, AND AIDING AND ABETTING A PERSON WITHOUT A LICENSE TO PRACTICE MEDICINE IN MONTANA.

HOPKINS, GARY L MD, DATE OF BIRTH APRIL 11, 1948, LICENSE NUMBER 0036207, OF 514 SOUTH MAIN ST, STEVENSVILLE, MT, WAS DISCIPLINED BY NEW JERSEY ON FEBRUARY 14, 1992.
DISCIPLINARY ACTION: SURRENDER OF LICENSE
OFFENSE: DISCIPLINARY ACTION BY ANOTHER STATE OR AGENCY
NOTES: DISCIPLINARY ACTION TAKEN AGAINST HIS LICENSE PRIVILEGES IN MONTANA. LICENSE PERMANENTLY SURRENDERED WITH PREJUDICE.

HOUSER, VICTOR CARL MD, DATE OF BIRTH NOVEMBER 30, 1951, LICENSE NUMBER 0007007, OF 355 1ST AVENUE W.N., KALISPELL, MT, WAS DISCIPLINED BY MONTANA ON MARCH 15, 1996.
DISCIPLINARY ACTION: FINE
OFFENSE: PROFESSIONAL MISCONDUCT
NOTES: FAILURE TO TRANSFER PATIENT RECORDS IN A TIMELY FASHION; FAILURE TO COOPERATE WITH A BOARD INVESTIGATION.

JOHNS, CHARLES BASIL DO, DATE OF BIRTH JANUARY 21, 1930, LICENSE NUMBER 0007380, OF 436 N. JACKSON, HELENA, MT, WAS DISCIPLINED BY MONTANA ON AUGUST 9, 1993.
NOTES: STIPULATION AND AGREEMENT; ORDER UNSPECIFIED.

KENCK, RALPH JOSEPH MD, DATE OF BIRTH APRIL 15, 1929, LICENSE NUMBER 0006821, OF 107 DILWORTH, GLENDIVE, MT, WAS DISCIPLINED BY MONTANA ON SEPTEMBER 5, 1991.
DISCIPLINARY ACTION: LICENSE SUSPENSION
OFFENSE: SUBSTANCE ABUSE
NOTES: CHEMICAL DEPENDENCY.

KENCK, RALPH JOSEPH MD, DATE OF BIRTH APRIL 15, 1929, LICENSE NUMBER 0006821, OF 108 SOUTH EAST AVE, OAK PARK, IL, WAS DISCIPLINED BY MONTANA ON APRIL 4, 1992.
OFFENSE: SUBSTANCE ABUSE
NOTES: FOUND GUILTY OF HABITUAL INTEMPERANCE OR EXCESSIVE USE OF ALCOHOL. EMERGENCY SUSPENSION OF 9/5/91 ON ALLEGATION OF ALCOHOL DEPENDENCE LIFTED FOLLOWING COMPLETION OF INPATIENT TREATMENT. CONTINUES AFTERCARE AGREEMENT WITH PROFESSIONAL ASSISTANCE PROGRAM. LICENSE RESTORED ON INACTIVE STATUS; IF HE RETURNS TO MONTANA MUST APPEAR BEFORE BOARD BEFORE PRACTICING.

KHALATIAN, SERGE MD, DATE OF BIRTH APRIL 20, 1942, OF 1935 N. BERENDO ST., LOS ANGELES, CA, WAS DISCIPLINED BY MONTANA ON APRIL 18, 1989.
DISCIPLINARY ACTION: DENIAL OF NEW LICENSE

KOHLI, SUBHASH C DR, DATE OF BIRTH MAY 19, 1940, LICENSE NUMBER 0006156, OF LOUTH COUNTY HOSPITAL, REPUBLIC OF IRELAND, WAS DISCIPLINED BY MONTANA ON OCTOBER 31, 1989.
DISCIPLINARY ACTION: REPRIMAND

KOON, RICHARD ETHEN MD, DATE OF BIRTH JANUARY 26, 1951, LICENSE NUMBER 0011497, WAS DISCIPLINED BY WEST VIRGINIA ON NOVEMBER 18, 1988.
DISCIPLINARY ACTION: EMERGENCY SUSPENSION
OFFENSE: SUBSTANCE ABUSE
NOTES: KOON HAD BEEN ABUSING DEXEDRINE; HE APPEARED DISORIENTED AND DISHEVELED DURING BUSINESS HOURS ON NOVEMBER 10, 1988. CASE OPEN AS OF DECEMBER 31, 1988; KANAWHA COUNTY CIRCUIT COURT DENIED KOON'S REQUEST FOR A WRIT OF PROHIBITION AGAINST THE SUMMARY SUSPENSION ON FEBRUARY 27, 1989. KOON HAD CLAIMED HE DID NOT PLAN TO TREAT PATIENTS THE DAY THE INVESTIGATOR CAME TO HIS OFFICE AND THAT HE WAS TAKING PRESCRIBED DEXEDRINE AS TREATMENT FOR A SEVERE DEPRESSION

KOON, RICHARD ETHEN MD, DATE OF BIRTH JANUARY 26, 1951, OF 1222 LEE STREET, CHARLESTON, WV, WAS DISCIPLINED BY DEA ON JANUARY 27, 1989.
DISCIPLINARY ACTION: SURRENDER OF CONTROLLED SUBSTANCE LICENSE
OFFENSE: PROFESSIONAL MISCONDUCT
NOTES: WEST VIRGINIA MEDICAL BOARD SUMMARILY SUSPENDED MEDICAL LICENSE. ARRESTED IN CHARLESTON, WEST VIRGINIA 12/88 FOR FORGED SCRIPT.

KOON, RICHARD ETHEN MD, DATE OF BIRTH JANUARY 26, 1951, LICENSE NUMBER 0011497, OF 308 WESTMORELAND DRIVE, DUNBAR, WV, WAS DISCIPLINED BY WEST VIRGINIA ON APRIL 6, 1989.
DISCIPLINARY ACTION: LICENSE SUSPENSION
OFFENSE: SUBSTANCE ABUSE
NOTES: LICENSE IMMEDIATELY SUSPENDED 11/18/88 BASED ON URINE SAMPLE REPORT. THIS WILL REMAIN IN EFFECT UNTIL HE SHOWS BOARD REPORT THAT HE HAS OBTAINED AN EVALUATION AND TREATMENT.

KOON, RICHARD ETHEN MD, DATE OF BIRTH JANUARY 26, 1951, LICENSE NUMBER 0005356, OF 1217 VIRGINIA ST. EAST, CHARLESTON, WV, WAS DISCIPLINED BY MONTANA ON APRIL 19, 1990.
DISCIPLINARY ACTION: LICENSE REVOCATION
OFFENSE: DISCIPLINARY ACTION BY ANOTHER STATE OR AGENCY
NOTES: SANCTIONED IN WEST VIRGINIA; VIOLATION OF PROBATION, AND MENTAL AND PHYSICAL IMPAIRMENT

KOON, RICHARD ETHEN MD, DATE OF BIRTH JANUARY 26, 1951, LICENSE NUMBER 0011497, OF 1319 QUARRIER STREET, CHARLESTON, WV, WAS DISCIPLINED BY WEST VIRGINIA ON OCTOBER 15, 1992.
DISCIPLINARY ACTION: 24-MONTH PROBATION; RESTRICTION PLACED ON LICENSE
NOTES: LICENSE WAS SUSPENDED IN APRIL 1989. MONTANA LICENSE REVOKED IN APRIL 1990. IN JUNE 1992 HE RECEIVED A PASSING SCORE ON THE SPEX EXAMINATION; LICENSE REINSTATED ON A PROBATIONARY STATUS SUBJECT TO THE FOLLOWING TERMS AND CONDITIONS: IS PROHIBITED FROM ENGAGING IN A SOLO OFFICE PRACTICE OF MEDICINE; PRACTICE MAY OCCUR ONLY UNDER THE SUPERVISION OF ANOTHER DULY LICENSED BOARD APPROVED PSYCHIATRIST WITH MONTHLY WRITTEN REPORTS; MUST SUBMIT TO RANDOM TESTING OF BODILY FLUIDS; MUST RECEIVE REGULAR CARE AND TREATMENT ON A MONTHLY BASIS BY A PSYCHIATRIST OTHER THAN THE SUPERVISING PSYCHIATRIST WHO WILL ALSO SUBMIT MONTHLY WRITTEN REPORTS TO THE BOARD; IS PROHIBITED FROM PRESCRIBING, DISPENSING, ADMINISTERING, MIXING, PREPARING, GIVING, OR DISTRIBUTING ANY CONTROLLED SUBSTANCES DESIGNATED AS SCHEDULE II; SHALL KEEP A LOG OF ALL

CONTROLLED SUBSTANCES HE PRESCRIBES; PROHIBITED FROM ADMINISTERING ANY SCHEDULED CONTROLLED SUBSTANCES TO HIMSELF WHICH ARE NOT PRESCRIBED BY HIS BOARD APPROVED TREATING PSYCHIATRIST; A COPY OF THIS CONSENT ORDER SHALL BE PROMPTLY PRESENTED TO ANY EMPLOYER, HEALTH CARE OR MEDICAL FACILITY WHERE HE SEEKS TO PRACTICE MEDICINE.

KOON, RICHARD ETHEN MD, DATE OF BIRTH JANUARY 26, 1951, LICENSE NUMBER 0011497, OF 1319 QUARRIER STREET, CHARLESTON, WV, WAS DISCIPLINED BY WEST VIRGINIA ON JUNE 25, 1993.
NOTES: LICENSE CHANGED TO THE INACTIVE STATUS AND HE IS UNABLE TO PRACTICE MEDICINE IN WEST VIRGINIA IN ANY MANNER WHATSOEVER.

KOON, RICHARD ETHEN MD, DATE OF BIRTH JANUARY 26, 1951, LICENSE NUMBER 0011497, OF 123 ½ 4TH AVENUE, SOUTH CHARLESTON, WV, WAS DISCIPLINED BY WEST VIRGINIA ON OCTOBER 1, 1993.
DISCIPLINARY ACTION: 24-MONTH PROBATION
NOTES: IN 6/93 LICENSE PLACED ON INACTIVE STATUS BASED ON NONCOMPLIANCE WITH 9/92 ORDER. REINSTATEMENT WITH FOLLOWING CONDITIONS: PROHIBITED FROM ENGAGING IN A SOLO OFFICE PRACTICE; SHALL BE EMPLOYED AT A SPECIFIED INSTITUTION WHERE HE MAY PRACTICE ONLY UNDER THE SUPERVISION OF ANOTHER DULY LICENSED PSYCHIATRIST APPROVED BY THE BOARD WHO WILL SUPERVISE HIS MEDICAL PRACTICE AND BE RESPONSIBLE FOR CARRYING OUT RANDOM, UNANNOUNCED TESTING OF HIS BODILY FLUIDS AND SUBMIT MONTHLY REPORTS TO THE BOARD; HE CAN ONLY PRACTICE MEDICINE IF HE RECEIVES REGULAR CARE AND TREATMENT AT LEAST ON A MONTHLY BASIS WITH MONTHLY WRITTEN REPORTS TO THE BOARD; HE SHALL UNDERGO RANDOM, UNANNOUNCED TESTING OF BODILY FLUIDS; HE IS PROHIBITED FROM PRESCRIBING, DISPENSING, ADMINISTERING, MIXING, PREPARING, GIVING OR DISTRIBUTING ANY CONTROLLED SUBSTANCES DESIGNATED AS SCHEDULE II; SHALL KEEP A LOG OF ANY AND ALL OTHER SCHEDULED CONTROLLED SUBSTANCES PRESCRIBED BY HIM TO ANY AND ALL PATIENTS; HE IS PROHIBITED FROM ADMINISTERING ANY SCHEDULED CONTROLLED SUBSTANCES TO HIMSELF WHICH ARE NOT PRESCRIBED BY A TREATING PHYSICIAN; AT THE END OR THE TWO-YEAR PROBATION PERIOD THIS ORDER OR A MODIFIED VERSION MAY BE ENTERED INTO; SHALL PROVIDE A COPY OF THIS ORDER TO ANY HEALTH CARE FACILITY WHERE HE PRACTICES OR SEEKS TO PRACTICE MEDICINE.

KOON, RICHARD ETHEN MD, DATE OF BIRTH JANUARY 26, 1951, OF 1530 NORWAY AVENUE, HUNTINGTON, WV, WAS DISCIPLINED BY DEA ON DECEMBER 12, 1993.
DISCIPLINARY ACTION: RESTRICTION PLACED ON CONTROLLED SUBSTANCE LICENSE
OFFENSE: CRIMINAL CONVICTION OR PLEA OF GUILTY, NOLO CONTENDERE, OR NO CONTEST TO A CRIME
NOTES: CONVICTED AND SENTENCED TO PROBATION FOR PRESCRIPTION FORGERY. APPLICATION FOR REGISTRATION. REGISTRATION APPROVED.

KRAFT, JEFFREY G DO, LICENSE NUMBER 0524228, OF 400 SOUTH SANTA FE, SALINA, KS, WAS DISCIPLINED BY KANSAS ON JANUARY 11, 1994.
DISCIPLINARY ACTION: MONITORING OF PHYSICIAN
OFFENSE: CRIMINAL CONVICTION OR PLEA OF GUILTY, NOLO CONTENDERE, OR NO CONTEST TO A CRIME
NOTES: ON 11/19/93 ENTERED A PLEA OF GUILTY TO THREE MISDEMEANOR COUNTS IN U.S. DISTRICT COURT INVOLVING DIVERSION OF PRESCRIPTION MEDICATIONS FOR OTHER THAN LEGITIMATE MEDICAL PURPOSES. AGREES TO REFRAIN FROM THE INGESTION, INHALATION, INJECTION OR OTHER USE OF ANY CONTROLLED SUBSTANCES UNLESS PRESCRIBED OR ADMINISTERED BY A LICENSED PHYSICIAN AND TO REFRAIN FROM THE INGESTION OF ALCOHOL; AGREES TO REFRAIN FROM THE INGESTION, INHALATION, INJECTION OR USE OF ANY ILLICIT, "STREET", ILLEGAL, AND/OR ANY TYPE OF DRUG NOT CURRENTLY CLASSIFIED BY THE FDA; AGREES THAT HE WILL NOT TRANSFER, GIVE, DISPENSE, SELL, ACCEPT OR TAKE ANY OF THE DRUGS DESCRIBED ABOVE EXCEPT TO THE PERSON FOR WHOM THE DRUG WAS ORIGINALLY AND PROPERLY PRESCRIBED; AGREES TO FULLY COMPLY WITH ANY AND ALL MONITORING CONTRACTS BETWEEN HIMSELF AND ANY STATE MEDICAL BOARD, MEDICAL ASSOCIATION OR OTHER PROFESSIONAL MONITORING GROUP INVOLVING THE TREATMENT OF ALCOHOL AND/OR DRUG ADDICTION AND HIS ABILITY TO SAFELY AND COMPETENTLY PRACTICE; AGREES TO SUBMIT TO RANDOM DRUG AND ALCOHOL SCREENS WHEN REQUESTED TO DO SO; AGREES THAT HIS PRIMARY PRACTICE SHALL BE LOCATED IN MONTANA AND 60 DAYS PRIOR TO PRACTICING IN KANSAS OR ANY OTHER LOCATION, HE SHALL NOTIFY THE BOARD OF HIS INTENTIONS; AGREES TO BE MONITORED BY THE KANSAS OSTEOPATHIC SOCIETY'S IMPAIRED PROVIDER PROGRAM AND TO RELEASE ALL INFORMATION REGARDING SAID MONITORING TO THE KANSAS BOARD IF HE SPENDS A SUBSTANTIAL AMOUNT OF TIME PRACTICING IN KANSAS; AGREES THAT IF HE MOVES HIS RESIDENCE TO KANSAS HE SHALL IMMEDIATELY ENTER INTO A CONTRACT WITH THE KANSAS OSTEOPATHIC ASSOCIATION'S IMPAIRED PROVIDER PROGRAM; UPON TERMINATION OF THE MONITORING CONTRACTS IN MONTANA MAY PETITION THE KANSAS BOARD FOR RESCISSION OF THIS STIPULATION.

KRAFT, JEFFREY G DO, LICENSE NUMBER 00N6066, OF 8401 W 17TH, WICHITA, KS, WAS DISCIPLINED BY ARKANSAS ON DECEMBER 20, 1994.
DISCIPLINARY ACTION: LICENSE REVOCATION

KRAFT, JEFFREY GALE DO, DATE OF BIRTH NOVEMBER 13, 1954, LICENSE NUMBER 0006218, OF 516 6TH STREET NORTH, GREAT FALLS, MT, WAS DISCIPLINED BY MONTANA ON AUGUST 10, 1994.
DISCIPLINARY ACTION: 60-MONTH PROBATION
OFFENSE: CRIMINAL CONVICTION OR PLEA OF GUILTY, NOLO CONTENDERE, OR NO CONTEST TO A CRIME
NOTES: MISDEMEANOR CONVICTION FOR PRESCRIPTION VIOLATIONS, CHEMICAL DEPENDENCY.

KRAFT, JEFFREY GALE DO, DATE OF BIRTH NOVEMBER 13, 1954, LICENSE NUMBER 0006218, OF 204 HILL LANE, ANACONDA, MT, WAS DISCIPLINED BY MONTANA ON JUNE 13, 1996.
DISCIPLINARY ACTION: PROBATION
OFFENSE: SUBSTANDARD CARE, INCOMPETENCE, OR NEGLIGENCE
NOTES: VIOLATION OF AGREEMENT WITH IMPAIRED PROFESSIONALS' PROGRAM; FAILURE TO MEET STANDARDS OF PRACTICE ON ONE PATIENT. REVOCATION STAYED AS LONG AS HE COMPLIES WITH PROBATION.

KRAFT, JEFFREY GALE DO, DATE OF BIRTH NOVEMBER 13, 1954, LICENSE NUMBER 0006218, OF 204 HILL LANE, ANACONDA, MT, WAS DISCIPLINED BY MONTANA ON AUGUST 21, 1996.
DISCIPLINARY ACTION: LICENSE REVOCATION
OFFENSE: FAILURE TO COMPLY WITH A PREVIOUS BOARD ORDER
NOTES: ALLEGATIONS OF DRINKING ALCOHOL IN VIOLATION OF HIS PROBATION. REVOCATION IN FULL FORCE AND EFFECT PENDING A HEARING ON THE ALLEGATIONS OF

- MONTANA -

PROBATION VIOLATION.

KRAUSE, ROBERT ALAN MD, DATE OF BIRTH MAY 6, 1947, LICENSE NUMBER 0004514, OF 4504 BLACKTAIL LANE, BUTTE, MT, WAS DISCIPLINED BY MONTANA ON APRIL 11, 1996.
DISCIPLINARY ACTION: EMERGENCY SUSPENSION
OFFENSE: SUBSTANCE ABUSE
NOTES: VIOLATED HIS MONTANA PROFESSIONAL ASSISTANCE PROGRAM AGREEMENT ENTERED INTO 1/24/96 FOR RECOVERY FROM ALCOHOL OR CHEMICAL DEPENDENCY; ON 3/13/96 INGESTED ALCOHOL AND DID NOT INFORM PROGRAM; IN 4/96 FAILED AND REFUSED TO REPORT FOR EVALUATION AND/OR TREATMENT AND FAILED TO REPORT TO A BOARD ORDERED EVALUATION; NOT IN RECOVERY OF HIS DISEASE OF ALCOHOLISM AND/OR CHEMICAL DEPENDENCY. SHALL SURRENDER LICENSE TO THE BOARD; AND SHALL CEASE AND DESIST FROM THE PRACTICE OF MEDICINE.

KRAUSE, ROBERT ALAN MD, DATE OF BIRTH MAY 6, 1947, LICENSE NUMBER 0004514, OF 4504 BLACKTAIL LANE, BUTTE, MT, WAS DISCIPLINED BY MONTANA ON JUNE 5, 1996.
DISCIPLINARY ACTION: 60-MONTH PROBATION
OFFENSE: SUBSTANCE ABUSE
NOTES: VIOLATED AGREEMENT WITH PROFESSIONAL ASSISTANCE PROGRAM; ALCOHOL ABUSE. HAS NOW UNDERGONE A BOARD APPROVED EVALUATION RECEIVING A DIAGNOSIS OF ALCOHOL ABUSE, WITH POSSIBLE ALCOHOL DEPENDENCE. CONDITIONS OF PROBATION: SHALL ENTER INTO A REVISED AGREEMENT WITH THE MONTANA PROFESSIONAL ASSISTANCE PROGRAM; SHALL ABSTAIN FROM ANY USE OF ALCOHOL, MIND-ALTERING OR POTENTIALLY ADDICTING DRUGS OR MEDICATIONS, EXCEPT WHEN PRESCRIBED BY HIS PRIMARY CARE PHYSICIAN; SHALL NOTIFY THE BOARD IN ADVANCE OF TAKING ANY MEDICATION, EXCEPT IN THE CASE OF MEDICAL EMERGENCY; SHALL INFORM HIS PRIMARY CARE PHYSICIAN, DENTIST, AND ANY OTHER HEALTH CARE PROVIDER OF THIS ORDER; SHALL NOT WRITE PRESCRIPTIONS FOR ANY MOOD-ALTERING, ALCOHOL BASED OR POTENTIALLY ADDICTING DRUGS FOR HIMSELF OR ANY MEMBER OF HIS FAMILY; SHALL SUBMIT TO RANDOM BODY FLUID ANALYSIS FOR A MINIMUM OF ONE YEAR UPON BOARD REQUEST; AND SHALL RENEW HIS LICENSE IN A TIMELY FASHION FROM YEAR TO YEAR, DURING THE PROBATIONARY PERIOD.

KRAUSE, ROBERT ALAN MD, DATE OF BIRTH MAY 6, 1947, LICENSE NUMBER 0004514, OF 4504 BLACKTAIL LANE, BUTTE, MT, WAS DISCIPLINED BY MONTANA ON JUNE 27, 1996.
DISCIPLINARY ACTION: EMERGENCY SUSPENSION
OFFENSE: FAILURE TO COMPLY WITH A PREVIOUS BOARD ORDER
NOTES: VIOLATION OF PROBATION BY INGESTING ALCOHOL ON 6/13/96; PRESENTLY IN RELAPSE. SHALL SURRENDER LICENSE TO THE BOARD; SHALL CEASE AND DESIST ENTIRELY FROM THE PRACTICE OF MEDICINE; SHALL PRESENT HIMSELF FOR COMPLETE MENTAL, PHYSICAL AND CHEMICAL DEPENDENCY EVALUATION AND COOPERATE FULLY WITH THE EVALUATION PROCESS; SHALL FULFILL ANY RECOMMENDATIONS FOR TREATMENT AND OBTAIN A SATISFACTORY MEDICAL DISCHARGE PRIOR TO SEEKING REINSTATEMENT OF LICENSE; AND SHALL PROVIDE THE BOARD WITH RELEASES AND AUTHORIZATIONS TO OBTAIN FULL AND COMPLETE COPIES OF ALL RECORDS, REPORTS OR OTHER DOCUMENTS REGARDING THIS EVALUATION.

KRAUSE, ROBERT ALAN MD, DATE OF BIRTH MAY 6, 1947, LICENSE NUMBER 0004514, OF 4504 BLACKTAIL LANE, BUTTE, MT, WAS DISCIPLINED BY MONTANA ON SEPTEMBER 27, 1996.
DISCIPLINARY ACTION: LICENSE REVOCATION
OFFENSE: FAILURE TO COMPLY WITH A PREVIOUS BOARD ORDER
NOTES: BASED ON ALLEGATIONS OF PROBATION VIOLATION. DEFAULT ACTION.

KURTZ, CURTIS G MD, DATE OF BIRTH JULY 19, 1940, LICENSE NUMBER 0003377, OF 300 N WILLSON #502E, BOZEMAN, MT, WAS DISCIPLINED BY MONTANA ON DECEMBER 13, 1990.
DISCIPLINARY ACTION: 60-MONTH MONITORING OF PHYSICIAN
OFFENSE: SUBSTANDARD CARE, INCOMPETENCE, OR NEGLIGENCE
NOTES: ALLEGED 23 COUNTS OF NEGLIGENCE AND MISPRESCRIBING CONTROLLED SUBSTANCES. ORDER OF SUPERVISION FOR FIVE YEARS. ON 12/05/91, AFTER PEER REVIEW, BOARD MODIFIED STIPULATION AND AGREEMENT. ORDER AMENDED AGAIN EFFECTIVE 11/30/92. ON 1/24/95 SUPERVISION REQUIREMENTS EXTENDED ONE YEAR. ON 11/13/95 REQUIREMENT INSTITUTED FOR CONTINUING MEDICAL EDUCATION IN SPECIFIC FIELDS.

KURTZ, CURTIS G MD, LICENSE NUMBER 0016817, OF 300 NORTH WILSON 502E, BOZEMAN, MT, WAS DISCIPLINED BY WISCONSIN ON AUGUST 27, 1991.
DISCIPLINARY ACTION: SURRENDER OF LICENSE
OFFENSE: DISCIPLINARY ACTION BY ANOTHER STATE OR AGENCY
NOTES: STIPULATED TO A FIVE YEAR LIMITATION OF MONTANA LICENSE ON 12/4/90; HAS NO INTENTION OF RETURNING TO WISCONSIN OR PRACTICING THERE.

KURTZ, GENE GAYLORD MD, DATE OF BIRTH JULY 16, 1935, LICENSE NUMBER 0003285, OF PO BOX 307 720 SUNSET DR, HAVRE, MT, WAS DISCIPLINED BY MONTANA ON MARCH 19, 1992.
DISCIPLINARY ACTION: EMERGENCY SUSPENSION
OFFENSE: SUBSTANCE ABUSE
NOTES: ALCOHOL RELAPSE.

KURTZ, GENE GAYLORD MD, DATE OF BIRTH JULY 16, 1935, LICENSE NUMBER 0003285, OF PO BOX 309, CHINOOK, MT, WAS DISCIPLINED BY MONTANA ON JUNE 29, 1993.
DISCIPLINARY ACTION: PROBATION
NOTES: ON 8/29/94 RESTRICTIONS ON LICENSE LIFTED. COMPLIED WITH TERMS OF PROBATION.

LEAL, JOSEPH MD, LICENSE NUMBER 0158478, OF 107 DILWORTH ST, GLENDIVE, MT, WAS DISCIPLINED BY NEW YORK ON MARCH 16, 1992.
OFFENSE: SUBSTANDARD CARE, INCOMPETENCE, OR NEGLIGENCE
NOTES: PLEADED GUILTY TO PRACTICING WITH GROSS NEGLIGENCE IN THE TREATMENT OF A PATIENT WITH AN ABDOMINAL DISTENTION. ONE-YEAR SUSPENSION, STAYED.

LEWIS, JIM EARL DO, DATE OF BIRTH JUNE 12, 1954, LICENSE NUMBER 0006123, OF 711 MAIN STREET SW, RONAN, MT, WAS DISCIPLINED BY MONTANA ON MAY 20, 1991.
NOTES: UNSPECIFIED AGREEMENT AND ORDER.

LEWIS, JIM EARL DO, DATE OF BIRTH JUNE 12, 1954, LICENSE NUMBER 0AA1903, OF PO BOX 82931, FAIRBANKS, AK, WAS DISCIPLINED BY ALASKA ON JUNE 6, 1991.
DISCIPLINARY ACTION: 60-MONTH PROBATION; MONITORING OF PHYSICIAN
NOTES: PRIOR PSYCHIATRIC TREATMENT AND CHEMICAL DEPENDENCY EVALUATION. CONDITIONS OF PROBATION: MUST CONSUME NO CONTROLLED DRUGS OR ALCOHOL; MUST PARTICIPATE IN BOARD APPROVED MONITORING PROGRAM; MUST RECEIVE PSYCHIATRIC CARE; MUST NOTIFY EMPLOYER/HOSPITALS OF ORDER; REPORTS TO BOARD; MUST NOTIFY BOARD OF CHANGE IN PERSONAL PHYSICIAN AND ABSENCES FROM STATE. ON 9/23/94 ORDER AMENDED TO DE-EMPHASIZE SUBSTANCE ABUSE AS IT RELATES TO HIS UNDERLYING MENTAL CONDITION.

- MONTANA -

LISTERUD, MARK BOYD MD, DATE OF BIRTH NOVEMBER 19, 1924, LICENSE NUMBER 0002797, OF 100 MAIN STREET, WOLF POINT, MT, WAS DISCIPLINED BY MONTANA ON FEBRUARY 23, 1993.
DISCIPLINARY ACTION: SURRENDER OF LICENSE; 4-MONTH RESTRICTION PLACED ON LICENSE
OFFENSE: SUBSTANDARD CARE, INCOMPETENCE, OR NEGLIGENCE
NOTES: ALLEGATIONS OF NEGLIGENT PRACTICE; CASE SETTLED WITHOUT ADMISSION OF WRONGDOING ON FOREGOING BASIS. FOUR MONTH RESTRICTED SURGICAL PRACTICE, THEN PERMANENT RETIREMENT.

LOVELL, RANDY J DO OF 907 MAIN BOX 969, THOMPSON FALLS, MT, WAS DISCIPLINED BY DEA ON APRIL 22, 1996.
DISCIPLINARY ACTION: RESTRICTION PLACED ON CONTROLLED SUBSTANCE LICENSE
NOTES: HISTORY OF ALLEGED DRUG VIOLATION.

MARTINI, STEVEN M MD, DATE OF BIRTH JANUARY 10, 1956, LICENSE NUMBER 0006097, OF 211 PARKWAY DRIVE, KALISPELL, MT, WAS DISCIPLINED BY MONTANA ON AUGUST 2, 1995.
DISCIPLINARY ACTION: 24-MONTH PROBATION
OFFENSE: PROVIDING FALSE INFORMATION TO THE BOARD
NOTES: GAVE FALSE INFORMATION ON APPLICATIONS FOR HOSPITAL PRIVILEGES.

MARTINI, STEVEN M MD, LICENSE NUMBER 0159250, OF 1036 S NUCLEUS AVENUE, COLUMBIA FALLS, MT, WAS DISCIPLINED BY NEW YORK ON OCTOBER 15, 1996.
DISCIPLINARY ACTION: LICENSE SUSPENSION
OFFENSE: DISCIPLINARY ACTION BY ANOTHER STATE OR AGENCY
NOTES: DISCIPLINED BY THE MONTANA BOARD FOR BEING A HABITUAL ABUSER OF ALCOHOL OR DRUGS; MAKING FRAUDULENT STATEMENTS ON HOSPITAL APPLICATIONS AND FAILING TO PROVIDE HOSPITALS WITH A COPY OF HIS AGREEMENT WITH THE MONTANA PROFESSIONAL ASSISTANCE PROGRAM. SUSPENSION UNTIL THE SUCCESSFUL COMPLETION OF A COURSE OF THERAPY OR TREATMENT AFTER WHICH THERE WILL BE A PROBATION FOR AT LEAST FIVE YEARS.

MCCORMICK, MICHAEL W B MD WAS DISCIPLINED BY IOWA ON NOVEMBER 12, 1987.
DISCIPLINARY ACTION: DENIAL OF NEW LICENSE

MCCORMICK, MICHAEL W B MD WAS DISCIPLINED BY IOWA ON FEBRUARY 22, 1988.
DISCIPLINARY ACTION: 60-MONTH PROBATION
OFFENSE: SUBSTANCE ABUSE
NOTES: DRUG USE. LICENSE GRANTED ON PROBATION.

MCCORMICK, MICHAEL W B MD, DATE OF BIRTH MARCH 17, 1952, LICENSE NUMBER 0026445, OF 2825 GETTYSBURG, EDMOND, OK, WAS DISCIPLINED BY IOWA ON APRIL 6, 1990.
DISCIPLINARY ACTION: 39-MONTH PROBATION
NOTES: ON 11/15/91, AMENDMENT TO CURRENT PROBATION; ALLOWED TO POSSESS TWO SYRINGES OF DIAZEPAM, AS PART OF A BANYAN STAT KIT. EFFECTIVE 11/29/93 PROBATION TERMINATED AND MEDICAL LICENSE RESTORED TO FULL PRIVILEGES.

MCCORMICK, MICHAEL W BYRON MD, LICENSE NUMBER 0011875, OF 1108 11TH AVE, DEWITT, IA, WAS DISCIPLINED BY OKLAHOMA ON OCTOBER 5, 1991.
DISCIPLINARY ACTION: 24-MONTH PROBATION; MONITORING OF PHYSICIAN
NOTES: FOLLOWING FEDERAL INCARCERATION HIS LICENSE WAS SUSPENDED ON 1/18/85 FOR THE PERIOD OF HIS INCARCERATION; WHEN HE WAS RELEASED, LICENSE REINSTATED TO FIVE YEAR PROBATION; PROBATION ENDED ON 1/22/88; LICENSE LAPSED BECAUSE OF NONRENEWAL; NOW WANTS TO SEEK TRAINING IN PATHOLOGY. PROBATION WITH FOLLOWING CONDITIONS: SHALL NOT PRESCRIBE, ADMINISTER OR DISPENSE ANY SCHEDULED DRUGS OR CONTROLLED DANGEROUS SUBSTANCES FOR HIS PERSONAL USE OR FOR OTHERS; SHALL NOTIFY ANY HOSPITAL WHERE HE HOLDS STAFF PRIVILEGES OR CLINIC OR GROUP OF THESE TERMS AND CONDITIONS; SHALL BE MONITORED ON PROFESSIONAL ACTIVITIES ON LEVEL III PROBATION; SHALL FURNISH BOARD WITH ADDRESS AND/OR CHANGE OF ADDRESS; SHALL APPEAR BEFORE BOARD UPON REQUEST.

MCCORMICK, MICHAEL W B MD, DATE OF BIRTH MARCH 17, 1952, LICENSE NUMBER 0004383, OF 1108 11TH STREET, DEWITT, IA, WAS DISCIPLINED BY MONTANA ON DECEMBER 31, 1991.
DISCIPLINARY ACTION: FINE
OFFENSE: PROVIDING FALSE INFORMATION TO THE BOARD
NOTES: FAILED TO DISCLOSE IOWA DISCIPLINARY ACTION ON 1991 MONTANA RENEWAL APPLICATION. LETTER OF CENSURE. AGREED HE WILL NOT SEEK RENEWAL OF MONTANA LICENSE IN 1992 OR THEREAFTER, NOR REAPPLY OR SEEK REINSTATEMENT OF LICENSE. $500 FINE.

MCCORMICK, MICHAEL W B MD OF 920 STANTON L. YOUNG RM. 920 BMS, OKLAHOMA CITY, OK, WAS DISCIPLINED BY DEA ON FEBRUARY 1, 1994.
DISCIPLINARY ACTION: RESTRICTION PLACED ON CONTROLLED SUBSTANCE LICENSE
OFFENSE: CRIMINAL CONVICTION OR PLEA OF GUILTY, NOLO CONTENDERE, OR NO CONTEST TO A CRIME
NOTES: CONVICTED 11/19/84 FOR KNOWINGLY AND INTENTIONALLY OMITTING MATERIAL INFORMATION FROM WRITTEN PRESCRIPTION FOR DILAUDID. RESTRICTION PLACED ON REGISTRATION. REGISTRATION PLACED ON PROBATION 04/06/90. FINED. IN 11/09/93 HEARING IN OKLAHOMA REGARDING FELONY COCAINE CONVICTION IN 1984, WAS PLACED ON PROBATION ENDING 11/9/94.

MILLER, JOHN J MD WAS DISCIPLINED BY NEVADA ON OCTOBER 17, 1995.
DISCIPLINARY ACTION: LICENSE REVOCATION
OFFENSE: DISCIPLINARY ACTION BY ANOTHER STATE OR AGENCY
NOTES: CONVICTION OF A FELONY; CHARGED WITH BEING FOUND GUILTY OF TWO FELONIES IN MONTANA; DISCIPLINARY ACTION AGAINST HIS LICENSE IN MONTANA; SUSPENSION OF LICENSE BY ANY OTHER JURISDICTION; FAILURE TO REPORT, WITHIN 30 DAYS, THE SUSPENSION OF HIS LICENSE TO PRACTICE MEDICINE IN ANOTHER JURISDICTION.

MILLER, JOHN J MD OF JACKSONVILLE, FL, WAS DISCIPLINED BY UTAH ON OCTOBER 28, 1995.
DISCIPLINARY ACTION: LICENSE REVOCATION; REVOCATION OF CONTROLLED SUBSTANCE LICENSE
OFFENSE: PHYSICAL OR MENTAL ILLNESS INHIBITING THE ABILITY TO PRACTICE WITH SKILL AND SAFETY
NOTES: ADMISSION OF INABILITY TO SAFELY ENGAGE IN THE PRACTICE OF MEDICINE BECAUSE OF A MENTAL OR PHYSICAL CONDITION.

MILLER, JOHN J MD, LICENSE NUMBER 0D27191, OF HIDDEN LAKE DRIVE, JACKSONVILLE, FL, WAS DISCIPLINED BY MARYLAND ON NOVEMBER 7, 1995.
DISCIPLINARY ACTION: PROBATION
OFFENSE: DISCIPLINARY ACTION BY ANOTHER STATE OR AGENCY
NOTES: ACTION BY MONTANA. REVOCATION STAYED.

MILLER, JOHN J MD, LICENSE NUMBER 0039841, OF DEER LODGE, MT, WAS DISCIPLINED BY FLORIDA ON MARCH 6, 1996.
DISCIPLINARY ACTION: LICENSE REVOCATION
OFFENSE: DISCIPLINARY ACTION BY ANOTHER STATE OR AGENCY

- MONTANA -

NOTES: CONVICTED OF A CRIME DIRECTLY RELATING TO THE PRACTICE OF MEDICINE.

MILLER, JOHN JOSEPH MD, DATE OF BIRTH FEBRUARY 14, 1942, LICENSE NUMBER 0003980, OF 310 SUNNYVIEW LANE, KALISPELL, MT, WAS DISCIPLINED BY MONTANA ON AUGUST 23, 1994.
DISCIPLINARY ACTION: EMERGENCY SUSPENSION
OFFENSE: SUBSTANCE ABUSE
NOTES: UNTREATED CHEMICAL DEPENDENCY. STIPULATION NOT TO SEEK REINSTATEMENT OF LICENSE UNTIL AFTER COMPLETION OF EVALUATION AND TREATMENT FOR ILLNESSES ON 8/31/94.

MILLER, JOHN JOSEPH MD, DATE OF BIRTH FEBRUARY 14, 1942, LICENSE NUMBER 00M5606, WAS DISCIPLINED BY IDAHO ON NOVEMBER 18, 1994.
DISCIPLINARY ACTION: LICENSE SUSPENSION
OFFENSE: DISCIPLINARY ACTION BY ANOTHER STATE OR AGENCY
NOTES: ON 8/24/94 MONTANA ORDERED THAT LICENSE BE PLACED ON EMERGENCY SUSPENSION; ALSO REQUIRED HIM TO HAVE A COMPLETE MENTAL AND PHYSICAL EXAMINATION. THE IDAHO BOARD FOR THE PURPOSE OF THIS RECIPROCAL DISCIPLINE INCORPORATES THE TERMS AND CONDITIONS OF THIS ORDER AND ORDERS HIM TO FULLY COMPLY WITH THEM.

MILLER, JOHN JOSEPH MD, DATE OF BIRTH FEBRUARY 14, 1942, LICENSE NUMBER 0021472, OF JACKSONVILLE, FL, WAS DISCIPLINED BY TENNESSEE ON FEBRUARY 23, 1995.
DISCIPLINARY ACTION: LICENSE REVOCATION
OFFENSE: DISCIPLINARY ACTION BY ANOTHER STATE OR AGENCY
NOTES: DISCIPLINARY ACTION TAKEN BY MONTANA BOARD. SUBSTANCE ABUSE. MUST APPEAR BEFORE BOARD IF REINSTATEMENT SOUGHT.

MILLER, JOHN JOSEPH MD, DATE OF BIRTH FEBRUARY 14, 1942, LICENSE NUMBER 00M5606, WAS DISCIPLINED BY IDAHO ON MAY 1, 1995.
DISCIPLINARY ACTION: LICENSE REVOCATION
OFFENSE: DISCIPLINARY ACTION BY ANOTHER STATE OR AGENCY
NOTES: IN 8/94 ENGAGED IN THE EXCESSIVE USE OF ALCOHOL OR OTHER SUBSTANCES TO THE EXTENT THAT THE USE IMPAIRED HIM PHYSICALLY OR MENTALLY; AS A RESULT HE WAS IN AN AUTO ACCIDENT WHICH CAUSED THE DEATH OF TWO PERSONS; LICENSE IN TENNESSEE WAS REVOKED ON 2/23/95. THE IDAHO BOARD ADOPTS THE FINDING OF THE TENNESSEE ORDER AND INCORPORATES ALL OF THE TERMS AND CONDITIONS OF THE TENNESSEE ORDER.

MILLER, JOHN JOSEPH MD, DATE OF BIRTH FEBRUARY 14, 1942, OF 215 SUNNYVIEW LANE #7, KALISPELL, MT, WAS DISCIPLINED BY MEDICARE ON MAY 4, 1995.
DISCIPLINARY ACTION: EXCLUSION FROM THE MEDICARE AND/OR MEDICAID PROGRAMS
OFFENSE: DISCIPLINARY ACTION BY ANOTHER STATE OR AGENCY
NOTES: LICENSE SUSPENDED FOR REASONS BEARING ON PROFESSIONAL PERFORMANCE.

MILLER, JOHN JOSEPH MD, DATE OF BIRTH FEBRUARY 14, 1942, LICENSE NUMBER 0003980, OF 3459 HIDDEN LAKE DRIVE WEST, JACKSONVILLE, FL, WAS DISCIPLINED BY MONTANA ON MAY 19, 1995.
DISCIPLINARY ACTION: PROBATION
OFFENSE: CRIMINAL CONVICTION OR PLEA OF GUILTY, NOLO CONTENDERE, OR NO CONTEST TO A CRIME
NOTES: CONVICTION OF FELONY; CHEMICAL DEPENDENCY. REVOCATION STAYED.

MILLER, JOHN JOSEPH MD, LICENSE NUMBER 0049431, OF JACKSONVILLE, FL, WAS DISCIPLINED BY VIRGINIA ON JUNE 13, 1995.
DISCIPLINARY ACTION: LICENSE SUSPENSION
OFFENSE: DISCIPLINARY ACTION BY ANOTHER STATE OR AGENCY
NOTES: REVOCATION BY TENNESSEE AND SUSPENSION BY MONTANA AFTER HE ENGAGED IN THE EXCESSIVE USE OF ALCOHOL OR OTHER SUBSTANCES.

MILLER, JOHN JOSEPH MD, DATE OF BIRTH FEBRUARY 14, 1942, LICENSE NUMBER 0031991, OF 3459 HIDDEN LAKE DR W, JACKSONVILLE, FL, WAS DISCIPLINED BY GEORGIA ON AUGUST 3, 1995.
DISCIPLINARY ACTION: LICENSE SUSPENSION
OFFENSE: CRIMINAL CONVICTION OR PLEA OF GUILTY, NOLO CONTENDERE, OR NO CONTEST TO A CRIME
NOTES: CONVICTION OF A CRIME. SUSPENDED INDEFINITELY.

MILLER, JOHN JOSEPH MD, DATE OF BIRTH FEBRUARY 14, 1942, LICENSE NUMBER 0009752, OF 3459 HIDDEN LAKE DRIVE WEST, JACKSONVILLE, FL, WAS DISCIPLINED BY WEST VIRGINIA ON NOVEMBER 20, 1995.
DISCIPLINARY ACTION: LICENSE REVOCATION
OFFENSE: DISCIPLINARY ACTION BY ANOTHER STATE OR AGENCY
NOTES: FOUND GUILTY OF TWO FELONY COUNTS OF NEGLIGENT HOMICIDE IN 2/95 IN MONTANA; HIS EXCESSIVE USE OF ALCOHOL CAUSED HIM TO BE IMPAIRED AND TO CAUSE THE DEATHS OF TWO PERSONS IN A MOTOR VEHICLE ACCIDENT. IN 2/95 THE TENNESSEE BOARD REVOKED HIS LICENSE. IN 11/94 THE IDAHO BOARD SUSPENDED HIS LICENSE AND IN 5/95 REVOKED HIS LICENSE. IN 8/94 MONTANA SUSPENDED HIS LICENSE AND IN 4/95 REVOKED HIS LICENSE AND THEN STAYED THE REVOCATION AS PROBATION UNDER SEVERAL TERMS AND CONDITIONS.

MILLER, JOHN JOSEPH MD, DATE OF BIRTH FEBRUARY 14, 1942, LICENSE NUMBER 0030589, WAS DISCIPLINED BY COLORADO ON JANUARY 11, 1996.
OFFENSE: CRIMINAL CONVICTION OR PLEA OF GUILTY, NOLO CONTENDERE, OR NO CONTEST TO A CRIME
NOTES: PLED GUILTY TO TWO FELONY CHARGES (NEGLIGENT HOMICIDE AS A RESULT OF A MOTOR VEHICLE ACCIDENT). ORDERED TO PERMANENTLY RELINQUISH HIS LICENSE TO PRACTICE MEDICINE IN COLORADO.

MILLER, JOHN JOSEPH MD, LICENSE NUMBER 0060453, OF DEER LODGE, MT, WAS DISCIPLINED BY OHIO ON FEBRUARY 14, 1996.
DISCIPLINARY ACTION: LICENSE REVOCATION
OFFENSE: DISCIPLINARY ACTION BY ANOTHER STATE OR AGENCY
NOTES: PRIOR ACTION BY MONTANA MEDICAL BOARD WHICH WAS BASED ON HIS ADMISSIONS THAT HE HAD ENGAGED IN EXCESSIVE USE OF ALCOHOL SO THAT HE WAS MENTALLY AND PHYSICALLY IMPAIRED AND THAT WHILE HE WAS IMPAIRED, HE WAS INVOLVED IN A MOTOR VEHICLE ACCIDENT THAT CAUSED THE DEATH OF TWO PEOPLE. CONVICTION OF TWO FELONY COUNTS OF NEGLIGENT HOMICIDE. PERMANENT REVOCATION.

MOTE, FREDERICK ANDREW MD, LICENSE NUMBER 0007573, OF PORTLAND, OR, WAS DISCIPLINED BY OREGON ON JULY 11, 1991.
DISCIPLINARY ACTION: RESTRICTION PLACED ON CONTROLLED SUBSTANCE LICENSE
NOTES: MUST PROVIDE TRIPLICATE COPIES OF CONTROLLED SUBSTANCE PRESCRIPTIONS; RESTRICTION ON SCHEDULES IV AND V; VOLUNTARY RESTRICTION ON SCHEDULES II AND III.

MOTE, FREDERICK ANDREW MD, DATE OF BIRTH JANUARY 21, 1936, LICENSE NUMBER 0009046, OF PO BOX 807, SUPERIOR, MT, WAS DISCIPLINED BY MONTANA ON OCTOBER 7, 1992.
DISCIPLINARY ACTION: 180-MONTH PROBATION; MONITORING OF PHYSICIAN
OFFENSE: CRIMINAL CONVICTION OR PLEA OF GUILTY, NOLO CONTENDERE, OR NO CONTEST TO A CRIME

- MONTANA -

NOTES: ON 7/1/92 PLED GUILTY TO A MISDEMEANOR, SEXUAL ABUSE OF MINOR; ADMITS HE IS A SEX OFFENDER AND SUFFERING FROM AN ATYPICAL SEXUAL DISORDER; HAS SOUGHT TREATMENT FOR THIS DISORDER; ENGAGED IN FRAUD ON LICENSE APPLICATION BY STATING THAT HE HAD NOT BEEN TREATED FOR A MENTAL ILLNESS. CONDITIONS OF PROBATION: SHALL ENTER INTO A SEX OFFENDER REHABILITATION PROGRAM APPROVED BY THE BOARD AND COMPLY WITH ALL REQUIREMENTS INCLUDING AT LEAST ONE GROUP THERAPY SESSION AND ONE INDIVIDUAL THERAPY SESSION PER WEEK; DIRECTOR OF THIS PROGRAM WILL PROVIDE THE BOARD WITH QUARTERLY REPORTS; DURING ALL PATIENT CONTACT WITH MINORS A THIRD PARTY SHALL BE IN THE ROOM; SHALL AVOID ANY UNCHAPERONED CONTACT WITH MINORS BOTH IN PROFESSIONAL AND PRIVATE LIFE; SHALL ABSTAIN FROM ANY SEXUAL CONTACT WITH MINORS OF EITHER SEX; SHALL ABSTAIN FROM SELF-MEDICATION IN ANY FORM AND SHALL OBTAIN ALL MEDICAL CARE FROM A BOARD APPROVED PHYSICIAN; SHALL SIGN ALL RELEASES NECESSARY FOR BOARD TO OBTAIN ALL RECORDS; SHALL INFORM EACH FACILITY WHERE HE PROVIDES SERVICES OF THE ORDER.

MOTE, FREDERICK ANDREW MD, DATE OF BIRTH JANUARY 21, 1936, LICENSE NUMBER 0009046, OF PO BOX 807, SUPERIOR, MT, WAS DISCIPLINED BY MONTANA ON DECEMBER 21, 1994.
DISCIPLINARY ACTION: PROBATION; RESTRICTION PLACED ON CONTROLLED SUBSTANCE LICENSE
OFFENSE: OVERPRESCRIBING OR MISPRESCRIBING DRUGS
NOTES: CONCERNING QUALITY OF CARE AND MANAGEMENT OF CHRONIC PAIN; PROBLEM WITH PRESCRIBING OF CONTROLLED SUBSTANCES. AMENDMENT TO STIPULATION FOR PROBATION ADDING REQUIREMENT FOR DUPLICATE PRESCRIPTIONS ON CONTROLLED SUBSTANCES, COMPLIANCE WITH CHARTING GUIDELINES, COOPERATION WITH PEER REVIEWS AND CONTINUING EDUCATION ON CHRONIC PAIN MANAGEMENT.

MULDOON, THOMAS MD, LICENSE NUMBER G018798, OF HOT SPRINGS, MT, WAS DISCIPLINED BY CALIFORNIA ON JUNE 13, 1987.
DISCIPLINARY ACTION: LICENSE REVOCATION
OFFENSE: CRIMINAL CONVICTION OR PLEA OF GUILTY, NOLO CONTENDERE, OR NO CONTEST TO A CRIME
NOTES: FEDERAL CONVICTION FOR ATTEMPTING TO MANUFACTURE METHAMPHETAMINE, RESULTING IN PRISON TERM.

OBYE, JOHN ROGER MD, LICENSE NUMBER 0003292, OF 5920 SW BURMA RD, LAKE OSWEGO, OR, WAS DISCIPLINED BY MONTANA ON APRIL 4, 1992.
DISCIPLINARY ACTION: LICENSE REVOCATION
OFFENSE: SUBSTANDARD CARE, INCOMPETENCE, OR NEGLIGENCE
NOTES: NEGLIGENCE, GROSS MALPRACTICE, MENTALLY AND PHYSICALLY UNABLE TO SAFELY ENGAGE IN THE PRACTICE OF MEDICINE.

OTT, JOHN DAVID DO, DATE OF BIRTH NOVEMBER 25, 1945, LICENSE NUMBER 0001494, OF 1336 ROSEARDEN DRIVE, FOREST GROVE, OR, WAS DISCIPLINED BY IOWA ON SEPTEMBER 4, 1991.
DISCIPLINARY ACTION: LICENSE SUSPENSION
NOTES: LICENSE INDEFINITELY SUSPENDED; DOCTOR AGREED TO NOT MAKE FURTHER APPLICATION FOR RENEWAL OR REINSTATEMENT OF MEDICAL LICENSE IN IOWA.

OTT, JOHN DAVID MD, DATE OF BIRTH NOVEMBER 25, 1945, WAS DISCIPLINED BY OREGON ON OCTOBER 10, 1991.
DISCIPLINARY ACTION: SURRENDER OF LICENSE
OFFENSE: SUBSTANDARD CARE, INCOMPETENCE, OR NEGLIGENCE
NOTES: ALLEGED INAPPROPRIATE CARE/INCOMPETENCE. RETIRE/SURRENDER IN LIEU OF DISCIPLINARY ACTION.

OTT, JOHN DAVID DO, DATE OF BIRTH NOVEMBER 25, 1945, LICENSE NUMBER 0009271, OF 1336 ROSEARDEN DR, FOREST GROVE, OR, WAS DISCIPLINED BY MONTANA ON MAY 26, 1992.
DISCIPLINARY ACTION: DENIAL OF NEW LICENSE
OFFENSE: PROFESSIONAL MISCONDUCT
NOTES: INADEQUATELY TREATED SEXUAL MISCONDUCT.

OTT, JOHN DAVID DO, DATE OF BIRTH NOVEMBER 25, 1945, LICENSE NUMBER 0009271, OF 1336 ROSEARDEN DRIVE, FOREST GROVE, OR, WAS DISCIPLINED BY MONTANA ON AUGUST 16, 1995.
DISCIPLINARY ACTION: RESTRICTION PLACED ON LICENSE
NOTES: ISSUED LICENSE WITH RESTRICTIONS. EVIDENCE OF REHABILITATION AND POSSIBILITY OF PRACTICE WITH REASONABLE SKILL AND SAFETY UNDER RESTRICTIONS.

OTT, JOHN DAVID MD, DATE OF BIRTH NOVEMBER 25, 1945, WAS DISCIPLINED BY WISCONSIN ON MAY 8, 1996.
DISCIPLINARY ACTION: DENIAL OF NEW LICENSE
OFFENSE: DISCIPLINARY ACTION BY ANOTHER STATE OR AGENCY
NOTES: ACTION IN IOWA, OREGON, MONTANA, AND PENNSYLVANIA. ON 9/04/91 HIS LICENSE TO PRACTICE MEDICINE AND SURGERY IN IOWA WAS INDEFINITELY SUSPENDED IN CONNECTION WITH ALLEGATIONS OF SEXUAL IMPROPRIETIES WITH PATIENTS. ON 10/10/91 HIS LICENSE TO PRACTICE MEDICINE IN OREGON WAS SURRENDERED. ON 5/26/92 HIS APPLICATION FOR LICENSURE IN MONTANA WAS DENIED. ON 7/12/95 HIS LICENSE IN PENNSYLVANIA WAS DENIED. AN EVALUATION CONCLUDED THAT ANY PRIVILEGE GRANTED TO DR. OTT TO PRACTICE MEDICINE SHOULD REQUIRE CONTINUED PARTICIPATION IN A PROGRAM, THAT A "MEDICAL SURVEILLANCE TEAM" SHOULD BE ORGANIZED TO OVERSEE HIS PRACTICE, THAT RANDOM PATIENT SURVEYS SHOULD BE PERFORMED TO MONITOR HIS BEHAVIOR WITH PATIENTS, AND THAT HE SHOULD BE SUBJECT TO QUARTERLY POLYGRAPH EXAMINATIONS.

PIGG, WILLIAM LARRY MD, LICENSE NUMBER 0040625, OF MELBOURNE, FL, WAS DISCIPLINED BY FLORIDA ON OCTOBER 26, 1988.
DISCIPLINARY ACTION: LICENSE SUSPENSION

PIGG, WILLIAM LARRY MD, DATE OF BIRTH FEBRUARY 13, 1946, OF 2601 MANORWOOD DRIVE, MELBOURNE, FL, WAS DISCIPLINED BY MEDICARE ON JULY 19, 1989.
DISCIPLINARY ACTION: EXCLUSION FROM THE MEDICARE AND/OR MEDICAID PROGRAMS
OFFENSE: DISCIPLINARY ACTION BY ANOTHER STATE OR AGENCY
NOTES: LICENSE REVOCATION OR SUSPENSION.

PIGG, WILLIAM LARRY MD OF ST MARIE, MT, WAS DISCIPLINED BY NORTH CAROLINA ON FEBRUARY 7, 1990.
DISCIPLINARY ACTION: LICENSE REVOCATION

PIZARRO, CECILIO D MD, LICENSE NUMBER 0059711, OF BUTTE, MT, WAS DISCIPLINED BY FLORIDA ON APRIL 15, 1994.
DISCIPLINARY ACTION: FINE; REPRIMAND
OFFENSE: FAILURE TO COMPLY WITH A PREVIOUS BOARD ORDER
NOTES: CHARGED WITH PAYING FOR HIS MEDICAL LICENSURE RENEWAL FEE WITH A BAD CHECK; VIOLATED AND IS VIOLATING PREVIOUS BOARD ORDER OF 9/21/92. $2,000 FINE.

PREBLE, PARKER E MD, DATE OF BIRTH MARCH 16, 1925, LICENSE NUMBER 0002588, OF 1031 ROBERTSON, FT. COLLINS, CO, WAS DISCIPLINED BY MONTANA ON FEBRUARY 8, 1989.
DISCIPLINARY ACTION: PROBATION; REPRIMAND
OFFENSE: DISCIPLINARY ACTION BY ANOTHER STATE OR AGENCY
NOTES: REPRIMAND FOR FAILURE TO FURNISH REQUIRED

- MONTANA -

INFORMATION IN RENEWING LICENSE; PROBATION PER COLORADO'S ORDER

RECKMANN, HEIMO W MD, DATE OF BIRTH NOVEMBER 13, 1917, LICENSE NUMBER 1025168, OF 279 IDLE HOUR DR, LEXINGTON, KY, WAS DISCIPLINED BY MICHIGAN ON MAY 19, 1995.
DISCIPLINARY ACTION: 24-MONTH PROBATION; RESTRICTION PLACED ON LICENSE
OFFENSE: DISCIPLINARY ACTION BY ANOTHER STATE OR AGENCY
NOTES: FAILURE TO REPORT/COMPLY.

RECKMANN, HEIMO W MD, LICENSE NUMBER 0024577, OF BARBOURVILLE, KY, WAS DISCIPLINED BY OHIO ON OCTOBER 17, 1995.
DISCIPLINARY ACTION: 3-MONTH LICENSE SUSPENSION; PROBATION
NOTES: REQUIRED TO NOTIFY BOARD AND OBTAIN APPROVAL FOR PLAN OF PRACTICE PRIOR TO PRACTICING IN OHIO. UPON RESUMPTION OF PRACTICE, LIMITED TO READING OF PLAIN FILMS AND SUBJECT TO PROBATIONARY TERMS AND CONDITIONS FOR AT LEAST EIGHT YEARS.

RECKMANN, HEIMO WALTER MD, DATE OF BIRTH NOVEMBER 13, 1917, LICENSE NUMBER 0018002, OF 279 IDLEHOUR DR, LEXINGTON, KY, WAS DISCIPLINED BY IOWA ON JULY 23, 1992.
DISCIPLINARY ACTION: SURRENDER OF LICENSE
NOTES: VOLUNTARY SURRENDER WHILE UNDER INVESTIGATION.

RECKMANN, HEIMO WALTER MD, DATE OF BIRTH NOVEMBER 13, 1917, LICENSE NUMBER 0013770, OF FAYETTE COUNTY, KY, WAS DISCIPLINED BY KENTUCKY ON JUNE 18, 1993.
DISCIPLINARY ACTION: LICENSE REVOCATION
OFFENSE: DISCIPLINARY ACTION BY ANOTHER STATE OR AGENCY
NOTES: DISCIPLINARY ACTION TAKEN BY WEST VIRGINIA BOARD OF MEDICINE AND KOSSUTH COUNTY HOSPITAL IN IOWA; FALSIFIED ANNUAL RENEWAL APPLICATION. CASE APPEALED TO JEFFERSON CIRCUIT COURT. ON 9/29/93 APPEAL RESOLVED. DURING PROBATION ALLOWED TO PRACTICE ONLY UNDER SUPERVISION OF 3 RADIOLOGISTS WITH BI-ANNUAL REPORTS PROVIDED; FINE ASSESSED. ORDER MODIFIED ON 6/03/96: REQUEST GRANTED THAT HIS PRACTICE BE SUPERVISED BY ONE RADIOLOGIST INSTEAD OF THREE.

RECKMANN, HEIMO WALTER MD, DATE OF BIRTH NOVEMBER 13, 1917, LICENSE NUMBER 0006977, OF 297 IDLE HOUR DRIVE, LEXINGTON, KY, WAS DISCIPLINED BY MONTANA ON JUNE 7, 1994.
DISCIPLINARY ACTION: PROBATION; RESTRICTION PLACED ON LICENSE
OFFENSE: DISCIPLINARY ACTION BY ANOTHER STATE OR AGENCY
NOTES: RECIPROCAL TO DISCIPLINARY ACTION TAKEN IN ANOTHER STATE. INDEFINITE PROBATION RESTRICTED TO RADIOLOGY AND SUPERVISED PRACTICE.

RECKMANN, HEIMO WALTER MD, DATE OF BIRTH NOVEMBER 13, 1917, LICENSE NUMBER 0043375, OF 279 IDLE HOUR DRIVE, LEXINGTON, KY, WAS DISCIPLINED BY VIRGINIA ON DECEMBER 21, 1994.
DISCIPLINARY ACTION: 60-MONTH PROBATION
OFFENSE: DISCIPLINARY ACTION BY ANOTHER STATE OR AGENCY
NOTES: ON 8/30/93 LICENSE RESTRICTED IN KENTUCKY. BASED ON DISCIPLINARY ACTION TAKEN AGAINST HIM BY A HOSPITAL AND FAILURE TO DISCLOSE THIS ON HIS LICENSE RENEWAL. SHALL ABIDE BY ALL TERMS OF THE PROBATION IMPOSED BY KENTUCKY BOARD. PROBATION SHALL RUN CONCURRENTLY WITH PROBATION IMPOSED BY KENTUCKY BOARD AND THUS IS RETROACTIVE TO 8/30/93. SHOULD PERIOD OF PROBATION BE SHORTENED BY THE KENTUCKY BOARD HIS PROBATION IN VIRGINIA SHALL BE SHORTENED.

SCEATS, DONALD J MD, DATE OF BIRTH MARCH 16, 1922, LICENSE NUMBER 0002648, OF 507 W. 14TH STREET, PUEBLO, CO, WAS DISCIPLINED BY MONTANA ON MAY 17, 1989.
DISCIPLINARY ACTION: RESTRICTION PLACED ON LICENSE; REPRIMAND
OFFENSE: DISCIPLINARY ACTION BY ANOTHER STATE OR AGENCY
NOTES: FOR FAILING TO DISCLOSE DISCIPLINARY ACTION IN ANOTHER STATE IN RENEWING LICENSE; RESTRICTIONS PER COLORADO ORDER

SCEATS, DONALD J MD, DATE OF BIRTH MARCH 16, 1922, LICENSE NUMBER C017014, OF PUEBLO, CO, WAS DISCIPLINED BY CALIFORNIA ON JULY 26, 1989.
DISCIPLINARY ACTION: SURRENDER OF LICENSE

SCEATS, DONALD J MD, DATE OF BIRTH MARCH 16, 1922, LICENSE NUMBER 0002648, OF 507 W. 14TH STREET, PUEBLO, CO, WAS DISCIPLINED BY MONTANA ON NOVEMBER 27, 1989.
DISCIPLINARY ACTION: SURRENDER OF LICENSE

SCEATS, DONALD J MD, LICENSE NUMBER 0013031, OF PUEBLO, CO, WAS DISCIPLINED BY COLORADO ON FEBRUARY 15, 1991.
OFFENSE: SUBSTANDARD CARE, INCOMPETENCE, OR NEGLIGENCE
NOTES: MAY NOT NOW OR IN THE FUTURE PRACTICE MEDICINE IN COLORADO WITHOUT MAKING APPLICATION AND RECEIVING BOARD'S APPROVAL.

SCEATS, DONALD J MD, DATE OF BIRTH MARCH 16, 1922, LICENSE NUMBER 0004683, OF PUEBLO, CO, WAS DISCIPLINED BY WASHINGTON ON MAY 18, 1991.
DISCIPLINARY ACTION: SURRENDER OF LICENSE
OFFENSE: DISCIPLINARY ACTION BY ANOTHER STATE OR AGENCY
NOTES: ON 8/14/87 COLORADO RESTRICTED HIS LICENSE BY PROHIBITING CARE OF LEVEL II OR III INFANTS AND FURTHER RESTRICTED HIS NEONATAL PRACTICE; ON 2/27/88, WHILE APPLYING FOR RENEWAL OF MONTANA LICENSE, STATED HE HAD NOT HAD ANY DISCIPLINARY ACTIONS TAKEN AGAINST HIM; MONTANA ENTERED INTO ORDER ON 5/17/89 REQUIRING HIM TO REPORT ANY DISCIPLINARY PROCEEDINGS OR VOLUNTARY LICENSE SURRENDERS WITHIN 30 DAYS; ACCEPTED THE SURRENDER OF HIS LICENSE ON 11/27/89 IN LIEU OF PROCEEDING TO HEARING ON CHARGES THAT HE HAD FAILED TO REPORT SURRENDERING HIS CALIFORNIA LICENSE WITHIN 30 DAYS; HE SURRENDERED CALIFORNIA LICENSE ON 6/7/89. AGREES NOT TO APPLY FOR REINSTATEMENT FOR AT LEAST ONE YEAR; MUST CONCLUDE ALL MEDICAL BUSINESS AND FORMALLY CLOSE PRACTICE WITHIN 90 DAYS.

SHEPARD, PHILLIP B MD OF HELENA, MT, WAS DISCIPLINED BY VIRGINIA ON OCTOBER 1, 1987.
DISCIPLINARY ACTION: LICENSE REVOCATION

SHEPARD, PHILLIP B MD, LICENSE NUMBER 0028735, WAS DISCIPLINED BY MICHIGAN ON OCTOBER 19, 1988.
DISCIPLINARY ACTION: LICENSE REVOCATION

SHEPARD, PHILLIP B MD, DATE OF BIRTH NOVEMBER 14, 1943, LICENSE NUMBER 0004524, OF 1206 EAST PIKE #505, SEATTLE, WA, WAS DISCIPLINED BY MONTANA ON SEPTEMBER 3, 1990.
DISCIPLINARY ACTION: LICENSE REINSTATEMENT; RESTRICTION PLACED ON LICENSE
OFFENSE: PROFESSIONAL MISCONDUCT
NOTES: VOLUNTARY SURRENDER ON 3/25/86 DUE TO BOARD'S INVESTIGATION INTO PRACTICE FOR DEVIATE SEXUAL CONDUCT. REINSTATEMENT WITH CONDITIONS: PATIENT CARE SHALL BE ONLY FOR ADULTS OR EMERGENCY ROOM/URGENT CARE; MAY DO AIDS COUNSELING OR RESEARCH; ALL PATIENT CONTACT SHALL HAVE THE PRESENCE OF A THIRD PARTY AT ALL TIMES; SHALL UNDERGO CONTINUAL PSYCHOTHERAPY WITH THERAPIST PROVIDING QUARTERLY REPORTS; SHALL

- MONTANA -

ENTER INTO A PERMANENT CONTRACT WITH THE MONTANA PROFESSIONAL ASSISTANCE PROGRAM; SHALL INFORM ANY FACILITY WHERE HE PROVIDES SERVICES OF THE ORDER. MODIFICATION OF CONDITIONS ON 3/23/92 TO PROVIDE CLARIFICATION.

SHOLLENBERGER, JOHN C MD, DATE OF BIRTH MARCH 13, 1942, LICENSE NUMBER 0004002, OF 7045 S CHRISTOPHER, BELEN, NM, WAS DISCIPLINED BY MONTANA ON JUNE 19, 1990.
DISCIPLINARY ACTION: SURRENDER OF LICENSE
OFFENSE: DISCIPLINARY ACTION BY ANOTHER STATE OR AGENCY
NOTES: SURRENDER PENDING DISCIPLINARY ACTION.

SHOLLENBERGER, JOHN C MD WAS DISCIPLINED BY NEW MEXICO ON DECEMBER 22, 1992.
DISCIPLINARY ACTION: LICENSE SUSPENSION
OFFENSE: FAILURE TO COMPLY WITH A PREVIOUS BOARD ORDER
NOTES: VIOLATION OF STIPULATION.

SHOLLENBERGER, JOHN C MD OF ALBUQUERQUE, NM, WAS DISCIPLINED BY NEW MEXICO ON SEPTEMBER 24, 1993.
DISCIPLINARY ACTION: LICENSE REVOCATION
OFFENSE: PROFESSIONAL MISCONDUCT

SHULL, THOMAS E MD, LICENSE NUMBER 0020297, OF TACOMA, PIERCE COUNTY, WA, WAS DISCIPLINED BY WASHINGTON ON MARCH 5, 1992.
DISCIPLINARY ACTION: EMERGENCY SUSPENSION
NOTES: ALLEGATIONS OF IMPAIRMENT.

SHULL, THOMAS E MD, LICENSE NUMBER 0020297, OF GOSHEN, IN, WAS DISCIPLINED BY WASHINGTON ON OCTOBER 22, 1992.
DISCIPLINARY ACTION: LICENSE SUSPENSION
OFFENSE: SUBSTANCE ABUSE
NOTES: MORAL TURPITUDE, CURRENT MISUSE OF ALCOHOL, AND ABUSE OF A CLIENT.

SHULL, THOMAS EARL MD, DATE OF BIRTH APRIL 26, 1929, LICENSE NUMBER 1037255, OF 1741 B COLLEGE MANOR DR, GOSHEN, IN, WAS DISCIPLINED BY INDIANA ON DECEMBER 17, 1992.
DISCIPLINARY ACTION: 3-MONTH EMERGENCY SUSPENSION
OFFENSE: DISCIPLINARY ACTION BY ANOTHER STATE OR AGENCY
NOTES: WHILE EMPLOYED AT A CLINIC IN WASHINGTON IN LATE 1991 HE EXHIBITED ERRATIC, ABERRANT AND HOSTILE BEHAVIOR TOWARDS PATIENTS AND FELLOW EMPLOYEES. ALCOHOL WAS REPEATEDLY SMELLED ON HIS BREATH. AFTER BEING FIRED FROM THE CLINIC HE MADE THREATS AGAINST FORMER EMPLOYERS. ALSO WROTE BAD CHECKS. WASHINGTON LICENSE SUMMARILY SUSPENDED 3/5/92, AND INDEFINITELY SUSPENDED 10/22/92. ORDERED TO UNDERGO PSYCHOLOGICAL AND SUBSTANCE ABUSE EVALUATION, WHICH HE HAD NOT DONE AS OF 12/17/92. AS OF 1/29/93 THE SUMMARY SUSPENSION IS CONTINUED IN FULL EFFECT WITH FOLLOWING CONDITIONS: HE MUST UNDERGO A PSYCHIATRIC AND SUBSTANCE ABUSE EVALUATION TO BE PERFORMED BY A BOARD APPROVED PSYCHIATRIST OR CERTIFIED ADDICTIONOLOGIST. THE BOARD WILL RECEIVE A REPORT, CONTAINING A HISTORY, EVALUATION, DIAGNOSIS, PROGNOSIS AND COURSE OF TREATMENT, IF ANY, FROM THE EXAMINING PHYSICIAN; SHALL ENTER INTO AN AGREEMENT WITH THE INDIANA STATE MEDICAL ASSOCIATION'S IMPAIRED PHYSICIAN PROGRAM AND ADHERE TO IT; A COPY OF THIS ORDER IS TO BE SENT TO THE MEDICAL LICENSING BOARDS OF OREGON, MONTANA, WASHINGTON, AND CALIFORNIA. EFFECTIVE 2/25/93, THE EMERGENCY SUSPENSION CONTINUES AS DOES CONDITION THAT HE SHALL ENTER INTO AN AGREEMENT WITH THE INDIANA STATE MEDICAL ASSOCIATION'S IMPAIRED PHYSICIAN PROGRAM AND ADHERE TO IT; EFFECTIVE 5/4/93, 6/10/93 AND 6/24/93 THE EMERGENCY SUSPENSION WAS CONTINUED FOR A PERIOD NOT TO EXCEED 90 DAYS.

SHULL, THOMAS EARL MD, DATE OF BIRTH APRIL 26, 1929, LICENSE NUMBER 0002894, OF 1741B COLLEGE MANOR DRIVE, GOSHEN, IN, WAS DISCIPLINED BY MONTANA ON FEBRUARY 10, 1993.
DISCIPLINARY ACTION: LICENSE REVOCATION
OFFENSE: DISCIPLINARY ACTION BY ANOTHER STATE OR AGENCY
NOTES: RECIPROCAL TO WASHINGTON'S ACTION.

SHULL, THOMAS EARL MD, DATE OF BIRTH APRIL 26, 1929, LICENSE NUMBER 1037255, OF 1741 B COLLEGE MANOR DRIVE, GOSHEN, IN, WAS DISCIPLINED BY INDIANA ON FEBRUARY 24, 1994.
DISCIPLINARY ACTION: LICENSE SUSPENSION; 120-MONTH PROBATION
OFFENSE: DISCIPLINARY ACTION BY ANOTHER STATE OR AGENCY
NOTES: AS OF 1/27/94 HE HAD NOT OBTAINED A STAY OF THE SUSPENSION ON HIS WASHINGTON LICENSE ALTHOUGH HE HAS INFORMED THE WASHINGTON BOARD OF HIS TREATMENT FOR ALCOHOL DEPENDENCE AND BIPOLAR DISORDER AND THAT HE WISHES TO REMAIN IN INDIANA; ON 2/10/93 IN A DEFAULT DECISION MONTANA LICENSE WAS REVOKED BASED ON THE WASHINGTON ACTION; ON 2/17/93 PLED GUILTY TO OPERATING A MOTOR VEHICLE WITH .10% OR MORE BLOOD ALCOHOL LEVEL; 60 DAY JAIL SENTENCE SUSPENDED WITH CONDITIONS; LETTERS FROM PHYSICIAN INDICATE HE HAS SUCCESSFULLY COMPLETED TREATMENT AND HE CONTINUES TO ACTIVELY PARTICIPATE IN RECOVERY ACTIVITIES INCLUDING AA MEETINGS AND A CONTRACT WITH MEDICAL ASSOCIATION. SUSPENSION INDEFINITE PENDING SUCCESSFUL COMPLETION OF SPEX EXAM. CONDITIONS OF PROBATION: SHALL ONLY WORK UNDER THE ON-SITE SUPERVISION OF A LICENSED PHYSICIAN; MAY ONLY WORK 30 HOURS PER WEEK; SHALL HAVE SUPERVISOR SUBMIT MONTHLY REPORTS TO THE BOARD; MAY NOT POSSESS DEA OR CONTROLLED SUBSTANCES REGISTRATION; SHALL ATTEND AT LEAST 3 AA/NARCOTICS ANONYMOUS OR CADUCEUS MEETINGS PER WEEK WITH QUARTERLY REPORTS TO THE BOARD; SHALL MAINTAIN AND COMPLY WITH HIS PHYSICIAN ASSISTANCE CONTRACT WITH MONTHLY REPORTS TO THE BOARD; SHALL HAVE PSYCHIATRIST SUBMIT MONTHLY REPORTS; SHALL NOTIFY THE BOARD OF A CHANGE IN TREATING PHYSICIANS; SHALL APPEAR BEFORE THE BOARD QUARTERLY. LICENSE AUTOMATICALLY REINSTATED ON PROBATION ON 9/8/94 AFTER HE PASSED THE SPEX EXAM. ORDER MODIFIED ON 2/15/95: THE REQUIREMENT TO WORK ONLY UNDER THE ON-SITE SUPERVISION OF A LICENSED PHYSICIAN IS DELETED; MAY WORK ONLY 40 HOURS PER WEEK; ALL OTHER TERMS AND CONDITIONS REMAIN IN FULL FORCE AND EFFECT.

SMITH, RENE Z DO, DATE OF BIRTH JANUARY 25, 1945, LICENSE NUMBER 0007854, OF 3313 NORTH COUNTRY CLUB RD, NEWCASTLE, OK, WAS DISCIPLINED BY MICHIGAN ON OCTOBER 13, 1992.
DISCIPLINARY ACTION: EMERGENCY SUSPENSION
OFFENSE: SUBSTANDARD CARE, INCOMPETENCE, OR NEGLIGENCE
NOTES: NEGLIGENCE AND INCOMPETENCE.

SMITH, RENE Z DR OF NEWCASTLE, OK, WAS DISCIPLINED BY ILLINOIS ON OCTOBER 1, 1993.
DISCIPLINARY ACTION: LICENSE SUSPENSION
OFFENSE: DISCIPLINARY ACTION BY ANOTHER STATE OR AGENCY
NOTES: DISCIPLINED IN MISSOURI. INDEFINITE SUSPENSION FOR A MINIMUM OF 5 YEARS.

SMITH, RENE Z DO, DATE OF BIRTH JANUARY 25, 1945, LICENSE NUMBER 0007854, OF C/O BECHTEL PO BOX 9729, AHMADI 61008 KUWAIT, WAS DISCIPLINED BY MICHIGAN ON NOVEMBER 24, 1993.

- MONTANA -

DISCIPLINARY ACTION: LICENSE REVOCATION
OFFENSE: SUBSTANDARD CARE, INCOMPETENCE, OR NEGLIGENCE
NOTES: NEGLIGENCE/INCOMPETENCE; LACK OF GOOD MORAL CHARACTER.

SMITH, RENE Z DO, DATE OF BIRTH JANUARY 25, 1945, OF 248 EAST KEY BOULEVARD, MIDWEST CITY, OK, WAS DISCIPLINED BY MONTANA ON SEPTEMBER 26, 1996.
DISCIPLINARY ACTION: DENIAL OF NEW LICENSE
OFFENSE: DISCIPLINARY ACTION BY ANOTHER STATE OR AGENCY
NOTES: DISCIPLINE IN OTHER STATE; UNPROFESSIONAL CONDUCT.

STEPHENSON, THOMAS R MD, LICENSE NUMBER 00G8862, OF LOS ANGELES, CA, WAS DISCIPLINED BY CALIFORNIA ON APRIL 11, 1994.
DISCIPLINARY ACTION: 4-MONTH LICENSE SUSPENSION; 116-MONTH PROBATION
OFFENSE: SUBSTANDARD CARE, INCOMPETENCE, OR NEGLIGENCE
NOTES: GROSS NEGLIGENCE, REPEATED NEGLIGENT ACTS, CREATING FALSE MEDICAL RECORDS, DISHONESTY, VIOLATING INSURANCE REQUIREMENTS, FALSE AND MISLEADING ADVERTISING IN THE CARE AND TREATMENT OF PLASTIC SURGERY PATIENTS. REVOCATION STAYED, PRIOR CONDITION.

STEPHENSON, THOMAS R MD, LICENSE NUMBER 0011349, OF HARLEM, MT, WAS DISCIPLINED BY FLORIDA ON JUNE 30, 1995.
DISCIPLINARY ACTION: LICENSE SUSPENSION; PROBATION
OFFENSE: DISCIPLINARY ACTION BY ANOTHER STATE OR AGENCY
NOTES: MEDICAL LICENSE SUSPENDED FOR 120 DAYS BY CALIFORNIA AND PLACED ON 10 YEARS PROBATION; FAILING TO REPORT THIS TO THE BOARD WITHIN 30 DAYS. SUSPENSION UNTIL SUCH TIME AS HIS CALIFORNIA LICENSE IS UNENCUMBERED AND UNTIL HE CAN APPEAR BEFORE THE BOARD AND ESTABLISH THAT HE CAN PRACTICE MEDICINE WITH REASONABLE SKILL AND SAFETY; UPON REINSTATEMENT, HIS LICENSE SHALL BE PLACED UPON PROBATION WITH TERMS AND CONDITIONS TO BE SET AT THAT TIME.

VASQUEZ, NED FRANCIS MD, DATE OF BIRTH MARCH 24, 1957, LICENSE NUMBER 0005353, OF PO BOX 7609, MISSOULA, MT, WAS DISCIPLINED BY MONTANA ON DECEMBER 20, 1993.
DISCIPLINARY ACTION: 60-MONTH PROBATION
OFFENSE: SEXUAL ABUSE OF OR SEXUAL MISCONDUCT WITH A PATIENT
NOTES: ADMITTED THAT HE ENGAGED IN SEXUAL CONDUCT WITH RESPECT TO ONE PATIENT. CONDITIONS OF PROBATION: SHALL ENTER INTO AN AGREEMENT WITH THE MONTANA PROFESSIONAL ASSISTANCE PROGRAM AND ABIDE BY ALL TERMS AND CONDITIONS; SHALL INFORM EACH FACILITY WHERE HE PROVIDES SERVICES OF THIS ORDER.

WHITE, MANUEL MD, DATE OF BIRTH JUNE 2, 1916, OF PO BOX 5058, HELENA, MT, WAS DISCIPLINED BY MONTANA ON SEPTEMBER 8, 1992.
DISCIPLINARY ACTION: DENIAL OF NEW LICENSE
OFFENSE: PROVIDING FALSE INFORMATION TO THE BOARD
NOTES: FRAUD ON APPLICATION, NEGLIGENCE, FALSIFICATION OF PATIENT RECORDS, MENTAL INABILITY TO SAFELY ENGAGE IN PRACTICE OF MEDICINE, LACK OF GOOD MORAL CHARACTER.

WHITE, MANUEL MD, LICENSE NUMBER 0004393, WAS DISCIPLINED BY WASHINGTON ON MARCH 19, 1993.
DISCIPLINARY ACTION: SURRENDER OF LICENSE
OFFENSE: SUBSTANDARD CARE, INCOMPETENCE, OR NEGLIGENCE
NOTES: BETWEEN 1986 AND 1991 HE FAILED TO CONFORM HIS CONDUCT TO GENERALLY ACCEPTED STANDARDS OF CLINICAL PROFESSIONAL PRACTICE IN THAT HE EXHIBITED IMPAIRED SURGICAL JUDGEMENT AND DIAGNOSTIC SKILLS, INAPPROPRIATE OR UNTIMELY WORK-UP OF PATIENTS, MEDICATION ERROR AND NON-STERILE TECHNIQUES AND COMMUNICATION PROBLEMS AFFECTING PATIENT CARE. RETIREMENT FROM PRACTICE IN WASHINGTON HAS ALREADY OCCURRED AND HE HAS NO PLANS TO RESUME PRACTICE; HE AGREES TO NOTIFY THE BOARD IF HE PLANS TO RESUME PRACTICE IN WASHINGTON.

WILLIAMS, JOYCE L MD OF NORTH BEND, KING COUNTY, WA, WAS DISCIPLINED BY WASHINGTON ON JANUARY 27, 1992.
DISCIPLINARY ACTION: LICENSE SUSPENSION

WILLIAMS, JOYCE L MD WAS DISCIPLINED BY WASHINGTON ON JULY 24, 1992.
DISCIPLINARY ACTION: RESTRICTION PLACED ON LICENSE
NOTES: REQUIRED TO MEET SPECIFIC TERMS AND CONDITIONS IN ORDER TO RECEIVE CONDITIONAL LICENSE. MODIFICATIONS TO THE ORDER MAY BE PETITIONED TO THE BOARD NO LESS THAN SIX MONTHS FROM THE DATE OF ORDER.

WILLIAMS, JOYCE LAREE MD, DATE OF BIRTH MAY 30, 1955, LICENSE NUMBER 0007542, OF 181-12TH STREET, SW, SIDNEY, MT, WAS DISCIPLINED BY MONTANA ON OCTOBER 6, 1993.
DISCIPLINARY ACTION: RESTRICTION PLACED ON LICENSE
OFFENSE: DISCIPLINARY ACTION BY ANOTHER STATE OR AGENCY
NOTES: ON 06/07/94, AFTER COMPLIANCE WITH ORIGINAL AGREEMENT, AMENDMENT ADDED TO ALLOW DR. WILLIAMS TO TAKE TEN INSTEAD OF SIX DELIVERIES A MONTH. ON 11/31/94 AMENDMENT REMOVED ALL RESTRICTIONS.

WINSTEAD, GLENN C MD, DATE OF BIRTH DECEMBER 17, 1944, LICENSE NUMBER 0006542, OF 2200 BOX ELDER, MILES CITY, MT, WAS DISCIPLINED BY MONTANA ON AUGUST 24, 1990.
DISCIPLINARY ACTION: PROBATION
OFFENSE: CRIMINAL CONVICTION OR PLEA OF GUILTY, NOLO CONTENDERE, OR NO CONTEST TO A CRIME
NOTES: FEDERAL FELONY CONVICTION INVOLVING MORAL TURPITUDE - COUNTERFEITING. PROBATION UNTIL FURTHER ORDER OF THE BOARD.

WINSTEAD, GLENN C MD, LICENSE NUMBER 00D9324, OF STEVENSVILLE, MT, WAS DISCIPLINED BY TEXAS ON FEBRUARY 22, 1991.
NOTES: MUST APPEAR BEFORE TEXAS BOARD AND RECEIVE APPROVAL BEFORE PRACTICING IN TEXAS.

WINSTEAD, GLENN C MD, LICENSE NUMBER 0021097, OF GREAT FALLS, MT, WAS DISCIPLINED BY VIRGINIA ON APRIL 19, 1993.
DISCIPLINARY ACTION: LICENSE REVOCATION
OFFENSE: CRIMINAL CONVICTION OR PLEA OF GUILTY, NOLO CONTENDERE, OR NO CONTEST TO A CRIME
NOTES: BASED ON FELONY CONVICTION.

ZELMAN, RUSSELL H MD, LICENSE NUMBER 0148542, OF HC 65 BOX 66, BOVIA, NY, WAS DISCIPLINED BY NEW YORK ON AUGUST 27, 1996.
DISCIPLINARY ACTION: 60-MONTH PROBATION; RESTRICTION PLACED ON LICENSE
OFFENSE: DISCIPLINARY ACTION BY ANOTHER STATE OR AGENCY
NOTES: ACTION IN MONTANA FOR FAILING TO PROPERLY DIAGNOSE AND TREAT SIX PATIENTS AND MAKING FALSE STATEMENTS REGARDING HIS CARE OF ONE PATIENT. MADE FALSE STATEMENTS ON BOTH HIS NEW YORK LICENSE REGISTRATION APPLICATION AND HIS APPLICATION FOR HOSPITAL PRIVILEGES. FIVE YEAR SUSPENSION, STAYED. WILL NOT ENGAGE IN THE PRACTICE OF SURGERY IN NEW YORK.

- MONTANA -

ZELMAN, RUSSELL HENRY MD, DATE OF BIRTH MAY 2, 1955, LICENSE NUMBER 0005358, OF PO BOX 859, MARGARETVILLE, NY, WAS DISCIPLINED BY MONTANA ON OCTOBER 9, 1992.
DISCIPLINARY ACTION: 60-MONTH PROBATION; RESTRICTION PLACED ON LICENSE
OFFENSE: SUBSTANDARD CARE, INCOMPETENCE, OR NEGLIGENCE
NOTES: PROCEEDINGS PENDING ON ALLEGATIONS OF NEGLIGENCE IN SURGICAL PRACTICE. RESTRICTIONS AFTER RETURN TO SURGICAL PRACTICE IN MONTANA. ON 5/21/97 PROBATION TERMINATED; HAS ELECTED NOT TO PRACTICE IN MONTANA.

ZUGAZA, ROMAN MD, LICENSE NUMBER 0149445, OF BUTTE, MT, WAS DISCIPLINED BY NEW YORK ON FEBRUARY 16, 1988.
NOTES: 2 YEAR SUSPENSION, STAYED.

OREGON

1996 serious action rate: 3.70/1000
1996 ranking: 29th

The Oregon Board of Medical Examiners provided copies of its quarterly cumulative listings of disciplinary reports from August 1989 through December 1996. These computer printouts list all doctors whose practice was somehow restricted by the Board at the time of the report. These reports list the physician's name, license number, city and state of residence, and the date and type of action taken. They provide information on modifications and terminations of board actions but not on court decisions affecting board actions. Oregon stated, however, that no such court decisions occurred.

Within the last two years, Oregon appears to have developed a policy of allowing doctors who are under investigation to surrender their licenses in lieu of further investigation and then labeling these surrenders "not a disciplinary action." In a letter sent to us, however, the Oregon board stated that "the licensee cannot reactivate their license without the completion of the original investigation." These physicians are not included in the Oregon listing of physicians.

The information provided covers disciplinary actions taken against allopathic physicians (MDs) and osteopathic physicians (DOs).

Besides disciplinary actions taken by the State Medical Board, this listing also includes actions taken by the Medicare/Medicaid programs, the FDA, and the DEA against physicians located in this state. Disciplinary actions taken by other states against physicians located in Oregon or that match to a physician disciplined by Oregon (see Appendix 2 for an explanation of the matching protocol) are also included.

Although we have made every effort to match physicians' names correctly, some materials we received did not include complete information on middle names, license numbers, birth dates or addresses. Therefore, consumers should remember that non-disciplined physicians and physicians with different disciplinary actions may have similar names to those disciplined physicians listed in this state. Consumers should also remember that if they want the most current information on the status on a physician's license, they should contact the medical board of the state in which the physician practices or had practiced.

According to the Federation of State Medical Boards, Oregon took 29 serious disciplinary actions against MDs and DOs in 1996. Compared to the 7,834 MDs licensed in the state, Oregon had a serious disciplinary action rate of 3.70 serious actions per 1,000 MDs and a ranking of 29th on that list (see Table A, Findings, pg. 14).

The tables below summarize the data Public Citizen received from Oregon.

Table I. Disciplinary Actions Against MDs and DOs August 1989 through December 1996*

Action	Number	Percent**
Revocation	12	3.9%
Surrender	13	4.2%
Suspension	31	10.0%
Probation	67	21.7%
Practice Restriction	56	18.1%
Action Taken Against Controlled Substance License	57	18.4%
Other Actions	73	23.6%
Total Actions	**309**	**100.0%**

* This table lists only the two most serious disciplinary actions taken against a physician
** Percentages may not total 100% due to rounding.

Table 2. Offenses for which MDs and DOs were Disciplined August 1989 through December 1996*

Offense	Number	Percent
Criminal Conviction	1	1.8%
Sexual Abuse of or Sexual Misconduct with a Patient	7	12.3%
Substandard Care, Incompetence or Negligence	10	17.5%
Misprescribing or Overprescribing Drugs	4	7.0%
Substance Abuse	16	28.1%
Disciplinary Action Taken Against License by Another State or Agency	1	1.8%
Other Offenses	18	31.6%
Total Records With Offense Listed	**57**	**100.0%**

* Includes only those actions for which an offense was listed and for which we had a corresponding term in our database.

Table 3. Disciplinary Actions Taken for Substandard Care, Incompetence or Negligence

Action	Number	Percent
Surrender	3	25.0%
Suspension	1	8.3%
Practice Restriction	1	8.3%
Fine	1	8.3%
Reprimand	5	41.7%
Other Actions	1	8.3%
Total Actions	**12**	**100.0%**

Table 4. Disciplinary Actions Taken for Substance Abuse

Action	Number	Percent
Suspension	4	22.2%
Emergency Suspension	1	5.6%
Probation	9	50.0%
Restriction of Controlled Substance License	1	5.6%
Other Actions	3	16.7%
Total Actions	**18**	**100.0%**

If you feel that your doctor has not given you proper medical care or has mistreated you in any way--whether or not he or she is listed in this report--it is important that you let your state medical board know. Even if they do not immediately act on your complaint, it is important that the information be recorded in their files because it is possible that other people may have filed or will file complaints about the same doctor. Send a brief written description of what occurred to the addresses below or call the phone numbers listed for more information on how to file a complaint.

Address
Oregon Board of Medical Examiners
Kathleen Haley, JD, Executive Director
620 Crown Plaza
1500 SW First Ave.
Portland, OR 97201-5826
(503) 229-5770

Listing of Doctors Sanctioned by Offense

Sexual Abuse of or Sexual Misconduct with a Patient
BECK, JONATHAN JAY
KESTER, EUGENE FRANCIS
KIMBERLEY, STEPHEN LANGTON
RICHARD, SAMUEL WILLIAM

Substandard Care, Incompetence, or Negligence
BOSS, ROBERT JOHN
BOYD, RALPH DEVEE
CLELAND, JOHN EASTMURE
GRIMWOOD, DAVID
HAEBERLIN, JAMES RICHARD
HARRIS, HARRY
HIKES, CHARLES EDWARD III
OTT, JOHN DAVID
VOELKER, GERALD BERNARD
WILTSE, WILLIAM EARLE

Criminal Conviction or Plea of Guilty, Nolo Contendere, or No Contest to a Crime
MURPHY, GEORGE BYRD JR

Misprescribing or Overprescribing Drugs
BUNNELL, HENRY KENDALL
JOHNSON, MARCUS PAUL
RASMUSSEN, CHESTER MURRAY
TYNER, SANDRA JEAN

Substance Abuse
CAESAR, RICHARD IRWIN
FAULK, CHARLES
LUNDY, THERESA MARIE
MASKELL, LAURA KATHLEEN
MCGOVERN, PETER JOHN
MILLER, ROBERT LESLIE
NEITLING, STANLEY JOSEPH JR
PRITCHARD, JAMES SCOTT
SKIPPER, GREGORY EARL
SMITH, CATHY SCHINDLER
VALENTINE, THOMAS V
WATKINS, ROBERT CAMP
WESTCOTT, GARY RAY
WILLIAMS, PAUL CARROLL

Caution: This list is designed to be used only in conjunction with the rest of this book which includes additional information on each physician such as license number, date of action and more complete descriptions of the offenses.

DISCIPLINARY ACTIONS

ACHORD, THADDEUS CLARR MD, DATE OF BIRTH SEPTEMBER 15, 1941, LICENSE NUMBER 0010474, OF 1962 NW KEARNEY STE L101, PORTLAND, OR, WAS DISCIPLINED BY OREGON ON OCTOBER 10, 1991.
DISCIPLINARY ACTION: SURRENDER OF LICENSE
OFFENSE: PROFESSIONAL MISCONDUCT
NOTES: ALLEGED SEXUAL MISCONDUCT. RETIRE/SURRENDER IN LIEU OF DISCIPLINARY ACTION.

ADAMS, GEORGE B MD, LICENSE NUMBER MD05855, OF SALEM, OR, WAS DISCIPLINED BY OREGON ON FEBRUARY 8, 1989.
DISCIPLINARY ACTION: RESTRICTION PLACED ON LICENSE

ANDERSON, WARREN LEROY MD OF 2800 N. VANCOUVER AVE., PORTLAND, OR, WAS DISCIPLINED BY DEA ON MAY 10, 1989.
DISCIPLINARY ACTION: RESTRICTION PLACED ON CONTROLLED SUBSTANCE LICENSE
OFFENSE: OVERPRESCRIBING OR MISPRESCRIBING DRUGS
NOTES: INAPPROPRIATE PRESCRIBING PRACTICES.

ASPER, PAUL ANSGAR MD, LICENSE NUMBER 0005557, OF WOODBURN, OR, WAS DISCIPLINED BY OREGON ON AUGUST 9, 1988.
DISCIPLINARY ACTION: RESTRICTION PLACED ON LICENSE
NOTES: VOLUNTARY LIMITATION, CONTINUING MEDICAL EDUCATION/NO PRESCRIBING FOR SPOUSE. NO LONGER RESTRICTED AS OF 10/13/92.

BALD, DOUGLAS MD, LICENSE NUMBER 0009634, OF PORTLAND, OR, WAS DISCIPLINED BY OREGON ON JANUARY 24, 1990.
DISCIPLINARY ACTION: RESTRICTION PLACED ON LICENSE
NOTES: MUST PROVIDE TRIPLICATE COPIES OF PRESCRIPTIONS. NO LONGER RESTRICTED AS OF 7/27/92.

BARNES, LAWRENCE RAY JR MD, LICENSE NUMBER MD09267, OF STAYTON, OR, WAS DISCIPLINED BY OREGON ON APRIL 9, 1987.
DISCIPLINARY ACTION: RESTRICTION PLACED ON LICENSE
NOTES: PSYCHIATRIC CARE REQUIRED. AS OF 3/3/97, NO LONGER LISTED AS RESTRICTED.

BARNES, LAWRENCE RAY JR MD OF 1371-10TH STREET, STAYTON, OR, WAS DISCIPLINED BY DEA ON SEPTEMBER 2, 1993.
DISCIPLINARY ACTION: RESTRICTION PLACED ON CONTROLLED SUBSTANCE LICENSE
OFFENSE: DISCIPLINARY ACTION BY ANOTHER STATE OR AGENCY
NOTES: PLACED ON VOLUNTARY LIMITATION WITH OREGON MEDICAL BOARD IN 1987.

BASSFORD, PAUL S JR MD, LICENSE NUMBER MD05442, OF EUGENE, OR, WAS DISCIPLINED BY OREGON ON OCTOBER 5, 1989.
DISCIPLINARY ACTION: RESTRICTION PLACED ON LICENSE
NOTES: VOLUNTARY LIMITATION. LICENSE NO LONGER RESTRICTED AS OF 5/7/90.

BECK, JONATHAN JAY MD, LICENSE NUMBER 0015406, OF WEST LINN, OR, WAS DISCIPLINED BY OREGON ON SEPTEMBER 21, 1995.
DISCIPLINARY ACTION: LICENSE SUSPENSION
OFFENSE: SEXUAL ABUSE OF OR SEXUAL MISCONDUCT WITH A PATIENT
NOTES: ALLEGED SEXUAL MISCONDUCT WITH FEMALE PATIENTS. INDEFINITE SUSPENSION. ON 12/26/95 INTERIM ORDER CONTINUING SUSPENSION. ON 5/1/96 ADDED $5,000 FINE. NO LONGER LISTED AS SUSPENDED AS OF 8/12/96.

BENDING, GLENVILLE C DR, LICENSE NUMBER 0015819, WAS DISCIPLINED BY MINNESOTA ON SEPTEMBER 11, 1993.
NOTES: STAYED SUSPENSION.

BENDING, GLENVILLE C MD, LICENSE NUMBER 0005453, OF TUCSON, AZ, WAS DISCIPLINED BY ARIZONA ON APRIL 14, 1994.
NOTES: SHALL NOT PRACTICE IN ARIZONA PRIOR TO MEETING WITH THE BOARD.

BENDING, GLENVILLE CHARLES MD, LICENSE NUMBER MD07773, OF NEWPORT, OR, WAS DISCIPLINED BY OREGON ON JULY 9, 1992.
DISCIPLINARY ACTION: RESTRICTION PLACED ON LICENSE

BENDING, GLENVILLE CHARLES MD, LICENSE NUMBER 0013279, WAS DISCIPLINED BY WASHINGTON ON MARCH 19, 1993.
DISCIPLINARY ACTION: RESTRICTION PLACED ON LICENSE
OFFENSE: DISCIPLINARY ACTION BY ANOTHER STATE OR AGENCY
NOTES: ON 7/8/92 OREGON LICENSE LIMITED IN THAT HE WILL OBTAIN A SECOND OPINION FOR PATIENTS FOR WHOM HE RECOMMENDS CATARACT SURGERY. LICENSE LIMITED INDEFINITELY AND HE SHALL COMPLY WITH THE TERMS OF THE VOLUNTARY LIMITATION OF HIS MEDICAL PRACTICE INTO WHICH HE ENTERED WITH THE OREGON BOARD SO LONG AS THAT VOLUNTARY LIMITATION IS IN EFFECT; IF HE ESTABLISHES A PRACTICE IN WASHINGTON THE BOARD MAY MAKE ANNOUNCED VISITS TO INSPECT OFFICE AND/OR MEDICAL RECORDS; INTERVIEW OFFICE STAFF OR SUPERVISORS; AND REVIEW OTHER ASPECTS OF HIS PRACTICE; SHALL ASSUME ALL COSTS; SHALL INFORM THE BOARD IN WRITING OF CHANGES IN HIS PRACTICE AND RESIDENCE ADDRESS.

BERSELLI, ROBERT ANDREW MD, LICENSE NUMBER 0007894, OF PORTLAND, OR, WAS DISCIPLINED BY OREGON ON JULY 14, 1995.
DISCIPLINARY ACTION: RESTRICTION PLACED ON CONTROLLED SUBSTANCE LICENSE
NOTES: MUST PROVIDE TRIPLICATE COPIES OF CONTROLLED SUBSTANCES PRESCRIPTIONS.

BERSELLI, ROBERT ANDREW MD, LICENSE NUMBER 0007894, OF PORTLAND, OR, WAS DISCIPLINED BY OREGON ON AUGUST 19, 1996.
DISCIPLINARY ACTION: RESTRICTION PLACED ON CONTROLLED SUBSTANCE LICENSE
NOTES: MUST PROVIDE TRIPLICATE COPIES OF CONTROLLED SUBSTANCES PRESCRIPTIONS.

BIDLEMAN, STEVEN KENT MD OF 2680 UHRMANN ROAD, KLAMATH FALLS, OR, WAS DISCIPLINED BY DEA ON JULY 31, 1989.
DISCIPLINARY ACTION: RESTRICTION PLACED ON CONTROLLED SUBSTANCE LICENSE
OFFENSE: OVERPRESCRIBING OR MISPRESCRIBING DRUGS
NOTES: INAPPROPRIATE PRESCRIBING PRACTICES.

BISCHEL, GEORGE WILLARD DO, LICENSE NUMBER DO06101, OF SALEM, OR, WAS DISCIPLINED BY OREGON ON MAY 18, 1993.
DISCIPLINARY ACTION: LICENSE SUSPENSION

BISKA, HAROLD V MD, LICENSE NUMBER MD05197, OF PORTLAND, OR, WAS DISCIPLINED BY OREGON ON OCTOBER 11, 1989.
DISCIPLINARY ACTION: RESTRICTION PLACED ON LICENSE
NOTES: LIMITED TO ADMINISTRATIVE MEDICINE. NOT RESTRICTED AS OF 2/8/90.

BOLIN, ROBERT BRUCE MD, LICENSE NUMBER 0014237, OF NORTH BEND, OR, WAS DISCIPLINED BY OREGON ON NOVEMBER 24, 1989.
DISCIPLINARY ACTION: 120-MONTH PROBATION; 120-MONTH RESTRICTION PLACED ON CONTROLLED SUBSTANCE LICENSE
NOTES: PRESCRIPTION RESTRICTION SCHEDULES II THROUGH V EXCEPT PATIENT HOSPITAL CHARTS. AS OF 3/10/94 NO LONGER LISTED AS ON PROBATION OR RESTRICTED.

BOND, RICHARD ALDEN MD, LICENSE NUMBER 0009466, OF CORVALIS, OR, WAS DISCIPLINED BY OREGON ON DECEMBER 7,

- OREGON -

1995.
DISCIPLINARY ACTION: LICENSE SUSPENSION
NOTES: STIPULATED ORDER OF SUSPENSION.

BOSLEY, LARRY LEE MD, LICENSE NUMBER 0032095, OF 8447 WILSHIRE 4TH FLR, BEVERLY HILLS, CA, WAS DISCIPLINED BY GEORGIA ON JUNE 8, 1989.
DISCIPLINARY ACTION: PROBATION
OFFENSE: DISCIPLINARY ACTION BY ANOTHER STATE OR AGENCY
NOTES: AS OF 8/7/91 PROBATION TERMINATED, HOLDS UNRESTRICTED LICENSE.

BOSLEY, LARRY LEE MD, LICENSE NUMBER MD05843, OF BEVERLY HILLS, CA, WAS DISCIPLINED BY OREGON ON AUGUST 17, 1993.
DISCIPLINARY ACTION: RESTRICTION PLACED ON LICENSE
NOTES: HAIR RESTORATION, TRANSPLANT AND MALE PATTERN BALDNESS REDUCTION.

BOSS, ROBERT JOHN MD, LICENSE NUMBER MD09837, OF BOARDMAN, OR, WAS DISCIPLINED BY OREGON ON APRIL 8, 1994.
DISCIPLINARY ACTION: FINE; REPRIMAND
OFFENSE: SUBSTANDARD CARE, INCOMPETENCE, OR NEGLIGENCE
NOTES: FAILURE TO DIAGNOSE PATIENT'S ECTOPIC PREGNANCY RESULTING IN DEATH. $2,500 FINE.

BOWEN, JAMES D MD OF ONTONAGON, MI, WAS DISCIPLINED BY MISSOURI ON SEPTEMBER 13, 1988.
DISCIPLINARY ACTION: LICENSE REVOCATION
OFFENSE: DISCIPLINARY ACTION BY ANOTHER STATE OR AGENCY
NOTES: CRIMINAL CONVICTION.

BOWEN, JAMES D MD, DATE OF BIRTH OCTOBER 31, 1939, LICENSE NUMBER 0038792, OF 2234 M-64, ONTONAGON, MI, WAS DISCIPLINED BY MICHIGAN ON OCTOBER 17, 1992.
DISCIPLINARY ACTION: LICENSE REVOCATION
OFFENSE: PHYSICAL OR MENTAL ILLNESS INHIBITING THE ABILITY TO PRACTICE WITH SKILL AND SAFETY
NOTES: MENTAL/PHYSICAL INCOMPETENCY.

BOWEN, JAMES D MD, DATE OF BIRTH OCTOBER 31, 1939, OF 6432 S E 134TH, PORTLAND, OR, WAS DISCIPLINED BY MEDICARE ON JUNE 30, 1993.
DISCIPLINARY ACTION: EXCLUSION FROM THE MEDICARE AND/OR MEDICAID PROGRAMS
OFFENSE: DISCIPLINARY ACTION BY ANOTHER STATE OR AGENCY
NOTES: LICENSE REVOKED FOR REASONS BEARING ON PROFESSIONAL COMPETENCE.

BOWEN, JAMES DAVID MD WAS DISCIPLINED BY HAWAII ON MARCH 16, 1988.
DISCIPLINARY ACTION: 12-MONTH LICENSE SUSPENSION

BOWEN, JAMES DAVID MD, LICENSE NUMBER 0012297, OF 401 S 7TH, ONTONAGON, MI, WAS DISCIPLINED BY GEORGIA ON MAY 23, 1988.
DISCIPLINARY ACTION: LICENSE SUSPENSION
OFFENSE: DISCIPLINARY ACTION BY ANOTHER STATE OR AGENCY

BOYD, RALPH DEVEE MD, LICENSE NUMBER MD16299, OF JOSEPH, OR, WAS DISCIPLINED BY OREGON ON APRIL 13, 1994.
DISCIPLINARY ACTION: REPRIMAND
OFFENSE: SUBSTANDARD CARE, INCOMPETENCE, OR NEGLIGENCE
NOTES: INADEQUATE TREATMENT OF 2 YEAR OLD BURN VICTIM.

BREMILLER, CLIFFORD EDWARD MD, LICENSE NUMBER MD06271, OF EUGENE, OR, WAS DISCIPLINED BY OREGON ON JULY 31, 1989.
DISCIPLINARY ACTION: RESTRICTION PLACED ON LICENSE
NOTES: ALLEGED PERSONAL SUBSTANCE ABUSE. MODIFICATION OF PROBATION/VOLUNTARY LIMITATION ON 10/11/91. AS OF 4/20/93 NO LONGER LISTED AS RESTRICTED.

BROOKHART, JOHN HOWARD MD, LICENSE NUMBER MD10528, OF ST HELENS, OR, WAS DISCIPLINED BY OREGON ON JULY 9, 1992.
DISCIPLINARY ACTION: 1-MONTH LICENSE SUSPENSION; 120-MONTH PROBATION
NOTES: SUSPENSION UNTIL 8/20/92; FINE; SCHEDULES II, III, IV AND V PRESCRIBING PRIVILEGES RESTRICTED.

BROWN, JOHN OLLIS JR MD, LICENSE NUMBER MD12045, OF PORTLAND, OR, WAS DISCIPLINED BY OREGON ON SEPTEMBER 10, 1988.
DISCIPLINARY ACTION: RESTRICTION PLACED ON LICENSE
NOTES: MUST PRACTICE ONLY IN SUPERVISED SETTING. PSYCHIATRIC REPORTS. AS OF 11/17/94 NO LONGER LISTED AS RESTRICTED.

BROWN, ROBERT MCDANNEL MD, LICENSE NUMBER MD07054, OF PORTLAND, OR, WAS DISCIPLINED BY OREGON ON APRIL 30, 1992.
DISCIPLINARY ACTION: 6-MONTH LICENSE SUSPENSION; FINE

BROWN, ROBERT MCDANNEL MD, LICENSE NUMBER MD07054, OF PORTLAND, OR, WAS DISCIPLINED BY OREGON ON APRIL 14, 1994.
DISCIPLINARY ACTION: SURRENDER OF LICENSE
NOTES: VOLUNTARY SURRENDER WHILE UNDER INVESTIGATION.

BRUST, RICHARD DUANE MD, LICENSE NUMBER MD06158, OF INDEPENDENCE, OR, WAS DISCIPLINED BY OREGON ON JUNE 1, 1993.
DISCIPLINARY ACTION: LICENSE SUSPENSION; PROBATION

BUCKMASTER, JOHN GILBERT MD, LICENSE NUMBER 0012764, OF PORTLAND, OR, WAS DISCIPLINED BY OREGON ON FEBRUARY 7, 1995.
NOTES: STIPULATED ORDER. INTERIM ORDER ALLOWING HIM TO RETURN TO PRACTICE SUBJECT TO TERMS OF ORDER AND FURTHER INVESTIGATION. NO LONGER LISTED AS RESTRICTED AS OF 11/27/95.

BUELL, JOHN WALTER DO, LICENSE NUMBER 0005982, OF DALLAS, IA, WAS DISCIPLINED BY OREGON ON FEBRUARY 22, 1990.
DISCIPLINARY ACTION: RESTRICTION PLACED ON LICENSE
NOTES: VOLUNTARY LIMITATION. ON 4/11/91 MODIFICATION OF PROBATION/VOLUNTARY LIMITATION. AS OF 3/3/97, NO LONGER LISTED AS RESTRICTED.

BUELL, JOHN WALTER DO WAS DISCIPLINED BY WASHINGTON ON AUGUST 16, 1991.
DISCIPLINARY ACTION: RESTRICTION PLACED ON LICENSE; MONITORING OF PHYSICIAN
OFFENSE: DISCIPLINARY ACTION BY ANOTHER STATE OR AGENCY
NOTES: ON 2/16/90 ACTION IN OREGON. WASHINGTON ORDER REQUIRES HIM TO COMPLY WITH OREGON ORDER INCLUDING: SHALL LIMIT HIS PRACTICE TO THE HOSPITAL EMERGENCY ROOM AND ANESTHESIA IN THE HOSPITAL; SHALL BE ALLOWED TO PERFORM PHYSICAL EXAMINATIONS OUTSIDE THE HOSPITAL SETTING ONLY FOR DEPARTMENT OF TRANSPORTATION PHYSICALS AND PILOT FLIGHT PHYSICALS; AGREES TO ATTEND THE NEXT AVAILABLE APPROPRIATE PRESCRIBING WORKSHOP; SHALL NOTIFY HIS HOSPITAL OR CHIEF OF STAFF OF ANY HEALTH CARE ENTITIES WHERE HE HAS PRIVILEGES OF THE TERMS OF THIS AGREEMENT; AND SHALL CAUSE REPORTS OF HIS PERFORMANCE TO BE SUBMITTED TO THE BOARD QUARTERLY. ADDITIONALLY SHALL SUBMIT IN WRITING TO THE BOARD ANY EMPLOYMENT OR RESIDENCE ADDRESS CHANGES IN WASHINGTON; AND SHALL SUBMIT COPIES OF ALL REPORTS SUBMITTED TO OREGON.

BULGER, ARTHUR R MD OF 11510 SE STARK, PORTLAND, OR, WAS DISCIPLINED BY DEA ON JULY 10, 1989.
DISCIPLINARY ACTION: RESTRICTION PLACED ON CONTROLLED SUBSTANCE LICENSE
OFFENSE: OVERPRESCRIBING OR MISPRESCRIBING DRUGS

- OREGON -

NOTES: INAPPROPRIATE PRESCRIBING PRACTICES

BUNNELL, HENRY KENDALL MD, LICENSE NUMBER MD07516, OF SODA SPRINGS, OR, WAS DISCIPLINED BY OREGON ON APRIL 20, 1994.
DISCIPLINARY ACTION: FINE
OFFENSE: OVERPRESCRIBING OR MISPRESCRIBING DRUGS
NOTES: INAPPROPRIATE PRESCRIBING OF CONTROLLED SUBSTANCES TO PATIENTS. $500 FINE.

BURGERT, PAUL JR DR OF 864 B REDDY AVENUE, KLAMATH FALLS, OR, WAS DISCIPLINED BY ILLINOIS ON MAY 1, 1988.
DISCIPLINARY ACTION: LICENSE SUSPENSION
OFFENSE: DISCIPLINARY ACTION BY ANOTHER STATE OR AGENCY
NOTES: INDEFINITE SUSPENSION; COLORADO LICENSE DISCIPLINED FOR SUBSTANCE ABUSE.

BURTON, THOMAS MD, LICENSE NUMBER 00G9416, OF SUN RIVER, OR, WAS DISCIPLINED BY CALIFORNIA ON OCTOBER 6, 1995.
DISCIPLINARY ACTION: 36-MONTH PROBATION
OFFENSE: DISCIPLINARY ACTION BY ANOTHER STATE OR AGENCY
NOTES: ACTION IN MINNESOTA. INAPPROPRIATE "FULL-BODY, FACE-TO-FACE" HUGS WITH FEMALE INPATIENTS IN HIS PSYCHIATRIC PRACTICE. REVOCATION, STAYED.

BURTON, TIMOTHY ANGUS MD, LICENSE NUMBER MD07992, OF HOOD RIVER, OR, WAS DISCIPLINED BY OREGON ON JANUARY 5, 1994.
DISCIPLINARY ACTION: 3-MONTH LICENSE SUSPENSION; FINE

BURTON, TIMOTHY ANGUS MD, LICENSE NUMBER MD07992, OF HOOD RIVER, OR, WAS DISCIPLINED BY OREGON ON JANUARY 14, 1994.
DISCIPLINARY ACTION: PROBATION

BUSENBARK, LINDA L MD OF 2726 45TH AVENUE SOUTH WEST, SEATTLE, WA, WAS DISCIPLINED BY DEA ON APRIL 16, 1996.
DISCIPLINARY ACTION: RESTRICTION PLACED ON CONTROLLED SUBSTANCE LICENSE
OFFENSE: PROFESSIONAL MISCONDUCT
NOTES: ALLEGED CONTROLLED SUBSTANCE VIOLATIONS.

BUSENBARK, LINDA LOUISE MD, LICENSE NUMBER MD13277, OF PORTLAND, OR, WAS DISCIPLINED BY OREGON ON AUGUST 17, 1992.
DISCIPLINARY ACTION: 120-MONTH PROBATION; FINE
NOTES: MUST PROVIDE TRIPLICATE COPIES OF CONTROLLED SUBSTANCE PRESCRIPTIONS FOR SCHEDULES III, IV AND V. AS OF 11/17/94 TERMS REVISED EXTENDING ORDER UNTIL 8/22/04. NO LONGER ON PROBATION AS OF 5/8/96.

BYRD, WALTON EDWARD MD OF 225 MADRONA SE, SALEM, OR, WAS DISCIPLINED BY DEA ON MAY 2, 1989.
DISCIPLINARY ACTION: RESTRICTION PLACED ON CONTROLLED SUBSTANCE LICENSE
OFFENSE: OVERPRESCRIBING OR MISPRESCRIBING DRUGS
NOTES: INAPPROPRIATE PRESCRIBING PRACTICES.

CAESAR, RICHARD IRWIN MD, LICENSE NUMBER 0012921, OF PORTLAND, OR, WAS DISCIPLINED BY OREGON ON FEBRUARY 6, 1995.
DISCIPLINARY ACTION: LICENSE SUSPENSION
OFFENSE: SUBSTANCE ABUSE
NOTES: HABITUAL OR EXCESSIVE USE OF DRUGS OR CONTROLLED SUBSTANCES.

CAESAR, RICHARD IRWIN MD, LICENSE NUMBER 0012921, OF PORTLAND, OR, WAS DISCIPLINED BY OREGON ON APRIL 13, 1995.
DISCIPLINARY ACTION: 120-MONTH PROBATION
OFFENSE: SUBSTANCE ABUSE

CAMPBELL, ROBERT PERRY MD, LICENSE NUMBER 0010884, OF PORTLAND, OR, WAS DISCIPLINED BY OREGON ON JANUARY 11, 1990.
DISCIPLINARY ACTION: 120-MONTH PROBATION
NOTES: NO LONGER ON PROBATION AS OF 7/27/92.

CARLSTROM, CHARLES H DO OF 14300 SE BAUMBACK RD, SANDY, OR, WAS DISCIPLINED BY DEA ON JULY 31, 1989.
DISCIPLINARY ACTION: RESTRICTION PLACED ON CONTROLLED SUBSTANCE LICENSE
OFFENSE: OVERPRESCRIBING OR MISPRESCRIBING DRUGS
NOTES: PRESCRIBED EXCESSIVE AMOUNTS OF SCHEDULE II SUBSTANCES.

CARLSTROM, CHARLES H DO OF 14300 SE BAUMBACK RD BOX 309, SANDY, OR, WAS DISCIPLINED BY DEA ON AUGUST 10, 1992.
DISCIPLINARY ACTION: RESTRICTION PLACED ON CONTROLLED SUBSTANCE LICENSE
NOTES: OREGON MEDICAL BOARD REQUESTED REVIEW OF HIS RECENT PURCHASES OF DEMEROL AND MORPHINE. SURRENDER OF DEA SCHEDULE II PRIVILEGES.

CARTER, JOHN L MD, LICENSE NUMBER 0008759, OF EUGENE, OR, WAS DISCIPLINED BY WASHINGTON ON JANUARY 27, 1995.
DISCIPLINARY ACTION: FINE
OFFENSE: DISCIPLINARY ACTION BY ANOTHER STATE OR AGENCY
NOTES: CONDITIONS PLACED ON LICENSE IN OREGON; AGREED TO COMPLY WITH THESE CONDITIONS AND APPEAR BEFORE THE BOARD PRIOR TO PRACTICE IN WASHINGTON. $100 FINE.

CARTER, JOHN LINUS MD, LICENSE NUMBER MD06964, OF EUGENE, OR, WAS DISCIPLINED BY OREGON ON JULY 17, 1993.
DISCIPLINARY ACTION: PROBATION; FINE
NOTES: $5,000 FINE.

CARTER, JOHN LINUS MD, LICENSE NUMBER MD06964, OF EUGENE, OR, WAS DISCIPLINED BY OREGON ON SEPTEMBER 15, 1993.
DISCIPLINARY ACTION: 2-MONTH LICENSE SUSPENSION

CASSIM, MUTHALIB M MD, LICENSE NUMBER MD11038, OF DALLAS, OR, WAS DISCIPLINED BY OREGON ON SEPTEMBER 12, 1987.
DISCIPLINARY ACTION: RESTRICTION PLACED ON LICENSE
NOTES: VOLUNTARY LIMITATION, NO ANTI-NEOPLASTIC MEDICINE

CHOONG, STEPHEN KHONG MING MD, LICENSE NUMBER 0010395, OF GRESHAM, OR, WAS DISCIPLINED BY OREGON ON AUGUST 24, 1990.
DISCIPLINARY ACTION: REPRIMAND

CLELAND, JOHN EASTMURE MD, LICENSE NUMBER 0005622, OF OREGON CITY, OR, WAS DISCIPLINED BY OREGON ON JANUARY 10, 1991.
DISCIPLINARY ACTION: RESTRICTION PLACED ON LICENSE; REQUIRED TO TAKE ADDITIONAL MEDICAL EDUCATION
OFFENSE: SUBSTANDARD CARE, INCOMPETENCE, OR NEGLIGENCE
NOTES: ALLEGED INAPPROPRIATE CARE/INCOMPETENCE. AGREED SETTLEMENT NOT TO PERFORM OBSTETRICS UNTIL HE PASSES A REFRESHER COURSE AND PASSES ORAL EXAM IN OBSTETRICS.

CLUNES, LINDSAY C DO, DATE OF BIRTH AUGUST 9, 1954, OF 2810 SW DEARMOND DRIVE, CORVALLIS, OR, WAS DISCIPLINED BY MEDICARE ON SEPTEMBER 10, 1996.
DISCIPLINARY ACTION: EXCLUSION FROM THE MEDICARE AND/OR MEDICAID PROGRAMS
OFFENSE: FAILURE TO COMPLY WITH A PROFESSIONAL RULE
NOTES: DEFAULTED ON PUBLIC HEALTH SERVICE EDUCATION LOAN.

COLASURDO, SUSAN GROVER MD, LICENSE NUMBER MD14419, OF EUGENE, OR, WAS DISCIPLINED BY OREGON ON OCTOBER 21, 1993.

- OREGON -

DISCIPLINARY ACTION: FINE; REPRIMAND
NOTES: $1,000 FINE.

CONRAD, ARTHUR KELLY JR MD, LICENSE NUMBER 0014553, OF BEND, OR, WAS DISCIPLINED BY OREGON ON NOVEMBER 24, 1995.
DISCIPLINARY ACTION: 120-MONTH PROBATION; FINE
NOTES: $5,000 FINE AS CONDITION OF STIPULATED PROBATION.

COOK, TED ALLEN MD, LICENSE NUMBER 0013047, OF PORTLAND, OR, WAS DISCIPLINED BY OREGON ON AUGUST 10, 1990.
DISCIPLINARY ACTION: 3-MONTH PROBATION; FINE
NOTES: NO LONGER LISTED ON PROBATION AS OF 2/16/96.

COOK, TED ALLEN MD, LICENSE NUMBER 00D1589, OF PORTLAND, OR, WAS DISCIPLINED BY TEXAS ON APRIL 20, 1991.
DISCIPLINARY ACTION: PROBATION
OFFENSE: DISCIPLINARY ACTION BY ANOTHER STATE OR AGENCY
NOTES: DISCIPLINARY ACTION TAKEN BY ANOTHER STATE FOR UNPROFESSIONAL CONDUCT. MUST COMPLY WITH ALL TERMS OF OREGON PROBATION; PRIOR TO PRACTICING IN TEXAS, MUST APPEAR BEFORE BOARD FOR APPROVAL. ON 10/5/96 PROBATION TERMINATED.

COULTER, JAMES A MD, LICENSE NUMBER MD09920, OF TURNER, OR, WAS DISCIPLINED BY OREGON ON JANUARY 8, 1987.
DISCIPLINARY ACTION: RESTRICTION PLACED ON LICENSE
NOTES: PRACTICE ONLY IN OFFICE SETTING

COUROGEN, WILLIAM PETER MD, LICENSE NUMBER 0008387, OF PORTLAND, OR, WAS DISCIPLINED BY OREGON ON JANUARY 10, 1991.
DISCIPLINARY ACTION: FINE; REPRIMAND
OFFENSE: PROFESSIONAL MISCONDUCT
NOTES: ALLEGED VIOLATION OF STATE/FEDERAL STATUTES.

CREGG, HUGH ANTHONY MD, LICENSE NUMBER MD17611, OF PORT ANGELES, OR, WAS DISCIPLINED BY OREGON ON DECEMBER 26, 1991.
DISCIPLINARY ACTION: RESTRICTION PLACED ON LICENSE

DEFRANK, LOUIS PAUL MD, LICENSE NUMBER MD06227, OF EUGENE, OR, WAS DISCIPLINED BY OREGON ON APRIL 9, 1988.
DISCIPLINARY ACTION: 120-MONTH PROBATION
NOTES: ON 10/10/91 TERMINATION OF PROBATION OR VOLUNTARY LIMITATION.

DENNIS, LAWRENCE A DO OF 621 S.E. MANCHESTER PLACE, PORTLAND, OR, WAS DISCIPLINED BY DEA ON DECEMBER 29, 1989.
DISCIPLINARY ACTION: RESTRICTION PLACED ON CONTROLLED SUBSTANCE LICENSE
OFFENSE: OVERPRESCRIBING OR MISPRESCRIBING DRUGS
NOTES: INAPPROPRIATE PRESCRIBING PRACTICES

DEWITT, PETER MD, LICENSE NUMBER 0004614, OF PORTLAND, OR, WAS DISCIPLINED BY OREGON ON JULY 5, 1990.
DISCIPLINARY ACTION: RESTRICTION PLACED ON CONTROLLED SUBSTANCE LICENSE
NOTES: MUST PROVIDE TRIPLICATE COPIES OF CONTROLLED SUBSTANCE PRESCRIPTIONS. NO LONGER RESTRICTED AS OF 1/28/92.

DIXON, HENRY HADLEY JR MD, LICENSE NUMBER MD05351, OF PORTLAND, OR, WAS DISCIPLINED BY OREGON ON JULY 13, 1989.
DISCIPLINARY ACTION: RESTRICTION PLACED ON CONTROLLED SUBSTANCE LICENSE
NOTES: MAY NOT PRESCRIBE SCHEDULE II OR III DRUGS. AS OF 5/25/94 NO LONGER LISTED AS RESTRICTED.

DOUGHTON, ROBERT P MD, LICENSE NUMBER MD06350, OF LAKE OSWEGO, OR, WAS DISCIPLINED BY OREGON ON NOVEMBER 17, 1987.
DISCIPLINARY ACTION: RESTRICTION PLACED ON LICENSE
NOTES: NO OBSTETRICS PRACTICE. NO LONGER LISTED AS RESTRICTED AS OF 5/8/96.

DOWSETT, PETER JOHN MD, LICENSE NUMBER MD07713, OF PORTLAND, OR, WAS DISCIPLINED BY OREGON ON JANUARY 15, 1993.
DISCIPLINARY ACTION: 120-MONTH PROBATION
NOTES: NO LONGER LISTED ON PROBATION AS OF 7/31/95.

DUNCAN, DAVID GALE MD OF 2400 N.E. ALBERTA, PORTLAND, OR, WAS DISCIPLINED BY DEA ON MAY 10, 1989.
DISCIPLINARY ACTION: RESTRICTION PLACED ON CONTROLLED SUBSTANCE LICENSE
OFFENSE: OVERPRESCRIBING OR MISPRESCRIBING DRUGS
NOTES: INAPPROPRIATE PRESCRIBING PRACTICES

DUNCAN, IAN ROBERT DO, LICENSE NUMBER DO10893, OF ATLANTA, GA, WAS DISCIPLINED BY OREGON ON DECEMBER 29, 1993.
DISCIPLINARY ACTION: 3-MONTH LICENSE SUSPENSION; PROBATION
NOTES: ALSO FINE; NO FEMALE PATIENTS. AS OF 8/18/94 MAY DIAGNOSE AND TREAT FEMALES REPENTANCE 65 WITH FEMALE CHAPERONE.

DYE, ROBERT A MD, LICENSE NUMBER 0016904, OF MESA, AZ, WAS DISCIPLINED BY ARIZONA ON JANUARY 20, 1993.
NOTES: FAILED THE OREGON SPEX EXAM. SHALL NOT PRACTICE MEDICINE IN ARIZONA UNTIL HE HAS TAKEN AND PASSED THE SPEX EXAM AND MET WITH THE BOARD.

DYE, ROBERT ARTHUR MD, LICENSE NUMBER MD16553, OF PARADISE VALLEY, OR, WAS DISCIPLINED BY OREGON ON MAY 16, 1990.
DISCIPLINARY ACTION: RESTRICTION PLACED ON LICENSE
NOTES: VOLUNTARY LIMITATION. AS OF 3/10/94 NO LONGER LISTED AS RESTRICTED.

EICKELBERG, STEVEN J MD, LICENSE NUMBER MD14222, OF TIGARD, OR, WAS DISCIPLINED BY OREGON ON JANUARY 7, 1988.
DISCIPLINARY ACTION: 120-MONTH PROBATION; 120-MONTH RESTRICTION PLACED ON CONTROLLED SUBSTANCE LICENSE
NOTES: RESTRICTION ON PRESCRIBING SCHEDULE II, III, IV OR V DRUGS. NO LONGER LISTED AS ON PROBATION AS OF 8/12/96.

EICKELBERG, STEVEN J MD OF 18270 UPPER MIDHILL DRIVE, WEST LINN, OR, WAS DISCIPLINED BY DEA ON AUGUST 2, 1989.
DISCIPLINARY ACTION: RESTRICTION PLACED ON CONTROLLED SUBSTANCE LICENSE
OFFENSE: OVERPRESCRIBING OR MISPRESCRIBING DRUGS
NOTES: INAPPROPRIATE PRESCRIBING PRACTICES

ELDER, TERRANCE O'DELL MD, LICENSE NUMBER MD18077, OF MYRTLE CREEK, OR, WAS DISCIPLINED BY OREGON ON JANUARY 14, 1993.
DISCIPLINARY ACTION: 132-MONTH PROBATION
NOTES: NO LONGER LISTED ON PROBATION AS OF 7/31/95.

ELDER, TERRANCE O'DELL MD, DATE OF BIRTH JANUARY 17, 1955, LICENSE NUMBER 0052509, OF 111 NORTON LANE, MYRTLE CREEK, OR, WAS DISCIPLINED BY NEW JERSEY ON JUNE 8, 1994.
DISCIPLINARY ACTION: 120-MONTH PROBATION
OFFENSE: SUBSTANCE ABUSE
NOTES: REVOCATION STAYED. PROBATION CONCURRENT WITH SUSPENSION IN OREGON. SHALL PROVIDE PROOF OF HIS COMPLIANCE WITH THE REQUIREMENTS OF THE OREGON BOARD ORDER AND APPEAR FOR A STATUS CONFERENCE WITH A COMMITTEE OF THE BOARD, PRIOR TO COMMENCING PRACTICE IN NEW JERSEY.

ELLIOTT, ROBERT MICHAEL MD, LICENSE NUMBER MD18653, OF

- OREGON -

PORTLAND, OR, WAS DISCIPLINED BY OREGON ON DECEMBER 27, 1993.
DISCIPLINARY ACTION: RESTRICTION PLACED ON LICENSE
NOTES: LIMITED TO HAIR TRANSPLANT AND MALE PATTERN BALDNESS.

ELLISON, JOHN HAROLD MD, LICENSE NUMBER 0006289, OF PORTLAND, OR, WAS DISCIPLINED BY OREGON ON OCTOBER 19, 1995.
DISCIPLINARY ACTION: 120-MONTH PROBATION

ELLISON, JOHN HAROLD MD, LICENSE NUMBER 0006289, OF HILLSBORO, OR, WAS DISCIPLINED BY OREGON ON JULY 8, 1996.
DISCIPLINARY ACTION: SURRENDER OF LICENSE
NOTES: VOLUNTARY RETIREMENT IN LIEU OF DISCIPLINARY ACTION.

EMETAROM, NNAMDI BENEDICT MD, LICENSE NUMBER 0009374, OF CLACKAMAS, OR, WAS DISCIPLINED BY OREGON ON MARCH 27, 1996.
DISCIPLINARY ACTION: 36-MONTH PROBATION; REQUIRED TO TAKE ADDITIONAL MEDICAL EDUCATION
NOTES: CONTINUING MEDICAL EDUCATION, SEMI-ANNUAL REPORTS FROM SUPERVISING PHYSICIAN; AND BIANNUAL INTERVIEWS BEFORE THE BOARD.

ERICKSON, KENNETH REED MD, LICENSE NUMBER MD13119, OF LAKE OSWEGO, OR, WAS DISCIPLINED BY OREGON ON APRIL 15, 1993.
DISCIPLINARY ACTION: RESTRICTION PLACED ON LICENSE
NOTES: VOLUNTARY LIMITATION.

EUBANKS, JAMES BRUCE DO, LICENSE NUMBER DO16596, OF PORTLAND, OR, WAS DISCIPLINED BY OREGON ON JANUARY 14, 1993.
DISCIPLINARY ACTION: 120-MONTH PROBATION; FINE
NOTES: $1,000 FINE.

EUBANKS, WILLIAM JAMES JR DO, LICENSE NUMBER DO12704, OF PORTLAND, OR, WAS DISCIPLINED BY OREGON ON JANUARY 14, 1993.
DISCIPLINARY ACTION: 120-MONTH PROBATION
NOTES: ON 7/19/94 PROBATION RESTARTED WITH NEW TERMS. NO LONGER LISTED ON PROBATION AS OF 5/8/96.

EUBANKS, WILLIAM JAMES JR DO, LICENSE NUMBER DO12704, OF PORTLAND, OR, WAS DISCIPLINED BY OREGON ON DECEMBER 2, 1993.
DISCIPLINARY ACTION: EMERGENCY SUSPENSION

EVERHART, FRANCIS JAMES MD, LICENSE NUMBER 0011936, OF HERMISTON, OR, WAS DISCIPLINED BY OREGON ON MAY 5, 1989.
DISCIPLINARY ACTION: RESTRICTION PLACED ON LICENSE
NOTES: PSYCHIATRIC CARE REQUIRED. NO LONGER RESTRICTED AS OF 1/28/92.

FABER, CLINTON MD, LICENSE NUMBER MD07900, OF REEDSPORT, OR, WAS DISCIPLINED BY OREGON ON APRIL 7, 1988.
DISCIPLINARY ACTION: RESTRICTION PLACED ON CONTROLLED SUBSTANCE LICENSE
NOTES: MAY NOT PRESCRIBE SCHEDULE II DRUGS. MUST PROVIDE TRIPLICATE COPIES OF PRESCRIPTIONS FOR STADOL AND NUBAIN, AND SCHEDULE III, IV AND V DRUGS. AS OF 2/22/95 NO LONGER LISTED AS ON RESTRICTION.

FAULK, CHARLES DR WAS DISCIPLINED BY OREGON ON JANUARY 10, 1991.
OFFENSE: SUBSTANCE ABUSE
NOTES: ALLEGED PERSONAL SUBSTANCE ABUSE. TERMINATION OF PROBATION OR VOLUNTARY LIMITATION.

FEENEY, ROBERT MD OF 825 WEST FRANCIS STREET, ROSEBURG, OR, WAS DISCIPLINED BY DEA ON MAY 8, 1989.
DISCIPLINARY ACTION: SURRENDER OF CONTROLLED SUBSTANCE LICENSE
OFFENSE: DISCIPLINARY ACTION BY ANOTHER STATE OR AGENCY
NOTES: ACTION BASED ON STATE REVOCATION FOR INCOMPETENCY TO PRACTICE MEDICINE.

FELDER, JERALD B MD, LICENSE NUMBER 0C25390, OF PENDLETON, OR, WAS DISCIPLINED BY CALIFORNIA ON JANUARY 2, 1996.
DISCIPLINARY ACTION: 60-MONTH PROBATION
OFFENSE: DISCIPLINARY ACTION BY ANOTHER STATE OR AGENCY
NOTES: SUPPLEMENTAL PRIVILEGES IN ENDOSCOPIC SINUS SURGERY REVOKED WHILE SERVING IN THE U.S. NAVY. SUSPENSION, STAYED.

FORTNER, LUCILLE LANIER MD, LICENSE NUMBER MD03688, OF TURNER, OR, WAS DISCIPLINED BY OREGON ON JANUARY 6, 1994.
DISCIPLINARY ACTION: EMERGENCY SUSPENSION
NOTES: NO LONGER LISTED ON SUSPENSION ON 8/18/94.

FULLER, STEPHEN MD, LICENSE NUMBER MD15877, OF LAKE OSWEGO, OR, WAS DISCIPLINED BY OREGON ON OCTOBER 12, 1988.
DISCIPLINARY ACTION: RESTRICTION PLACED ON LICENSE
NOTES: NO SURGERY. NO LONGER RESTRICTED AS OF FEBRUARY 8, 1990

GAMBEE, JOHN E MD OF 66 CLUB ROAD #140, EUGENE, OR, WAS DISCIPLINED BY DEA ON MARCH 24, 1995.
DISCIPLINARY ACTION: SURRENDER OF CONTROLLED SUBSTANCE LICENSE
OFFENSE: DISCIPLINARY ACTION BY ANOTHER STATE OR AGENCY
NOTES: STATE BOARD.

GAMBEE, JOHN EDWIN MD, LICENSE NUMBER MD09526, OF EUGENE, OR, WAS DISCIPLINED BY OREGON ON DECEMBER 31, 1994.
DISCIPLINARY ACTION: LICENSE REVOCATION
OFFENSE: PROFESSIONAL MISCONDUCT

GARCIA, RANDAL LEE MD, LICENSE NUMBER MD13361, OF BROOKINGS, OR, WAS DISCIPLINED BY OREGON ON JULY 13, 1988.
DISCIPLINARY ACTION: 120-MONTH PROBATION; REQUIRED TO TAKE ADDITIONAL MEDICAL EDUCATION
NOTES: MUST PROVIDE TRIPLICATE COPIES OF CONTROLLED SUBSTANCE PRESCRIPTIONS. MUST ATTEND COURSES ON PROPER PRESCRIBING OF CONTROLLED SUBSTANCES

GARCIA, RANDAL LEE MD, LICENSE NUMBER G044501, OF BROOKINGS, OR, WAS DISCIPLINED BY CALIFORNIA ON JANUARY 30, 1991.
DISCIPLINARY ACTION: LICENSE REVOCATION
OFFENSE: DISCIPLINARY ACTION BY ANOTHER STATE OR AGENCY
NOTES: DISCIPLINED BY OREGON BOARD FOR EXCESSIVE USE OF ULTRASOUND, UNNECESSARY LAB AND X-RAY WORK, AND INAPPROPRIATE PRESCRIBING.

GARCIA, RANDAL LEE MD OF 446 OAK STREET PO BOX 1119, BROOKINGS, OR, WAS DISCIPLINED BY DEA ON AUGUST 28, 1993.
DISCIPLINARY ACTION: RESTRICTION PLACED ON CONTROLLED SUBSTANCE LICENSE
OFFENSE: DISCIPLINARY ACTION BY ANOTHER STATE OR AGENCY
NOTES: ON PROBATION AND PRESCRIPTION RESTRICTION FOR SCHEDULES III, IV, V PER OREGON MEDICAL BOARD ORDER JUNE/JULY 1989. 1990 DEA RENEWAL LIABILITY QUESTIONS ANSWERED FALSELY.

GARNER, FRANK A MD OF 1561 S.W. BIRDIE DRIVE, CORVALLIS, OR, WAS DISCIPLINED BY DEA ON OCTOBER 31, 1994.
DISCIPLINARY ACTION: RESTRICTION PLACED ON CONTROLLED

- OREGON -

SUBSTANCE LICENSE
OFFENSE: OVERPRESCRIBING OR MISPRESCRIBING DRUGS
NOTES: QUESTIONABLE PRESCRIBING PRACTICES.

GARNER, FRANK A MD OF SANDY, UT, WAS DISCIPLINED BY UTAH ON AUGUST 1, 1996.
OFFENSE: DISCIPLINARY ACTION BY ANOTHER STATE OR AGENCY
NOTES: ACTION IN OREGON. UTAH SUSPENSION STAYED AS LONG AS HE REMAINS IN FULL COMPLIANCE WITH THE TERMS AND CONDITIONS OF HIS OREGON PROBATION.

GARNER, FRANK ALFRED MD, LICENSE NUMBER 0014325, OF CORVALLIS, OR, WAS DISCIPLINED BY OREGON ON JULY 19, 1990.
DISCIPLINARY ACTION: RESTRICTION PLACED ON CONTROLLED SUBSTANCE LICENSE
NOTES: VOLUNTARY LIMITATION. NO SCHEDULE II OR III PRESCRIBING EXCEPT INSTITUTIONAL PATIENTS.

GARNER, FRANK ALFRED MD, LICENSE NUMBER MD14325, OF CORVALLIS, OR, WAS DISCIPLINED BY OREGON ON APRIL 15, 1994.
DISCIPLINARY ACTION: 120-MONTH PROBATION; RESTRICTION PLACED ON LICENSE
NOTES: LIMITED TO PSYCHIATRY IN APPROVED SETTING; 50 HOURS OF CONTINUING MEDICAL EDUCATION; NO PSYCHOPHARMOCOLOGICAL DRUGS WITHOUT APPROVAL.

GERRITZ, GLENN A JR MD OF 4677 CARNES ROAD, ROSEBURG, OR, WAS DISCIPLINED BY DEA ON SEPTEMBER 27, 1994.
DISCIPLINARY ACTION: RESTRICTION PLACED ON CONTROLLED SUBSTANCE LICENSE
OFFENSE: DISCIPLINARY ACTION BY ANOTHER STATE OR AGENCY
NOTES: STATE BOARD.

GERRITZ, GLENN ALBERT JR MD, LICENSE NUMBER 0009686, OF GRAND RONDE, OR, WAS DISCIPLINED BY OREGON ON JANUARY 9, 1992.
DISCIPLINARY ACTION: 36-MONTH RESTRICTION PLACED ON CONTROLLED SUBSTANCE LICENSE
NOTES: TRIPLICATE COPIES OF PRESCRIPTIONS FOR SCHEDULE II, III AND IV DRUGS. NO LONGER LISTED AS RESTRICTED AS OF 5/16/95.

GIROD, JOHN COOPER MD OF SALEM, OR, WAS DISCIPLINED BY VERMONT ON MARCH 9, 1987.
NOTES: MUST APPEAR BEFORE THE BOARD BEFORE REACTIVATING INACTIVE LICENSE

GIROD, JOHN COOPER MD, LICENSE NUMBER 0012930, OF SALEM, OR, WAS DISCIPLINED BY OREGON ON JANUARY 12, 1989.
DISCIPLINARY ACTION: RESTRICTION PLACED ON CONTROLLED SUBSTANCE LICENSE
NOTES: MUST PROVIDE TRIPLICATE COPIES OF CONTROLLED SUBSTANCE PRESCRIPTIONS. NO LONGER RESTRICTED AS OF 7/27/92.

GOWEN, DALE RUSSELL MD, LICENSE NUMBER 0013553, OF TILLAMOOK, OR, WAS DISCIPLINED BY OREGON ON AUGUST 18, 1989.
DISCIPLINARY ACTION: RESTRICTION PLACED ON LICENSE
NOTES: VOLUNTARY LIMITATION; NO LONGER RESTRICTED AS OF 2/8/90.

GOWEN, DALE RUSSELL MD, LICENSE NUMBER 0013553, OF HOOD RIVER, OR, WAS DISCIPLINED BY OREGON ON JUNE 13, 1990.
DISCIPLINARY ACTION: RESTRICTION PLACED ON LICENSE
NOTES: VOLUNTARY LIMITATION; NO SURGERY/STEROIDS. NO LONGER LISTED AS RESTRICTED AS OF 5/8/96.

GREWE, RAY VICTOR MD, LICENSE NUMBER 0004216, OF PORTLAND, OR, WAS DISCIPLINED BY OREGON ON NOVEMBER 5, 1990.
DISCIPLINARY ACTION: RESTRICTION PLACED ON CONTROLLED SUBSTANCE LICENSE
NOTES: MUST PROVIDE TRIPLICATE COPIES OF CONTROLLED SUBSTANCE PRESCRIPTIONS. NO LONGER RESTRICTED AS OF 1/28/92.

GRIFFITH, WARREN G DO, LICENSE NUMBER 0134211, OF OAKRIDGE, OR, WAS DISCIPLINED BY NEW YORK ON JULY 22, 1987.
DISCIPLINARY ACTION: REPRIMAND

GRIMWOOD, DAVID DR WAS DISCIPLINED BY OREGON ON MAY 1, 1991.
DISCIPLINARY ACTION: SURRENDER OF LICENSE
OFFENSE: SUBSTANDARD CARE, INCOMPETENCE, OR NEGLIGENCE
NOTES: ALLEGED INAPPROPRIATE CARE/INCOMPETENCE. RETIRE/SURRENDER IN LIEU OF DISCIPLINARY ACTION.

GRITZKA, THOMAS L MD, LICENSE NUMBER MD08117, OF PORTLAND, OR, WAS DISCIPLINED BY OREGON ON JULY 13, 1988.
DISCIPLINARY ACTION: 120-MONTH PROBATION
NOTES: ON 7/11/91 TERMINATION OF PROBATION OR VOLUNTARY LIMITATION.

GRUBER, MATTHEW MD, LICENSE NUMBER MD04652, OF SALEM, OR, WAS DISCIPLINED BY OREGON ON OCTOBER 13, 1994.
DISCIPLINARY ACTION: RESTRICTION PLACED ON LICENSE; MONITORING OF PHYSICIAN
NOTES: NO PEDIATRICS, OBSTETRICS, MAJOR SURGERY; CLINIC PRACTICE UNDER SUPERVISION; NO HOSPITAL PATIENTS. NO LONGER LISTED AS RESTRICTED AS OF 2/22/95.

HAEBERLIN, JAMES RICHARD MD, LICENSE NUMBER 0011816, OF CORVALLIS, OR, WAS DISCIPLINED BY OREGON ON NOVEMBER 1, 1991.
DISCIPLINARY ACTION: REPRIMAND
OFFENSE: SUBSTANDARD CARE, INCOMPETENCE, OR NEGLIGENCE
NOTES: ALLEGED INAPPROPRIATE CARE/INCOMPETENCE.

HALVERSON, HAROLD W MD, LICENSE NUMBER MD04437, OF PORTLAND, OR, WAS DISCIPLINED BY OREGON ON JANUARY 22, 1987.
DISCIPLINARY ACTION: 120-MONTH PROBATION; 120-MONTH RESTRICTION PLACED ON CONTROLLED SUBSTANCE LICENSE
NOTES: RESTRICTION ON PRESCRIBING SCHEDULE II AND III DRUGS. NO LONGER ON PROBATION AS OF 11/15/89

HARRIS, HARRY DR WAS DISCIPLINED BY OREGON ON APRIL 16, 1991.
DISCIPLINARY ACTION: SURRENDER OF LICENSE
OFFENSE: SUBSTANDARD CARE, INCOMPETENCE, OR NEGLIGENCE
NOTES: ALLEGED INAPPROPRIATE CARE/INCOMPETENCE. RETIRE/SURRENDER IN LIEU OF DISCIPLINARY ACTION.

HARRIS, HENRY FREEMAN MD OF 4309 OAKRIDGE ROAD, LAKE OSWEGO, OR, WAS DISCIPLINED BY DEA ON SEPTEMBER 29, 1989.
DISCIPLINARY ACTION: RESTRICTION PLACED ON CONTROLLED SUBSTANCE LICENSE
OFFENSE: OVERPRESCRIBING OR MISPRESCRIBING DRUGS
NOTES: DEA RESTRICTION DUE TO INAPPROPRIATE PRESCRIBING PRACTICES

HARTMANN, RONALD ALLAN MD, LICENSE NUMBER 0008811, OF SWEET HOME, OR, WAS DISCIPLINED BY OREGON ON APRIL 7, 1989.
DISCIPLINARY ACTION: RESTRICTION PLACED ON CONTROLLED SUBSTANCE LICENSE
NOTES: MUST PROVIDE TRIPLICATE COPIES OF CONTROLLED SUBSTANCE PRESCRIPTIONS. NO LONGER RESTRICTED AS OF 1/28/92.

HAYES, DANIEL PETER MD, LICENSE NUMBER MD08354, OF

- OREGON -

TUALATIN, OR, WAS DISCIPLINED BY OREGON ON FEBRUARY 26, 1994.
DISCIPLINARY ACTION: LICENSE REVOCATION

HAYES, DANIEL PETER MD, DATE OF BIRTH DECEMBER 2, 1943, OF 18604 UPPER MIDHILL ROAD, WEST LINN, OR, WAS DISCIPLINED BY NORTH DAKOTA ON JULY 26, 1996.
DISCIPLINARY ACTION: DENIAL OF NEW LICENSE
OFFENSE: DISCIPLINARY ACTION BY ANOTHER STATE OR AGENCY
NOTES: ACTION IN OREGON FOR ENGAGING IN A SEXUAL RELATIONSHIP WITH A NUMBER OF HIS PATIENTS.

HAYES, JEFFREY BENTON MD, LICENSE NUMBER MD12570, OF SCAPPOOSE, OR, WAS DISCIPLINED BY OREGON ON OCTOBER 8, 1992.
DISCIPLINARY ACTION: PROBATION; FINE
NOTES: SCHEDULES II AND III PRESCRIBING PRIVILEGES RESTRICTED.

HAYES, JEFFREY BENTON MD, LICENSE NUMBER MD12570, OF SCAPPOOSE, OR, WAS DISCIPLINED BY OREGON ON MAY 17, 1994.
DISCIPLINARY ACTION: LICENSE SUSPENSION
OFFENSE: FAILURE TO COMPLY WITH A PREVIOUS BOARD ORDER
NOTES: VIOLATED PROBATION.

HAYES, JEFFREY BENTON MD, LICENSE NUMBER 0012570, OF PORTLAND, OR, WAS DISCIPLINED BY OREGON ON APRIL 25, 1995.
DISCIPLINARY ACTION: PROBATION; RESTRICTION PLACED ON CONTROLLED SUBSTANCE LICENSE
OFFENSE: FAILURE TO COMPLY WITH A PREVIOUS BOARD ORDER
NOTES: SUBSTANCE ABUSE. VIOLATION OF PROBATION. CANNOT PRESCRIBE SCHEDULE II, III OR IV CONTROLLED SUBSTANCES EXCEPT FOR HOSPITAL PATIENTS.

HAYES, JEFFREY BENTON MD OF 33721 E COLUMBIA AVE PO BOX 979, SCAPPOOSE, OR, WAS DISCIPLINED BY DEA ON JUNE 28, 1995.
DISCIPLINARY ACTION: SURRENDER OF CONTROLLED SUBSTANCE LICENSE
NOTES: IN LIEU OF ORDER TO SHOW CAUSE.

HENRY, THOMAS PAUL MD, LICENSE NUMBER MD11446, OF PORTLAND, OR, WAS DISCIPLINED BY OREGON ON AUGUST 4, 1989.
DISCIPLINARY ACTION: 121-MONTH PROBATION
NOTES: NO LONGER LISTED ON PROBATION AS OF 1/21/93.

HIKES, CHARLES E III MD WAS DISCIPLINED BY WASHINGTON ON AUGUST 20, 1993.
DISCIPLINARY ACTION: RESTRICTION PLACED ON LICENSE
OFFENSE: DISCIPLINARY ACTION BY ANOTHER STATE OR AGENCY
NOTES: ON 7/17/91 OREGON LICENSE RESTRICTED FOR 10 YEARS. SHALL COMPLY WITH THE TERMS, CONDITIONS, AND RESTRICTIONS IMPOSED ON HIS MEDICAL LICENSE IN OREGON; SHALL PETITION BOARD IN WRITING AND APPEAR BEFORE THE BOARD IF HE WISHES TO PRACTICE IN WASHINGTON.

HIKES, CHARLES E III MD OF 2450 SE TWELFTH STREET, SALEM, OR, WAS DISCIPLINED BY DEA ON NOVEMBER 20, 1993.
DISCIPLINARY ACTION: RESTRICTION PLACED ON CONTROLLED SUBSTANCE LICENSE
OFFENSE: DISCIPLINARY ACTION BY ANOTHER STATE OR AGENCY
NOTES: OREGON MEDICAL BOARD PLACED MEDICAL LICENSE ON PROBATION 07/17/91 TO CONTINUE UNTIL 2001.

HIKES, CHARLES E MD OF 2450 SOUTH EAST 12TH STREET, SALEM, OR, WAS DISCIPLINED BY DEA ON MAY 10, 1994.
DISCIPLINARY ACTION: RESTRICTION PLACED ON CONTROLLED SUBSTANCE LICENSE
OFFENSE: DISCIPLINARY ACTION BY ANOTHER STATE OR AGENCY
NOTES: STATE BOARD.

HIKES, CHARLES EDWARD III MD, LICENSE NUMBER 0009100, OF SALEM, OR, WAS DISCIPLINED BY OREGON ON JULY 17, 1991.
DISCIPLINARY ACTION: 120-MONTH PROBATION; FINE
OFFENSE: PROFESSIONAL MISCONDUCT
NOTES: FINE PAYABLE IN 90 DAYS; REVOCATION STAYED.

HIKES, CHARLES EDWARD III MD, LICENSE NUMBER 0009100, OF SALEM, OR, WAS DISCIPLINED BY OREGON ON AUGUST 15, 1991.
DISCIPLINARY ACTION: 3-MONTH LICENSE SUSPENSION
OFFENSE: SUBSTANDARD CARE, INCOMPETENCE, OR NEGLIGENCE
NOTES: ALLEGED INAPPROPRIATE CARE/INCOMPETENCE.

HILL, ROBERT D MD, LICENSE NUMBER 00C6143, OF ODESSA, TX, WAS DISCIPLINED BY TEXAS ON JANUARY 6, 1995.
DISCIPLINARY ACTION: 60-MONTH PROBATION; REQUIRED TO TAKE ADDITIONAL MEDICAL EDUCATION
OFFENSE: LOSS OR RESTRICTION OF HOSPITAL PRIVILEGES
NOTES: ON 4/7/92 A HOSPITAL SUMMARILY SUSPENDED HIS PRIVILEGES DUE TO THE FOLLOWING: HE EXAMINED A NEWBORN INFANT WHO HIS NOTES REFLECTED WAS NORMAL, A POOR EATER, AND STATED "WATCH"; NURSES' NOTES REFLECT THE BABY WAS SPITTING UP EMESIS, REFUSING TO NURSE, WAS NOT STOOLING AND WAS NOT AROUSABLE; IN SPITE OF THIS DR. HILL DISCHARGED PATIENT AND ADVISED PARENTS TO CALL IF EATING DID NOT IMPROVE; THEY DID CALL LATER THAT DAY AND HE REFUSED TO SEE THE CHILD AS HE BELIEVED THE PROBLEM WOULD RESOLVE ITSELF; ANOTHER PHYSICIAN HOSPITALIZED THE INFANT THAT SAME DAY; THE INFANT WAS DIAGNOSED WITH CYSTIC FIBROSIS. HE RESIGNED FROM THE HOSPITAL AFTER BEING ADVISED THAT THE HOSPITAL'S EXECUTIVE COMMITTEE WOULD RECOMMEND A PERMANENT SUSPENSION. SUSPENSION STAYED. CONDITIONS OF PROBATION: SHALL HAVE A BOARD-APPROVED MONITORING PHYSICIAN WITH MONTHLY REPORTS; SHALL ATTEND AT LEAST 50 HOURS PER YEAR OF CONTINUING MEDICAL EDUCATION; SHALL APPEAR BEFORE THE BOARD ONCE A YEAR; SHALL COOPERATE WITH THE BOARD IN VERIFYING COMPLIANCE; SHALL INFORM BOARD OF CHANGE OF ADDRESS WITHIN 10 DAYS OR IF HE LEAVES THE STATE; TIME SPENT OUT OF TEXAS DOES NOT COUNT TOWARD PROBATION. SHALL NOT SEEK MODIFICATION FOR ONE YEAR. ON 3/2/96 REQUEST TO TERMINATE ORDER DENIED BUT ORDER MODIFIED SO HE SHALL PROVIDE WRITTEN REPORTS TO STAFF WHICH REFLECT THE LEVEL OF HIS PRACTICE SKILLS FROM ALL FACILITIES WHERE HE PRACTICES UPON BOARD REQUEST IN LIEU OF PREVIOUS REQUIREMENT FOR A MONITOR; MAY REQUEST MODIFICATION EVERY SIX MONTHS. PROBATION TERMINATED ON 8/17/96.

HILL, ROBERT DIXON MD, LICENSE NUMBER MD16554, OF CRESWELL, OR, WAS DISCIPLINED BY OREGON ON NOVEMBER 1, 1993.
DISCIPLINARY ACTION: 24-MONTH RESTRICTION PLACED ON LICENSE; 24-MONTH RESTRICTION PLACED ON CONTROLLED SUBSTANCE LICENSE
NOTES: NO SCHEDULE II DRUGS EXCEPT FOR HOSPITAL PATIENTS; TRIPLICATE COPIES OF CONTROLLED SUBSTANCE PRESCRIPTIONS MUST BE PROVIDED FOR SCHEDULE III DRUGS; BOTH CONDITIONS SUBJECT TO REVIEW. VOLUNTARY LIMITATION SUBJECT TO REVIEW ON 11/1/95. NO LONGER LISTED ON PROBATION AS OF 11/27/95.

HILL, ROBERT DIXON MD, LICENSE NUMBER 0027422, OF CRESWELL, OR, WAS DISCIPLINED BY WASHINGTON ON JUNE 2, 1995.
DISCIPLINARY ACTION: RESTRICTION PLACED ON CONTROLLED SUBSTANCE LICENSE
NOTES: AGREED ORDER RESTRICTING HIS PRESCRIBING OF

- OREGON -

CONTROLLED SUBSTANCES.

HILL, ROBERT DIXON MD, LICENSE NUMBER 0G13809, OF CREWELL, OR, WAS DISCIPLINED BY CALIFORNIA ON MARCH 4, 1996.
DISCIPLINARY ACTION: LICENSE REVOCATION
OFFENSE: DISCIPLINARY ACTION BY ANOTHER STATE OR AGENCY
NOTES: ACTION IN OREGON. VOLUNTARY LIMITATION FILED LIMITING LICENSE TO PRACTICE MEDICINE WITH RESPECT TO SCHEDULES II AND III CONTROLLED SUBSTANCES. DEFAULT ACTION.

HITZ, MICHAEL E MD, LICENSE NUMBER MD16249, OF PORTLAND, OR, WAS DISCIPLINED BY OREGON ON JULY 25, 1989.
DISCIPLINARY ACTION: RESTRICTION PLACED ON LICENSE
NOTES: NO LONGER RESTRICTED AS OF 11/15/89

HUMISTON, KARL E MD, LICENSE NUMBER 0142429, OF NEW YORK, NY, WAS DISCIPLINED BY NEW YORK ON AUGUST 30, 1989.
DISCIPLINARY ACTION: LICENSE REVOCATION

HUMISTON, KARL E MD OF 15-15 HAZEN STREET, EAST ELMHURST, NY, WAS DISCIPLINED BY DEA ON FEBRUARY 26, 1990.
DISCIPLINARY ACTION: SURRENDER OF CONTROLLED SUBSTANCE LICENSE
NOTES: LICENSE REVOKED.

HUMISTON, KARL E MD, DATE OF BIRTH JUNE 14, 1930, OF PO BOX 2035, ALBANY, OR, WAS DISCIPLINED BY MEDICARE ON JUNE 26, 1991.
DISCIPLINARY ACTION: EXCLUSION FROM THE MEDICARE AND/OR MEDICAID PROGRAMS
OFFENSE: DISCIPLINARY ACTION BY ANOTHER STATE OR AGENCY
NOTES: LICENSE REVOCATION OR SUSPENSION.

HUNG, SIAN-MING MD, LICENSE NUMBER MD08062, OF PORTLAND, OR, WAS DISCIPLINED BY OREGON ON JULY 31, 1992.
DISCIPLINARY ACTION: LICENSE REVOCATION

HUNG, SIAN-MING MD, LICENSE NUMBER 0011180, OF VANCOUVER, WA, WAS DISCIPLINED BY WASHINGTON ON JANUARY 31, 1994.
DISCIPLINARY ACTION: RESTRICTION PLACED ON LICENSE
OFFENSE: PROFESSIONAL MISCONDUCT
NOTES: SHALL RETAIN A MEDICAL LICENSE BUT MUST LIMIT HIS PRACTICE TO ACUPUNCTURE. ON 12/11/95 HIS REQUEST TO MODIFY THIS ORDER WAS DENIED. ON 12/9/96 HIS REQUEST TO MODIFY ORDER GRANTED AND THE REQUIREMENT THAT HE APPEAR BEFORE BOARD ON AN ANNUAL BASIS WAS ELIMINATED.

HUNT, CLYDE ERNEST MD, LICENSE NUMBER MD10058, OF TILLAMOOK, OR, WAS DISCIPLINED BY OREGON ON JULY 9, 1987.
DISCIPLINARY ACTION: RESTRICTION PLACED ON LICENSE
NOTES: NO ALCOHOL.

HUTCHINSON, ALFRED CHARETTE MD, LICENSE NUMBER 0003690, OF PORTLAND, OR, WAS DISCIPLINED BY OREGON ON JULY 14, 1995.
DISCIPLINARY ACTION: 12-MONTH SURRENDER OF LICENSE
NOTES: VOLUNTARY SURRENDER. NOT A DISCIPLINARY ORDER. EMERGENCY SUSPENSION TERMINATED.

IANORA, ALFRED A MD, LICENSE NUMBER 0096150, OF 25800 VERA LANE, VENETA, OR, WAS DISCIPLINED BY NEW YORK ON MAY 6, 1994.
DISCIPLINARY ACTION: LICENSE REVOCATION
OFFENSE: DISCIPLINARY ACTION BY ANOTHER STATE OR AGENCY
NOTES: FOUND GUILTY OF PROFESSIONAL MISCONDUCT BY THE OREGON BOARD.

IANORA, ALFRED ANTHONY JR MD, LICENSE NUMBER MD07243, OF EUGENE, OR, WAS DISCIPLINED BY OREGON ON JANUARY 15, 1993.
DISCIPLINARY ACTION: EMERGENCY SUSPENSION

IANORA, ALFRED ANTHONY JR MD OF 1661-68 HIGH STREET, EUGENE, OR, WAS DISCIPLINED BY DEA ON AUGUST 2, 1993.
DISCIPLINARY ACTION: SURRENDER OF CONTROLLED SUBSTANCE LICENSE
OFFENSE: DISCIPLINARY ACTION BY ANOTHER STATE OR AGENCY
NOTES: EMERGENCY SUSPENSION OF OREGON MEDICAL LICENSE 01/15/93.

IANORA, ALFRED ANTHONY JR MD, LICENSE NUMBER MD07243, OF EUGENE, OR, WAS DISCIPLINED BY OREGON ON NOVEMBER 8, 1993.
DISCIPLINARY ACTION: LICENSE REVOCATION

IRONSIDE, ROBERT BRUCE MD, LICENSE NUMBER 0008396, OF PORTLAND, OR, WAS DISCIPLINED BY OREGON ON SEPTEMBER 10, 1990.
DISCIPLINARY ACTION: RESTRICTION PLACED ON CONTROLLED SUBSTANCE LICENSE
NOTES: MUST PROVIDE TRIPLICATE COPIES OF CONTROLLED SUBSTANCE PRESCRIPTIONS. NO LONGER RESTRICTED AS OF 1/28/92.

JACOB, STANLEY WALLACE MD, LICENSE NUMBER 0006134, OF PORTLAND, OR, WAS DISCIPLINED BY OREGON ON JANUARY 19, 1995.
DISCIPLINARY ACTION: REPRIMAND
OFFENSE: FAILURE TO COMPLY WITH A PROFESSIONAL RULE
NOTES: FAILURE TO FOLLOW ACCEPTED STANDARDS FOR MEDICAL RECORD KEEPING ON A PATIENT.

JANZEN, GAYLORD DEAN DO, LICENSE NUMBER 0007570, OF ESTACADA, OR, WAS DISCIPLINED BY OREGON ON OCTOBER 4, 1989.
DISCIPLINARY ACTION: RESTRICTION PLACED ON CONTROLLED SUBSTANCE LICENSE
NOTES: MUST PROVIDE TRIPLICATE COPIES OF CONTROLLED SUBSTANCES PRESCRIPTIONS. NO LONGER RESTRICTED AS OF 1/28/92.

JARRETT, JOHN R MD, LICENSE NUMBER 0008191, OF EUGENE, OR, WAS DISCIPLINED BY OREGON ON MARCH 6, 1990.
DISCIPLINARY ACTION: PROBATION

JOHNSON, MARCUS PAUL MD, LICENSE NUMBER 0008971, OF LINCOLN CITY, OR, WAS DISCIPLINED BY OREGON ON APRIL 11, 1991.
DISCIPLINARY ACTION: RESTRICTION PLACED ON LICENSE; RESTRICTION PLACED ON CONTROLLED SUBSTANCE LICENSE
OFFENSE: OVERPRESCRIBING OR MISPRESCRIBING DRUGS
NOTES: ALLEGED INAPPROPRIATE PRESCRIBING. VOLUNTARY LIMITATION; NO SCHEDULED DRUGS; PRACTICE LIMITED TO RADIOLOGY.

JOHNSON, RICHARD H MD, LICENSE NUMBER MD08061, OF PENDLETON, OR, WAS DISCIPLINED BY OREGON ON JANUARY 21, 1987.
DISCIPLINARY ACTION: 60-MONTH PROBATION

JOHNSTON, JAMES C MD, LICENSE NUMBER 0022573, WAS DISCIPLINED BY ARIZONA ON OCTOBER 18, 1995.
NOTES: SHALL NOT PRACTICE MEDICINE IN ARIZONA PRIOR TO MEETING WITH THE BOARD.

JOHNSTON, JAMES CHRISTOPHER MD, DATE OF BIRTH NOVEMBER 20, 1959, LICENSE NUMBER 00G8880, OF NACOGDOCHES, TX, WAS DISCIPLINED BY TEXAS ON JUNE 22, 1994.
DISCIPLINARY ACTION: RESTRICTION PLACED ON LICENSE
OFFENSE: SEXUAL ABUSE OF OR SEXUAL MISCONDUCT WITH A PATIENT
NOTES: AS RECENTLY AS 6/8/94 CRIMINAL COMPLAINTS WERE FILED AGAINST HIM ALLEGING HE ENGAGED IN BEHAVIOR CONSTITUTING ATTEMPTED SEXUAL ASSAULT

- OREGON -

AGAINST INDIVIDUALS WHO WERE PATIENTS; DENIES ALLEGATIONS; BECAUSE HE DESIRES TO FOCUS RESOURCES AND TIME ON DEFENSE OF THE CRIMINAL CASE. AGREES TO THIS ORDER WITH THE BOARD. LICENSE IS RESTRICTED AS FOLLOWS: SHALL NOT EXAMINE OR TREAT PATIENTS AFTER THE ORDER DATE; WITHIN 30 DAYS SHALL SUBMIT HIMSELF FOR ASSESSMENT THROUGH THE BEHAVIOR CARE NETWORK PROGRAM OR OTHER BOARD-APPROVED PROGRAM WHICH WILL FOCUS ON THE DISPARITY BETWEEN THE COMPLAINTS AGAINST HIM AND HIS OWN VERSION OF EVENTS AND ATTEMPT TO DETERMINE THE DEGREE OF RISK TO THE PUBLIC INVOLVED IN HIS CONTINUED PRACTICE; SHOULD THIS EVALUATION INDICATE HIS PRACTICE CONSTITUTES NO THREAT TO THE PUBLIC HEALTH HE SHALL BE PERMITTED TO RESUME PRACTICE PENDING FURTHER ORDER OF THE BOARD PROVIDED HE SEES PATIENTS ONLY WHEN ACCOMPANIED BY A CHAPERONE APPROVED IN ADVANCE WHO WILL SIGN ALL CHARTS TO INDICATE PRESENCE; SHALL COOPERATE WITH THE BOARD IN VERIFYING COMPLIANCE; SHALL INFORM BOARD OF CHANGE OF ADDRESS WITHIN 10 DAYS.

JOHNSTON, JAMES CHRISTOPHER MD, LICENSE NUMBER 00M5411, WAS DISCIPLINED BY IDAHO ON DECEMBER 14, 1994.
DISCIPLINARY ACTION: RESTRICTION PLACED ON LICENSE; MONITORING OF PHYSICIAN
OFFENSE: DISCIPLINARY ACTION BY ANOTHER STATE OR AGENCY
NOTES: ON 9/30/94 TEXAS RESTRICTED HIS LICENSE BASED ON CRIMINAL ALLEGATIONS THAT HE HAD ENGAGED IN BEHAVIOR CONSTITUTING ATTEMPTED SEXUAL ASSAULT AGAINST PATIENTS. IDAHO BOARD ADOPTS AND INCORPORATES ALL TERMS AND CONDITIONS OF THE TEXAS ORDER WHICH INCLUDE: SHALL NOT EXAMINE OR TREAT ANY PATIENTS WITHOUT BEING ACCOMPANIED AT ALL TIMES BY A PROCTOR OR CHAPERONE APPROVED BY THE BOARD; SHALL OBTAIN AN EXAM TABLE THAT IS SPECIFICALLY DESIGNED FOR THE PERFORMANCE OF ELECTROMYOGRAPHY WITH A STANDARD ARM BOARD AND THE ABILITY TO ELEVATE THE HEAD OF THE PATIENT; SHALL REPOSITION HIS EXAMINATION TABLE SO THAT HE MAY WALK BEHIND PATIENTS TO EXAMINE THE SHOULDER AND PROXIMAL AREAS; SHALL NOT PLACE A PAGER OR INSTRUMENTS IN HIS POCKETS DURING EXAMINATION OF PATIENTS; PATIENTS SHALL BE REPOSITIONED DURING EVALUATIONS ONLY BY A NURSE OR TECHNICIAN; SHALL EXPLAIN TO ALL PATIENTS THOSE PROCEDURES WHICH INVOLVE CONTACT WITH HIM PRIOR TO SUCH CONTACT; SHALL ASK PATIENTS IN DETAIL REGARDING ANY PROBLEMS OR CONCERNS WHICH THEY MIGHT HAVE CONCERNING HIS EXAMINATIONS OR ANY PROCEDURES PERFORMED; SHALL UNDERGO ADDITIONAL PHALLOMETRIC TESTING WITHIN 60 DAYS.

JOHNSTON, JAMES CHRISTOPHER MD, LICENSE NUMBER 0A44527, OF NACOGDOCHES, TX, WAS DISCIPLINED BY CALIFORNIA ON DECEMBER 30, 1995.
DISCIPLINARY ACTION: SURRENDER OF LICENSE
NOTES: WHILE CHARGES PENDING.

JOHNSTON, JAMES CHRISTOPHER MD, LICENSE NUMBER 0018716, OF SAN ANTONIO, TX, WAS DISCIPLINED BY OREGON ON NOVEMBER 4, 1996.
DISCIPLINARY ACTION: SURRENDER OF LICENSE
NOTES: VOLUNTARY SURRENDER.

JURA, RANDELL PETER MD, LICENSE NUMBER MD12431, OF GRESHAM, OR, WAS DISCIPLINED BY OREGON ON OCTOBER 6, 1988.
DISCIPLINARY ACTION: PROBATION

JURA, RANDELL PETER MD, LICENSE NUMBER MD12431, OF GRESHAM, OR, WAS DISCIPLINED BY OREGON ON OCTOBER 19, 1993.
DISCIPLINARY ACTION: FINE
NOTES: $2,500 FINE.

KATTENHORN, LOWELL D MD OF 1215 N.E. SEVENTH STREET, GRANTS PASS, OR, WAS DISCIPLINED BY DEA ON MARCH 15, 1996.
DISCIPLINARY ACTION: SURRENDER OF CONTROLLED SUBSTANCE LICENSE
OFFENSE: DISCIPLINARY ACTION BY ANOTHER STATE OR AGENCY
NOTES: STATE BOARD.

KATTENHORN, LOWELL DEAN MD, LICENSE NUMBER MD07834, OF GRANTS PASS, OR, WAS DISCIPLINED BY OREGON ON FEBRUARY 5, 1990.
DISCIPLINARY ACTION: RESTRICTION PLACED ON LICENSE
NOTES: MUST PROVIDE TRIPLICATE COPIES OF PRESCRIPTIONS FOR SCHEDULES III, IV, AND V. AS OF 5/25/94 LICENSE LAPSED DUE TO NONPAYMENT OF FEES. AS OF 11/17/94 LICENSE LISTED AS ACTIVE AGAIN ALTHOUGH STILL RESTRICTED.

KATTENHORN, LOWELL DEAN MD, LICENSE NUMBER 0007834, OF GRANTS PASS, OR, WAS DISCIPLINED BY OREGON ON OCTOBER 19, 1995.
DISCIPLINARY ACTION: 12-MONTH SURRENDER OF LICENSE
NOTES: VOLUNTARY SURRENDER WHILE UNDER INVESTIGATION.

KEHRLI, MARTIN ALAN MD, LICENSE NUMBER 0013978, OF SALEM, OR, WAS DISCIPLINED BY OREGON ON JANUARY 10, 1991.
DISCIPLINARY ACTION: 120-MONTH PROBATION
NOTES: TERMINATION OF SUSPENSION; REVOCATION STAYED.

KEITH, DOUGLAS SCOTT MD, LICENSE NUMBER 0020075, OF VANCOUVER, OR, WAS DISCIPLINED BY OREGON ON JUNE 6, 1996.
DISCIPLINARY ACTION: RESTRICTION PLACED ON LICENSE
NOTES: VOLUNTARY LIMITATION. AS OF 5/27/97, NO LONGER LISTED AS RESTRICTED.

KELLY, RONALD K MD, LICENSE NUMBER MD15540, OF DIXON, OR, WAS DISCIPLINED BY OREGON ON MAY 10, 1988.
DISCIPLINARY ACTION: RESTRICTION PLACED ON LICENSE

KELLY, RONALD K MD, DATE OF BIRTH APRIL 15, 1953, OF DAVIS, CA, WAS DISCIPLINED BY CALIFORNIA ON MARCH 1, 1992.
DISCIPLINARY ACTION: DENIAL OF NEW LICENSE
NOTES: DEFAULT DECISION.

KELLY, RONALD K MD WAS DISCIPLINED BY NEVADA ON MARCH 20, 1996.
DISCIPLINARY ACTION: EMERGENCY SUSPENSION
NOTES: COMPLAINT FILED ALLEGING THE CONTINUED PRACTICE OF MEDICINE WOULD ENDANGER THE HEALTH, SAFETY AND WELFARE OF HIS PATIENTS.

KELLY, RONALD K MD WAS DISCIPLINED BY NEVADA ON JULY 2, 1996.
DISCIPLINARY ACTION: LICENSE REVOCATION
OFFENSE: CRIMINAL CONVICTION OR PLEA OF GUILTY, NOLO CONTENDERE, OR NO CONTEST TO A CRIME
NOTES: FOUND GUILTY OF CONVICTION OF A FELONY; INABILITY TO PRACTICE MEDICINE WITH REASONABLE SKILL AND SAFETY BECAUSE OF ILLNESS, A MENTAL OR PHYSICAL CONDITION OR THE USE OF ALCOHOL, DRUGS, NARCOTICS, OR ANY OTHER SUBSTANCE; RENDERING PROFESSIONAL SERVICES TO A PATIENT WHILE THE PHYSICIAN IS UNDER THE INFLUENCE OF ALCOHOL OR ANY CONTROLLED SUBSTANCE. SHALL REIMBURSE THE BOARD FOR ALL EXPENSES INCURRED IN THE INVESTIGATION AND HEARING PROCESS.

- OREGON -

KESTER, EUGENE FRANCIS MD, DATE OF BIRTH JULY 20, 1938, LICENSE NUMBER MD11529, OF PO BOX 215, BEAVERTON, OR, WAS DISCIPLINED BY OREGON ON JUNE 30, 1994.
DISCIPLINARY ACTION: LICENSE SUSPENSION
OFFENSE: SEXUAL ABUSE OF OR SEXUAL MISCONDUCT WITH A PATIENT
NOTES: ON 6/13/94 HE ADMITTED TO BOARD THAT HE HAD SEXUAL INTERCOURSE WITH FIVE OF HIS ADULT FEMALE PATIENTS AND INAPPROPRIATE SEXUAL CONTACT WITH ANOTHER ADULT FEMALE PATIENT. LICENSE SUSPENDED UNTIL 7/16/94.

KESTER, EUGENE FRANCIS MD, LICENSE NUMBER MD11529, OF PO BOX 215, BEAVERTON, OR, WAS DISCIPLINED BY OREGON ON JULY 15, 1994.
DISCIPLINARY ACTION: EMERGENCY SUSPENSION
OFFENSE: SEXUAL ABUSE OF OR SEXUAL MISCONDUCT WITH A PATIENT
NOTES: ON 6/13/94 HE ADMITTED TO HAVING SEXUAL INTERCOURSE WITH FIVE OF HIS ADULT FEMALE PATIENTS AND INAPPROPRIATE SEXUAL CONTACT WITH ANOTHER ADULT FEMALE PATIENT.

KESTER, EUGENE FRANCIS MD OF 10490 SW EASTRIDGE, PORTLAND, OR, WAS DISCIPLINED BY DEA ON NOVEMBER 30, 1994.
DISCIPLINARY ACTION: SURRENDER OF CONTROLLED SUBSTANCE LICENSE
OFFENSE: DISCIPLINARY ACTION BY ANOTHER STATE OR AGENCY
NOTES: STATE BOARD.

KESTER, EUGENE FRANCIS MD, DATE OF BIRTH JULY 20, 1938, LICENSE NUMBER MD11529, OF PO BOX 215, BEAVERTON, OR, WAS DISCIPLINED BY OREGON ON JANUARY 19, 1995.
DISCIPLINARY ACTION: LICENSE REVOCATION
OFFENSE: SEXUAL ABUSE OF OR SEXUAL MISCONDUCT WITH A PATIENT
NOTES: ENGAGED IN SEXUAL MISCONDUCT WITH SEVEN ADULT FEMALE PATIENTS.

KESTER, EUGENE FRANCIS MD, LICENSE NUMBER 0016979, OF PORTLAND, OR, WAS DISCIPLINED BY WASHINGTON ON JUNE 22, 1995.
DISCIPLINARY ACTION: EMERGENCY SUSPENSION
OFFENSE: DISCIPLINARY ACTION BY ANOTHER STATE OR AGENCY
NOTES: ALLEGATIONS OF ACTION IN ANOTHER STATE.

KESTER, EUGENE FRANCIS MD, LICENSE NUMBER 0016979, OF PORTLAND, OR, WAS DISCIPLINED BY WASHINGTON ON APRIL 19, 1996.
DISCIPLINARY ACTION: LICENSE SUSPENSION
NOTES: INDEFINITE SUSPENSION PENDING THE COMPLETION OF A NUMBER OF CONDITIONS.

KIMBERLEY, STEPHEN L MD OF 2050 NW LOVEJOY, PORTLAND, OR, WAS DISCIPLINED BY DEA ON MARCH 30, 1995.
DISCIPLINARY ACTION: SURRENDER OF CONTROLLED SUBSTANCE LICENSE
OFFENSE: DISCIPLINARY ACTION BY ANOTHER STATE OR AGENCY
NOTES: STATE BOARD.

KIMBERLEY, STEPHEN LANGTON MD, DATE OF BIRTH JUNE 6, 1951, LICENSE NUMBER MD12797, OF PORTLAND, OR, WAS DISCIPLINED BY OREGON ON NOVEMBER 3, 1994.
DISCIPLINARY ACTION: EMERGENCY SUSPENSION
OFFENSE: SEXUAL ABUSE OF OR SEXUAL MISCONDUCT WITH A PATIENT
NOTES: ADMITTED FOR EVALUATION FOR CHEMICAL DEPENDENCY ON 9/2/94 AND FOR TREATMENT ON 11/2/94; ADMITTED TO INAPPROPRIATE SEXUAL BEHAVIOR WITH PATIENTS DURING EXAMINATIONS, INCLUDING INAPPROPRIATE SEXUAL COMMENTS TO ONE OF HIS ADULT FEMALE PATIENTS DURING PELVIC EXAMS.

KIMBERLEY, STEPHEN LANGTON MD, DATE OF BIRTH JUNE 6, 1951, LICENSE NUMBER MD12797, OF 85296 RIDGETOP DRIVE, EUGENE, OR, WAS DISCIPLINED BY OREGON ON JULY 24, 1995.
DISCIPLINARY ACTION: LICENSE REVOCATION
OFFENSE: SEXUAL ABUSE OF OR SEXUAL MISCONDUCT WITH A PATIENT
NOTES: HABITUAL OR EXCESSIVE USE OF INTOXICANTS, DRUGS OR CONTROLLED SUBSTANCES; SEXUALLY MOLESTED TWO, AND MADE INAPPROPRIATE SEXUAL COMMENTS TO ONE OF HIS ADULT FEMALE PATIENTS DURING PELVIC EXAMS. SHALL NOT APPLY FOR RESTORATION OF HIS LICENSE FOR TWO YEARS.

KIMBERLEY, STEPHEN LANGTON MD, LICENSE NUMBER 0G42400, OF EUGENE, OR, WAS DISCIPLINED BY CALIFORNIA ON JUNE 28, 1996.
DISCIPLINARY ACTION: SURRENDER OF LICENSE
NOTES: WHILE CHARGES PENDING.

KING, ALBERT DR WAS DISCIPLINED BY OREGON ON OCTOBER 22, 1991.
DISCIPLINARY ACTION: DENIAL OF NEW LICENSE

KNOWER, MICHAEL EDWARD MD, LICENSE NUMBER 0015601, OF PRINEVILLE, OR, WAS DISCIPLINED BY OREGON ON JUNE 4, 1996.
DISCIPLINARY ACTION: 12-MONTH REPRIMAND

KOCH, RICHARD A MD OF 110 SOUTH ALDER STREET, PILOT ROCK, OR, WAS DISCIPLINED BY DEA ON APRIL 11, 1995.
DISCIPLINARY ACTION: RESTRICTION PLACED ON CONTROLLED SUBSTANCE LICENSE
OFFENSE: PROFESSIONAL MISCONDUCT
NOTES: ALLEGED CONTROLLED SUBSTANCE VIOLATIONS.

KOCH, RICHARD ARTHUR MD, LICENSE NUMBER MD05203, OF PILOT ROCK, OR, WAS DISCIPLINED BY OREGON ON JULY 15, 1993.
DISCIPLINARY ACTION: RESTRICTION PLACED ON LICENSE; RESTRICTION PLACED ON CONTROLLED SUBSTANCE LICENSE
NOTES: SCHEDULE II AND III PRESCRIBING PRIVILEGES RESTRICTED EXCEPT AT UMATILLA COUNTY JAIL, EOCC AND HOSPITALS.

KRAUSE, HENRY A DO OF 10529 NE HALSEY, PORTLAND, OR, WAS DISCIPLINED BY DEA ON DECEMBER 13, 1989.
DISCIPLINARY ACTION: RESTRICTION PLACED ON CONTROLLED SUBSTANCE LICENSE
OFFENSE: OVERPRESCRIBING OR MISPRESCRIBING DRUGS
NOTES: INAPPROPRIATE PRESCRIBING PRACTICES NOTED BY OREGON BOARD OF MEDICAL EXAMINERS.

LARSON, WILBUR LINUS EDMUND MD, LICENSE NUMBER MD04495, OF PORTLAND, OR, WAS DISCIPLINED BY OREGON ON OCTOBER 13, 1994.
DISCIPLINARY ACTION: RESTRICTION PLACED ON CONTROLLED SUBSTANCE LICENSE
NOTES: RESTRICTED FROM PRESCRIBING SCHEDULE II DRUGS. AS OF 9/30/97, NO LONGER LISTED AS RESTRICTED.

LASERSOHN, WILLIAM B MD, LICENSE NUMBER 0G47192, OF SALEM, OR, WAS DISCIPLINED BY CALIFORNIA ON MARCH 30, 1988.
DISCIPLINARY ACTION: 60-MONTH PROBATION
OFFENSE: DISCIPLINARY ACTION BY ANOTHER STATE OR AGENCY
NOTES: OREGON LICENSE DISCIPLINED BY THAT STATE. REVOCATION STAYED.

LAYNE, GREGORY DAVID MD, LICENSE NUMBER 0010517, OF HILLSBORO, OR, WAS DISCIPLINED BY OREGON ON JULY 9, 1987.
DISCIPLINARY ACTION: 120-MONTH PROBATION
NOTES: NO LONGER ON PROBATION AS OF 7/27/92.

- OREGON -

LEFEVRE, JOHN DR WAS DISCIPLINED BY OREGON ON JULY 11, 1991.
DISCIPLINARY ACTION: DENIAL OF NEW LICENSE

LEIBOLD, WERNER MD, LICENSE NUMBER MD11787, OF CANYONVILLE, OR, WAS DISCIPLINED BY OREGON ON SEPTEMBER 12, 1987.
DISCIPLINARY ACTION: 120-MONTH PROBATION
NOTES: ON 12/31/91, TERMINATION OF PROBATION OR VOLUNTARY LIMITATION.

LEIBOLD, WERNER MD OF 251 N. MAIN ST, CANYONVILLE, OR, WAS DISCIPLINED BY ILLINOIS ON SEPTEMBER 1, 1989.
DISCIPLINARY ACTION: PROBATION
OFFENSE: DISCIPLINARY ACTION BY ANOTHER STATE OR AGENCY
NOTES: OREGON LICENSE WAS DISCIPLINED

LEIBOLD, WERNER MD, LICENSE NUMBER A026223, OF CANYONVILLE, OR, WAS DISCIPLINED BY CALIFORNIA ON SEPTEMBER 20, 1989.
DISCIPLINARY ACTION: LICENSE REVOCATION
OFFENSE: DISCIPLINARY ACTION BY ANOTHER STATE OR AGENCY
NOTES: DISCIPLINED BY OREGON MEDICAL BOARD FOR VIOLATING LIMITATIONS ON OBSTETRICAL PRACTICE

LIBENSON, BRADLEY NEAL DO, LICENSE NUMBER 0017979, OF HAVERHILL, OR, WAS DISCIPLINED BY OREGON ON APRIL 13, 1995.
DISCIPLINARY ACTION: REPRIMAND; MONITORING OF PHYSICIAN
NOTES: REQUIREMENT FOR FEMALE CHAPERONE FOR ALL FEMALE PATIENTS. MONITOR NO LONGER LISTED AS OF 5/8/96.

LINDNER, DANIEL JOHN MD, LICENSE NUMBER MD13271, OF PORTLAND, OR, WAS DISCIPLINED BY OREGON ON JANUARY 13, 1989.
DISCIPLINARY ACTION: PROBATION
NOTES: NO LONGER ON PROBATION AS OF 2/4/91.

LINEHAN, CHARLES K MD, LICENSE NUMBER MD05254, OF ASTORIA, OR, WAS DISCIPLINED BY OREGON ON APRIL 9, 1988.
DISCIPLINARY ACTION: RESTRICTION PLACED ON CONTROLLED SUBSTANCE LICENSE
NOTES: RESTRICTION ON PRESCRIBING SCHEDULE II AND III DRUGS AND PROPOXYPHENE. AS OF SEPTEMBER 7, 1988, MUST ALSO PROVIDE TRIPLICATE COPIES OF PRESCRIPTIONS FOR SCHEDULE II-V DRUGS. NO LONGER RESTRICTED AS OF 2/4/91.

LINEHAN, CHARLES K MD, LICENSE NUMBER A016426, OF ASTORIA, OR, WAS DISCIPLINED BY CALIFORNIA ON FEBRUARY 11, 1991.
DISCIPLINARY ACTION: 60-MONTH PROBATION
OFFENSE: DISCIPLINARY ACTION BY ANOTHER STATE OR AGENCY
NOTES: DISCIPLINED BY OREGON BOARD. REVOCATION STAYED.

LONG, ERIC WILLIAM MD OF 6485 SW BORLAND RD SUITE G, TUALATIN, OR, WAS DISCIPLINED BY DEA ON MARCH 13, 1992.
DISCIPLINARY ACTION: RESTRICTION PLACED ON CONTROLLED SUBSTANCE LICENSE
OFFENSE: OVERPRESCRIBING OR MISPRESCRIBING DRUGS
NOTES: INAPPROPRIATE PRESCRIBING PRACTICES.

LOOSLI, CHARLES GARY MD, LICENSE NUMBER MD06086, OF ST HELENS, OR, WAS DISCIPLINED BY OREGON ON NOVEMBER 1, 1988.
DISCIPLINARY ACTION: 12-MONTH RESTRICTION PLACED ON CONTROLLED SUBSTANCE LICENSE; FINE
NOTES: $2000 FINE. NO PRESCRIBING FOR FAMILY MEMBERS. MUST PROVIDE TRIPLICATE COPIES OF CONTROLLED DRUG PRESCRIPTIONS. NO LONGER RESTRICTED AS OF 11/15/89.

LOOSLI, CHARLES GARY MD OF 525 NORTH HIGHWAY, ST HELENS, OR, WAS DISCIPLINED BY DEA ON JUNE 2, 1989.
DISCIPLINARY ACTION: RESTRICTION PLACED ON CONTROLLED SUBSTANCE LICENSE
OFFENSE: OVERPRESCRIBING OR MISPRESCRIBING DRUGS
NOTES: PLACED ON RESTRICTION FROM PRESCRIBING SCHEDULES II THROUGH V CONTROLLED SUBSTANCES TO FAMILY FOR 1 YEAR.

LUBER, JOHN M MD, LICENSE NUMBER 0010106, OF PORTLAND, OR, WAS DISCIPLINED BY OREGON ON AUGUST 9, 1990.
DISCIPLINARY ACTION: FINE; REPRIMAND

LUNDY, THERESA MARIE MD, LICENSE NUMBER MD13681, OF ROSEBURG, OR, WAS DISCIPLINED BY OREGON ON AUGUST 4, 1994.
DISCIPLINARY ACTION: EMERGENCY SUSPENSION

LUNDY, THERESA MARIE MD, LICENSE NUMBER MD13681, OF ROSEBURG, OR, WAS DISCIPLINED BY OREGON ON OCTOBER 18, 1994.
DISCIPLINARY ACTION: 120-MONTH PROBATION
OFFENSE: SUBSTANCE ABUSE

MACGREGOR, MALCOLM MD, DATE OF BIRTH DECEMBER 9, 1925, OF 495 N E BEECH STREET, GRESHAM, OR, WAS DISCIPLINED BY MEDICARE ON JUNE 7, 1989.
DISCIPLINARY ACTION: EXCLUSION FROM THE MEDICARE AND/OR MEDICAID PROGRAMS
OFFENSE: DISCIPLINARY ACTION BY ANOTHER STATE OR AGENCY
NOTES: LICENSE REVOCATION OR SUSPENSION.

MACK, DONALD MD, LICENSE NUMBER 0A17918, OF PORTLAND, OR, WAS DISCIPLINED BY CALIFORNIA ON APRIL 25, 1988.
DISCIPLINARY ACTION: 60-MONTH PROBATION
OFFENSE: DISCIPLINARY ACTION BY ANOTHER STATE OR AGENCY
NOTES: REVOCATION STAYED; DISCIPLINED BY OREGON BOARD FOR VIOLATING DRUG RESTRICTION

MALEY, JOSEPH CLIFT MD, LICENSE NUMBER 0008291, OF CORVALLIS, OR, WAS DISCIPLINED BY OREGON ON SEPTEMBER 11, 1990.
DISCIPLINARY ACTION: PROBATION; FINE
NOTES: NO LONGER LISTED ON PROBATION AS OF 5/8/96.

MANDELBLATT, STEVEN JAY MD, LICENSE NUMBER MD13180, OF PORTLAND, OR, WAS DISCIPLINED BY OREGON ON NOVEMBER 12, 1992.
DISCIPLINARY ACTION: 1-MONTH LICENSE SUSPENSION; FINE

MANHART, MARK W DO, DATE OF BIRTH OCTOBER 22, 1954, OF 17198 S CHAPIN WAY, LAKE OSWEGO, OR, WAS DISCIPLINED BY MEDICARE ON MAY 26, 1993.
DISCIPLINARY ACTION: EXCLUSION FROM THE MEDICARE AND/OR MEDICAID PROGRAMS
OFFENSE: FAILURE TO COMPLY WITH A PROFESSIONAL RULE
NOTES: DEFAULTED ON HEALTH EDUCATION ASSISTANCE LOAN. REINSTATED ON 6/12/97.

MASKELL, LAURA KATHLEEN MD, LICENSE NUMBER 0015244, OF SEASIDE, OR, WAS DISCIPLINED BY OREGON ON DECEMBER 6, 1990.
DISCIPLINARY ACTION: LICENSE SUSPENSION

MASKELL, LAURA KATHLEEN MD, LICENSE NUMBER 0015244, WAS DISCIPLINED BY OREGON ON SEPTEMBER 6, 1991.
DISCIPLINARY ACTION: PROBATION
OFFENSE: SUBSTANCE ABUSE
NOTES: ALLEGED PERSONAL SUBSTANCE ABUSE. REVOCATION STAYED; TERMINATION OF SUSPENSION.

MASKELL, LAURA KATHLEEN MD, LICENSE NUMBER MD15244, OF ST HELENS, OR, WAS DISCIPLINED BY OREGON ON MAY 17, 1994.

- OREGON -

DISCIPLINARY ACTION: LICENSE SUSPENSION
OFFENSE: FAILURE TO COMPLY WITH A PREVIOUS BOARD ORDER
NOTES: VIOLATED PROBATION; SUSPENSION UNTIL 6/9/94.

MASKELL, LAURA KATHLEEN MD, LICENSE NUMBER MD15244, OF ST HELENS, OR, WAS DISCIPLINED BY OREGON ON JULY 14, 1994.
DISCIPLINARY ACTION: 120-MONTH PROBATION
NOTES: PROBATION STARTED ON 9/5/91 EXTENDED ANOTHER 10 YEARS.

MASKELL, LAURA KATHLEEN MD, LICENSE NUMBER 0015244, OF ST HELENS, OR, WAS DISCIPLINED BY OREGON ON JANUARY 30, 1996.
DISCIPLINARY ACTION: 120-MONTH PROBATION

MATSUDA, ARTHUR TORU MD, LICENSE NUMBER 0005178, OF BEAVERTON, OR, WAS DISCIPLINED BY OREGON ON JUNE 12, 1991.
DISCIPLINARY ACTION: EMERGENCY SUSPENSION
NOTES: NO LONGER SUSPENDED AS OF 1/28/92.

MAURER, JOHN GAFFNEY MD, LICENSE NUMBER 0009713, OF ASHLAND, OR, WAS DISCIPLINED BY OREGON ON OCTOBER 7, 1991.
DISCIPLINARY ACTION: 12-MONTH RESTRICTION PLACED ON CONTROLLED SUBSTANCE LICENSE
NOTES: MUST PROVIDE TRIPLICATE COPIES OF CONTROLLED SUBSTANCE PRESCRIPTIONS. NO LONGER RESTRICTED AS OF 1/28/92.

MAYER, BARRY S MD, LICENSE NUMBER 0034125, OF LAKE OSWEGO, OR, WAS DISCIPLINED BY FLORIDA ON FEBRUARY 15, 1991.
DISCIPLINARY ACTION: FINE; REPRIMAND
OFFENSE: PROVIDING FALSE INFORMATION TO THE BOARD
NOTES: FOUND GUILTY OF LICENSE RENEWAL BY FRAUDULENT MISREPRESENTATION IN THAT HE FALSELY CERTIFIED THAT HE HAD COMPLETED THE CONTINUING MEDICAL EDUCATION REQUIREMENTS FOR LICENSE RENEWAL; VIOLATED A BOARD RULE IN THAT HE FAILED TO SUBMIT DOCUMENTATION VERIFYING RISK MANAGEMENT REQUIREMENT OF CONTINUING MEDICAL EDUCATION IN RESPONSE TO BOARD'S RANDOM AUDIT. HE MUST PAY $1000 FINE AND SUBMIT DOCUMENTATION OF COMPLETION OF ALL CONTINUING MEDICAL EDUCATION REQUIREMENTS FOR THE 1986-1987 AND 1988-89 LICENSING BIENNIUMS WITHIN SIX MONTHS; MUST COMPLETE FIVE ADDITIONAL HOURS CATEGORY I CONTINUING MEDICAL EDUCATION IN RISK MANAGEMENT WITHIN SIX MONTHS; MUST SUBMIT DOCUMENTATION OF COMPLETION OF THESE REQUIREMENTS WITH CERTIFICATES FOR 1990-91 BIENNIUM; REPRIMAND.

MCCULLOUGH, LESLIE LEE MD, LICENSE NUMBER MD11227, OF ROSEBURG, OR, WAS DISCIPLINED BY OREGON ON JULY 13, 1989.
DISCIPLINARY ACTION: RESTRICTION PLACED ON LICENSE
NOTES: ON 12/31/91 PROBATION/LIMITATION WAS MODIFIED. AS OF 8/1/93 NO LONGER LISTED ON PROBATION OR LIMITATION.

MCDONALD, PATRICK CHARLES MD, LICENSE NUMBER 0013817, OF WOODBURN, OR, WAS DISCIPLINED BY OREGON ON AUGUST 20, 1990.
DISCIPLINARY ACTION: RESTRICTION PLACED ON CONTROLLED SUBSTANCE LICENSE
NOTES: VOLUNTARY LIMITATION; LIMITED SCHEDULE II'S; MUST PROVIDE TRIPLICATE COPIES OF CONTROLLED SUBSTANCE PRESCRIPTIONS. NO LONGER RESTRICTED AS OF 7/27/92.

MCDONALD, ROBERT WILSON MD, LICENSE NUMBER MD12644, OF MT ANGEL, OR, WAS DISCIPLINED BY OREGON ON NOVEMBER 13, 1991.
DISCIPLINARY ACTION: 24-MONTH RESTRICTION PLACED ON LICENSE
NOTES: ALLEGED INAPPROPRIATE CARE/INCOMPETENCE. VOLUNTARY LIMITATION. AS OF 3/10/94 NO LONGER LISTED AS RESTRICTED.

MCGOVERN, PETER JOHN MD, LICENSE NUMBER MD09904, OF PORTLAND, OR, WAS DISCIPLINED BY OREGON ON JULY 13, 1989.
DISCIPLINARY ACTION: 120-MONTH PROBATION
OFFENSE: SUBSTANCE ABUSE
NOTES: ALLEGED PERSONAL SUBSTANCE ABUSE. ON 1/10/91 MODIFICATION OF PROBATION/VOLUNTARY LIMITATION.

MCGOVERN, PETER JOHN MD, LICENSE NUMBER MD09904, OF PORTLAND, OR, WAS DISCIPLINED BY OREGON ON MAY 26, 1994.
DISCIPLINARY ACTION: LICENSE SUSPENSION
OFFENSE: PHYSICAL OR MENTAL ILLNESS INHIBITING THE ABILITY TO PRACTICE WITH SKILL AND SAFETY
NOTES: AUTOMATIC SUSPENSION FOR MENTAL ILLNESS. NO LONGER SUSPENDED AS OF 8/12/96.

MCGOVERN, PETER JOHN MD OF 6441 SW CANYON CT #100, PORTLAND, OR, WAS DISCIPLINED BY DEA ON MAY 8, 1995.
DISCIPLINARY ACTION: SURRENDER OF CONTROLLED SUBSTANCE LICENSE
OFFENSE: DISCIPLINARY ACTION BY ANOTHER STATE OR AGENCY
NOTES: STATE BOARD.

MCGREGOR, MALCOLM DR WAS DISCIPLINED BY OREGON ON DECEMBER 31, 1991.
DISCIPLINARY ACTION: DENIAL OF NEW LICENSE

MCKAY, LORNE D MD, LICENSE NUMBER 0023456, OF CT, WAS DISCIPLINED BY MINNESOTA ON JANUARY 10, 1987.
DISCIPLINARY ACTION: FINE; RESTRICTION PLACED ON LICENSE
OFFENSE: SUBSTANDARD CARE, INCOMPETENCE, OR NEGLIGENCE
NOTES: OPHTHALMOLOGIST OBTAINED "LOANS" FROM A VULNERABLE ADULT WITHOUT ANY DOCUMENTATION OR REPAYMENT SCHEDULE; FAILED TO PROPERLY SUBMIT MEDICARE FORMS FOR REIMBURSEMENT OF SAME PATIENT; IMPROPER MANAGEMENT OF MEDICAL RECORDS, SUBSTANDARD TREATMENT OF A PATIENT; MAY NOT PRACTICE IN MINNESOTA WITHOUT BOARD APPROVAL OF PRACTICE SETTING; AND MUST BE BOARD ELIGIBLE IN OPHTHALMOLOGY AT TIME OF REQUEST AND HAVE ENGAGED AN OFFICE MANAGEMENT CONSULTING FIRM TO ASSIST IN ADMINISTERING OF BILLING, RECORD KEEPING AND OTHER OFFICE FUNCTIONS; MONTHLY REPORTS FROM CURRENT CONNECTICUT FELLOWSHIP PROGRAM; PROHIBITED FROM RECEIVING ANY LOANS, GIFTS, FAVORS OR GRATUITIES FROM PATIENTS; PENALTY OF $10,000

MCKAY, LORNE D MD OF GRESHAM, OR, WAS DISCIPLINED BY NORTH DAKOTA ON MARCH 11, 1988.
DISCIPLINARY ACTION: LICENSE REVOCATION
OFFENSE: PROFESSIONAL MISCONDUCT
NOTES: DISHONEST, UNETHICAL AND UNPROFESSIONAL CONDUCT LIKELY TO DECEIVE, DEFRAUD AND HARM THE PUBLIC

MEAD, RICHARD JOSEPH MD, LICENSE NUMBER 0011683, OF SALEM, OR, WAS DISCIPLINED BY OREGON ON OCTOBER 19, 1995.
DISCIPLINARY ACTION: 36-MONTH PROBATION; FINE
NOTES: $1,000 FINE; MUST SUCCESSFULLY COMPLETE PROGRAM OF RE-EDUCATION AND TRAINING DURING PROBATION.

MEIER, WERNER RICHARD MD, LICENSE NUMBER 0008801, OF PORTLAND, OR, WAS DISCIPLINED BY OREGON ON SEPTEMBER 12, 1990.
DISCIPLINARY ACTION: REPRIMAND

- OREGON -

MENKES, ALAN LEWIS DO, LICENSE NUMBER DO11453, OF UPLAND, OR, WAS DISCIPLINED BY OREGON ON OCTOBER 6, 1988.
DISCIPLINARY ACTION: RESTRICTION PLACED ON LICENSE
NOTES: OFFICE BASED PRACTICE ONLY. AS OF 5/25/94 LICENSE LAPSED DUE TO NONPAYMENT OF FEES.

MENTZER, RICHARD LYNN JR MD, LICENSE NUMBER 0008548, OF BLACHLY, OR, WAS DISCIPLINED BY OREGON ON OCTOBER 8, 1990.
DISCIPLINARY ACTION: RESTRICTION PLACED ON CONTROLLED SUBSTANCE LICENSE
NOTES: MUST PROVIDE TRIPLICATE COPIES OF CONTROLLED SUBSTANCE PRESCRIPTIONS. NO LONGER RESTRICTED AS OF 1/28/92.

METTLER, DONALD C MD, LICENSE NUMBER MD05332, OF PORTLAND, OR, WAS DISCIPLINED BY OREGON ON JULY 14, 1988.
DISCIPLINARY ACTION: RESTRICTION PLACED ON CONTROLLED SUBSTANCE LICENSE
NOTES: NO PRESCRIBING DERMATRON OR PHENOLIC COMPOUNDS

MICHAELS, ROBIN R MD, LICENSE NUMBER MDO9558, OF SALEM, OR, WAS DISCIPLINED BY OREGON ON APRIL 9, 1988.
DISCIPLINARY ACTION: RESTRICTION PLACED ON LICENSE
NOTES: PSYCHIATRIC CARE REQUIRED

MICKEL, STEPHEN DALE MD, LICENSE NUMBER MD12725, OF THE DALLES, OR, WAS DISCIPLINED BY OREGON ON APRIL 25, 1989.
DISCIPLINARY ACTION: 120-MONTH PROBATION; 120-MONTH RESTRICTION PLACED ON CONTROLLED SUBSTANCE LICENSE
NOTES: NO PRESCRIBING SCHEDULE II, III, IV AND V DRUGS EXCEPT IN THE EMERGENCY ROOM. AS OF 8/1/93 NO LONGER LISTED AS ON PROBATION AND RESTRICTED.

MILLER, ROBERT L MD, LICENSE NUMBER 0090798, OF 898 LAKE ROAD, PENN YAN, NY, WAS DISCIPLINED BY NEW YORK ON MARCH 23, 1993.
DISCIPLINARY ACTION: SURRENDER OF LICENSE
OFFENSE: PROFESSIONAL MISCONDUCT
NOTES: WILLFULLY PHYSICALLY ABUSED A PATIENT.

MILLER, ROBERT L MD OF 3414 N KAISER CENTER DRIVE, PORTLAND, OR, WAS DISCIPLINED BY DEA ON MARCH 27, 1995.
DISCIPLINARY ACTION: SURRENDER OF CONTROLLED SUBSTANCE LICENSE
OFFENSE: DISCIPLINARY ACTION BY ANOTHER STATE OR AGENCY
NOTES: STATE BOARD.

MILLER, ROBERT LESLIE MD, LICENSE NUMBER MD07875, OF PORTLAND, OR, WAS DISCIPLINED BY OREGON ON OCTOBER 13, 1994.
DISCIPLINARY ACTION: LICENSE SUSPENSION; 120-MONTH PROBATION
OFFENSE: SUBSTANCE ABUSE
NOTES: ALCOHOL ABUSE. SUSPENSION INDEFINITE PENDING SUCCESSFUL DIVERSION REPORT. CONDITIONS OF PROBATION: MONITORED TREATMENT; QUARTERLY APPEARANCES BEFORE BOARD.

MILLER, ROBERT LESLIE MD, LICENSE NUMBER 0007875, OF PORTLAND, OR, WAS DISCIPLINED BY OREGON ON AUGUST 29, 1996.
DISCIPLINARY ACTION: 120-MONTH PROBATION; RESTRICTION PLACED ON CONTROLLED SUBSTANCE LICENSE
NOTES: CONDITIONS OF PROBATION: ADMINISTRATIVE MEDICINE ONLY; SHALL NOT PRESCRIBE SCHEDULE II, III OR IV DRUGS.

MILTON, ROBERT E MD, LICENSE NUMBER 0A19222, OF REDDING, CA, WAS DISCIPLINED BY CALIFORNIA ON FEBRUARY 9, 1996.
DISCIPLINARY ACTION: SURRENDER OF LICENSE
NOTES: WHILE CHARGES PENDING.

MILTON, ROBERT E MD OF 844 HARTNELL, REDDING, CA, WAS DISCIPLINED BY DEA ON MARCH 12, 1996.
DISCIPLINARY ACTION: SURRENDER OF CONTROLLED SUBSTANCE LICENSE
OFFENSE: DISCIPLINARY ACTION BY ANOTHER STATE OR AGENCY
NOTES: STATE BOARD.

MILTON, ROBERT ELWIN MD, LICENSE NUMBER MD11519, OF REDDING, OR, WAS DISCIPLINED BY OREGON ON OCTOBER 13, 1994.
DISCIPLINARY ACTION: LICENSE REVOCATION
OFFENSE: PROFESSIONAL MISCONDUCT
NOTES: FRAUDULENT BILLING; AIDING AND ABETTING NON-LICENSED TO PRACTICE MEDICINE. DEFAULT HEARING.

MINSKY, FRANCES M MD, LICENSE NUMBER MD15504, OF HOOD RIVER, OR, WAS DISCIPLINED BY OREGON ON NOVEMBER 2, 1989.
DISCIPLINARY ACTION: LICENSE SUSPENSION
NOTES: NOT SUSPENDED AS OF 2/8/90

MINSKY, FRANCES M MD, DATE OF BIRTH MAY 19, 1952, OF P O BOX 1253, TAHOE CITY, CA, WAS DISCIPLINED BY MEDICARE ON APRIL 4, 1991.
DISCIPLINARY ACTION: EXCLUSION FROM THE MEDICARE AND/OR MEDICAID PROGRAMS
OFFENSE: DISCIPLINARY ACTION BY ANOTHER STATE OR AGENCY
NOTES: LICENSE REVOCATION OR SUSPENSION.

MINSKY, FRANCES M MD, LICENSE NUMBER 0G50322, OF TRUCKEE, CA, WAS DISCIPLINED BY CALIFORNIA ON APRIL 25, 1991.
DISCIPLINARY ACTION: 120-MONTH PROBATION
OFFENSE: DISCIPLINARY ACTION BY ANOTHER STATE OR AGENCY
NOTES: DISCIPLINED BY OREGON BOARD FOR DRUG ABUSE AND MENTAL ILLNESS; CRIMINAL CONVICTION IN CALIFORNIA FOR OBTAINING CONTROLLED SUBSTANCES BY FRAUD. REVOCATION STAYED.

MINSKY, FRANCES M MD, LICENSE NUMBER 0G50322, OF SAN DIEGO, CA, WAS DISCIPLINED BY CALIFORNIA ON DECEMBER 15, 1991.
DISCIPLINARY ACTION: LICENSE REVOCATION
OFFENSE: FAILURE TO COMPLY WITH A PREVIOUS BOARD ORDER
NOTES: PROBATION VIOLATIONS. DEFAULT DECISION.

MIRACLE, MAX VERNON MD, LICENSE NUMBER MD05610, OF PORTLAND, OR, WAS DISCIPLINED BY OREGON ON SEPTEMBER 12, 1987.
DISCIPLINARY ACTION: 120-MONTH PROBATION; 120-MONTH RESTRICTION PLACED ON CONTROLLED SUBSTANCE LICENSE
NOTES: RESTRICTION ON PRESCRIBING SCHEDULE II, III, IV AND V DRUGS; PRESCRIPTION RESTRICTION MODIFIED ON 11/15/88 TO REQUIRE ONLY TRIPLICATE COPIES OF CONTROLLED SUBSTANCE PRESCRIPTIONS. AS OF 5/27/97, NO LONGER LISTED AS ON PROBATION; RESTRICTION STILL IN EFFECT.

MIRACLE, MAX VERNON MD, LICENSE NUMBER A018031, OF TROUTDALE, OR, WAS DISCIPLINED BY CALIFORNIA ON OCTOBER 13, 1989.
DISCIPLINARY ACTION: LICENSE REVOCATION
OFFENSE: DISCIPLINARY ACTION BY ANOTHER STATE OR AGENCY
NOTES: DEFAULT DECISION; DISCIPLINED BY OREGON MEDICAL BOARD FOR INAPPROPRIATE PRESCRIBING OF RITALIN TO HYPERACTIVE PUPILS WITHOUT EXAM AND INDEPENDENT EVALUATION

MISKO, JOHN CHARLES MD, LICENSE NUMBER 0005892, OF PORTLAND, OR, WAS DISCIPLINED BY OREGON ON MAY 6, 1991.
DISCIPLINARY ACTION: RESTRICTION PLACED ON CONTROLLED SUBSTANCE LICENSE
NOTES: MUST PROVIDE TRIPLICATE COPIES OF CONTROLLED

- OREGON -

SUBSTANCE PRESCRIPTIONS. NO LONGER RESTRICTED AS OF 1/28/92.

MOORE, RAYMOND EDMOND MD, LICENSE NUMBER 0005208, OF PORTLAND, OR, WAS DISCIPLINED BY OREGON ON JULY 11, 1991.
DISCIPLINARY ACTION: RESTRICTION PLACED ON CONTROLLED SUBSTANCE LICENSE
NOTES: MUST PROVIDE TRIPLICATE COPIES OF CONTROLLED SUBSTANCE PRESCRIPTIONS. NO LONGER RESTRICTED AS OF 1/28/92.

MORRIS, TRACY LEE MD, LICENSE NUMBER MD16369, OF PORTLAND, OR, WAS DISCIPLINED BY OREGON ON OCTOBER 11, 1989.
DISCIPLINARY ACTION: RESTRICTION PLACED ON LICENSE
NOTES: LIMITED TO A SETTING WITH MEDICAL SUPERVISION. AS OF 5/27/97, NO LONGER LISTED AS RESTRICTED.

MORSE, HOWARD T MD, DATE OF BIRTH DECEMBER 31, 1932, OF 30 MONTGOMERY COURT, PORT LUDLOW, OR, WAS DISCIPLINED BY MEDICARE ON JUNE 27, 1996.
DISCIPLINARY ACTION: EXCLUSION FROM THE MEDICARE AND/OR MEDICAID PROGRAMS
OFFENSE: DISCIPLINARY ACTION BY ANOTHER STATE OR AGENCY
NOTES: LICENSE SURRENDERED FOR REASONS BEARING ON PROFESSIONAL COMPETENCE.

MORSE, HOWARD TILTON MD, LICENSE NUMBER 0A18547, OF PASADENA, CA, WAS DISCIPLINED BY CALIFORNIA ON APRIL 20, 1995.
DISCIPLINARY ACTION: SURRENDER OF LICENSE
NOTES: VOLUNTARY SURRENDER WHILE CHARGES PENDING.

MOTE, FREDERICK ANDREW MD, LICENSE NUMBER 0007573, OF PORTLAND, OR, WAS DISCIPLINED BY OREGON ON JULY 11, 1991.
DISCIPLINARY ACTION: RESTRICTION PLACED ON CONTROLLED SUBSTANCE LICENSE
NOTES: MUST PROVIDE TRIPLICATE COPIES OF CONTROLLED SUBSTANCE PRESCRIPTIONS; RESTRICTION ON SCHEDULES IV AND V; VOLUNTARY RESTRICTION ON SCHEDULES II AND III.

MOTE, FREDERICK ANDREW MD, DATE OF BIRTH JANUARY 21, 1936, LICENSE NUMBER 0009046, OF PO BOX 807, SUPERIOR, MT, WAS DISCIPLINED BY MONTANA ON OCTOBER 7, 1992.
DISCIPLINARY ACTION: 180-MONTH PROBATION; MONITORING OF PHYSICIAN
OFFENSE: CRIMINAL CONVICTION OR PLEA OF GUILTY, NOLO CONTENDERE, OR NO CONTEST TO A CRIME
NOTES: ON 7/1/92 PLED GUILTY TO A MISDEMEANOR, SEXUAL ABUSE OF MINOR; ADMITS HE IS A SEX OFFENDER AND SUFFERING FROM AN ATYPICAL SEXUAL DISORDER; HAS SOUGHT TREATMENT FOR THIS DISORDER; ENGAGED IN FRAUD ON LICENSE APPLICATION BY STATING THAT HE HAD NOT BEEN TREATED FOR A MENTAL ILLNESS. CONDITIONS OF PROBATION: SHALL ENTER INTO A SEX OFFENDER REHABILITATION PROGRAM APPROVED BY THE BOARD AND COMPLY WITH ALL REQUIREMENTS INCLUDING AT LEAST ONE GROUP THERAPY SESSION AND ONE INDIVIDUAL THERAPY SESSION PER WEEK; DIRECTOR OF THIS PROGRAM WILL PROVIDE THE BOARD WITH QUARTERLY REPORTS; DURING ALL PATIENT CONTACT WITH MINORS A THIRD PARTY SHALL BE IN THE ROOM; SHALL AVOID ANY UNCHAPERONED CONTACT WITH MINORS BOTH IN PROFESSIONAL AND PRIVATE LIFE; SHALL ABSTAIN FROM ANY SEXUAL CONTACT WITH MINORS OF EITHER SEX; SHALL ABSTAIN FROM SELF-MEDICATION IN ANY FORM AND SHALL OBTAIN ALL MEDICAL CARE FROM A BOARD APPROVED PHYSICIAN; SHALL SIGN ALL RELEASES NECESSARY FOR BOARD TO OBTAIN ALL RECORDS; SHALL INFORM EACH FACILITY WHERE HE PROVIDES SERVICES OF THE ORDER.

MOTE, FREDERICK ANDREW MD, DATE OF BIRTH JANUARY 21, 1936, LICENSE NUMBER 0009046, OF PO BOX 807, SUPERIOR, MT, WAS DISCIPLINED BY MONTANA ON DECEMBER 21, 1994.
DISCIPLINARY ACTION: PROBATION; RESTRICTION PLACED ON CONTROLLED SUBSTANCE LICENSE
OFFENSE: OVERPRESCRIBING OR MISPRESCRIBING DRUGS
NOTES: CONCERNING QUALITY OF CARE AND MANAGEMENT OF CHRONIC PAIN; PROBLEM WITH PRESCRIBING OF CONTROLLED SUBSTANCES. AMENDMENT TO STIPULATION FOR PROBATION ADDING REQUIREMENT FOR DUPLICATE PRESCRIPTIONS ON CONTROLLED SUBSTANCES, COMPLIANCE WITH CHARTING GUIDELINES, COOPERATION WITH PEER REVIEWS AND CONTINUING EDUCATION ON CHRONIC PAIN MANAGEMENT.

MUMFORD, D CURTIS MD, LICENSE NUMBER 0029419, OF PORTLAND, OR, WAS DISCIPLINED BY WASHINGTON ON MAY 31, 1996.
DISCIPLINARY ACTION: SURRENDER OF LICENSE
NOTES: AGREED TO RETIRE IN CONSIDERATION OF TERMINATING A PENDING INVESTIGATION.

MUMFORD, DWIGHT CURTIS MD, LICENSE NUMBER MD08485, OF BEAVERTON, OR, WAS DISCIPLINED BY OREGON ON JANUARY 13, 1994.
DISCIPLINARY ACTION: RESTRICTION PLACED ON LICENSE
NOTES: SHALL NOT ENGAGE IN THE PRACTICE OF MEDICINE. NO LONGER LISTED AS RESTRICTED AS OF 8/12/96.

MURPHY, GEORGE B MD OF 7591-C CRATER LAKE HIGHWAY, WHITE CITY, OR, WAS DISCIPLINED BY DEA ON APRIL 20, 1994.
DISCIPLINARY ACTION: SURRENDER OF CONTROLLED SUBSTANCE LICENSE
NOTES: IN LIEU OF PUBLIC INTEREST REVOCATION.

MURPHY, GEORGE B JR MD, LICENSE NUMBER 0023930, OF 2600 NORTH VALLEY VIEW RD, ASHLAND, OR, WAS DISCIPLINED BY MASSACHUSETTS ON JUNE 14, 1995.
DISCIPLINARY ACTION: SURRENDER OF LICENSE
NOTES: RESIGNATION.

MURPHY, GEORGE BYRD JR MD, LICENSE NUMBER MD12748, OF ASHLAND, OR, WAS DISCIPLINED BY OREGON ON JULY 15, 1994.
DISCIPLINARY ACTION: LICENSE REVOCATION
OFFENSE: CRIMINAL CONVICTION OR PLEA OF GUILTY, NOLO CONTENDERE, OR NO CONTEST TO A CRIME
NOTES: CONVICTION FOR WRONGFUL CLAIMS.

NEAL, STANLEY KING MD, LICENSE NUMBER 0009527, OF ALBANY, OR, WAS DISCIPLINED BY OREGON ON AUGUST 14, 1991.
DISCIPLINARY ACTION: RESTRICTION PLACED ON CONTROLLED SUBSTANCE LICENSE
NOTES: MUST PROVIDE TRIPLICATE COPIES OF CONTROLLED SUBSTANCE PRESCRIPTIONS. NO LONGER RESTRICTED AS OF 1/28/92.

NEITLING, STANLEY JOSEPH JR MD, LICENSE NUMBER MD13059, OF ALOHA, OR, WAS DISCIPLINED BY OREGON ON OCTOBER 13, 1994.
DISCIPLINARY ACTION: LICENSE SUSPENSION
OFFENSE: SUBSTANCE ABUSE
NOTES: ADDICTION TO CONTROLLED SUBSTANCES.

NEITLING, STANLEY JOSEPH JR MD, LICENSE NUMBER 0013059, OF ALOHA, OR, WAS DISCIPLINED BY OREGON ON JANUARY 19, 1995.
DISCIPLINARY ACTION: 120-MONTH PROBATION
OFFENSE: SUBSTANCE ABUSE
NOTES: ALCOHOL DEPENDENCE.

NICKELS, RUSSELL A MD, DATE OF BIRTH JUNE 11, 1939, OF 415

- OREGON -

HIGHLAND AVENUE, SMITH RIVER, CA, WAS DISCIPLINED BY MEDICARE ON DECEMBER 30, 1992.
DISCIPLINARY ACTION: EXCLUSION FROM THE MEDICARE AND/OR MEDICAID PROGRAMS
OFFENSE: DISCIPLINARY ACTION BY ANOTHER STATE OR AGENCY
NOTES: LICENSE SURRENDERED IN OREGON WHILE A FORMAL DISCIPLINARY HEARING WAS PENDING.

NICKELS, RUSSELL A MD, LICENSE NUMBER 0030241, OF BROOKINGS, OR, WAS DISCIPLINED BY OHIO ON APRIL 17, 1996.
DISCIPLINARY ACTION: 72-MONTH PROBATION; RESTRICTION PLACED ON LICENSE
OFFENSE: PROVIDING FALSE INFORMATION TO THE BOARD
NOTES: CERTIFIED ON LICENSE RENEWAL APPLICATION THAT HE HAD COMPLETED REQUIRED CONTINUING MEDICAL EDUCATION HOURS WHEN HE HAD NOT COMPLETED THOSE HOURS AT THE TIME OF CERTIFICATION. REQUIRED HOURS WERE SUBSEQUENTLY COMPLETED.

NICKELS, RUSSELL A MD, LICENSE NUMBER 0C30675, OF BROOKINGS, OR, WAS DISCIPLINED BY CALIFORNIA ON JUNE 7, 1996.
DISCIPLINARY ACTION: 3-MONTH LICENSE SUSPENSION; 81-MONTH PROBATION
OFFENSE: DISCIPLINARY ACTION BY ANOTHER STATE OR AGENCY
NOTES: ACTION IN OREGON. VOLUNTARY SURRENDER TO PRACTICE MEDICINE FOR PERFORMING MEDICAL TREATMENT ON PATIENTS THAT WAS CONTRARY TO ACCEPTABLE MEDICAL STANDARDS, THAT CONSTITUTED A DANGER TO PATIENTS AND WAS INAPPROPRIATE AND/OR UNNECESSARY. REVOCATION, STAYED.

NOVAK, FREDDIE MD WAS DISCIPLINED BY OREGON ON DECEMBER 23, 1991.
DISCIPLINARY ACTION: LICENSE SUSPENSION
NOTES: NO LONGER SUSPENDED AS OF 1/28/92.

NOVAK, FREDDIE P MD, LICENSE NUMBER 0G61059, OF PORTLAND, OR, WAS DISCIPLINED BY CALIFORNIA ON MAY 26, 1994.
DISCIPLINARY ACTION: 60-MONTH PROBATION
OFFENSE: DISCIPLINARY ACTION BY ANOTHER STATE OR AGENCY
NOTES: DISCIPLINE BY OREGON BOARD FOR IMPAIRMENT DUE TO EXCESSIVE USE OF CONTROLLED DRUGS. REVOCATION STAYED.

NOVAK, FREDDIE PATRICK DOUGLAS MD, LICENSE NUMBER 0015427, OF PORTLAND, OR, WAS DISCIPLINED BY OREGON ON AUGUST 23, 1991.
DISCIPLINARY ACTION: EMERGENCY SUSPENSION
NOTES: NO LONGER SUSPENDED AS OF 1/28/92.

NOVAK, FREDDIE PATRICK MD, LICENSE NUMBER 0028055, OF 1848 N WINCHELL ST, PORTLAND, OR, WAS DISCIPLINED BY GEORGIA ON JULY 1, 1992.
DISCIPLINARY ACTION: NONRENEWAL OF LICENSE
OFFENSE: DISCIPLINARY ACTION BY ANOTHER STATE OR AGENCY
NOTES: LICENSE SUSPENDED IN OREGON 1/9/92. REVOKED FOR NONRENEWAL.

NOVAK, FREDDIE PATRICK MD, LICENSE NUMBER 0025150, OF OR, WAS DISCIPLINED BY WASHINGTON ON DECEMBER 17, 1992.
DISCIPLINARY ACTION: EMERGENCY SUSPENSION
OFFENSE: DISCIPLINARY ACTION BY ANOTHER STATE OR AGENCY
NOTES: SUSPENSION/REVOCATION AND OR RESTRICTION OF HIS LICENSE TO PRACTICE IN ANOTHER JURISDICTION AND BEING UNABLE TO PRACTICE WITH REASONABLE SKILL AND SAFETY.

NOVAK, FREDDIE PATRICK MD, LICENSE NUMBER 0025150, WAS DISCIPLINED BY WASHINGTON ON MARCH 19, 1993.
DISCIPLINARY ACTION: PROBATION; FINE
OFFENSE: DISCIPLINARY ACTION BY ANOTHER STATE OR AGENCY
NOTES: ON 8/23/91 OREGON LICENSE SUSPENDED BASED ON EXCESSIVE USE OF CONTROLLED SUBSTANCES; URINE SAMPLE TESTED POSITIVE FOR COCAINE ON 11/29/91; SURRENDERED OREGON LICENSE IN LIEU OF FURTHER PROCEEDINGS IN 1/92. PROBATION SUBJECT TO TERMS AND CONDITIONS AS FOLLOWS: SHALL NOT PRACTICE MEDICINE IN WASHINGTON UNTIL HE UNDERGOES A PSYCHOLOGICAL AND PHYSICAL EXAMINATION; SHALL APPEAR BEFORE THE BOARD AND BE REQUIRED TO PRESENT EVIDENCE OF HIS RECOVERY FROM HIS ADDICTION TO DRUGS AND ALCOHOL, INCLUDING THE RESULTS OF THE PSYCHOLOGICAL AND PHYSICAL EXAMINATION; SHALL INFORM THE BOARD IN WRITING OF CHANGES IN PRACTICE AND/OR RESIDENCE ADDRESS; SHALL PAY A $250 FINE. ON 3/23/95 HIS REQUEST FOR MODIFICATION OF THIS ORDER WAS DENIED.

NOVAK, FREDDIE PATRICK MD WAS DISCIPLINED BY NEVADA ON JUNE 30, 1993.
DISCIPLINARY ACTION: LICENSE REVOCATION
OFFENSE: DISCIPLINARY ACTION BY ANOTHER STATE OR AGENCY
NOTES: ON 03/05/93 CHARGED WITH FAILING TO REPORT WITHIN 30 DAYS, AND CONTINUAL FAILURE TO REPORT TO THE BOARD, THE SUSPENSION AND SURRENDER OF HIS OREGON LICENSE TO PRACTICE MEDICINE.

NOVAK, FREDDIE PATRICK DOUGLAS MD, LICENSE NUMBER 0015427, OF PORTLAND, OR, WAS DISCIPLINED BY OREGON ON MAY 17, 1995.
DISCIPLINARY ACTION: 120-MONTH PROBATION; RESTRICTION PLACED ON CONTROLLED SUBSTANCE LICENSE
NOTES: CANNOT PRESCRIBE SCHEDULE II CONTROLLED SUBSTANCES; MUST PROVIDE TRIPLICATE COPIES OF SCHEDULE III AND IV CONTROLLED SUBSTANCES PRESCRIPTIONS UNDER SUPERVISION OF HOSPITAL IN WHICH HE HAS PRIVILEGES.

NOVAK, FREDDIE PATRICK DOUGLAS MD, LICENSE NUMBER 0015427, OF PORTLAND, OR, WAS DISCIPLINED BY OREGON ON FEBRUARY 1, 1996.
DISCIPLINARY ACTION: EMERGENCY SUSPENSION

O'GARA, MICHAEL T DO, LICENSE NUMBER DO08605, OF GOLD BEACH, OR, WAS DISCIPLINED BY OREGON ON OCTOBER 6, 1988.
DISCIPLINARY ACTION: EMERGENCY SUSPENSION

O'GARA, MICHAEL T DO, LICENSE NUMBER DO08605, OF GOLD BEACH, OR, WAS DISCIPLINED BY OREGON ON JULY 13, 1989.
DISCIPLINARY ACTION: 120-MONTH PROBATION; RESTRICTION PLACED ON CONTROLLED SUBSTANCE LICENSE
NOTES: NO PRESCRIBING SCHEDULE II OR III DRUGS EXCEPT IN THE HOSPITAL. ON 1/10/91 DENIAL OF REQUEST FOR TERMINATION OR MODIFICATION OF PROBATION/VOLUNTARY LIMITATION.

O'GARA, MICHAEL T DO, LICENSE NUMBER 113911D, OF 65 W 4TH STREET, GOLD BEACH, OR, WAS DISCIPLINED BY NEW YORK ON JUNE 20, 1994.
DISCIPLINARY ACTION: SURRENDER OF LICENSE
OFFENSE: DISCIPLINARY ACTION BY ANOTHER STATE OR AGENCY
NOTES: DID NOT CONTEST CHARGES THAT HE HAD BEEN FOUND GUILTY OF MISCONDUCT BY THE OREGON BOARD.

O'GARA, MICHAEL THOMAS DO OF 165 WEST 4TH STREET, GOLD BEACH, OR, WAS DISCIPLINED BY DEA ON MARCH 15, 1996.
DISCIPLINARY ACTION: RESTRICTION PLACED ON CONTROLLED SUBSTANCE LICENSE
OFFENSE: DISCIPLINARY ACTION BY ANOTHER STATE OR AGENCY
NOTES: STATE BOARD.

OBYE, JOHN ROGER MD, LICENSE NUMBER 0003292, OF 5920 SW

- OREGON -

BURMA RD, LAKE OSWEGO, OR, WAS DISCIPLINED BY MONTANA ON APRIL 4, 1992.
DISCIPLINARY ACTION: LICENSE REVOCATION
OFFENSE: SUBSTANDARD CARE, INCOMPETENCE, OR NEGLIGENCE
NOTES: NEGLIGENCE, GROSS MALPRACTICE, MENTALLY AND PHYSICALLY UNABLE TO SAFELY ENGAGE IN THE PRACTICE OF MEDICINE.

OELKE, DAVID EDWARD MD, LICENSE NUMBER 0008951, OF COOS BAY, OR, WAS DISCIPLINED BY OREGON ON FEBRUARY 4, 1987.
DISCIPLINARY ACTION: RESTRICTION PLACED ON CONTROLLED SUBSTANCE LICENSE
NOTES: MUST PROVIDE TRIPLICATE COPIES OF CONTROLLED SUBSTANCE PRESCRIPTIONS. NO LONGER RESTRICTED AS OF 1/28/92.

OGARA, MICHAEL THOMAS DO, LICENSE NUMBER 0008605, OF GOLD BEACH, OR, WAS DISCIPLINED BY OREGON ON JANUARY 18, 1996.
DISCIPLINARY ACTION: RESTRICTION PLACED ON CONTROLLED SUBSTANCE LICENSE
NOTES: CANNOT PRESCRIBE SCHEDULE II CONTROLLED SUBSTANCES EXCEPT PATIENT CHARTS IN HOSPITAL; MUST PROVIDE TRIPLICATE COPIES OF SCHEDULE III CONTROLLED SUBSTANCE PRESCRIPTIONS.

OLBRICH, GARY D MD, LICENSE NUMBER 0G31633, OF EUGENE, OR, WAS DISCIPLINED BY CALIFORNIA ON JUNE 19, 1992.
DISCIPLINARY ACTION: 60-MONTH PROBATION
OFFENSE: DISCIPLINARY ACTION BY ANOTHER STATE OR AGENCY
NOTES: DISCIPLINE BY OREGON BOARD. REVOCATION, STAYED. PROBATION WITH TERMS AND CONDITIONS.

OLBRICH, GARY DAVID MD, LICENSE NUMBER 0016466, OF EUGENE, OR, WAS DISCIPLINED BY OREGON ON JANUARY 16, 1990.
DISCIPLINARY ACTION: RESTRICTION PLACED ON LICENSE
NOTES: NO LONGER RESTRICTED AS OF 7/27/92.

OTT, JOHN DAVID DO, DATE OF BIRTH NOVEMBER 25, 1945, LICENSE NUMBER 0001494, OF 1336 ROSEARDEN DRIVE, FOREST GROVE, OR, WAS DISCIPLINED BY IOWA ON SEPTEMBER 4, 1991.
DISCIPLINARY ACTION: LICENSE SUSPENSION
NOTES: LICENSE INDEFINITELY SUSPENDED; DOCTOR AGREED TO NOT MAKE FURTHER APPLICATION FOR RENEWAL OR REINSTATEMENT OF MEDICAL LICENSE IN IOWA.

OTT, JOHN DAVID MD, DATE OF BIRTH NOVEMBER 25, 1945, WAS DISCIPLINED BY OREGON ON OCTOBER 10, 1991.
DISCIPLINARY ACTION: SURRENDER OF LICENSE
OFFENSE: SUBSTANDARD CARE, INCOMPETENCE, OR NEGLIGENCE
NOTES: ALLEGED INAPPROPRIATE CARE/INCOMPETENCE. RETIRE/SURRENDER IN LIEU OF DISCIPLINARY ACTION.

OTT, JOHN DAVID DO, DATE OF BIRTH NOVEMBER 25, 1945, LICENSE NUMBER 0009271, OF 1336 ROSEARDEN DR, FOREST GROVE, OR, WAS DISCIPLINED BY MONTANA ON MAY 26, 1992.
DISCIPLINARY ACTION: DENIAL OF NEW LICENSE
OFFENSE: PROFESSIONAL MISCONDUCT
NOTES: INADEQUATELY TREATED SEXUAL MISCONDUCT.

OTT, JOHN DAVID DO, DATE OF BIRTH NOVEMBER 25, 1945, LICENSE NUMBER 0009271, OF 1336 ROSEARDEN DRIVE, FOREST GROVE, OR, WAS DISCIPLINED BY MONTANA ON AUGUST 16, 1995.
DISCIPLINARY ACTION: RESTRICTION PLACED ON LICENSE
NOTES: ISSUED LICENSE WITH RESTRICTIONS. EVIDENCE OF REHABILITATION AND POSSIBILITY OF PRACTICE WITH REASONABLE SKILL AND SAFETY UNDER RESTRICTIONS.

OTT, JOHN DAVID MD, DATE OF BIRTH NOVEMBER 25, 1945, WAS DISCIPLINED BY WISCONSIN ON MAY 8, 1996.
DISCIPLINARY ACTION: DENIAL OF NEW LICENSE
OFFENSE: DISCIPLINARY ACTION BY ANOTHER STATE OR AGENCY
NOTES: ACTION IN IOWA, OREGON, MONTANA, AND PENNSYLVANIA. ON 9/04/91 HIS LICENSE TO PRACTICE MEDICINE AND SURGERY IN IOWA WAS INDEFINITELY SUSPENDED IN CONNECTION WITH ALLEGATIONS OF SEXUAL IMPROPRIETIES WITH PATIENTS. ON 10/10/91 HIS LICENSE TO PRACTICE MEDICINE IN OREGON WAS SURRENDERED. ON 5/26/92 HIS APPLICATION FOR LICENSURE IN MONTANA WAS DENIED. ON 7/12/95 HIS LICENSE IN PENNSYLVANIA WAS DENIED. AN EVALUATION CONCLUDED THAT ANY PRIVILEGE GRANTED TO DR. OTT TO PRACTICE MEDICINE SHOULD REQUIRE CONTINUED PARTICIPATION IN A PROGRAM, THAT A "MEDICAL SURVEILLANCE TEAM" SHOULD BE ORGANIZED TO OVERSEE HIS PRACTICE, THAT RANDOM PATIENT SURVEYS SHOULD BE PERFORMED TO MONITOR HIS BEHAVIOR WITH PATIENTS, AND THAT HE SHOULD BE SUBJECT TO QUARTERLY POLYGRAPH EXAMINATIONS.

PACHOT, JOHN REED MD, LICENSE NUMBER 0011353, OF TUALATIN, OR, WAS DISCIPLINED BY OREGON ON APRIL 28, 1987.
DISCIPLINARY ACTION: RESTRICTION PLACED ON CONTROLLED SUBSTANCE LICENSE
NOTES: MUST PROVIDE TRIPLICATE COPIES OF CONTROLLED SUBSTANCE PRESCRIPTIONS. NO LONGER RESTRICTED AS OF 10/13/92.

PALTROW, KENNETH GUY MD, LICENSE NUMBER 0006784, OF PORTLAND, OR, WAS DISCIPLINED BY OREGON ON OCTOBER 26, 1987.
DISCIPLINARY ACTION: RESTRICTION PLACED ON CONTROLLED SUBSTANCE LICENSE
NOTES: MUST PROVIDE TRIPLICATE COPIES OF CONTROLLED SUBSTANCE PRESCRIPTIONS. AS OF 8/1/93 NO LONGER LISTED AS RESTRICTED.

PAROSA, JAMES FRANCIS MD, LICENSE NUMBER 0011110, OF SALEM, OR, WAS DISCIPLINED BY OREGON ON JANUARY 28, 1987.
DISCIPLINARY ACTION: 120-MONTH PROBATION
NOTES: AS OF 8/1/93 NO LONGER LISTED AS ON PROBATION.

PAROSA, JAMES FRANCIS MD, LICENSE NUMBER 0011110, OF SALEM, OR, WAS DISCIPLINED BY OREGON ON APRIL 7, 1988.
DISCIPLINARY ACTION: RESTRICTION PLACED ON CONTROLLED SUBSTANCE LICENSE
NOTES: MUST PROVIDE TRIPLICATE COPIES OF CONTROLLED SUBSTANCE PRESCRIPTIONS. ON 8/1/93 NO LONGER LISTED AS ON RESTRICTION.

PARSONS, REX RICHARD MD, LICENSE NUMBER MD12968, OF TILLAMOOK, OR, WAS DISCIPLINED BY OREGON ON JULY 13, 1989.
DISCIPLINARY ACTION: RESTRICTION PLACED ON LICENSE
NOTES: ON 10/10/91 TERMINATION OF PROBATION OR VOLUNTARY LIMITATION.

PATTON, PHILLIP EDWARD MD, LICENSE NUMBER 0014787, OF TROUTDALE, OR, WAS DISCIPLINED BY OREGON ON APRIL 18, 1996.
DISCIPLINARY ACTION: 12-MONTH REPRIMAND
OFFENSE: PROFESSIONAL MISCONDUCT
NOTES: UNPROFESSIONAL AND DISHONORABLE CONDUCT.

PEACOCK, WILLIS EDWARD MD, LICENSE NUMBER 0006389, OF SALEM, OR, WAS DISCIPLINED BY OREGON ON OCTOBER 10, 1991.
DISCIPLINARY ACTION: LICENSE SUSPENSION

PEACOCK, WILLIS EDWARD MD, LICENSE NUMBER MD06389, OF SALEM, OR, WAS DISCIPLINED BY OREGON ON APRIL 9, 1992.
DISCIPLINARY ACTION: 120-MONTH PROBATION; 120-MONTH RESTRICTION PLACED ON CONTROLLED SUBSTANCE LICENSE
NOTES: SCHEDULE II PRESCRIBING PRIVILEGES RESTRICTED; MUST PROVIDE TRIPLICATE COPIES OF CONTROLLED SUBSTANCE PRESCRIPTIONS FOR SCHEDULES III, IV AND V.

- OREGON -

PETERS, BRUCE ALFRED MD, LICENSE NUMBER MD06296, OF PORTLAND, OR, WAS DISCIPLINED BY OREGON ON OCTOBER 9, 1987.
DISCIPLINARY ACTION: RESTRICTION PLACED ON LICENSE
NOTES: NO ANESTHESIOLOGY

PETROSKE, JAMES L MD OF 2250 NW FLANDERS, #103, PORTLAND, OR, WAS DISCIPLINED BY DEA ON APRIL 27, 1989.
DISCIPLINARY ACTION: SURRENDER OF CONTROLLED SUBSTANCE LICENSE
OFFENSE: OVERPRESCRIBING OR MISPRESCRIBING DRUGS
NOTES: PRESCRIBED EXCESSIVE AMOUNTS OF METHYLPHENIDATE. SURRENDERED LICENSE TO PRACTICE MEDICINE IN OREGON FOLLOWED BY VOLUNTARY SURRENDER OF CONTROLLED SUBSTANCE REGISTRATION.

PETROSKE, JAMES L MD WAS DISCIPLINED BY WASHINGTON ON MARCH 15, 1990.
DISCIPLINARY ACTION: EMERGENCY SUSPENSION

PETROSKE, JAMES L MD WAS DISCIPLINED BY WASHINGTON ON JUNE 22, 1990.
DISCIPLINARY ACTION: LICENSE REVOCATION
OFFENSE: DISCIPLINARY ACTION BY ANOTHER STATE OR AGENCY
NOTES: OREGON BOARD RESTRICTED LICENSE 7/13/88 AND ON 1/25/89 ACCEPTED SURRENDER OF LICENSE IN LIEU OF PROCEEDING TO A CONTESTED HEARING ON POSSIBLE REVOCATION OF HIS LICENSE. MAY PETITION FOR REINSTATEMENT AT ANY TIME.

PETROSKE, JAMES LAWRENCE MD, DATE OF BIRTH MAY 11, 1933, LICENSE NUMBER 0015511, OF PO BOX 2908, PORTLAND, OR, WAS DISCIPLINED BY MINNESOTA ON JANUARY 28, 1991.
DISCIPLINARY ACTION: LICENSE REVOCATION
OFFENSE: DISCIPLINARY ACTION BY ANOTHER STATE OR AGENCY
NOTES: VIOLATING FEDERAL LAW RELATING TO THE PRACTICE OF MEDICINE; ENGAGING IN UNETHICAL AND UNPROFESSIONAL CONDUCT; INABILITY TO PRACTICE MEDICINE WITH REASONABLE SKILL AND SAFETY BY REASON OF CHEMICALS; BECOMING HABITUATED TO INTOXICANTS; PRESCRIBING DRUGS FOR OTHER THAN MEDICALLY ACCEPTED THERAPEUTIC PURPOSES; ENGAGING IN CONDUCT WITH PATIENTS WHICH IS SEXUAL.

PETROSKE, JAMES LAWRENCE MD, DATE OF BIRTH MAY 11, 1933, OF 2250 N W FLANDERS, PORTLAND, OR, WAS DISCIPLINED BY MEDICARE ON JULY 24, 1991.
DISCIPLINARY ACTION: EXCLUSION FROM THE MEDICARE AND/OR MEDICAID PROGRAMS
OFFENSE: DISCIPLINARY ACTION BY ANOTHER STATE OR AGENCY
NOTES: LICENSE REVOCATION OR SUSPENSION.

PINNEY, CHARLES TANNERT JR MD, LICENSE NUMBER 0015755, OF PORTLAND, OR, WAS DISCIPLINED BY OREGON ON OCTOBER 14, 1991.
DISCIPLINARY ACTION: 120-MONTH PROBATION; 120-MONTH RESTRICTION PLACED ON CONTROLLED SUBSTANCE LICENSE
OFFENSE: PROFESSIONAL MISCONDUCT
NOTES: REVOCATION STAYED; NO SCHEDULE II, III, AND IV PRESCRIBING PRIVILEGES. AS OF 8/18/94 HAD SCHEDULE II, III AND IV PRIVILEGES FOR PATIENTS IN EMERGENCY ROOMS. NO LONGER LISTED AS ON PROBATION AS OF 11/27/95.

PRITCHARD, JAMES SCOTT DO, LICENSE NUMBER 0013835, OF PORTLAND, OR, WAS DISCIPLINED BY OREGON ON MARCH 30, 1995.
DISCIPLINARY ACTION: LICENSE SUSPENSION
OFFENSE: SUBSTANCE ABUSE
NOTES: INDEFINITE SUSPENSION.

PUZISS, ABE MD, LICENSE NUMBER 0003388, OF PORTLAND, OR, WAS DISCIPLINED BY OREGON ON APRIL 12, 1995.
DISCIPLINARY ACTION: SURRENDER OF LICENSE
NOTES: VOLUNTARY SURRENDER. THIS IS NOT A DISCIPLINARY ACTION.

QUINN, KEVIN T MD OF PORTLAND, OR, WAS DISCIPLINED BY NORTH DAKOTA ON JULY 21, 1989.
DISCIPLINARY ACTION: MONITORING OF PHYSICIAN
NOTES: MUST NOTIFY THE BOARD OF ANY INTENTION TO PRACTICE MEDICINE IN THE STATE AND MUST SUBMIT TO CHEMICAL DEPENDENCY MONITORING UPON HIS RETURN

QUINN, KEVIN THOMAS MD, LICENSE NUMBER MD16252, OF BEND, OR, WAS DISCIPLINED BY OREGON ON JULY 19, 1989.
DISCIPLINARY ACTION: 120-MONTH PROBATION
NOTES: AS OF 8/1/93 NO LONGER LISTED AS ON PROBATION.

RASMUSSEN, CHESTER MURRAY DO, LICENSE NUMBER 0005601, OF JUNCTION CITY, OR, WAS DISCIPLINED BY OREGON ON JANUARY 11, 1991.
DISCIPLINARY ACTION: RESTRICTION PLACED ON CONTROLLED SUBSTANCE LICENSE
OFFENSE: OVERPRESCRIBING OR MISPRESCRIBING DRUGS
NOTES: ALLEGED INAPPROPRIATE PRESCRIBING. NO DEA PRIVILEGES. ON 7/11/91 DENIAL OF REQUEST FOR TERMINATION OR MODIFICATION OF PROBATION/VOLUNTARY LIMITATION.

RASMUSSEN, CHESTER MURRAY DO OF 1020 WEST 6TH, JUNCTION CITY, OR, WAS DISCIPLINED BY DEA ON DECEMBER 10, 1993.
DISCIPLINARY ACTION: SURRENDER OF CONTROLLED SUBSTANCE LICENSE
OFFENSE: DISCIPLINARY ACTION BY ANOTHER STATE OR AGENCY
NOTES: MEDICAL BOARD SUSPENDED LICENSE ON 11/01/91.

REDFIELD, JOHN T MD, LICENSE NUMBER 0095091, OF 1065 EAST 22ND AVENUE, EUGENE, OR, WAS DISCIPLINED BY NEW YORK ON AUGUST 8, 1996.
DISCIPLINARY ACTION: LICENSE REVOCATION
OFFENSE: DISCIPLINARY ACTION BY ANOTHER STATE OR AGENCY
NOTES: ACTION IN OREGON FOR BEING UNABLE TO SAFELY AND COMPETENTLY PRACTICE MEDICINE BECAUSE OF A PSYCHIATRIC CONDITION.

REDFIELD, JOHN THOMAS MD, LICENSE NUMBER 0006844, OF EUGENE, OR, WAS DISCIPLINED BY OREGON ON NOVEMBER 14, 1995.
DISCIPLINARY ACTION: LICENSE SUSPENSION
NOTES: MUST SUCCESSFULLY PASS PANEL EXAM IN HIS SPECIALTY ADMINISTERED BY BOARD.

REILLY, DENNIS EUGENE DO, LICENSE NUMBER DO13019, OF THE DALLES, OR, WAS DISCIPLINED BY OREGON ON APRIL 9, 1992.
DISCIPLINARY ACTION: PROBATION; FINE

RICHARD, SAMUEL DR WAS DISCIPLINED BY OREGON ON NOVEMBER 5, 1991.
DISCIPLINARY ACTION: FINE; REPRIMAND
OFFENSE: PROFESSIONAL MISCONDUCT
NOTES: ALLEGED SEXUAL MISCONDUCT.

RICHARD, SAMUEL WILLIAM MD, DATE OF BIRTH DECEMBER 20, 1952, LICENSE NUMBER 0014970, OF OHSU HEALTH CENTER, PORTLAND, OR, WAS DISCIPLINED BY OREGON ON JULY 11, 1991.
DISCIPLINARY ACTION: FINE; REPRIMAND
OFFENSE: SEXUAL ABUSE OF OR SEXUAL MISCONDUCT WITH A PATIENT
NOTES: ADMITTED THAT HAD SEXUAL RELATIONS WITH AN ADULT, FEMALE PATIENT. REPRIMANDED FOR UNPROFESSIONAL CONDUCT; $1,000 FINE; SHALL ENTER

- OREGON -

INTO AN OUTPATIENT PROGRAM OF PSYCHOTHERAPY UNDER THE CARE AND TREATMENT OF A BOARD APPROVED PSYCHIATRIST.

RIDGWAY, DERRY LEE MD, LICENSE NUMBER 0010816, OF PORTLAND, OR, WAS DISCIPLINED BY OREGON ON OCTOBER 11, 1991.
DISCIPLINARY ACTION: 99-MONTH PROBATION
OFFENSE: PROFESSIONAL MISCONDUCT
NOTES: REVOCATION STAYED.

ROBINSON, TAYLOR MD, LICENSE NUMBER MD15910, OF EUGENE, OR, WAS DISCIPLINED BY OREGON ON JULY 31, 1993.
DISCIPLINARY ACTION: LICENSE REVOCATION

ROBINSON, TAYLOR MD, LICENSE NUMBER 0044899, OF 1442 PEARL STREET, EUGENE, OR, WAS DISCIPLINED BY MASSACHUSETTS ON MAY 11, 1994.
DISCIPLINARY ACTION: LICENSE REVOCATION
OFFENSE: DISCIPLINARY ACTION BY ANOTHER STATE OR AGENCY
NOTES: DISCIPLINE BY OREGON; SEXUAL RELATIONS.

ROSENCRANTZ, DAVID RICHARD MD, LICENSE NUMBER 0007089, OF PORTLAND, OR, WAS DISCIPLINED BY OREGON ON JULY 19, 1996.
DISCIPLINARY ACTION: PROBATION; FINE
NOTES: MUST PROVIDE TRIPLICATE COPIES OF CONTROLLED SUBSTANCES PRESCRIPTIONS. $5,000 FINE.

ROSS, TIMOTHY TODD MD, LICENSE NUMBER 0012417, OF PORTLAND, OR, WAS DISCIPLINED BY OREGON ON OCTOBER 12, 1987.
DISCIPLINARY ACTION: RESTRICTION PLACED ON CONTROLLED SUBSTANCE LICENSE
NOTES: RESTRICTION ON PRESCRIBING SCHEDULE II DRUGS. MUST PROVIDE TRIPLICATE COPIES OF CONTROLLED SUBSTANCE PRESCRIPTIONS. ON 7/11/91 VOLUNTARY LIMITATION WAS TERMINATED. NO LONGER RESTRICTED AS OF 1/28/92.

RUE, GEORGE H JR MD, LICENSE NUMBER 0004440, OF PORTLAND, OR, WAS DISCIPLINED BY OREGON ON APRIL 12, 1990.
DISCIPLINARY ACTION: LICENSE SUSPENSION

RUE, GEORGE H JR MD OF TAYLORS, SC, WAS DISCIPLINED BY WASHINGTON ON OCTOBER 7, 1991.
DISCIPLINARY ACTION: SURRENDER OF LICENSE
OFFENSE: DISCIPLINARY ACTION BY ANOTHER STATE OR AGENCY
NOTES: UNDER INVESTIGATION BY BOARD CONCERNING ALLEGATIONS OF UNPROFESSIONAL CONDUCT RELATING TO ACTIONS TAKEN AGAINST LICENSE BY OTHER STATE, AND FURTHER ALLEGATIONS OF PHYSICAL AND MENTAL IMPAIRMENT. RETIREMENT FROM PRACTICE EFFECTIVE IMMEDIATELY.

RUTTLE, PAUL EDWARD MD, LICENSE NUMBER MD13325, OF RIVERTON, OR, WAS DISCIPLINED BY OREGON ON OCTOBER 6, 1988.
DISCIPLINARY ACTION: RESTRICTION PLACED ON LICENSE
NOTES: NO SURGERY EXCEPT TO ASSIST QUALIFIED SURGEONS. NO LONGER LISTED AS RESTRICTED AS OF 1/28/92.

SAKS, SELDON KEITH MD, LICENSE NUMBER 0015511, OF PORTLAND, OR, WAS DISCIPLINED BY OREGON ON OCTOBER 20, 1995.
DISCIPLINARY ACTION: 6-MONTH RESTRICTION PLACED ON CONTROLLED SUBSTANCE LICENSE; REQUIRED TO TAKE ADDITIONAL MEDICAL EDUCATION
NOTES: MUST PROVIDE TRIPLICATE COPIES OF PRESCRIPTIONS FOR SCHEDULE III, IV AND V CONTROLLED SUBSTANCES. MUST ATTEND A WORKSHOP IN APPROPRIATE PRESCRIBING, A TWO DAY COURSE. NO LONGER LISTED AS RESTRICTED AS OF 8/12/96.

SCOTT, PETER NORMAN MD, LICENSE NUMBER 0014756, OF PORTLAND, OR, WAS DISCIPLINED BY OREGON ON JANUARY 10, 1991.
DISCIPLINARY ACTION: 120-MONTH PROBATION
OFFENSE: PROFESSIONAL MISCONDUCT
NOTES: REVOCATION STAYED. AS OF 4/20/93 NO LONGER LISTED AS ON PROBATION.

SHAH, ASHVIN NATVARLAL MD OF 3040 SCOTT CRESCENT DRIVE, FLOSSMOOR, IL, WAS DISCIPLINED BY DEA ON JULY 18, 1995.
DISCIPLINARY ACTION: SURRENDER OF CONTROLLED SUBSTANCE LICENSE
NOTES: IN LIEU OF ORDER TO SHOW CAUSE.

SHAH, ASHVIN NATVARLAL MD, LICENSE NUMBER 0011420, OF CHICAGO, IL, WAS DISCIPLINED BY OREGON ON FEBRUARY 29, 1996.
DISCIPLINARY ACTION: LICENSE SUSPENSION
OFFENSE: DISCIPLINARY ACTION BY ANOTHER STATE OR AGENCY
NOTES: AUTOMATIC SUSPENSION FOR ACTION TAKEN IN ANOTHER STATE.

SHEINKOPF, RUSSELL HENDEL MD, LICENSE NUMBER 0013043, OF PORTLAND, OR, WAS DISCIPLINED BY OREGON ON OCTOBER 11, 1990.
DISCIPLINARY ACTION: FINE; REPRIMAND

SHEPPARD, STEPHEN A MD, LICENSE NUMBER 0A27522, OF BROOKINGS, OR, WAS DISCIPLINED BY CALIFORNIA ON DECEMBER 30, 1994.
DISCIPLINARY ACTION: 60-MONTH PROBATION
OFFENSE: CRIMINAL CONVICTION OR PLEA OF GUILTY, NOLO CONTENDERE, OR NO CONTEST TO A CRIME
NOTES: CONVICTION OF FURNISHING A CONTROLLED SUBSTANCE TO A PERSON NOT UNDER HIS TREATMENT FOR A PATHOLOGY OR CONDITION. PRESCRIBING WITHOUT A GOOD FAITH PRIOR EXAM AND MEDICAL INDICATION THEREFOR. REVOCATION STAYED.

SHEPPARD, STEPHEN ALLEN MD, DATE OF BIRTH JUNE 6, 1920, OF 3737 MORAGA AVE SUITE A5, SAN DIEGO, CA, WAS DISCIPLINED BY MEDICARE ON AUGUST 19, 1992.
DISCIPLINARY ACTION: 36-MONTH EXCLUSION FROM THE MEDICARE AND/OR MEDICAID PROGRAMS
OFFENSE: CRIMINAL CONVICTION OR PLEA OF GUILTY, NOLO CONTENDERE, OR NO CONTEST TO A CRIME
NOTES: CONVICTION RELATING TO CONTROLLED SUBSTANCES.

SISLER, FRANK OSCAR MD, LICENSE NUMBER MD04160, OF PORTLAND, OR, WAS DISCIPLINED BY OREGON ON OCTOBER 13, 1994.
DISCIPLINARY ACTION: RESTRICTION PLACED ON LICENSE; RESTRICTION PLACED ON CONTROLLED SUBSTANCE LICENSE
NOTES: NO SCHEDULE II AND III PRESCRIBING PRIVILEGES; MUST PROVIDE TRIPLICATE COPIES FOR SCHEDULE IVS; PATIENTS MUST HAVE PRIMARY PHYSICIAN; VOLUNTARY LIMITATION.

SISLER, FRANK OSCAR MD, LICENSE NUMBER 0004160, OF PORTLAND, OR, WAS DISCIPLINED BY OREGON ON JANUARY 15, 1996.
DISCIPLINARY ACTION: 12-MONTH SURRENDER OF LICENSE
NOTES: VOLUNTARY SURRENDER.

SKACH, LORRAINE E MD, LICENSE NUMBER MD15334, OF SALEM, OR, WAS DISCIPLINED BY OREGON ON OCTOBER 8, 1987.
DISCIPLINARY ACTION: RESTRICTION PLACED ON LICENSE
NOTES: PSYCHIATRIC CARE REQUIRED. AS OF 2/22/95 NO LONGER LISTED AS RESTRICTED.

SKIPPER, GREGORY EARL MD, LICENSE NUMBER 0012011, OF NEWBERG, OR, WAS DISCIPLINED BY OREGON ON DECEMBER 6,

- OREGON -

1990.
DISCIPLINARY ACTION: LICENSE SUSPENSION

SKIPPER, GREGORY EARL MD, LICENSE NUMBER 0012011, OF NEWBERG, OR, WAS DISCIPLINED BY OREGON ON JULY 25, 1991.
DISCIPLINARY ACTION: PROBATION; RESTRICTION PLACED ON CONTROLLED SUBSTANCE LICENSE
OFFENSE: SUBSTANCE ABUSE
NOTES: ALLEGED PERSONAL SUBSTANCE ABUSE. PRESCRIPTION RESTRICTION: NO SCHEDULE II, III, IV, OR V PRESCRIBING PRIVILEGES. REVOCATION STAYED; TERMINATION OF SUSPENSION. AS OF 8/18/94 HAD SCHEDULE II AND III PRESCRIBING PRIVILEGES WITH HOSPITAL PATIENTS; SCHEDULES IV AND V DRUGS ALLOWED WITH TRIPLICATE PRESCRIPTIONS ONLY. AS OF 5/27/97, NO LONGER LISTED AS RESTRICTED AND NO LONGER ON PROBATION.

SMITH, CATHY SCHINDLER MD, LICENSE NUMBER 0015784, OF HILLSBORO, OR, WAS DISCIPLINED BY OREGON ON JULY 25, 1988.
DISCIPLINARY ACTION: RESTRICTION PLACED ON LICENSE
OFFENSE: SUBSTANCE ABUSE
NOTES: NO LONGER RESTRICTED AS OF 10/13/92.

SMITH, DAVID LLOYD MD OF 2883 RAWHIDE COURT, WEST LINN, OR, WAS DISCIPLINED BY DEA ON FEBRUARY 3, 1995.
DISCIPLINARY ACTION: SURRENDER OF CONTROLLED SUBSTANCE LICENSE
NOTES: IN LIEU OF ORDER TO SHOW CAUSE.

SPRAY, CHARLES DR WAS DISCIPLINED BY OREGON ON OCTOBER 10, 1991.
NOTES: TERMINATION OF PROBATION OR VOLUNTARY LIMITATION. RETIRE/SURRENDER IN LIEU OF DISCIPLINARY ACTION.

STANFORD, GARY E MD OF DETROIT, OR, WAS DISCIPLINED BY DEA ON APRIL 16, 1993.
DISCIPLINARY ACTION: REVOCATION OF CONTROLLED SUBSTANCE LICENSE
OFFENSE: DISCIPLINARY ACTION BY ANOTHER STATE OR AGENCY
NOTES: ON 8/15/85 MEDICAL LICENSE IN OREGON RESTRICTED FOR SIX MONTHS AS A RESULT OF HIS CONVICTION FOR NEGLIGENT HOMICIDE; ON 8/19/86 MEDICAL LICENSE IN ILLINOIS WAS SUSPENDED INDEFINITELY; APPLICATION TO PRACTICE MEDICINE WAS DENIED IN WASHINGTON ON 12/21/87; USED COCAINE FOR PERSONAL USE; ALLEGATIONS REGARDING FALSIFICATION OF A HOSPITAL RECORD AND ACCOUNTABILITY FOR AN OFFICE SUPPLY OF CONTROLLED SUBSTANCES; IN 1988, VIOLATED TERMS OF PROBATION FROM NEGLIGENT HOMICIDE CONVICTION BY USING SERAX AND XANAX.

STAWARSKI, SANDRA J MD, LICENSE NUMBER 0139651, OF 108 NE SAVAGE ST, GRANTS PASS, OR, WAS DISCIPLINED BY NEW YORK ON FEBRUARY 7, 1992.
DISCIPLINARY ACTION: LICENSE REVOCATION
OFFENSE: DISCIPLINARY ACTION BY ANOTHER STATE OR AGENCY
NOTES: THE OREGON BOARD TOOK ACTION ON HER LICENSE AFTER SHE ADMITTED TO HABITUAL AND EXCESSIVE USE OF ALCOHOL AND CONTROLLED SUBSTANCES. ALSO KNOWN AS: SANDRA FORREST TYNER, MD.

STOELK, EUGENE MERLE MD, LICENSE NUMBER 0014983, OF PORTLAND, OR, WAS DISCIPLINED BY OREGON ON FEBRUARY 13, 1996.
DISCIPLINARY ACTION: 120-MONTH PROBATION; FINE
NOTES: $5,000 FINE WITHIN TEN DAYS OF ORDER. 1000 HOURS COMMUNITY SERVICE, CONTINUING MEDICAL EDUCATION, RANDOM REVIEW OF CHARTS AND AUDITS.

STONEBROOK, PHILIP R MD, LICENSE NUMBER MD08422, OF ASHLAND, OR, WAS DISCIPLINED BY OREGON ON DECEMBER 5, 1989.
DISCIPLINARY ACTION: 120-MONTH PROBATION
NOTES: NO LONGER LISTED ON PROBATION AS OF 1/21/93.

STRINGHAM, CHARLES H MD OF 260 MILLER STREET SOUTH, SALEM, OR, WAS DISCIPLINED BY DEA ON MAY 31, 1996.
DISCIPLINARY ACTION: RESTRICTION PLACED ON CONTROLLED SUBSTANCE LICENSE
OFFENSE: DISCIPLINARY ACTION BY ANOTHER STATE OR AGENCY
NOTES: STATE BOARD.

STRINGHAM, CHARLES HOWARD MD OF 260 MILLER STREET S, SALEM, OR, WAS DISCIPLINED BY DEA ON MARCH 16, 1993.
DISCIPLINARY ACTION: RESTRICTION PLACED ON CONTROLLED SUBSTANCE LICENSE
OFFENSE: OVERPRESCRIBING OR MISPRESCRIBING DRUGS
NOTES: INAPPROPRIATE PRESCRIBING PRACTICES WHICH WERE NOTED BY AN OREGON BOARD OF MEDICAL EXAMINERS INVESTIGATION.

STRINGHAM, CHARLES HOWARD MD, LICENSE NUMBER MD09749, OF SALEM, OR, WAS DISCIPLINED BY OREGON ON APRIL 6, 1994.
DISCIPLINARY ACTION: RESTRICTION PLACED ON LICENSE
NOTES: VOLUNTARY LIMITATION.

SUTHERLAND, DANIEL L MD, LICENSE NUMBER MD11075, OF GRANTS PASS, OR, WAS DISCIPLINED BY OREGON ON OCTOBER 12, 1989.
DISCIPLINARY ACTION: LICENSE SUSPENSION
NOTES: NOT SUSPENDED AS OF 2/8/90

SUTHERLAND, DANIEL L MD OF 5555 PEACHTREE DUNWOOD RD STE312, ATLANTA, GA, WAS DISCIPLINED BY DEA ON JUNE 17, 1994.
DISCIPLINARY ACTION: SURRENDER OF CONTROLLED SUBSTANCE LICENSE
OFFENSE: DISCIPLINARY ACTION BY ANOTHER STATE OR AGENCY
NOTES: STATE BOARD/UNLAWFUL DISTRIBUTION.

SUTHERLAND, DANIEL LAWRENCE MD, DATE OF BIRTH JUNE 7, 1923, LICENSE NUMBER 0025973, OF 8213 HWY 85 #1204, RIVERDALE, GA, WAS DISCIPLINED BY IOWA ON MARCH 4, 1991.
DISCIPLINARY ACTION: SURRENDER OF LICENSE
OFFENSE: DISCIPLINARY ACTION BY ANOTHER STATE OR AGENCY

SUTHERLAND, DANIEL LAWRENCE MD, DATE OF BIRTH JUNE 7, 1923, OF PO BOX 91624, ATLANTA, GA, WAS DISCIPLINED BY MEDICARE ON NOVEMBER 6, 1991.
DISCIPLINARY ACTION: EXCLUSION FROM THE MEDICARE AND/OR MEDICAID PROGRAMS
OFFENSE: DISCIPLINARY ACTION BY ANOTHER STATE OR AGENCY
NOTES: LICENSE REVOCATION OR SUSPENSION.

SUTHERLAND, DANIEL LAWRENCE MD, DATE OF BIRTH JUNE 7, 1923, LICENSE NUMBER 0030679, OF PO BOX 2212, SMYRNA, GA, WAS DISCIPLINED BY GEORGIA ON AUGUST 4, 1994.
DISCIPLINARY ACTION: SURRENDER OF LICENSE
OFFENSE: OVERPRESCRIBING OR MISPRESCRIBING DRUGS

TAKLA, GAMIL NASSIF MD, LICENSE NUMBER MD06550, OF BEAVERTON, OR, WAS DISCIPLINED BY OREGON ON JULY 15, 1993.
DISCIPLINARY ACTION: RESTRICTION PLACED ON LICENSE
NOTES: VOLUNTARY LIMITATION.

THAYER, JAMES ROBERT MD, LICENSE NUMBER 0013684, OF GRESHAM, OR, WAS DISCIPLINED BY OREGON ON JUNE 9, 1990.
DISCIPLINARY ACTION: LICENSE SUSPENSION

THAYER, JAMES ROBERT MD, LICENSE NUMBER 0013684, OF PORTLAND, OR, WAS DISCIPLINED BY OREGON ON APRIL 9, 1992.
DISCIPLINARY ACTION: 120-MONTH PROBATION; 120-MONTH RESTRICTION PLACED ON CONTROLLED SUBSTANCE LICENSE

- OREGON -

NOTES: MUST PROVIDE TRIPLICATE COPIES OF CONTROLLED SUBSTANCES PRESCRIPTIONS FOR SCHEDULES II THROUGH V. AS OF 8/18/94 NO LONGER LISTED AS ON PROBATION OR RESTRICTED.

THOMAS, STEPHEN JOHN JR MD, LICENSE NUMBER 0008290, OF ALOHA, OR, WAS DISCIPLINED BY OREGON ON SEPTEMBER 9, 1989.
DISCIPLINARY ACTION: RESTRICTION PLACED ON CONTROLLED SUBSTANCE LICENSE
NOTES: MUST PROVIDE TRIPLICATE COPIES OF CONTROLLED SUBSTANCE PRESCRIPTIONS. NO LONGER RESTRICTED AS OF 1/28/92.

TOKAR, RONALD LEE MD, LICENSE NUMBER 0017543, OF WALLA WALLA, WA, WAS DISCIPLINED BY OREGON ON OCTOBER 4, 1991.
DISCIPLINARY ACTION: RESTRICTION PLACED ON LICENSE
NOTES: VOLUNTARY LIMITATION.

TREW, GEORGE MD, LICENSE NUMBER MD10301, OF MEDFORD, OR, WAS DISCIPLINED BY OREGON ON JANUARY 4, 1990.
DISCIPLINARY ACTION: EMERGENCY SUSPENSION

TREW, GEORGE DR WAS DISCIPLINED BY OREGON ON APRIL 15, 1991.
DISCIPLINARY ACTION: SURRENDER OF LICENSE
OFFENSE: FAILURE TO COMPLY WITH A PREVIOUS BOARD ORDER
NOTES: ALLEGED VIOLATION PROBATION/VOLUNTARY LIMITATION.

TREW, GEORGE MD, LICENSE NUMBER 0024024, OF MEDFORD, OR, WAS DISCIPLINED BY WASHINGTON ON APRIL 22, 1991.
DISCIPLINARY ACTION: EMERGENCY SUSPENSION
OFFENSE: DISCIPLINARY ACTION BY ANOTHER STATE OR AGENCY
NOTES: ON 8/9/90 OREGON MEDICAL LICENSE WAS REVOKED, REVOCATION STAYED, AND HE WAS PLACED ON 10 YEARS PROBATION WHEN HE WAS FOUND TO HAVE ENGAGED IN THE HABITUAL USE OF ALCOHOL. ON 1/8/90 HE ENTERED AN INPATIENT TREATMENT PROGRAM FOR ALCOHOL ABUSE; WAS DISCHARGED FROM THE PROGRAM ON 2/12/90.

TREW, GEORGE MD, LICENSE NUMBER 0024024, OF MEDFORD, OR, WAS DISCIPLINED BY WASHINGTON ON OCTOBER 2, 1991.
DISCIPLINARY ACTION: LICENSE REVOCATION
OFFENSE: DISCIPLINARY ACTION BY ANOTHER STATE OR AGENCY
NOTES: ON 4/10/91 OREGON ACCEPTED THE SURRENDER OF HIS LICENSE IN LIEU OF FURTHER DISCIPLINARY ACTION FOR VIOLATION OF THE PROVISION OF PREVIOUS BOARD ORDER REQUIRING THAT HE COMPLETELY REFRAIN FROM THE USE OF ALCOHOLIC BEVERAGES.

TREW, GEORGE MD OF LOS ALAMOS, NM, WAS DISCIPLINED BY NEW MEXICO ON DECEMBER 15, 1993.
DISCIPLINARY ACTION: DENIAL OF NEW LICENSE
OFFENSE: PROFESSIONAL MISCONDUCT

TROCHMANN, REBEKAH ANN MD, LICENSE NUMBER MD15248, OF BEAVERTON, OR, WAS DISCIPLINED BY OREGON ON JULY 15, 1994.
DISCIPLINARY ACTION: RESTRICTION PLACED ON CONTROLLED SUBSTANCE LICENSE
NOTES: NO SCHEDULE II PRESCRIBING; MUST PROVIDE TRIPLICATE COPIES OF PRESCRIPTIONS FOR ALL SCHEDULE III DRUGS. NO LONGER LISTED AS RESTRICTED AS OF 2/22/95.

TYNER, SANDRA DR WAS DISCIPLINED BY OREGON ON JANUARY 10, 1991.
NOTES: DENIAL OF REQUEST FOR TERMINATION OR MODIFICATION OF PROBATION/VOLUNTARY LIMITATION.

TYNER, SANDRA JEAN MD, LICENSE NUMBER 0012361, OF GRANTS PASS, OR, WAS DISCIPLINED BY OREGON ON APRIL 9, 1987.
DISCIPLINARY ACTION: RESTRICTION PLACED ON CONTROLLED SUBSTANCE LICENSE
OFFENSE: OVERPRESCRIBING OR MISPRESCRIBING DRUGS
NOTES: PRESCRIPTION RESTRICTION; MUST PROVIDE TRIPLICATE COPIES OF CONTROLLED SUBSTANCE PRESCRIPTIONS FOR SCHEDULES III, IV, AND V. NO SCHEDULE II PRESCRIBING. AS OF 8/12/96, NO LONGER LISTED AS RESTRICTED.

TYNER, SANDRA JEAN MD, LICENSE NUMBER 0012361, OF GRANTS PASS, OR, WAS DISCIPLINED BY OREGON ON JANUARY 19, 1995.
DISCIPLINARY ACTION: 26-MONTH PROBATION
NOTES: ORDER TO IMPLEMENT PROBATION TERMS. NO LONGER LISTED ON PROBATION AS OF 8/12/96.

TYNER, SANDRA JEAN MD, LICENSE NUMBER 0012361, OF GRANTS PASS, OR, WAS DISCIPLINED BY OREGON ON MAY 1, 1996.
DISCIPLINARY ACTION: LICENSE SUSPENSION
NOTES: INTERIM ORDER OF SUSPENSION. NO LONGER SUSPENDED AS OF 8/12/96.

VALENTINE, THOMAS V MD, LICENSE NUMBER MD15787, OF SEASIDE, OR, WAS DISCIPLINED BY OREGON ON JULY 26, 1988.
DISCIPLINARY ACTION: MONITORING OF PHYSICIAN
OFFENSE: SUBSTANCE ABUSE
NOTES: MUST PROVIDE TRIPLICATE COPIES OF CONTROLLED SUBSTANCE PRESCRIPTIONS. LICENSE NO LONGER UNDER CONDITIONS AS OF 8/10/90.

VANLOON, GLEN DR WAS DISCIPLINED BY OREGON ON MARCH 4, 1991.
DISCIPLINARY ACTION: DENIAL OF NEW LICENSE

VISTICA, MARY FRANCIS DR OF 3101 SW 13TH ST, PORTLAND, OR, WAS DISCIPLINED BY ILLINOIS ON JANUARY 1, 1988.
DISCIPLINARY ACTION: 5-MONTH PROBATION
OFFENSE: PRACTICING WITHOUT A VALID LICENSE
NOTES: TEMPORARY LICENSE FOR POSTGRAD CLINICAL TRAINING ISSUED

VOELKER, GERALD BERNARD MD, LICENSE NUMBER 0006299, OF TIGARD, OR, WAS DISCIPLINED BY OREGON ON AUGUST 23, 1991.
DISCIPLINARY ACTION: REPRIMAND
OFFENSE: SUBSTANDARD CARE, INCOMPETENCE, OR NEGLIGENCE
NOTES: ALLEGED INAPPROPRIATE CARE/INCOMPETENCE.

VOLP, HEINRICH MD, LICENSE NUMBER DU00264, OF BURNS, OR, WAS DISCIPLINED BY OREGON ON SEPTEMBER 28, 1987.
DISCIPLINARY ACTION: LICENSE REVOCATION

VONHIPPEL, JOSEPHINE BARON RASKIND MD, LICENSE NUMBER 0007058, OF EUGENE, OR, WAS DISCIPLINED BY OREGON ON DECEMBER 6, 1990.
DISCIPLINARY ACTION: RESTRICTION PLACED ON CONTROLLED SUBSTANCE LICENSE
NOTES: MUST PROVIDE TRIPLICATE COPIES OF CONTROLLED SUBSTANCE PRESCRIPTIONS. NO LONGER RESTRICTED AS OF 1/28/92.

VU, DAM MD, LICENSE NUMBER MD12474, OF PORTLAND, OR, WAS DISCIPLINED BY OREGON ON JANUARY 25, 1994.
DISCIPLINARY ACTION: LICENSE REVOCATION

VU, DAM MD, LICENSE NUMBER 0018907, OF BEAVERTON, OR, WAS DISCIPLINED BY WASHINGTON ON DECEMBER 16, 1994.
DISCIPLINARY ACTION: SURRENDER OF LICENSE

VU, DAM MD, DATE OF BIRTH SEPTEMBER 9, 1953, OF 15474 NW WHITE FOX DRIVE, BEAVERTON, OR, WAS DISCIPLINED BY MEDICARE ON AUGUST 3, 1995.
DISCIPLINARY ACTION: 36-MONTH EXCLUSION FROM THE MEDICARE AND/OR MEDICAID PROGRAMS

- OREGON -

OFFENSE: CRIMINAL CONVICTION OR PLEA OF GUILTY, NOLO CONTENDERE, OR NO CONTEST TO A CRIME
NOTES: CONVICTED OF A CRIME RELATED TO THE DELIVERY OF HEALTH CARE OR FINANCIAL MISCONDUCT INVOLVING A GOVERNMENT-OPERATED PROGRAM.

WALTERS, MARC DR WAS DISCIPLINED BY OREGON ON JANUARY 24, 1991.
DISCIPLINARY ACTION: DENIAL OF NEW LICENSE
OFFENSE: PROFESSIONAL MISCONDUCT

WALTERS, MARC H MD, DATE OF BIRTH JULY 4, 1957, LICENSE NUMBER 0027837, OF 16455 SW ESTUARY DR #101, BEAVERTON, OR, WAS DISCIPLINED BY WISCONSIN ON JULY 18, 1990.
DISCIPLINARY ACTION: SURRENDER OF LICENSE
OFFENSE: CRIMINAL CONVICTION OR PLEA OF GUILTY, NOLO CONTENDERE, OR NO CONTEST TO A CRIME
NOTES: CONVICTED OF 4TH DEGREE SEXUAL ASSAULT OF A MENTALLY RETARDED PATIENT ON 4/27/89. HAS NOT PRACTICED MEDICINE IN WISCONSIN SINCE 9/88. HE HAS SUFFERED FROM A PSYCHIATRIC ILLNESS AND HAS BEEN TREATED IN 5/82, 8/86, AND 10/88. THE CONDUCT WHICH LED TO HIS CONVICTION WAS DUE, AT LEAST IN PART, TO HIS PSYCHIATRIC ILLNESS.

WATKINS, ROBERT C MD OF 3414 N KAISER CTR DR, PORTLAND, OR, WAS DISCIPLINED BY DEA ON MARCH 30, 1995.
DISCIPLINARY ACTION: SURRENDER OF CONTROLLED SUBSTANCE LICENSE
OFFENSE: DISCIPLINARY ACTION BY ANOTHER STATE OR AGENCY
NOTES: STATE BOARD.

WATKINS, ROBERT CAMP MD, LICENSE NUMBER MD12030, OF CLACKAMAS, OR, WAS DISCIPLINED BY OREGON ON NOVEMBER 3, 1994.
DISCIPLINARY ACTION: EMERGENCY SUSPENSION
OFFENSE: SUBSTANCE ABUSE

WEEKS-ALLGOOD, MELANIE SUE MD, LICENSE NUMBER MD13267, OF PENDLETON, OR, WAS DISCIPLINED BY OREGON ON SEPTEMBER 3, 1992.
DISCIPLINARY ACTION: EMERGENCY SUSPENSION

WEEKS-ALLGOOD, MELANIE SUE MD, LICENSE NUMBER MD13267, OF PENDLETON, OR, WAS DISCIPLINED BY OREGON ON JANUARY 14, 1993.
DISCIPLINARY ACTION: 120-MONTH PROBATION; 120-MONTH RESTRICTION PLACED ON CONTROLLED SUBSTANCE LICENSE
NOTES: CANNOT PRESCRIBE SCHEDULES II, III AND IV. AS OF 2/22/95 NO LONGER LISTED AS ON PROBATION OR RESTRICTED.

WENBERG, KENNETH F MD, LICENSE NUMBER 0025365, OF CAMANO, WA, WAS DISCIPLINED BY WASHINGTON ON JANUARY 18, 1994.
OFFENSE: DISCIPLINARY ACTION BY ANOTHER STATE OR AGENCY
NOTES: VOLUNTARY LIMITATION IMPOSED ON HIS LICENSE BY OREGON. MUST COMPLY WITH ALL TERMS AND CONDITIONS IMPOSED BY THE STATE OF OREGON.

WENBERG, KENNETH FRED MD, LICENSE NUMBER MD14131, OF STANWOOD, OR, WAS DISCIPLINED BY OREGON ON JANUARY 18, 1989.
DISCIPLINARY ACTION: RESTRICTION PLACED ON LICENSE

WENBERG, KENNETH FRED MD, LICENSE NUMBER MD14131, OF HEPPNER, OR, WAS DISCIPLINED BY OREGON ON FEBRUARY 8, 1989.
DISCIPLINARY ACTION: RESTRICTION PLACED ON LICENSE
NOTES: NO OBSTETRICS PRACTICE. NO LONGER RESTRICTED AS OF 1/28/92.

WESTCOTT, GARY RAY MD, LICENSE NUMBER 0019199, OF PORTLAND, OR, WAS DISCIPLINED BY OREGON ON JANUARY 30, 1995.
DISCIPLINARY ACTION: 120-MONTH PROBATION
OFFENSE: SUBSTANCE ABUSE
NOTES: ALCOHOLISM. MUST MAKE QUARTERLY APPEARANCES BEFORE BOARD; SHALL HAVE MONITORING PHYSICIAN; HEALTH PROFESSIONALS TREATMENT PROGRAM; URINE AND/OR BLOOD SPECIMENS VOLUNTARILY RANDOM.

WESTCOTT, GARY RAY MD, LICENSE NUMBER 0019199, OF PORTLAND, OR, WAS DISCIPLINED BY OREGON ON AUGUST 2, 1996.
DISCIPLINARY ACTION: LICENSE SUSPENSION

WESTCOTT, GARY RAY MD, LICENSE NUMBER 0019199, OF PORTLAND, OR, WAS DISCIPLINED BY OREGON ON NOVEMBER 4, 1996.
DISCIPLINARY ACTION: 120-MONTH PROBATION
NOTES: NEW TERMS REPLACE OLD PROBATION TERMS.

WEYL, ALLAN D MD, LICENSE NUMBER 0020437, OF COLTON, OR, WAS DISCIPLINED BY FLORIDA ON JUNE 21, 1988.
DISCIPLINARY ACTION: LICENSE REVOCATION

WHANG, EDWARD KEESAN MD, LICENSE NUMBER 0010381, OF PORTLAND, OR, WAS DISCIPLINED BY OREGON ON SEPTEMBER 10, 1990.
DISCIPLINARY ACTION: RESTRICTION PLACED ON CONTROLLED SUBSTANCE LICENSE
NOTES: MUST PROVIDE TRIPLICATE COPIES OF CONTROLLED PRESCRIPTIONS. NO LONGER RESTRICTED AS OF 1/28/92.

WICHSER, JAMES ALLEN MD, LICENSE NUMBER MD09860, OF NORTH OAKS, OR, WAS DISCIPLINED BY OREGON ON JULY 13, 1988.
DISCIPLINARY ACTION: 60-MONTH RESTRICTION PLACED ON CONTROLLED SUBSTANCE LICENSE
NOTES: RESTRICTION ON PRESCRIBING SCHEDULE II DRUGS. MUST PROVIDE TRIPLICATE COPIES OF SCHEDULE III-V PRESCRIPTIONS. AS OF 8/1/93 NO LONGER LISTED AS RESTRICTED.

WILLIAMS, PAUL C MD, LICENSE NUMBER 0014868, WAS DISCIPLINED BY ARIZONA ON JANUARY 19, 1990.
DISCIPLINARY ACTION: 60-MONTH PROBATION; REQUIRED TO ENTER AN IMPAIRED PHYSICIAN PROGRAM OR DRUG OR ALCOHOL TREATMENT
OFFENSE: FAILURE TO COMPLY WITH A PREVIOUS BOARD ORDER
NOTES: VIOLATED 5/24/89 ORDER IN THE FOLLOWING WAYS: IN 10/89 A BLOOD SAMPLE TESTED POSITIVE FOR ALCOHOL; ALSO FAILED TO OBTAIN A BOARD-APPROVED TREATING PHYSICIAN AND MAINTAIN A LOG OF ALL MEDICATIONS TAKEN. CONDITIONS OF PROBATION: MUST IMMEDIATELY ENROLL IN THE LEVEL III AFTERCARE PROGRAM OF NAVAL HOSPITAL AND ATTEND 4 12-STEP AA WEEKLY MEETINGS; WEEKLY MEETINGS WITH AFTERCARE PROGRAM MANAGER; MANDATORY URINALYSIS TWICE WEEKLY; MANDATORY USE OF ANTABUSE. MUST CONTINUE TO PARTICIPATE IN A SUBSTANCE ABUSE TREATMENT PROGRAM EVEN WHEN FORMAL REGIMEN ENDS ON 12/11/90. QUARTERLY REPORTS MUST BE SUBMITTED TO BOARD BY PROGRAM OR THERAPIST; WILL ALSO ABIDE BY TERMS OF 5/24/89 ORDER.

WILLIAMS, PAUL C MD, DATE OF BIRTH DECEMBER 4, 1942, LICENSE NUMBER 0017317, OF LAKE OSWEGO, OR, WAS DISCIPLINED BY COLORADO ON JULY 12, 1991.
DISCIPLINARY ACTION: 60-MONTH PROBATION; REQUIRED TO ENTER AN IMPAIRED PHYSICIAN PROGRAM OR DRUG OR ALCOHOL TREATMENT
OFFENSE: SUBSTANCE ABUSE
NOTES: HABITUAL INTEMPERANCE, ALCOHOL ABUSE AND

ALCOHOL DEPENDENCE. ALCOHOL TREATMENT AND MONITORING AND PRACTICE MONITORING. IN ABEYANCE.

WILLIAMS, PAUL CARROLL MD, LICENSE NUMBER 0017419, OF PORTLAND, OR, WAS DISCIPLINED BY OREGON ON AUGUST 15, 1991.
DISCIPLINARY ACTION: 120-MONTH PROBATION
OFFENSE: SUBSTANCE ABUSE
NOTES: ALLEGED PERSONAL SUBSTANCE ABUSE. REVOCATION STAYED. AS OF 2/22/95 NO LONGER LISTED AS ON PROBATION.

WILLIAMS, PAUL CARROLL MD, LICENSE NUMBER 0C34650, OF LAKE OSWEGO, OR, WAS DISCIPLINED BY CALIFORNIA ON JUNE 18, 1992.
DISCIPLINARY ACTION: 60-MONTH PROBATION
OFFENSE: DISCIPLINARY ACTION BY ANOTHER STATE OR AGENCY
NOTES: DISCIPLINED BY ARIZONA BOARD RELATED TO ALCOHOL ABUSE. REVOCATION, STAYED. PROBATION WITH TERMS AND CONDITIONS.

WILLIAMS, VERN RANDAL MD, LICENSE NUMBER MD14502, OF BEAVERTON, OR, WAS DISCIPLINED BY OREGON ON FEBRUARY 8, 1989.
DISCIPLINARY ACTION: 120-MONTH PROBATION

WILLIAMS, VERN RANDAL MD, LICENSE NUMBER 0014502, OF PORTLAND, OR, WAS DISCIPLINED BY OREGON ON AUGUST 29, 1990.
DISCIPLINARY ACTION: FINE

WILLIAMS, VERN RANDAL MD, LICENSE NUMBER 0014502, OF PORTLAND, OR, WAS DISCIPLINED BY OREGON ON NOVEMBER 4, 1996.
DISCIPLINARY ACTION: RESTRICTION PLACED ON CONTROLLED SUBSTANCE LICENSE
NOTES: MUST PROVIDE TRIPLICATE COPIES OF SCHEDULED III CONTROLLED SUBSTANCES PRESCRIPTIONS.

WILLIS, DONALD CLYDE MD, LICENSE NUMBER MD10994, OF PORTLAND, OR, WAS DISCIPLINED BY OREGON ON AUGUST 18, 1994.
DISCIPLINARY ACTION: RESTRICTION PLACED ON LICENSE
NOTES: VOLUNTARY LIMITATION.

WILSON, JOHN D MD, LICENSE NUMBER 0C42303, OF EUGENE, OR, WAS DISCIPLINED BY CALIFORNIA ON JUNE 24, 1994.
DISCIPLINARY ACTION: REPRIMAND
OFFENSE: DISCIPLINARY ACTION BY ANOTHER STATE OR AGENCY
NOTES: DISCIPLINE BY OREGON BOARD.

WILSON, JOHN DAVID MD, LICENSE NUMBER 0010554, OF EUGENE, OR, WAS DISCIPLINED BY OREGON ON AUGUST 27, 1990.
DISCIPLINARY ACTION: REPRIMAND

WILSON, JOHN DAVID MD, LICENSE NUMBER 1024019, OF 1162 WILLIAMETTE ST, EUGENE, OR, WAS DISCIPLINED BY INDIANA ON JUNE 29, 1992.
DISCIPLINARY ACTION: REPRIMAND
OFFENSE: DISCIPLINARY ACTION BY ANOTHER STATE OR AGENCY
NOTES: ON AUGUST 27, 1990, HE WAS FINED $500 AND REPRIMANDED BY THE BOARD OF MEDICAL EXAMINERS OF OREGON FOR REVEALING CONFIDENTIAL PATIENT INFORMATION WITHOUT LEGAL RIGHT OR PATIENT AUTHORIZATION. WILL APPEAR BEFORE THE BOARD PRIOR TO PRACTICING IN THE STATE.

WILSON, WILLIAM S MD, LICENSE NUMBER MD08244, OF SALEM, OR, WAS DISCIPLINED BY OREGON ON JANUARY 8, 1987.
DISCIPLINARY ACTION: RESTRICTION PLACED ON LICENSE
NOTES: PSYCHIATRIC CARE REQUIRED; 3RD PERSON IN ROOM DURING EXAMINATIONS

WILTSE, WILLIAM EARLE MD, LICENSE NUMBER 0005389, OF DRAIN, OR, WAS DISCIPLINED BY OREGON ON APRIL 11, 1991.
DISCIPLINARY ACTION: REPRIMAND
OFFENSE: SUBSTANDARD CARE, INCOMPETENCE, OR NEGLIGENCE
NOTES: ALLEGED INAPPROPRIATE CARE; INCOMPETENCE.

WINANS, WILLIAM EDWARD DO, LICENSE NUMBER DO07880, OF TIGARD, OR, WAS DISCIPLINED BY OREGON ON JULY 9, 1992.
DISCIPLINARY ACTION: RESTRICTION PLACED ON LICENSE
NOTES: ON 10/14/93 LIMITATION AMENDED.

WINANS, WILLIAM EDWARD DO, LICENSE NUMBER 0007880, OF TIGARD, OR, WAS DISCIPLINED BY OREGON ON OCTOBER 14, 1993.
DISCIPLINARY ACTION: RESTRICTION PLACED ON LICENSE
NOTES: VOLUNTARY LIMITATION. AMENDED VOLUNTARY LIMITATION TO REPLACE PRIOR ORDER.

WINKLER, ALBERT JR MD, LICENSE NUMBER MD06800, OF MCMINNVILLE, OR, WAS DISCIPLINED BY OREGON ON NOVEMBER 1, 1989.
DISCIPLINARY ACTION: PROBATION
NOTES: 10-YEAR PROBATION IMPOSED ON 4/13/79. PROBATION EXTENDED SOMETIME DURING 1989 AND MADE OPEN-ENDED. NO LONGER ON PROBATION AS OF 2/8/90.

WINSLOW, HOMER LLAROY MD, LICENSE NUMBER 0006066, OF OREGON CITY, OR, WAS DISCIPLINED BY OREGON ON AUGUST 5, 1991.
DISCIPLINARY ACTION: RESTRICTION PLACED ON CONTROLLED SUBSTANCE LICENSE
NOTES: MUST PROVIDE TRIPLICATE COPIES OF CONTROLLED SUBSTANCE PRESCRIPTIONS. NO LONGER RESTRICTED AS OF 1/28/92.

WOLFENSON, ELENA HERNANDEZ MD, LICENSE NUMBER MD17700, OF PORTLAND, OR, WAS DISCIPLINED BY OREGON ON OCTOBER 13, 1994.
DISCIPLINARY ACTION: LICENSE REVOCATION
OFFENSE: FAILURE TO COMPLY WITH A PROFESSIONAL RULE
NOTES: FAILED A BOARD-ORDERED COMPETENCY EXAM IN HER FIELD OF SPECIALTY.

YAP-CHIONGCO, BASILIO M MD, LICENSE NUMBER 0089450, OF 399 SUNWOOD DRIVE NW, SALEM, OR, WAS DISCIPLINED BY NEW YORK ON APRIL 17, 1996.
DISCIPLINARY ACTION: SURRENDER OF LICENSE
OFFENSE: DISCIPLINARY ACTION BY ANOTHER STATE OR AGENCY
NOTES: ACTION IN CALIFORNIA FOR GROSS NEGLIGENCE INVOLVING ONE SURGICAL PATIENT.

YOUNG, GEORGE MD, LICENSE NUMBER MD18219, OF ASTORIA, OR, WAS DISCIPLINED BY OREGON ON APRIL 15, 1993.
DISCIPLINARY ACTION: RESTRICTION PLACED ON LICENSE
NOTES: VOLUNTARY LIMITATION.

YOUNG, GEORGE DR, LICENSE NUMBER 0023689, WAS DISCIPLINED BY MINNESOTA ON MAY 14, 1994.
NOTES: STAYED SUSPENSION.

YOUNG, GEORGE MD, LICENSE NUMBER 0G41318, OF SEASIDE, OR, WAS DISCIPLINED BY CALIFORNIA ON MAY 24, 1995.
DISCIPLINARY ACTION: 120-MONTH PROBATION
OFFENSE: DISCIPLINARY ACTION BY ANOTHER STATE OR AGENCY
NOTES: DISCIPLINES BY WASHINGTON AND OREGON BOARDS RELATED TO ALCOHOL PROBLEMS. REVOCATION STAYED.

ZELLER, WERNER EMANUEL MD, LICENSE NUMBER 0003269, OF PORTLAND, OR, WAS DISCIPLINED BY OREGON ON JANUARY 18, 1996.
DISCIPLINARY ACTION: 12-MONTH SURRENDER OF LICENSE
NOTES: VOLUNTARY SURRENDER WHILE UNDER INVESTIGATION.

WASHINGTON
1996 serious action rate: 3.09/1000
1996 ranking: 40th

The Washington Medical Board sent board orders from 1987 through 1996. The orders include the physician's name, degree, date and type of action taken and the reason for the action. The board also sent monthly summaries of its actions which covered 1991 through 1996, listing the physician's name, degree, license number, city and state of residence, date and type of action taken, and reason for the action. The orders contain information on modifications and terminations of board actions but not on court decisions which affect board actions.

The Washington State Board of Osteopathic Medicine sent orders for actions taken from 1991 through 1996 which include the physician's name, degree, date and type of action and the reason for the action. These contain information on modifications and terminations of board orders but not on court decisions that affect board actions. Many orders are consent agreements between the physician and the board prior to final board action.

The information provided covers disciplinary actions taken against allopathic physicians (MDs) and osteopathic physicians (DO).

Besides disciplinary actions taken by the State Medical Boards, this listing also includes actions taken by the Medicare/Medicaid programs, the FDA, and the DEA against physicians located in this state. Disciplinary actions taken by other states against physicians located in Washington or that match a physician disciplined by Washington (see Appendix 2 for an explanation of the matching protocol) are also included.

> Although we have made every effort to match physicians' names correctly, some materials we received did not include complete information on middle names, license numbers, birth dates or addresses. Therefore, consumers should remember that non-disciplined physicians and physicians with different disciplinary actions may have similar names to those disciplined physicians listed in this state. Consumers should also remember that if they want the most current information on the status on a physician's license, they should contact the medical board of the state in which the physician practices or had practiced.

According to the Federation of State Medical Boards, Washington took 43 serious disciplinary actions against MDs in 1996. Compared to the 13,931 MDs licensed in the state, Washington had a serious disciplinary action rate of 3.09 serious action per 1,000 MDs and a ranking of 40th on that list (see Table A, Findings, pg. 14).

The tables below summarize the data Public Citizen received from Washington.

Table I. Disciplinary Actions Against MDs and DOs 1987 through 1996*

Actions	Number	Percent**
Revocation	27	4.8%
Surrender	72	12.9%
Suspension	26	4.7%
Probation	86	15.4%
Practice Restriction	68	12.2%
Action Taken Against Controlled Substance License	27	4.8%
Other Actions	253	45.3%
Total Actions	**559**	**100.0%**

* This table lists only the two most serious disciplinary actions taken against a physician.
** Percentages may not total 100% due to rounding.

Table 2. Offenses for which MDs and DOs were Disciplined 1987 through 1996*

Offense	Number	Percent
Criminal Conviction	8	3.0%
Sexual Abuse of or Sexual Misconduct with a Patient	26	9.7%
Substandard Care, Incompetence or Negligence	59	22.1%
Misprescribing or Overprescribing Drugs	33	12.4%
Substance Abuse	21	7.9%
Disciplinary Action Taken Against License by Another State or Agency	40	15.0%
Other Offenses	80	30.0%
Total Records With Offense Listed	**267**	**100.0%**

* Includes only those actions for which an offense was listed and for which we had a corresponding term in our database.

Table 3. Disciplinary Actions Taken for Sexual Abuse of or Sexual Misconduct with a Patient

Action	Number	Percent
Revocation	2	4.8%
Surrender	4	9.5%
Suspension	1	2.4%
Emergency Suspension	3	7.1%
Probation	10	23.8%
Fine	14	33.3%
Other Actions	8	19.0%
Total Actions	**42**	**100.0%**

Table 4. Disciplinary Actions Taken for Substandard Care, Incompetence or Negligence

Action	Number	Percent
Revocation	6	7.0%
Surrender	5	6.2%
Suspension	1	12.0%
Emergency Suspension	6	7.4%
Probation	14	17.3%
Practice Restriction	17	21.0%
Fine	13	16.0%
Reprimand	3	3.7%
Other Actions	16	19.8%
Total Actions	**81**	**100.0%**

Table 5. Disciplinary Actions Taken for Criminal Conviction

Action	Number	Percent
Revocation	4	30.8%
Surrender	1	7.7%
Suspension	1	7.7%
Probation	1	7.7%
Practice Restriction	1	7.7%
Fine	3	23.1%
Other Actions	2	15.4%
Total Actions	**13**	**100.0%**

Table 6. Disciplinary Actions Taken for Misprescribing or Overprescribing Drugs

Action	Number	Percent
Revocation	2	3.8%
Surrender	4	7.5%
Revocation, Surrender, or Suspension of Controlled Substance License	1	1.9%
Emergency Suspension	2	3.8%
Probation	9	17.0%
Restriction of Controlled Substance License	10	18.9%
Fine	7	13.2%
Education	7	13.2%
Other Actions	11	20.8%
Total Actions	**53**	**100.0%**

Table 7. Disciplinary Actions Taken for Substance Abuse

Action	Number	Percent
Revocation	2	6.5%
Surrender	1	3.2%
Suspension	3	9.7%
Emergency Suspension	6	19.4%
Probation	7	22.6%
Fine	3	9.7%
Restriction of Controlled Substance License	2	6.5%
Other Actions	7	22.6%
Total Actions	**31**	**100.0%**

If you feel that your doctor has not given you proper medical care or has mistreated you in any way--whether or not he or she is listed in this report--it is important that you let your state medical board know. Even if they do not immediately act on your complaint, it is important that the information be recorded in their files because it is possible that other people may have filed or will file complaints about the same doctor. Send a brief written description of what occurred to the addresses below or call the phone numbers listed for more information on how to file a complaint.

Address
Washington Medical Quality Assurance Commission &
Washington State Board of Osteopathic Medicine and Surgery
Keith O. Shafer, Executive Director
PO Box 47866
Olympia, WA 98504-7866
(360) 753-2287
DO: (360) 586-8438
Internet: http://www.doh.wa.gov
> This internet address is being provided as an additional source for consumer information on DOs. Those state licensing boards with websites make independent choices about the type of information to be included on their site and how often it is updated. Please contact the board directly to receive the most current information on a particular physician or disciplinary action.

Listing of Doctors Sanctioned by Offense

Sexual Abuse of or Sexual Misconduct with a Patient

ACHARI, NARAYANA K
BREDA, URI W
BUSCHER, DAVID S
CALABRIA, JACK J
CARNINE, KENNETH S
CASTELL, HUGH M
CHIAROTTINO, GARY D
COOK, STUART J
DE HART, COR
DOCKUM, JOHN G
EDIBIOKPO, EMMANUEL A
HOPFNER, EDWARD A
HUMMEL, RALPH T
MOORE, CLOISE BARTON
NAKATA, KENNETH M
NEWTON, DOUGLAS E
NGHIEM, THIEU LENH
PARK, JAMES F
STANK, THOMAS MARK
STANLEY, JOHN L
STRANGE, MEL K
TRUSCHEL, TIMOTHY L
WIMBERGER, HERBERT C
ZEILENGA, DONALD W
MONTOJO, PEDRO M
NGUYEN, BANG DUY
OLLEE, HENRY P
OPPENHEIM, ELLIOTT B
ORAVETZ, JAN
PARK, JOHN C
REITER, JACK M
RESOL, JUAN H
SAYRE, MICHAEL C
SEVERSON, JEWELL A
SHINKOSKEY, ALMON C
STANSFIELD, STEPHEN J
STAUDINGER, SUZANNE
STOWENS, DANIEL W
THOMAS, GORDON G
THOMPSON, SHAHNAZ
THORNTON, DELL
VISKOVITCH, BORKO
WARNER, GLENN A
WATTS, ARTHUR B
WHITE, MANUEL
WOLNER-HANSSEN, PAL
WRIGHT, VIRGIL G
YOUNG, TIMOTHY G

Substandard Care, Incompetence, or Negligence

AMEND, DEXTER R
ANDERSON, ROBERT A
BALLARD, JACK D
BATEY, GEORGE R
BHASKAR, PADMINI
BLACK, MURRAY L
BOYD, HERSCHELL
BUCK, HARPER J
BURKE, EDMUND L
CENAC, PAUL E
CHIAROTTINO, GARY D
COSTLEIGH, ROBERT J
DAHL, CHRISTIAN WILLIAM
DAVIS, FREDERICK B
DILLER, JOHN L
DRUMHELLER, GLENN W
DUDLEY, DONALD L
EKLAND, DAVID A
FAIRFAX, GEORGE T
FOWLER, FRANKLIN S JR
FREDRIKSON, STEVEN E
GILES, ROY C
HALEY, JAMES C
HARRIS, STANLEY E
HELLER, HOWARD F
HOPFNER, EDWARD A
IP, STANLEY S
JOHNSON, CLIFFORD J
KAO, CARL C
LOWDEN, ROBERT
MCDONNELL, THOMAS R
MCINTYRE, DAVID J

Criminal Conviction or Plea of Guilty, Nolo Contendere, or No Contest to a Crime

CARNINE, KENNETH S
HOLLINGSWORTH, LYMAN B
HUYNH, TRONG V
LITTGE, ROGER O
MARASHI, S MOHAMMAD
MARGOLIS, RONALD C
SPRINGEL, RONALD D
WILSON, DAVID Q

Misprescribing or Overprescribing Drugs

ATESER, COSKUN R
AXFORD, GLEN V
BATEY, GEORGE R
BLOOM, ALLAN I
BUNCH, DAVID C
CLAUSING, VERNON D
DENGLER, GEORGE W
DURHAM, STANLEY
FERNANDEZ, CEFERINO
FIELDS, ALVIN
GAHRINGER, JOHN E
GEHLEN, CHARLES J
GLEESON, FRANK G
HANSON, KEITH L
HELLER, HOWARD F
HILLMAN, STEVEN K
LANDON, JOHN W
MOFFETT, CHARLES
MOSS, NORMAN W
PATEL, BHAGWAT
PHELPS, JANICE K

Caution: This list is designed to be used only in conjunction with the rest of this book which includes additional information on each physician such as license number, date of action and more complete descriptions of the offenses.

Misprescribing or Overprescribing Drugs (cont'd)

PLASTINO, JOHN P
PLAYER, GLENN S
RENDELL, HEIDI S
RICE, JAMES W
SAID, MOHAMMAD H
SATO, KENNETH K
SUTHERLAND, ELEANOR I
TUURA, JAMES L
WALLACE, JAMES F
YOUNG, TIMOTHY G

Substance Abuse

BOURNE, MARVIN L
BURKS, DONALD E
DUTTON, EDWARD W
ERICKSON, CLAYTON D
FRIEDLAND, THOMAS
HARTHCOCK, KERRY A
HAUTMAN, BARBARA A
JOHNSON, HAROLD Z
MCDONNELL, THOMAS R
MESSNER, ROBERT C
MORRISON, KENNETH J
NORMAN, CINDY RAE
RAY, LANCE I
REICHMANN, FRANK J
SHULL, THOMAS E
TREPP, ROBERT D
WALLS, DAVID
WILLIAMS, VIRGINIA

Caution: This list is designed to be used only in conjunction with the rest of this book which includes additional information on each physician such as license number, date of action and more complete descriptions of the offenses.

DISCIPLINARY ACTIONS

ACHARI, NARAYANA K MD, LICENSE NUMBER 0013338, OF PASCO, WA, WAS DISCIPLINED BY WASHINGTON ON OCTOBER 25, 1994.
DISCIPLINARY ACTION: RESTRICTION PLACED ON LICENSE
OFFENSE: SEXUAL ABUSE OF OR SEXUAL MISCONDUCT WITH A PATIENT
NOTES: ALLEGATIONS OF MORAL TURPITUDE AND SEXUAL CONTACT WITH PATIENTS. EMERGENCY ACTION ORDERING HE MUST HAVE A CHAPERONE WHEN TREATING FEMALE PATIENTS.

ACHARI, NARAYANA K MD WAS DISCIPLINED BY WASHINGTON ON APRIL 18, 1996.
DISCIPLINARY ACTION: RESTRICTION PLACED ON LICENSE; MONITORING OF PHYSICIAN
OFFENSE: SEXUAL ABUSE OF OR SEXUAL MISCONDUCT WITH A PATIENT
NOTES: BETWEEN 8/92 AND 5/94 TOUCHED FIVE PATIENTS IN A NON-THERAPEUTIC MANNER WITH AN INTIMATE PART OF HIS BODY AGAINST INTIMATE AND NON-INTIMATE PARTS OF THEIR BODIES WITH THE PURPOSE OR INTENT TO GRATIFY HIS SEXUAL DESIRE CONSTITUTING UNPROFESSIONAL CONDUCT; HE DENIED THESE CHARGES. INDEFINITE SUSPENSION STAYED ON CONDITIONS: SHALL HAVE A TRAINED CHAPERONE PRESENT DURING HIS EXAMINATION OR TREATMENT OF ALL FEMALE PATIENTS IN AN OFFICE SETTING; THE CHAPERONE SHALL NOTE HIS/HER PRESENCE IN THE PATIENTS' CHARTS; SHALL MAKE COMPLIANCE APPEARANCES BEFORE THE BOARD IN SIX MONTHS AND YEARLY THEREAFTER; BOARD SHALL MAKE UNANNOUNCED VISITS PRIOR TO EACH COMPLIANCE HEARING TO REVIEW MEDICAL RECORDS, INTERVIEW OFFICE STAFF, AND OTHERWISE MONITOR COMPLIANCE. MAY NOT PETITION FOR MODIFICATION OF THIS ORDER FOR FIVE YEARS.

ADATIA, ALNASIR H DO WAS DISCIPLINED BY WASHINGTON ON AUGUST 16, 1991.
DISCIPLINARY ACTION: FINE; REQUIRED TO TAKE ADDITIONAL MEDICAL EDUCATION
NOTES: SHALL COMPLETE AT LEAST 10 HOURS OF CREDITABLE CONTINUING PROFESSIONAL EDUCATION REGARDING THE PROPER THERAPEUTIC USE OF STEROIDS WITHIN SIX MONTHS; SHALL SUBMIT WRITTEN DOCUMENTATION TO THE BOARD OF THE COURSE CONTENT AND HIS ATTENDANCE AND PARTICIPATION; SHALL MAINTAIN ACCURATE AND COMPLETE RECORDS REGARDING PATIENTS HE HAS TREATED AND SHALL ACCURATELY REPORT THE INFORMATION IN THOSE RECORDS WHEN REQUIRED TO RELEASE THAT INFORMATION TO OTHER TREATING PRACTITIONERS OR IN ACCORDANCE WITH APPLICABLE LAWS; AND SHALL FULLY INFORM HIMSELF OF THE STANDARD OF CARE FOR THE APPROPRIATE USE OF STEROID MEDICATIONS AND SHALL CONFORM HIS USE OF THESE DRUGS TO THAT STANDARD. $1000 CIVIL PENALTY.

ADATIA, ALNASIR H DO WAS DISCIPLINED BY WASHINGTON ON FEBRUARY 25, 1994.
DISCIPLINARY ACTION: PROBATION; FINE
NOTES: ONE YEAR SUSPENSION, STAYED FOR AT LEAST THREE YEAR PROBATION UNDER TERMS AND CONDITIONS: SHALL SUBMIT QUARTERLY DECLARATIONS UNDER PENALTY OF PERJURY STATING COMPLIANCE; SHALL SUBMIT IN WRITING TO THE BOARD ANY EMPLOYMENT OR RESIDENCE ADDRESS CHANGE; SHALL APPEAR BEFORE THE BOARD UPON REQUEST; SHALL RETURN ALL FEES CHARGED ONE PATIENT FROM 5/92 THROUGH 12/92 AND ALL FEES CHARGES ANOTHER PATIENT FROM 7/91 THROUGH 7/92; SHALL PROVIDE THE BOARD WITH A FULL ACCOUNTING OF FEES CHARGED THE TWO PATIENTS; SHALL PERMIT THE DEPARTMENT OF HEALTH TO AUDIT RECORDS AND REVIEW PRACTICE ON AN ANNOUNCED BASIS A MINIMUM OF TWO TIMES A YEAR; SHALL OBTAIN SECOND OPINIONS FROM A BOARD APPROVED AND CERTIFIED OBSTETRICIAN OR GYNECOLOGIST ON ALL GYNECOLOGY AND/OR OBSTETRICS PATIENTS FOR CASES INVOLVING SUSPECTED CERVICAL DYSPLASIA, OVARIAN DISEASE, OR DYSFUNCTIONAL UTERINE BLEEDING; SHALL MAINTAIN HEALTH CARE RECORDS ACCORDING TO A SPECIFIED PLAN; SHALL HAVE A BOARD APPROVED THIRD PARTY PRESENT WHILE EXAMINING OR TREATING FEMALE PATIENTS WHO IS FAMILIAR WITH THIS ORDER AND WHO SHALL SUBMIT QUARTERLY REPORTS TO THE BOARD; WITHIN 60 DAYS SHALL SUBMIT TO THE BOARD FOR ITS PRIOR APPROVAL, A PROGRAM OF REMEDIAL EDUCATION WHICH SHALL INCLUDE EIGHT HOURS ON MAINTAINING PROPER BOUNDARIES IN PHYSICIAN/PATIENT RELATIONSHIPS AND AVOIDING INAPPROPRIATE SEXUAL COMMENTS, EIGHT HOURS ON MEDICAL RECORD KEEPING/TREATMENT DOCUMENTATION, AND FOUR HOURS OF APPROPRIATE REFERRAL TO SPECIALISTS; THIS SHALL BE COMPLETED WITHIN 18 MONTHS. $2,000 ADMINISTRATIVE FINE.

AHLERS, BRYSON DR OF SOUTH 19TH AND UNION, TACOMA, WA, WAS DISCIPLINED BY ILLINOIS ON OCTOBER 1, 1988.
DISCIPLINARY ACTION: LICENSE SUSPENSION
OFFENSE: DISCIPLINARY ACTION BY ANOTHER STATE OR AGENCY
NOTES: INDEFINITE SUSPENSION AFTER HE WAS DISCIPLINED BY WASHINGTON STATE FOR INCOMPETENT OR NEGLIGENT PRACTICE OF MEDICINE

AHMAD, MIR LATIF MD, LICENSE NUMBER 0MC1658, OF LONGVIEW, WA, WAS DISCIPLINED BY WASHINGTON ON JULY 25, 1996.
DISCIPLINARY ACTION: DENIAL OF NEW LICENSE

ALLISON, A REID JR MD WAS DISCIPLINED BY MAINE ON MAY 14, 1996.
DISCIPLINARY ACTION: FINE; REPRIMAND
OFFENSE: PROVIDING FALSE INFORMATION TO THE BOARD
NOTES: FRAUD/DECEIT IN APPLICATION FOR LICENSE; AND FAILED TO DISCLOSE A HOSPITAL SANCTION.

ALLISON, A REID JR MD OF HILTON HEAD, SC, WAS DISCIPLINED BY WASHINGTON ON SEPTEMBER 25, 1996.
DISCIPLINARY ACTION: DENIAL OF NEW LICENSE
OFFENSE: PROFESSIONAL MISCONDUCT
NOTES: COMMITTED UNPROFESSIONAL CONDUCT.

ALLISON, STANLEY C MD, LICENSE NUMBER 0C29575, OF TACOMA, WA, WAS DISCIPLINED BY CALIFORNIA ON MARCH 30, 1988.
DISCIPLINARY ACTION: LICENSE REVOCATION
OFFENSE: DISCIPLINARY ACTION BY ANOTHER STATE OR AGENCY
NOTES: DISCIPLINED BY WASHINGTON STATE MEDICAL BOARD. DEFAULT DECISION.

ALLISON, STANLEY C MD, LICENSE NUMBER 00D2339, OF OLYMPIA, WA, WAS DISCIPLINED BY TEXAS ON OCTOBER 24, 1988.
DISCIPLINARY ACTION: SURRENDER OF LICENSE
OFFENSE: DISCIPLINARY ACTION BY ANOTHER STATE OR AGENCY
NOTES: DISCIPLINED IN WASHINGTON AND CALIFORNIA

ALTMAN, MILTON E MD OF 2060 DELLESTA DRIVE, BELLINGHAM, WA, WAS DISCIPLINED BY DEA ON DECEMBER 17, 1993.
DISCIPLINARY ACTION: SURRENDER OF CONTROLLED SUBSTANCE LICENSE
OFFENSE: DISCIPLINARY ACTION BY ANOTHER STATE OR AGENCY
NOTES: BASED ON LACK OF STATE AUTHORIZATION TO HANDLE

- WASHINGTON -

CONTROLLED SUBSTANCES.

AMEND, DEXTER R MD, LICENSE NUMBER 0003501, OF SPOKANE, WA, WAS DISCIPLINED BY WASHINGTON ON DECEMBER 30, 1996.
DISCIPLINARY ACTION: FINE; REQUIRED TO TAKE ADDITIONAL MEDICAL EDUCATION
OFFENSE: SUBSTANDARD CARE, INCOMPETENCE, OR NEGLIGENCE
NOTES: COMMITTED SEVERAL ACTS OF NEGLIGENCE. REQUIRED TO TAKE 20 CONTINUING MEDICAL EDUCATION HOURS. $1,000 FINE.

ANCIER, STEPHEN L MD, DATE OF BIRTH MAY 1, 1949, LICENSE NUMBER 0025753, OF UPPER MONTCLAIR, NJ, WAS DISCIPLINED BY COLORADO ON OCTOBER 13, 1993.
DISCIPLINARY ACTION: LICENSE REVOCATION
OFFENSE: CRIMINAL CONVICTION OR PLEA OF GUILTY, NOLO CONTENDERE, OR NO CONTEST TO A CRIME
NOTES: CONVICTION OF AN OFFENSE INVOLVING MORAL TURPITUDE; RESORTING TO FRAUD, MISREPRESENTATION OR DECEPTION IN APPLYING FOR, SECURING AND SEEKING REINSTATEMENT OF A LICENSE TO PRACTICE MEDICINE IN COLORADO. THIS CASE WAS ON APPEAL TO THE COLORADO COURT OF APPEALS AS OF 8/94.

ANCIER, STEPHEN L MD, LICENSE NUMBER 0019001, OF UPPER MONTCLAIR, NJ, WAS DISCIPLINED BY WASHINGTON ON MARCH 8, 1996.
NOTES: SUSPENSION, STAYED UNDER SEVERAL CONDITIONS.

ANCIER, STEPHEN LEE MD, LICENSE NUMBER 0163647, OF UPPER MONTCLAIR, NJ, WAS DISCIPLINED BY NEW YORK ON MAY 24, 1989.
DISCIPLINARY ACTION: 12-MONTH PROBATION
NOTES: SUSPENSION 1 YEAR, STAYED.

ANCIER, STEPHEN LEE MD, LICENSE NUMBER 032139E, OF UPPER MONTCLAIR, NJ, WAS DISCIPLINED BY PENNSYLVANIA ON JULY 25, 1989.
DISCIPLINARY ACTION: 3-MONTH LICENSE SUSPENSION; FINE
OFFENSE: DISCIPLINARY ACTION BY ANOTHER STATE OR AGENCY
NOTES: FAILED TO REPORT TO THE BOARD REVOCATION BY THE COLORADO MEDICAL BOARD ON 9/4/87; DID REPORT A CONVICTION IN CANADA OF THREE COUNTS OF FORGERY AND ONE COUNT OF MAKING A FALSE STATEMENT. RECEIVED A PARDON FROM THE CANADIAN GOVERNOR GENERAL ON 1/18/82 FOR THIS CONVICTION. $2,000 FINE.

ANCIER, STEPHEN LEE MD, DATE OF BIRTH JANUARY 5, 1947, LICENSE NUMBER 032139E, OF 21 BROOKFIELD ROAD, PO BOX 4351, UPPER MONTCLAIR, NJ, WAS DISCIPLINED BY PENNSYLVANIA ON FEBRUARY 7, 1995.
DISCIPLINARY ACTION: LICENSE REVOCATION
OFFENSE: DISCIPLINARY ACTION BY ANOTHER STATE OR AGENCY
NOTES: RECIPROCAL ACTION FROM COLORADO; TWO COUNTS OF FRAUDULENT REPRESENTATIONS; TWO COUNTS OF IMMORAL CONDUCT; MAKING FALSE BIENNIAL REGISTRATION.

ANCIER, STEPHEN LEE MD, LICENSE NUMBER 0163647, OF PO BOX 4351 21 BROOKFIELD RD, UPPER MOUNTCLAIR, NJ, WAS DISCIPLINED BY NEW YORK ON APRIL 17, 1995.
DISCIPLINARY ACTION: LICENSE REVOCATION
OFFENSE: DISCIPLINARY ACTION BY ANOTHER STATE OR AGENCY
NOTES: CONVICTED UNDER THE NEW ZEALAND CRIMES ACT OF 1961 FOR FORGING AIRLINE TICKETS, CREDIT CARD FORGERY AND MARIJUANA POSSESSION. DISCIPLINED BY COLORADO AND PENNSYLVANIA FOR FILING FALSE INFORMATION ON LICENSE APPLICATIONS.

ANCIER, STEPHEN LEE MD, DATE OF BIRTH JANUARY 5, 1947, OF 21 BROOKFIELD ROAD, PO BOX 43451, UPPER MONTCLAIR, NJ, WAS DISCIPLINED BY MEDICARE ON SEPTEMBER 9, 1996.
DISCIPLINARY ACTION: EXCLUSION FROM THE MEDICARE AND/OR MEDICAID PROGRAMS
OFFENSE: DISCIPLINARY ACTION BY ANOTHER STATE OR AGENCY
NOTES: LICENSE REVOKED FOR REASONS BEARING ON PROFESSIONAL PERFORMANCE. REINSTATED ON 9/26/96.

ANDERSON, CHARLES L MD, LICENSE NUMBER 0012729, OF TACOMA, WA, WAS DISCIPLINED BY WASHINGTON ON MAY 31, 1996.
DISCIPLINARY ACTION: RESTRICTION PLACED ON LICENSE; REQUIRED TO TAKE ADDITIONAL MEDICAL EDUCATION
NOTES: RESTRICTED FROM PROVIDING TREATMENT FOR SEXUAL DEVIANCY OR RECOVERY FROM SEXUAL ASSAULT UNTIL HE COMPLETES REMEDIAL EDUCATION.

ANDERSON, KENNETH MD WAS DISCIPLINED BY WASHINGTON ON JULY 20, 1990.
DISCIPLINARY ACTION: 60-MONTH PROBATION; RESTRICTION PLACED ON LICENSE
OFFENSE: PROFESSIONAL MISCONDUCT
NOTES: CHARGED WITH SEXUALLY HARASSING STAFF AND EMPLOYEES, BOTH ON AND OFF THE JOB, WHICH SUBSTANTIALLY INTERFERED WITH THEIR WORK, AND CONSISTED OF COMMENTS OF A SEXUALLY SUGGESTIVE NATURE, PHYSICAL TOUCHING, AND THE COMMMUNICATION OF AN IMPLIED CONDITION OF EMPLOYMENT THAT THESE WOMEN SUBMIT TO SEXUAL HARASSMENT. TERMS OF PROBATION: FEMALE CHAPERONE MUST BE PRESENT AT ALL TIMES WHEN HE IS SEEING A FEMALE PATIENT; MUST INFORM HIS PRESENT AND FUTURE OFFICE STAFF THAT BOARD REQUIRES HIM TO HAVE A FEMALE CHAPERONE PRESENT AT ALL TIMES WHEN HE'S SEEING A FEMALE PATIENT; SHALL CONTINUE IN TREATMENT AND FOLLOW RECOMMENDATIONS WITH ANNUAL REPORTS TO THE BOARD; SHALL SUBMIT TO ANNUAL REVIEW OF OFFICE PROCEDURES REGARDING CHAPERONAGE; SHALL MAKE ANNUAL APPEARANCES BEFORE THE BOARD DOCUMENTING COMPLIANCE; REPRESENTATIVES OF BOARD MAY MAKE ANNOUNCED VISITS TO REVIEW PRACTICE; SHALL NOTIFY BOARD IF HE MOVES OR RESIDES OUT OF STATE; MAY NOT PETITION FOR MODIFICATION FOR ONE YEAR. ON 8/20/93 HE WAS IN COMPLIANCE WITH THIS ORDER AND THE BOARD TERMINATED ITS JURISDICTION OVER HIM.

ANDERSON, KENNETH N MD, LICENSE NUMBER 0C26306, OF SEATTLE, WA, WAS DISCIPLINED BY CALIFORNIA ON AUGUST 26, 1992.
DISCIPLINARY ACTION: SURRENDER OF LICENSE
NOTES: VOLUNTARY SURRENDER WHILE CHARGES PENDING.

ANDERSON, ROBERT A MD WAS DISCIPLINED BY WASHINGTON ON JULY 20, 1990.
DISCIPLINARY ACTION: 36-MONTH PROBATION; REQUIRED TO TAKE ADDITIONAL MEDICAL EDUCATION
OFFENSE: SUBSTANDARD CARE, INCOMPETENCE, OR NEGLIGENCE
NOTES: ON 1/29/90 BOARD ISSUED A STATEMENT OF CHARGES ASSERTING THAT HE FAILED TO TIMELY DIAGNOSE CARCINOMA OF THE RECTOSIGMOID IN ONE PATIENT AND FAILED TO TIMELY DIAGNOSE BREAST CANCER IN ANOTHER PATIENT. CONDITIONS OF PROBATION: SHALL COMPLETE 50 HOURS OF BOARD APPROVED CONTINUING MEDICAL EDUCATION IN THE AREA OF DIAGNOSIS OF CANCER OF THE COLON AND BREAST WITHIN 2 YEARS; SHALL SUBMIT A SUMMARY OF MATERIAL PRESENTED IN THESE COURSES; SHALL RECOMMEND APPROPRIATE SCREENING, PER AMERICAN CANCER SOCIETY PROTOCOL, TO ALL HIS PATIENTS WHO FALL WITHIN THE GUIDELINES; SHALL MAINTAIN A LIST OF ALL HIS BREAST AND COLON

WASHINGTON

CANCER PATIENTS AND ALL PATIENTS WHO FALL WITHIN NOTED GUIDELINES FOR ANNUAL REVIEW; SHALL APPEAR ANNUALLY BEFORE THE BOARD AND PRESENT PROOF OF COMPLIANCE WITH ORDER; A REPRESENTATIVE OF THE BOARD MAY MAKE ANNOUNCED VISITS TO INSPECT PRACTICE; SHALL INFORM THE BOARD IF HE CHANGES ADDRESS OR MOVES OUT OF STATE; TIME OF PROBATION NOT COUNTED IF OUT OF STATE. ON 9/17/92 REQUEST FOR RELEASE FROM PROBATION DENIED.

ANDREW, CURTIS C MD WAS DISCIPLINED BY WASHINGTON ON JUNE 28, 1993.
DISCIPLINARY ACTION: REPRIMAND
OFFENSE: PROFESSIONAL MISCONDUCT
NOTES: ON 11/28/90 HE LEFT HIS PRACTICE IN PORT ANGELES WITHOUT NOTICE TO AND WITHOUT ARRANGING COVERAGE FOR HIS PATIENTS, INCLUDING ONE PATIENT HOSPITALIZED AT OLYMPIC MEMORIAL HOSPITAL.

ANDREW, CURTIS C MD, LICENSE NUMBER 0037463, OF MAUI, HI, WAS DISCIPLINED BY FLORIDA ON NOVEMBER 10, 1994.
DISCIPLINARY ACTION: FINE
OFFENSE: DISCIPLINARY ACTION BY ANOTHER STATE OR AGENCY
NOTES: FAILED TO REPORT TO THE BOARD IN WRITING AND WITHIN 30 DAYS, DISCIPLINARY ACTION TAKEN AGAINST HIS LICENSE BY ANOTHER JURISDICTION; VIOLATED A BOARD RULE IN THAT HE FAILED TO NOTIFY THE AGENCY OF HIS CURRENT MAILING ADDRESS. $1,250 FINE.

ARAGON, PERRY REAS MD, LICENSE NUMBER 0022588, OF WAPATO, WA, WAS DISCIPLINED BY WASHINGTON ON MAY 31, 1996.
DISCIPLINARY ACTION: RESTRICTION PLACED ON CONTROLLED SUBSTANCE LICENSE; MONITORING OF PHYSICIAN
NOTES: RESTRICTION OF HIS PRESCRIBING OF CONTROLLED SUBSTANCES; SHALL MAINTAIN COMPLETE HEALTH CARE RECORDS; SHALL PRACTICE UNDER A PRECEPTOR; SHALL UNDERGO A PROFESSIONAL ASSESSMENT EVALUATION.

ARAGON, PERRY REAS MD, LICENSE NUMBER 0022588, OF WAPATO, WA, WAS DISCIPLINED BY WASHINGTON ON NOVEMBER 19, 1996.
DISCIPLINARY ACTION: LICENSE SUSPENSION
OFFENSE: FAILURE TO COMPLY WITH A PREVIOUS BOARD ORDER
NOTES: OUT OF COMPLIANCE WITH THE ORDER DATED 5/31/96. STAY OF SUSPENSION LIFTED.

ARONOFF, RONALD G MD, LICENSE NUMBER 0015003, WAS DISCIPLINED BY WASHINGTON ON MAY 21, 1993.
DISCIPLINARY ACTION: RESTRICTION PLACED ON LICENSE
OFFENSE: PHYSICAL OR MENTAL ILLNESS INHIBITING THE ABILITY TO PRACTICE WITH SKILL AND SAFETY
NOTES: UNABLE TO PRACTICE MEDICINE WITH REASONABLE SKILL AND SAFETY TO CONSUMERS DUE TO A CLOSED HEAD INJURY SUFFERED IN 5/84; EVALUATIONS REVEAL HE SUFFERS FROM MILD CEREBRAL DYSFUNCTION, DIFFICULTY DEALING WITH STRESS AND EASY FATIGUABILITY. HIS PRACTICE SHALL BE RESTRICTED: SHALL NOT ENGAGE IN ANY UNAPPROVED FORM OF PRACTICE INVOLVING PATIENT CARE; SHALL BE LIMITED TO THE PRACTICE OF ADMINISTRATIVE MEDICINE OR OTHER AVENUES OF PRACTICE THAT DO NOT INVOLVE PATIENT CARE; SHALL OBTAIN ADVANCE BOARD APPROVAL OF ANY CLINICAL PRACTICE. IF HE WISHES TO RETURN TO THE PRACTICE OF UNRESTRICTED CLINICAL MEDICINE THEN HE MUST SATISFY SPECIFIED CONDITIONS. SHALL APPEAR BEFORE THE BOARD UPON REQUEST; MAY PETITION FOR A CHANGE IN TERMS IN NO SOONER THAN ONE YEAR; SHALL INFORM THE BOARD IN WRITING OF CHANGES IN HIS PRACTICE AND RESIDENCE ADDRESS; SHALL INFORM THE BOARD IF HE LEAVES WASHINGTON. ON 5/6/95, THE COMMISSION DENIED HIS REQUEST TO PERMIT HIM TO WORK WITH A MENTOR BUT GRANTED HIS REQUEST TO ALLOW HIM TO ARRANGE A PRECEPTORSHIP PLAN OUTSIDE A TEACHING INSTITUTIONAL SETTING UNDER CERTAIN CONDITIONS. ON 1/8/96 BOARD GRANTED HIS REQUEST TO EXTEND THIS PRECEPTORSHIP PLAN. ON 9/7/96 HIS REQUEST FOR AN UNCONDITIONAL LICENSE WAS GRANTED AND LICENSE IS NOW UNRESTRICTED.

ARONOFF, RONALD G MD, LICENSE NUMBER 0G60761, OF OLYMPIA, WA, WAS DISCIPLINED BY CALIFORNIA ON MAY 12, 1995.
DISCIPLINARY ACTION: 36-MONTH PROBATION
OFFENSE: DISCIPLINARY ACTION BY ANOTHER STATE OR AGENCY
NOTES: RESTRICTION BY WASHINGTON STATE BOARD BECAUSE OF HEAD INJURIES FROM AUTO ACCIDENT DIMINISHING ABILITY TO PRACTICE SAFELY. REVOCATION STAYED.

ATESER, COSKIN R MD OF 6200 LAKESHORE DRIVE S, SEATTLE, WA, WAS DISCIPLINED BY MEDICARE ON MAY 5, 1987.
DISCIPLINARY ACTION: 120-MONTH EXCLUSION FROM THE MEDICARE AND/OR MEDICAID PROGRAMS
OFFENSE: SUBSTANDARD CARE, INCOMPETENCE, OR NEGLIGENCE
NOTES: HE DID NOT PROVIDE ADEQUATE OR PROPER DOCUMENTATION WITH REGARDS TO 25 MEDICAL RECORDS SELECTED FOR REVIEW. SOME OF THE SERVICES PROVIDED MAY HAVE BEEN EXTREMELY EXCESSIVE AND SOMETIMES UNNECESSARY.

ATESER, COSKUN R MD WAS DISCIPLINED BY WASHINGTON ON SEPTEMBER 15, 1989.
DISCIPLINARY ACTION: EMERGENCY SUSPENSION
OFFENSE: OVERPRESCRIBING OR MISPRESCRIBING DRUGS
NOTES: ALLEGEDLY OVERPRESCRIBED CONTROLLED SUBSTANCES TO CHRONIC PAIN PATIENTS THROUGH WRITING DUPLICATE PRESCRIPTIONS AND NOTING ONLY ONE IN RECORDS.

ATESER, COSKUN R MD WAS DISCIPLINED BY WASHINGTON ON JANUARY 19, 1990.
DISCIPLINARY ACTION: SURRENDER OF CONTROLLED SUBSTANCE LICENSE; FINE
OFFENSE: OVERPRESCRIBING OR MISPRESCRIBING DRUGS
NOTES: HIS PRESCRIBING OF CONTROLLED SUBSTANCES FOR PATIENTS WAS IN A NONTHERAPEUTIC MANNER IN THAT HE PRESCRIBED LARGE AMOUNTS OF CONTROLLED SUBSTANCES WITHOUT OBTAINING APPROPRIATE CONSULTATION WITH SPECIALISTS AND WITHOUT ADEQUATE DOCUMENTATION OF PHYSICAL EXAMINATIONS TO SUBSTANTIATE THE NEED FOR THE PRESCRIPTION OR DOCUMENTATION OF THE PATIENT'S ABILITY TO FUNCTION APPROPRIATELY UNDER HIS TREATMENT PROGRAM; THE AMOUNT OF CONTROLLED SUBSTANCES PRESCRIBED FOR PATIENTS PRESENTED A DANGER OF PATIENT HARM BY ADDICTING THE PATIENT TO CONTROLLED SUBSTANCES, AND IN TURN, CAUSING WITHDRAWAL SYMPTOMS UPON CURTAILMENT OF THE CONTROLLED SUBSTANCES; EVIDENCE SUGGESTS THAT HE IS NAIVE AND LACKS AWARENESS OF THE MANIPULATION ENGAGED IN BY SUBSTANCE ABUSERS TO ACQUIRE CONTROLLED SUBSTANCES FROM PHYSICIANS; HE WAS EASILY MANIPULATED BY SUBSTANCE ABUSERS DUE TO HIS LACK OF AWARENESS AND AS A RESULT OF THE CARELESS AND SLOPPY PROTOCOLS AND RECORD KEEPING MAINTAINED IN HIS OFFICE; THESE PRESCRIBING PRACTICES WERE NEGLIGENT AND INCOMPETENT. TEN YEAR MINUMUM SUSPENSION, STAYED UNDER THE FOLLOWING TERMS AND CONDITIONS: SHALL IMMEDIATELY SURRENDER HIS DEA REGISTRATION AND

– WASHINGTON –

SHALL NOT PRESCRIBE ANY CONTROLLED SUBSTANCES; SHALL PROVIDE EVIDENCE SATISFACTORY TO THE BOARD OF ATTENDING A SEMINAR ON CHRONIC PAIN MANAGEMENT WITHIN 12 MONTHS; SHALL COOPERATE IN FULL WITH A PRACTICE REVIEW BY THE BOARD WHICH SHALL OCCUR AT LEAST ONCE DURING THE 12 MONTHS IMMEDIATELY FOLLOWING THE DATE OF THIS ORDER AND WHICH SHALL OCCUR AT LEAST ONCE BIENNIALLY THEREAFTER; SHALL MAINTAIN PATIENT CHARTS IN SUCH A FASHION THAT, FOR EACH PATIENT, THERE IS A HISTORY, PHYSICAL, CLINICAL IMPRESSION, PLAN OF TREATMENT, AND DOCUMENTATION OF ANY AND ALL CONSULTATIONS; SHALL APPEAR BEFORE THE BOARD FOR A COMPLIANCE REVIEW IN 12 MONTHS; MAY NOT PETITION FOR MODIFICATION OF ANY PROVISION OF THIS ORDER FOR 60 MONTHS AND THEN MUST PROVIDE SATISFACTORY PROOF TO THE BOARD THAT HE HAS TAKEN AFFIRMATIVE ACTION TO PREVENT REPETITION OF THE CONDUCT WHICH RESULTED IN THE ORDER; SHALL PAY A FINE OF $3,000.

ATESER, COSKUN R MD, LICENSE NUMBER 0009603, OF RENTON, WA, WAS DISCIPLINED BY WASHINGTON ON DECEMBER 19, 1992.
DISCIPLINARY ACTION: LICENSE SUSPENSION
OFFENSE: FAILURE TO COMPLY WITH A PREVIOUS BOARD ORDER
NOTES: HE DID NOT COMPLY WITH THE CONDITIONS OF 1/90 ORDER.

AXFORD, GLEN V MD WAS DISCIPLINED BY WASHINGTON ON SEPTEMBER 17, 1993.
DISCIPLINARY ACTION: SURRENDER OF LICENSE
OFFENSE: OVERPRESCRIBING OR MISPRESCRIBING DRUGS
NOTES: UNDER INVESTIGATION BY THE BOARD CONCERNING HIS PRESCRIPTION PRACTICE WITH PATIENTS, IN PARTICULAR HIS PRESCRIPTION OF CONTROLLED SUBSTANCES FOR SEVERAL PATIENTS. VOLUNTARY RETIREMENT EFFECTIVE 10/01/93: HAS NO PLANS TO RESUME PRACTICE SUBSEQUENT TO HIS DATE OF RETIREMENT; HIS RETIREMENT SHALL BE PERMANENT; MAY RESUME PRACTICE IN THIS STATE ONLY WITH THE PRIOR BOARD APPROVAL; SHALL NOTIFY THE BOARD IF HE PLANS TO RESUME PRACTICE IN THIS OR ANY OTHER JURISDICTION. THE INVESTIGATION WAS TERMINATED.

BAILEY, HARRY K MD WAS DISCIPLINED BY WASHINGTON ON JANUARY 21, 1994.
DISCIPLINARY ACTION: SURRENDER OF LICENSE
NOTES: UNDER INVESTIGATION BY THE BOARD CONCERNING HIS ABILITY TO PRACTICE MEDICINE WITH REASONABLE SKILL AND SAFETY TO PATIENTS. VOLUNTARY RETIREMENT EFFECTIVE 5/15/93: HAS NO PLANS TO RESUME PRACTICE SUBSEQUENT TO HIS DATE OF RETIREMENT; HIS RETIREMENT SHALL BE PERMANENT; MAY RESUME PRACTICE ONLY WITH PRIOR BOARD APPROVAL; SHALL NOTIFY THE BOARD IF HE PLANS TO RESUME PRACTICE IN THIS OR ANY OTHER JURISDICTION.

BALLARD, JACK D MD WAS DISCIPLINED BY WASHINGTON ON APRIL 16, 1993.
DISCIPLINARY ACTION: REPRIMAND
OFFENSE: SUBSTANDARD CARE, INCOMPETENCE, OR NEGLIGENCE
NOTES: ON 1/22/91 HE REMOVED A PATIENT'S SPLEEN AND DID NOT ADMINISTER A PNEUMOCOCCAL VACCINATION WHICH CREATED AN UNREASONABLE RISK OF HARM; SIX MONTHS LATER THE PATIENT DIED OF PNEUMOCOCCAL SEPSIS.

BARNERT, ANTHONY L MD, LICENSE NUMBER 0G26816, OF VALENCIA, CA, WAS DISCIPLINED BY CALIFORNIA ON JULY 5, 1993.
DISCIPLINARY ACTION: PROBATION
NOTES: REVOCATION STAYED; LIFETIME PROBATION.

BARNERT, ANTHONY LEWIS MD, LICENSE NUMBER 0033239, OF TARZANA, CA, WAS DISCIPLINED BY WASHINGTON ON OCTOBER 6, 1995.
DISCIPLINARY ACTION: MONITORING OF PHYSICIAN
NOTES: GRANTED A LICENSE UNDER TERMS AND CONDITIONS TO MONITOR BIPOLAR DISORDER.

BASS, R LAMAR MD, LICENSE NUMBER 0010454, OF BELLEVUE, WA, WAS DISCIPLINED BY WASHINGTON ON MARCH 28, 1996.
DISCIPLINARY ACTION: PROBATION
OFFENSE: PROFESSIONAL MISCONDUCT
NOTES: AT LEAST TWO YEAR PROBATION UNDER SEVERAL CONDITIONS.

BATEY, GEORGE R MD, LICENSE NUMBER 0005278, OF TACOMA, WA, WAS DISCIPLINED BY WASHINGTON ON JANUARY 2, 1991.
DISCIPLINARY ACTION: EMERGENCY SUSPENSION
OFFENSE: OVERPRESCRIBING OR MISPRESCRIBING DRUGS
NOTES: ALLEGATIONS OF PRESCRIBING CONTROLLED SUBSTANCES AND/OR LEGEND DRUGS TO 14 PATIENTS IN NON-THERAPEUTIC AMOUNTS, SOME OF WHOM EXHIBITED DRUG-SEEKING BEHAVIOR; ALSO TREATED AND/OR PRESCRIBED FOR PATIENTS WITHOUT PERFORMING THOROUGH PHYSICAL EXAMINATIONS, CREATING AN UNREASONABLE RISK. IN 12/90 THE PIERCE COUNTY SHERIFF'S DEPARTMENT SEARCHED HIS OFFICE AND RECOVERED STOLEN GOODS FROM HIS OFFICE.

BATEY, GEORGE R MD, LICENSE NUMBER 0005278, OF TACOMA, PIERCE COUNTY, WA, WAS DISCIPLINED BY WASHINGTON ON AUGUST 21, 1992.
DISCIPLINARY ACTION: LICENSE REVOCATION
OFFENSE: SUBSTANDARD CARE, INCOMPETENCE, OR NEGLIGENCE
NOTES: CHARGES OF INAPPROPRIATE PRESCRIBING MAINTAINING INADEQUATE MEDICAL RECORDS, FAILURE TO PERFORM THOROUGH EXAMINATIONS AND RECORDING TESTS THAT WERE NOT PERFORMED. REVOCATION EFFECTIVE NO LATER THAN 90 DAYS OF THE DATE OF ORDER. MAY NOT APPLY FOR WASHINGTON LICENSE AT ANY TIME IN THE FUTURE.

BAUER, LESTER E MD WAS DISCIPLINED BY WASHINGTON ON MARCH 16, 1990.
DISCIPLINARY ACTION: SURRENDER OF LICENSE
NOTES: RETIRED FROM PRACTICE EFFECTIVE 1/1/89, WHICH WILL BE CONSIDERED PERMANENT; CHARGES ARE WITHDRAWN.

BAUSHER, JOHN CHARLES MD, LICENSE NUMBER 0017464, OF ABERDEEN, WA, WAS DISCIPLINED BY WASHINGTON ON JANUARY 25, 1993.
DISCIPLINARY ACTION: REPRIMAND
OFFENSE: PROFESSIONAL MISCONDUCT
NOTES: BASED ON ALLEGATIONS OF MORAL TURPITUDE AND SEXUAL RELATIONSHIP WITH EMPLOYEE WHOSE CHILDREN WERE PATIENTS OF DR. BAUSHER. WILL COMPLY WITH TERMS AS STATED IN THE ORDER.

BEATTY, HUGH T MD, LICENSE NUMBER 0022359, OF OAK HARBOR ISLAND COUNTY, WA, WAS DISCIPLINED BY WASHINGTON ON JANUARY 17, 1992.
DISCIPLINARY ACTION: PROBATION
OFFENSE: PROVIDING FALSE INFORMATION TO THE BOARD
NOTES: KNOWINGLY SUPPLIED FALSE INFORMATION IN AN APPLICATION AND NEGLIGENTLY PRESCRIBED CONTROLLED SUBSTANCES. FIVE-YEAR SUSPENSION SHALL BE STAYED PROVIDING HE ABIDED BY TERMS AND CONDITIONS.

BEATTY, HUGH T MD, LICENSE NUMBER 0022359, OF OAK HARBOR, WA, WAS DISCIPLINED BY WASHINGTON ON JANUARY 24, 1993.

- WASHINGTON -

OFFENSE: FAILURE TO COMPLY WITH A PREVIOUS BOARD ORDER
NOTES: THE BOARD FOUND HIM DEFICIENT IN HIS COMPLIANCE WITH ALL TERMS AND CONDITIONS OF HIS JANUARY 1992 ORDER. HE SHALL FOLLOW THE TERMS AND CONDITIONS OF THIS ORDER TO BRING HIMSELF INTO FULL COMPLIANCE.

BEATTY, HUGH T MD WAS DISCIPLINED BY WASHINGTON ON SEPTEMBER 20, 1993.
DISCIPLINARY ACTION: SURRENDER OF CONTROLLED SUBSTANCE LICENSE
OFFENSE: FAILURE TO COMPLY WITH A PREVIOUS BOARD ORDER
NOTES: NONCOMPLIANCE TO A PREVIOUS BOARD ORDER DATED 1/17/92 WHICH SUSPENDED HIS LICENSE TO PRACTICE MEDICINE FOR A PERIOD OF FIVE YEARS, STAYED UNDER CERTAIN TERMS AND CONDITIONS. ON 1/14/93 THE BOARD FOUND THAT HE HAD BEEN DEFICIENT IN HIS COMPLIANCE WITH THIS ORDER; SIX MONTHS LATE IN PAYMENT OF FINE; FAILED TO SEEK PRIOR APPROVAL OF CONTINUING MEDICAL EDUCATION HE DID OBTAIN AND EVEN THAT DID NOT CONSTITUTE THE REQUIRED 25 HOURS. ON 8/20/93 HE ACKNOWLEDGED TO THE BOARD THAT WITH RESPECT TO AT LEAST THREE PATIENTS, HE WAS OUT OF COMPLIANCE WITH THAT PORTION OF THE ORDER RELATED TO BENZODIAZEPINES IN THAT HE HAS ISSUED MULTIPLE PRESCRIPTIONS COVERING PERIODS LONGER THAN THREE WEEKS, HE DID NOT USE TRIPLICATE PRESCRIPTIONS WHEN WRITING PRESCRIPTIONS FOR NURSING HOME PATIENTS, AND HE HAD NOT FORWARDED MONTHLY REPORTS WITH RESPECT TO HIS EFFORTS TO OBTAIN CONTINUING MEDICAL EDUCATION CREDITS. MAY NOT PRESCRIBE, ADMINISTER, DISPENSE, OR ORDER ANY CONTROLLED SUBSTANCES FOR ANY PATIENTS FROM AND AFTER THE EFFECTIVE DATE OF THIS ORDER; SHALL SURRENDER HIS DEA PERMIT, WHICH AUTHORIZES HIM TO PRESCRIBE CONTROLLED SUBSTANCES; SHALL APPEAR BEFORE THE BOARD FOR FURTHER COMPLIANCE REVIEW IN SIX MONTHS; IN ALL OTHER RESPECTS THE ORDER OF 1/17/92 AND 1/14/93 SHALL REMAIN IN FULL FORCE AND EFFECT.

BEATTY, HUGH T MD OF 27500 102ND N.W., STANWOOD, WA, WAS DISCIPLINED BY DEA ON OCTOBER 22, 1993.
DISCIPLINARY ACTION: SURRENDER OF CONTROLLED SUBSTANCE LICENSE
OFFENSE: FAILURE TO COMPLY WITH A PREVIOUS BOARD ORDER
NOTES: HE FAILED TO COMPLY WITH PRIOR MEDICAL BOARD ORDER DATED 11/92. ON 10/20/93 BOARD ORDERED THAT HE MAY NOT HAVE CONTROLLED SUBSTANCES PRIVILEGES.

BEATTY, HUGH T MD, LICENSE NUMBER 0022359, OF OAK HARBOR, WA, WAS DISCIPLINED BY WASHINGTON ON DECEMBER 16, 1994.
DISCIPLINARY ACTION: SURRENDER OF LICENSE

BENDING, GLENVILLE C DR, LICENSE NUMBER 0015819, WAS DISCIPLINED BY MINNESOTA ON SEPTEMBER 11, 1993.
NOTES: STAYED SUSPENSION.

BENDING, GLENVILLE C MD, LICENSE NUMBER 0005453, OF TUCSON, AZ, WAS DISCIPLINED BY ARIZONA ON APRIL 14, 1994.
NOTES: SHALL NOT PRACTICE IN ARIZONA PRIOR TO MEETING WITH THE BOARD.

BENDING, GLENVILLE CHARLES MD, LICENSE NUMBER MD07773, OF NEWPORT, OR, WAS DISCIPLINED BY OREGON ON JULY 9, 1992.
DISCIPLINARY ACTION: RESTRICTION PLACED ON LICENSE

BENDING, GLENVILLE CHARLES MD, LICENSE NUMBER 0013279, WAS DISCIPLINED BY WASHINGTON ON MARCH 19, 1993.
DISCIPLINARY ACTION: RESTRICTION PLACED ON LICENSE

OFFENSE: DISCIPLINARY ACTION BY ANOTHER STATE OR AGENCY
NOTES: ON 7/8/92 OREGON LICENSE LIMITED IN THAT HE WILL OBTAIN A SECOND OPINION FOR PATIENTS FOR WHOM HE RECOMMENDS CATARACT SURGERY. LICENSE LIMITED INDEFINITELY AND HE SHALL COMPLY WITH THE TERMS OF THE VOLUNTARY LIMITATION OF HIS MEDICAL PRACTICE INTO WHICH HE ENTERED WITH THE OREGON BOARD SO LONG AS THAT VOLUNTARY LIMITATION IS IN EFFECT; IF HE ESTABLISHES A PRACTICE IN WASHINGTON THE BOARD MAY MAKE ANNOUNCED VISITS TO INSPECT OFFICE AND/OR MEDICAL RECORDS; INTERVIEW OFFICE STAFF OR SUPERVISORS; AND REVIEW OTHER ASPECTS OF HIS PRACTICE; SHALL ASSUME ALL COSTS; SHALL INFORM THE BOARD IN WRITING OF CHANGES IN HIS PRACTICE AND RESIDENCE ADDRESS.

BENITEZ, FRANCO B MD WAS DISCIPLINED BY WASHINGTON ON MAY 9, 1988.
DISCIPLINARY ACTION: SURRENDER OF LICENSE

BERECZ, ROBERT JAMES MD, LICENSE NUMBER 0016918, OF 105 BROOK DRIVE, CHEHALIS, WA, WAS DISCIPLINED BY WISCONSIN ON JULY 23, 1987.
OFFENSE: DISCIPLINARY ACTION BY ANOTHER STATE OR AGENCY
NOTES: DISCIPLINED BY WASHINGTON STATE FOR ENGAGING IN UNSAFE PRACTICES. MUST PASS AN ORAL EXAM BEFORE APPLYING FOR RE-REGISTRATION IN WISCONSIN.

BERGMAN, SANDER MD, LICENSE NUMBER 0015161, OF BREMERTON, WA, WAS DISCIPLINED BY WASHINGTON ON NOVEMBER 13, 1992.
DISCIPLINARY ACTION: EMERGENCY SUSPENSION
OFFENSE: PROFESSIONAL MISCONDUCT
NOTES: ALLEGATIONS OF MORAL TURPITUDE AND ABUSE OF A CLIENT.

BERGMAN, SANDER MD, LICENSE NUMBER 0G24765, OF BREMERTON, WA, WAS DISCIPLINED BY CALIFORNIA ON MAY 27, 1994.
DISCIPLINARY ACTION: SURRENDER OF LICENSE
NOTES: VOLUNTARY SURRENDER OF LICENSE WHILE CHARGES PENDING.

BERGMAN, SANDER E MD, LICENSE NUMBER 0015161, OF BREMERTON, WA, WAS DISCIPLINED BY WASHINGTON ON OCTOBER 6, 1995.
DISCIPLINARY ACTION: LICENSE REVOCATION

BERMAN, BENNETT I MD OF PORT LUDLOW, JEFFERSON CO, WA, WAS DISCIPLINED BY WASHINGTON ON MAY 21, 1992.
DISCIPLINARY ACTION: DENIAL OF NEW LICENSE

BEYMER, CHARLES H MD OF BOISE, ID, WAS DISCIPLINED BY WASHINGTON ON JANUARY 13, 1992.
DISCIPLINARY ACTION: RESTRICTION PLACED ON LICENSE
NOTES: CONDITIONAL LICENSE ISSUED WITH SPECIFIC CONDITIONS.

BHASKAR, PADMINI MD WAS DISCIPLINED BY WASHINGTON ON SEPTEMBER 29, 1993.
DISCIPLINARY ACTION: RESTRICTION PLACED ON LICENSE; FINE
OFFENSE: SUBSTANDARD CARE, INCOMPETENCE, OR NEGLIGENCE
NOTES: PERFORMED UNNECESSARY FERTILITY SURGERY THAT WAS NOT MEDICALLY INDICATED WHICH CONSTITUTES NEGLIGENCE, INCOMPETENCE OR MALPRACTICE AND CREATES UNREASONABLE RISK THAT A PATIENT MAY BE HARMED IN ONE CASE. GUILTY OF "UNBUNDLING" WHICH IS A MISREPRESENTATION OF THE USUAL AND CUSTOMARY BILLING PROCEDURE IN A MANNER CALCULATED TO RECEIVE EXCESSIVE REIMBURSEMENT;

CHARGED INDIVIDUAL PROCEDURES WHICH WERE AN INTEGRAL PART OF PERFORMING OTHER PROCEDURES INSTEAD OF CHARGING A SINGLE, ALL-INCLUSIVE FEE, WHICH WOULD PROPERLY INCLUDE HOSPITAL ADMISSION, PROCEDURES, HISTORY AND PHYSICAL, AND HOSPITAL DISCHARGE IN TWO CASES; SHOWED ONE PATIENT A PORTION OF ANOTHER PATIENT'S MEDICAL RECORDS. RESTRICTED LICENSE: SHALL USE A BOARD APPROVED BILLING AND ACCOUNTING FIRM FOR ALL OF HER MEDICAL BILLINGS FOR A MINIMUM OF 10 YEARS; SHALL OBTAIN PRIOR BOARD APPROVAL IF SHE JOINS A GROUP PRACTICE; SHALL OBTAIN A SECOND OPINION FROM A BOARD APPROVED CONSULTANT OR CONSULTANTS WHEN PERFORMING ANY TUBAL SURGERY INVOLVING THE CLEARING OF BLOCKAGE OF THE FALLOPIAN TUBES AND SHALL RETAIN A COPY OF THOSE SECOND OPINIONS FOR REVIEW BY THE BOARD UNTIL OTHERWISE ORDERED; SHALL COMPLETE A MINIMUM OF A 14 HOUR BOARD APPROVED COURSE ON ETHICS WHICH MAY BE TAILORED SPECIFICALLY TO ADDRESS THE BILLING, REPRESENTATION, AND BREACH OF PATIENT-PHYSICIAN PRIVILEGE CONCERNS; SHALL COOPERATE IN FULL WITH A PRACTICE REVIEW CONDUCTED A MINIMUM OF ONCE ANNUALLY; SHALL APPEAR BEFORE THE BOARD FOR A COMPLIANCE APPEARANCE AT LEAST ANNUALLY; SHALL PAY A FINE OF $5,000.

BHASKAR, PADMINI MD, LICENSE NUMBER 0117331, OF 18314 142ND AVENUE SE, RENTON, WA, WAS DISCIPLINED BY NEW YORK ON MAY 23, 1995.
DISCIPLINARY ACTION: 24-MONTH PROBATION
OFFENSE: DISCIPLINARY ACTION BY ANOTHER STATE OR AGENCY
NOTES: ACTION BY WASHINGTON BOARD FOR EXCESSIVE FEES "UNBUNDLING", PERFORMING FERTILITY SURGERY NOT MEDICALLY INDICATED AND FOR BREACHING PATIENT CONFIDENTIALITY. TWO YEAR SUSPENSION, STAYED AS PROBATION UPON COMMENCING PRACTICE IN NEW YORK.

BHASKAR, PADMINI MD OF RENTON, WA, WAS DISCIPLINED BY OHIO ON DECEMBER 11, 1995.
DISCIPLINARY ACTION: DENIAL OF NEW LICENSE
OFFENSE: DISCIPLINARY ACTION BY ANOTHER STATE OR AGENCY
NOTES: PRIOR ACTION BY WASHINGTON'S MEDICAL BOARD BASED ON BILLING PRACTICES; FAILURE TO LIST FOUR FLEX EXAMS ON LICENSURE APPLICATION WHICH SHE HAD PREVIOUSLY TAKEN; SHOWING A PATIENT'S MEDICAL RECORDS TO ANOTHER PATIENT; PERFORMING SURGERY THAT WAS NOT MEDICALLY INDICATED AND LACK OF THE FULL, UNLIMITED LICENSE REQUIRED FOR ENDORSEMENT.

BIHLER, DAVID ANTHONY MD, LICENSE NUMBER 0018975, OF PORT ANGELES, WA, WAS DISCIPLINED BY WASHINGTON ON FEBRUARY 15, 1991.
DISCIPLINARY ACTION: MONITORING OF PHYSICIAN
OFFENSE: FAILURE TO COMPLY WITH A PREVIOUS BOARD ORDER
NOTES: ON 12/14/85 BOARD ISSUED AN ORDER OF SUSPENSION, WHICH WAS STAYED SUBJECT TO CERTAIN TERMS AND CONDITIONS, INCLUDING PARTICIPATION IN THE WASHINGTON MONITORED TREATMENT PROGRAM, AS A RESULT OF HIS DIVERSION OF CONTROLLED SUBSTANCES FOR HIS OWN NONTHERAPEUTIC USE. HE RELAPSED IN 8/90 AND WAS FOUND OUT OF COMPLIANCE WITH THE PROGRAM; RECEIVED TREATMENT AND A PSYCHOLOGICAL EVALUATION FROM 9/27/90 TO 10/24/90. MINIMUM FIVE YEAR SUSPENSION STAYED ON FOLLOWING CONDITIONS: MUST PARTICIPATE IN PSYCHOTHERAPY ON A WEEKLY BASIS; SHALL SUBMIT TO MONTHLY RANDOM URINE TESTS, WITH QUARTERLY REPORTS TO THE BOARD; MUST PARTICIPATE WITH NARCOTICS ANONYMOUS WEEKLY WITH QUARTERLY REPORTS TO THE BOARD; SHALL ABSTAIN FROM ALL MIND ALTERING AND POTENTIALLY ADDICTIVE DRUGS INCLUDING ALCOHOL; MUST PROVIDE A COPY OF THE ORDER TO PSYCHIATRIST AND THERAPIST, HIS OFFICE STAFF, ANY PHYSICIAN WITH WHOM HE HAS A PROFESSIONAL RELATIONSHIP, AND THE CHIEF OF STAFF OF ANY HOSPITAL WHERE HE HAS PRIVILEGES; MUST APPEAR BEFORE THE BOARD FOR COMPLIANCE HEARINGS IN 6 MONTHS AND ANNUALLY THEREAFTER; SHALL INFORM BOARD IF HE LEAVES THE STATE; MAY NOT PETITION FOR MODIFICATION OF TERMS OF ORDER FOR TWO YEARS. ON 12/11/95 ORDER TERMINATED AND LICENSE UNRESTRICTED.

BLACK, MURRAY L DO WAS DISCIPLINED BY WASHINGTON ON JANUARY 6, 1994.
DISCIPLINARY ACTION: EMERGENCY SUSPENSION
NOTES: ON 1/20/94 SUMMARY SUSPENSION MODIFIED: HIS CONTROLLED SUBSTANCE PRIVILEGES SHALL BE SUSPENDED; SHALL OBTAIN CONSULTATION OR SECOND OPINIONS ON ALL PAIN MANAGEMENT PATIENTS FROM A BOARD CERTIFIED FAMILY PRACTICE OR INTERNAL MEDICINE PHYSICIAN; SHALL MAINTAIN HEALTH CARE RECORDS ACCORDING TO A SPECIFIED PLAN.

BLACK, MURRAY L DO WAS DISCIPLINED BY WASHINGTON ON APRIL 22, 1994.
DISCIPLINARY ACTION: 24-MONTH PROBATION; FINE
OFFENSE: SUBSTANDARD CARE, INCOMPETENCE, OR NEGLIGENCE
NOTES: ALLEGATIONS THAT HIS MEDICAL MANAGEMENT OF TWO PATIENTS WAS BELOW THE STANDARD OF CARE. CONDITIONS OF PROBATION: HIS PRIVILEGES FOR SCHEDULE II AND III CONTROLLED SUBSTANCES ARE SUSPENDED; SHALL OBTAIN CONSULTATION OR SECOND OPINIONS FROM A BOARD APPROVED PHYSICIAN ON ALL PAIN MANAGEMENT PATIENTS; SHALL MAINTAIN HEALTH CARE RECORDS ACCORDING TO A SPECIFIED PLAN; SHALL TAKE AND PASS THE SPEX; MAY PETITION THE BOARD FOR RELEASE NO SOONER THAN ONE YEAR; SHALL INFORM THE BOARD, IN WRITING, OF CHANGES IN HIS PRACTICE AND RESIDENCE ADDRESS; SHALL NOTIFY THE BOARD OF DEPARTURE AND RETURN FROM WASHINGTON; THE PERIOD OF PROBATION SHALL BE TOLLED FOR ANY TIME OF RESIDENCE AND PRACTICE OUTSIDE OF WASHINGTON; AND SHALL COMPLETE AT LEAST EIGHT COURSE HOURS OF BOARD APPROVED CONTINUING PROFESSIONAL EDUCATION IN PAIN MANAGEMENT AND THE THERAPEUTIC USE OF CONTROLLED SUBSTANCES AND AT LEAST FOUR HOURS EACH ON MEDICAL DIAGNOSIS AND PATIENT RECORD KEEPING; MUST SUBMIT PROOF OF COMPLETION. $5,000 FINE.

BLACK, MURRAY L DO WAS DISCIPLINED BY WASHINGTON ON NOVEMBER 23, 1994.
DISCIPLINARY ACTION: RESTRICTION PLACED ON LICENSE; MONITORING OF PHYSICIAN
OFFENSE: FAILURE TO COMPLY WITH A PREVIOUS BOARD ORDER
NOTES: IN NONCOMPLIANCE WITH THE 4/22/94 ORDER. FAILED THE SPEX EXAMINATION AND HAS NOT OFFERED ANY OTHER SUBSTANTIAL OR SUFFICIENT EVIDENCE OF CURRENT GENERAL COMPETENCE. INDEFINITE SUSPENSION STAYED, UNDER TERMS AND CONDITIONS: SHALL BE LIMITED TO TREATMENT OF ALLERGY PATIENTS, ENVIRONMENTAL/ECOLOGICAL MEDICINE, AND OSTEOPATHIC MANIPULATION; PRIOR TO RECEIVING ANY TREATMENT FROM HIM, EACH PATIENT SHALL RECEIVE A COMPREHENSIVE HISTORY AND PHYSICAL EXAMINATION BY ANOTHER PHYSICIAN AND A WRITTEN REPORT SHALL BE PROVIDED TO HIM AND PLACED IN THE PATIENT'S FILE; ALL PATIENTS SHALL BE

REEXAMINED BY ANOTHER PHYSICIAN ANNUALLY AND A NEW REPORT PROVIDED TO HIM; HIS RECORDS SHALL BE AVAILABLE UPON REASONABLE NOTICE FOR CHART REVIEW BY THE DEPARTMENT OF HEALTH; MAY PETITION FOR MODIFICATION AFTER HE TAKES AND PASSES THE SPEX; ALL OTHER TERMS OF 4/22/94 ORDER REMAIN IN EFFECT.

BLACK, MURRAY L MD, LICENSE NUMBER 0A28862, OF YAKIMA, WA, WAS DISCIPLINED BY CALIFORNIA ON AUGUST 27, 1996.
DISCIPLINARY ACTION: SURRENDER OF LICENSE
NOTES: WHILE CHARGES PENDING.

BLACK, MURRAY LEE DO OF 609 SOUTH 48TH AVENUE, YAKIMA, WA, WAS DISCIPLINED BY DEA ON APRIL 11, 1995.
DISCIPLINARY ACTION: SURRENDER OF CONTROLLED SUBSTANCE LICENSE
OFFENSE: DISCIPLINARY ACTION BY ANOTHER STATE OR AGENCY
NOTES: STATE BOARD.

BLOOM, ALLAN MD, LICENSE NUMBER FE13852, OF REDMOND, WA, WAS DISCIPLINED BY CALIFORNIA ON MAY 27, 1995.
DISCIPLINARY ACTION: SURRENDER OF LICENSE
NOTES: WHILE CHARGES PENDING.

BLOOM, ALLAN I MD, LICENSE NUMBER 0017888, OF BELLEVUE KING COUNTY, WA, WAS DISCIPLINED BY WASHINGTON ON JANUARY 17, 1992.
DISCIPLINARY ACTION: PROBATION
OFFENSE: OVERPRESCRIBING OR MISPRESCRIBING DRUGS
NOTES: NEGLIGENTLY PRESCRIBED CONTROLLED SUBSTANCES. FIVE-YEAR SUSPENSION SHALL BE STAYED PROVIDING HE ABIDES BY TERMS AND CONDITIONS. EFFECTIVE 6/14/93 BOARD ACCEPTS HIS RETIREMENT WHICH SHALL BE PERMANENT; HE MAY RESUME PRACTICE IN THIS STATE ONLY WITH PRIOR BOARD APPROVAL; HE WILL NOTIFY THE BOARD IF HE PLANS TO RESUME PRACTICE OR APPLY FOR LICENSURE IN ANY OTHER JURISDICTION.

BLUM, JACK MD, DATE OF BIRTH JANUARY 9, 1934, LICENSE NUMBER 0C28144, OF FAIR OAKS, CA, WAS DISCIPLINED BY CALIFORNIA ON JUNE 22, 1990.
DISCIPLINARY ACTION: SURRENDER OF LICENSE
NOTES: VOLUNTARY SURRENDER ACCEPTED WHILE CHARGES PENDING.

BLUM, JACK MD, LICENSE NUMBER 0006978, OF CONROE, TX, WAS DISCIPLINED BY MISSISSIPPI ON NOVEMBER 21, 1991.
DISCIPLINARY ACTION: SURRENDER OF LICENSE
OFFENSE: DISCIPLINARY ACTION BY ANOTHER STATE OR AGENCY
NOTES: ACTION TAKEN IN CALIFORNIA.

BLUM, JACK MD, DATE OF BIRTH JANUARY 9, 1934, LICENSE NUMBER 0005293, WAS DISCIPLINED BY ARIZONA ON JANUARY 23, 1992.
DISCIPLINARY ACTION: PROBATION
OFFENSE: DISCIPLINARY ACTION BY ANOTHER STATE OR AGENCY
NOTES: CALIFORNIA LICENSE SURRENDERED EFFECTIVE 6/22/90 IN CONJUCTION WITH DISCIPLINARY PROCEEDINGS PENDING AGAINST HIM IN CALIFORNIA. ADMITTED THAT HE USED OR ADMINISTERED TO HIMSELF CONTROLLED SUBSTANCES AND DANGEROUS DRUGS WHICH CAUSED URINE SAMPLES TO TEST POSITIVE ON SIX TESTS DURING THE PERIOD FROM 4/18/88 THROUGH 6/22/89. DR. BLUM IS GUILTY OF UNPROFESSIONAL CONDUCT FOR USE OF CONTROLLED SUBSTANCES EXCEPT IF PRESCRIBED BY ANOTHER PHYSICIAN FOR USE DURING A PRESCRIBED COURSE OF TREATMENT. SHALL MEET WITH THE ARIZONA BOARD PRIOR TO PRACTICING MEDICINE IN ARIZONA AND SHALL BE SUBJECT TO ANY PSYCHIATRIC, PSYCHOMETRIC AND PHYSICAL EVALUATION OR COMPETENCY TESTS THAT THE BOARD MAY DEEM NECESSARY PRIOR TO PERMITTING HIM TO PRACTICE MEDICINE.

BLUM, JACK MD, DATE OF BIRTH JANUARY 9, 1934, LICENSE NUMBER 0003057, OF DALLAS, TX, WAS DISCIPLINED BY VERMONT ON OCTOBER 15, 1992.
OFFENSE: DISCIPLINARY ACTION BY ANOTHER STATE OR AGENCY
NOTES: SURRENDERED LICENSE IN CALIFORNIA ON 3/29/90. DISCIPLINED FOR UNPROFESSIONAL CONDUCT, IN THAT HE ADMITTED HE USED OR ADMINISTERED TO HIMSELF CONTROLLED SUBSTANCES AND DANGEROUS DRUGS WHICH CAUSED URINE SAMPLES TO TEST POSITIVE BETWEEN 1/19/89 AND 6/22/89. IF HE SHOULD REAPPLY FOR LICENSURE IN CALIFORNIA, HIS APPLICATION SHALL BE TREATED AS AN ORIGINAL APPLICATION AND HE SHALL BE REQUIRED TO MEET ALL THE REQUIREMENTS OF A NEW APPLICANT. BEFORE PRACTICING IN VERMONT, WILL APPEAR BEFORE THE BOARD AND BE SUBJECT TO ANY COMPETENCY TESTS THEY DEEM NECESSARY.

BLUM, JACK MD, LICENSE NUMBER 0013563, OF DALLAS, TX, WAS DISCIPLINED BY WASHINGTON ON NOVEMBER 20, 1992.
DISCIPLINARY ACTION: PROBATION
OFFENSE: DISCIPLINARY ACTION BY ANOTHER STATE OR AGENCY
NOTES: CHARGES OF SUSPENSION, REVOCATION, OR RESTRICTION OF THE LICENSE TO PRACTICE IN ANOTHER JURISDICTION. UNABLE TO PRACTICE IN WASHINGTON UNTIL CERTAIN CONDITIONS ARE MET.

BLUM, JACK MD, DATE OF BIRTH JANUARY 9, 1934, LICENSE NUMBER 00D2660, OF 10044 INWOOD ROAD, DALLAS, TX, WAS DISCIPLINED BY TEXAS ON JANUARY 29, 1993.
DISCIPLINARY ACTION: 60-MONTH PROBATION; RESTRICTION PLACED ON CONTROLLED SUBSTANCE LICENSE
OFFENSE: DISCIPLINARY ACTION BY ANOTHER STATE OR AGENCY
NOTES: DISCIPLINED BY CALIFORNIA BOARD FOR SELF-ADMINISTRATION OF DANGEROUS OR CONTROLLED SUBSTANCES LEADING TO SURRENDER OF HIS LICENSE; MISSISSIPPI LICENSE ALSO SURRENDERED ALTHOUGH HE HAD NEVER PRACTICED THERE; DISCIPLINED BY ARIZONA BOARD ALTHOUGH HE NEVER PRACTICED THERE; SELF-ADMINISTERED DIAZEPAM, CODEINE, PHENERGAN, AND PROCARDIA; CURRENTLY PRACTICING IN GEORGIA. 5 YEAR SUSPENSION STAYED. CONDITIONS OF PROBATION: SHALL PARTICIPATE IN ACTIVITIES OF A PHYSICIAN HEALTH AND REHABILITATION COMMITTEE AND ATTEND WEEKLY MEETINGS WITH QUARTERLY REPORTS; SHALL PARTICIPATE IN AA'S 12 STEP PROGRAM NOT LESS THAN 2 TIMES A WEEK WITH QUARTERLY REPORTS; SHALL FURNISH THE BOARD WITH WRITTEN REPORTS ON HIS MEDICAL CONDITION AND COMPLIANCE WITH THIS ORDER WHEN REQUESTED; SHALL ABSTAIN FROM THE CONSUMPTION OF ALCOHOL/CONTROLLED SUBSTANCES IN ANY FORM; SHALL SUBMIT HIMSELF FOR APPROPRIATE EXAMS INCLUDING DRUG OR ALCOHOL SCREENS; SHALL NOT TREAT OR OTHERWISE SERVE AS THE PHYSICIAN, PRESCRIBE, DISPENSE OR ADMINISTER DRUGS THAT MAY BE SUBJECT TO ABUSE TO HIMSELF OR ANY MEMBER OF HIS FAMILY; SHALL NOT POSSESS, ADMINISTER, DISPENSE OR PRESCRIBE SCHEDULE II OR IIN CONTROLLED SUBSTANCES OUTSIDE OF A HOSPITAL SETTING; SHALL MAINTAIN A SEPARATE LOG OF ALL PRESCRIPTIONS WRITTEN FOR CONTROLLED SUBSTANCES WHICH SHALL BE AVAILABLE FOR INSPECTION; SHALL OBTAIN THE SERVICES OF A PRIMARY CARE PHYSICIAN WHO SHALL RELEASE INFORMATION TO THE BOARD; BOARD WILL BE INFORMED IF ANY DRUG HAVING ADDICTION-FORMING OR ADDICTION-SUSTAINING LIABILITY IS PRESCRIBED; SHALL OBTAIN NO PRESCRIPTIONS FROM ANY OTHER

PHYSICIAN UNLESS IT IS APPROVED IN WRITING WITHIN 24 HOURS; ANY PRESCRIPTIONS WRITTEN CAN BE FILLED ONLY AT BOARD-APPROVED PHARMACIES; SHALL BE EVALUATED BY A BOARD-APPROVED PSYCHIATRIST TO WHOM HE WILL PROVIDE A COPY OF THE ORDER; SHALL COOPERATE WITH THE BOARD IN VERIFYING COMPLIANCE; SHALL INFORM BOARD OF CHANGE OF ADDRESS WITHIN 10 DAYS; TIME SPENT OUT OF TEXAS OR GEORGIA DOES NOT COUNT TOWARD PROBATION; SHALL APPEAR BEFORE THE BOARD ONCE A YEAR; SHALL APPEAR BEFORE THE BOARD PRIOR TO PRACTICING IN TEXAS. SHALL NOT SEEK MODIFICATION UNTIL FEBRUARY 6, 1994.

BLUM, JACK MD, DATE OF BIRTH JANUARY 9, 1934, LICENSE NUMBER 0016004, OF 101 BOWENS MILL ROAD, DOUGLAS, GA, WAS DISCIPLINED BY GEORGIA ON JUNE 28, 1993.
DISCIPLINARY ACTION: EMERGENCY SUSPENSION
NOTES: IMPAIRMENT.

BLUM, JACK MD, DATE OF BIRTH JANUARY 9, 1934, LICENSE NUMBER 0016004, OF 10044 INWOOD ROAD, DALLAS, TX, WAS DISCIPLINED BY GEORGIA ON OCTOBER 7, 1993.
DISCIPLINARY ACTION: LICENSE SUSPENSION
NOTES: IMPAIRMENT; SHALL NOT ENGAGE IN OR RETURN TO PRACTICE OF MEDICINE IN GEORGIA UNTIL FURTHER ORDER OF THE BOARD.

BLUM, JACK MD, DATE OF BIRTH JANUARY 9, 1934, LICENSE NUMBER 00D2660, OF DALLAS, TX, WAS DISCIPLINED BY TEXAS ON OCTOBER 14, 1993.
DISCIPLINARY ACTION: EMERGENCY SUSPENSION
OFFENSE: FAILURE TO COMPLY WITH A PREVIOUS BOARD ORDER
NOTES: VIOLATED 1/29/93 ORDER IN THAT HE REFUSED TO SUPPLY A URINE SAMPLE IN 8/93 AND INGESTED CONTROLLED SUBSTANCES IN 9/93.

BLUM, JACK MD OF 10044 INWOOD ROAD, DALLAS, TX, WAS DISCIPLINED BY DEA ON NOVEMBER 24, 1993.
DISCIPLINARY ACTION: SURRENDER OF CONTROLLED SUBSTANCE LICENSE
NOTES: CONTINUES TO ATTEMPT TO OBTAIN CONTROLLED SUBSTANCES BY CALL-IN PRESCRIPTIONS.

BLUM, JACK MD, DATE OF BIRTH JANUARY 9, 1934, LICENSE NUMBER 00D2660, OF DALLAS, TX, WAS DISCIPLINED BY TEXAS ON JUNE 22, 1994.
DISCIPLINARY ACTION: PROBATION
OFFENSE: FAILURE TO COMPLY WITH A PREVIOUS BOARD ORDER
NOTES: VIOLATED 1/29/93 TEXAS ORDER IN THAT HE REFUSED TO SUPPLY A URINE SAMPLE ON 8/26/93, INGESTED CONTROLLED SUBSTANCES THREE TIMES IN 9/93; SURRENDERED HIS DEA CONTROLLED SUBSTANCES REGISTRATION ON 11/22/93. SUSPENSION STAYED. CONDITIONS OF INDEFINITE PROBATION: SHALL NOT PRACTICE MEDICINE UNTIL HE HAS UNDERGONE A 72 HOUR INPATIENT EVALUATION FOR CHEMICAL DEPENDENCY, HAS OBTAINED A COMPLETE NEUROLOGIC EXAM FROM A BOARD APPROVED PSYCHIATRIST, CAN DEMONSTRATE COMPLIANCE WITH THIS PSYCHIATRIST'S RECOMMENDATIONS AND APPEARS BEFORE THE BOARD TO REQUEST PERMISSION TO PRACTICE. UPON AN ADEQUATE SHOWING BEFORE THE BOARD THAT HE IS ABLE TO SAFELY PRACTICE MEDICINE, HE SHALL BE ALLOWED TO RESUME THE PRACTICE OF MEDICINE UNDER VARIOUS TERMS AND CONDITIONS.

BLUM, JACK MD, DATE OF BIRTH JANUARY 9, 1934, LICENSE NUMBER 00D2660, WAS DISCIPLINED BY TEXAS ON JANUARY 5, 1995.
DISCIPLINARY ACTION: 120-MONTH PROBATION; RESTRICTION PLACED ON CONTROLLED SUBSTANCE LICENSE
OFFENSE: FAILURE TO COMPLY WITH A PREVIOUS BOARD ORDER
NOTES: SUSPENSION STAYED. CONDITIONS OF PROBATION: SHALL ABSTAIN FROM THE CONSUMPTION OR ALCOHOL OR CONTROLLED SUBSTANCES IN ANY FORM UNLESS PRESCRIBED BY ANOTHER PHYSICIAN FOR A LEGITIMATE AND THERAPEUTIC PURPOSE; SHALL SUBMIT HIMSELF FOR APPROPRIATE EXAMS INCLUDING DRUG OR ALCOHOL SCREENS; SHALL NOT TREAT OR OTHERWISE SERVE AS PHYSICIAN FOR HIMSELF OR ANY MEMBER OF HIS FAMILY AND SHALL NOT PRESCRIBE, DISPENSE OR ADMINISTER ANY DRUGS THAT MAY BE SUBJECT TO ABUSE TO HIMSELF OR ANY MEMBER OF HIS FAMILY; SHALL ONLY ORDER AND ADMINISTER CONTROLLED SUBSTANCES FOR PERSONS UNDERGOING INPATIENT PROCEDURES AND/OR TREATMENTS AT A HOSPITAL FOR PURPOSES OF INPATIENT CARE; SHALL SURRENDER ALL UNUSED TRIPLICATE PRESCRIPTION FORMS AND CONTROLLED SUBSTANCES IN HIS POSSESSION INCLUDING SAMPLES; SHALL BE MONITORED BY A BOARD-APPROVED PHYSICIAN WITH QUARTERLY REPORTS TO THE BOARD; SEPARATE FROM PATIENT RECORDS SHALL MAINTAIN A FILE OF EVERY PRESCRIPTION WRITTEN FOR DANGEROUS DRUGS WHICH SHALL BE AVAILABLE FOR REVIEW; SHALL NOT TELEPHONE ANY PRESCRIPTION TO A PHARMACY FOR DANGEROUS DRUGS THAT MAY BE HABIT-FORMING; SHALL PARTICIPATE IN THE ACTIVITIES OF A PHYSICIANS' HEALTH AND REHABILITATION COMMITTEE AND ABIDE BY TERMS OF AN AFTERCARE PROGRAM CONTRACT WITH QUARTERLY REPORTS; SHALL PARTICIPATE IN AA'S PROGRAMS NOT LESS THAN THREE TIMES A WEEK WITH QUARTERLY REPORTS TO THE BOARD; SHALL SUBMIT HIMSELF FOR EVALUATION AND TREATMENT TO A BOARD-APPROVED PSYCHIATRIST WITH QUARTERLY REPORTS; SHALL ATTEND AT LEAST 40 HOURS OF CONTINUING MEDICAL EDUCATION PER YEAR; SHALL APPEAR BEFORE THE BOARD TWICE A YEAR; SHALL GIVE A COPY OF THIS ORDER TO ANY HEALTH CARE ENTITY WHERE HE HAS PRIVILEGES; SHALL COOPERATE WITH THE BOARD IN VERIFYING COMPLIANCE; SHALL INFORM BOARD OF CHANGE OF ADDRESS WITHIN 10 DAYS OR IF HE LEAVES THE STATE; TIME SPENT OUT OF TEXAS DOES NOT COUNT TOWARD PROBATION. SHALL NOT SEEK MODIFICATION FOR ONE YEAR.

BLUM, JACK MD, DATE OF BIRTH JANUARY 9, 1934, LICENSE NUMBER 00D2660, WAS DISCIPLINED BY TEXAS ON JUNE 28, 1995.
DISCIPLINARY ACTION: LICENSE REVOCATION
OFFENSE: FAILURE TO COMPLY WITH A PREVIOUS BOARD ORDER
NOTES: BETWEEN 10/6/94 AND 1/5/95 DIAGNOSED, TREATED, AND PRESCRIBED TO PATIENTS IN VIOLATION OF ORDER; NONCOMPLIANCE TO 1/05/95 ORDER IN THAT HE FAILED TO CAUSE HIS TREATING PHYSICIAN TO REPORT THE INGESTION OF FIORCET AND DIRECTED A MEDICAL ASSISTANT OF HIS MONITORING PHYSICIAN TO PREPARE PRESCRIPTIONS OF CHLORAL HYDRATE AND DIAZEPAM IN HIS WIFE'S NAME WHICH HE TRIED TO FILL, NEITHER OF WHICH WERE AUTHORIZED OR DIRECTED BY HIS MONITORING PHYSICIAN.

BLUM, JACK MD, DATE OF BIRTH JANUARY 9, 1934, LICENSE NUMBER 0003057, OF DALLAS, TX, WAS DISCIPLINED BY VERMONT ON NOVEMBER 3, 1995.
DISCIPLINARY ACTION: LICENSE REVOCATION
OFFENSE: DISCIPLINARY ACTION BY ANOTHER STATE OR AGENCY
NOTES: TEXAS BOARD TOOK DISCIPLINARY ACTION AGAINST HIS MEDICAL LICENSE; ON HIS 1994-1996 LICENSE RENEWAL APPLICATION HE FALSELY ANSWERED "NO" TO A QUESTION REGARDING DISCIPLINARY ACTION TAKEN BY ANOTHER STATE WHEN HE HAD ACTIONS TAKEN BY

SEVERAL STATES BETWEEN 1990 AND 1993; ALSO ANSWERED "NO" TO A QUESTION REGARDING REDUCTION, SUSPENSION OR REVOCATION OF STAFF PRIVILEGES, EMPLOYMENT OR APPOINTMENT IN A HOSPITAL OR OTHER HEALTH CARE INSTITUTION WHEN HE HAD RESIGNED FROM A HOSPITAL IN GEORGIA IN 4/93.

BLUM, JACK MD, DATE OF BIRTH JANUARY 9, 1934, LICENSE NUMBER 0005293, WAS DISCIPLINED BY ARIZONA ON JANUARY 19, 1996.
DISCIPLINARY ACTION: LICENSE REVOCATION
OFFENSE: DISCIPLINARY ACTION BY ANOTHER STATE OR AGENCY
NOTES: VIOLATED TERMS OF TEXAS PROBATION OF 1/93 IN THAT HE REFUSED TO SUPPLY A URINE SAMPLE AT THE REQUEST OF A COMPLIANCE OFFICER IN 8/93; IN 9/93, INGESTED CHLORAL HYDRATE, CODEINE, AND XANAX WITHOUT A PRESCRIPTION FROM HIS PRIMARY PHYSICIAN AS REQUIRED BY PROBATION TERMS; SURRENDERED HIS DEA CONTROLLED SUBSTANCES REGISTRATION ON 11/22/93; PLACED ON 10 YEAR PROBATION IN TEXAS IN 1/95 BASED ON NONCOMPLIANCE. IN 1993,1994 AND 1995 APPLICATIONS FOR LICENSE RENEWAL IN ARIZONA, HE DENIED ANY DISCIPLINARY ACTION TAKEN AGAINST HIS LICENSE DURING THE REGISTRATION PERIODS AND DENIED ANY DENIAL, RESTRICTION, SUSPENSION, OR LOSS/REVOCATION OF DEA OR PRESCRIPTION PERMIT, DESPITE ACTIONS BY ARIZONA, TEXAS AND SURRENDER OF HIS DEA REGISTRATION DURING THOSE PERIODS. PERMANENT REVOCATION; FINAL DECISION WITH NO OPPORTUNITY FOR REHEARING OR REVIEW.

BOLLES, LEO JOSEPH MD, LICENSE NUMBER 0004165, OF BELLEVUE, WA, WAS DISCIPLINED BY WASHINGTON ON DECEMBER 15, 1995.
DISCIPLINARY ACTION: RESTRICTION PLACED ON LICENSE
NOTES: SHALL REFER ALL PATIENTS WITH ADRENAL OR THYROID PROBLEMS TO A BOARD-CERTIFIED ENDOCRINOLOGIST FOR CONSULTATION.

BONNINGTON, WILLIAM MD, LICENSE NUMBER 0031783, OF VANCOUVER, WA, WAS DISCIPLINED BY WASHINGTON ON AUGUST 23, 1996.
DISCIPLINARY ACTION: SURRENDER OF LICENSE
NOTES: AGREEMENT TO RETIRE.

BOUCHER-LEIF, JEANNE MD WAS DISCIPLINED BY WASHINGTON ON MARCH 16, 1990.
DISCIPLINARY ACTION: SURRENDER OF LICENSE
NOTES: UNDER INVESTIGATION BY THE BOARD CONCERNING HER ABILITY TO PRACTICE MEDICINE WITH REASONABLE SKILL AND SAFETY TO PATIENTS. VOLUNTARY RETIREMENT EFFECTIVE 5/01/90: HAS NO PLANS TO RESUME PRACTICE SUBSEQUENT TO THAT DATE; AGREES THAT HER RETIREMENT SHALL BE PERMANENT AND THAT SHE MAY RESUME PRACTICE IN THIS STATE ONLY WITH PRIOR APPROVAL OF THE BOARD; AGREES THAT IF SHE PLANS TO RESUME PRACTICE IN THIS OR ANY OTHER JURISDICTION SHE WILL INFORM THE BOARD. INVESTIGATION WAS TERMINATED.

BOURNE, MARVIN MD, LICENSE NUMBER 0009339, OF TACOMA, WA, WAS DISCIPLINED BY WASHINGTON ON OCTOBER 30, 1992.
DISCIPLINARY ACTION: EMERGENCY SUSPENSION
NOTES: ALLEGATIONS THAT HE MAY BE UNABLE TO PRACTICE MEDICINE WITH REASONABLE SKILL AND SAFETY.

BOURNE, MARVIN L MD WAS DISCIPLINED BY WASHINGTON ON APRIL 16, 1993.
DISCIPLINARY ACTION: EMERGENCY SUSPENSION; MONITORING OF PHYSICIAN

OFFENSE: SUBSTANCE ABUSE
NOTES: ALLEGATIONS THAT HE IS UNABLE TO PRACTICE WITH REASONABLE SKILL AND SAFETY BY REASON OF A MENTAL OR PHYSICAL CONDITION AND CURRENT MISUSE OF ALCOHOL. AS OF 9/28/92 HIS TREATING PSYCHIATRIST DIAGNOSED HIM WITH ALCOHOLISM, POORLY CONTROLLED, DYSTHYMIA, HYPERTENSION AND ARTHRITIS. HE HAS BEEN A PARTICIPANT IN THE WASHINGTON PHYSICIAN'S HEALTH PROGRAM (WPHP) SINCE 9/90, BUT RELAPSED WITH ALCOHOL USE ABOUT THE LAST WEEK OF 9/92. HIS TREATING PSYCHIATRIST REPORTED THAT HE CONTINUED TO HAVE EPISODES OF BINGE DRINKING.THE 10/20/92 SUMMARY SUSPENSION SHALL REMAIN IN EFFECT UNTIL FURTHER ORDER OF THE BOARD; SHALL ENTER INTO AN AGREEMENT WITH WPHP AND FULLY COMPLY WITH ALL THE REQUIREMENTS; SHALL AUTHORIZE AND REQUEST THEM TO PREPARE REPORTS TO THE BOARD; SHALL NOT POSSESS OR USE LEGEND DRUGS OR CONTROLLED SUBSTANCES, INCLUDING ALCOHOL, UNLESS THEY ARE PRESCRIBED BY ANOTHER PHYSICIAN FOR LEGITIMATE THERAPEUTIC PURPOSES AND SAID PRESCRIPTION IS APPROVED BY THE WPHP; AGREES TO SUBMIT TO RANDOM AND OBSERVED URINALYSIS AND/OR BLOOD TESTS; SHALL REMAIN UNDER THE CARE AND TREATMENT OF HIS PRESENT TREATING PSYCHIATRIST; MAY PETITION THE BOARD FOR A CHANGE IN THE TERMS/CONDITIONS OF THE ORDER IN NO SOONER THAN TWO YEARS; SHALL INFORM THE BOARD IN WRITING, OF CHANGES IN HIS PRACTICE AND RESIDENCE ADDRESS; MUST NOTIFY THE BOARD IN WRITING IF HE LEAVES WASHINGTON; THE PERIOD OF PROBATION/SUSPENSION SHALL BE TOLLED FOR ANY TIME PERIOD DURING WHICH HE RESIDES AND/OR PRACTICES OUTSIDE OF WASHINGTON.

BOWDEN, THOMAS MD WAS DISCIPLINED BY WASHINGTON ON AUGUST 20, 1993.
DISCIPLINARY ACTION: SURRENDER OF LICENSE
NOTES: UNDER INVESTIGATION BY THE BOARD CONCERNING HIS ABILITY TO PRACTICE MEDICINE WITH REASONABLE SKILL AND SAFETY TO PATIENTS. VOLUNTARY RETIREMENT EFFECTIVE THE SUMMER OF 1992 IN LIEU OF FURTHER INVESTIGATION: HAS NO PLANS TO RESUME PRACTICE; HIS RETIREMENT SHALL BE PERMANENT; MAY RESUME PRACTICE IN THIS STATE ONLY WITH THE PRIOR BOARD APPROVAL; SHALL NOTIFY THE BOARD IF HE PLANS TO RESUME PRACTICE IN THIS OR ANY OTHER JURISIDICTION. THE INVESTIGATION WAS TERMINATED.

BOYD, HERSCHELL MD, LICENSE NUMBER 0005419, OF SEATTLE, WA, WAS DISCIPLINED BY WASHINGTON ON NOVEMBER 20, 1992.
DISCIPLINARY ACTION: RESTRICTION PLACED ON LICENSE
OFFENSE: SUBSTANDARD CARE, INCOMPETENCE, OR NEGLIGENCE
NOTES: NEGLIGENTLY PERFORMING RADIAL KERATOTOMY SURGERY; PUBLISHING MISLEADING ADVERTISEMENTS; MAKING MISLEADING STATEMENTS AND ALTERING MEDICAL RECORDS. SHALL NOT PRACTICE ANY SURGERY.

BRANDT, CORNELIS D MD, LICENSE NUMBER 0005282, OF YAKIMA, WA, WAS DISCIPLINED BY WASHINGTON ON JANUARY 27, 1995.
DISCIPLINARY ACTION: FINE; RESTRICTION PLACED ON LICENSE
NOTES: AGREED NOT TO TREAT NURSING HOME PATIENTS; SHALL COMPLETE CONTINUING MEDICAL EDUCATION; $1,000 FINE. ON 2/25/97 BOARD GRANTED HIS REQUEST TO TERMINATE ORDER AND LICENSE IS UNRESTRICTED.

BREDA, URI MD WAS DISCIPLINED BY WASHINGTON ON JUNE 17, 1989.
DISCIPLINARY ACTION: PROBATION; FINE

OFFENSE: PROFESSIONAL MISCONDUCT
NOTES: BETWEEN 10/86 AND 1/89 WITH REGARD TO 35 PATIENTS PROVIDED TREATMENT THAT WAS NOT INDICATED AND/OR PERFORMED SURGERY THAT WAS NOT INDICATED AND/OR PERFORMED SURGERY IN HIS OFFICE THAT SHOULD NOT HAVE BEEN PERFORMED IN AN OFFICE SETTING AND/OR REQUESTED UNNECESSARY LABORATORY TESTS; ADMINISTERED MEDICATIONS THAT WERE CONTRAINDICATED AND/OR PRESCRIBED UNNECESSARY MEDICATIONS AND/OR IMPROPERLY ADMINISTERED MEDICATIONS; OVERCHARGED OR SUBMITTED EXCESSIVE BILLS TO PATIENTS AND/OR THEIR INSURANCE COMPANIES. 10 YEAR SUSPENSION STAYED TO PROBATION UNDER THE FOLLOWING TERMS AND CONDITIONS: SHALL NOT PERFORM ANY SURGERY WHATSOEVER, EITHER IN HIS OFFICE OR ELSEWHERE; SHALL BE ALLOWED TO PERFORM AS A SURGICAL ASSISTANT; IF HE PROVIDES SURVICES AS A SURGICAL ASSISTANT, ANY SUBMITTED BILL TO ANY PATIENT OR HEALTH INSURANCE PROVIDER MUST RECEIVE PRIOR APPROVAL FROM THE PRIMARY SURGEON ON THE CASE; SHALL MAINTAIN A LIST OF ALL CASES IN WHICH HE PERFORMS AS A SURGICAL ASSISTANT AND SHALL BE SUBMITTED TO THE BOARD AT THE INTERVAL DESIGNATED FOR THE PRACTICE REVIEWS; SHALL LIMIT HIS CHARGES FOR MEDICAL SERVICES TO AMOUNTS THAT ARE REASONABLE AND CONSISTENT WITH THE GENERAL STANDARDS OF THE MEDICAL COMMUNITY; HIS PATIENT RECORDS AND BILLING RECORDS SHALL BE REGULARLY REVIEWED AT LEAST ONCE EVERY SIX MONTHS; SHALL APPEAR BEFORE THE BOARD ONCE A YEAR FROM THE DATE OF THIS ORDER AND PRESENT PROOF THAT HE IS COMPLYING WITH THE ORDER; MAY PETITION THE BOARD TO MODIFY ANY OF THE CONDITIONS OF THIS ORDER IN NO SOONER THAN THREE YEARS; MUST NOTIFY THE BOARD IN WRITING IF HE LEAVES WASHINGTON AND PRACTICE OUTSIDE OF WASHINGTON WILL NOT APPLY TO THE REDUCTION OF THE PROBATIONARY PERIOD; $1,000 FINE.

BREDA, URI W MD, LICENSE NUMBER 0009433, OF RENTON, WA, WAS DISCIPLINED BY WASHINGTON ON JUNE 25, 1991.
DISCIPLINARY ACTION: EMERGENCY SUSPENSION
OFFENSE: FAILURE TO COMPLY WITH A PREVIOUS BOARD ORDER
NOTES: ALLEGATIONS OF SEXUAL CONTACT WITH FOUR PATIENTS, DISPENSING EXPIRED, INEFFECTIVE PRESCRIPTION DRUGS, NEGLIGENTLY PERFORMING A PELVIC EXAM ON A FIFTH PATIENT, CREATING A RISK OF INFECTION TO THIS PATIENT AND OTHER PATIENTS, AND NEGLIGENTLY COMPLETING PATIENT CHARTS. VIOLATED TERMS AND CONDITIONS OF A 6/13/89 BOARD ORDER GRANTING PROBATION.

BREDA, URI W MD, LICENSE NUMBER 0009433, OF RENTON, WA, WAS DISCIPLINED BY WASHINGTON ON NOVEMBER 14, 1991.
DISCIPLINARY ACTION: SURRENDER OF LICENSE
OFFENSE: SEXUAL ABUSE OF OR SEXUAL MISCONDUCT WITH A PATIENT
NOTES: ALLEGATIONS THAT HE HAD SEXUAL CONTACT WITH FOUR PATIENTS; PERFORMED EXAMINATIONS THAT EXPOSED PATIENTS TO INFECTION CREATING AN UNREASONABLE RISK THAT A PATIENT MAY BE HARMED; HE IS UNABLE TO PRACTICE WITH REASONABLE SAFETY AND SKILL AND MAY NOT BE AMENABLE TO TREATMENT; NEGLIGENTLY OR INCOMPETENTLY CHARTED PATIENTS' COMPLAINTS, PHYSICAL FINDINGS AND DIAGNOSIS. HE REPRESENTS HE HAS BEEN RETIRED SINCE 6/25/91 AND HAS NO PLANS TO RESUME PRACTICE. RETIREMENT SHALL BE PERMANENT AND HE WILL NOT REAPPLY TO PRACTICE MEDICINE IN THIS STATE. HE MUST NOTIFY THE BOARD IF HE PLANS TO RESUME PRACTICE IN ANY OTHER JURISDICTION. VOLUNTARY SURRENDER IN LIEU OF FURTHER PROCEEDINGS.

BROOKS, BANCROFT MD, LICENSE NUMBER 0027849, OF TACOMA, WA, WAS DISCIPLINED BY COLORADO ON FEBRUARY 8, 1991.
DISCIPLINARY ACTION: LICENSE REVOCATION
OFFENSE: SUBSTANDARD CARE, INCOMPETENCE, OR NEGLIGENCE
NOTES: ACTION BASED ON DIAGNOSIS AND TREATMENT OF PSYCHIATRIC PATIENTS AT COLORADO STATE HOSPITAL.

BROOKS, BANCROFT MD OF ALBUQUERQUE, NM, WAS DISCIPLINED BY MISSOURI ON NOVEMBER 2, 1992.
DISCIPLINARY ACTION: LICENSE REVOCATION
OFFENSE: DISCIPLINARY ACTION BY ANOTHER STATE OR AGENCY
NOTES: NO REAPPLICATION FOR FIVE YEARS.

BROWN, CYNTHIA A MD, LICENSE NUMBER 0D26655, OF 16816 5TH AVENUE SE, BUTHELL, WA, WAS DISCIPLINED BY MARYLAND ON MARCH 12, 1990.
DISCIPLINARY ACTION: SURRENDER OF LICENSE; SURRENDER OF CONTROLLED SUBSTANCE LICENSE
OFFENSE: SUBSTANDARD CARE, INCOMPETENCE, OR NEGLIGENCE
NOTES: HAS NOT PRACTICED IN MARYLAND SINCE 10/26/88; LICENSED IN TEXAS AND HAS APPLIED IN WASHINGTON STATE; MAY APPLY FOR REINSTATEMENT UPON COMPLETION OF A BOARD-APPROVED TRAINING PROGRAM

BROWN, CYNTHIA A MD, LICENSE NUMBER 00D8160, OF BOTHELL, WA, WAS DISCIPLINED BY TEXAS ON FEBRUARY 22, 1991.
NOTES: MAY NOT PRACTICE IN TEXAS UNTIL THE MARYLAND BOARD HAS ACTED ON ANY PETITION SHE HAS FILED OR MAY FILE FOR REINSTATEMENT OF HER LICENSE; RECEIVE PERMISSION OF TEXAS BOARD BEFORE RETURNING TO PRACTICE MEDICINE IN TEXAS AND BE SUBJECT TO ANY TERMS IMPOSED

BROWN, DENNIS B DR WAS DISCIPLINED BY WASHINGTON ON APRIL 4, 1988.
DISCIPLINARY ACTION: CEASE AND DESIST ORDER
OFFENSE: FAILURE TO COMPLY WITH A PROFESSIONAL RULE
NOTES: SHALL NOT ADVERTISE THAT CARE AND TREATMENT WILL BE AT NO COST WHEN THERE ARE CIRCUMSTANCES UNDER WHICH PATIENT MAY BE REQUIRED TO PAY ALL OR PART OF THE FEE; DID NOT ADMIT TO ANY VIOLATIONS

BROWN, THOMAS E MD, LICENSE NUMBER 0026638, OF SEATTLE, WA, WAS DISCIPLINED BY WASHINGTON ON MARCH 21, 1994.
DISCIPLINARY ACTION: SURRENDER OF LICENSE
NOTES: SUBSEQUENT TO INVESTIGATION REGARDING ABILITY TO PRACTICE WITH REASONABLE SKILL AND SAFETY.

BRYANT, MARY M MD, LICENSE NUMBER 0033408, OF PUYALLUP, WA, WAS DISCIPLINED BY WASHINGTON ON AUGUST 23, 1996.
DISCIPLINARY ACTION: SURRENDER OF LICENSE

BRYANT, MARY MADELINE MD, LICENSE NUMBER 0003899, WAS DISCIPLINED BY SOUTH DAKOTA ON DECEMBER 4, 1996.
DISCIPLINARY ACTION: SURRENDER OF LICENSE
OFFENSE: SUBSTANCE ABUSE
NOTES: IN 1988 VOLUNTARILY UNDERWENT TREATMENT FOR ALCOHOL ABUSE; IN 1989 GRANTED A LICENSE TO PRACTICE IN TEXAS AND ENTERED INTO AN AGREEMENT TO ABSTAIN FROM ALCOHOL AND PARTICIPATE IN AA; IN JANUARY AND FEBRUARY 1996 A MEDICAL ASSISTANT SMELLED ALCOHOL ON HER BREATH WHILE SHE WAS TREATING PATIENTS ON FOUR OR FIVE OCCASIONS; ON 5/02/96 SEVERAL STAFF MEMBERS SMELLED ALCOHOL ON HER BREATH WHILE SHE WAS TREATING PATIENTS AND WHEN SHE UNDERWENT A BREATH-ALCOHOL

TEST AND A BLOOD-ALCOHOL TEST AND BOTH TEST RESULTS WERE POSITIVE FOR THE PRESENCE OF ALCOHOL; ON 7/10/96 SHE ENTERED SPRINGBROOK NORTHWEST FOR TREATMENT AND EVALUATION OF ALCOHOL ABUSE; SHE LEFT SPRINGBROOK NORTHWEST AGAINST MEDICAL ADVICE AND WITHOUT COMPLETING TREATMENT OR EVALUATION.

BUCK, HARPER J MD WAS DISCIPLINED BY NEBRASKA ON AUGUST 31, 1990.
DISCIPLINARY ACTION: PROBATION
OFFENSE: DISCIPLINARY ACTION BY ANOTHER STATE OR AGENCY
NOTES: UNPROFESSIONAL CONDUCT, ALCOHOL IMPAIRMENT.

BUCK, HARPER J MD WAS DISCIPLINED BY WASHINGTON ON SEPTEMBER 17, 1993.
DISCIPLINARY ACTION: 60-MONTH PROBATION; FINE
OFFENSE: SUBSTANDARD CARE, INCOMPETENCE, OR NEGLIGENCE
NOTES: INCOMPETENCE, NEGLIGENCE OR MALPRACTICE IN ONE CASE IN 8/92 WHERE A PATIENT WAS TAKEN TO THE MEDICAL CLINIC COMPLAINING OF CHEST PAIN. THE NURSE CALLED HIM AND HE DIRECTED HER TO OBSERVE THE PATIENT, TO PERFORM AN ELECTROCARDIOGRAM, AND CALL HIM BACK. HE DID NOT ORDER OXYGEN, THE PLACEMENT OF AN INTRAVENOUS LINE, OR THE ADMINISTRATION OF MORPHINE. THE NURSE ADMINISTERED MILK OF MAGNESIA WHICH HAD NO EFFECT. HE LATER ARRIVED AT THE CLINIC AND AFTER CALLING FOR A HELICOPTER EVACUATION NOTICED THE PATIENT WAS OBTUNDED, BEGAN ADMINISTRATION OF OXYGEN, AND INSTALLED AN INTRAVENOUS LINE. HE DID NOT ADMINISTER MEDICATIONS SUCH A EPINEPHRINE OR LIDOCAINE OR ADMINISTER ELECTRICAL DEFIBRILLATION. THE PATIENT DIED 25 MINUTES LATER. FIVE YEAR SUSPENSION, STAYED UNDER THE FOLLOWING TERMS AND CONDITIONS: SHALL OBTAIN CERTIFICATION IN ADVANCED CARDIAC LIFE SUPPORT WITHIN THREE MONTHS AND SHALL MAINTAIN SUCH CERTIFICATION DURING THE STAYED SUSPENSION; SHALL SUBMIT PROOF OF SUCH CERTIFICATION AND OF EACH RECERTIFICATION; SHALL ATTEND A BOARD APPROVED REVIEW COURSE IN FAMILY PRACTICE AND/OR EMERGENCY MEDICINE WHICH MUST CONSIST OF 35 OR MORE COURSE HOURS WITHIN ONE YEAR; SHALL APPEAR BEFORE THE BOARD IN ONE YEAR TO PRESENT PROOF OF THAT HE IS IN COMPLIANCE AND SHALL CONTINUE TO MAKE SUCH COMPLIANCE APPEARANCE ANNUALLY UNTIL PROBATION IS LIFTED; THE BOARD MAY MAKE ANNOUNCED OR UNANNOUNCED VISITS ANNUALLY TO INSPECT OFFICE OR MEDICAL RECORDS, INTERVIEW OFFICE STAFF OR SUPERVISORS, OR REVIEW OTHER ASPECTS OF HIS PRACTICE; SHALL INFORM THE BOARD IN WRITING OF CHANGES OF HIS PRACTICE AND RESIDENCE ADDRESS; MUST NOTIFY THE BOARD IN WRITING IF HE LEAVES WASHINGTON; THE PERIOD OF PROBATION/SUSPENSION SHALL BE TOLLED FOR ANY TIME PERIOD DURING WHICH HE RESIDES AND/OR PRACTICES OUTSIDE OF WASHINTON; MAY PETITION THE BOARD FOR A CHANGE IN THE TERMS AND CONDITIONS IN NO SOONER THAN ONE YEAR; $1,000 FINE. ON 11/4/94 HIS REQUEST TO MODIFY THIS ORDER WAS DENIED.

BELL, JOHN WALTER DO, LICENSE NUMBER 0005982, OF DALLAS, IA, WAS DISCIPLINED BY OREGON ON FEBRUARY 22, 1990.
DISCIPLINARY ACTION: RESTRICTION PLACED ON LICENSE
NOTES: VOLUNTARY LIMITATION. ON 4/11/91 MODIFICATION OF PROBATION/VOLUNTARY LIMITATION. AS OF 3/3/97, NO LONGER LISTED AS RESTRICTED.

BUELL, JOHN WALTER DO WAS DISCIPLINED BY WASHINGTON ON AUGUST 16, 1991.
DISCIPLINARY ACTION: RESTRICTION PLACED ON LICENSE; MONITORING OF PHYSICIAN
OFFENSE: DISCIPLINARY ACTION BY ANOTHER STATE OR AGENCY
NOTES: ON 2/16/90 ACTION IN OREGON. WASHINGTON ORDER REQUIRES HIM TO COMPLY WITH OREGON ORDER INCLUDING: SHALL LIMIT HIS PRACTICE TO THE HOSPITAL EMERGENCY ROOM AND ANESTHESIA IN THE HOSPITAL; SHALL BE ALLOWED TO PERFORM PHYSICAL EXAMINATIONS OUTSIDE THE HOSPITAL SETTING ONLY FOR DEPARTMENT OF TRANSPORTATION PHYSICALS AND PILOT FLIGHT PHYSICALS; AGREES TO ATTEND THE NEXT AVAILABLE APPROPRIATE PRESCRIBING WORKSHOP; SHALL NOTIFY HIS HOSPITAL OR CHIEF OF STAFF OF ANY HEALTH CARE ENTITIES WHERE HE HAS PRIVILEGES OF THE TERMS OF THIS AGREEMENT; AND SHALL CAUSE REPORTS OF HIS PERFORMANCE TO BE SUBMITTED TO THE BOARD QUARTERLY. ADDITIONALLY SHALL SUBMIT IN WRITING TO THE BOARD ANY EMPLOYMENT OR RESIDENCE ADDRESS CHANGES IN WASHINGTON; AND SHALL SUBMIT COPIES OF ALL REPORTS SUBMITTED TO OREGON.

BUNCH, DAVID C MD WAS DISCIPLINED BY WASHINGTON ON MARCH 24, 1990.
DISCIPLINARY ACTION: FINE; RESTRICTION PLACED ON CONTROLLED SUBSTANCE LICENSE
OFFENSE: OVERPRESCRIBING OR MISPRESCRIBING DRUGS
NOTES: PRESCRIBED FIORINAL AND EMPIRIN #3 TO ONE PATIENT FROM 1/86 TO 5/88 FOR OTHER THAN LEGITIMATE THERAPEUTIC PURPOSES. RESTRICTIONS ON LICENSE INCLUDE: SHALL SUBMIT TRIPLICATE PRESCRIPTIONS ON ALL CONTROLLED SUBSTANCES SCHEDULE II THROUGH V; SHALL NOT PRESCRIBE SCHEDULE II DRUGS FOR MORE THAN 3 DAYS EXCEPT FOR TERMINALLY ILL CANCER PATIENTS; SHALL NOT PRESCRIBE SCHEDULE III DRUGS FOR MORE THAN THREE WEEKS AND SCHEDULE IV AND V DRUGS FOR MORE THAN FOUR WEEKS; SHALL PERMIT COMPREHENSIVE PRACTICE REVIEW BY THE BOARD; SHALL COMPLETE 50 HOURS OF CONTINUING MEDICAL EDUCATION IN THE AREA OF DRUG ADDICTION AND CHRONIC PAIN MANAGEMENT; $350 FINE; SHALL APPEAR BEFORE BOARD IN FIVE YEARS TO PROVE COMPLIANCE.

BURKE, EDMUND L MD, LICENSE NUMBER 0005531, OF YAKIMA, WA, WAS DISCIPLINED BY WASHINGTON ON MARCH 11, 1993.
DISCIPLINARY ACTION: SURRENDER OF LICENSE
OFFENSE: SUBSTANDARD CARE, INCOMPETENCE, OR NEGLIGENCE
NOTES: INVESTIGATION CONCERNING DELAYED OR INAPPROPRIATE DIAGNOSIS AND TREATMENT AND HIS PHYSICAL HEALTH. BOARD ACCEPTS HIS RETIREMENT WHICH SHALL BE PERMANENT; HE MAY RESUME PRACTICE IN THIS STATE ONLY WITH PRIOR BOARD APPROVAL AND HE WILL NOTIFY THE BOARD IF HE PLANS TO RESUME PRACTICE OR APPLY FOR LICENSURE IN THIS OR ANY OTHER JURISDICTION.

BURKS, DONALD E MD, LICENSE NUMBER 0018394, OF ARLINGTON, WA, WAS DISCIPLINED BY WASHINGTON ON MAY 17, 1991.
DISCIPLINARY ACTION: LICENSE SUSPENSION; FINE
OFFENSE: SUBSTANCE ABUSE
NOTES: PERSONALLY USED CONTROLLED SUBSTANCES IN 1989 AND 1990 IN A WAY OTHER THAN FOR LEGITIMATE OR THERAPEUTIC PURPOSES; FAILED AN ATTEMPT AT TREATMENT WITH THE WASHINGTON MONITORED TREATMENT PROGRAM FOR HIS ADDICTION TO CONTROLLED SUBSTANCES; TESTED POSITIVE FOR METHADONE AND BENZODIAZEPINES IN A URINE DRUG SCREEN IN 4/90 AND WAS DIAGNOSED IN 4/90 AS HAVING A SUBSTANCE ABUSE DISORDER THAT SUBSTANTIALLY COMPROMISED HIS ABILITY TO EXERCISE THE

JUDGMENT REQUIRED TO PRACTICE MEDICINE. SUSPENSION STAYED WHEN THE FOLLOWING TERMS AND CONDITIONS ARE MET: SHALL CEASE TREATMENT OF PATIENTS IMMEDIATELY; SHALL CONCLUDE ALL BUSINESS AND CLOSE HIS PRACTICE NO LATER THAN 90 DAYS; MAY NOT APPLY FOR REINSTATEMENT FOR 3 YEARS; $100 FINE. ON 12/11/95 REQUEST FOR REINSTATEMENT OF LICENSE DENIED.

BURKS, DONALD E MD, DATE OF BIRTH SEPTEMBER 9, 1948, OF 22512 15TH NE, ARLINGTON, VA, WAS DISCIPLINED BY MEDICARE ON MAY 8, 1992.
DISCIPLINARY ACTION: EXCLUSION FROM THE MEDICARE AND/OR MEDICAID PROGRAMS
OFFENSE: DISCIPLINARY ACTION BY ANOTHER STATE OR AGENCY
NOTES: LICENSE REVOCATION OR SUSPENSION.

BURNS, BRUCE MD, LICENSE NUMBER 0019452, WAS DISCIPLINED BY WASHINGTON ON AUGUST 16, 1990.
DISCIPLINARY ACTION: LICENSE SUSPENSION
OFFENSE: DISCIPLINARY ACTION BY ANOTHER STATE OR AGENCY
NOTES: ON 12/16/86 PLED GUILTY TO THREE COUNTS OF GRAND LARCENY BASED ON STEALING $3,500 FROM MEDICAID, $7,000 FROM MEDICARE, AND $25,000 FROM BLUE SHIELD BY FALSELY BILLING FOR PSYCHOTHERAPY SERVICES WHICH WERE NEVER PROVIDED; SURRENDERED LICENSE IN NEW YORK ON 11/23/87 BASED ON HIS INABILITY TO PRACTICE BECAUSE OF MENTAL DISABILITY; DIAGNOSED AS HAVING BIPOLAR DISORDER, WHICH WAS TREATED WITH LITHIUM, WHICH HE NO LONGER TAKES. TO QUALIFY FOR A STAY OF SUSPENSION HE SHALL OBTAIN AN EVALUATION FROM BOARD APPROVED PSYCHOLOGIST OR PSYCHIATRIST AND A PHYSICAL EVALUATION WITHIN ONE YEAR, AND IF REVIEW RAISES NO CONCERNS ABOUT ABILITY TO PRACTICE, SUSPENSION SHALL BE STAYED. ON 06/20/91 THE RESULTS OF THESE EVALUATIONS WERE SUBMITTED. SUSPENSION IS NOW STAYED AND HE MUST COMPLY WITH TERMS OF THE ORDER.

BUSCHER, DAVID S MD, LICENSE NUMBER 0017080, OF BELLEVUE, WA, WAS DISCIPLINED BY WASHINGTON ON FEBRUARY 21, 1992.
DISCIPLINARY ACTION: PROBATION; FINE
OFFENSE: SEXUAL ABUSE OF OR SEXUAL MISCONDUCT WITH A PATIENT
NOTES: CHARGES OF SEXUAL CONTACT WITH A PATIENT. PROBATIONARY STATUS FOR AT LEAST THREE YEARS ON CONDITION THAT HE COMPLIES WITH CERTAIN TERMS; $1,000 FINE; ANNUAL COMPLIANCE HEARINGS; PROOF OF CONTINUING MEDICAL EDUCATION CREDITS; PERIODIC PRACTICE REVIEWS. ON 5/31/96 THIS ORDER WAS TERMINATED.

BUSENBARK, LINDA L MD OF 2726 45TH AVENUE SOUTH WEST, SEATTLE, WA, WAS DISCIPLINED BY DEA ON APRIL 16, 1996.
DISCIPLINARY ACTION: RESTRICTION PLACED ON CONTROLLED SUBSTANCE LICENSE
OFFENSE: PROFESSIONAL MISCONDUCT
NOTES: ALLEGED CONTROLLED SUBSTANCE VIOLATIONS.

BUSENBARK, LINDA LOUISE MD, LICENSE NUMBER MD13277, OF PORTLAND, OR, WAS DISCIPLINED BY OREGON ON AUGUST 17, 1992.
DISCIPLINARY ACTION: 120-MONTH PROBATION; FINE
NOTES: MUST PROVIDE TRIPLICATE COPIES OF CONTROLLED SUBSTANCE PRESCRIPTIONS FOR SCHEDULES III, IV AND V. AS OF 11/17/94 TERMS REVISED EXTENDING ORDER UNTIL 8/22/04. NO LONGER ON PROBATION AS OF 5/8/96.

CALABRIA, JACK J DO WAS DISCIPLINED BY WASHINGTON ON AUGUST 17, 1994.
DISCIPLINARY ACTION: FINE; RESTRICTION PLACED ON LICENSE
OFFENSE: SEXUAL ABUSE OF OR SEXUAL MISCONDUCT WITH A PATIENT
NOTES: ENGAGED IN INAPPROPRIATE SEXUAL CONTACT WITH THREE FEMALE PATIENTS ON 11/27/91, 1/02/92, AND 10/15/93 WITHOUT OSTEOPATHIC MEDICAL JUSTIFICATION; AND ATTEMPTED TO DO SO WITH A FOURTH ON 4/24/93 WHEN HE FAILED TO EXPLAIN THE MEDICAL NECESSITY OF A PELVIC EXAMINATION TO A PATIENT DURING THE TREATMENT OF UPPER BACK PAIN RESULTING FROM AN AUTO ACCIDENT, THE PATIENT REFUSED THE EXAMINATION. TWO YEAR SUSPENSION, STAYED UNDER TERMS AND CONDITIONS: SHALL EMPLOY A BOARD APPROVED FEMALE ATTENDANT TO BE PRESENT IN THE ROOM AT ALL TIMES WHEN HE EXAMINES, TREATS, OR COUNSELS ANY FEMALE PATIENT; SHALL PROVIDE EACH MUSCLE ENERGY TECHNIQUE PATIENTS WITH A MUSCLE ENERGY TECHNIQUE BROCHURE; SHALL SUBMIT FOR BOARD APPROVAL A NOTICE STATEMENT WHICH SHALL BE PROVIDED TO ALL FEMALE PATIENTS ADVISING THEM THAT AN ATTENDANT SHALL BE PRESENT DURING THE EXAMINATION OF AND CONSULTATION WITH ANY FEMALE PATIENT; SHALL UNDERTAKE AN EVALUATION BY A QUALIFIED HEALTH CARE PROVIDER BEFORE PETITIONING THE BOARD FOR MODIFICATION; SHALL SUBMIT QUARTERLY DECLARATIONS UNDER PENALTY OF PERJURY REGARDING COMPLIANCE; SHALL NOTIFY THE BOARD OF DEPARTURE AND RETURN FROM WASHINGTON; SHALL PROVIDE THE BOARD WITH A CURRENT HOME AND BUSINESS ADDRESS AND ANY CHANGES OF ADDRESS; TIME SPENT OUTSIDE WASHINGTON WILL NOT APPLY TO THE REDUCTION OF THE SUSPENSION; $3,000 FINE.

CALKINS, GREGORY P MD, DATE OF BIRTH NOVEMBER 23, 1950, LICENSE NUMBER 0025811, OF JOLIET, IL, WAS DISCIPLINED BY KENTUCKY ON JANUARY 4, 1990.
DISCIPLINARY ACTION: 24-MONTH PROBATION; FINE
NOTES: FINE $500.00. PROBATION TERMINATED ON 1/15/92.

CALKINS, GREGORY P MD OF CINCINNATI, OH, WAS DISCIPLINED BY OHIO ON MARCH 19, 1990.
DISCIPLINARY ACTION: 1-MONTH LICENSE SUSPENSION; 60-MONTH PROBATION
OFFENSE: CRIMINAL CONVICTION OR PLEA OF GUILTY, NOLO CONTENDERE, OR NO CONTEST TO A CRIME
NOTES: FELONY CONVICTION (INCOME TAX EVASION); REVOCATION STAYED

CALKINS, GREGORY P MD, DATE OF BIRTH NOVEMBER 23, 1950, LICENSE NUMBER 0026343, OF 817 GLENWOOD AVENUE, JOLIET, IL, WAS DISCIPLINED BY IOWA ON DECEMBER 23, 1991.
DISCIPLINARY ACTION: SURRENDER OF LICENSE
OFFENSE: DISCIPLINARY ACTION BY ANOTHER STATE OR AGENCY

CALKINS, GREGORY PAUL MD, LICENSE NUMBER 00G8583, OF JOLIET, IL, WAS DISCIPLINED BY TEXAS ON SEPTEMBER 24, 1988.
OFFENSE: CRIMINAL CONVICTION OR PLEA OF GUILTY, NOLO CONTENDERE, OR NO CONTEST TO A CRIME
NOTES: MUST NOTIFY BOARD WITHIN 10 DAYS FROM DATE ON WHICH HE IS NOTIFIED BY ANY STATE WHERE LICENSED OF ANY DISCIPLINARY ACTION ARISING OUT OF HIS INCOME TAX EVASION CONVICTION.

CALKINS, GREGORY PAUL MD, LICENSE NUMBER 0015302, OF IN, WAS DISCIPLINED BY WEST VIRGINIA ON JUNE 16, 1989.
OFFENSE: CRIMINAL CONVICTION OR PLEA OF GUILTY, NOLO CONTENDERE, OR NO CONTEST TO A CRIME
NOTES: CONVICTED IN HAMMOND INDIANA FOR INCOME TAX EVASION, A FELONY. TEXAS ATTACHED CONDITIONS ON HIS LICENSE ON 9/24/88. HE MUST NOTIFY BOARD IN WRITING OF ANY DISCIPLINARY ACTIONS TAKEN BY

- WASHINGTON -

OTHER STATES WHERE HE IS LICENSED AS A RESULT OF INCOME TAX EVASION CONVICTION. MUST NOTIFY THE BOARD OF ANY CHANGE OF ADDRESS.

CALKINS, GREGORY PAUL MD, LICENSE NUMBER 040120E, WAS DISCIPLINED BY PENNSYLVANIA ON JANUARY 26, 1990.
DISCIPLINARY ACTION: REPRIMAND

CALKINS, GREGORY PAUL MD, LICENSE NUMBER 0017859, WAS DISCIPLINED BY ARIZONA ON JUNE 30, 1990.
DISCIPLINARY ACTION: EMERGENCY SUSPENSION
OFFENSE: CRIMINAL CONVICTION OR PLEA OF GUILTY, NOLO CONTENDERE, OR NO CONTEST TO A CRIME
NOTES: PLED GUILTY TO INCOME TAX EVASION IN INDIANA 10/28/87 AND PLACED ON CRIMINAL PROBATION FOR FIVE YEARS WITH A $1000 FINE AND 500 HOURS OF COMMUNITY SERVICE. TEXAS BOARD ALSO REQUIRED HIM TO INFORM THEM OF ANY ACTION TAKEN BASED ON THIS CONVICTION.

CALKINS, GREGORY PAUL MD WAS DISCIPLINED BY HAWAII ON JULY 18, 1990.
DISCIPLINARY ACTION: LICENSE REVOCATION

CALKINS, GREGORY PAUL MD WAS DISCIPLINED BY WASHINGTON ON OCTOBER 19, 1990.
OFFENSE: DISCIPLINARY ACTION BY ANOTHER STATE OR AGENCY
NOTES: CONVICTED IN U.S. DISTRICT COURT FOR THE NORTHERN DISTRICT OF INDIANA OF INCOME TAX EVASION ON 12/18/87; TEXAS RESTRICTED HIS LICENSE ON 9/24/88. MUST COMPLY WITH TEXAS AND DISTRICT COURT ORDERS; MUST APPEAR BEFORE THE BOARD BEFORE PRACTICING IN WASHINGTON; MUST ADVISE BOARD OF ANY CHANGE OF ADDRESS.

CARNINE, KENNETH S MD, LICENSE NUMBER 0010798, OF MT VERNON, WA, WAS DISCIPLINED BY WASHINGTON ON MARCH 11, 1993.
DISCIPLINARY ACTION: EMERGENCY SUSPENSION
OFFENSE: SEXUAL ABUSE OF OR SEXUAL MISCONDUCT WITH A PATIENT
NOTES: ALLEGATIONS OF MORAL TURPITUDE, ABUSE AND/OR SEXUAL CONTACT WITH A PATIENT.

CARNINE, KENNETH S MD, LICENSE NUMBER 00D4946, OF MT VERNON, WA, WAS DISCIPLINED BY TEXAS ON SEPTEMBER 30, 1994.
DISCIPLINARY ACTION: SURRENDER OF LICENSE
OFFENSE: DISCIPLINARY ACTION BY ANOTHER STATE OR AGENCY
NOTES: ALLEGATIONS OF DISCIPLINARY ACTION BY ANOTHER STATE OR BY THE UNIFORMED SERVICES OF THE U.S. SURRENDER IN LIEU OF FURTHER INVESTIGATION; SHALL NOT PETITION FOR REINSTATEMENT OF LICENSE.

CARNINE, KENNETH S MD, LICENSE NUMBER 0010798, OF MOUNT VERNON, WA, WAS DISCIPLINED BY WASHINGTON ON APRIL 21, 1995.
DISCIPLINARY ACTION: SURRENDER OF LICENSE; FINE
OFFENSE: CRIMINAL CONVICTION OR PLEA OF GUILTY, NOLO CONTENDERE, OR NO CONTEST TO A CRIME
NOTES: PLED GUILTY TO ONE COUNT OF FOURTH DEGREE ASSAULT, DESCRIBED AS INTENTIONAL OR OFFENSIVE CONTACT WITH ANOTHER PERSON WITHOUT THE PERMISSION OF THAT PERSON AND NOT IN SELF DEFENSE; THE VICTIM WAS A FEMALE PATIENT; A JAIL SENTENCE AND FINE OF $2,500 WAS IMPOSED; FROM APPROXIMATELY 1975 UNTIL 1993, HE PERFORMED BREAST OR PELVIC EXAMINATIONS ON 25 FEMALE PATIENTS WHICH DID NOT MEET THE STANDARD OF A REASONABLY PRUDENT PHYSICIAN PRACTICING IN WASHINGTON. SHALL PERMANENTLY SURRENDER HIS WASHINGTON LICENSE, NEVER TO PRACTICE MEDICINE OR SURGERY IN THIS STATE; $1,000 FINE.

CARNINE, KENNETH S MD, DATE OF BIRTH DECEMBER 20, 1941, OF PO BOX 2662, RANCHO MIRAGE, CA, WAS DISCIPLINED BY MEDICARE ON APRIL 9, 1996.
DISCIPLINARY ACTION: 60-MONTH EXCLUSION FROM THE MEDICARE AND/OR MEDICAID PROGRAMS
OFFENSE: CRIMINAL CONVICTION OR PLEA OF GUILTY, NOLO CONTENDERE, OR NO CONTEST TO A CRIME
NOTES: CONVICTED OF A CRIME RELATED TO PATIENT ABUSE OR NEGLECT.

CARRON, WILLIAM CLARK MD, LICENSE NUMBER 0G47837, OF SEATTLE, WA, WAS DISCIPLINED BY CALIFORNIA ON JULY 8, 1996.
DISCIPLINARY ACTION: 60-MONTH PROBATION
OFFENSE: CRIMINAL CONVICTION OR PLEA OF GUILTY, NOLO CONTENDERE, OR NO CONTEST TO A CRIME
NOTES: CONVICTED OF STALKING. REVOCATION, STAYED.

CARTER, JOHN L MD, LICENSE NUMBER 0008759, OF EUGENE, OR, WAS DISCIPLINED BY WASHINGTON ON JANUARY 27, 1995.
DISCIPLINARY ACTION: FINE
OFFENSE: DISCIPLINARY ACTION BY ANOTHER STATE OR AGENCY
NOTES: CONDITIONS PLACED ON LICENSE IN OREGON; AGREED TO COMPLY WITH THESE CONDITIONS AND APPEAR BEFORE THE BOARD PRIOR TO PRACTICE IN WASHINGTON. $100 FINE.

CARTER, JOHN LINUS MD, LICENSE NUMBER MD06964, OF EUGENE, OR, WAS DISCIPLINED BY OREGON ON JULY 17, 1993.
DISCIPLINARY ACTION: PROBATION; FINE
NOTES: $5,000 FINE.

CARTER, JOHN LINUS MD, LICENSE NUMBER MD06964, OF EUGENE, OR, WAS DISCIPLINED BY OREGON ON SEPTEMBER 15, 1993.
DISCIPLINARY ACTION: 2-MONTH LICENSE SUSPENSION

CASTELL, HUGH M MD, LICENSE NUMBER 0009937, OF BELLEVUE, WA, WAS DISCIPLINED BY WASHINGTON ON DECEMBER 17, 1993.
DISCIPLINARY ACTION: PROBATION; FINE
OFFENSE: SEXUAL ABUSE OF OR SEXUAL MISCONDUCT WITH A PATIENT
NOTES: ALLEGATIONS THAT FROM 1974 TO 1983 HAD A SEXUAL RELATIONSHIP WITH A FORMER PATIENT, WHICH MAY HAVE BEGUN DURING THERAPY. HE DENIES THESE ALLEGATIONS AND CONTENDS THAT THE SEXUAL RELATIONSHIP BEGAN SHORTLY AFTER THERAPY ENDED, AND AFTER THE PATIENT WAS REFERRED TO ANOTHER THERAPIST FOR TREATMENT. OTHER ALLEGATIONS THAT DURING THE LATER 1980S AND/OR THE EARLY 1990S, HE HAD A SEXUAL RELATIONSHIP WITH ANOTHER FORMER PATIENT WHO HAD BEEN REFERRED TO ANOTHER THERAPIST FOR TREATMENT. HE STATES THAT THE SEXUAL RELATIONSHIP MAY NOT HAVE BEGUN FOR AT LEAST THREE YEARS AFTER THE THERAPY HAD ENDED, AND THAT THE FORMER PATIENT WAS IN THERAPY WITH ANOTHER THERAPIST. INDEFINITE SUSPENSION; STAYED. CONDITIONS OF PROBATION: SHALL APPEAR BEFORE THE BOARD SIX MONTHS FROM THE DATE OF THIS ORDER AND ANNUALLY THEREAFTER FOR COMPLIANCE HEARINGS; SHALL VIDEOTAPE ALL SESSIONS WITH FEMALE PATIENTS WITH CONTROLS HANDLED BY ANOTHER OFFICE WORKER; SHALL BE SUBJECTED TO OFFICE INSPECTIONS; SHALL INFORM ALL CURRENT AND FUTURE FEMALE PATIENTS OF THESE RESTRICTIONS; SHALL PROVIDE A COPY OF THIS ORDER TO ANY HEALTH CARE ENTITY WHERE HE HAS PRIVILEGES; SHALL CONTINUE IN THERAPY WITH A BOARD APPROVED THERAPIST WITH QUARTERLY REPORTS; SHALL BE INVOLVED IN A PROFESSIONAL CONSULTATION GROUP WITH HIS COLLEAGUES AND AN ORGANIZED

- WASHINGTON -

CONTINUING EDUCATION PROGRAM; SHALL INFORM THE BOARD OF ANY CHANGE OF ADDRESS OR IF HE LEAVES THE STATE; TIME SPENT OUT OF STATE DOES NOT COUNT TOWARD PROBATION; SHALL EMPLOY A SUPERVISING PSYCHIATRIST. MAY NOT SEEK MODIFICATION FOR ONE YEAR. $2,000 FINE.

CASTELL, HUGH M MD, LICENSE NUMBER 0009937, OF BELLEVUE, WA, WAS DISCIPLINED BY WASHINGTON ON JUNE 10, 1994.
DISCIPLINARY ACTION: EMERGENCY SUSPENSION
OFFENSE: FAILURE TO COMPLY WITH A PREVIOUS BOARD ORDER
NOTES: FAILED TO COMPLY WITH BOARD'S 12/17/93 ORDER; ENGAGED IN A SEXUAL RELATIONSHIP WITH SEVERAL PATIENTS.

CASTELL, HUGH M MD, LICENSE NUMBER 0009937, OF BELLEVUE, WA, WAS DISCIPLINED BY WASHINGTON ON DECEMBER 16, 1994.
DISCIPLINARY ACTION: SURRENDER OF LICENSE
OFFENSE: FAILURE TO COMPLY WITH A PREVIOUS BOARD ORDER
NOTES: DID NOT COMPLY WITH CONDITIONS OF A 12/17/93 AGREED ORDER THAT HE WOULD VIDEOTAPE ALL SESSIONS WITH FEMALE PATIENTS FOR BOARD REVIEW NOR DID HE COMPLY WITH CONDITION THAT REQUIRED HIM TO INFORM ALL FEMALE PATIENTS OF THE CONDITIONS OF THAT ORDER; THE EFFECTIVE DATE OF THE ORDER WAS 12/27/93 BUT HE DID NOT BEGIN VIDEOTAPING UNTIL 2/14/94 AND DID SEE PATIENTS BETWEEN THOSE TWO DATES; ENGAGED IN HUGGING AND KISSING WITH ONE PATIENT OFF CAMERA, SPECIFICALLY INSTRUCTING HER NOT TO ASK FOR HUGS ON CAMERA; A REVIEW OF HIS PRACTICE CONDUCTED ON 4/4/94 REVEALED THAT HE TREATED AT LEAST FOUR PATIENTS WITHOUT INFORMING THEM OF THE 12/17/93 ORDER AND HAVING THEIR NOTIFICATION SHEET SIGNED AND PLACED IN THEIR FILE AS REQUIRED BY THE ORDER. HE ADVISED THE BOARD THAT HE HAS RETIRED FROM MEDICAL PRACTICE EFFECTIVE 6/94 AND HAS NO PLANS TO RESUME PRACTICE. RETIREMENT SHALL BE CONSIDERED PERMANENT; MAY NOT PETITION FOR REINSTATEMENT OF PERMISSION TO PRACTICE FOR 10 YEARS; SHALL NOTIFY BOARD IF HE PLANS TO PRACTICE IN ANOTHER JURISDICTION.

CASTELL, HUGH MCFARLANE MD OF 1370 116TH AVE NE, BELLEVUE, WA, WAS DISCIPLINED BY DEA ON MARCH 20, 1995.
DISCIPLINARY ACTION: SURRENDER OF CONTROLLED SUBSTANCE LICENSE
OFFENSE: DISCIPLINARY ACTION BY ANOTHER STATE OR AGENCY
NOTES: STATE BOARD.

CENAC, PAUL E MD, LICENSE NUMBER 0027568, OF BELLINGHAM, WA, WAS DISCIPLINED BY WASHINGTON ON OCTOBER 26, 1994.
DISCIPLINARY ACTION: RESTRICTION PLACED ON LICENSE
OFFENSE: SUBSTANDARD CARE, INCOMPETENCE, OR NEGLIGENCE
NOTES: ALLEGED NEGLIGENCE. EMERGENCY ACTION TAKEN SUMMARILY RESTRICTING HIS LICENSE TO PROHIBIT HIM FROM PERFORMING CERTAIN TYPES OF SURGERY. ON 12/1/94 HIS MOTION TO MODIFY THE ORDER OF SUMMARY LIMITATION WAS DENIED.

CENAC, PAUL E MD, LICENSE NUMBER 0027568, OF BELLINGHAM, WA, WAS DISCIPLINED BY WASHINGTON ON AUGUST 25, 1995.
DISCIPLINARY ACTION: 60-MONTH PROBATION; FINE
NOTES: PROBATION UNDER THE FOLLOWING TERMS AND CONDITIONS: SHALL OBTAIN COUNSELING OR THERAPY; SHALL SUBMIT TO AN EVALUATION BY A PSYCHOLOGIST OR PSYCHIATRIST; SHALL PRACTICE UNDER SUPERVISION; SHALL CONSULT WITH A MENTOR; SHALL REFRAIN FROM TREATING PERSONS WITH WHICH HE HAS A CLOSE RELATIONSHIP; SHALL TAKE ADDITIONAL CONTINUING MEDICAL EDUCATION COURSES; SHALL PAY A FINE. ON 3/25/96 THE BOARD MODIFIED AND CLARIFIED THE ORDER: REQUIRED TO CEASE FROM BEGINNING ANY SURGICAL PROCEDURES UNLESS A BOARD-CERTIFIED PLASTIC SURGEON IS PRESENT; SHALL NOT HAVE NURSES OR OTHER PRACTITIONERS INITIATE CONSCIOUS SEDATION OF A SURGICAL PATIENT UNLESS HE AND/OR A BOARD-CERTIFIED SURGEON IS PRESENT; SHALL NOT TREAT RELATIVES. ON 5/30/96 REITERATED THESE RESTRICTIONS. HE WAS FOUND TO BE IN COMPLIANCE WITH THE ORDER AT BOTH OF THESE REVIEWS.

CHANG, JONATHAN H MD, LICENSE NUMBER 0016997, OF 6602 59TH ST. COURT WEST, TACOMA, WA, WAS DISCIPLINED BY OKLAHOMA ON OCTOBER 22, 1995.
DISCIPLINARY ACTION: LICENSE REVOCATION
OFFENSE: DISCIPLINARY ACTION BY ANOTHER STATE OR AGENCY
NOTES: ON 11/23/93 THE UNITED STATES ARMY REVOKED HIS CLINICAL PRIVILEGES FOR HIS UNSATISFACTORY PERFORMANCE OF HIS DUTIES AS AN ANESTHESIOLOGIST.

CHIAROTTINO, GARY D MD, LICENSE NUMBER 0011022, OF BELLINGHAM, WA, WAS DISCIPLINED BY WASHINGTON ON OCTOBER 25, 1991.
DISCIPLINARY ACTION: EMERGENCY SUSPENSION
OFFENSE: SEXUAL ABUSE OF OR SEXUAL MISCONDUCT WITH A PATIENT
NOTES: CHARGES BASED UPON ALLEGATIONS OF INAPPROPRIATE SEXUAL CONTACT WITH TWO PATIENTS. THURSTON COUNTY SUPERIOR COURT ISSUED AN ORDER ON 11/8/91 WHICH PROVIDES HE MAY PRACTICE MEDICINE WITH CERTAIN REQUIREMENTS. DECISION SUBJECT TO FURTHER REVIEW.

CHIAROTTINO, GARY D MD, LICENSE NUMBER 0011022, OF BELLINGHAM, WA, WAS DISCIPLINED BY WASHINGTON ON FEBRUARY 15, 1993.
DISCIPLINARY ACTION: FINE; RESTRICTION PLACED ON LICENSE
OFFENSE: SUBSTANDARD CARE, INCOMPETENCE, OR NEGLIGENCE
NOTES: SEXUAL CONTACT, ABUSE OF A PATIENT, MORAL TURPITUDE AND INCOMPETENCE/NEGLIGENCE. BETWEEN 6/89 AND 4/91 MADE INAPPROPRIATE COMMENTS AND PERFORMED INAPPROPRIATE ACTIONS DURING A PELVIC EXAMINATION, CONSTITUTING UNPROFESSIONAL CONDUCT WITH THREE PATIENTS; SEXUALLY ABUSED AND ENGAGED IN MORAL TURPITUDE WITH TWO OF THEM DURING PELVIC EXAMINATIONS; AND PERFORMED A BREAST EXAMINATION IN AN INAPPROPRIATE AND ABUSIVE MANNER WITH THE THIRD; ENGAGED IN A NEGLIGENT ACT BY FAILING TO PERFORM A PROPER EXAMINATION OF ONE OF THE PATIENTS WHOSE COMPLAINT WAS POSSIBLE BRONCHITIS. SUSPENSION STAYED. HE SHALL COMPLY WITH THE FOLLOWING CONDITIONS: SHALL NOT PROVIDE MEDICAL SERVICES TO FEMALE PATIENTS UNTIL HE ENTERS A BOARD APPROVED MENTAL HEALTH PROGRAM AND MAKES SUFFICIENT PROGRESS TO RECEIVE THE BOARD'S APPROVAL; UPON SUCH APPROVAL SHALL ONLY PROVIDE SERVICES TO FEMALE PATIENTS WITH A CHAPERONE PRESENT; SHALL PROVIDE BOARD APPROVED DISCLOSURE STATEMENTS TO ALL OFFICE STAFF MEMBERS, ALL FACILITIES WHERE HE PROVIDES CARE, AND FEMALE PATIENTS; BOARD SHALL CONDUCT PERIODIC ON-SITE INSPECTIONS; SHALL PAY $11,000 FINE; MAY NOT PETITION FOR MODIFICATION FOR 24 MONTHS. REQUEST FOR BOARD APPROVAL TO TREAT FEMALE PATIENTS DENIED ON 12/17/93. ON 5/27/94, THE BOARD GRANTED HIS REQUEST FOR APPROVAL TO TREAT FEMALE PATIENTS, PROVIDED THAT A FEMALE CHAPERONE IS PRESENT AT ALL TIMES.

CHIAROTTINO, GARY D MD, LICENSE NUMBER 0C27432, OF

WASHINGTON

BELLINGHAM, WA, WAS DISCIPLINED BY CALIFORNIA ON JANUARY 19, 1996.
DISCIPLINARY ACTION: SURRENDER OF LICENSE
NOTES: WHILE CHARGES PENDING.

CHUNG, DONG I MD OF CHICAGO, IL, WAS DISCIPLINED BY ILLINOIS ON FEBRUARY 1, 1990.
DISCIPLINARY ACTION: LICENSE REVOCATION; REVOCATION OF CONTROLLED SUBSTANCE LICENSE
OFFENSE: OVERPRESCRIBING OR MISPRESCRIBING DRUGS
NOTES: ALLEGED TO HAVE ENGAGED IN THE NONTHERAPEUTIC PRESCRIPTION AND DISPENSING OF MEDICINE, INEFFECTIVE CONTROLS AGAINST THE DIVERSION OF CONTROLLED SUBSTANCES, UNAUTHORIZED DELIVERY AND DISPENSION UNDER THE CONTROLLED SUBSTANCES ACT AND UNPROFESSIONAL CONDUCT

CHUNG, DONG I MD WAS DISCIPLINED BY WASHINGTON ON AUGUST 20, 1993.
DISCIPLINARY ACTION: REQUIRED TO TAKE ADDITIONAL MEDICAL EDUCATION
OFFENSE: DISCIPLINARY ACTION BY ANOTHER STATE OR AGENCY
NOTES: HIS LICENSE WAS REVOKED IN ILLINOIS ON 2/09/90 FOR NON-THERAPEUTIC PRESCRIPTION AND DISPENSING OF MEDICINE, INEFFECTIVE CONTROLS AGAINST THE DIVERSION OF CONTROLLED SUBSTANCES, UNAUTHORIZED DELIVERY AND DISPENSING UNDER THE CONTROLLED SUBSTANCES ACT, AND UNPROFESSIONAL CONDUCT. SHALL NOT PRACTICE MEDICINE IN WASHINGTON UNTIL HE APPEARS BEFORE THE BOARD AT WHICH TIME HE SHALL PRESENT THE FOLLOWING EVIDENCE: COMPLIANCE WITH ALL TERMS IMPOSED ON HIM BY THE ILLINOIS BOARD; THAT ON OR BEFORE 2/10/94 HE HAS RENEWED HIS CURRENTLY EXPIRED WASHINGTON LICENSE BY COMPLYING WITH THE RENEWAL REQUIREMENTS; SHALL ENROLL IN AND COMPLETE 50 HOURS OF CONTINUING MEDICAL EDUCATION IN APPROPRIATE PRESCRIBING OF CONTROLLED SUBSTANCES; SHALL INFORM THE BOARD IN WRITING OF CHANGES IN HIS PRACTICE AND RESIDENCE ADDRESS.

CLANCY, JOHN MD WAS DISCIPLINED BY WASHINGTON ON MARCH 28, 1990.
DISCIPLINARY ACTION: SURRENDER OF LICENSE
NOTES: RETIRED FROM MEDICAL PRACTICE EFFECTIVE 2/28/87 WITH NO PLANS TO RESUME PRACTICE; AGREES THAT RETIREMENT SHALL BE PERMANENT AND THAT HE SHALL RESUME PRACTICE ONLY WITH PRIOR BOARD APPROVAL; SHALL INFORM BOARD IF HE PRACTICES IN ANY OTHER JURISDICTION.

CLARK, EDWARD L MD OF SEATTLE, WA, WAS DISCIPLINED BY WASHINGTON ON JANUARY 17, 1991.
DISCIPLINARY ACTION: LICENSE REINSTATEMENT; 60-MONTH PROBATION
NOTES: LICENSE REVOKED 4/16/77. HAS NOT PRACTICED MEDICINE AND SURGERY SINCE 1977 OR COMPLETED ANY CATEGORY I CONTINUING MEDICAL EDUCATION SINCE 1978. REINSTATEMENT SHALL BE GRANTED WHEN HE PASSES THE ENTIRE FLEX EXAM AND EITHER SUCCESSFULLY COMPLETES A ONE YEAR ROTATING INTERNSHIP, OR COMPLETES THE LAST TWO YEARS OF AN ACCREDITED MEDICAL SCHOOL PROGRAM WITHIN 4 YEARS; SHALL PRACTICE ONLY IN A BOARD APPROVED SUPERVISED ENVIRONMENT; SHALL APPEAR BEFORE BOARD THREE MONTHS AFTER LICENSURE TO SUBMIT REPORT DETAILING PLANS FOR PRACTICE; SHALL NOT PRESCRIBE OR DISPENSE ANY CONTROLLED SUBSTANCES NOR OBTAIN REGISTRATION FROM DEA; SHALL REPORT TO THE BOARD AS DIRECTED.

CLAUSING, VERNON D DO OF 13624 1ST SOUTH, SEATTLE, WA, WAS DISCIPLINED BY DEA ON MARCH 7, 1988.
DISCIPLINARY ACTION: DENIAL OF NEW LICENSE
OFFENSE: DISCIPLINARY ACTION BY ANOTHER STATE OR AGENCY
NOTES: IN NOV 1979 A HOSPITAL BARRED CLAUSING FROM PRESCRIBING SCHEDULE II AND III CONTROLLED SUBSTANCES AND WAS REQUIRED TO UNDERGO PSYCHIATRIC COUNSELING; HE SUBSEQUENTLY LOST HIS ADMITTING PRIVILEGES THERE. WASHINGTON CONTROLLED SUBSTANCE LICENSE SUSPENDED ON MARCH 7,1981, WITH REVOCATION OF OSTEOPATHIC LICENSE STAYED. SUSPENSION WAS ABATED AS TO CERTAIN SCHEDULE IV AND ALL SCHEDULE V DRUGS ON AUG 8, 1985. HE OVERPRESCRIBED CONTROLLED SUBSTANCES TO ADDICTS AND TO PEOPLE WHO WERE DIVERTING THE DRUGS TO ILLEGAL CHANNELS, INCLUDING PRESCRIBING LARGE QUANTITIES OF PERCODAN AND VALIUM TO A PREGNANT WOMAN, WHOSE BABY WAS BORN SHOWING SIGNS OF ADDICTION. WASHINGTON STATE DEPARTMENT OF LABOR AND INDUSTRIES BARRED CLAUSING FROM PARTICIPATION IN THE WORKERS COMPENSATION PROGRAM IN 1984, BASED ON HIS OVERPRESCRIPTION OF DEPENDENCY-INDUCING DRUGS. ON OCT 20, 1983, HE WAS CONVICTED IN WASHINGTON STATE SUPERIOR COURT FOR KING COUNTY FOR FAILING TO REPORT CHILD ABUSE OF AN INFANT WHO SUBSEQUENTLY DIED FROM THAT ABUSE. HE WAS FINED $1500. THE STATE OSTEOPATHIC BOARD THEN RESTRICTED HIM FROM TREATING PATIENTS UNDER 10, WITH A SUSPENSION STAYED. CLAUSING WAS HOSPITALIZED IN 1962 FOR PSYCHIATRIC TREATMENT FOLLOWING INGESTION OF LSD. HE WAS DIAGNOSED IN 1981 WITH A PARANOID PERSONALITY DISORDER.

CLAUSING, VERNON D DO WAS DISCIPLINED BY WASHINGTON ON JANUARY 25, 1995.
DISCIPLINARY ACTION: RESTRICTION PLACED ON CONTROLLED SUBSTANCE LICENSE
OFFENSE: OVERPRESCRIBING OR MISPRESCRIBING DRUGS
NOTES: ALLEGED OVERPRESCRIBING OF SIX DRUGS WHICH CONSTITUTES EVIDENCE OF IMMINENT DANGER OF HARM TO HIS PATIENTS AND THE GENERAL PUBLIC: DID NOT ALLOW RECORDS TO BE EXAMINED BY THE BOARD. SUMMARILY RESTRICTED PENDING FINAL DISPOSITION: SHALL NOT PRESCRIBE THE LISTED LEGEND DRUGS, OR ANY OF THEIR GENERIC EQUIVALENTS: NALBUPHINE HCl INJECTABLE, BRAND NAME OF NUBAIN; STADOL INJECTABLE AND NASAL SOLUTION; CARISOPRODOL, BRAND NAME SOMA; BUTALBITAL/APAP/CAFFEINE TABLETS, BRAND NAME FIORICET; PHRENALIN TABLETS; AND PROMETHAZINE INJECTABLE AND/OR TABLETS, BRAND NAME PHENERGAN.

CLAUSING, VERNON D DO WAS DISCIPLINED BY WASHINGTON ON APRIL 22, 1995.
DISCIPLINARY ACTION: LICENSE REVOCATION; FINE
OFFENSE: OVERPRESCRIBING OR MISPRESCRIBING DRUGS
NOTES: PRESCRIBED FOR USE, OR DISTRIBUTION OF LEGEND DRUGS IN ANY WAY OTHER THAN FOR LEGITIMATE OR THERAPEUTIC PURPOSES IN THE CASES OF 25 PATIENTS BETWEEN 1/01/92 AND 12/31/93 PRESCRIBED THE FOLLOWING DRUGS IN ABOVE AVERAGE QUANTITIES, FREQUENCIES OR DURATIONS: NUBAIN, STADOL, SOMA, FIORICET, PHRENITIN AND PHENERGAN; ALSO IN SEVEN OF THESE CASES RECORDS WERE FOUND TO BE INADEQUATE, AND TREATMENT WAS BELOW STANDARDS OF CARE; AND FAILURE TO COOPERATE WITH THE DISCIPLINING AUTHORITY BY NOT FURNISHING PAPERS OR DOCUMENTS. MAY NOT PETITION FOR REINSTATEMENT FOR 10 YEARS; AND SHALL SURRENDER ALL COPIES OF HIS LICENSE TO PRACTICE

- WASHINGTON -

OSTEOPATHIC MEDICINE AND SURGERY. $25,000 FINE.

CLAUSING, VERNON D DO, DATE OF BIRTH SEPTEMBER 16, 1922, OF 13627 OCCIDENTAL S, SEATTLE, WA, WAS DISCIPLINED BY MEDICARE ON OCTOBER 10, 1995.
DISCIPLINARY ACTION: EXCLUSION FROM THE MEDICARE AND/OR MEDICAID PROGRAMS
OFFENSE: DISCIPLINARY ACTION BY ANOTHER STATE OR AGENCY
NOTES: LICENSE REVOKED FOR REASONS BEARING ON PROFESSIONAL PERFORMANCE.

COOK, STUART J MD, LICENSE NUMBER 0012500, OF OLYMPIA, THURSTON COUNTY, WA, WAS DISCIPLINED BY WASHINGTON ON MAY 15, 1992.
DISCIPLINARY ACTION: SURRENDER OF LICENSE
OFFENSE: SEXUAL ABUSE OF OR SEXUAL MISCONDUCT WITH A PATIENT
NOTES: ALLEGATIONS OF UNPROFESSIONAL CONDUCT REGARDING SEXUAL CONTACT WITH THREE PATIENTS DURING PATIENT PHYSICAL EXAMINATIONS. RETIREMENT SHALL BE PERMANENT; SHALL IMMEDIATELY SURRENDER TO THE BOARD CURRENT MEDICAL LICENSE AND DEA REGISTRATION AND SHALL NOT RENEW HIS LICENSE.

COOKE, THOMAS R DO, LICENSE NUMBER 00E6056, OF CHEHALIS, WA, WAS DISCIPLINED BY TEXAS ON FEBRUARY 22, 1991.
NOTES: MUST COMPLY WITH WASHINGTON STATE BOARD ORDER; RECEIVE PERMISSION OF TEXAS BOARD BEFORE RETURNING TO PRACTICE OF OBSTETRICS IN TEXAS AND BE SUBJECT TO ANY TERMS IMPOSED.

CORELL, WILLIAM F MD, LICENSE NUMBER 0017781, OF SPOKANE, WA, WAS DISCIPLINED BY WASHINGTON ON AUGUST 19, 1994.
DISCIPLINARY ACTION: 60-MONTH PROBATION; FINE
OFFENSE: PROFESSIONAL MISCONDUCT
NOTES: USED AN ILLEGAL DEVICE TO TREAT A PATIENT. MUST CEASE USING THE ECLOSION EPEX BIOFEEDBACK DEVICE AND SHALL OBEY RESTRICTIONS PLACED BY THE COMMISSION CONCERNING FDA REGULATIONS ON ALL OTHER DEVICES; MUST RETURN FEES CHARGED TO THE PATIENT'S INSURER FOR USE OF THE ECLOSION DEVICE IN THIS CASE WITHIN 90 DAYS; SHALL SUBMIT ALL WRITTEN ADVERTISEMENTS FOR HIS PRACTICE TO THE COMMISSION AND OBEY COMMISSION RESTRICTIONS CONCERNING REPRESENTATIONS MADE TO PATIENTS; SHALL PERMIT SEMI-ANNUAL COMPLIANCE AUDITS OF HIS PRACTICE; SHALL APPEAR BEFORE THE COMMISSION ANNUALLY AND PAY A $2500 FINE WITHIN 90 DAYS. ON 9/25/96 HIS REQUEST TO TERMINATE THIS ORDER GRANTED AND LICENSE UNRESTRICTED.

COSTLEIGH, ROBERT J MD, LICENSE NUMBER 0009976, OF SILVERDALE, WA, WAS DISCIPLINED BY WASHINGTON ON MARCH 4, 1994.
DISCIPLINARY ACTION: 36-MONTH PROBATION; FINE
OFFENSE: SUBSTANDARD CARE, INCOMPETENCE, OR NEGLIGENCE
NOTES: FAILING TO DIAGNOSE APPENDICITIS IN A PATIENT. MUST UNDERGO SEMI-ANNUAL PRACTICE REVIEWS, APPEAR ANNUALLY BEFORE THE BOARD AND PAY A $1000 FINE.

CUMBERBATCH, RUDOLPH S MD, LICENSE NUMBER 0010191, OF TOPEKA, KS, WAS DISCIPLINED BY WASHINGTON ON AUGUST 16, 1991.
DISCIPLINARY ACTION: SURRENDER OF LICENSE
NOTES: RETIRED STATUS AGREEMENT WITHOUT FINDINGS; RETIREMENT FROM PRACTICE IN WASHINGTON SHALL BE PERMANENT.

DAHL, CHRISTIAN WILLIAM MD, LICENSE NUMBER 0023715, OF KENT, WA, WAS DISCIPLINED BY WASHINGTON ON NOVEMBER 20, 1992.
OFFENSE: SUBSTANDARD CARE, INCOMPETENCE, OR NEGLIGENCE
NOTES: NEGLIGENCE. AGREED ORDER, UNSPECIFIED. ON 3/3/94 ORDER TERMINATED. LICENSE REINSTATED IN FULL.

DAHL, CHRISTIAN WILLIAM MD, LICENSE NUMBER 0023715, OF KENT, WA, WAS DISCIPLINED BY WASHINGTON ON APRIL 19, 1996.
DISCIPLINARY ACTION: RESTRICTION PLACED ON LICENSE; MONITORING OF PHYSICIAN
NOTES: RESTRICTION OF LICENSE; SHALL REVIEW MEDICAL LITERATURE AND PREPARE A PAPER ON CARDIOVASCULAR EMERGENCIES; SHALL HAVE A CONSULTANT REVIEW HOSPITAL CHARTS OF ALL PATIENTS HE ADMITS TO THE HOSPITAL.

DAVIS, DANIEL MD, LICENSE NUMBER 0037838, OF 34 CHURCH STREET, GREENFIELD, MA, WAS DISCIPLINED BY MASSACHUSETTS ON MARCH 9, 1994.
DISCIPLINARY ACTION: LICENSE SUSPENSION
OFFENSE: PROFESSIONAL MISCONDUCT
NOTES: ALSO SEXUAL MISCONDUCT. EFFECTIVE 2/23/94.

DAVIS, DANIEL MD, DATE OF BIRTH NOVEMBER 23, 1942, OF 34 CHURCH STREET, GREENFIELD, MA, WAS DISCIPLINED BY MEDICARE ON JUNE 30, 1994.
DISCIPLINARY ACTION: EXCLUSION FROM THE MEDICARE AND/OR MEDICAID PROGRAMS
OFFENSE: DISCIPLINARY ACTION BY ANOTHER STATE OR AGENCY
NOTES: LICENSE SUSPENDED FOR REASONS BEARING ON PROFESSIONAL PERFORMANCE. REINSTATED ON 10/16/95.

DAVIS, DANIEL MD, LICENSE NUMBER 0119816, OF 43 CRESCENT STREET, GREENFIELD, MA, WAS DISCIPLINED BY NEW YORK ON FEBRUARY 28, 1995.
DISCIPLINARY ACTION: SURRENDER OF LICENSE
OFFENSE: DISCIPLINARY ACTION BY ANOTHER STATE OR AGENCY
NOTES: ACTION IN MASSACHUSETTS. HE ADMITTED TO ASKING PATIENTS INAPPROPRIATE SEXUAL QUESTIONS WHICH HAD NO LEGITIMATE MEDICAL PURPOSE.

DAVIS, DANIEL MD, DATE OF BIRTH NOVEMBER 23, 1942, LICENSE NUMBER 0006700, OF 34 CHURCH STREET, GREENFIELD, MA, WAS DISCIPLINED BY VERMONT ON MAY 5, 1995.
DISCIPLINARY ACTION: 60-MONTH LICENSE SUSPENSION
OFFENSE: DISCIPLINARY ACTION BY ANOTHER STATE OR AGENCY
NOTES: ENGAGED IN INAPPROPRIATE TOUCHING AND QUESTIONING OF PATIENTS IN MASSACHUSETTS. DUE TO THIS, EFFECTIVE 2/23/94 THE MASSACHUSETTS BOARD SUSPENDED HIS LICENSE TO PRACTICE MEDICINE FOR FIVE YEARS WITH A PROVISION THAT HE MAY FILE A PETITION FOR REINSTATEMENT AT THE CONCLUSION OF ONE YEAR FROM THE EFFECTIVE DATE OF THE SUSPENSION. HIS VERMONT MEDICAL LICENSE IS SUSPENDED RETROACTIVE TO THE DATE OF THE MASSACHUSETTS ACTION. UPON REINSTATEMENT OF HIS MASSACHUSETTS MEDICAL LICENSE HE MAY APPLY FOR REINSTATEMENT OF HIS LICENSE IN VERMONT. IF HE RETURNED TO ACTIVE STATUS HIS VERMONT LICENSE WOULD BE SUBJECT TO SUCH CONDITIONS AND RESTRICTIONS AS THE BOARD DEEMS NECESSARY. WILL PROVIDE A COPY OF THIS ORDER ANYPLACE WHERE HE HAS PRIVILEGES OR TO ANY STATE BOARD WHERE HE HAS PRIVILEGES WITHIN 10 DAYS.

DAVIS, DANIEL MD, LICENSE NUMBER 0037838, OF 34 CHURCH ST, GREENFIELD, MA, WAS DISCIPLINED BY MASSACHUSETTS ON JULY 12, 1995.
DISCIPLINARY ACTION: PROBATION
OFFENSE: PROFESSIONAL MISCONDUCT
NOTES: SEXUAL MISCONDUCT. SUSPENSION STAYED.

DAVIS, DANIEL MD, LICENSE NUMBER 0011190, OF GREENFIELD, MA,

WAS DISCIPLINED BY WASHINGTON ON AUGUST 30, 1995.
DISCIPLINARY ACTION: SURRENDER OF LICENSE
NOTES: VOLUNTARY SURRENDER.

DAVIS, DANIEL MD, LICENSE NUMBER 0006700, OF 34 CHURCH STREET, GREENFIELD, MA, WAS DISCIPLINED BY VERMONT ON FEBRUARY 8, 1996.
DISCIPLINARY ACTION: PROBATION
NOTES: CONDITIONED LICENSE.

DAVIS, FREDERICK B MD, LICENSE NUMBER 0010139, OF SEATTLE, WA, WAS DISCIPLINED BY WASHINGTON ON DECEMBER 18, 1992.
DISCIPLINARY ACTION: RESTRICTION PLACED ON LICENSE
OFFENSE: SUBSTANDARD CARE, INCOMPETENCE, OR NEGLIGENCE
NOTES: CHARGES OF NEGLIGENCE, WILLFUL BETRAYAL OF A PRACTITIONER-PATIENT PRIVILEGE AND ABUSE OF A CLIENT OR PATIENT. SHALL NOT EVALUATE VICTIMS OF SEXUAL ABUSE.

DAVIS, FREDERICK B MD, LICENSE NUMBER 0C29811, OF SEATTLE, WA, WAS DISCIPLINED BY CALIFORNIA ON JULY 10, 1995.
DISCIPLINARY ACTION: 60-MONTH PROBATION
OFFENSE: DISCIPLINARY ACTION BY ANOTHER STATE OR AGENCY
NOTES: DISCIPLINED BY THE WASHINGTON STATE BOARD FOR IMPROPERLY PERFORMING, IN TWO SEPARATE CASES, DEFENSE PSYCHIATRIC EVALUATIONS OF TWO MINORS ALLEGED TO BE SEXUALLY ABUSED BY THEIR FATHERS. REVOCATION STAYED.

DAVIS, MCWILLIAM H MD WAS DISCIPLINED BY WASHINGTON ON AUGUST 18, 1989.
OFFENSE: LOSS OR RESTRICTION OF HOSPITAL PRIVILEGES
NOTES: ABOUT 7/19/85 NAVAL HOSPITAL, BEAUFORT, SOUTH CAROLINA, REVOKED HIS PRIVILEGES FOR THE PRACTICE OF MEDICINE AT THE HOSPITAL. ON 2/14/85 HE DID NOT COME TO THE HOSPITAL AT 2:00 A.M. WHEN A NURSE INFORMED HIM THE PATIENT'S PO2 DROPPED TO 50 AND IN 5/85 A PATIENT HAD TRANSIENT DIFFICULTY WITH SPEECH AND NUMBNESS OF THE LEFT ARM; DID NOT DOCUMENT THAT HE TOLD THE PATIENT TO RETURN IF THERE WERE FURTHER PROBLEMS. THE HOSPITAL'S ACTION WAS UPHELD ON APPEALS. SHALL NOT PRACTICE MEDICINE IN WASHINGTON UNLESS AND UNTIL HE APPEARS PERSONALLY BEFORE THE BOARD AND OBTAINS WRITTEN PERMISSION AT WHICH TIME HE SHALL PROVIDE WRITTEN COPIES OF EVALUATIONS AND RECOMMENDATIONS FROM EACH PSYCHIATRIST WHO EVALUATED HIM AFTER 5/16/89, IF ANY.

DE HART, COR MD, LICENSE NUMBER 0029654, OF SEATTLE, WA, WAS DISCIPLINED BY WASHINGTON ON NOVEMBER 28, 1993.
DISCIPLINARY ACTION: 36-MONTH PROBATION; FINE
OFFENSE: SEXUAL ABUSE OF OR SEXUAL MISCONDUCT WITH A PATIENT
NOTES: ALLEGATIONS THAT HE COMMENCED A SEXUAL RELATIONSHIP WITH A WOMAN PATIENT WHOM HE HAD BEEN PROVIDING PSYCHIATRIC TREATMENT BEGINNING IN OCTOBER 1985; KISSED HER IN 11/86 AND KISSED AND FONDLED HER IN 12/86 DURING TREATMENT; SHE ALLEGES THEY BEGAN HAVING INTERCOURSE ON OR ABOUT 12/17/86 THROUGH 6/92. HE DENIES THE RELATIONSHIP OCCURRED WHILE HE WAS PROVIDING TREATMENT TO THE PATIENT, AND STATES THAT THE SEXUAL RELATIONSHIP BEGAN AFTER THE PHYSICIAN-PATIENT RELATIONSHIP HAD TERMINATED. PROBATION UNDER THE FOLLOWING TERMS AND CONDITIONS: SHALL ENSURE THAT A LICENSED FEMALE HEALTH CARE PROFESSIONAL IS PRESENT IN THE ROOM WHENEVER HE SEES A FEMALE PATIENT; THIS PROFESSIONAL SHALL INDICATE THAT SHE WAS PRESENT ON THE PATIENT'S CHART; SHALL PROVIDE WRITTEN NOTICE TO ALL CURRENT AND FUTURE FEMALE PATIENTS THAT HE IS UNDER DISCIPLINARY RESTRICTIONS; SHALL PROVIDE A COPY OF THIS STIPULATION AND AGREED ORDER TO ANY HEALTH CARE ENTITY WHERE HE HAS PRIVILEGES; SHALL HAVE NO SOCIAL OR SEXUAL CONTACT WITH ANY PAST, CURRENT OR FUTURE FEMALE PATIENTS; SHALL COMMENCE THERAPY WITH A BOARD APPROVED THERAPIST WITH QUARTERLY REPORTS; SHALL UNDERGO FIVE MEDICAL ETHICS CONSULTATIONS WITH A MEDICAL ETHICIST; SHALL APPEAR BEFORE THE BOARD SIX MONTHS FROM THE DATE OF THIS ORDER AND ANNUALLY THEREAFTER FOR COMPLIANCE REVIEWS; SHALL HAVE ANNOUNCED OFFICE INSPECTIONS; SHALL INFORM THE BOARD OF CHANGE OF ADDRESS OR IF HE LEAVES THE STATE; TIME SPENT OUT OF WASHINGTON DOES NOT COUNT TOWARD PROBATION. $1,000 FINE. MAY NOT SEEK MODIFICATION FOR TWO YEARS. ON 5/19/95 REQUEST FOR MODIFICATION DENIED.

DE HART, COR MD, LICENSE NUMBER 0000678, OF 3032 37TH AVENUE, SEATTLE, WA, WAS DISCIPLINED BY DELAWARE ON OCTOBER 4, 1994.
DISCIPLINARY ACTION: 72-MONTH LICENSE SUSPENSION; RESTRICTION PLACED ON LICENSE
OFFENSE: SEXUAL ABUSE OF OR SEXUAL MISCONDUCT WITH A PATIENT
NOTES: SEXUAL LIAISON WITH PATIENT; EXPLOITED THE PATIENT PRIVILEGE FOR SEXUAL GRATIFICATION; LACK OF REMORSE AND LACK OF RECOGNITION FOR WHAT HE HAD DONE IN THAT HE ATTEMPTED TO BLAME THE VICTIM AND HER HUSBAND. PERMANENT RESTRICTION ON FUTURE REINSTATEMENT INCLUDES A PROHIBITION ON TREATING WOMEN AND MINORS UNDER 21.

DENGLER, GEORGE W MD, LICENSE NUMBER 0007069, OF LOPEZ ISLAND, WA, WAS DISCIPLINED BY WASHINGTON ON FEBRUARY 16, 1990.
DISCIPLINARY ACTION: 60-MONTH RESTRICTION PLACED ON CONTROLLED SUBSTANCE LICENSE; REQUIRED TO TAKE ADDITIONAL MEDICAL EDUCATION
OFFENSE: OVERPRESCRIBING OR MISPRESCRIBING DRUGS
NOTES: TREATED ONE PATIENT AND PRESCRIBED SCHEDULE II DRUGS WHEN PATIENT WAS RECEIVING SIMILAR DRUGS FROM OTHERS; FAILED TO MONITOR THE USE OF SUCH DRUGS, WHICH RESULTED IN PATIENT RECEIVING AMOUNTS WHICH EXCEEDED THERAPEUTIC REQUIREMENTS. LICENSE RESTRICTED SUCH THAT: SHALL ONLY PRESCRIBE SCHEDULE II DRUGS IN AN ACUTE SITUATION FOR 3 WEEKS OR LESS OR AS NEEDED TO CONTROL PAIN ASSOCIATED WITH MALIGNANCY; SHALL MAINTAIN A LOG OF ALL SUCH PRESCRIPTIONS; SHALL SUBMIT TRIPLICATE PRESCRIPTIONS ON SCHEDULES III-V DRUGS; SHALL ALLOW BOARD TO MAKE ANNOUNCED VISITS TO INSPECT RECORDS; SHALL SUBMIT VERIFICATION OF ATTENDANCE AT 25 HOURS PER YEAR OF CONTINUING MEDICAL EDUCATION REGARDING PAIN CONTROL AND/OR USE OF SCHEDULED DRUGS TO CONTROL CHRONIC PAIN; SHALL APPEAR BEFORE BOARD TO PROVE COMPLIANCE; MAY APPLY FOR MODIFICATION AFTER ONE YEAR. LICENSE REINSTATED IN FULL AS OF 4/30/92.

DILLER, JOHN L MD, LICENSE NUMBER 0013892, OF PUYALLUP, WA, WAS DISCIPLINED BY WASHINGTON ON DECEMBER 17, 1993.
DISCIPLINARY ACTION: 24-MONTH PROBATION; RESTRICTION PLACED ON CONTROLLED SUBSTANCE LICENSE
OFFENSE: SUBSTANDARD CARE, INCOMPETENCE, OR NEGLIGENCE
NOTES: PRESCRIBED WEIGHT LOSS DRUGS AND BIRTH CONTROL PILLS TO A PATIENT AND CONTINUED TO PRESCRIBE WEIGHT LOSS MEDICATION DESPITE THE

FACT THAT THE PATIENT EXPERIENCED NO MEDICAL BENEFIT; FAILED TO MONITOR AND/OR RECORD THE BLOOD PRESSURE OF THIS PATIENT DESPITE THE FACT HE WAS PRESCRIBING TWO MEDICATIONS WHICH CONTRIBUTE TO AN INCREASED RISK OF HIGH BLOOD PRESSURE AND STROKE; PATIENT SUFFERED A STROKE ON 5/11/91; AFTER LEARNING OF THIS PATIENT'S STROKE, HE MADE FIVE RETROACTIVE NOTATIONS OF NORMAL BLOOD PRESSURE READINGS ON THE PATIENT'S MEDICAL CHART. CONDITIONS OF PROBATION ARE AS FOLLOWS: SHALL NOT PRESCRIBE WEIGHT LOSS MEDICATION; SHALL DICTATE HIS NOTES AND HAVE THEM TRANSCRIBED IN A TIMELY MANNER; SHALL TAKE OR HAVE TAKEN BLOOD PRESSURE READINGS FOR HIS PATIENTS FOR WHICH MEDICAL PRACTICE DEEMS IT APPROPRIATE AND SHALL RECORD THESE READINGS WITHIN 24 HOURS; SHALL APPEAR BEFORE THE BOARD IN ONE YEAR; AGREES TO AN ANNOUNCED BOARD VISIT WITHIN 90 DAYS AND THEREAFTER SEMI-ANNUALLY TO INSPECT OFFICE AND REVIEW OTHER ASPECTS OF HIS PRACTICE; SHALL INFORM THE BOARD OF CHANGES IN HIS PRACTICE AND RESIDENCE ADDRESS; MUST NOTIFY THE BOARD IF HE LEAVES WASHINGTON TO PRACTICE OUTSIDE THE STATE; THE PROBATION PERIOD SHALL BE TOLLED FOR ANY TIME PERIOD DURING WHICH HE RESIDES AND/OR PRACTICES OUTSIDE WASHINGTON; SHALL PAY A $500 FINE. LICENSE UNRESTRICTED ON 1/8/96.

DOCKUM, JOHN G MD, LICENSE NUMBER 0026645, OF KENNEWICK, WA, WAS DISCIPLINED BY WASHINGTON ON DECEMBER 27, 1994.
DISCIPLINARY ACTION: EMERGENCY SUSPENSION
OFFENSE: SEXUAL ABUSE OF OR SEXUAL MISCONDUCT WITH A PATIENT
NOTES: ALLEGATIONS OF MORAL TURPITUDE AND SEXUAL CONTACT WITH PATIENTS. NO FINAL ACTION TAKEN AS OF 4/23/97.

DOREY, LEE R MD, LICENSE NUMBER 0017078, OF TACOMA, WA, WAS DISCIPLINED BY WASHINGTON ON OCTOBER 6, 1995.
DISCIPLINARY ACTION: PROBATION; RESTRICTION PLACED ON LICENSE
NOTES: PROBATION UNDER THE FOLLOWING TERMS AND CONDITIONS: MUST REQUIRE PATIENTS TO GET SECOND OPINIONS BEFORE HE PREFORMS SPINAL SURGERY; RESTRICTION OF HIS PRESCRIBING OF CONTROLLED DANGEROUS SUBSTANCES.

DORSEY, CHARLES L MD, LICENSE NUMBER 0C43037, OF SPOKANE, WA, WAS DISCIPLINED BY CALIFORNIA ON AUGUST 25, 1992.
DISCIPLINARY ACTION: 60-MONTH PROBATION
NOTES: 5-YEAR PROBATIONARY CERTIFICATE GRANTED.

DOUGLASS, ROBERT E MD WAS DISCIPLINED BY WASHINGTON ON SEPTEMBER 8, 1992.
DISCIPLINARY ACTION: RESTRICTION PLACED ON LICENSE
NOTES: CONDITIONAL LICENSE ISSUED WITH SPECIFIC CONDITIONS.

DRUMHELLER, GLENN W DO WAS DISCIPLINED BY WASHINGTON ON JULY 8, 1994.
DISCIPLINARY ACTION: PROBATION; FINE
OFFENSE: SUBSTANDARD CARE, INCOMPETENCE, OR NEGLIGENCE
NOTES: COMMITTED UNPROFESSIONAL CONDUCT BY NEGLIGENTLY LEAVING SURGICAL TUBING IN THE BODY OF A PATIENT SUBSEQUENT TO OTOLARYNGOLOGICAL SURGERY ON 4/30/91 WHICH RESULTED IN NUMEROUS INFECTIONS AND EXTENDED PAIN AND SUFFERING TO THAT PATIENT AND WHICH RESULTED IN A $20,000 MALPRACTICE PAYMENT. PROBATIONARY STATUS UNTIL SUCCESSFUL COMPLETION OF THE CONDITIONS: SHALL SUBMIT FOR APPROVAL TO THE BOARD, A STATEMENT OF POLICIES AND PROCEDURES OF ACCOUNTABILITY FOR AND DOCUMENTATION OF SURGICAL IMPLANT DEVICES AND ALL OTHER SURGICAL SUPPLIES AND EQUIPMENT WHICH WILL PREVENT FOREIGN BODIES FROM BEING LEFT IN THE PATIENTS AFTER SURGERY. $500 ADMINISTRATIVE FINE. SHALL NOTIFY THE BOARD OF CURRENT HOME AND BUSINESS ADDRESS OR ANY CHANGES IN ADDRESS. ON 1/20/95 RELEASED FROM PROBATION.

DU, EDWARD L MD, DATE OF BIRTH OCTOBER 16, 1937, OF 5410 CALIFORNIA AVE, SW, SEATTLE, WA, WAS DISCIPLINED BY MEDICARE ON JANUARY 28, 1991.
DISCIPLINARY ACTION: EXCLUSION FROM THE MEDICARE AND/OR MEDICAID PROGRAMS
NOTES: PEER REVIEW ORGANIZATION RECOMMENDATION.

DU, EDWARD L MD, LICENSE NUMBER 0013461, OF RENTON, KING COUNTY, WA, WAS DISCIPLINED BY WASHINGTON ON MARCH 20, 1992.
DISCIPLINARY ACTION: LICENSE SUSPENSION
OFFENSE: PROFESSIONAL MISCONDUCT
NOTES: CHARGES OF UNPROFESSIONAL CONDUCT, AND REASONABLE GROUNDS TO BELIEVE THAT HE MAY BE UNABLE TO PRACTICE MEDICINE WITH REASONABLE SKILL AND SAFETY. SUSPENDED INDEFINITELY.

DUDLEY, DONALD L MD, LICENSE NUMBER 0012695, OF SEATTLE, WA, WAS DISCIPLINED BY WASHINGTON ON FEBRUARY 16, 1994.
DISCIPLINARY ACTION: LICENSE SUSPENSION
OFFENSE: SUBSTANDARD CARE, INCOMPETENCE, OR NEGLIGENCE
NOTES: MORAL TURPITUDE AND INCOMPETENCE. LICENSE SUSPENDED INDEFINITELY. IF HE WISHES TO HAVE HIS LICENSE REINSTATED IN THE FUTURE, SHALL PETITION THE BOARD IN WRITING.

DUDLEY, DONALD L MD, LICENSE NUMBER 0012695, OF GIG HARBOR, WA, WAS DISCIPLINED BY WASHINGTON ON JUNE 13, 1996.
DISCIPLINARY ACTION: MONITORING OF PHYSICIAN
NOTES: THE COMMISSION GRANTED HIS REQUEST TO LIFT THE SUSPENSION OF HIS LICENSE BUT PLACED CONDITIONS ON HIS PRACTICE, INCLUDING REQUIRING HIM TO SUBMIT A PLAN FOR SUPERVISION OF HIS PRACTICE FOR BOARD APPROVAL.

DUNCAN, WILLIAM R MD, LICENSE NUMBER 0002600, OF PORT ANGELES, WA, WAS DISCIPLINED BY WASHINGTON ON MAY 2, 1996.
DISCIPLINARY ACTION: SURRENDER OF LICENSE
NOTES: AGREED TO RETIRE.

DUNLAP, JAMES P MD WAS DISCIPLINED BY WASHINGTON ON SEPTEMBER 11, 1990.
DISCIPLINARY ACTION: SURRENDER OF LICENSE
OFFENSE: FAILURE TO COMPLY WITH A PREVIOUS BOARD ORDER
NOTES: BOARD ISSUED STATEMENT OF CHARGES 08/29/90 ALLEGING THAT HE FAILED TO COMPLY WITH ORDER REQUIRING A PHYSICAL AND PSYCHIATRIC EVALUATION WITHIN THE TIME FRAME SPECIFIED. RETIRED ON 5/16/90 AND HAS NO PLANS TO RESUME PRACTICE; RETIREMENT SHALL BE PERMANENT.

DURHAM, STANLEY MD WAS DISCIPLINED BY WASHINGTON ON JANUARY 16, 1987.
DISCIPLINARY ACTION: REPRIMAND; REQUIRED TO TAKE ADDITIONAL MEDICAL EDUCATION
OFFENSE: OVERPRESCRIBING OR MISPRESCRIBING DRUGS
NOTES: DURING 1983, 1984 AND 1985 EXCESSIVELY PRESCRIBED STADOL FOR A PATIENT IN SUCH A MANNER AS TO CREATE AND MAINTAIN A STATE OF ADDICTION IN THAT PATIENT; FAILED TO INITIATE CONFERENCES WITH HER OTHER PHYSICIANS TO DISCUSS A UNIFIED TREATMENT

- WASHINGTON -

PROGRAM; SHALL OBTAIN CONTINUING MEDICAL EDUCATION IN THE SUBJECT OF MANAGEMENT OF CHRONIC PAIN WITHIN 6 MONTHS; SHALL NOT DISPENSE CONTROLLED SUBSTANCES TO THIS PARTICULAR PATIENT; SHALL SUBMIT TO THE BOARD A LIST OF CHRONIC PAIN PATIENTS FOR WHOM HE IS PRESCRIBING CONTROLLED SUBSTANCES OR NON-NARCOTIC ANALGESICS; SHALL APPEAR BEFORE THE BOARD IN 6 MONTHS;

DUTTON, EDWARD W MD, LICENSE NUMBER 0012214, OF CLINTON, ISLAND COUNTY, WA, WAS DISCIPLINED BY WASHINGTON ON JULY 20, 1992.
NOTES: SUSPENSION, STAYED CONDITIONED ON HIS COMPLIANCE WITH THE TERMS AND CONDITIONS IN ORDER.

DUTTON, EDWARD W MD, LICENSE NUMBER 0012214, OF BLAINE, WA, WAS DISCIPLINED BY WASHINGTON ON FEBRUARY 10, 1993.
DISCIPLINARY ACTION: EMERGENCY SUSPENSION
OFFENSE: FAILURE TO COMPLY WITH A PREVIOUS BOARD ORDER
NOTES: BASED ON ALLEGATIONS OF IMPAIRMENT AND FAILURE TO COMPLY WITH AN ORDER.

DUTTON, EDWARD W MD, LICENSE NUMBER 0012214, OF BLAINE, WA, WAS DISCIPLINED BY WASHINGTON ON MARCH 4, 1993.
DISCIPLINARY ACTION: MONITORING OF PHYSICIAN
OFFENSE: FAILURE TO COMPLY WITH A PREVIOUS BOARD ORDER
NOTES: ALLEGATIONS OF IMPAIRMENT AND VIOLATION OF A 7/92 ORDER. REQUIRED TO ENTER INTO A CONTRACT WITH WASHINGTON PHYSICIAN'S HEALTH PROGRAM; APPEAR FOR A REVIEW OF THE SUMMARY SUSPENSION; AND SHALL ENTER AND SUCCESSFULLY COMPLETE AN ALCOHOL AND SUBSTANCE ABUSE PROGRAM. ON 11/30/93 SUSPENSION STAYED PERMITTING HIM TO PRACTICE AS LONG AS HE ADHERES TO TERMS AND CONDITIONS.

DUTTON, EDWARD W MD, LICENSE NUMBER 0012214, WAS DISCIPLINED BY WASHINGTON ON NOVEMBER 30, 1993.
DISCIPLINARY ACTION: RESTRICTION PLACED ON LICENSE; REQUIRED TO ENTER AN IMPAIRED PHYSICIAN PROGRAM OR DRUG OR ALCOHOL TREATMENT
OFFENSE: SUBSTANCE ABUSE
NOTES: SUCCESSFULLY COMPLETED AN ALCOHOL AND SUBSTANCE ABUSE TREATMENT PROGRAM AND HAS ENTERED INTO A CONTRACT WITH THE WASHINGTON PHYSICIANS HEALTH PROGRAM (WPHP). SUSPENSION STAYED UNDER THE FOLLOWING RESTRICTIONS: PERMITTED TO PRACTICE MEDICINE AT THE SOUTH SEATTLE MEDICAL CLINIC AND MUST OBTAIN APPROVAL OF THE BOARD, OF ALL OTHER EMPLOYMENT SITUATIONS INCLUDING CHANGES IN HIS WORK SITUATION, PRIOR TO BEGINNING SUCH EMPLOYMENT OR CHANGE IN WORK CONDITION; SHALL COMPLY WITH WPHP DECISION AS TO WHETHER HE MUST NOTIFY THE SOUTH SEATTLE MEDICAL CLINIC OF HIS CHEMICAL DEPENDENCY AND/OR PROVIDE COPIES OF THIS BOARD ORDER; ALL OTHER EMPLOYERS AND FUTURE EMPLOYERS MUST BE NOTIFIED OF HIS CHEMICAL DEPENDENCY AND HE MUST PROVIDE THEM WITH A COPY OF THIS BOARD ORDER PRIOR TO THE START OF HIS EMPLOYMENT; SHALL CONTINUE IN TREATMENT AND MONITORING WITH WPHP WITH REPORTS SUBMITTED EVERY SIX MONTHS; SHALL NOT POSSESS OR USE LEGEND DRUGS OR CONTROLLED SUBSTANCES, INCLUDING ALCOHOL, UNLESS PRESCRIBED BY ANOTHER PHYSICIAN FOR A LEGITIMATE THERAPEUTIC PURPOSE; SHALL FULLY COMPLY WITH ALL CONDITIONS AND REQUIREMENTS OF THE 7/20/92 BOARD ORDER; SHALL APPEAR BEFORE THE BOARD AT ITS 12/93 MEETING.

DUTTON, EDWARD WAYNE MD, DATE OF BIRTH FEBRUARY 13, 1940, LICENSE NUMBER 0038658, OF 408 PEACOCK STREET, COCHRAN, GA, WAS DISCIPLINED BY GEORGIA ON JULY 7, 1994.
DISCIPLINARY ACTION: 60-MONTH PROBATION
NOTES: IMPAIRMENT. LICENSED WITH CONDITIONS.

EARLY, RONALD G MD, LICENSE NUMBER 0015403, OF SEATTLE, WA, WAS DISCIPLINED BY WASHINGTON ON JULY 1, 1992.
DISCIPLINARY ACTION: PROBATION; FINE
OFFENSE: PROFESSIONAL MISCONDUCT
NOTES: ALLEGATIONS OF MORAL TURPITUDE AND FALSE INFORMATION ON A REPORT; SEXUAL CONTACT WITH A FORMER PATIENT FROM ABOUT 1981 THROUGH 1986. SUSPENSION, STAYED PROVIDED HE COMPLIES WITH TERMS AND CONDITIONS WHICH ARE AS FOLLOWS: SHALL NOT HAVE ANY ONGOING OR MORE THAN CASUAL CONTACT OR ANY SEXUAL CONTACT WITH ANY CURRENT PATIENTS, FORMER PATIENTS OR IMMEDIATE RELATIVES WITH THE EXCEPTION OF HIS WIFE; SHALL NOT PROVIDE ANY MEDICAL SERVICES IN EXCHANGE FOR IN-KIND SERVICES; SHALL CONTINUE IN INDIVIDUAL CONSULTATION WITH PSYCHIATRIST OR PSYCHOLOGIST APPROVED BY THE BOARD AT LEAST ON A MONTHLY BASIS WHO SHALL PROVIDE REPORTS TO THE BOARD AT LEAST TWO TIMES PER YEAR; SHALL PERMIT A REPRESENTATIVE OF THE DEPARTMENT OF HEALTH TO MAKE ANNOUNCED OR UNANNOUNCED VISITS AT LEAST YEARLY TO INSPECT AND REVIEW HIS OFFICE AND MEDICAL RECORDS, INTERVIEW STAFF AND OTHERWISE REVIEW HIS PRACTICE; SHALL NOTIFY ALL HOSPITALS AND/OR CLINICS AT WHICH HE CURRENTLY PRACTICES OR WHERE HE OBTAINS PRIVILEGES OF THE CONDITIONS OF THIS ORDER; SHALL NOT PRESCRIBE TO ANY CURRENT OR FORMER PATIENT ANY CONTROLLED SUBSTANCES OR LEGEND DRUGS EXCEPT FOR THERAPEUTIC PURPOSES; SHALL PAY A FINE OF $2,000; ON 5/27/94 BOARD GRANTED HIS REQUEST FOR TERMINATION AND LICENSE WAS REINSTATED IN FULL.

EDGREN, CLAUDE GORDON MD WAS DISCIPLINED BY WASHINGTON ON DECEMBER 29, 1988.
DISCIPLINARY ACTION: EMERGENCY SUSPENSION
OFFENSE: DISCIPLINARY ACTION BY ANOTHER STATE OR AGENCY
NOTES: ON 12/04/86 HIS LICENSE IN IDAHO WAS REVOKED.

EDIBIOKPO, EMMANUEL A DO WAS DISCIPLINED BY WASHINGTON ON MARCH 8, 1994.
DISCIPLINARY ACTION: LICENSE REVOCATION; FINE
OFFENSE: SEXUAL ABUSE OF OR SEXUAL MISCONDUCT WITH A PATIENT
NOTES: INAPPROPRIATE SEXUAL CONTACT WITH A PATIENT'S MOTHER WHICH IS AN ACT OF MORAL TURPITUDE AND COULD HAVE BEEN PREVENTED BY SIMPLE MEANS; UNPROFESSIONAL CONDUCT WITH REGARDS TO A 16-YEAR-OLD EMPLOYEE WHO HE ASKED TO RUB HIS NECK; CONDUCTED A MEDICALLY UNNECESSARY VAGINAL EXAMINATION AND REMOVED THE PATIENT'S CLOTHING HIMSELF CONSTITUTING SEXUAL CONTACT AND INAPPROPRIATE COMMENTS TO ANOTHER PATIENT; AIDED AND ABETTED UNLICENSED PERSONS TO ADMINISTER INJECTIONS; AND DEMONSTRATED A REPEATED INABILITY TO RECOGNIZE AND MAINTAIN APPROPRIATE BOUNDARIES IN HIS PROFESSIONAL AND PERSONAL LIFE BY PROVIDING MEDICAL SERVICES TO EMPLOYEES AND PERSONS WITH WHOM HE HAS A DATING RELATIONSHIP; FAILURE TO CLEARLY COMMUNICATE WITH PATIENTS AND OFFICE PERSONNEL. REVOCATION FOR A MINIMUM OF 10 YEARS; AT LEAST SIX MONTH SHALL BE SERVED WITHOUT A STAY. A STAY SHALL BE GRANTED UPON COMPLETION OF CONDITIONS: SHALL PRESENT TO THE BOARD AN EVALUATION BY A BOARD APPROVED

MENTAL HEALTH PRACTITIONER SKILLED IN EVALUATION OF HEALTH CARE PRACTITIONERS ENGAGING IN SEXUAL MISCONDUCT; SHALL PROVIDE THE BOARD WITH EVIDENCE OF HAVING COMMENCED THERAPY; WITHIN 12 MONTHS SHALL EARN 25 CONTINUING MEDICAL EDUCATION CREDITS OF WHICH AT LEAST EIGHT HOURS SHALL BE IN MEDICAL ETHICS AND THE REMAINDER IN THE AREA OF OFFICE MANAGEMENT AND PERSONNEL MANAGEMENT AND PROVIDE PROOF OF COMPLETION TO THE BOARD; SHALL PARTICIPATE IN MENTAL HEALTH COUNSELING WITH A MENTAL HEALTH PRACTITIONER SKILLED IN THE TREATMENT OF HEALTH CARE PRACTITIONERS WHO HAVE BOUNDARY ISSUES AND WHO SHALL SUBMIT QUARTERLY PROGRESS REPORTS TO THE BOARD; SHALL NOT DATE OR HAVE SEXUAL RELATIONSHIPS WITH ANY OFFICE EMPLOYEE OR PRESENT OR PAST PATIENT; SHALL NOT HIRE ANY PRESENT OR FORMER PATIENT; SHALL NOT PROVIDE MEDICAL CARE TO ANY OFFICE PERSONNEL EXCEPT AS MAY BE REQUIRED BY OFFICE EMERGENCIES; SHALL NOT TREAT ANY INDIVIDUAL WITH WHOM HE HAS HAD A DATING OR SEXUAL RELATIONSHIP EXCEPT AS MAY BE REQUIRED BY EMERGENCY SITUATIONS; SHALL SUBMIT TO THE BOARD PERSONAL QUARTERLY REPORTS DESCRIBING STRESSES HE FACES AND HIS METHODS OF DEALING WITH THEM; SHALL PROVIDE TO THE BOARD A CURRENT HOME AND BUSINESS ADDRESS AND ANY CHANGE OF ADDRESS; SHALL MAKE HIS OFFICE AND OFFICE RECORDS AVAILABLE FOR PERIODIC BOARD INSPECTIONS; MAY PETITION FOR MODIFICATION NO SOONER THAN FIVE YEARS; AND MAY APPLY FOR REINSTATEMENT NO SOONER THAN 10 YEARS. $5,000 FINE.

EDIBIOKPO, EMMANUEL A DO WAS DISCIPLINED BY WASHINGTON ON JANUARY 20, 1995.
DISCIPLINARY ACTION: FINE; 120-MONTH REQUIRED TO TAKE ADDITIONAL MEDICAL EDUCATION
OFFENSE: SEXUAL ABUSE OF OR SEXUAL MISCONDUCT WITH A PATIENT
NOTES: HE APPEALED THE 3/8/94 ORDER TO SUPERIOR COURT. THE ORDER WAS STAYED ON 4/28/94. ON 1/20/95 IN LIEU OF FURTHER JUDICIAL PROCEEDINGS THE PREVIOUS ORDER WAS WITHDRAWN AND THE FOLLOWING ORDER WAS AGREED TO: LICENSE SUBJECT TO THE FOLLOWING CONDITIONS FOR THE NEXT 10 YEARS: SHALL EMPLOY A BOARD APPROVED, REGISTERED NURSE OF LICENSED PRACTICAL NURSE DURING ALL REGULAR CLINIC HOURS AND DURING ANY OTHER PERIODS IN WHICH HE TREATS FEMALE PATIENTS; THE NURSE SHALL MAINTAIN A LOG OF FEMALE PATIENTS AND TO CERTIFY THAT SHE WAS PRESENT DURING THE EXAMINATION, TREATMENT, COUNSELING, OR MEETING OF THOSE PATIENTS; SHALL REVIEW AND INITIAL THE LOG EACH DAY HE SEES PATIENTS IN HIS OFFICE; SHALL ESTABLISH, AS AN EMPLOYMENT RESPONSIBILITY OF THE NURSE, THE DUTY TO REPORT TO THE BOARD ANY FAILURE BY HIM TO COMPLY WITH THE LOG-KEEPING REQUIREMENT; SHALL PROVIDE A COPY OF THIS ORDER TO ALL OFFICE PERSONNEL CURRENTLY EMPLOYED AND EACH FUTURE EMPLOYEE; THE LOG SHALL BE AVAILABLE FOR PERIODIC INSPECTION BY THE DEPARTMENT OF HEALTH AND FORWARDED TO THEM AT THE END OF EACH MONTH; SHALL MAKE HIS OFFICE AND OFFICE RECORDS AVAILABLE FOR PERIODIC BOARD INSPECTION; SHALL REQUIRE AND VERIFY THAT ALL STAFF RESPONSIBLE FOR GIVING INJECTIONS HAVE THE APPROPRIATE LICENSE OR CERTIFICATION IN WASHINGTON; SHALL INFORM THE BOARD, IN WRITING, OF CHANGES OF HIS PRACTICE AND RESIDENCE ADDRESS; SHALL NOTIFY THE BOARD IN WRITING OF THE DATES OF DEPARTURE AND RETURN TO WASHINGTON; SHALL COMPLETE BOARD APPROVED, EIGHT COURSE HOURS OF CONTINUING PROFESSIONAL EDUCATION IN MEDICAL ETHICS AND SUBMIT PROOF OF COMPLETION WITHIN TWO YEARS; SHALL FILE QUARTERLY DECLARATIONS UNDER PENALTY OF PERJURY REGARDING COMPLIANCE; AND IF SUCCESSFULLY COMPLIES FOR FIVE YEARS, MAY PETITION THE BOARD FOR MODIFICATION. $1,500 FINE.

EHSAN, MIKE MD, LICENSE NUMBER 0103360, OF EVERETT, WA, WAS DISCIPLINED BY NEW YORK ON AUGUST 30, 1989.
DISCIPLINARY ACTION: LICENSE REVOCATION

EICHMEIER, JAMES F MD, DATE OF BIRTH AUGUST 11, 1945, LICENSE NUMBER 0030730, OF 2934 MT HOPE ROAD, OKEMOS, MI, WAS DISCIPLINED BY MICHIGAN ON JANUARY 20, 1995.
DISCIPLINARY ACTION: 6-MONTH LICENSE SUSPENSION; 12-MONTH PROBATION
OFFENSE: SUBSTANDARD CARE, INCOMPETENCE, OR NEGLIGENCE
NOTES: NEGLIGENCE/INCOMPETENCE. LIMITED 3 YEARS; $1,000 FINE.

EICHMEIER, JAMES F MD, DATE OF BIRTH AUGUST 11, 1945, LICENSE NUMBER 1030730, OF 2934 MT HOPE RD, OKEMOS, MI, WAS DISCIPLINED BY MICHIGAN ON FEBRUARY 1, 1995.
DISCIPLINARY ACTION: REVOCATION OF CONTROLLED SUBSTANCE LICENSE
OFFENSE: PROFESSIONAL MISCONDUCT
NOTES: CONTROLLED SUBSTANCES VIOLATIONS.

EICHMEIER, JAMES F MD, LICENSE NUMBER 0015404, OF OKEMOS, MI, WAS DISCIPLINED BY WASHINGTON ON JANUARY 26, 1996.
NOTES: HIS LICENSE EXPIRED. HE AGREED THAT PRIOR TO COMMENCING PRACTICE IN WASHINGTON HE WOULD APPLY FOR A LICENSE AND APPEAR PERSONALLY BEFORE THE BOARD.

EISENBERG, JEFFREY I MD WAS DISCIPLINED BY WASHINGTON ON SEPTEMBER 25, 1992.
DISCIPLINARY ACTION: DENIAL OF NEW LICENSE
NOTES: MAY MAKE APPLICATION AGAIN NO SOONER THAN TWO YEARS FROM DATE OF ORDER.

EISENBERG, JEFFREY I MD, DATE OF BIRTH DECEMBER 15, 1953, LICENSE NUMBER 041036L, OF PO BOX 379, RIDLEY PARK, PA, WAS DISCIPLINED BY PENNSYLVANIA ON AUGUST 23, 1995.
DISCIPLINARY ACTION: PROBATION
OFFENSE: SUBSTANCE ABUSE
NOTES: PAST USE OF DRUGS AND ALCOHOL; IMPAIRMENT BY MENTAL ILLNESS. REVOCATION STAYED IN FAVOR OF PROBATION WITH SPECIFIED CONDITIONS; HE MAY APPLY FOR REINSTATEMENT AFTER FIVE YEARS HAVE LAPSED.

EK, THEODORE W MD, LICENSE NUMBER 0011027, OF BREMERTON, WA, WAS DISCIPLINED BY WASHINGTON ON APRIL 22, 1991.
DISCIPLINARY ACTION: EMERGENCY SUSPENSION
OFFENSE: FAILURE TO COMPLY WITH A PREVIOUS BOARD ORDER
NOTES: ALLEGATION OF A FAILURE TO SUBMIT TO A PSYCHOLOGICAL AND PHYSICAL EXAM AS ORDERED BY THE BOARD 11/11/90.

EK, THEODORE W MD, LICENSE NUMBER 0011027, OF BREMERTON, WA, WAS DISCIPLINED BY WASHINGTON ON JUNE 21, 1991.
DISCIPLINARY ACTION: PROBATION; FINE
OFFENSE: FAILURE TO COMPLY WITH A PREVIOUS BOARD ORDER
NOTES: AGREED THAT HE FAILED TO SUBMIT TO THE PSYCHOLOGICAL AND PHYSICAL EVALUATION ORDERED BY THE BOARD IN THE INTERIM ORDER ISSUED 11/11/90. SUBSEQUENT TO SUMMARY SUSPENSION OF 4/22/91 HE WAS DIAGNOSED AS HAVING ALCOHOL ABUSE AND DEPENDENCY; ENTERED INPATIENT TREATMENT FOR

THIS IN OREGON AND WAS DISCHARGED WITH FAVORABLE REPORTS CONCERNING RECOVERY. SUSPENSION WILL BE STAYED TO PROBATION PROVIDING HE ABIDES BY THE FOLLOWING CONDITIONS: MUST NOT PRESCRIBE CONTROLLED SUBSTANCES FOR HIMSELF OR ANY MEMBER OF HIS FAMILY; SHALL NOT POSSESS OR USE CONTROLLED SUBSTANCES INCLUDING ALCOHOL; SHALL COMPLY WITH REQUIREMENTS OF THE WASHINGTON MONITORED TREATMENT PROGRAM AND THE CONTRACT ENTERED INTO WITH THEM; MUST SUBMIT TO RANDOM OBSERVED TESTING OF BODILY FLUIDS IF REQUESTED; RESULTS OF TREATMENT PROGRAM SHALL BE SHARED WITH HOSPITAL AND THE BOARD; SHALL OBTAIN BOARD APPROVAL BEFORE CHANGING PRACTICE; WILL OBTAIN A WRITTEN REPORT FROM HIS SUPERVISOR AND THE WASHINGTON MONITORED TREATMENT PROGRAM EVERY SIX MONTHS WHICH HE SHALL SUBMIT TO THE BOARD; MUST APPEAR BEFORE THE BOARD EVERY SIX MONTHS; MAY NOT REQUEST A MODIFICATION OF ORDER FOR ONE YEAR; MUST NOTIFY THE BOARD IF HE LEAVES THE STATE OR IF HE CHANGES ADDRESS; $500 FINE. ON 10/18/96 HIS REQUEST TO TERMINATE THIS ORDER GRANTED AND LICENSE UNRESTRICTED.

EKLAND, DAVID A MD WAS DISCIPLINED BY WASHINGTON ON FEBRUARY 20, 1987.
DISCIPLINARY ACTION: REPRIMAND
OFFENSE: SUBSTANDARD CARE, INCOMPETENCE, OR NEGLIGENCE
NOTES: ENGAGED IN UNSAFE AND UNPROFESSIONAL CONDUCT BY FAILING TO OPEN PACK A CONTAMINATED WOUND; FAILING TO ADMINISTER ANTIBIOTICS IN LIGHT OF OBVIOUS CONTAMINATION; FAILED TO PROVIDE FOLLOW-UP CARE WHEN PATIENT RETURNED TO HOSPITAL COMPLAINING OF PAIN; RESULT WAS DEATH OF THE PATIENT; BOARD ACTION RESULT OF MALPRACTICE SETTLEMENT; SHALL PREPARE A WRITTEN STATEMENT OF CURRENTLY ACCEPTED PROTOCOL FOR THE TREATMENT OF CONTAMINATED TRAUMATIC INJURIES

ELLOWAY, SIMON MD WAS DISCIPLINED BY WASHINGTON ON FEBRUARY 20, 1987.
DISCIPLINARY ACTION: RESTRICTION PLACED ON LICENSE
NOTES: SHALL NOT PERFORM ANY BREACH DELIVERIES; SHALL NOT RESUME THE PRACTICE OF OBSTETRICS WITHOUT AUTHORIZATION FROM THE BOARD WHICH WILL BE GRANTED WHEN THE BOARD RECEIVES DOCUMENTATION THAT HE HAS HAD ADEQUATE TRAINING IN HIGH RISK OBSTETRICS. ON 6/21/90 LIMITATIONS ON LICENSE REMOVED THAT PROHIBITED HIM FROM PERFORMING BREECH DELIVERIES AND FROM RESUMING THE PRACTICE OF OBSTETRICS WITHOUT BOARD ORDER.

EMERSON, LUTHER L MD, LICENSE NUMBER 0005316, OF BRATTLEBORO, VT, WAS DISCIPLINED BY VERMONT ON DECEMBER 2, 1992.
DISCIPLINARY ACTION: 6-MONTH LICENSE SUSPENSION; 36-MONTH PROBATION
OFFENSE: SUBSTANDARD CARE, INCOMPETENCE, OR NEGLIGENCE
NOTES: UNPROFESSIONAL CONDUCT IN THAT HIS METHADONE TREATMENT OF 18 HEROIN ADDICTS WAS WRONG AND ILLEGAL; SOUNDNESS OF MEDICAL JUDGEMENT IS QUESTIONABLE; SOMETIMES FAILS TO RECOGNIZE OR REACT TO SERIOUS DISEASE; EXHIBITED GROSS FAILURE TO USE AND EXERCISE THAT DEGREE OF CARE, SKILL, AND PROFICIENCY BY PRESCRIBING METHADONE FOR PATIENTS. LICENSE SUSPENDED FOR A PERIOD OF THREE YEARS, ALL STAYED BUT FOR A PERIOD OF SIX MONTHS. SHALL REMAIN ON PROBATION FOR THE ENTIRE THREE-YEAR PERIOD. LICENSE CONDITIONED AS FOLLOWS: SHALL FILE DUPLICATE PRESCRIPTIONS WITH THE BOARD FOR SCHEDULE II THROUGH IV CONTROLLED DRUGS; SHALL ATTEND CONTINUING MEDICAL EDUCATION PROGRAMS IN THE PROPER PRESCRIBING OF CONTROLLED SUBSTANCES AND INTERNAL MEDICINE; SHALL MAKE HIS MEDICAL RECORDS AVAILABLE TO A SPECIALIST IN INTERNAL MEDICINE WHO WILL REPORT QUARTERLY TO THE BOARD; SHALL COOPERATE WITH THE BRATTLEBORO MEDICAL COMMUNITY AND AREA NURSING HOME ADMINISTRATORS TO ALLEVIATE LOCAL NURSING HOME ADMITTING PROBLEMS. MAY PETITION FOR REMOVAL OF CONDITIONS IN THREE YEARS. THIS ORDER TAKES EFFECT IN 60 DAYS. HEARING PANEL STAYED ORDER PENDING APPEAL TO APPELLATE OFFICER ON 12/22/92. ON 8/11/93 ORDER REMANDED TO THE BOARD TO RECONSIDER ITS ORIGINAL ORDER AND TO MAKE ADDITIONAL FINDINGS. ON 12/9/93 BOARD REISSUED THE ORDER UNDER THE SAME CONDITIONS. CONDITIONS REMOVED ON 11/6/96.

EMERSON, LUTHER L MD OF 2201 S.W. HOLDEN ST. APT. D-208, SEATTLE, WA, WAS DISCIPLINED BY DEA ON DECEMBER 22, 1994.
DISCIPLINARY ACTION: RESTRICTION PLACED ON CONTROLLED SUBSTANCE LICENSE
OFFENSE: DISCIPLINARY ACTION BY ANOTHER STATE OR AGENCY
NOTES: STATE BOARD.

EMERSON, LUTHER LEE MD, LICENSE NUMBER 0115535, OF 2201 SW HOLDEN STREET, SEATTLE, WA, WAS DISCIPLINED BY NEW YORK ON AUGUST 24, 1995.
DISCIPLINARY ACTION: PROBATION
OFFENSE: DISCIPLINARY ACTION BY ANOTHER STATE OR AGENCY
NOTES: ACTION IN VERMONT FOR EXCESSIVELY AND IMPROPERLY PRESCRIBING METHADONE TO PATIENTS AND FILED A FALSE PHYSICAL FITNESS REPORT WHICH STATED THAT THE PATIENT WAS FREE OF ANY ADDICTIVE DRUGS. SHALL COMPLY WITH ANY PENALTY AND PROBATION TERMS IMPOSED BY ANY OTHER STATE BOARD UPON COMMENCING THE PRACTICE OF MEDICINE IN NEW YORK BEFORE THE YEAR 2000. PROBATION FOR A PERIOD OF TWO YEARS OR UNTIL THE YEAR 2000 WHICHEVER IS LONGER IN DURATION.

ENRILE, RODOLFO C MD WAS DISCIPLINED BY WISCONSIN ON AUGUST 30, 1994.
DISCIPLINARY ACTION: DENIAL OF NEW LICENSE
OFFENSE: PROVIDING FALSE INFORMATION TO THE BOARD
NOTES: ON 1/18/94 FALSIFIED HIS APPLICATION BY FAILING TO DISCLOSE THAT HE WAS A NAMED DEFENDANT IN A NEW YORK MALPRACTICE ACTION.

ENRILE, RODOLFO C MD OF ELMHURST, NY, WAS DISCIPLINED BY WASHINGTON ON SEPTEMBER 30, 1996.
DISCIPLINARY ACTION: REQUIRED TO TAKE ADDITIONAL MEDICAL EDUCATION
NOTES: LICENSE DISCIPLINED IN ANOTHER JURISDICTION. GRANTED A LICENSE TO PRACTICE MEDICINE, BUT PROHIBITED FROM DOING SO UNTIL HE COMPLETES 12 MONTHS OF POST-GRADUATE CLINICAL TRAINING.

EPSTEIN, H STEPHEN MD, LICENSE NUMBER 0010796, OF SEATTLE, WA, WAS DISCIPLINED BY WASHINGTON ON APRIL 21, 1995.
DISCIPLINARY ACTION: SURRENDER OF LICENSE
NOTES: AGREED TO RETIRE.

EPSTEIN, H STEPHEN MD, LICENSE NUMBER 0005178, OF 13030 MILITARY ROAD SOUTH, SEATTLE, WA, WAS DISCIPLINED BY HAWAII ON OCTOBER 30, 1996.
DISCIPLINARY ACTION: LICENSE REVOCATION
OFFENSE: SUBSTANDARD CARE, INCOMPETENCE, OR NEGLIGENCE
NOTES: PERFORMED SURGERIES THAT FAILED TO MEET THE

STANDARDS OF CARE OF A REASONABLY PRUDENT PHYSICIAN; VOLUNTARILY RETIRED FROM PRACTICE IN WASHINGTON ON 4/21/95. FAILED TO INFORM THE HAWAII BOARD OF THE WASHINGTON ORDER; AND DISCLOSED THAT HE SUFFERS FROM TOURRETTE'S SYNDROME THAT RENDERS HIM UNABLE TO PRACTICE MEDICINE WITH REASONABLE SKILL. SHALL NOT APPLY FOR REINSTATEMENT FOR AT LEAST FIVE YEARS; AND SHALL TURN IN ALL INDICIA OF LICENSURE TO THE BOARD WITHIN 30 DAYS.

ERICKSON, CLAYTON D MD WAS DISCIPLINED BY WASHINGTON ON APRIL 14, 1993.
DISCIPLINARY ACTION: EMERGENCY SUSPENSION
OFFENSE: SUBSTANCE ABUSE
NOTES: SINCE 9/8/89 HAD AN AGREEMENT WITH THE WASHINGTON MONITORED TREATMENT PROGRAM (WMTP) FOR ALCOHOL ABUSE; RELAPSED IN 10/92; IN 8-9/92 HE OBTAINED CONTROLLED SUBSTANCES, INCLUDING BUT NOT NECESSARILY LIMITED TO, APPROXIMATELY 20 VICODIN TABLETS, APPROXIMATELY 12 TYLOX CAPLETS AND APPROXIMATELY FIVE, 0.5 ML MORPHINE TUBEX SYRINGES CONTAINING 10 MG/ML OR MORPHINE FOR HIS OWN USE AND WITHOUT AUTHORIZATION OR PRESCRIPTION; FOLLOWING THIS RELAPSE HE ENTERED INPATIENT ALCOHOL TREATMENT ON 11/06/92 AND WAS DISCHARGED ON 2/25/93. ON 4/18/93 WMTP REPORTED HE HAD AGAIN RELAPSED.

ERICKSON, CLAYTON D MD, LICENSE NUMBER 0014951, OF SEATTLE, WA, WAS DISCIPLINED BY WASHINGTON ON MARCH 10, 1995.
DISCIPLINARY ACTION: LICENSE SUSPENSION
NOTES: INDEFINITE SUSPENSION. SHALL ENTER INTO A CONTRACT WITH THE PHYSICIAN'S HEALTH PROGRAM.

ERICKSON, CLAYTON DALE MD OF 624 DALEY STREET #2, EDMONDS, WA, WAS DISCIPLINED BY DEA ON JULY 27, 1995.
DISCIPLINARY ACTION: SURRENDER OF CONTROLLED SUBSTANCE LICENSE
OFFENSE: DISCIPLINARY ACTION BY ANOTHER STATE OR AGENCY
NOTES: STATE BOARD.

ESPINOSA, KARLA MARIE MD WAS DISCIPLINED BY WASHINGTON ON JUNE 16, 1992.
DISCIPLINARY ACTION: RESTRICTION PLACED ON LICENSE
NOTES: CONDITIONAL LICENSE ISSUED WITH SPECIFIC CONDITIONS.

FAIRFAX, GEORGE T MD WAS DISCIPLINED BY WASHINGTON ON MAY 21, 1993.
DISCIPLINARY ACTION: SURRENDER OF LICENSE
OFFENSE: SUBSTANDARD CARE, INCOMPETENCE, OR NEGLIGENCE
NOTES: BOARD INVESTIGATION BASED UPON THE MANDATORY REPORT BY HIS PROFESSIONAL liability INSURANCE CARRIER REGARDING THE RESULT OF A SETTLEMENT REACHED IN A PROFESSIONAL LAWSUIT BROUGHT AGAINST HIM ALLEGING A LACK OF REASONABLE PRUDENCE IN PROVIDING MEDICAL CARE. IT IS SPECIFICALLY AGREED AND UNDERSTOOD BY THE PARTIES THAT THIS ORDER SHALL NOT BE CONSTRUED AS AN ADMISSION OF GUILT, LIABILITY, OR WRONG DOING. VOLUNTARY RETIREMENT EFFECTIVE 4/19/93 AND HAS NO PLANS TO RESUME PRACTICE SUBSEQUENT TO THAT DATE: RETIREMENT SHALL BE PERMANENT; MAY RESUME PRACTICE ONLY WITH PRIOR BOARD APPROVAL; SHALL NOTIFY THE BOARD IF HE PLANS TO RESUME PRACTICE IN THIS STATE OR ANY OTHER JURISDICTION; BOARD MAY RELEASE ANY INFORMATION RELATING TO THE INVESTIGATION TO THE PROPER LICENSING AUTHORITIES IN ANY JURISDICTION. INVESTIGATION SHALL BE TERMINATED.

FARLEY, PATRICK CLARE MD, LICENSE NUMBER 0030541, OF SEATTLE, WA, WAS DISCIPLINED BY WASHINGTON ON JULY 27, 1994.
DISCIPLINARY ACTION: EMERGENCY SUSPENSION
OFFENSE: PHYSICAL OR MENTAL ILLNESS INHIBITING THE ABILITY TO PRACTICE WITH SKILL AND SAFETY
NOTES: UNABLE TO PRACTICE WITH REASONABLE SKILL AND SAFETY DUE TO A MENTAL OR PHYSICAL CONDITION, HE HAS COMMITTED ACTS OF MORAL TURPITUDE AND HE MISREPRESENTED A FACT IN HIS APPLICATION FOR A LICENSE TO PRACTICE MEDICINE.

FARLEY, PATRICK CLARE MD, LICENSE NUMBER 00G2696, OF SEATTLE, WA, WAS DISCIPLINED BY TEXAS ON OCTOBER 27, 1994.
DISCIPLINARY ACTION: EMERGENCY SUSPENSION
OFFENSE: DISCIPLINARY ACTION BY ANOTHER STATE OR AGENCY
NOTES: AVAILABLE EVIDENCE AND INFORMATION INDICATE THE FOLLOWING: HAS ENGAGED IN CONDUCT INDICATIVE OF A MENTAL CONDITION WHICH CAUSES HIM TO BE UNABLE TO PRACTICE WITH REASONABLE SKILL AND SAFETY; HAS UNDERGONE AN INDEPENDENT PSYCHIATRIC EXAM WHICH LED TO A DIAGNOSIS OF SUCH A MENTAL CONDITION; ON 7/27/94 WASHINGTON SUMMARILY SUSPENDED HIS LICENSE BASED ON THIS.

FARLEY, PATRICK CLARE MD, LICENSE NUMBER 0030541, OF EL PASO, TX, WAS DISCIPLINED BY WASHINGTON ON APRIL 19, 1996.
DISCIPLINARY ACTION: LICENSE SUSPENSION
NOTES: INDEFINITE SUSPENSION PENDING THE COMPLETION OF A NUMBER OF CONDITIONS.

FARLEY, PATRICK CLARE MD, LICENSE NUMBER 00G2696, WAS DISCIPLINED BY TEXAS ON AUGUST 17, 1996.
DISCIPLINARY ACTION: 60-MONTH PROBATION; REQUIRED TO TAKE ADDITIONAL MEDICAL EDUCATION
OFFENSE: PHYSICAL OR MENTAL ILLNESS INHIBITING THE ABILITY TO PRACTICE WITH SKILL AND SAFETY
NOTES: ON 10/27/94 TEMPORARILY SUSPENDED BY THE TEXAS BOARD BASED ON AN ASSAULT AND CRIMINAL TRESPASS CONVICTION IN SEATTLE IN 1994 AND INABILITY TO PRACTICE BY REASON OF A MENTAL CONDITION; AFTER 7/27/94 ENTERED TREATMENT FOR BI-POLAR DISORDER; THREE PHYSICIANS ON 4/05/96, 7/09/96, AND 7/22/96 EXPRESSED THEIR OPINION THAT HE IS ABLE TO PRACTICE MEDICINE; MET ALL REQUIREMENTS SET FOR THE LIFTING OF SUSPENSION OF WASHINGTON ACTION. SUSPENSION STAYED. CONDITIONS OF PROBATION: SHALL NOT PRACTICE MEDICINE IN TEXAS UNTIL HE REQUESTS IN WRITING TO THE BOARD TO RESUME THE PRACTICE OF MEDICINE IN TEXAS AND PROVIDES SUFFICIENT EVIDENCE AND INFORMATION WHICH INDICATES THAT THE SUSPENSION PREVIOUSLY IMPOSED ON HIS WASHINGTON LICENSE HAS BEEN STAYED OR LIFTED; SHALL CONTINUE TO RECEIVE CARE AND TREATMENT FROM A BOARD APPROVED PSYCHIATRIST NO LESS THAN ONCE PER MONTH WHO SHALL PROVIDE QUARTERLY REPORTS; SHALL PARTICIPATE IN ALCOHOL OR DRUG SCREENS; HIS MEDICAL PRACTICE, INCLUDING ANY OFFICE AND SURGICAL PRACTICE, SHALL BE MONITORED BY A BOARD APPROVED TEXAS PHYSICIAN WITH QUARTERLY REPORTS TO THE BOARD; SHALL OBTAIN AT LEAST 50 HOURS PER YEAR OF CONTINUING MEDICAL EDUCATION; SHALL APPEAR BEFORE THE BOARD AT LEAST ONE TIME PER YEAR OR UPON REQUEST; SHALL COOPERATE WITH THE BOARD IN VERIFYING COMPLIANCE INCLUDING PROVIDING COPIES OF MEDICAL RELEASES UPON REQUEST; SHALL COMPLY WITH THE WASHINGTON ORDER; SHALL GIVE A COPY OF THIS ORDER TO ANY HEALTH CARE ENTITY WHERE HE HAS PRIVILEGES; SHALL PROVIDE A COPY OF THIS ORDER TO ANYONE REQUESTING IT WITHIN 10 DAYS; TIME PERIOD OUT OF

TEXAS DOES NOT COUNT TOWARD RESTRICTION; SHALL INFORM THE BOARD OF CHANGE OF ADDRESS WITHIN 10 DAYS OR IF HE LEAVES THE STATE; SHALL NOT SEEK MODIFICATION FOR ONE YEAR.

FARLEY, PATRICK CLARE MD, LICENSE NUMBER 0030541, OF EL PASO, TX, WAS DISCIPLINED BY WASHINGTON ON SEPTEMBER 25, 1996.
NOTES: PREVIOUS SUSPENSION NOW RESTRICTED TO THE TERMS OF THE 4/96 CONSENT ORDER.

FELDZAMEN, ALVIN N DO WAS DISCIPLINED BY WASHINGTON ON MAY 18, 1993.
OFFENSE: DISCIPLINARY ACTION BY ANOTHER STATE OR AGENCY
NOTES: ACTION IN CALIFORNIA CONCERNING THE ISSUANCE OF CONTROLLED SUBSTANCE PRESCRIPTIONS WITHOUT LEGITIMATE MEDICAL PURPOSE AND NO MEDICAL INDICATION FOR THE PRESCRIPTION WHICH RESULTED IN REVOCATION, STAYED WITH CONDITIONS. IN WASHINGTON SUSPENSION STAYED; PRIOR TO ACTIVE PRACTICE IN WASHINGTON, MUST APPEAR BEFORE THE BOARD FOR A HEARING REGARDING HIS COMPLIANCE WITH THE CALIFORNIAN CONDITIONS; AND MAY PETITION THE BOARD FOR FULL REINSTATEMENT OF LICENSURE UPON SUCCESSFUL COMPLETION WITH THE TERMS OF PROBATION IN CALIFORNIA. LICENSE BASED ON 8/12/94 CALIFORNIA REINSTATEMENT. WASHINGTON LICENSE REINSTATED ON 10/14/94. SHALL PROVIDE THE BOARD WITH CURRENT HOME AND BUSINESS ADDRESSES AND CHANGE OF ADDRESS.

FERNANDEZ, CEFERINO MD WAS DISCIPLINED BY WASHINGTON ON JUNE 8, 1987.
DISCIPLINARY ACTION: RESTRICTION PLACED ON CONTROLLED SUBSTANCE LICENSE; MONITORING OF PHYSICIAN
OFFENSE: OVERPRESCRIBING OR MISPRESCRIBING DRUGS
NOTES: ALLEGEDLY PRESCRIBED FOR NONTHERAPEUTIC USE TO NUMEROUS PATIENTS IN 1985 AND 1986 INCLUDING TYLENOL 4 AND AMBENYL; SHALL NOT PRESCRIBE ANY CLASS II OR III NARCOTICS UNLESS HE RECEIVES PERMISSION FROM BOARD PRIOR TO PRESCRIBING AND WILL APPEAR IN PERSON TO REQUEST SUCH PERMISSION; AGREES TO PRACTICE REVIEW IN THREE MONTHS

FERNANDEZ, CEFERINO A MD, LICENSE NUMBER 0045790, OF SEATTLE, WA, WAS DISCIPLINED BY FLORIDA ON DECEMBER 19, 1990.
DISCIPLINARY ACTION: SURRENDER OF LICENSE
NOTES: IN LIEU OF FURTHER PROSECUTION, AGREED TO NEVER AGAIN APPLY FOR LICENSURE IN FLORIDA.

FERNANDEZ, CEFERINO A MD OF 7909 RAINIER AVENUE SOUTH, SEATTLE, WA, WAS DISCIPLINED BY DEA ON NOVEMBER 9, 1995.
DISCIPLINARY ACTION: RESTRICTION PLACED ON CONTROLLED SUBSTANCE LICENSE
OFFENSE: PROFESSIONAL MISCONDUCT
NOTES: ALLEGED CONTROLLED SUBSTANCE VIOLATIONS.

FIELDS, ALVIN MD, LICENSE NUMBER 0003751, OF SEATTLE, WA, WAS DISCIPLINED BY WASHINGTON ON OCTOBER 19, 1990.
DISCIPLINARY ACTION: 36-MONTH PROBATION; RESTRICTION PLACED ON LICENSE
OFFENSE: OVERPRESCRIBING OR MISPRESCRIBING DRUGS
NOTES: PRESCRIBED BIPHETAMINE 20, IONAMIN 30 AND/OR DIDREX 50 MG FOR ONE PATIENT FROM 8/76 THROUGH 3/1/85 IN DOSAGES IN EXCESS OF THE NORMAL RECOMMENDED AMOUNT. CONDITIONS OF PROBATION: SHALL SUBMIT TRIPLICATE PRESCRIPTIONS ON ALL CONTROLLED SUBSTANCES SCHEDULE II THROUGH V; SHALL NOT PRESCRIBE SCHEDULE II DRUGS FOR MORE THAN THREE DAYS, WITH RENEWALS ONLY AFTER APPROPRIATE CONSULTATION; SHALL NOT PRESCRIBE AMPHETAMINES; SHALL COMPLETE 50 HOURS OF CONTINUING MEDICAL EDUCATION IN THE AREA OF CHEMICAL DEPENDENCY; SHALL OBTAIN PRIOR APPROVAL TO PRACTICE IN ANY SETTING OTHER THAN CHEC MEDICAL CENTERS; SHALL APPEAR ANNUALLY BEFORE BOARD TO PROVE COMPLIANCE; BOARD MAY INSPECT RECORDS AND REVIEW OTHER ASPECTS OF PRACTICE; SHALL INFORM BOARD IF HE CHANGES ADDRESS OR LEAVES THE STATE; MAY NOT REQUEST MODIFICATION FOR ONE YEAR. ON 1/15/93 FOUND IN COMPLIANCE WITH THIS ORDER; ORDER MODIFIED SO HE SHALL COMPLETE 50 HOURS OF CONTINUING MEDICAL EDUCATION CREDITS IN CATEGORY I, II OR V WHICH SPECIFICALLY DEAL WITH CHEMICAL DEPENDENCY DURING THIS PENDENCY OF PROBATION IN ADDITION TO THE CONTINUING EDUCATION REQUIRED FOR LICENSURE RENEWAL.

FLEMING, PETER V MD, LICENSE NUMBER 0029039, OF NEW YORK, NY, WAS DISCIPLINED BY WASHINGTON ON MAY 31, 1996.
OFFENSE: DISCIPLINARY ACTION BY ANOTHER STATE OR AGENCY
NOTES: ACTION IN NEW YORK. AGREED ORDER REQUIRING HIM TO COMPLY WITH THE TERMS AND CONDITIONS OF AN ORDER OF THE NEW YORK BOARD. ON 7/10/97 BOARD GRANTED HIS REQUEST TO TERMINATE THIS ORDER AND LICENSE IS UNRESTRICTED.

FOWLER, FRANKLIN S JR MD, LICENSE NUMBER 0012057, OF STANWOOD, WA, WAS DISCIPLINED BY WASHINGTON ON MAY 3, 1991.
DISCIPLINARY ACTION: EMERGENCY SUSPENSION
OFFENSE: SUBSTANDARD CARE, INCOMPETENCE, OR NEGLIGENCE
NOTES: ALLEGATIONS OF PERFORMING AN IN-OFFICE OPEN BREAST BIOPSY USING RESULTS OF ULTRASOUND/SONOGRAPHIC TESTING RATHER THAN AVAILABLE MAMMOGRAPHY X-RAY PROCEDURES; THIS PATIENT WAS NOT TRANSFERRED TO HOSPITAL IN A TIMELY MANNER AND CONTINUED TO HEMORRHAGE WITHOUT TREATMENT FOR CONTINUING BLOOD LOSS AND LOW BLOOD PRESSURE, RESULTING IN A BLOOD LOSS SHOCK CONDITION; SECOND PATIENT SEEN FIVE TIMES FOR COMPLAINTS OF ABDOMINAL PAIN WAS NOT CORRECTLY DIAGNOSED OR TREATED; A THIRD PATIENT WITH A HISTORY OF CONGESTIVE HEART FAILURE WAS NOT DIAGNOSED OR TREATED CORRECTLY; CONTROLLED SUBSTANCES PURCHASED OVER A PERIOD OF SEVEN MONTHS WERE NOT PROPERLY RECORDED, AND DARVON, NOR WERE DISPENSING RECORDS MAINTAINED.

FOWLER, FRANKLIN S JR MD, LICENSE NUMBER 0012057, OF STANWOOD, WA, WAS DISCIPLINED BY WASHINGTON ON JULY 24, 1991.
DISCIPLINARY ACTION: LICENSE REVOCATION
OFFENSE: SUBSTANDARD CARE, INCOMPETENCE, OR NEGLIGENCE
NOTES: PHYSICIAN CANNOT PRACTICE WITHOUT UNDUE RISK OF HARM TO PATIENTS (INCLUDING INJURY TO ONE PATIENT AND DEATH OF ANOTHER), NEGLIGENCE, INCOMPETENCE AND/OR MALPRACTICE; AND VIOLATIONS RELATING TO DRUG DISPENSING AND PRESCRIBING. IF HE DOES NOT SURRENDER HIS LICENSE WITHIN 10 DAYS OF THE RECEIPT OF THIS ORDER, HIS LICENSE WILL BE REVOKED, WITH NO RIGHT TO REAPPLY FOR A MINIMUM OF TWO YEARS FROM THE DATE OF THIS ORDER, AND UNTIL HE CAN PROVIDE EVIDENCE OF REHABILITATION TO THE BOARD WHICH SHALL INCLUDE: SUCCESSFUL COMPLETION OF A REMEDIAL EDUCATION PROGRAM APPROVED BY THE BOARD; PASSAGE OF THE SPEX EXAMINATION; PROOF OF REHABILITATION. HE APPEALED THE BOARD'S ORDER TO THE SNOHOMISH COUNTY SUPERIOR COURT. BY

ORAL DECISION IN 4/92 THE COURT REMANDED THIS MATTER TO THE BOARD FOR REVIEW OF THE PREVIOUS SANCTIONS. EFFECTIVE 5/15/92, THE BOARD ORDERED THAT HIS LICENSE BE SUSPENDED UNTIL HE HAD COMPLIED WITH CERTAIN CONDITIONS.

FOWLER, FRANKLIN S MD, LICENSE NUMBER 0G17405, OF STANWOOD, WA, WAS DISCIPLINED BY CALIFORNIA ON JUNE 25, 1993.
DISCIPLINARY ACTION: LICENSE SUSPENSION
NOTES: SUSPENSION WITH CONDITIONS PRECEDENT.

FREDRIKSON, STEVEN E MD, LICENSE NUMBER 0017093, OF PORT ORCHARD, WA, WAS DISCIPLINED BY WASHINGTON ON DECEMBER 18, 1992.
DISCIPLINARY ACTION: RESTRICTION PLACED ON LICENSE
OFFENSE: SUBSTANDARD CARE, INCOMPETENCE, OR NEGLIGENCE
NOTES: NEGLIGENCE. SHALL BECOME RE-CERTIFIED IN FAMILY PRACTICE MEDICINE. ON 10/9/95 FOUND IN COMPLIANCE WITH THIS ORDER BUT ORDER MODIFIED TO REQUIRE ADDITIONAL REVIEW OF HIS CHARTS BY ANOTHER PHYSICIAN. ON 11/8/96 HIS REQUEST TO TERMINATE THIS ORDER GRANTED AND LICENSE UNRESTRICTED.

FRIEDLAND, THOMAS MD WAS DISCIPLINED BY WASHINGTON ON SEPTEMBER 7, 1989.
DISCIPLINARY ACTION: EMERGENCY SUSPENSION
OFFENSE: SUBSTANCE ABUSE
NOTES: ALLEGATIONS OF ALCOHOL ADDICTION.

FRIEDLAND, THOMAS MD WAS DISCIPLINED BY WASHINGTON ON NOVEMBER 22, 1989.
DISCIPLINARY ACTION: MONITORING OF PHYSICIAN
OFFENSE: SUBSTANCE ABUSE
NOTES: IMPAIRED PHYSICIAN BY VIRTUE OF ALCOHOL ADDICTION. FIVE YEAR SUSPENSION STAYED UNDER THE FOLLOWING TERMS AND CONDITIONS: SHALL ENTER INTO A CONTRACT WITH THE WASHINGTON MONITORED TREATMENT PROGRAM (WMTP) AND COMPLY WITH ITS CONDITIONS FOR A PERIOD OF NO LESS THAN THE TIME DURING WHICH HIS LICENSE SHALL REMAIN SUSPENDED WITH REPORTS EVERY SIX MONTHS; SHALL BE SUBJECT TO PRACTICE REVIEWS UPON REQUEST WITH REPORTS EVERY SIX MONTHS; SHALL APPEAR ONCE EVERY SIX MONTHS BEFORE THE BOARD FOR REVIEWS OF HIS PROGRESS AND COMPLIANCE WITH THE CONDITIONS OF THIS ORDER.

FROMMLET, MICHAEL MD OF CAMAS, WA, WAS DISCIPLINED BY WASHINGTON ON OCTOBER 27, 1995.
DISCIPLINARY ACTION: DENIAL OF NEW LICENSE

GAHRINGER, JOHN E MD, LICENSE NUMBER 0004174, WAS DISCIPLINED BY WASHINGTON ON DECEMBER 14, 1989.
DISCIPLINARY ACTION: RESTRICTION PLACED ON LICENSE; RESTRICTION PLACED ON CONTROLLED SUBSTANCE LICENSE
OFFENSE: OVERPRESCRIBING OR MISPRESCRIBING DRUGS
NOTES: PRESCRIBED VARIOUS DRUGS FOR PATIENTS IN EXCESSIVE AMOUNTS, FOR EXCESSIVE PERIODS OF TIME, AND IN CONTRAINDICATED CONSIDERATIONS; HIS MEDICAL RECORDS FOR PATIENTS REVEAL EXCESSIVE ADMINISTRATION OF CONTROLLED SUBSTANCES, INCLUDING BUT NOT LIMITED TO EXCESSIVE PRESCRIBING AND ADMINISTRATION OF DEMEROL, AND OTHER LEGEND DRUGS; USE OF BICILLIN INJECTION IN CONJUNCTION WITH ORAL PENICILLIN A COMBINATION OF DRUGS WHICH RAISES THE BOARD'S CONCERN WITH HIS PRESCRIBING PRACTICE; THE PROLONGED USE OF METHADONE ON AT LEAST ONE PATIENT WHEN HE IS NOT OFFICIALLY RECOGNIZED AS A METHADONE PROGRAM RAISES BOARD CONCERN; HIS MEDICAL RECORDS ARE INADEQUATE WITH RESPECT TO DESCRIBING THE CLINICAL IMPRESSIONS AND MEDICAL INDICATIONS FOR THE MEDICATIONS BEING PRESCRIBED, DISPENSED, AND ADMINISTERED; RECORDS ARE DEVOID OF OR SUBSTANTIALLY LIMITED IN DEMONSTRATING ANY FINDING UPON PHYSICAL EXAMINATION OF PATIENTS AND INADEQUATE IN THEIR FAILURE TO DEMONSTRATE MONITORING OF THE PATIENTS ON MEDICATIONS PRESCRIBED, DISPENSED, OR ADMINISTERED; RECORDS FAIL TO INCLUDE A PLAN OF TREATMENT; HAS VOLUNTARILY CEASED PRESCRIBING SCHEDULE II AND III CONTROLLED SUBSTANCES IN 1988; UPON RENEWAL OF DEA APPLICATION, APPLIED ONLY FOR ABILITY TO PRESCRIBE SCHEDULE IV AND V CONTROLLED SUBSTANCES. LICENSE SUSPENSION FOR A MINIMUM OF 10 YEARS, STAYED UNDER THE FOLLOWING TERMS AND CONDITIONS: SHALL SURRENDER HIS DEA REGISTRATION WITH THE EXCEPTION OF SCHEDULE V CONTROLLED SUBSTANCES, WHICH HE MAY PRESCRIBE AND ADMINISTER WITH THE LIMITATION OF NO PRESCRIBING, DISPENSING, OR ADMINISTERING OF DIHYDROCODEINE COUGH SYRUPS AND LOMOTIL, IN ITS BRAND NAME OR GENERIC FORM; SHALL ADMINISTER NO INJECTIONS IN HIS OFFICE PRACTICE, WITH THE EXCEPTION OF IMMUNIZATIONS, UNLESS HE FIRST RECEIVES A RECOMMENDATION AND AUTHORIZATION FROM A CONSULTANT AND THE RECOMMENDATION AND AUTHORIZATION SHALL BE DOCUMENTED IN THE PATIENTS' CHARTS; SHALL USE TRIPLICATE PRESCRIPTION SCRIPTS FOR ALL MEDICATIONS PRESCRIBED; SHALL FOR EVERY NEW PATIENT, OBTAIN A COMPLETE HISTORY, PERFORM A PHYSICAL, AND DOCUMENT HIS FINDINGS ON THE PATIENTS' CHARTS; SHALL COOPERATE IN FULL WITH RANDOM PRACTICE REVIEWS CONDUCTED A MINIMUM OF FOUR TIMES PER YEAR; MAY PETITION FOR MODIFICATION OF THE TERMS AND CONDITIONS IN NO LESS THAN 24 MONTHS; SHALL PERSONALLY APPEAR BEFORE THE BOARD IN SIX MONTHS; MUST SUBMIT SATISFACTORY PROOF TO THE BOARD THAT HE HAS TAKEN ACTIONS TO PREVENT THE CONDUCT WHICH RESULTED IN THIS ORDER PRIOR TO GRANTING REINSTATEMENT OF HIS LICENSE.

GAHRINGER, JOHN E MD, LICENSE NUMBER 0004174, OF EAST WENATCHEE, WA, WAS DISCIPLINED BY WASHINGTON ON AUGUST 16, 1991.
DISCIPLINARY ACTION: EMERGENCY SUSPENSION
OFFENSE: FAILURE TO COMPLY WITH A PREVIOUS BOARD ORDER
NOTES: MAY HAVE VIOLATED BOARD ORDER ISSUED ON 12/14/89 BY INJECTING MEDICATIONS; HIS MANNER OF PRESCRIBING, ADMINISTERING, OR DISPENSING MEDICATIONS INDICATED BY THE RECORDS REVIEWED AND BASED UPON HIS TESTIMONY AT THE COMPLIANCE HEARING POSE A DANGER TO THE PUBLIC HEALTH, SAFETY AND WELFARE SUFFICIENT TO WARRANT IMMEDIATE ACTION.

GAHRINGER, JOHN E MD, LICENSE NUMBER 0004174, OF EAST WENATCHEE, WA, WAS DISCIPLINED BY WASHINGTON ON NOVEMBER 15, 1991.
DISCIPLINARY ACTION: SURRENDER OF LICENSE
NOTES: RETIREMENT TO BECOME EFFECTIVE 10 DAYS FROM DATE OF ORDER. AGREES THAT RETIREMENT SHALL BE PERMANENT, AND SHALL NOT RENEW OR REAPPLY FOR LICENSURE.

GANTI, SHASHI DR, DATE OF BIRTH MARCH 15, 1954, LICENSE NUMBER 0059944, OF 2035 HAMBURG TURNPIKE, WAYNE, NJ, WAS DISCIPLINED BY NEW JERSEY ON JANUARY 10, 1995.
DISCIPLINARY ACTION: LICENSE SUSPENSION
OFFENSE: DISCIPLINARY ACTION BY ANOTHER STATE OR AGENCY
NOTES: PENDING ACTION BY THE CALIFORNIA BOARD. THIS

- WASHINGTON -

SUSPENSION PENDING RESOLUTION OF THE CALIFORNIA MATTER. UPON RESOLUTION SHALL NOTIFY BOARD TO DETERMINE WHETHER THE SUSPENSION SHOULD BE LIFTED. SHALL SUBMIT WRITTEN REPORTS OF PROGRESS OF CALIFORNIA ACTION EVERY SIX MONTHS.

GANTI, SHASHI MD, LICENSE NUMBER 0162239, OF BOX 53264, BELLEVUE, WA, WAS DISCIPLINED BY NEW YORK ON JULY 25, 1995.
DISCIPLINARY ACTION: SURRENDER OF LICENSE
OFFENSE: DISCIPLINARY ACTION BY ANOTHER STATE OR AGENCY
NOTES: ACTION IN CALIFORNIA FOR COMMITTING SEXUAL ASSAULT AND FOR HIS NEGLIGENT CARE AND TREATMENT OF A PATIENT.

GARCIA, GEORGE L MD, LICENSE NUMBER 0026827, OF TRENTON, MO, WAS DISCIPLINED BY WASHINGTON ON DECEMBER 15, 1995.
NOTES: AGREED TO SEVERAL TERMS AND CONDITIONS, INCLUDING COMPLYING WITH A CONTRACT SIGNED WITH THE MISSOURI PHYSICIANS' HEALTH PROGRAM.

GEHLEN, CHARLES J MD, LICENSE NUMBER 0005295, OF SEATTLE, WA, WAS DISCIPLINED BY WASHINGTON ON MARCH 4, 1994.
DISCIPLINARY ACTION: PROBATION; FINE
OFFENSE: OVERPRESCRIBING OR MISPRESCRIBING DRUGS
NOTES: ALLEGATIONS OF NON-THERAPEUTIC PRESCRIBING. FIVE YEAR SUSPENSION STAYED. PRESCRIBING PRIVILEGES ARE LIMITED AND ALL PRESCRIPTIONS MUST BE WRITTEN ON TRIPLICATE PRESCRIPTION FORMS. MUST APPEAR ANNUALLY BEFORE BOARD, UNDERGO QUARTERLY PRACTICE REVIEWS AND PAY A $5000 FINE.

GILES, ROY C MD, LICENSE NUMBER 0008708, OF BELLINGHAM, WA, WAS DISCIPLINED BY WASHINGTON ON MARCH 11, 1991.
DISCIPLINARY ACTION: EMERGENCY SUSPENSION
OFFENSE: SUBSTANDARD CARE, INCOMPETENCE, OR NEGLIGENCE
NOTES: ALLEGATIONS OF NONRESPONSIVENESS AS AN ANESTHESIOLOGIST DURING A C-SECTION, CREATING AN UNREASONABLE RISK FOR THE PATIENT; ALSO FAILED TO PROVIDE A FULL AND COMPLETE EXPLANATION OF THE SITUATION.

GLEESON, FRANK G MD, LICENSE NUMBER 0005873, OF SEATTLE, WA, WAS DISCIPLINED BY WASHINGTON ON SEPTEMBER 21, 1990.
DISCIPLINARY ACTION: 60-MONTH PROBATION
OFFENSE: OVERPRESCRIBING OR MISPRESCRIBING DRUGS
NOTES: PROBLEMS WITH PRESCRIBING PRACTICES. ON 10/15/92 BOARD ORDERED THAT HE SHALL COMPLY WITH THE CLARIFIED TERMS OF THIS ORDER. ON 3/18/93 ORDER MODIFIED TO REDUCE THE NUMBER OF CONTINUING MEDICAL EDUCATION HOURS ON THE SUBJECT OF PAIN AND ADDICTION FROM 50 TO 20 TO BE COMPLETED BY 2/6/94 AND THAT HE SHALL APPEAR BEFORE THE BOARD FOR A COMPLIANCE APPEARANCE IN 12 MONTHS. ON 5/27/94 HE WAS FOUND TO BE IN COMPLIANCE WITH THIS ORDER WITH THE EXCEPTION OF THE PRESCRIPTION REQUIREMENT. FURTHER PRESCRIPTION REQUIREMENTS WERE ORDERED AND HE SHALL APPEAR BEFORE THE BOARD AS REQUIRED. ON 12/9/96 HIS REQUEST TO TERMINATE THIS ORDER GRANTED AND LICENSE UNRESTRICTED.

GOSS, SANDRA G MD, LICENSE NUMBER 0028791, OF EDMONDS, WA, WAS DISCIPLINED BY WASHINGTON ON MARCH 8, 1996.
DISCIPLINARY ACTION: REQUIRED TO TAKE ADDITIONAL MEDICAL EDUCATION; MONITORING OF PHYSICIAN
NOTES: FIVE YEAR RESTRICTED LICENSE: SHALL ATTEND AN EXTENDED REFRESHER COURSE IN OBSTETRICS; SHALL RETAIN A PRECEPTOR FOR THE PURPOSE OF IMPROVING AND MONITORING HIS OBSTETRICAL PRACTICE.

GRADIN, WESLEY C MD, LICENSE NUMBER 0024901, OF PUYALLUP, WA, WAS DISCIPLINED BY WASHINGTON ON AUGUST 19, 1994.
DISCIPLINARY ACTION: 36-MONTH PROBATION; FINE
OFFENSE: PROFESSIONAL MISCONDUCT
NOTES: ALLOWED OFFICE PERSONNEL TO SEE PATIENTS IN HIS ABSENCE FOR SEVERAL DAYS WITHOUT THE SUPERVISION OF A LICENSED MEDICAL DOCTOR, CERTIFIED PHYSICIAN ASSISTANT, OR CERTIFIED FAMILY NURSE PRACTITIONER. SHALL REFUND OR CREDIT WITHIN 90 DAYS ALL FEES CHARGED THE PATIENTS SEEN BY HIS STAFF DURING HIS ABSENCE. SHALL PROVIDE ADEQUATE COVERAGE AND SUPERVISION OF HIS PRACTICE DURING ANY FUTURE ABSENCES AND SHALL SUBMIT REQUIRED DOCUMENTATION CONCERNING HIS PRACTICE TO THE COMMISSION AS ORDERED. SHALL APPEAR BEFORE THE COMMISSION IN SIX MONTHS, SHALL ALLOW COMPLIANCE AUDITS OF HIS PRACTICE, SHALL COMPLETE 10 CONTINUING MEDICAL EDUCATION HOURS IN THE AREA OF MEDICAL ETHICS, AND SHALL PAY A $5000 FINE WITHIN 90 DAYS. ON 11/7/95 REQUEST TO TERMINATE THIS ORDER DENIED ON 4/4/96 REQUEST TO TERMINATE ORDER GRANTED AND LICENSE UNRESTRICTED.

GRAY, CARROL LEE MD, LICENSE NUMBER 0020594, OF LACEY, WA, WAS DISCIPLINED BY WASHINGTON ON JUNE 28, 1994.
DISCIPLINARY ACTION: LICENSE SUSPENSION
NOTES: MAY APPLY FOR REINSTATEMENT AFTER HE HAS SATISFIED THE TREATMENT AND MONITORING REQUIREMENTS AND SUBMITS PROOF HE IS FIT TO PRACTICE.

GRAY, CARROLL LEE MD, LICENSE NUMBER 0020594, OF LACEY, WA, WAS DISCIPLINED BY WASHINGTON ON DECEMBER 14, 1993.
DISCIPLINARY ACTION: EMERGENCY SUSPENSION
NOTES: ALLEGATIONS OF IMPAIRMENT. INDEFINITE SUSPENSION. ON 6/28/94, BOARD DECIDED THAT HE MAY APPLY FOR REINSTATEMENT AFTER HE HAS SATISFIED THE TREATMENT AND MONITORING REQUIREMENTS SET FORTH BY THE WASHINGTON PHYSICIAN'S HEALTH PROGRAM AND SUBMITS PROOF THAT HE IS FIT TO PRACTICE. THE BOARD MAY IMPOSE OTHER CONDITIONS OR RESTRICTIONS WHEN OR IF IT DECIDES TO REINSTATE HIS LICENSE.

GRAY, CARROLL LEE MD, DATE OF BIRTH SEPTEMBER 8, 1940, LICENSE NUMBER 0015078, OF SEATTLE, WA, WAS DISCIPLINED BY NORTH CAROLINA ON JUNE 5, 1995.
DISCIPLINARY ACTION: LICENSE SUSPENSION
NOTES: INDEFINITE SUSPENSION.

GRUNNER, ANTONIN J MD WAS DISCIPLINED BY WASHINGTON ON NOVEMBER 8, 1990.
NOTES: SHALL COMPLY WITH THE SUMMARY SUSPENSION ORDER OF 7/13/90 IN FULL, INCLUDING LOCATING AND SURRENDERING BOTH PARTS OF HIS LICENSE AND COOPERATING IN FULL WITH RANDOM, UNANNOUNCED INSPECTIONS BY BOARD STAFF TO CONFIRM COMPLIANCE.

GRUNNER, ANTONIN J MD, LICENSE NUMBER 0021250, OF BELLINGHAM, WA, WAS DISCIPLINED BY WASHINGTON ON FEBRUARY 20, 1991.
DISCIPLINARY ACTION: LICENSE REVOCATION
OFFENSE: FAILURE TO COMPLY WITH A PREVIOUS BOARD ORDER
NOTES: FAILURE TO COMPLY WITH PREVIOUS BOARD ORDERS, INCLUDING ORDER OF 10/15/87, INABILITY TO TELL THE TRUTH, THE POSSIBILITY OF MENTAL IMPAIRMENT IN ADDITION TO ALCOHOL ADDICTION, AND SEVERAL FAILED ATTEMPTS AT HIS TREATMENT FOR ADDICTION. MAY NOT REAPPLY FOR LICENSURE FOR A MINIMUM OF TWO YEARS FROM THE DATE OF THIS ORDER AND UNTIL

HE CAN PROVIDE SATISFACTORY EVIDENCE OF REHABILITATION, INCLUDING: MUST SUCCESSFULLY COMPLETE A LONG-TERM INPATIENT ALCOHOL/SUBSTANCE ABUSE TREATMENT PROGRAM OF AT LEAST SIX MONTHS AND, PREFERABLY, OF ONE YEAR DURATION; A THOROUGH PSYCHIATRIC OR PSYCHOLOGICAL EVALUATION, INCLUDING POSSIBLE SEXUAL DEVIANCY, TO EVALUATE IF RESPONDENT HAS A MENTAL HEALTH DISORDER, WHETHER TREATMENT IS INDICATED, AND THE PROGNOSIS.

HAINER, JAMES W MD WAS DISCIPLINED BY WASHINGTON ON NOVEMBER 20, 1987.
DISCIPLINARY ACTION: SURRENDER OF LICENSE

HALEY, JAMES C MD WAS DISCIPLINED BY WASHINGTON ON JUNE 19, 1987.
DISCIPLINARY ACTION: RESTRICTION PLACED ON LICENSE; REQUIRED TO TAKE ADDITIONAL MEDICAL EDUCATION
OFFENSE: SUBSTANDARD CARE, INCOMPETENCE, OR NEGLIGENCE
NOTES: RENDERED INCOMPETENT MEDICAL TREATMENT - FIRST PATIENT HAD AN ABRUPTIO PLACENTAL COMPLICATION, BLOOD LOSS AND HYPOXIA IN 1978 RESULTING IN NEUROLOGICAL DAMAGE; ASSISTED IN A CHOLECYSTECTOMY ON A SECOND PATIENT IN 1982 WHERE THE PRIMARY SURGEON SEVERED THE COMMON BILE DUCT; SEVERED A THIRD PATIENT'S COMMON DUCT DURING A ROUTINE CHOLECYSTECTOMY IN 1982; FAILED TO DIAGNOSE TENDON INJURIES ON A FOURTH PATIENT IN 1983 RESULTING IN LATER CORRECTIVE PROCEDURES AND COMPLICATED RECOVERY; FAILED TO RESPOND PROPERLY TO FETAL DISTRESS DURING LABOR AND FETAL DAMAGE FROM A FORCEP DELIVERY RESULTING IN FETAL DEATH IN 1983; FAILED TO RECOGNIZE AND RESPOND TO A SIXTH PATIENT'S HIGH-RISK PREGNANCY WITH LARGE FETUS, RESULTING IN A COMPLICATED DELIVERY AND DAMAGED NEWBORN IN 1984; RESTRICTIONS: SHALL NOT ACT AS PRIMARY SURGEON IN SURGERY OR DELIVERIES UNTIL HE COMPLETES A ONE-YEAR PRECEPTORSHIP IN OBSTETRICS AND ONE IN GENERAL SURGERY; SHALL APPEAR BEFORE BOARD AFTER COMPLETION BEFORE PRACTICING. ON 2/12/96 HIS REQUEST TO TERMINATE THIS ORDER WAS DENIED BUT THE REQUEST WILL BE CONSIDERED AFTER THE BOARD RECEIVES ADDITIONAL INFORMATION. ON 6/7/96 HIS REQUEST TO TERMINATE ORDER GRANTED AND LICENSE IS UNRESTRICTED.

HALEY, JAMES CLACK MD WAS DISCIPLINED BY INDIANA ON FEBRUARY 26, 1987.
DISCIPLINARY ACTION: DENIAL OF NEW LICENSE
OFFENSE: DISCIPLINARY ACTION BY ANOTHER STATE OR AGENCY
NOTES: REQUEST FOR TEMPORARY MEDICAL PERMIT DENIED; DISCIPLINE BY WASHINGTON STATE, MALPRACTICE JUDGEMENTS

HALEY, THEODORE R MD WAS DISCIPLINED BY WASHINGTON ON JULY 21, 1990.
DISCIPLINARY ACTION: MONITORING OF PHYSICIAN
NOTES: INITIALLY SUSPENDED FOR TEN YEARS BY ORDER DATED 9/15/89, SUSPENSION STAYED UPON COMPLIANCE WITH CERTAIN TERMS. AMENDED ORDER OF 11/07/89 TO BE MODIFIED AS FOLLOWS: MONITORING BY SUPERVISOR OF ONE-YEAR FELLOWSHIP PROGRAM IN SURGICAL CRITICAL CARE AT COOK COUNTY HOSPITAL WITH QUARTERLY REPORTS TO WASHINGTON AND ILLINOIS BOARDS; SHALL SUBMIT TO MONTHLY PSYCHIATRIC OR PSYCHOLOGICAL EVALUATIONS WITH QUARTERLY REPORTS TO THE BOARD; HE SHALL IMMEDIATELY NOTIFY BOARD OF HAVING OBTAINED LICENSURE IN ILLINOIS; BOARD SHALL OBTAIN ADDITIONAL INFORMATION BEFORE APPROVING A PSYCHIATRIST. ALL OTHER CONDITIONS OF 9/15/89 AND 11/7/89 ORDERS REMAIN IN EFFECT.

HALEY, THEODORE R MD OF CHICAGO, IL, WAS DISCIPLINED BY ILLINOIS ON SEPTEMBER 1, 1990.
DISCIPLINARY ACTION: 24-MONTH PROBATION
OFFENSE: DISCIPLINARY ACTION BY ANOTHER STATE OR AGENCY
NOTES: LICENSE IN WASHINGTON WAS SUSPENDED FOR 10 YEARS, STAYED UPON COMPLIANCE WITH CONDITIONS. ILLINOIS PHYSICIAN LICENSE APPROVED AND PLACED ON INDEFINITE PROBATION FOR A MINIMUM OF TWO YEARS.

HALEY, THEODORE R MD OF 950 MATTHEW DR PO BOX 590, WAYNESBORO, MS, WAS DISCIPLINED BY DEA ON NOVEMBER 15, 1990.
DISCIPLINARY ACTION: SURRENDER OF CONTROLLED SUBSTANCE LICENSE
NOTES: SUSPENSION OF LICENSE 11/16/89 INCLUDED TEN YEARS SUSPENSION AND TEN YEARS PROBATION. MEDICAL LICENSE REVOKED 11/16/89 IN MISSISSIPPI. ILLINOIS PHYSICIAN LICENSE ISSUED 09/27/90 WITH TWO YEAR PROBATION CLAUSE; ILLINOIS CONTROLLED SUBSTANCE LICENSE ISSUED 12/04/90.

HAMACHER, EDWARD N MD WAS DISCIPLINED BY WASHINGTON ON NOVEMBER 18, 1993.
DISCIPLINARY ACTION: SURRENDER OF LICENSE
OFFENSE: PROFESSIONAL MISCONDUCT
NOTES: UNDER INVESTIGATION BY THE BOARD CONCERNING A MANDATORY REPORT OF A SETTLEMENT OF MALPRACTICE SUIT AGAINST HIM CONCERNING COMPLICATIONS FOLLOWING A MAMMOPLASTY AND BREAST IMPLANTATION. VOLUNTARY RETIREMENT EFFECTIVE 1/31/91: HAS NO PLANS TO RESUME PRACTICE; SHALL RETIRE PERMANENTLY; MAY RESUME PRACTICE ONLY WITH PRIOR BOARD APPROVAL; WILL NOTIFY THE BOARD IF HE PLANS TO RESUME PRACTICE OR APPLY FOR LICENSURE IN ANY OTHER JURISDICTION. THE INVESTIGATION WAS TERMINATED.

HANSON, KEITH L MD, LICENSE NUMBER 0025353, WAS DISCIPLINED BY WASHINGTON ON JULY 14, 1995.
DISCIPLINARY ACTION: 60-MONTH PROBATION; FINE
OFFENSE: OVERPRESCRIBING OR MISPRESCRIBING DRUGS
NOTES: BETWEEN 4/29/92 AND 10/3/94 OVERPRESCRIBED VICODIN TABLETS TO ONE OF HIS PATIENTS. CONDITIONS OF PROBATION ARE AS FOLLOWS: SHALL COMPLETE 25 HOURS OF CONTINUING MEDICAL EDUCATION IN PRESCRIBING CONTROLLED SUBSTANCES AND SUBSTANCE ABUSE WITHIN ONE YEAR; SHALL WRITE ALL PRESCRIPTIONS FOR CONTROLLED SUBSTANCES ON SERIALLY NUMBERED TRIPLICATE PRESCRIPTION PADS AND SHALL SUBMIT THIRD COPIES OF ALL SUCH PRESCRIPTIONS QUARTERLY TO THE BOARD; SHALL PRESCRIBE CONTROLLED SUBSTANCES FOR PAIN ONLY UNDER SPECIFIED CONDITIONS; SHALL NOTE SPECIFIED INFORMATION IN THE PATIENTS CHART; SHALL APPEAR BEFORE THE BOARD EVERY SIX MONTHS FOR THE FIRST YEAR AND ANNUALLY THEREAFTER; A REPRESENTATIVE OF THE BOARD MAY MAKE ANNOUNCED VISITS SEMIANNUALLY TO HIS PRACTICE; MAY PETITION THE BOARD FOR A CHANGE IN THE TERMS/CONDITIONS OF THIS ORDER IN NO SOONER THAN TWO YEARS; SHALL INFORM THE BOARD IN WRITING OF HIS CHANGE IN PRACTICE AND RESIDENCE ADDRESS; ANY TIME PERIOD DURING WHICH HE RESIDES AND/OR PRACTICES OUTSIDE WASHINGTON SHALL NOT APPLY TO THE REDUCTION OF THE DURATION OF THE PROBATION; SHALL PAY A $1,000 FINE. ON 2/12/96 THE BOARD DENIED HIS REQUEST TO PERMIT

HIM TO PETITION FOR EARLY TERMINATION OF THE ORDER. ON 6/15/96 REQUEST TO TERMINATE THIS ORDER GRANTED; LICENSE IS UNRESTRICTED.

HARRIS, STANLEY E MD, LICENSE NUMBER 0008613, OF SEATTLE, WA, WAS DISCIPLINED BY WASHINGTON ON OCTOBER 16, 1992.
DISCIPLINARY ACTION: RESTRICTION PLACED ON LICENSE
OFFENSE: SUBSTANDARD CARE, INCOMPETENCE, OR NEGLIGENCE
NOTES: NEGLIGENCE. UNABLE TO PRACTICE OBSTETRICS FOR A MINIMUM OF THREE YEARS. ON 11/16/94 WAS IN COMPLIANCE WITH THE ORDER. HIS REQUEST FOR AN UNRESTRICTED LICENSE WAS DENIED.

HART, BURTON B DO WAS DISCIPLINED BY WASHINGTON ON APRIL 28, 1995.
DISCIPLINARY ACTION: 24-MONTH PROBATION; FINE
OFFENSE: PROFESSIONAL MISCONDUCT
NOTES: ADVERTISING WHICH IS FALSE, FRAUDULENT OR MISLEADING. SHALL IMMEDIATELY CEASE AND REFRAIN FROM USING, ADVISING, PRESCRIBING, OR TREATING PATIENTS WITH INTRAVENOUS OR ORAL USE OF HYDROGEN PEROXIDE AND SHALL NOT ALLOW ANY AUXILIARY STAFF TO PERFORM OR CONSULT WITH OR TREAT PATIENTS WITH HYDROGEN PEROXIDE; SHALL MAKE HIS OFFICE AND OFFICE RECORDS AVAILABLE FOR PERIODIC BOARD INSPECTION; SHALL COMPLY WITH THE BOARD'S COMPLIANCE SURVEILLANCE PROGRAM INCLUDING SUBMITTING QUARTERLY DECLARATIONS WITH ALL THE CONDITIONS OF PROBATION AND APPEARING IN PERSON FOR COMPLIANCE INTERVIEWS; SHALL PROVIDE THE BOARD CURRENT HOME AND BUSINESS ADDRESSES AND ANY CHANGES IN ADDRESS; AND TIME NOT SPENT PRACTICING SHALL BE TOLLED. $1,500 FINE.

HART, BURTON B DO WAS DISCIPLINED BY IDAHO ON DECEMBER 11, 1995.
DISCIPLINARY ACTION: DENIAL OF NEW LICENSE
OFFENSE: DISCIPLINARY ACTION BY ANOTHER STATE OR AGENCY
NOTES: PRACTICE INCLUDES THE USE OF UNACCEPTED AND UNCONVENTIONAL MEDICAL PRACTICES INCLUDING SCLERA, EDTA, AND CHELATION THERAPIES; DISCIPLINED BY WASHINGTON BOARD FOR UNCONVENTIONAL AND UNACCEPTED USE OF HYDROGEN PEROXIDE; LIED ON IDAHO APPLICATION WHEN HE SAID HIS LICENSE WAS NOT RESTRICTED IN ANOTHER STATE; ADMITTED TO WASHINGTON BOARD THAT HE ENGAGED IN FALSE, FRAUDULENT OR MISLEADING ADVERTISING AND PROMOTING UNNECESSARY OR INEFFICACIOUS DRUGS, DEVICES, TREATMENTS, PROCEDURES AND SERVICES FOR PERSONAL GAIN.

HARTHCOCK, KERRY A MD WAS DISCIPLINED BY WASHINGTON ON APRIL 15, 1988.
DISCIPLINARY ACTION: PROBATION; REQUIRED TO ENTER AN IMPAIRED PHYSICIAN PROGRAM OR DRUG OR ALCOHOL TREATMENT
OFFENSE: SUBSTANCE ABUSE
NOTES: LICENSE ISSUED ON INDEFINITE PROBATION; RANDOM URINE TESTS; SHALL PARTICIPATE IN NARCOTICS ANONYMOUS OR AA TWICE WEEKLY WITH QUARTERLY REPORTS TO THE BOARD; REGULAR INTERVIEWS WITH THE BOARD; SHALL SUBMIT QUARTERLY PROGRESS REPORTS TO THE BOARD. MONITORED TREATMENT PROGRAM HAD BEEN REQUIRED BY PREVIOUS BOARD ORDER.

HARTHCOCK, KERRY ALFRED MD, LICENSE NUMBER 00G1428, OF SEATTLE, WA, WAS DISCIPLINED BY TEXAS ON JANUARY 26, 1990.
OFFENSE: DISCIPLINARY ACTION BY ANOTHER STATE OR AGENCY
NOTES: STIPULATED ORDER. SHALL COMPLY WITH PROBATIONARY REQUIREMENTS OF WASHINGTON BOARD ORDER, TEXAS BOARD TO HAVE ACCESS TO WASHINGTON BOARD DOCUMENTS, MUST OBTAIN APPROVAL FROM TEXAS BOARD PRIOR TO PRACTICING IN TEXAS. AS OF 4/20/91 PROBATION TERMINATED; LICENSE FREE OF ANY RESTRICTION OR LIMITATION.

HAUTMAN, BARBARA A MD WAS DISCIPLINED BY WASHINGTON ON APRIL 10, 1990.
DISCIPLINARY ACTION: PROBATION; FINE
OFFENSE: SUBSTANCE ABUSE
NOTES: SUFFERS FROM AN ADDICTIVE DISEASE WHICH HAS LED TO HER DIVERSION AND USE OF FENTANYL IN THE PAST. SUSPENSION STAYED BASED ON COMPLIANCE WITH THE FOLLOWING CONDITIONS OF PROBATION: HAS DIVERTED FENTANYL FOR HER OWN USE IN 7 AND/OR 8/88 AND IN 9/89. SUSPENSION STAYED; CONDITIONS OF PROBATION: SHALL NOT PRESCRIBE CONTROLLED SUBSTANCES FOR HER OWN USE OR MEMBER OF HER FAMILY; SHALL NOT POSSESS CONTROLLED SUBSTANCES, INCLUDING ALCOHOL; SHALL COMPLY WITH REQUIREMENTS OF THE WASHINGTON MONITORED TREATMENT PROGRAM AND CONTRACT WITH PLACE OF EMPLOYMENT; RANDOM TESTS OF BODILY FLUIDS; REPORTS FROM TREATMENT PROGRAM AND EMPLOYER TO THE BOARD EVERY SIX MONTHS; SHALL OBTAIN BOARD APPROVAL BEFORE CHANGING EMPLOYMENT; MAY NOT REQUEST MODIFICATION FOR TWO YEARS; SHALL INFORM BOARD IF SHE MOVES OUT OF STATE AND OF ANY CHANGE OF ADDRESS; $500 FINE. ON 2/15/91 THE BOARD DENIED A REQUEST TO EXPAND HER JOB RESPONSIBILITIES AT THE UNIVERSITY OF WASHINGTON. ON 9/13/91 ORDER MODIFIED WITH THE FOLLOWING CONDITIONS: MUST NOTIFY THE BOARD IF SHE CHOOSES TO PRACTICE IN ANOTHER JURISDICTION; MUST COMPLETELY ABSTAIN FROM THE USE OF FENTANYL AND ITS COGENERS; SHALL PROVIDE A COPY OF THIS ORDER TO HER PERSONAL PHYSICIAN AND ANY HOSPITAL WHERE SHE WORKS, OR TO ANYONE ELSE SHE PRACTICES MEDICINE WITH; MUST TAKE A THERAPEUTIC DOSE OF NALTREXONE ON A REGULAR SCHEDULE AS PRESCRIBED BY HER PERSONAL PHYSICIAN; SHALL ATTEND A MINIMUM OF THREE AA/NARCOTICS ANONYMOUS MEETINGS PER WEEK AND SHALL KEEP A LOG OF ATTENDANCE; SHALL SUBMIT TO AN INITIAL EVALUATION WITHIN 60 DAYS BY A BOARD APPROVED PSYCHIATRIST; MAY TAKE A MAXIMUM OF 8 WEEKS VACATION AND/OR CONTINUING MEDICAL EDUCATION EACH CALENDAR YEAR; MUST SEE A THERAPIST ON A WEEKLY BASIS WITH QUARTERLY REPORTS TO THE BOARD; MAY NOT APPLY FOR MODIFICATION FOR ONE YEAR. MUST APPEAR BEFORE THE BOARD IN SIX MONTHS TO VERIFY COMPLIANCE; BOARD MAY MAKE UNANNOUNCED VISITS TO INSPECT PRACTICE. ON 10/15/92 BOARD FOUND HER TO BE IN COMPLIANCE WITH THIS ORDER AND MODIFIED CERTAIN CONDITIONS OF THE ORDER WHICH SHE IS REQUIRED TO COMPLY WITH IN FULL. ON 6/17/93 PROBATION TERMINATED.

HAUTMAN, BARBARA A MD, LICENSE NUMBER 0A44852, OF SEATTLE, WA, WAS DISCIPLINED BY CALIFORNIA ON JULY 7, 1993.
DISCIPLINARY ACTION: 60-MONTH PROBATION
NOTES: REVOCATION STAYED.

HAUTMAN, BARBARA ANN MD, LICENSE NUMBER 0030784, OF 2500 CANTERBURY LN EAST STE 306, SEATTLE, WA, WAS DISCIPLINED BY GEORGIA ON JULY 8, 1991.
DISCIPLINARY ACTION: NONRENEWAL OF LICENSE
OFFENSE: DISCIPLINARY ACTION BY ANOTHER STATE OR AGENCY
NOTES: DISCIPLINARY ACTION IN WASHINGTON. ADMINISTRATIVE REVOCATION FOR FAILURE TO RENEW.

- WASHINGTON -

HAUTMAN, BARBARA ANN MD, DATE OF BIRTH OCTOBER 20, 1951, LICENSE NUMBER 0048719, OF 15320 ELLEN DRIVE, LIVONIA, MI, WAS DISCIPLINED BY MICHIGAN ON NOVEMBER 12, 1993.
DISCIPLINARY ACTION: REPRIMAND
OFFENSE: SUBSTANCE ABUSE
NOTES: $250 ADMINISTRATIVE COSTS.

HELLER, HOWARD F MD WAS DISCIPLINED BY WASHINGTON ON FEBRUARY 20, 1987.
DISCIPLINARY ACTION: REQUIRED TO TAKE ADDITIONAL MEDICAL EDUCATION; MONITORING OF PHYSICIAN
OFFENSE: OVERPRESCRIBING OR MISPRESCRIBING DRUGS
NOTES: ALLEGEDLY HAS ENGAGED IN NONTHERAPEUTIC PRESCRIBING OF CONTROLLED SUBSTANCES TO AT LEAST ONE PATIENT IN 1983 AND 1984 INCLUDING BUT NOT LIMITED TO MORPHINE SULFATE, DILAUDID, DEMEROL, VISTARIL AND NORFLEX; SHALL ATTEND A PROFESSIONAL SEMINAR ON TREATMENT OF PAIN WITH MEDICATION WITHIN 12 MONTHS; PRESCRIPTIONS FOR SCHEDULE II DRUGS WILL FOR TWO YEARS BE REVIEWED QUARTERLY BY HOSPITAL STAFF WITH QUARTERLY REPORTS TO BOARD; ALL PRESCRIPTIONS FOR SCHEDULE II AND III DRUGS WILL BE IN TRIPLICATE WITH COPIES IN QUARTERLY REPORT. ON 9/26/89 RELEASED FROM THE TERMS OF THIS BOARD ORDER.

HELLER, HOWARD F MD, LICENSE NUMBER 0018533, OF SEATTLE, WA, WAS DISCIPLINED BY WASHINGTON ON FEBRUARY 19, 1993.
DISCIPLINARY ACTION: RESTRICTION PLACED ON LICENSE; REQUIRED TO TAKE ADDITIONAL MEDICAL EDUCATION
OFFENSE: SUBSTANDARD CARE, INCOMPETENCE, OR NEGLIGENCE
NOTES: IN 1/91 EXAMINED A PATIENT IN EMERGENCY ROOM WITH COMPLAINTS OF DIARRHEA, NAUSEA, AND VOMITING AND RELEASED THE PATIENT WITHOUT ANY LAB WORK, X-RAYS OR HYDRATION; PATIENT RETURNED TO EMERGENCY ROOM 17 HOURS LATER IN SEPTIC SHOCK AND REQUIRED TREATMENT AT AN ACUTE CARE FACILITY; ATTRIBUTES HIS ERRORS TO DEPRESSION FOR WHICH HE OBTAINED TREATMENT VIA THERAPY. CONDITIONS OF RESTRICTION ARE AS FOLLOWS: SHALL NOT PRACTICE IN ANY SETTING WHERE HE WOULD BE WORKING IN EMERGENCY MEDICINE; SHALL APPEAR BEFORE THE BOARD ANNUALLY FOR A COMPLIANCE APPEARANCE WITH THE FIRST APPEARANCE TO BE IN ONE YEAR; SHALL BRING WITH HIM TO THE COMPLIANCE APPEARANCE DOCUMENTATION REGARDING HIS ATTENDANCE AT 50 HOURS OF CONTINUING MEDICAL EDUCATION; MAY PETITION TO REMOVE THE RESTRICTIONS NO EARLIER THAN 12 MONTHS. REQUEST TO TERMINATE ORDER GRANTED 3/4/94; LICENSE REINSTATED IN FULL.

HIKES, CHARLES E III MD WAS DISCIPLINED BY WASHINGTON ON AUGUST 20, 1993.
DISCIPLINARY ACTION: RESTRICTION PLACED ON LICENSE
OFFENSE: DISCIPLINARY ACTION BY ANOTHER STATE OR AGENCY
NOTES: ON 7/17/91 OREGON LICENSE RESTRICTED FOR 10 YEARS. SHALL COMPLY WITH THE TERMS, CONDITIONS, AND RESTRICTIONS IMPOSED ON HIS MEDICAL LICENSE IN OREGON; SHALL PETITION BOARD IN WRITING AND APPEAR BEFORE THE BOARD IF HE WISHES TO PRACTICE IN WASHINGTON.

HIKES, CHARLES E III MD OF 2450 SE TWELFTH STREET, SALEM, OR, WAS DISCIPLINED BY DEA ON NOVEMBER 20, 1993.
DISCIPLINARY ACTION: RESTRICTION PLACED ON CONTROLLED SUBSTANCE LICENSE
OFFENSE: DISCIPLINARY ACTION BY ANOTHER STATE OR AGENCY
NOTES: OREGON MEDICAL BOARD PLACED MEDICAL LICENSE ON PROBATION 07/17/91 TO CONTINUE UNTIL 2001.

HIKES, CHARLES EDWARD III MD, LICENSE NUMBER 0009100, OF SALEM, OR, WAS DISCIPLINED BY OREGON ON JULY 17, 1991.
DISCIPLINARY ACTION: 120-MONTH PROBATION; FINE
OFFENSE: PROFESSIONAL MISCONDUCT
NOTES: FINE PAYABLE IN 90 DAYS; REVOCATION STAYED.

HIKES, CHARLES EDWARD III MD, LICENSE NUMBER 0009100, OF SALEM, OR, WAS DISCIPLINED BY OREGON ON AUGUST 15, 1991.
DISCIPLINARY ACTION: 3-MONTH LICENSE SUSPENSION
OFFENSE: SUBSTANDARD CARE, INCOMPETENCE, OR NEGLIGENCE
NOTES: ALLEGED INAPPROPRIATE CARE/INCOMPETENCE.

HILL, ROBERT D MD, LICENSE NUMBER 00C6143, OF ODESSA, TX, WAS DISCIPLINED BY TEXAS ON JANUARY 6, 1995.
DISCIPLINARY ACTION: 60-MONTH PROBATION; REQUIRED TO TAKE ADDITIONAL MEDICAL EDUCATION
OFFENSE: LOSS OR RESTRICTION OF HOSPITAL PRIVILEGES
NOTES: ON 4/7/92 A HOSPITAL SUMMARILY SUSPENDED HIS PRIVILEGES DUE TO THE FOLLOWING: HE EXAMINED A NEWBORN INFANT WHO HIS NOTES REFLECTED WAS NORMAL, A POOR EATER, AND STATED "WATCH"; NURSES' NOTES REFLECT THE BABY WAS SPITTING UP EMESIS, REFUSING TO NURSE, WAS NOT STOOLING AND WAS NOT AROUSABLE; IN SPITE OF THIS DR. HILL DISCHARGED PATIENT AND ADVISED PARENTS TO CALL IF EATING DID NOT IMPROVE; THEY DID CALL LATER THAT DAY AND HE REFUSED TO SEE THE CHILD AS HE BELIEVED THE PROBLEM WOULD RESOLVE ITSELF; ANOTHER PHYSICIAN HOSPITALIZED THE INFANT THAT SAME DAY; THE INFANT WAS DIAGNOSED WITH CYSTIC FIBROSIS. HE RESIGNED FROM THE HOSPITAL AFTER BEING ADVISED THAT THE HOSPITAL'S EXECUTIVE COMMITTEE WOULD RECOMMEND A PERMANENT SUSPENSION. SUSPENSION STAYED. CONDITIONS OF PROBATION: SHALL HAVE A BOARD-APPROVED MONITORING PHYSICIAN WITH MONTHLY REPORTS; SHALL ATTEND AT LEAST 50 HOURS PER YEAR OF CONTINUING MEDICAL EDUCATION; SHALL APPEAR BEFORE THE BOARD ONCE A YEAR; SHALL COOPERATE WITH THE BOARD IN VERIFYING COMPLIANCE; SHALL INFORM BOARD OF CHANGE OF ADDRESS WITHIN 10 DAYS OR IF HE LEAVES THE STATE; TIME SPENT OUT OF TEXAS DOES NOT COUNT TOWARD PROBATION. SHALL NOT SEEK MODIFICATION FOR ONE YEAR. ON 3/2/96 REQUEST TO TERMINATE ORDER DENIED BUT ORDER MODIFIED SO HE SHALL PROVIDE WRITTEN REPORTS TO STAFF WHICH REFLECT THE LEVEL OF HIS PRACTICE SKILLS FROM ALL FACILITIES WHERE HE PRACTICES UPON BOARD REQUEST IN LIEU OF PREVIOUS REQUIREMENT FOR A MONITOR; MAY REQUEST MODIFICATION EVERY SIX MONTHS. PROBATION TERMINATED ON 8/17/96.

HILL, ROBERT DIXON MD, LICENSE NUMBER MD16554, OF CRESWELL, OR, WAS DISCIPLINED BY OREGON ON NOVEMBER 1, 1993.
DISCIPLINARY ACTION: 24-MONTH RESTRICTION PLACED ON LICENSE; 24-MONTH RESTRICTION PLACED ON CONTROLLED SUBSTANCE LICENSE
NOTES: NO SCHEDULE II DRUGS EXCEPT FOR HOSPITAL PATIENTS; TRIPLICATE COPIES OF CONTROLLED SUBSTANCE PRESCRIPTIONS MUST BE PROVIDED FOR SCHEDULE III DRUGS; BOTH CONDITIONS SUBJECT TO REVIEW. VOLUNTARY LIMITATION SUBJECT TO REVIEW ON 11/1/95. NO LONGER LISTED ON PROBATION AS OF 11/27/95.

HILL, ROBERT DIXON MD, LICENSE NUMBER 0027422, OF CRESWELL, OR, WAS DISCIPLINED BY WASHINGTON ON JUNE 2, 1995.
DISCIPLINARY ACTION: RESTRICTION PLACED ON CONTROLLED SUBSTANCE LICENSE
NOTES: AGREED ORDER RESTRICTING HIS PRESCRIBING OF

- WASHINGTON -

CONTROLLED SUBSTANCES.

HILL, ROBERT DIXON MD, LICENSE NUMBER 0G13809, OF CREWELL, OR, WAS DISCIPLINED BY CALIFORNIA ON MARCH 4, 1996.
DISCIPLINARY ACTION: LICENSE REVOCATION
OFFENSE: DISCIPLINARY ACTION BY ANOTHER STATE OR AGENCY
NOTES: ACTION IN OREGON. VOLUNTARY LIMITATION FILED LIMITING LICENSE TO PRACTICE MEDICINE WITH RESPECT TO SCHEDULES II AND III CONTROLLED SUBSTANCES. DEFAULT ACTION.

HILLMAN, STEVEN K MD, LICENSE NUMBER 0022616, OF SEQUIM, WA, WAS DISCIPLINED BY WASHINGTON ON NOVEMBER 4, 1994.
DISCIPLINARY ACTION: PROBATION
OFFENSE: OVERPRESCRIBING OR MISPRESCRIBING DRUGS
NOTES: ALLEGATIONS THAT HE PRESCRIBED MEDICATION FOR A PATIENT IN A NON-THERAPEUTIC MANNER. PROBATION FOR 3-5 YEARS WITH CERTAIN CONDITIONS. ON 10/25/95 HIS REQUEST TO TERMINATE THIS ORDER WAS GRANTED AND HE HAS AN UNRESTRICTED LICENSE.

HOLLINGSWORTH, LYMAN B MD, DATE OF BIRTH DECEMBER 16, 1909, OF 3651 N E 169TH, SEATTLE, WA, WAS DISCIPLINED BY MEDICARE ON AUGUST 9, 1990.
DISCIPLINARY ACTION: 120-MONTH EXCLUSION FROM THE MEDICARE AND/OR MEDICAID PROGRAMS
OFFENSE: CRIMINAL CONVICTION OR PLEA OF GUILTY, NOLO CONTENDERE, OR NO CONTEST TO A CRIME
NOTES: CONVICTION RELATING TO CONTROLLED SUBSTANCES.

HOLLINGSWORTH, LYMAN B MD WAS DISCIPLINED BY WASHINGTON ON OCTOBER 19, 1990.
DISCIPLINARY ACTION: LICENSE REVOCATION; FINE
OFFENSE: CRIMINAL CONVICTION OR PLEA OF GUILTY, NOLO CONTENDERE, OR NO CONTEST TO A CRIME
NOTES: FAILED TO COMPLY WITH PREVIOUS BOARD ORDER OF 2/15/85 RESTRICTING PRESCRIBING AND DISPENSING OF PHENDIMETRAZINE, AND WAS CONVICTED OF DISTRIBUTING THE DRUG FOR OTHER THAN LEGITIMATE MEDICAL PURPOSES 9/14/89. SHALL CEASE CARE AND TREATMENT OF PATIENTS IMMEDIATELY AND FORMALLY CLOSE PRACTICE WITHIN 90 DAYS; SHALL INFORM THE BOARD IF CHANGES ADDRESS OR LEAVES THE STATE.

HOLLINGSWORTH, LYMAN B DR OF SEATTLE, WA, WAS DISCIPLINED BY ILLINOIS ON JUNE 1, 1994.
DISCIPLINARY ACTION: LICENSE SUSPENSION
OFFENSE: DISCIPLINARY ACTION BY ANOTHER STATE OR AGENCY
NOTES: DISCIPLINED IN WASHINGTON. INDEFINITE SUSPENSION.

HOLMES, THOMAS STEPHENSON MD, LICENSE NUMBER 0012396, OF BELLEVUE, WA, WAS DISCIPLINED BY WASHINGTON ON OCTOBER 6, 1995.
DISCIPLINARY ACTION: 60-MONTH PROBATION
NOTES: PROBATION UNDER SEVERAL TERMS AND CONDITIONS. ORDER MODIFIED ON 5/01/96 TO PERMIT HIM TO PROVIDE PSYCHOTHERAPY OR COUNSELING DIRECTLY TO PATIENTS, BUT CANNOT PROVIDE INTENSIVE, LONG-TERM PSYCHOTHERAPY OR COUNSELING TO PATIENTS.

HOOVER, LARRY C DO WAS DISCIPLINED BY WASHINGTON ON NOVEMBER 3, 1995.
DISCIPLINARY ACTION: 24-MONTH PROBATION; FINE
NOTES: UNPROFESSIONAL CONDUCT. CONDITIONS OF PROBATION: SHALL MAINTAIN MALPRACTICE INSURANCE AT A MINIMUM OF $100,000.00 INDIVIDUAL AND $300,000.00 ANNUAL AGGREGATE; WITHIN 12 MONTHS, SHALL COMPLETE CONTINUING MEDICAL EDUCATION CONSISTING OF 16 COURSE HOURS IN APPROPRIATE PRESCRIBING, INCLUDING IDENTIFICATION OF DRUG SEEKING PATIENTS, FOUR HOURS OF MEDICAL RECORD KEEPING, 4 HOURS OF APPROPRIATE REFERRALS AND/OR CONSULTATIONS, AND AT A MINIMUM, 124 HOURS OF CONTINUING MEDICAL EDUCATION IN 24 MONTHS; COURSES MUST BE BOARD APPROVED; SHALL MAINTAIN HEALTH CARE RECORDS IN A SPECIFIED MANNER; SHALL SUBMIT QUARTERLY REPORTS REGARDING COMPLIANCE; SHALL BE SUBJECT TO A REVIEW OF PATIENT CHARTS UPON BOARD REQUEST; SHALL NOTIFY THE BOARD IN WRITING OF DEPARTURE AND RETURN FROM WASHINGTON; TIME SPENT OUT OF WASHINGTON DOES NOT COUNT TOWARD PROBATION; SHALL PROVIDE BOARD WITH CURRENT HOME AND BUSINESS ADDRESSES AND ANY CHANGE IN ADDRESS; $2,000 ADMINISTRATIVE FINE.

HOPFNER, EDWARD A MD, LICENSE NUMBER 0008237, OF PORT ANGELES, WA, WAS DISCIPLINED BY WASHINGTON ON NOVEMBER 12, 1993.
DISCIPLINARY ACTION: EMERGENCY SUSPENSION
OFFENSE: SUBSTANDARD CARE, INCOMPETENCE, OR NEGLIGENCE
NOTES: ALLEGATIONS OF MORAL TURPITUDE/NEGLIGENCE, SEXUAL CONTACT WITH A PATIENT, AND INFLUENCE AND INTERFERENCE WITH AN INVESTIGATION.

HOPFNER, EDWARD A MD, LICENSE NUMBER 0008237, OF PORT ANGELES, WA, WAS DISCIPLINED BY WASHINGTON ON JANUARY 17, 1994.
DISCIPLINARY ACTION: PROBATION; FINE
OFFENSE: SEXUAL ABUSE OF OR SEXUAL MISCONDUCT WITH A PATIENT
NOTES: SEXUAL CONTACT WITH A PATIENT AND AN OFFER OF MONEY TO THE COMPLAINANT IN EXCHANGE FOR WITHDRAWAL OF COMPLAINT AGAINST HIM TO THE MEDICAL DISCIPLINARY BOARD. SUSPENSION OF FIVE YEARS STAYED ON CONDITIONS: $5,000 FINE; SHALL HAVE A LICENSED MONITOR PRESENT WHEN TREATING FEMALE PATIENTS; SHALL DISSEMINATE THE ORDER TO FACILITIES WHERE HE HAS PRIVILEGES; SHALL HAVE QUARTERLY REPORTS FROM THERAPIST AND AN ANNUAL REPORT FROM AN EVALUATOR TREATING PATIENTS WTH SEXUAL PROBLEMS; PERIODIC REPORTS OF PRESCRIBING PRACTICE. ON 9/6/94 COMMISSION DETERMINED THAT HE WAS IN COMPLIANCE WITH THIS ORDER. HIS MODIFICATION REQUEST WAS DENIED. ON 12/9/96 COMPLIANCE HEARINGS WERE REDUCED TO ONCE A YEAR, AND HE WAS PERMITTED TO PROVIDE SAMPLES OF LEGEND DRUGS TO PATIENTS WITHOUT RESTRICTIONS.

HUEMER, RICHARD P MD, LICENSE NUMBER 0026944, OF BRUSH PRAIRIE, WA, WAS DISCIPLINED BY WASHINGTON ON SEPTEMBER 30, 1994.
DISCIPLINARY ACTION: FINE
NOTES: ENTERED INTO AN AGREED ORDER IN WHICH HE AGREED TO NOT PRESCRIBE, ORDER OR ADMINISTER ANY HORMONAL EXTRACT NOT APPROVED BY THE FDA AND HE SHALL PAY A $120 FINE.

HUEMER, RICHARD P MD, LICENSE NUMBER 0A18706, OF BRUSH PRAIRIE, WA, WAS DISCIPLINED BY CALIFORNIA ON SEPTEMBER 1, 1995.
DISCIPLINARY ACTION: REPRIMAND
OFFENSE: DISCIPLINARY ACTION BY ANOTHER STATE OR AGENCY
NOTES: ACTION IN WASHINGTON FOR INJECTING PATIENTS WITH A NEW DRUG, A HORMONAL EXTRACT, ADRENAL CORTICAL EXTRACT AND THYMUS EXTRACT, NOT YET APPROVED BY THE FDA OR WASHINGTON STATE.

HUMMEL, RALPH T MD, LICENSE NUMBER 0008239, OF OLYMPIA, WA, WAS DISCIPLINED BY WASHINGTON ON DECEMBER 17, 1993.
DISCIPLINARY ACTION: PROBATION; FINE
OFFENSE: SEXUAL ABUSE OF OR SEXUAL MISCONDUCT WITH A

- WASHINGTON -

PATIENT
NOTES: SEXUAL CONTACT WITH A PATIENT. SHALL COMPLY WITH TERMS AND CONDITIONS AS STATED IN THE ORDER TO INCLUDE CEASING TREATMENT OF FEMALE PATIENTS WITH LIMITED, SPECIFIED EXCEPTIONS FOR COUNSELING OF COUPLES AND SPECIFIED PATIENTS, WHO WILL ALWAYS BE ACCOMPANIED BY A CAREGIVER; HE SHALL PROVIDE A COPY OF THIS ORDER TO HIS OFFICE STAFF; SHALL HAVE NO SEXUAL OR SOCIAL CONTACT WITH FEMALE PATIENTS PAST, CURRENT, OR FUTURE; SHALL MAKE COMPLIANCE APPEARANCES; ALLOW PRACTICE REVIEW; AND PAY A FINE.

HUNG, SIAN-MING MD, LICENSE NUMBER MD08062, OF PORTLAND, OR, WAS DISCIPLINED BY OREGON ON JULY 31, 1992.
DISCIPLINARY ACTION: LICENSE REVOCATION

HUNG, SIAN-MING MD, LICENSE NUMBER 0011180, OF VANCOUVER, WA, WAS DISCIPLINED BY WASHINGTON ON JANUARY 31, 1994.
DISCIPLINARY ACTION: RESTRICTION PLACED ON LICENSE
OFFENSE: PROFESSIONAL MISCONDUCT
NOTES: SHALL RETAIN A MEDICAL LICENSE BUT MUST LIMIT HIS PRACTICE TO ACUPUNCTURE. ON 12/11/95 HIS REQUEST TO MODIFY THIS ORDER WAS DENIED. ON 12/9/96 HIS REQUEST TO MODIFY ORDER GRANTED AND THE REQUIREMENT THAT HE APPEAR BEFORE BOARD ON AN ANNUAL BASIS WAS ELIMINATED.

HUYNH, PAUL T MD, DATE OF BIRTH JUNE 2, 1930, OF 1815 S 17TH AVENUE, SEATTLE, WA, WAS DISCIPLINED BY MEDICARE ON JULY 18, 1995.
DISCIPLINARY ACTION: 180-MONTH EXCLUSION FROM THE MEDICARE AND/OR MEDICAID PROGRAMS
OFFENSE: CRIMINAL CONVICTION OR PLEA OF GUILTY, NOLO CONTENDERE, OR NO CONTEST TO A CRIME
NOTES: CONVICTED OF A CRIME INVOLVING THE MEDICARE, MEDICAID, MATERNAL AND CHILD HEALTH SERVICES BLOCK GRANT OR BLOCK GRANTS TO STATES FOR SOCIAL SERVICES PROGRAMS.

HUYNH, TRONG V MD, LICENSE NUMBER 0022380, OF SEATTLE, WA, WAS DISCIPLINED BY WASHINGTON ON NOVEMBER 4, 1996.
DISCIPLINARY ACTION: LICENSE REVOCATION
OFFENSE: CRIMINAL CONVICTION OR PLEA OF GUILTY, NOLO CONTENDERE, OR NO CONTEST TO A CRIME
NOTES: COMMITTED ACTS OF MORAL TURPITUDE AND MISREPRESENTATION; AND CONVICTION OF A FELONY. DEFAULT ACTION.

HWANG, AURORA G MD, LICENSE NUMBER 0A40850, OF LINDSAY, CA, WAS DISCIPLINED BY CALIFORNIA ON AUGUST 9, 1995.
DISCIPLINARY ACTION: 36-MONTH PROBATION
OFFENSE: SUBSTANDARD CARE, INCOMPETENCE, OR NEGLIGENCE
NOTES: INCOMPETENCE IN THE CARE AND TREATMENT OF THREE ADULT PATIENTS: MISDIAGNOSED MALIGNANT CHEST TUMOR, UNDERESTIMATED CARDIAC CONDITION; MISMANAGED DIABETES LEADING TO FOOT GANGRENE. REVOCATION, STAYED.

HWANG, AURORA GRACE MD, LICENSE NUMBER 0020304, OF LINDSAY, CA, WAS DISCIPLINED BY WASHINGTON ON DECEMBER 23, 1996.
DISCIPLINARY ACTION: LICENSE REVOCATION
OFFENSE: DISCIPLINARY ACTION BY ANOTHER STATE OR AGENCY
NOTES: DISCIPLINED IN ANOTHER STATE. DEFAULT ACTION.

IP, STANLEY S MD, LICENSE NUMBER 0024910, OF PUYALLUP, WA, WAS DISCIPLINED BY WASHINGTON ON DECEMBER 17, 1993.
OFFENSE: SUBSTANDARD CARE, INCOMPETENCE, OR NEGLIGENCE
NOTES: ALLEGATIONS OF NEGLIGENCE. MUST COMPLY WITH TERMS AND CONDITIONS OF THE UNSPECIFIED ORDER. ON 5/1/96 HIS REQUEST TO TERMINATE THIS ORDER WAS GRANTED AND LICENSE IS UNRESTRICTED.

IP, STANLEY SHUI-WAH MD, LICENSE NUMBER 0A40498, OF TACOMA, WA, WAS DISCIPLINED BY CALIFORNIA ON JUNE 12, 1995.
DISCIPLINARY ACTION: SURRENDER OF LICENSE
NOTES: WHILE CHARGES PENDING.

JAIN, NARENDER MD, LICENSE NUMBER 0022269, OF GREEN BAY, WI, WAS DISCIPLINED BY WASHINGTON ON MARCH 9, 1994.
DISCIPLINARY ACTION: FINE; REPRIMAND
OFFENSE: PROVIDING FALSE INFORMATION TO THE BOARD
NOTES: ALLEGATIONS OF PROVIDING MISLEADING OR INACCURATE INFORMATION TO THE BOARD AND TWO EMERGENCY RESIDENCY PROGRAMS. MUST PAY A $2000 FINE. ON 11/7/95 HIS REQUEST TO TERMINATE THIS ORDER WAS GRANTED AND IS HIS LICENSE IS NOW UNRESTRICTED.

JAMES, HELEN A MD, LICENSE NUMBER 0020348, OF BELLINGHAM, WA, WAS DISCIPLINED BY WASHINGTON ON APRIL 3, 1995.
DISCIPLINARY ACTION: RESTRICTION PLACED ON LICENSE; REQUIRED TO TAKE ADDITIONAL MEDICAL EDUCATION
NOTES: RESTRICTED LICENSE BY REQUIRING COMPLIANCE WITH CERTAIN CONDITIONS, INCLUDING THE COMPLETION OF A TWO-WEEK MINI-RESIDENCY.

JENKS, MICHAEL J MD, LICENSE NUMBER 0018129, OF EVERETT, WA, WAS DISCIPLINED BY WASHINGTON ON AUGUST 25, 1995.
DISCIPLINARY ACTION: PROBATION; FINE
NOTES: PROBATION UNDER THE FOLLOWING TERMS AND CONDITIONS: SHALL SUBMIT TO RECORDS AUDITS; SHALL TAKE ADDITIONAL COURSES IN CONTINUING MEDICAL EDUCATION; SHALL USE TRIPLICATE PRESCRIPTION FORMS; SHALL PAY A FINE. ON 9/11/97 BOARD GRANTED HIS REQUEST TO TERMINATE THIS ORDER.

JENSEN, ERIC MD, LICENSE NUMBER 0008566, OF SEATTLE, WA, WAS DISCIPLINED BY WASHINGTON ON MARCH 21, 1994.
DISCIPLINARY ACTION: RESTRICTION PLACED ON LICENSE
NOTES: ENTERED INTO AN AGREEMENT RETIRING FROM THE PRACTICE OF OBSTETRICS.

JOHNSON, CLIFFORD J DO WAS DISCIPLINED BY WASHINGTON ON MAY 3, 1996.
DISCIPLINARY ACTION: 36-MONTH PROBATION; FINE
OFFENSE: SUBSTANDARD CARE, INCOMPETENCE, OR NEGLIGENCE
NOTES: FROM 12/11/92 TO 12/18/92 TREATED A PATIENT FOR WHOM HE DID NOT PERFORM AN EKG OR REFER TO A CARDIOLOGIST TO DETERMINE WHETHER HIS PATIENT WAS SUFFERING FROM A CARDIAC RELATED CONDITION. THE PATIENT WAS LATER DIAGNOSED WITH MYOCARDIAL INFARCTION AND PASSED AWAY AT A LATER DATE DUE TO COMPLICATIONS FROM SURGERY RELATED TO HIS CARDIAC CONDITION. THE BOARD MAY CONDUCT A MINIMUM OF TWO UNANNOUNCED PRACTICE REVIEWS OF HIS MEDICAL CHARTS AND RECORDS WHICH SHALL FOCUS ON MEDICAL RECORD KEEPING, COMPLETE AND APPROPRIATE DOCUMENTATION, AND THE IDENTIFICATION OF SYMPTOMS OF CARDIAC DISEASE; SHALL COMPLETE EIGHT HOURS OF BOARD APPROVED CONTINUING MEDICAL EDUCATION IN THE TOPICS OF RECOGNIZING AND DIAGNOSING CARDIAC DISEASES AND MEDICAL RECORD KEEPING; ALL PATIENTS SHALL HAVE ACCURATE AND ADEQUATE RECORDS KEPT IN A SPECIFIED MANNER; SHALL SUBMIT A REPORT TO THE BOARD VERIFYING COMPLIANCE EVERY 90 DAYS; $5,000 FINE; AND MAY NOT PETITION FOR MODIFICATION FOR AT LEAST TWO YEARS.

JOHNSON, ERIC C MD WAS DISCIPLINED BY WASHINGTON ON MAY

- WASHINGTON -

21, 1993.
DISCIPLINARY ACTION: SURRENDER OF LICENSE
NOTES: UNDER INVESTIGATION CONCERNING HIS ABILITY TO PRACTICE MEDICINE WITH REASONABLE SKILL AND SAFETY TO PATIENTS. VOLUNTARY RETIREMENT EFFECTIVE 4/15/93 AND HAS NO PLANS TO RESUME PRACTICE SUBSEQUENT TO THAT DATE: RETIREMENT SHALL BE PERMANENT; MAY RESUME PRACTICE ONLY WITH PRIOR BOARD APPROVAL; SHALL NOTIFY THE BOARD IF HE PLANS TO PRACTICE IN THIS OR ANY OTHER JURISDICTION. INVESTIGATION SHALL BE TERMINATED.

JOHNSON, H RICHARD MD, LICENSE NUMBER 0018130, OF TACOMA, WA, WAS DISCIPLINED BY WASHINGTON ON JUNE 1, 1992.
DISCIPLINARY ACTION: EMERGENCY SUSPENSION
OFFENSE: PROFESSIONAL MISCONDUCT
NOTES: ALLEGATIONS OF MORAL TURPITUDE AND ABUSE OF A CLIENT.

JOHNSON, H RICHARD MD, LICENSE NUMBER 0018130, OF TACOMA, WA, WAS DISCIPLINED BY WASHINGTON ON JANUARY 15, 1993.
DISCIPLINARY ACTION: FINE; RESTRICTION PLACED ON LICENSE
OFFENSE: PROFESSIONAL MISCONDUCT
NOTES: HE HAD SEXUAL RELATIONSHIPS WITH EIGHT PATIENTS BETWEEN 1985 AND 1991. LICENSE SHALL REMAIN SUSPENDED INDEFINITELY AND THE SUSPENSION STAYED WITH PROBATION GRANTED PROVIDED HE COMPLIES WITH TERMS AND CONDITIONS OF ORDER INCLUDING: SHALL NOT SEE AND/OR TREAT FEMALE PATIENTS; SHALL CONTINUE IN WEEKLY THERAPY WITH A BOARD APPROVED THERAPIST WITH QUARTERLY REPORTS TO THE BOARD; SHALL NOT ENGAGE IN ANY SOCIAL OR SEXUAL CONTACT WITH PATIENTS OR STAFF UNDER HIS SUPERVISION OR PAST PATIENTS; SHALL NOT MAKE HOUSE CALLS OR BE ON CALL IF HE IS PART OF A GROUP PRACTICE; HOSPITAL PRACTICE LIMITED TO ONE SPECIFIED HOSPITAL, WITH QUARTERLY REPORTS REQUIRED; SHALL PROVIDE THE BOARD WITH HIS MEDICAL RECORDS; SHALL UNDERGO FIVE MEDICAL ETHICS CONSULTATIONS; SHALL APPEAR BEFORE THE BOARD EVERY SIX MONTHS; BOARD MAY MAKE ANNOUNCED VISITS TO INSPECT HIS PRACTICE; SHALL INFORM THE BOARD OF CHANGE OF ADDRESS OR IF HE LEAVES THE STATE; TIME SPENT OUT OF WASHINGTON DOES NOT COUNT TOWARD PROBATION. ON 6/23/93 ORDER MODIFIED TO ALLOW HIM TO PRACTICE AT ADDITIONAL HOSPITALS AND TO ALLOW HIM TO ASSIST IN SURGERY ON FEMALE PATIENTS; SHALL NOT PROVIDE ANY FOLLOW UP CARE OR TREATMENT FOR SUCH PATIENTS; SHALL APPEAR BEFORE THE BOARD IN SIX MONTHS TO PRESENT PROOF OF COMPLIANCE. ON 1/21/94 THE BOARD DETERMINED THAT HE WAS IN COMPLIANCE AND MODIFIED THE ORDER AS FOLLOWS: HE MAY TREAT FEMALE PATIENTS AS LONG AS A FEMALE HEALTH CARE PROFESSIONAL IN THE ROOM AT ALL TIMES AND INDICATES HER PRESENCE ON THE PATIENT'S CHART; HE MAY BE ON CALL IF HE JOINS A GROUP PRACTICE; HE MUST PROVIDE A COPY OF HIS ORDERS TO ALL PRESENT AND FUTURE FEMALE PATIENTS; HE MUST PARTICIPATE IN A RELAPSE PREVENTION PROGRAM. ON 6/20/94 MODIFICATION TO CHAPERONE REQUIREMENTS GRANTED; HOSPITAL LIST WHERE HE MAY PRACTICE EXPANDED; REQUEST TO TREAT ATHLETES AT SPORTING EVENTS IS DENIED. ON 1/20/95, ORDER MODIFIED ELIMINATING THE REQUIREMENT THAT HE ENGAGE IN PSYCHOTHERAPY. THE BOARD TERMINATED JURISDICTION OF THIS ORDER ON 2/8/96, EFFECTIVE 1/26/96, AND HE WAS ISSUED AN UNRESTRICTED LICENSE.

JOHNSON, H RICHARD MD, LICENSE NUMBER 0022011, WAS DISCIPLINED BY MINNESOTA ON MAY 8, 1993.
NOTES: STAYED SUSPENSION.

JOHNSON, HAROLD Z MD WAS DISCIPLINED BY WASHINGTON ON SEPTEMBER 8, 1989.
DISCIPLINARY ACTION: EMERGENCY SUSPENSION
OFFENSE: SUBSTANCE ABUSE
NOTES: HAS BEEN OBSERVED EXHIBITING SIGNS OF SUBSTANCE ABUSE AND/OR A PHYSICAL OR MENTAL IMPAIRMENT WHICH RENDERS HIM INCAPABLE OF PRACTICING; ALLEGEDLY PROVIDED INCOMPETENT, NEGLIGENT OR SUBSTANDARD MEDICAL SERVICE TO 25 PATIENTS

JOHNSON, HAROLD Z MD, LICENSE NUMBER 00D0926, OF ADA, OK, WAS DISCIPLINED BY TEXAS ON JUNE 10, 1991.
OFFENSE: DISCIPLINARY ACTION BY ANOTHER STATE OR AGENCY
NOTES: SHOULD HE DESIRE TO PRACTICE MEDICINE IN TEXAS, MUST DEMONSTRATE TO BOARD HIS CAPACITY TO PRACTICE WITH REASONABLE SKILL AND SAFETY AND PROVIDE STATUS REPORT OF WASHINGTON LICENSE; IF TEXAS GRANTS HIM PERMISSION TO PRACTICE, TEXAS BOARD MAY IMPOSE ADDITIONAL PROBATIONARY TERMS.

JOHNSON, HAROLD ZAY MD, LICENSE NUMBER 0G18683, OF LONG BEACH, CA, WAS DISCIPLINED BY CALIFORNIA ON MAY 1, 1994.
DISCIPLINARY ACTION: LICENSE REVOCATION
OFFENSE: DISCIPLINARY ACTION BY ANOTHER STATE OR AGENCY
NOTES: DISCIPLINED BY WASHINGTON STATE BOARD BASED ON ALLEGED IMPAIRMENT DUE TO ALCOHOLISM. TEXAS DISCIPLINE BASED ON ABOVE ACTION. DEFAULT DECISION.

JOLLEY, TIMOTHY B MD WAS DISCIPLINED BY WASHINGTON ON SEPTEMBER 13, 1991.
DISCIPLINARY ACTION: LICENSE SUSPENSION; RESTRICTION PLACED ON LICENSE
OFFENSE: FAILURE TO COMPLY WITH A PREVIOUS BOARD ORDER
NOTES: ON 2/20/87 HIS LICENSE WAS SUSPENDED FOR FIVE YEARS WITH SUSPENSION STAYED PENDING CONDITIONS; CONDITIONS WERE MODIFIED ON 5/26/88. ONE CONDITION OF THE 5/26/88 ORDER REQUIRED THAT WHENEVER HE WAS WITH A FEMALE PATIENT, A FEMALE MEDICAL PRACTITIONER HAD TO BE PRESENT AT ALL TIMES; HE TESTIFIED THERE HAD BEEN OCCASIONS WHEN THE NURSE WAS OUT OF THE ROOM BUT SHE HAD NOT BEEN OUT OF SIGHT AND THE DOOR HAD BEEN OPEN. THIS ORDER ALSO PROVIDED THAT WITHIN 2 YEARS HE WAS REQUIRED TO ESTABLISH A SHARED PRACTICE WITH ANOTHER PHYSICIAN; HE HAD NOT ESTABLISHED SUCH A SHARED PRACTICE. SUSPENSION EXTENDED FOR AT LEAST ONE YEAR DUE TO HIS LACK OF COMPLIANCE WITH PREVIOUS ORDERS; MAY NOT BE IN SOLO PRACTICE BEYOND 9/1/92; MUST PERSONALLY APPEAR FOR COMPLIANCE REVIEW IN ONE YEAR.

KAO, CARL C MD WAS DISCIPLINED BY WASHINGTON ON SEPTEMBER 21, 1990.
DISCIPLINARY ACTION: RESTRICTION PLACED ON LICENSE; MONITORING OF PHYSICIAN
OFFENSE: SUBSTANDARD CARE, INCOMPETENCE, OR NEGLIGENCE
NOTES: STATEMENTS OF CHARGES ISSUED BY BOARD ON 7/6/89 AND 10/13/89 ALLEGED SURGERY PERFORMED ON 50 PATIENTS CONSTITUTED UNPROFESSIONAL CONDUCT; HE AGREED THAT THE INTERCOSTAL TO CAUDA EQUINA ANASTOMOSIS PERFORMED ON 4 PATIENTS SHOULD NOT HAVE BEEN PERFORMED IN ANY SETTING OTHER THAN UNDER AN EXPERIMENTAL PROTOCOL IN A MAJOR MEDICAL CENTER, AND THAT HE PERFORMED THEM AT DAYTON GENERAL HOSPITAL, WHICH IS NOT A MAJOR MEDICAL CENTER AND DID NOT HAVE AN EXPERIMENTAL PROTOCOL FOR THESE PROCEDURES. FIVE YEAR

- WASHINGTON -

SUSPENSION STAYED ON CONDITIONS: SHALL ALLOW BOARD REPRESENTATIVE TO MAKE UNANNOUNCED OR ANNOUNCED VISITS TO OFFICES; SHALL NOT PERFORM INTERCOSTAL TO CAUDA EQUINA ANASTOMOSES WITHOUT PRIOR APPROVAL OF BOARD; ON PATIENTS WITH SPINAL CORD INJURY, SHALL OBTAIN WRITTEN PREAPPROVAL FROM SPECIFIED PHYSICIAN BEFORE PERFORMING A VARIETY OF SPECIFIED PROCEDURES, WITH COPIES OF THE OPERATIVE REPORT SUBMITTED TO BOARD; SHALL PAY COSTS OF $2,000; SHALL SEND REPORTS TWICE A YEAR TO THE BOARD DOCUMENTING THE SPINAL CORD INJURED PATIENTS UPON WHOM HE HAS PERFORMED SURGERY.

KAO, CARL C MD, DATE OF BIRTH MARCH 1, 1935, OF 1012 S THIRD STREET, DAYTON, WA, WAS DISCIPLINED BY MEDICARE ON SEPTEMBER 24, 1990.
DISCIPLINARY ACTION: 60-MONTH EXCLUSION FROM THE MEDICARE AND/OR MEDICAID PROGRAMS
OFFENSE: SUBSTANDARD CARE, INCOMPETENCE, OR NEGLIGENCE
NOTES: PEER REVIEW ORGANIZATION RECOMMENDATION. ON 09/21/90 AGREED TO VOLUNTARILY EXCLUDE HIMSELF FROM THE MEDICARE PROGRAM.

KAO, CHUN CHING MD, DATE OF BIRTH MARCH 1, 1935, LICENSE NUMBER 0018328, OF 11510 SWAIN LOCK TERRACE, POTOMAC, MD, WAS DISCIPLINED BY IOWA ON AUGUST 4, 1992.
DISCIPLINARY ACTION: PROBATION
OFFENSE: DISCIPLINARY ACTION BY ANOTHER STATE OR AGENCY
NOTES: INDEFINITE PROBATION. ALSO KNOWN AS CARL KAO, MD.

KARPILOW, CRAIG MD, LICENSE NUMBER 0018887, OF SEATTLE, WA, WAS DISCIPLINED BY WASHINGTON ON NOVEMBER 4, 1994.
DISCIPLINARY ACTION: FINE; REPRIMAND
OFFENSE: PROFESSIONAL MISCONDUCT
NOTES: AIDING AND ABETTING AN UNLICENSED PERSON TO PRACTICE MEDICINE. MUST PAY A $1,000 FINE. ON 5/11/95 BOARD GRANTED HIS REQUEST TO TERMINATE JURISDICTION UNDER THIS ORDER; LICENSE IS UNRESTRICTED.

KEEHAN, MICHAEL F MD WAS DISCIPLINED BY WASHINGTON ON SEPTEMBER 25, 1992.
DISCIPLINARY ACTION: DENIAL OF NEW LICENSE
NOTES: MAY MAKE APPLICATION AGAIN NO SOONER THAN TWO YEARS FROM DATE OF ORDER.

KELLY, FRANCIS WILLIAM MD, DATE OF BIRTH SEPTEMBER 1, 1947, LICENSE NUMBER 0013147, OF 514 N. BIRCH, BOX 3262, OWAK, WA, WAS DISCIPLINED BY WEST VIRGINIA ON JUNE 6, 1993.
DISCIPLINARY ACTION: LICENSE SUSPENSION; REQUIRED TO TAKE ADDITIONAL MEDICAL EDUCATION
OFFENSE: DISCIPLINARY ACTION BY ANOTHER STATE OR AGENCY
NOTES: AGREEMENT ON 5/27/93 WITH THE DEPARTMENT OF HEALTH AND HUMAN SERVICES SUSPENDING HIS PRIVILEGES UNTIL HE COMPLETES A SPECIFIED RESIDENCY PROGRAM. WEST VIRGINIA LICENSE SUSPENDED INDEFINITELY UNTIL THE FOLLOWING OCCURS: MUST SUCCESSFULLY COMPLETE A RESIDENCY PROGRAM IN A PROGRAM APPROVED BY THE ACCREDITATION COUNCIL FOR GRADUATE MEDICAL EDUCATION; REQUESTS REINSTATEMENT OF HIS MEDICAL LICENSE AND APPEARS BEFORE MEMBERS OF THE BOARD FOR A FULL DISCUSSION OF HIS REQUEST.

KESTER, EUGENE FRANCIS MD, DATE OF BIRTH JULY 20, 1938, LICENSE NUMBER MD11529, OF PO BOX 215, BEAVERTON, OR, WAS DISCIPLINED BY OREGON ON JUNE 30, 1994.
DISCIPLINARY ACTION: LICENSE SUSPENSION
OFFENSE: SEXUAL ABUSE OF OR SEXUAL MISCONDUCT WITH A PATIENT
NOTES: ON 6/13/94 HE ADMITTED TO BOARD THAT HE HAD SEXUAL INTERCOURSE WITH FIVE OF HIS ADULT FEMALE PATIENTS AND INAPPROPRIATE SEXUAL CONTACT WITH ANOTHER ADULT FEMALE PATIENT. LICENSE SUSPENDED UNTIL 7/16/94.

KESTER, EUGENE FRANCIS MD, LICENSE NUMBER MD11529, OF PO BOX 215, BEAVERTON, OR, WAS DISCIPLINED BY OREGON ON JULY 15, 1994.
DISCIPLINARY ACTION: EMERGENCY SUSPENSION
OFFENSE: SEXUAL ABUSE OF OR SEXUAL MISCONDUCT WITH A PATIENT
NOTES: ON 6/13/94 HE ADMITTED TO HAVING SEXUAL INTERCOURSE WITH FIVE OF HIS ADULT FEMALE PATIENTS AND INAPPROPRIATE SEXUAL CONTACT WITH ANOTHER ADULT FEMALE PATIENT.

KESTER, EUGENE FRANCIS MD OF 10490 SW EASTRIDGE, PORTLAND, OR, WAS DISCIPLINED BY DEA ON NOVEMBER 30, 1994.
DISCIPLINARY ACTION: SURRENDER OF CONTROLLED SUBSTANCE LICENSE
OFFENSE: DISCIPLINARY ACTION BY ANOTHER STATE OR AGENCY
NOTES: STATE BOARD.

KESTER, EUGENE FRANCIS MD, DATE OF BIRTH JULY 20, 1938, LICENSE NUMBER MD11529, OF PO BOX 215, BEAVERTON, OR, WAS DISCIPLINED BY OREGON ON JANUARY 19, 1995.
DISCIPLINARY ACTION: LICENSE REVOCATION
OFFENSE: SEXUAL ABUSE OF OR SEXUAL MISCONDUCT WITH A PATIENT
NOTES: ENGAGED IN SEXUAL MISCONDUCT WITH SEVEN ADULT FEMALE PATIENTS.

KESTER, EUGENE FRANCIS MD, LICENSE NUMBER 0016979, OF PORTLAND, OR, WAS DISCIPLINED BY WASHINGTON ON JUNE 22, 1995.
DISCIPLINARY ACTION: EMERGENCY SUSPENSION
OFFENSE: DISCIPLINARY ACTION BY ANOTHER STATE OR AGENCY
NOTES: ALLEGATIONS OF ACTION IN ANOTHER STATE.

KESTER, EUGENE FRANCIS MD, LICENSE NUMBER 0016979, OF PORTLAND, OR, WAS DISCIPLINED BY WASHINGTON ON APRIL 19, 1996.
DISCIPLINARY ACTION: LICENSE SUSPENSION
NOTES: INDEFINITE SUSPENSION PENDING THE COMPLETION OF A NUMBER OF CONDITIONS.

KETTING, EFFIE J MD, LICENSE NUMBER 0019749, OF KENNEWICK, WA, WAS DISCIPLINED BY WASHINGTON ON NOVEMBER 17, 1995.
DISCIPLINARY ACTION: RESTRICTION PLACED ON LICENSE
NOTES: AGREED NOT TO PRACTICE OBSTETRICS OR PROVIDE PRENATAL CARE.

KINANE, THOMAS J MD, LICENSE NUMBER 0159679, OF ENUMCLAW, WA, WAS DISCIPLINED BY NEW YORK ON NOVEMBER 10, 1987.
DISCIPLINARY ACTION: 17-MONTH PROBATION
NOTES: 1 YEAR SUSPENSION STAYED

KINCAID, JOSEPH P MD WAS DISCIPLINED BY ARIZONA ON DECEMBER 10, 1991.
DISCIPLINARY ACTION: REQUIRED TO ENTER AN IMPAIRED PHYSICIAN PROGRAM OR DRUG OR ALCOHOL TREATMENT; MONITORING OF PHYSICIAN
OFFENSE: SUBSTANCE ABUSE
NOTES: VOLUNTARILY ENTERED A TREATMENT PROGRAM FOR ALCOHOL ABUSE. MUST IMMEDIATELY PARTICIPATE IN A BOARD-APPROVED MONITORED AFTERCARE TREATMENT PROGRAM WHOSE THERAPIST MUST SUBMIT QUARTERLY REPORTS; MUST PARTICIPATE IN 90 12-STEP MEETINGS FOR SUBSTANCE ABUSE WITHIN 90 DAYS; MUST THEN PARTICIPATE IN A 12-STEP RECOVERY PROGRAM AS DETERMINED BY HIS TREATING THERAPIST AND ATTEND AT LEAST THREE WEEKLY

- WASHINGTON -

MEETINGS; SHALL OBTAIN A BOARD-APPROVED TREATING PHYSICIAN; SHALL ABSTAIN COMPLETELY FROM THE CONSUMPTION OF ALCOHOLIC BEVERAGES AND DRUGS EXCEPT WHEN PRESCRIBED BY HIS TREATING PHYSICIAN; MUST SUBMIT TO WITNESSED RANDOM BIOLOGICAL FLUID COLLECTION; KEEP A LOG OF ANY AND ALL MEDICATIONS PRESCRIBED FOR HIM; SHALL SUBMIT TO ANY EXAMINATIONS OR THERAPY ORDERED BY BOARD; SHALL APPEAR BEFORE BOARD FOR INTERVIEWS UPON REQUEST; SHALL INFORM BOARD OF CHANGE OF ADDRESS OR IF AWAY FOR MORE THAN 5 DAYS. ORDER TERMINATED ON 4/16/96.

KINCAID, JOSEPH P MD WAS DISCIPLINED BY WASHINGTON ON JULY 13, 1992.
DISCIPLINARY ACTION: RESTRICTION PLACED ON LICENSE
NOTES: CONDITIONAL LICENSE ISSUED WITH SPECIFIC CONDITIONS.

KLOPFENSTEIN, KARL MD WAS DISCIPLINED BY WASHINGTON ON JANUARY 15, 1993.
DISCIPLINARY ACTION: SURRENDER OF LICENSE
NOTES: UNDER INVESTIGATION BY THE BOARD CONCERNING HIS ABILITY TO PRACTICE MEDICINE WITH REASONABLE SKILL AND SAFETY TO PATIENTS. VOLUNTARY RETIREMENT EFFECTIVE 3/01/89: HAS NO PLANS TO RESUME PRACTICE IN THE FUTURE; HIS RETIREMENT SHALL BE PERMANENT; MAY RESUME PRACTICE ONLY WITH PRIOR BOARD APPROVAL; WILL NOTIFY THE BOARD IF HE PLANS TO RESUME PRACTICE IN THIS OR ANY OTHER JURISDICTION.

KNUDSEN, DENNIS W DO OF 5559 N. 62 DRIVE, GLENDALE, AZ, WAS DISCIPLINED BY MEDICARE ON OCTOBER 7, 1987.
DISCIPLINARY ACTION: EXCLUSION FROM THE MEDICARE AND/OR MEDICAID PROGRAMS
OFFENSE: FAILURE TO COMPLY WITH A PREVIOUS BOARD ORDER
NOTES: EXCLUDED FROM MEDICARE UNTIL PAYS PREVIOUSLY-IMPOSED FINE.

KNUDSEN, DENNIS W DO WAS DISCIPLINED BY WASHINGTON ON MAY 17, 1991.
DISCIPLINARY ACTION: 60-MONTH LICENSE SUSPENSION
OFFENSE: DISCIPLINARY ACTION BY ANOTHER STATE OR AGENCY
NOTES: ACTION IN UTAH. CONDITIONS OF SUSPENSION: SHALL COMPLY WITH ANY TERMS OR CONDITIONS FROM UTAH; THE BOARD SHALL BE ENTITLED TO REVIEW ANY RECORD OR REPORT, INCLUDING COPIES OF ANY PSYCHIATRIC OR PSYCHOLOGICAL EVALUATION, MADE ON THE UTAH ORDER; SHALL NOT PRACTICE IN WASHINGTON PRIOR TO APPEARANCE BEFORE THE BOARD; AND AFTER FIVE YEARS OF COMPLIANCE SHALL BE SUBJECT TO PETITION FOR REINSTATEMENT.

KOHLBERG, IRVING J MD OF 10126 NE 132ND ST., STE.B, KIRKLAND, WA, WAS DISCIPLINED BY DEA ON OCTOBER 6, 1989.
DISCIPLINARY ACTION: RESTRICTION PLACED ON CONTROLLED SUBSTANCE LICENSE
OFFENSE: PROFESSIONAL MISCONDUCT
NOTES: EXCESSIVE PURCHASE; ACCOUNTABILITY INVESTIGATION REVEALED SHORTAGE OF APPROXIMATELY 11,596 DOSAGE UNITS; VOLUNTARY RESTRICTION OF REGISTRATION.

KOMARNISKI, ED A MD OF 17601 NORTH ROAD, BOTHELL, WA, WAS DISCIPLINED BY DEA ON NOVEMBER 27, 1995.
DISCIPLINARY ACTION: SURRENDER OF CONTROLLED SUBSTANCE LICENSE
NOTES: IN LIEU OF ORDER TO SHOW CAUSE.

KOMARNISKI, EDWARD A MD, LICENSE NUMBER 0007038, OF SEATTLE, WA, WAS DISCIPLINED BY WASHINGTON ON MARCH 10, 1995.
DISCIPLINARY ACTION: SURRENDER OF LICENSE
NOTES: AGREED TO RETIRE FROM THE PRACTICE OF MEDICINE.

KOO, YOUNG S MD OF HAMMOND, IN, WAS DISCIPLINED BY ILLINOIS ON APRIL 1, 1993.
DISCIPLINARY ACTION: LICENSE REVOCATION
OFFENSE: DISCIPLINARY ACTION BY ANOTHER STATE OR AGENCY
NOTES: DISCIPLINED IN INDIANA.

KOO, YOUNG SOO MD OF 6429 KENNEDY AVE., HAMMOND, IL, WAS DISCIPLINED BY ILLINOIS ON SEPTEMBER 1, 1989.
DISCIPLINARY ACTION: 12-MONTH PROBATION; FINE
OFFENSE: PRACTICING WITHOUT A VALID CONTROLLED SUBSTANCE LICENSE
NOTES: CHARGED WITH IMPROPERLY EXAMINING A FEMALE PATIENT AND ISSUED PRESCRIPTIONS WITHOUT A CURRENT ILLINOIS CONTROLLED SUBSTANCES LICENSE; FINED $1500

KOO, YOUNG SOO MD, LICENSE NUMBER 1028341, OF 530 TURNBERRY STREET, SCHERERVILLE, IN, WAS DISCIPLINED BY INDIANA ON JANUARY 24, 1991.
DISCIPLINARY ACTION: 3-MONTH EMERGENCY SUSPENSION
OFFENSE: DISCIPLINARY ACTION BY ANOTHER STATE OR AGENCY
NOTES: ON 1/17/91 HE WAS CHARGED WITH RAPE DURING A PELVIC EXAM HE PERFORMED ON 3/30/89; ILLINOIS LICENSE WAS PLACED ON PROBATION THROUGH A CONSENT ORDER OF 9/1/89, IN WHICH HE ADMITTED THAT HIS CONDUCT WITH A FEMALE PATIENT ON 7/11/88 WAS UNPROFESSIONAL AND IMMORAL AND THAT HE ENGAGED IN PRESCRIPTION IMPROPRIETIES; HE HAS FAILED TO COMPLY WITH ILLINOIS CONSENT ORDER AND LICENSE IS NO LONGER CURRENT IN ILLINOIS.

KOO, YOUNG SOO MD, LICENSE NUMBER 1028341, OF 530 TURNBERRY STREET, SCHERERVILLE, IN, WAS DISCIPLINED BY INDIANA ON JANUARY 29, 1991.
DISCIPLINARY ACTION: RESTRICTION PLACED ON LICENSE
OFFENSE: DISCIPLINARY ACTION BY ANOTHER STATE OR AGENCY
NOTES: LICENSE REINSTATED FROM EMERGENCY SUSPENSION ORDERED ON 1/24/91 DUE TO HIS FAILURE TO COMPLY WITH TERMS OF CONSENT ORDER WITH ILLINOIS. MAY NOT PERFORM ANY PELVIC EXAMINATIONS ON FEMALE PATIENTS; MUST HAVE ANOTHER OFFICE STAFF PERSON OR MEMBER OF PATIENT'S FAMILY PRESENT DURING EXAMINATION OF FEMALE PATIENTS IF DISROBING IS REQUIRED; SHALL PROVIDE WRITTEN REPORTS TO THE BOARD ON A MONTHLY BASIS CONCERNING PHYSICAL EXAMINATIONS. PATIENTS MUST SIGN CONSENT FORM ATTACHED TO ILLINOIS CONSENT ORDER OF 1989 PRIOR TO EXAMINATION. SHALL MAKE DILIGENT EFFORT TO OBTAIN AN ILLINOIS MEDICAL LICENSE; COSTS OF $479.00 ASSESSED.

KOO, YOUNG SOO MD, LICENSE NUMBER 1028341, OF 6429 KENNEDY BOX 2336, HAMMOND, IN, WAS DISCIPLINED BY INDIANA ON AUGUST 20, 1992.
DISCIPLINARY ACTION: 3-MONTH EMERGENCY SUSPENSION
OFFENSE: CRIMINAL CONVICTION OR PLEA OF GUILTY, NOLO CONTENDERE, OR NO CONTEST TO A CRIME
NOTES: 7/30/92: FOUND GUILTY OF FELONY RAPE OF A PATIENT IN HIS OFFICE. ON 11/2/92, 6/1/93, 8/2/93, 10/13/93, 12/6/93, 2/28/94 AND 4/27/94 EMERGENCY SUSPENSION CONTINUED FOR A PERIOD NOT TO EXCEED 90 DAYS.

KOO, YOUNG SOO MD, DATE OF BIRTH AUGUST 23, 1940, OF 6429 KENNEDY AVENUE, HAMMOND, IN, WAS DISCIPLINED BY MEDICARE ON AUGUST 29, 1993.
DISCIPLINARY ACTION: 240-MONTH EXCLUSION FROM THE MEDICARE AND/OR MEDICAID PROGRAMS
OFFENSE: CRIMINAL CONVICTION OR PLEA OF GUILTY, NOLO

- WASHINGTON -

CONTENDERE, OR NO CONTEST TO A CRIME
NOTES: CONVICTED OF A CRIME RELATED TO PATIENT ABUSE.

KOO, YOUNG SOO MD, LICENSE NUMBER 1028341, OF 2293 NORTH MAIN STREET, CROWN POINT, IN, WAS DISCIPLINED BY INDIANA ON DECEMBER 15, 1994.
DISCIPLINARY ACTION: LICENSE REVOCATION
OFFENSE: CRIMINAL CONVICTION OR PLEA OF GUILTY, NOLO CONTENDERE, OR NO CONTEST TO A CRIME
NOTES: ON 3/30/89 HE RAPED A PATIENT IN HIS OFFICE AFTER INJECTING HER WITH VALIUM; WAS CONVICTED OF THE CHARGE IN 7/92 AND THE INDIANA COURT OF APPEALS UNANIMOUSLY AFFIRMED CONVICTION ON 9/22/94; HAD ENTERED CONSENT ORDER WITH ILLINOIS BOARD ON 9/1/89 AFTER ADMITTING THAT HIS CONDUCT WITH A FEMALE PATIENT WAS OF SUCH A NATURE THAT COULD REASONABLY BE CONSTRUED AS UNPROFESSIONAL AND IMMORAL AND THAT HE ENGAGED IN IMPROPRIETIES REGARDING THE PRESCRIPTION OF CONTROLLED SUBSTANCES; BECAUSE OF VIOLATIONS OF THIS CONSENT ORDER AND CONVICTION OF RAPE ILLINOIS LICENSE REVOKED ON 4/6/93; IN 5/92 HE VIOLATED 1/29/91 INTERIM ORDER BY SEEING A FEMALE PATIENT ALONE AND INAPPROPRIATELY TOUCHING HER.

KOO, YOUNG SOO MD, LICENSE NUMBER 0017043, OF WESTVILLE, IN, WAS DISCIPLINED BY WASHINGTON ON OCTOBER 3, 1996.
DISCIPLINARY ACTION: LICENSE REVOCATION
OFFENSE: DISCIPLINARY ACTION BY ANOTHER STATE OR AGENCY
NOTES: DISCIPLINED IN ANOTHER STATE: COMMITTED AN ACT OF MORAL TURPITUDE; AND CONVICTED OF A FELONY. DEFAULT ACTION.

KRANZ, ERIC MD WAS DISCIPLINED BY OHIO ON JUNE 18, 1987.
DISCIPLINARY ACTION: DENIAL OF NEW LICENSE
NOTES: PERMANENT DENIAL

KRANZ, ERIC MD, LICENSE NUMBER 0013367, OF 2924 JACKSON AVENUE, POINT PLEASANT, WV, WAS DISCIPLINED BY WEST VIRGINIA ON MARCH 26, 1988.
DISCIPLINARY ACTION: LICENSE REVOCATION
OFFENSE: DISCIPLINARY ACTION BY ANOTHER STATE OR AGENCY
NOTES: KRANZ WAS DENIED A LICENSE IN OHIO ON JUNE 19, 1987 BECAUSE HE LIED ON HIS APPLICATION AND HAD TRIED TO SELL ANSWERS TO TWO LICENSURE EXAMS. HE HAD PREVIOUSLY BEEN DENIED LICENSURE IN PENNSYLVANIA AND OKLAHOMA. HE LIED ABOUT ALL THESE DENIALS TO THE WEST VIRGINIA BOARD. KRANZ ALSO PLEADED NOLO CONTENDERE ON APRIL 10, 1987 TO MISDEMEANOR BATTERY CHARGES FOR VERBALLY ABUSING AND FONDLING A FEMALE EMPLOYEE OF PLEASANT VALLEY HOSPITAL. BOARD'S DECISION WAS AFFIRMED BY KANAWHACOUNT CIRCUIT COURT ON 3/28/90

KRANZ, ERIC MD, LICENSE NUMBER 0014602, OF 1716 JEFFERSON AVE, POINT PLEASANT, WV, WAS DISCIPLINED BY OKLAHOMA ON FEBRUARY 9, 1989.
DISCIPLINARY ACTION: LICENSE REVOCATION
OFFENSE: DISCIPLINARY ACTION BY ANOTHER STATE OR AGENCY
NOTES: ON OR AROUND 6/19/87 DENIED LICENSURE BY THE OHIO BOARD DUE TO FAILURE TO DISCLOSE PREVIOUS DENIAL OF HIS APPLICATIONS IN OKLAHOMA IN 1983 AND IN PENNSYLVANIA IN 1981 AND MISREPRESENTATION IN CLAIMING TO BE A 1978 LICENTIATE OF THE MEDICAL COUNCIL OF CANADA WHEN HE WAS NOT AND NEVER HAD BEEN; ON OR AROUND 3/18/88 HIS WEST VIRGINIA LICENCE WAS REVOKED BASED IN PART ON HIS PLEA OF NOLO CONTENDERE TO A CRIMINAL CHARGE OF BATTERY MISDEMEANOR ASSOCIATED WITH A CHARGE OF FIRST DEGREE SEXUAL ABUSE FILED BY A MARRIED WOMAN ALLEGING HE MADE VARIOUS SEXUAL INNUENDOS, VERBAL ABUSE, AND UNINVITED FONDLING AT THE PLEASANT VALLEY HOSPITAL WHERE SHE WAS EMPLOYED. ON 3/8/90 MOTION FOR RECONSIDERATION DENIED.

KRANZ, ERIC MD OF 614 G ST SE, WASHINGTON, DC, WAS DISCIPLINED BY VIRGINIA ON JULY 31, 1989.
DISCIPLINARY ACTION: DENIAL OF NEW LICENSE
OFFENSE: PROVIDING FALSE INFORMATION TO THE BOARD
NOTES: LICENSE DENIED FOR APPLICATION FRAUD AND UNPROFESSIONAL CONDUCT.

KRANZ, ERIC MD, LICENSE NUMBER 032661E, OF SCRANTON, PA, WAS DISCIPLINED BY PENNSYLVANIA ON MARCH 29, 1990.
DISCIPLINARY ACTION: FINE; REPRIMAND
OFFENSE: DISCIPLINARY ACTION BY ANOTHER STATE OR AGENCY
NOTES: DISCIPLINARY ACTION TAKEN AGAINST HIS LICENSE IN WEST VIRGINIA AND IN OKLAHOMA, BASED ON HIS PLEA OF NOLO CONTENDERE IN WEST VIRGINIA TO A MISDEMEANOR RELATING TO MEDICINE, AND IN OKLAHOMA, BASED ON THEIR FINDING HIM GUILTY OF THE COMMISSION OF ANY ACT WHICH IS A VIOLATION OF THE CRIMINAL LAW OF OKLAHOMA WHEN CONNECTED WITH THE PHYSICIAN'S PRACTICE OF MEDICINE.

KRANZ, ERIC MD, DATE OF BIRTH MARCH 18, 1946, OF 1616 DICKSON AVE, SCRANTON, PA, WAS DISCIPLINED BY MEDICARE ON SEPTEMBER 24, 1990.
DISCIPLINARY ACTION: EXCLUSION FROM THE MEDICARE AND/OR MEDICAID PROGRAMS
OFFENSE: DISCIPLINARY ACTION BY ANOTHER STATE OR AGENCY
NOTES: LICENSE REVOCATION OR SUSPENSION. NO LONGER LISTED AS EXCLUDED AS OF 9/30/92.

KRANZ, ERIC MD, LICENSE NUMBER 0426384, OF BALTIMORE, MD, WAS DISCIPLINED BY VERMONT ON JUNE 5, 1991.
DISCIPLINARY ACTION: LICENSE REVOCATION
OFFENSE: DISCIPLINARY ACTION BY ANOTHER STATE OR AGENCY
NOTES: ON 6/18/87 OHIO DENIED HIS LICENSE APPLICATION; ON 4/10/87 HE WAS CONVICTED OF A BATTERY MISDEMEANOR INVOLVING MAKING UNWANTED SEXUAL ADVANCES TO A FEMALE NURSE IN THE HOSPITAL WHERE HE WORKED; WEST VIRGINIA REVOKED HIS LICENSE ON 3/18/88; OKLAHOMA REVOKED HIS LICENSE ON 2/9/89. ON HIS 10/87 RENEWAL APPLICATION IN VERMONT HE ANSWERED NO TO QUESTIONS ASKING IF HE HAD ACTIONS AGAINST HIS LICENSE OR HAD ANY CONVICTIONS.

KRANZ, ERIC MD, LICENSE NUMBER 0023597, WAS DISCIPLINED BY WASHINGTON ON FEBRUARY 21, 1992.
NOTES: SUSPENSION, STAYED ON CONDITIONS THAT HE SHALL NOT PRACTICE IN WASHINGTON STATE WITHOUT PRIOR APPROVAL OF THE BOARD.

KROLL, KENNETH M MD, LICENSE NUMBER 0012526, OF CARMEL, CA, WAS DISCIPLINED BY WASHINGTON ON JANUARY 27, 1995.
DISCIPLINARY ACTION: SURRENDER OF LICENSE
NOTES: AGREED TO RETIRE FROM THE PRACTICE OF MEDICINE. THE BOARD WITHDREW PREVIOUSLY ISSUED FORMAL CHARGES.

KUTZNER, ROBERT R MD, DATE OF BIRTH MARCH 17, 1951, LICENSE NUMBER 0037012, OF 608 W OCEAN FRONT, BALBOA, CA, WAS DISCIPLINED BY GEORGIA ON MARCH 6, 1995.
DISCIPLINARY ACTION: EMERGENCY SUSPENSION
OFFENSE: FAILURE TO COMPLY WITH A PREVIOUS BOARD ORDER
NOTES: FAILURE TO COMPLY WITH BOARD ORDERED EVALUATION.

KUTZNER, ROBERT R MD, DATE OF BIRTH MARCH 17, 1951, LICENSE NUMBER 1040297, OF 144 GLOVERS GATEWAY, HAMILTON, GA, WAS

- WASHINGTON -

DISCIPLINED BY INDIANA ON MARCH 23, 1995.
DISCIPLINARY ACTION: 3-MONTH EMERGENCY SUSPENSION
OFFENSE: DISCIPLINARY ACTION BY ANOTHER STATE OR AGENCY
NOTES: SUMMARY SUSPENSION IN GEORGIA ON 3/6/95 BASED ON ALLEGATIONS THAT ON 1/13/95, GEORGIA BOARD ISSUED AN EVALUATION ORDER FOR A MENTAL/PHYSICAL EXAMINATION WHICH HE NEVER OBTAINED. ORDERED TO IMMEDIATELY SURRENDER HIS LICENSE, ALL CONTROLLED SUBSTANCES IN HIS POSSESSION AND ALL PRESCRIPTION PADS IN HIS POSSESSION. ON 6/7/95 AND 8/4/95, EMERGENCY SUSPENSION CONTINUED FOR 90 DAYS.

KUTZNER, ROBERT R MD, LICENSE NUMBER 0028069, OF SAN DIMAS, CA, WAS DISCIPLINED BY WASHINGTON ON NOVEMBER 8, 1996.
DISCIPLINARY ACTION: LICENSE REVOCATION
OFFENSE: DISCIPLINARY ACTION BY ANOTHER STATE OR AGENCY
NOTES: DISCIPLINED IN ANOTHER STATE. DEFAULT ACTION.

KUTZNER, ROBERT RUSSELL MD, LICENSE NUMBER 0G52483, OF SANTA MARIA, CA, WAS DISCIPLINED BY CALIFORNIA ON FEBRUARY 21, 1996.
DISCIPLINARY ACTION: LICENSE REVOCATION
OFFENSE: DISCIPLINARY ACTION BY ANOTHER STATE OR AGENCY
NOTES: DISCIPLINARY ACTION IN GEORGIA. REVOCATION AFTER A CONTESTED HEARING.

LACE, JOHN W MD WAS DISCIPLINED BY WASHINGTON ON JULY 14, 1992.
DISCIPLINARY ACTION: RESTRICTION PLACED ON LICENSE
NOTES: CONDITIONAL LICENSE ISSUED WITH SPECIFIC CONDITIONS.

LADERAS, TEOFILO G MD, LICENSE NUMBER 0011668, OF VANCOUVER, WA, WAS DISCIPLINED BY WASHINGTON ON MARCH 4, 1994.
DISCIPLINARY ACTION: SURRENDER OF LICENSE
NOTES: SUBSEQUENT TO INVESTIGATION CONCERNING ABILITY TO PRACTICE WITH REASONABLE SKILL AND SAFETY.

LADERAS, TEOFILO G JR MD, LICENSE NUMBER 0034945, OF VANCOUVER, WA, WAS DISCIPLINED BY OHIO ON SEPTEMBER 26, 1995.
DISCIPLINARY ACTION: SURRENDER OF LICENSE
NOTES: PERMANENT VOLUNTARY RETIREMENT ACCEPTED IN LIEU OF FURTHER FORMAL DISCIPLINARY PROCEEDINGS.

LAMBERT, PAUL W MD, LICENSE NUMBER 0014916, OF CLARKSTON, WA, WAS DISCIPLINED BY WASHINGTON ON SEPTEMBER 8, 1994.
DISCIPLINARY ACTION: 60-MONTH PROBATION; FINE
NOTES: PROBATION HAS FOLLOWING TERMS AND CONDITIONS: SHALL UTILIZE A "SOAP" CHARTING FORMAT FOR ALL PATIENT FILES, SHALL WRITE ALL PRESCRIPTIONS FOR CONTROLLED SUBSTANCES FOR OUT-PATIENT USAGE ON SERIALLY NUMBERED TRIPLICATE PRESCRIPTION PADS, SHALL COMPLETE 25 HOURS OF CATEGORY I CONTINUING MEDICAL EDUCATION IN THE AREAS OF PRESCRIBING CONTROLLED SUBSTANCES, ADDICTION OR SUBSTANCE ABUSE AND SHALL PAY A $500 FINE. ON 5/11/95 HIS REQUEST WAS GRANTED TO HAVE A COMMISSION REPRESENTATIVE MAKE ANNUAL RATHER THAN SEMI-ANNUAL VISITS TO HIS PRACTICE. ON 9/11/97 BOARD GRANTED HIS REQUEST TO TERMINATE THIS ORDER.

LAMBERT, PAUL W MD, LICENSE NUMBER 00M4794, WAS DISCIPLINED BY IDAHO ON NOVEMBER 21, 1994.
DISCIPLINARY ACTION: PROBATION; REQUIRED TO TAKE ADDITIONAL MEDICAL EDUCATION
OFFENSE: DISCIPLINARY ACTION BY ANOTHER STATE OR AGENCY
NOTES: ON 9/8/94 WASHINGTON BOARD ACTION ISSUED FIVE YEAR SUSPENSION WHICH WAS STAYED WITH TERMS AND CONDITIONS BASED ON HIS PRESCRIBING EXCESSIVE AMOUNTS OF DANGEROUS DRUGS AND FAILING TO RECORD PRESCRIPTIONS FOR SIX PATIENTS BETWEEN 5/91 AND 2/93. THE IDAHO BOARD ADOPTS THIS RECIPROCAL DISCIPLINE, INCORPORATING THE TERMS AND CONDITIONS OF THE WASHINGTON ORDER WHICH INCLUDE PROBATION WITH THE FOLLOWING CONDITIONS: SHALL UTILIZE A SOAP CHARTING FORMAT FOR ALL PATIENT FILES; SHALL WRITE ALL PRESCRIPTIONS FOR CONTROLLED SUBSTANCES OF OUTPATIENT USAGE ON SERIALLY NUMBERED TRIPLICATE PRESCRIPTION PADS; SHALL NOT PRESCRIBE SCHEDULED DRUGS FOR MORE THAN TWO WEEKS FOR ANY SINGLE DIAGNOSIS OR COMPLAINT OR TO ANY PATIENT WITH AN ADDICTION HISTORY OR SUSPECTED ADDITION PROBLEM; SHALL COMPLETE 25 HOURS OF CATEGORY I CONTINUING MEDICAL EDUCATION IN THE AREAS OF PRESCRIBING CONTROLLED SUBSTANCES AND ADDICTION OR SUBSTANCE ABUSE; 13 OF THE HOURS MUST BE COMPLETED WITHIN ONE YEAR OF THE EFFECTIVE DATE OF THIS ORDER; THE REMAINING 12 HOURS SHALL BE COMPLETED WITHIN 24 MONTHS OF THE EFFECTIVE DATE OF THIS ORDER; SHALL APPEAR BEFORE THE COMMISSION SIX MONTHS FROM EFFECTIVE DATE; A REPRESENTATIVE OF THE COMMISSION MAY MAKE ANNOUNCED VISITS SEMI-ANNUALLY TO HIS PRACTICE TO REVIEW RECORDS AND OTHER ASPECTS OF HIS PRACTICE; SHALL INFORM THE BOARD OF ANY CHANGES IN HIS PRACTICE OR RESIDENCE ADDRESS. $500 FINE.

LAMBERT, PAUL W MD, LICENSE NUMBER 0C16439, OF CLARKSTON, WA, WAS DISCIPLINED BY CALIFORNIA ON SEPTEMBER 7, 1995.
DISCIPLINARY ACTION: SURRENDER OF LICENSE
NOTES: WHILE CHARGES PENDING.

LANDON, JOHN W MD, LICENSE NUMBER 0016925, OF SEATTLE, WA, WAS DISCIPLINED BY WASHINGTON ON JUNE 27, 1994.
DISCIPLINARY ACTION: 36-MONTH PROBATION; RESTRICTION PLACED ON CONTROLLED SUBSTANCE LICENSE
OFFENSE: OVERPRESCRIBING OR MISPRESCRIBING DRUGS
NOTES: ALLEGATIONS OF INAPPROPRIATE PRESCRIBING. CONDITIONS OF PROBATION ARE AS FOLLOWS: MUST USE TRIPLICATE PRESCRIPTION BLANKS WHEN PRESCRIBING CONTROLLED SUBSTANCES; ABIDE BY RESTRICTIONS ON PRESCRIBING OF CONTROLLED SUBSTANCES; MAKE REGULAR COMPLIANCE APPEARANCES BEFORE BOARD; ALLOW INSPECTIONS OF HIS OFFICE AND RECORDS; COMPLETE 25 HOURS OF CONTINUING MEDICAL EDUCATION WITHIN 12 MONTHS AND PAY $2000 IN COSTS WITHIN 16 MONTHS.

LANDON, JOHN W MD, LICENSE NUMBER 0016925, OF SEATTLE, WA, WAS DISCIPLINED BY WASHINGTON ON OCTOBER 6, 1995.
DISCIPLINARY ACTION: SURRENDER OF LICENSE
NOTES: AGREED TO RETIRE. THE BOARD WITHDREW THE FORMAL CHARGES.

LAVIGNE, JEFFREY E MD, DATE OF BIRTH JULY 2, 1944, LICENSE NUMBER 0026988, OF 630 1ST AVENUE #11D, NEW YORK, NY, WAS DISCIPLINED BY NEW JERSEY ON AUGUST 28, 1989.
DISCIPLINARY ACTION: RESTRICTION PLACED ON LICENSE
OFFENSE: DISCIPLINARY ACTION BY ANOTHER STATE OR AGENCY
NOTES: ACTION BASED ON STATE OF WASHINGTON SANCTION FOR PERFORMING SURGICAL PROCEDURES WITHOUT A FULL EVALUATION OF PATIENT, PERFORMING PROCEDURES NEVER PERFORMED IN A HOSPITAL, AND NOT OBTAINING FULL INFORMED CONSENT. SHALL PERFORM NO SURGERY IN NJ OTHER THAN MINOR PROCEDURES APPROVED BY THE BOARD TO BE DONE IN

AN OFFICE SETTING. PRIOR TO OBTAINING THIS APPROVAL, LICENSEE MUST APPEAR BEFORE A BOARD COMMITTEE FOR A STATUS CONFERENCE.

LAVIGNE, JEFFREY E MD WAS DISCIPLINED BY VERMONT ON AUGUST 1, 1990.
DISCIPLINARY ACTION: RESTRICTION PLACED ON LICENSE
OFFENSE: DISCIPLINARY ACTION BY ANOTHER STATE OR AGENCY
NOTES: DISCIPLINED BY WASHINGTON STATE IN 4/88 ON ALLEGATIONS OF POOR SURGICAL TECHNIQUE ON SIX PATIENTS AND FAILURE TO APPROPRIATELY EVALUATE PATIENTS PRIOR TO SURGERY AND/OR TO CONSULT WITH OTHER PHYSICIANS. SHALL NOT PRACTICE MEDICINE IN VERMONT WITHOUT FIRST RENEWING HIS LICENSE AND NOTIFYING THE BOARD OF HIS INTENT TO PRACTICE IN THE STATE; SHALL PERFORM NO SURGERY OTHER THAN MINOR PROCEDURES APPROVED BY THE BOARD WHICH MAY BE PERFORMED IN AN OFFICE SETTING.

LAVIGNE, JEFFREY E MD, LICENSE NUMBER 0018248, OF NY, WAS DISCIPLINED BY WASHINGTON ON JULY 2, 1992.
DISCIPLINARY ACTION: SURRENDER OF LICENSE

LAVIGNE, JEFFREY E MD, LICENSE NUMBER 0G26459, OF NEW YORK, NY, WAS DISCIPLINED BY CALIFORNIA ON OCTOBER 15, 1992.
DISCIPLINARY ACTION: SURRENDER OF LICENSE
NOTES: VOLUNTARY SURRENDER WHILE CHARGES PENDING.

LAVIGNE, JEFFREY E MD, LICENSE NUMBER 0114611, OF 7 EAST 68TH STREET, NEW YORK, NY, WAS DISCIPLINED BY NEW YORK ON SEPTEMBER 28, 1994.
DISCIPLINARY ACTION: LICENSE REVOCATION; FINE
OFFENSE: PROFESSIONAL MISCONDUCT
NOTES: $40,000 FINE.

LAVIGNE, JEFFREY ELLIOTT MD, DATE OF BIRTH JULY 2, 1944, LICENSE NUMBER 0020438, OF NEW YORK, NY, WAS DISCIPLINED BY IOWA ON NOVEMBER 2, 1990.
DISCIPLINARY ACTION: SURRENDER OF LICENSE
OFFENSE: DISCIPLINARY ACTION BY ANOTHER STATE OR AGENCY

LAVIGNE, JEFFREY ELLIOTT MD, DATE OF BIRTH JULY 2, 1944, LICENSE NUMBER 0026988, OF 259 SOUTH WEST 193RD PLACE, NORMONDEY PARK, WA, WAS DISCIPLINED BY NEW JERSEY ON MAY 9, 1996.
DISCIPLINARY ACTION: LICENSE REVOCATION
OFFENSE: DISCIPLINARY ACTION BY ANOTHER STATE OR AGENCY
NOTES: ACTION IN WASHINGTON AND NEW YORK.

LAVIOLETTE, RODNEY MD, LICENSE NUMBER 0005245, OF HARTFORD, KY, WAS DISCIPLINED BY WASHINGTON ON OCTOBER 7, 1995.
DISCIPLINARY ACTION: LICENSE REVOCATION
NOTES: DEFAULT ACTION.

LAZACHEK, GARY W MD, LICENSE NUMBER 0023998, WAS DISCIPLINED BY MINNESOTA ON FEBRUARY 20, 1989.
DISCIPLINARY ACTION: LICENSE REVOCATION
OFFENSE: DISCIPLINARY ACTION BY ANOTHER STATE OR AGENCY
NOTES: LICENSE REVOKED IN NEW YORK BASED ON FRAUDULENT PRACTICE, GROSS NEGLIGENCE RELATING TO DIAGNOSTIC AND THERAPEUTIC MEASURES, UNPROFESSIONAL CONDUCT; NEGLIGENCE AND INCOMPETENCE; ALSO REVOKED IN WASHINGTON AND CALIFORNIA BASED ON NEW YORK ACTION

LAZACHEK, GARY W MD, DATE OF BIRTH SEPTEMBER 23, 1943, LICENSE NUMBER 0021365, OF 600 FIRST AVENUE, SEATTLE, WA, WAS DISCIPLINED BY WISCONSIN ON MAY 24, 1989.
DISCIPLINARY ACTION: LICENSE REVOCATION
OFFENSE: DISCIPLINARY ACTION BY ANOTHER STATE OR AGENCY
NOTES: LICENSE REVOKED IN NEW YORK ON MAY 2, 1983 BASED ON PRACTICING PROFESSION FRAUDULENTLY, WITH GROSS NEGLIGENCE AND OR INCOMPETENCE ON MORE THAN ONE OCCASION AND COMMITTING UNPROFESSIONAL CONDUCT; ALSO REVOKED IN CALIFORNIA ON APRIL 21, 1986 AND WASHINGTON ON FEBRUARY 24, 1984; WILL PAY COSTS OF PROCEEDING

LAZACHEK, GARY W MD, LICENSE NUMBER 0021000, OF SEATTLE, WA, WAS DISCIPLINED BY CONNECTICUT ON JUNE 21, 1990.
DISCIPLINARY ACTION: LICENSE REVOCATION
OFFENSE: SUBSTANDARD CARE, INCOMPETENCE, OR NEGLIGENCE
NOTES: INCOMPETENCE/NEGLIGENCE.

LEVITT, GILBERT MD, LICENSE NUMBER 0093256, OF 2500 81ST AVENUE, MERCER ISLAND, WA, WAS DISCIPLINED BY NEW YORK ON OCTOBER 18, 1995.
DISCIPLINARY ACTION: SURRENDER OF LICENSE
OFFENSE: DISCIPLINARY ACTION BY ANOTHER STATE OR AGENCY
NOTES: ACTION IN WASHINGTON AND CALIFORNIA FOR HAVING A MENTAL AND/OR PHYSICAL CONDITION WHICH PREVENTS HIM FROM PRACTICING SURGERY, PROVIDING ON-CALL SERVICE OR PROVIDING EMERGENCY CARE WITH REASONABLE SKILL AND SAFETY.

LEVITT, GILBERT W MD WAS DISCIPLINED BY WASHINGTON ON AUGUST 20, 1993.
DISCIPLINARY ACTION: RESTRICTION PLACED ON LICENSE; MONITORING OF PHYSICIAN
OFFENSE: PHYSICAL OR MENTAL ILLNESS INHIBITING THE ABILITY TO PRACTICE WITH SKILL AND SAFETY
NOTES: HE SUFFERS FROM PHYSICAL AND PSYCHOLOGICAL CONDITIONS THAT CAUSE HIM TO SUFFER CHEST PAIN DURING STRESSFUL SITUATIONS, AND THAT CHEST PAIN REQUIRES HIM TO CEASE THE STRESS-INDUCING ACTIVITIES. HAS VOLUNTARILY LIMITED HIS PRACTICE SINCE 1990. HIS PRACTICE SHALL BE LIMITED: SHALL NOT PERFORM SURGERY, PROVIDE ON-CALL SERVICE, OR PROVIDE EMERGENCY CARE; SHALL NOTIFY THE BOARD OF THE TYPE AND SCOPE OF HIS PRACTICE AND OF ANY CHANGES IN THE TYPE AND SCOPE OF HIS PRACTICE; THIS LIMITATION SHALL CONTINUE INDEFINITELY; SHALL APPEAR BEFORE THE BOARD UPON REQUEST; THE BOARD MAY MAKE ANNOUNCED OR UNANNOUNCED VISITS TO INSPECT OFFICE AND/OR MEDICAL RECORDS, INTERVIEW STAFF OR SUPERVISORS, REVIEW OTHER ASPECTS OF HIS PRACTICE INCLUDING DIRECT OBSERVATION OF HIS PERFORMANCE IN HIS PRACTICE SETTING; MAY PETITION THE BOARD FOR A CHANGE IN TERMS OR CONDITIONS IN NO SOONER THAN ONE YEAR; SHALL INFORM THE BOARD, IN WRITING, OF CHANGES IN HIS PRACTICE AND RESIDENCE ADDRESS; MUST NOTIFY THE BOARD IN WRITING IF HE LEAVES WASHINGTON.

LEVITT, GILBERT W MD, LICENSE NUMBER 0C29050, OF MERCER ISLAND, WA, WAS DISCIPLINED BY CALIFORNIA ON FEBRUARY 22, 1995.
DISCIPLINARY ACTION: SURRENDER OF LICENSE
NOTES: VOLUNTARY SURRENDER WHILE CHARGES PENDING.

LEWIS, RICHARD D MD, LICENSE NUMBER 0017808, OF ABERDEEN, WA, WAS DISCIPLINED BY WASHINGTON ON DECEMBER 18, 1992.
DISCIPLINARY ACTION: REPRIMAND
OFFENSE: PROFESSIONAL MISCONDUCT
NOTES: MORAL TURPITUDE AND ABUSE OF A CLIENT.

LIES, BERT A MD, LICENSE NUMBER 0029966, OF SANTA FE, NM, WAS DISCIPLINED BY WASHINGTON ON NOVEMBER 15, 1996.
DISCIPLINARY ACTION: PROBATION

- WASHINGTON -

NOTES: PROBATION UNDER TERMS AND CONDITIONS.

LIM, KHENG B MD WAS DISCIPLINED BY WASHINGTON ON AUGUST 20, 1993.
DISCIPLINARY ACTION: FINE; REQUIRED TO TAKE ADDITIONAL MEDICAL EDUCATION
OFFENSE: DISCIPLINARY ACTION BY ANOTHER STATE OR AGENCY
NOTES: ACTION IN FLORIDA IN 9/16/91 RESTRICTING HIS LICENSE. SHALL WRITE AN ARTICLE ON HOW TO REACT TO CARDIORESPIRATORY ARREST IN THE OPERATING ROOM WITHIN ONE YEAR FOR THE WASHINGTON AND FLORIDA BOARD; SHALL INFORM THE BOARD IN WRITING OF THE CHANGES IN HIS PRACTICE AND RESIDENCE ADDRESS; SHALL COMPLETE 50 HOURS BOARD APPROVED CONTINUING MEDICAL EDUCATION IN THE AREAS OF ANESTHESIOLOGY, RISK MANAGEMENT AND/OR RECORD KEEPING WITHIN 15 MONTHS; MAY SUBMIT FOR APPROVAL THOSE COURSE HOURS COMPLETED IN COMPLIANCE WITH THE FLORIDA BOARD; MAY PETITION THE BOARD FOR A CHANGE IN THE TERMS/CONDITIONS IN NO SOONER THAN ONE YEAR; SHALL NOT PRACTICE IN WASHINGTON UNTIL HE FILES A WRITTEN PETITION AND APPEARS PERSONALLY BEFORE THE BOARD; SHALL PAY A $100 FINE.

LIM, KHENG BEE MD, LICENSE NUMBER 0A39726, OF NEW SMYRNA BEACH, FL, WAS DISCIPLINED BY CALIFORNIA ON MAY 18, 1995.
DISCIPLINARY ACTION: REPRIMAND
OFFENSE: DISCIPLINARY ACTION BY ANOTHER STATE OR AGENCY
NOTES: DISCIPLINE BY FLORIDA INVOLVING ANESTHESIOLOGY PRACTICE.

LIN, JANG-BOR MD, LICENSE NUMBER 0A35329, OF VISALIA, CA, WAS DISCIPLINED BY CALIFORNIA ON OCTOBER 7, 1993.
DISCIPLINARY ACTION: 1-MONTH LICENSE SUSPENSION; 59-MONTH PROBATION
OFFENSE: SUBSTANDARD CARE, INCOMPETENCE, OR NEGLIGENCE
NOTES: GROSS NEGLIGENCE IN ATTEMPTED VAGINAL DELIVERY OF MACROSOMIC FETUS (14 POUNDS. STILLBORN) REVOCATION STAYED.

LIN, JANG-BOR MD, LICENSE NUMBER 0018143, OF VISALIA, CA, WAS DISCIPLINED BY WASHINGTON ON DECEMBER 16, 1994.
DISCIPLINARY ACTION: FINE
NOTES: REQUIRED TO PETITION THE COMMISSION FOR PERMISSION TO PRACTICE MEDICINE IN WASHINGTON STATE BEFORE COMING BACK TO WASHINGTON. SHALL PAY A $500 FINE.

LIN, JANG-BOR MD, LICENSE NUMBER 0003755, OF 1626 SOUTH COURT STREET, VISALIA, CA, WAS DISCIPLINED BY HAWAII ON AUGUST 16, 1995.
OFFENSE: DISCIPLINARY ACTION BY ANOTHER STATE OR AGENCY
NOTES: ACTION IN CALIFORNIA. AGREE THAT HE WILL FULLY COMPLY WITH ALL THE TERMS AND CONDITIONS OF THE CALIFORNIA BOARD ORDER OF 9/7/93 INCLUDING SPECIFIED EXAMS AND CONTINUING EDUCATION, THAT 50 PERCENT OF PATIENTS SHALL BE MEDI-CAL PATIENTS, SHALL NOT SUPERVISE PHYSICIAN ASSISTANTS AND SHALL APPEAR BEFORE BOARD UPON REQUEST; SHALL NOTIFY HAWAII OF ANY MODIFICATIONS OR INFRACTIONS WITHIN 30 DAYS; SHALL NOTIFY HAWAII A MINIMUM OF 60 DAYS PRIOR TO COMMENCEMENT OF PRACTICE IN HAWAII; SHALL NOTIFY THE BOARD ON ANY CHANGE IN HIS EMPLOYMENT, BUSINESS ADDRESS, BUSINESS TELEPHONE NUMBER, RESIDENCE ADDRESS OR RESIDENCE TELEPHONE NUMBER WITHIN 14 DAYS OF OCCURRENCE.

LIN, JANG-BOR MD, LICENSE NUMBER 1029705, OF 1626 SOUTH COURT STREET, VISALIA, CA, WAS DISCIPLINED BY INDIANA ON JULY 30, 1996.
DISCIPLINARY ACTION: PROBATION; MONITORING OF PHYSICIAN
OFFENSE: DISCIPLINARY ACTION BY ANOTHER STATE OR AGENCY
NOTES: ON 2/12/93 REVOCATION OF LICENSE IN CALIFORNIA STAYED AS FIVE YEAR PROBATION FOR GROSS NEGLIGENCE IN HIS CARE AND TREATMENT OF A PATIENT IN THAT HE ATTEMPTED VAGINAL DELIVERY AT TERM OF A MACROSOMIC FETUS; AND DID NOT CORRECTLY ASSESS THE FETUS' WEIGHT AND SIZE PRIOR TO INDUCING LABOR TO A DIABETIC PATIENT, WHO WAS IN HER SECOND PREGNANCY, AND WHO PREVIOUSLY DELIVERED A MACROSOMIC INFANT WITH SHOULDER DYSTOCIA; THE INFANT WAS STILLBORN; ON 12/09/94 ENTERED INTO AN AGREEMENT IN WASHINGTON THAT HE WAS TO ABIDE BY THE CALIFORNIA ORDER; ENTERED INTO AN AGREEMENT IN HAWAII THAT HE WAS TO ABIDE BY THE CALIFORNIA ORDER. INDEFINITE PROBATION IN INDIANA UNDER TERMS AND CONDITIONS: SHALL NOT HAVE THE RIGHT TO PETITION THE BOARD FOR WITHDRAWAL OF PROBATION UNTIL HE SUCCESSFULLY COMPLETES THE PROBATION IMPOSED BY THE CALIFORNIA BOARD; SHALL INFORM THE BOARD OF HIS ADDRESSES AND TELEPHONE NUMBERS AND ANY CHANGES; SHALL PROVIDE THE BOARD WITH COPIES OF ALL REPORTS THAT HE SUBMITS TO THE CALIFORNIA BOARD WHICH SHALL INCLUDE DOCUMENTATION OF HIS CONTINUING MEDICAL EDUCATION AND QUARTERLY REPORTS VERIFYING HIS PROBATION COMPLIANCE; AND SHALL INFORM THE BOARD PRIOR TO ENGAGING IN ANY MEDICAL PRACTICE IN INDIANA. $275.50 ASSESSED COSTS.

LITTGE, ROGER O MD, DATE OF BIRTH JUNE 26, 1947, OF 2005 COURT STREET, REDDING, CA, WAS DISCIPLINED BY MEDICARE ON AUGUST 2, 1993.
DISCIPLINARY ACTION: 36-MONTH EXCLUSION FROM THE MEDICARE AND/OR MEDICAID PROGRAMS
OFFENSE: CRIMINAL CONVICTION OR PLEA OF GUILTY, NOLO CONTENDERE, OR NO CONTEST TO A CRIME
NOTES: CONVICTED OF MULTIPLE FELONY AND MISDEMEANOR COUNTS RELATED TO THE UNLAWFUL PRESCRIPTION AND DISPENSING OF CONTROLLED SUBSTANCES.

LITTGE, ROGER O MD, LICENSE NUMBER 0030084, OF REDDING, CA, WAS DISCIPLINED BY WASHINGTON ON MARCH 6, 1995.
DISCIPLINARY ACTION: LICENSE REVOCATION
OFFENSE: CRIMINAL CONVICTION OR PLEA OF GUILTY, NOLO CONTENDERE, OR NO CONTEST TO A CRIME
NOTES: CONVICTION OF SEVERAL CRIMES INVOLVING CONTROLLED SUBSTANCES IN CALIFORNIA. DEFAULT DECISION.

LITTGE, ROGER O MD OF STATE HWY 44 SHINGLETOWN, SHINGLETOWN, CA, WAS DISCIPLINED BY DEA ON MAY 7, 1995.
DISCIPLINARY ACTION: SURRENDER OF CONTROLLED SUBSTANCE LICENSE
OFFENSE: DISCIPLINARY ACTION BY ANOTHER STATE OR AGENCY
NOTES: STATE BOARD.

LONG, WALTER K JR MD, LICENSE NUMBER 0015287, OF KINGWOOD, TX, WAS DISCIPLINED BY WASHINGTON ON NOVEMBER 17, 1995.
NOTES: SHALL NOT PRACTICE IN WASHINGTON UNTIL HE APPEARS BEFORE THE BOARD AND PRESENTS EVIDENCE THAT HE CAN PRACTICE MEDICINE WITH REASONABLE SKILL AND SAFETY.

LONG, WALTER KEIRN JR MD, LICENSE NUMBER 00C4177, OF KINGWOOD, TX, WAS DISCIPLINED BY TEXAS ON APRIL 15, 1994.
DISCIPLINARY ACTION: RESTRICTION PLACED ON LICENSE
OFFENSE: SUBSTANDARD CARE, INCOMPETENCE, OR NEGLIGENCE
NOTES: ADMITTED THAT PATIENTS UNDER HIS TREATMENT HAD

DEVELOPED COMPLICATIONS RELATED TO GASTRIC STAPLING PROCEDURES; SUCH COMPLICATIONS ARE COMMON AND ARE NOT INDICATIVE OF NEGLIGENCE PER SE; PROFESSIONAL FAILURE TO PRACTICE MEDICINE IN AN ACCEPTABLE MANNER CONSISTENT WITH PUBLIC HEALTH AND WELFARE. SHALL NOT PERFORM ANY GASTRIC REDUCTION SURGERY FOR OBESITY; SHALL GIVE A COPY OF THIS ORDER TO ANY HEALTH CARE ENTITY WHERE HE HAS PRIVILEGES; SHALL COOPERATE WITH THE BOARD IN VERIFYING COMPLIANCE; SHALL INFORM BOARD OF CHANGE OF ADDRESS WITHIN 10 DAYS. SHALL NOT SEEK MODIFICATION FOR ONE YEAR.

LOPEZ-SAMAYOA, OMAR E MD, LICENSE NUMBER 0029282, OF LOMA LINDA, CA, WAS DISCIPLINED BY WASHINGTON ON MAY 31, 1996.
DISCIPLINARY ACTION: 60-MONTH PROBATION
NOTES: PROBATION UNDER TERMS AND CONDITIONS INCLUDING A PROFESSIONAL ASSESSMENT EVALUATION.

LOWDEN, ROBERT MD WAS DISCIPLINED BY WASHINGTON ON FEBRUARY 21, 1987.
DISCIPLINARY ACTION: RESTRICTION PLACED ON LICENSE
OFFENSE: SUBSTANDARD CARE, INCOMPETENCE, OR NEGLIGENCE
NOTES: SUBSTANDARD CARE OF ONE PATIENT FROM 1978-80, FAILED TO PERFORM A SUFFICIENT DIAGNOSTIC WORK-UP PRIOR TO A UTERINE SUSPENSION, SUCH THAT THE INDICATIONS FOR THIS RARELY USED PROCEDURE WERE NOT PRESENT, RESULTING IN SERIOUS HARM TO THE PATIENT; SHALL NOT PERFORM MAJOR SURGERY UNLESS THE PATIENT HAS RECEIVED A SECOND OPINION FROM ANOTHER PHYSICIAN; SHALL NOT PERFORM MINOR SURGERY UNLESS PATIENT HAS BEEN RECOMMENDED TO SEEK A SECOND OPINION FROM ANOTHER PHYSICIAN

LUPU, MARIAN F MD OF STORM LAKE, LA, WAS DISCIPLINED BY WASHINGTON ON MARCH 27, 1992.
DISCIPLINARY ACTION: DENIAL OF NEW LICENSE

MABUNGA, ROGELIO FLORES MD, LICENSE NUMBER 0018554, OF SEATTLE, WA, WAS DISCIPLINED BY WASHINGTON ON JANUARY 20, 1990.
DISCIPLINARY ACTION: PROBATION; RESTRICTION PLACED ON CONTROLLED SUBSTANCE LICENSE
OFFENSE: DISCIPLINARY ACTION BY ANOTHER STATE OR AGENCY
NOTES: ON 10/10/87 OREGON LICENSE WAS REVOKED; PRESCRIBED MEDICATIONS FOR NONTHERAPEUTIC REASONS TO TWO PATIENTS, ONE OF WHOM DISPLAYED DRUG SEEKING BEHAVIOR BETWEEN 3/87 AND 8/88. INDEFINITE PERIOD OF SUSPENSION, STAYED AS PROBATION UNDER THE FOLLOWING TERMS AND CONDITIONS: SHALL PERMIT THE BOARD TO MAKE UNANNOUNCED VISITS TO INSPECT RECORDS, INTERVIEW STAFF, AND REVIEW HIS PRACTICE TO MONITOR COMPLIANCE WITH THIS ORDER; SHALL NOT PRESCRIBE ANY SCHEDULE II, III, IV, OR V DRUGS; SHALL APPEAR BEFORE THE BOARD IN ONE YEAR AND PRESENT PROOF THAT HE IS IN COMPLIANCE AND APPEAR ANNUALLY AFTER THAT; MAY REQUEST A CHANGE IN ANY OF THE CONDITIONS AT ANY TIME AFTER IT IS SIGNED; SHALL ATTEND A BOARD APPROVED THREE DAY CONTINUING MEDICAL EDUCATION COURSE ON PAIN THERAPY AND CHRONIC PAIN MANAGEMENT; SHALL WRITE A ONE TO TWO PAGE THESIS ON HOW THE REQUIRED COURSE HELPS HIM IMPROVE HIS PRESCRIBING PRACTICES AND SHALL SUBMIT THIS THESIS TO THE BOARD FOR APPROVAL; SHALL WRITE SYNOPSES OF FOUR TO FIVE DIFFERENT PAIN MANAGEMENT ARTICLES PUBLISHED IN MEDICAL JOURNALS IN THE PAST THREE YEARS AND SHALL SUBMIT THEM TO THE BOARD; SHALL WRITE PARAGRAPHS ON BOTH DEXEDRINE AND RITALIN SUMMARIZING THE INDICATIONS FOR EACH, IF ANY AND SHALL SUBMIT THEM TO THE BOARD; MUST NOTIFY THE BOARD IN WRITING IF HE LEAVES WASHINGTON OR IF HE CHANGES HIS ADDRESSES; ON 6/13/96 THE COMMISSION DENIED HIS REQUEST TO TERMINATE JURISDICTION UNDER THIS ORDER. ON 10/16/96 FOUND NOT IN COMPLIANCE WITH THE ORDER AND DENIED HIS REQUEST TO TERMINATE THE TERMS AND CONDITIONS.

MAERCKS, RALPH OWEN MD OF COCONUT GROVE, FL, WAS DISCIPLINED BY NORTH CAROLINA ON OCTOBER 14, 1987.
DISCIPLINARY ACTION: SURRENDER OF LICENSE

MAERCKS, RALPH OWEN MD, LICENSE NUMBER 0023467, OF MIAMI, FL, WAS DISCIPLINED BY WASHINGTON ON MAY 18, 1991.
DISCIPLINARY ACTION: LICENSE SUSPENSION
OFFENSE: DISCIPLINARY ACTION BY ANOTHER STATE OR AGENCY
NOTES: ENTERED INTO AN AGREEMENT WITH THE FLORIDA BOARD OF MEDICINE VOLUNTARILY RELINQUISHING HIS LICENSE TO PRACTICE MEDICINE AND SURGERY IN THAT STATE ON 11/04/86.

MALDEN, MARCEL MD, LICENSE NUMBER 0005482, OF TACOMA, WA, WAS DISCIPLINED BY WASHINGTON ON JUNE 27, 1991.
DISCIPLINARY ACTION: SURRENDER OF LICENSE
NOTES: ENTERED INTO RETIRED STATUS AGREEMENT WITHOUT FINDINGS; EFFECTIVE DATE OF RETIREMENT 7/31/91. HE AGREED THAT RETIREMENT SHALL BE PERMANENT AND SHALL NOT REAPPLY WITHOUT PRIOR APPROVAL OF THE BOARD; SHALL INFORM THE BOARD IF HE INTENDS TO PRACTICE IN ANY OTHER JURISDICTION.

MALISZEWSKI, BOGDAN F MD, LICENSE NUMBER 0021751, WAS DISCIPLINED BY WASHINGTON ON JANUARY 15, 1993.
DISCIPLINARY ACTION: REPRIMAND
OFFENSE: DISCIPLINARY ACTION BY ANOTHER STATE OR AGENCY
NOTES: MORAL TURPITUDE AND MISREPRESENTATION AND SUSPENSION/REVOCATION OF A LICENSE TO PRACTICE IN ANOTHER JURISDICTION.

MANDEVILLE, JOHN W MD WAS DISCIPLINED BY WASHINGTON ON DECEMBER 13, 1989.
DISCIPLINARY ACTION: SURRENDER OF LICENSE
NOTES: RETIRED EFFECTIVE 6/11/87: ADVISED THAT HE IS UNDER INVESTIGATION BY THE BOARD CONCERNING HIS ABILITY TO PRACTICE MEDICINE WITH REASONABLE SKILL AND SAFETY TO PATIENTS; HE HAS NO PLANS TO RESUME PRACTICE AND RETIREMENT WILL BE PERMANENT. SHALL NOTIFY THE BOARD IF HE PLANS PRACTICE IN THIS OR ANY JURISDICTION.

MANN, DENNIS S DO OF 12345 30TH N.E., SEATTLE, WA, WAS DISCIPLINED BY WASHINGTON ON JUNE 29, 1992.
OFFENSE: PRACTICING WITHOUT A VALID LICENSE
NOTES: PRACTICED MEDICINE WITHOUT A LICENSE AFTER HE DID NOT RENEW HIS LICENSE WHICH EXPIRED ON 11/22/91. SHALL CEASE AND DESIST FROM THE PRACTICE OF OSTEOPATHIC MEDICINE AND SURGERY.

MANN, DENNIS S DO WAS DISCIPLINED BY WASHINGTON ON MAY 18, 1993.
DISCIPLINARY ACTION: PROBATION; FINE
OFFENSE: FAILURE TO COMPLY WITH A PROFESSIONAL RULE
NOTES: FAILED TO COMPLETE THE RENEWAL PROCESS. 30 DAY SUSPENSION, STAYED UNDER THE FOLLOWING TERMS AND CONDITIONS: SHALL PAY FULL FEES FOR RENEWAL OF HIS LICENSE AND COMPLY WITH THE CONTINUING MEDICAL EDUCATION REQUIREMENT; SHALL SUBMIT QUARTERLY REPORTS UNDER PENALTY OF PERJURY REGARDING COMPLIANCE; SHALL NOTIFY THE BOARD IN WRITING OF DEPARTURE AND RETURN DATES FROM

- WASHINGTON -

WASHINGTON; SHALL NOTIFY BOARD OF CHANGE OF ADDRESS; MAY PETITION THE BOARD FOR MODIFICATION AFTER ONE YEAR; TIME SPENT OUT OF WASHINGTON DOES NOT COUNT TOWARD THE TIME OF THIS ORDER; AND SHALL PAY A $1,000 CIVIL PENALTY.

MANN, DENNIS S DO WAS DISCIPLINED BY WASHINGTON ON AUGUST 31, 1993.
OFFENSE: FAILURE TO COMPLY WITH A PREVIOUS BOARD ORDER
NOTES: SHALL IMMEDIATELY CEASE AND DESIST FROM THE PRACTICE OF OSTEOPATHIC MEDICINE AND SURGERY UNTIL HE COMPLIES WITH ALL LEGAL REQUIREMENTS FOR THE RENEWAL OF HIS LICENSE UNDER THE TERMS SET OUT IN HIS STIPULATED ORDER OF PROBATION.

MARASHI, S MOHAMMAD MD, LICENSE NUMBER 0011128, OF SPOKANE, WA, WAS DISCIPLINED BY WASHINGTON ON MARCH 15, 1991.
DISCIPLINARY ACTION: PROBATION; FINE
OFFENSE: CRIMINAL CONVICTION OR PLEA OF GUILTY, NOLO CONTENDERE, OR NO CONTEST TO A CRIME
NOTES: ON 5/1/89 WAS CONVICTED IN U.S DISTRICT COURT, EASTERN DISTRICT OF WASHINGTON, OF WILLFULLY ATTEMPTING TO EVADE OR DEFEAT TAX DUE FOR THE CALENDAR YEARS 1981, 1982, AND 1983 BY FILING A FRAUDULENT TAX RETURN, AND FOR FILING A FALSE TAX RETURN FOR FISCAL YEAR ENDING 9/30/81. SUSPENSION STAYED; CONDITIONS OF PROBATION: SHALL COMPLETE 14 COURSE HOURS OF AMERICAN MEDICAL ASSOCIATION APPROVED CATEGORY I CONTINUING MEDICAL EDUCATION IN THE AREA OF MEDICAL ETHICS WITHIN THREE YEARS; $500 FINE; MAY PETITION FOR MODIFICATION OF THIS ORDER THREE YEARS FROM BOARD ORDER, OR UPON TERMINATION OF FEDERAL PROBATION, WHICHEVER IS SOONER; SHALL INFORM THE BOARD OF A CHANGE OF ADDRESS OR IF HE LEAVES THE STATE. PROBATION TERMINATED AS OF 8/20/93.

MARASHI, S MOHAMMAD MD, LICENSE NUMBER 0100715, OF WEST 105 8TH AVENUE, SPOKANE, WA, WAS DISCIPLINED BY NEW YORK ON JANUARY 30, 1995.
DISCIPLINARY ACTION: 12-MONTH PROBATION
OFFENSE: CRIMINAL CONVICTION OR PLEA OF GUILTY, NOLO CONTENDERE, OR NO CONTEST TO A CRIME
NOTES: CONVICTED OF A FELONY FOR FILING FALSE AND FRAUDULENT INCOME TAX RETURNS. ONE YEAR SUSPENSION STAYED.

MARGOLIS, RONALD C DO WAS DISCIPLINED BY WASHINGTON ON JANUARY 26, 1990.
DISCIPLINARY ACTION: RESTRICTION PLACED ON LICENSE
OFFENSE: PROFESSIONAL MISCONDUCT
NOTES: IF ALLEGATIONS ARE TRUE, IT WOULD MEAN THAT THE PATIENT'S HEALTH WOULD BE AT RISK FROM THE USE OF UNSTERILE SUPPLIES AND EQUIPMENT AND THE ADMINISTRATION OF OUT OF DATE MEDICATION. EMERGENCY RESTRICTION PENDING HEARING: SHALL NOT DIRECTLY OR INDIRECTLY THROUGH AN AGENT OR EMPLOYEE PERFORM ANY IN-OFFICE SURGICAL OR INVASIVE PROCEDURE INCLUDING ANY ABORTIONS, INJECTIONS, OR ANY PROCEDURE REQUIRING THE SEVERING OR PENETRATION OF HUMAN TISSUE. ON 3/12/90 THE RESTRICTIONS ARE LIFTED UNDER THE FOLLOWING CONDITIONS STILL PENDING A HEARING: SHALL INSURE THAT ALL MEDICATIONS DISPENSED OR USED IN HIS OFFICE WILL BE CURRENT; HIS OFFICE SHALL BE INSPECTED BY DEPARTMENT OF HEALTH OFFICIALS TO VERIFY THAT ALL MEDICATIONS FOR PATIENT USE ARE WITHIN CURRENT EXPIRATION DATES AND THAT HE HAS A FULLY STOCKED EMERGENCY KIT; SHALL USE ONLY STERILE DISPOSABLE NEEDLES, SYRINGES, CANNULAS, AND LAMINARIA AND WILL USE THEM ONLY ONCE, DISPOSING OF EACH ITEM USED; SHALL HIRE A NURSE WHO WILL BE IN CHARGE OF OVERSEEING OFFICE STERILITY AND WHO SHALL REPORT UPON REQUEST TO THE DEPARTMENT OF HEALTH REGARDING ADHERENCE TO STERILE PROCEDURE IN THE OFFICE; SHALL PERFORM, IN HIS OFFICE ONLY, SUCH NECESSARY BLOOD TEST AS RH, PREGNANCY, AND WET MOUNT FOR BACTERIAL INFECTIONS; ALL OTHER TESTS SHALL BE SENT TO A PATHOLOGY LABORATORY AND THE PATIENT WILL BE CHARGED ACCORDING TO LABORATORY CHARGE; ULTRASOUNDS WILL BE PERFORMED AS NEEDED; HIS OFFICE AND ROOMS SHALL BE OPEN TO REGULAR OR RANDOM INSPECTIONS; ALONG WITH HIS STAFF, SHALL DRAW UP AN OFFICE PROTOCOL FOR ALL TO FOLLOW REGARDING ROTATION OF MEDICATION, OFFICE STERILIZATION PROCEDURES, CHARTING PROCEDURES, AND MACHINE MAINTENANCE WHICH SHALL BE MADE AVAILABLE UPON BOARD REQUEST. NOTHING IN THIS ORDER SHALL BE CONSTRUED AS AN ADMISSION OF ANY WRONG-DOING OR GUILT.

MARGOLIS, RONALD C DO, DATE OF BIRTH FEBRUARY 15, 1942, OF 945 ELFORD DRIVE NW, SEATTLE, WA, WAS DISCIPLINED BY MEDICARE ON MARCH 16, 1992.
DISCIPLINARY ACTION: 120-MONTH EXCLUSION FROM THE MEDICARE AND/OR MEDICAID PROGRAMS
OFFENSE: CRIMINAL CONVICTION OR PLEA OF GUILTY, NOLO CONTENDERE, OR NO CONTEST TO A CRIME
NOTES: PROGRAM-RELATED CONVICTION.

MARGOLIS, RONALD C DO WAS DISCIPLINED BY WASHINGTON ON AUGUST 7, 1992.
DISCIPLINARY ACTION: 36-MONTH LICENSE SUSPENSION; MONITORING OF PHYSICIAN
OFFENSE: CRIMINAL CONVICTION OR PLEA OF GUILTY, NOLO CONTENDERE, OR NO CONTEST TO A CRIME
NOTES: ON 4/29/91 PLED GUILTY TO MEDICAL CARE FALSE STATEMENT; AND ADMITTED TO KNOWINGLY MAKING FALSE REPRESENTATIONS OF MATERIAL FACT IN APPLYING FOR PAYMENT FOR TREATING MEDICAID RECIPIENTS. SUSPENSION WILL BE STAYED UNDER TERMS AND CONDITIONS: SHALL DEVELOP A WRITTEN PROTOCOL OUTLINING HIS ABORTION PROCEDURES AND ANY OTHER MEDICAL PROCEDURES COMMONLY PERFORMED IN HIS OFFICES; SHALL DEVELOP A WRITTEN PROTOCOL WITH RESPECT TO RECORD KEEPING WHICH SHALL INSURE THAT ALL PROCEDURES FOR WHICH BILLING IS SUBMITTED ARE CLEARLY IDENTIFIED AND SUBSTANTIATED AND THE MANNER IN WHICH BILLS ARE TO BE PREPARED AND SUBMITTED; SHALL BE SUBJECT TO UNANNOUNCED INSPECTIONS FOR THE PURPOSE OF DETERMINING HIS COMPLIANCE; SHALL NOTIFY THE BOARD IN WRITING OF CHANGES IN ADDRESS; SHALL NOTIFY THE BOARD IN WRITING DATES OF DEPARTURE AND RETURN FROM WASHINGTON; TIME SPENT OUT OF WASHINGTON DOES NOT COUNT TOWARD PROBATION; AND MAY PETITION THE BOARD FOR REINSTATEMENT IN NO SOONER THAN THREE YEARS. ON 2/08/96 RELEASED FROM THE ORDER AND ISSUED AN UNRESTRICTED AND UNCONDITIONAL LICENSE PROVIDED THAT HIS ANNUAL LICENSEE FEES HAVE BEEN PAID.

MARGOLIS, RONALD C DO, LICENSE NUMBER 0109159, OF 9730 3RD AVENUE NORTHEAST #201, SEATTLE, WA, WAS DISCIPLINED BY NEW YORK ON FEBRUARY 22, 1994.
DISCIPLINARY ACTION: 60-MONTH LICENSE SUSPENSION
OFFENSE: DISCIPLINARY ACTION BY ANOTHER STATE OR AGENCY
NOTES: CONVICTED OF MEDICAID FRAUD; HAD DISCIPLINARY ACTION TAKEN AGAINST HIS WASHINGTON LICENSE.

- WASHINGTON -

MARGOLIS, RONALD C DO, LICENSE NUMBER 20A4455, OF SEATTLE, WA, WAS DISCIPLINED BY CALIFORNIA ON NOVEMBER 4, 1994.
DISCIPLINARY ACTION: LICENSE REVOCATION
OFFENSE: DISCIPLINARY ACTION BY ANOTHER STATE OR AGENCY
NOTES: ACTION IN WASHINGTON FOR CONVICTION OF A FELONY IN BILLING MEDICAL PROGRAM.

MARGOLIS, RONALD C DO, LICENSE NUMBER 0109159, OF 9730 3RD AVENUE NORTH EAST, SEATTLE, WA, WAS DISCIPLINED BY NEW YORK ON FEBRUARY 22, 1995.
DISCIPLINARY ACTION: 60-MONTH LICENSE SUSPENSION
OFFENSE: CRIMINAL CONVICTION OR PLEA OF GUILTY, NOLO CONTENDERE, OR NO CONTEST TO A CRIME
NOTES: PLED GUILTY IN WASHINGTON SUPREME COURT OF KNOWINGLY MAKING OR CAUSING TO BE MADE FALSE STATEMENTS IN APPLICATIONS FOR PAYMENT TO A MEDICAID PROGRAM.

MATHEWS, JOHN WAYNE MD, LICENSE NUMBER 0017392, OF BELLEVUE, WA, WAS DISCIPLINED BY WASHINGTON ON JANUARY 18, 1991.
DISCIPLINARY ACTION: PROBATION; FINE
OFFENSE: LOSS OR RESTRICTION OF HOSPITAL PRIVILEGES
NOTES: IN 8/89 HIS PRIVILEGES TO PRACTICE AT OVERLAKE HOSPITAL AND MEDICAL CENTER WERE SUMMARILY SUSPENDED DUE TO FALSIFICATION AND/OR FAILING TO PROVIDE INFORMATION ON HIS REAPPOINTMENT APPLICATION REGARDING THE FACT HE HAD BEEN NAMED IN A LAWSUIT BY A FORMER PATIENT IN MASSACHUSETTS; HAD A ROMANTIC SEXUALIZED RELATIONSHIP WITH A PATIENT STARTING IN 1979, AND HAD A ROMANTIC RELATIONSHIP AND SEXUAL CONTACT WITH A PATIENT STARTING IN 1988. REVOCATION STAYED; CONDITIONS OF PROBATION: SHALL HAVE A FEMALE CO-THERAPIST PRESENT WHENEVER HE CONSULTS WITH OR TREATS A FEMALE PATIENT OR RELATIVE, OR SHALL HAVE FEMALE PATIENT CONSENT IN WRITING TO HAVE SESSION VIDEOTAPED, WHICH WILL THEN BE REVIEWED BY CO-THERAPIST; ALL PATIENTS AND FACILITIES WHERE HE WORKS SHALL RECEIVE A LETTER DESCRIBING THE MONITORING CONDITION AND THE REASONS FOR IT; SHALL NOT HAVE SEXUAL CONTACT OR SEXUALLY ORIENTED CONDUCT WITH ANY PATIENT, FORMER PATIENT, IMMEDIATE RELATIVES OR FRIENDS OF PATIENTS WITH ONE EXCEPTION; SHALL NOT DIAGNOSE, TREAT OR PRESCRIBE MEDICATION FOR ANY FEMALE WITH WHOM HE HAS HAD A ROMANTIC OR SEXUAL RELATIONSHIP, OR HER FAMILY MEMBERS; SHALL CONTINUE WITH BOARD APPROVED THERAPIST TWICE A WEEK AND ONE HOUR SESSIONS WITH PSYCHIATRIC COLLEAGUES BIWEEKLY; SHALL CONTINUE TO HAVE ONE HOUR SUPERVISION OF THERAPY CASES BIWEEKLY; SHALL PROVIDE QUARTERLY REPORTS TO BOARD FROM SUPERVISOR AND THERAPIST; SHALL UNDERGO POLYGRAPH EXAMS; SHALL PERMIT A BOARD REPRESENTATIVE TO MAKE UNANNOUNCED INSPECTIONS OF PRACTICE AT LEAST YEARLY; SHALL APPEAR BEFORE THE BOARD EVERY SIX MONTHS FOR THE FIRST YEAR, AND YEARLY THEREAFTER, FOR COMPLIANCE REVIEW; SHALL PROVIDE COPY OR ORDER TO ALL HOSPITALS AND CLINICS WHERE HE HAS PRIVILEGES AND ALL PROFESSIONAL STAFF IN HIS OFFICE; $1000 FINE; SHALL INFORM THE BOARD IF HE LEAVES THE STATE; MAY NOT REQUEST TERMINATION OF THE ORDER FOR FIVE YEARS. ON 4/10/92, A COMPLIANCE/PROGRESS REVIEW WAS HELD AND HE WAS FOUND OUT OF COMPLIANCE WITH BOARDS PREVIOUS ORDER. REQUEST FOR MODIFICATION OF ORDER DENIED. DEPARTMENT SHALL MAKE AN ANNOUNCED OR UNANNOUNCED VISIT TO INSPECT HIS OFFICE AND MEDICAL RECORDS. PRIOR TO NEXT REVIEW, SHALL SUBMIT REPORTS FROM TWO DOCTORS ADDRESSING HIS PROGRESS IN THERAPY AND HIS ABILITY TO PRACTICE MEDICINE IN A SAFE MANNER. ON 5/27/94 FOUND TO BE IN COMPLIANCE WITH THIS ORDER AND IT WAS AMENDED, LIFTING THE MONITORING REQUIREMENT PROVIDING HE PREPARES AND PROVIDES A DISCLOSURE STATEMENT OUTLINING THE TERMS OF THE ORDER TO ALL FEMALE PATIENTS, WHICH THEY WILL SIGN AND HAVE PLACED IN THEIR RECORDS. ON 3/27/95 ORDER MODIFIED SUCH THAT SUPERVISION AND PSYCHOTHERAPY REQUIREMENTS REDUCED. ON 4/4/96 REQUEST FOR RELEASE FROM JURISIDICTION DENIED; SHALL OBTAIN AN INDEPENDENT EVALUATION BY A COMMISSION APPROVED SPECIALIST WHO DEALS WITH SEXUAL PROBLEMS WITHIN FOUR MONTHS.

MATHEWS, JOHN WAYNE MD, LICENSE NUMBER 0031852, OF 27 100TH AVE NE MEYDENBAUER BLDG, -BELLEVUE, WA, WAS DISCIPLINED BY MASSACHUSETTS ON SEPTEMBER 23, 1992.
DISCIPLINARY ACTION: NONRENEWAL OF LICENSE
OFFENSE: DISCIPLINARY ACTION BY ANOTHER STATE OR AGENCY
NOTES: DISCIPLINARY ACTION BY OTHER JURISDICTION; IMPROPER PRESCRIBING FOR SELF; SEXUAL MISCONDUCT. REVOCATION OF INCHOATE RIGHT TO RENEW.

MCCUIN, JEROME MD OF EDMONDS, CA, WAS DISCIPLINED BY WASHINGTON ON MAY 21, 1992.
DISCIPLINARY ACTION: DENIAL OF NEW LICENSE
NOTES: MAY NOT APPLY FOR A LICENSE FOR A MINIMUM OF TEN YEARS FROM THE DATE OF THE ORDER.

MCCUIN, JEROME ELLIS MD, LICENSE NUMBER 0C36270, OF INGLEWOOD, CA, WAS DISCIPLINED BY CALIFORNIA ON FEBRUARY 11, 1987.
DISCIPLINARY ACTION: 4-MONTH LICENSE SUSPENSION; 116-MONTH PROBATION
OFFENSE: INSURANCE, MEDICARE, OR MEDICAID FRAUD
NOTES: REVOCATION STAYED; FALSE INSURANCE BILLING FOR COSMETIC SURGERY AND ANESTHESIA SERVICES

MCCUIN, JEROME ELLIS MD, LICENSE NUMBER 0016516, OF 5601 6TH AVENUE, TACOMA, WA, WAS DISCIPLINED BY GEORGIA ON JULY 14, 1988.
DISCIPLINARY ACTION: LICENSE REVOCATION
OFFENSE: DISCIPLINARY ACTION BY ANOTHER STATE OR AGENCY

MCCUIN, JEROME ELLIS MD OF 3839 W FIRST ST B8, SANTA ANA, CA, WAS DISCIPLINED BY DEA ON APRIL 1, 1992.
DISCIPLINARY ACTION: RESTRICTION PLACED ON CONTROLLED SUBSTANCE LICENSE
OFFENSE: SUBSTANCE ABUSE
NOTES: VOLUNTARILY SURRENDERED GEORGIA MEDICAL LICENSE. CURRENTLY ON TEN YEAR PROBATION FOR FALSIFYING MEDICAL AND INSURANCE RECORDS. REQUIRED TO ENTER DIVERSION PROGRAM FOR COCAINE ADDICTION. INCARCERATED 10/26/87 IN BORON, CALIFORNIA FOR COCAINE ADDICTION; RELEASED 6/89. APPROVAL OF APPLICATION FOR SCHEDULES IV AND V FOR THREE YEAR PERIOD.

MCCUIN, JEROME ELLIS MD, LICENSE NUMBER 0C36270, OF CARSON, CA, WAS DISCIPLINED BY CALIFORNIA ON FEBRUARY 18, 1993.
DISCIPLINARY ACTION: EMERGENCY SUSPENSION
NOTES: TEMPORARY RESTRAINING ORDER ISSUED.

MCCUIN, JEROME ELLIS MD, LICENSE NUMBER 0C36270, OF CARSON, CA, WAS DISCIPLINED BY CALIFORNIA ON SEPTEMBER 17, 1993.
DISCIPLINARY ACTION: LICENSE REVOCATION
OFFENSE: FAILURE TO COMPLY WITH A PREVIOUS BOARD ORDER
NOTES: COCAINE ABUSE, FALSE RECORDS IN VIOLATION OF

- WASHINGTON -

FEDERAL PROBATION FOR PRIOR CONVICTION FOR BANK FRAUD SCHEME; AND IN VIOLATION OF PROBATION OF PRIOR BOARD DISCIPLINE.

MCDONNELL, THOMAS R MD WAS DISCIPLINED BY WASHINGTON ON AUGUST 16, 1989.
DISCIPLINARY ACTION: 120-MONTH PROBATION; RESTRICTION PLACED ON CONTROLLED SUBSTANCE LICENSE
OFFENSE: SUBSTANCE ABUSE
NOTES: SUFFERS FROM THE DISEASE OF CHEMICAL DEPENDENCY AS A RESULT OF WHICH, ON A REGULAR AND FREQUENT BASIS, PERSONALLY USED CONTROLLED SUBSTANCES FOR NONTHERAPEUTIC PURPOSES DURING AND AFTER HIS OFFICE HOURS WHILE ENGAGED IN THE PRACTICE OF MEDICINE; PRESCRIBED CONTROLLED SUBSTANCES IN A NONTHERAPEUTIC MANNER; AND USED HIS POSITION AS A PHYSICIAN TO OBTAIN LARGE QUANTITIES OF CONTROLLED SUBSTANCES BY FRAUD. SUMMARY SUSPENSION DATED 6/2/86 IS STAYED TO 10 YEAR PROBATION UNDER THE FOLLOWING TERMS AND CONDITIONS: SHALL HAVE A BOARD APPROVED SUPERVISORY PHYSICIAN WHO SHALL SUBMIT REPORTS TO THE BOARD QUARTERLY FOR TWO YEARS AND EVERY SIX MONTHS THEREAFTER; SHALL BE MONITORED BY THE WASHINGTON MONITORED TREATMENT PROGRAM (WMTP) AND SHALL COMPLY WITH ALL CONDITIONS IN THE CONTRACT WHICH SHALL INCLUDE RANDOM URINE TESTING WITH QUARTERLY REPORTS FOR TWO YEARS AND EVERY SIX MONTHS THEREAFTER; SHALL APPEAR BEFORE THE BOARD EACH YEAR OR UPON BOARD REQUEST; SHALL REQUEST IN WRITING APPROVAL FROM THE BOARD PRIOR TO ENGAGING IN ANY MEDICAL PRACTICE; SHALL PERMIT THE BOARD TO MAKE UNANNOUNCED VISITS TO INSPECT RECORDS INCLUDING MEDICAL RECORDS, INTERVIEW STAFF AND SUPERVISORS, AND OTHERWISE REVIEW HIS PRACTICE TO MONITOR FOR COMPLIANCE WITH THIS ORDER; SHALL PRESCRIBE CONTROLLED SUBSTANCES TO HOSPITALIZED PATIENTS ONLY; MAY REQUEST A CHANGE IN ANY OF THE ABOVE CONDITIONS OF PROBATION IN NO SOONER THAN TWO YEARS; MUST NOTIFY THE BOARD IN WRITING IF HE LEAVES WASHINGTON; MAY REQUEST THE BOARD IN FIVE YEARS TO TERMINATE ITS PROBATION AND END JURISDICTION IN THIS CASE. ON 5/26/93 LICENSE FULLY REINSTATED.

MCDONNELL, THOMAS R MD, LICENSE NUMBER 0010443, OF SPANAWAY, WA, WAS DISCIPLINED BY WASHINGTON ON APRIL 8, 1996.
DISCIPLINARY ACTION: EMERGENCY SUSPENSION
OFFENSE: SUBSTANDARD CARE, INCOMPETENCE, OR NEGLIGENCE
NOTES: ALLEGED NEGLIGENCE. SUMMARILY SUSPENDED.

MCDONNELL, THOMAS R MD, LICENSE NUMBER 00M4828, WAS DISCIPLINED BY IDAHO ON AUGUST 13, 1996.
DISCIPLINARY ACTION: EMERGENCY SUSPENSION
OFFENSE: DISCIPLINARY ACTION BY ANOTHER STATE OR AGENCY
NOTES: EMERGENCY SUSPENSION IN WASHINGTON 4/08/96 FOR FAILING TO ADEQUATELY SUPERVISE NURSING STAFF AND MID-LEVEL HEALTH CARE PROVIDERS UNDER HIS SUPERVISION TO SUCH A DEGREE THAT CERTAIN PATIENTS AND EMPLOYEES HAVE BEEN EXPOSED TO AN UNREASONABLE RISK OF HARM; AND FELL BELOW THE STANDARD OF CARE OF A REASONABLY PRUDENT PHYSICIAN, THEREBY EXPOSING CERTAIN PATIENTS AND EMPLOYEES TO AN UNREASONABLE RISK OF HARM. THE IDAHO BOARD ADOPTS AND INCORPORATES THE TERMS AND CONDITIONS THE WASHINGTON ORDER.

MCGUIRE, JAMES R MD WAS DISCIPLINED BY ALASKA ON FEBRUARY 10, 1994.
DISCIPLINARY ACTION: LICENSE SUSPENSION; RESTRICTION PLACED ON LICENSE
OFFENSE: SEXUAL ABUSE OF OR SEXUAL MISCONDUCT WITH A PATIENT
NOTES: SEXUAL MISCONDUCT WITH A FEMALE PATIENT. BECAUSE OF SEXUAL MISCONDUCT WITH FEMALE PATIENT OVER ABOUT A FIVE AND A HALF YEAR PERIOD, BOARD ISSUED HIS LICENSE SUSPENDED UNTIL BOARD RECEIVES PROOF THAT HE IS ABLE TO PRACTICE SAFELY.

MCGUIRE, JAMES R MD, LICENSE NUMBER 0015236, OF STEILACOOM, WA, WAS DISCIPLINED BY WASHINGTON ON JULY 10, 1995.
DISCIPLINARY ACTION: FINE; RESTRICTION PLACED ON LICENSE
OFFENSE: DISCIPLINARY ACTION BY ANOTHER STATE OR AGENCY
NOTES: ACTION IN ALASKA WHERE HIS LICENSE WAS SUSPENDED. SHALL RESTRICT HIS PRACTICE TO THE TREATMENT OF ADULT MALES AT MCNEIL ISLAND CORRECTIONS CENTER; SHALL PRACTICE UNDER SUPERVISION; SHALL CONTINUE THERAPY AND HAVE A PHYSICAL EXAMINATION; SHALL REFRAIN FROM ALCOHOL AND MOOD-ALTERING SUBSTANCES; SHALL APPEAR BEFORE THE BOARD FOR A COMPLIANCE REVIEW IN SIX MONTHS. $1,000 FINE.

MCGUIRE, TERENCE F MD, LICENSE NUMBER 00E5845, OF EDMONDS, WA, WAS DISCIPLINED BY TEXAS ON MARCH 4, 1995.
DISCIPLINARY ACTION: REPRIMAND
OFFENSE: PROFESSIONAL MISCONDUCT
NOTES: BETWEEN 1989 AND 1991, FAILED TO MAINTAIN APPROPRIATE PHYSICIAN-PATIENT BOUNDARIES IN THE COURSE OF PSYCHIATRIC CARE OF AN ADULT FEMALE PATIENT: ALLOWED A PERSONAL RELATIONSHIP TO DEVELOP AND CONTINUE WHICH HAD AN ADVERSE IMPACT ON PATIENT CARE AND INCLUDED INAPPROPRIATE PHYSICAL CONTACT; OVER THE COURSE OF SEVERAL YEARS, FAILED TO KEEP ADEQUATE RECORDS OF PSYCHIATRIC CARE AND COUNSELING OF VARIOUS PATIENTS; HE REPORTS HIS LACK OF DOCUMENTATION WAS INTENTIONAL IN AN EFFORT TO PROTECT THE CONFIDENTIALITY OF PATIENTS AND FAMILY MEMBERS INVOLVED IN CRITICAL WORK FOR THE GOVERNMENT.

MCINTYRE, DAVID J MD, LICENSE NUMBER 0008243, OF BELLEVUE, WA, WAS DISCIPLINED BY WASHINGTON ON FEBRUARY 18, 1993.
DISCIPLINARY ACTION: 36-MONTH PROBATION
OFFENSE: SUBSTANDARD CARE, INCOMPETENCE, OR NEGLIGENCE
NOTES: INCOMPETENCE/NEGLIGENCE/MALPRACTICE. ON 5/21/93 HIS MOTION FOR RECONSIDERATION WAS DENIED. ON 7/27/95 HIS REQUEST WAS GRANTED TO ELIMINATE THAT HE OBTAIN SECOND OPINIONS ON CERTAIN SURGERIES. ON 6/16/96 HIS REQUEST TO TERMINATE THIS ORDER GRANTED AND LICENSE UNRESTRICTED.

MCNAMARA, JOHN E MD WAS DISCIPLINED BY WASHINGTON ON AUGUST 21, 1990.
DISCIPLINARY ACTION: SURRENDER OF LICENSE
NOTES: UNDER INVESTIGATION CONCERNING COMPLIANCE WITH A PREVIOUS BOARD ORDER. RETIREMENT SHALL BE PERMANENT; HAS NO PLANS TO RESUME PRACTICE SUBSEQUENT TO 8/21/90.

MCNAMARA, JOHN E MD OF YELM MEMORIAL CLINIC, YELM, WA, WAS DISCIPLINED BY DEA ON DECEMBER 6, 1990.
DISCIPLINARY ACTION: SURRENDER OF CONTROLLED SUBSTANCE LICENSE
OFFENSE: DISCIPLINARY ACTION BY ANOTHER STATE OR AGENCY
NOTES: DEA RECEIVED INFORMATION ON 10/22/90 THAT HE ENTERED STIPULATED RETIREMENT AGREEMENT WITH

- WASHINGTON -

WASHINGTON MEDICAL BOARD, WHICH TERMINATED HIS AUTHORIZATION TO PRESCRIBE, ADMINISTER, OR DISPENSE CONTROLLED SUBSTANCES.

MCNAUGHTON, MARSE L MD, LICENSE NUMBER 0015856, OF TACOMA, WA, WAS DISCIPLINED BY WASHINGTON ON MAY 31, 1996.
DISCIPLINARY ACTION: RESTRICTION PLACED ON CONTROLLED SUBSTANCE LICENSE; REQUIRED TO TAKE ADDITIONAL MEDICAL EDUCATION
NOTES: RESTRICTED HIS PRESCRIBING OF CONTROLLED SUBSTANCES AND REQUIRED HIM TO TAKE A PROGRAM OF REMEDIAL EDUCATION PRESCRIBING CONTROLLED SUBSTANCES.

MCNICHOL, STANLEY P DO WAS DISCIPLINED BY WASHINGTON ON NOVEMBER 30, 1990.
DISCIPLINARY ACTION: SUSPENSION OF CONTROLLED SUBSTANCE LICENSE
OFFENSE: PHYSICAL OR MENTAL ILLNESS INHIBITING THE ABILITY TO PRACTICE WITH SKILL AND SAFETY
NOTES: ALLEGATIONS OF A MENTAL CONDITION RESULTING IN DEFECTS IN HIS JUDGMENT AND HIS ABILITY TO PRACTICE PSYCHIATRY. LICENSE PLACED ON INACTIVE STATUS UNDER TERMS AND CONDITIONS: SHALL NOT ENGAGE IN THE PRACTICE OF OSTEOPATHIC MEDICINE AND SURGERY, INCLUDING PSYCHIATRY; IN ORDER TO PROVIDE CONTINUED THERAPY TO HIS CURRENT PATIENTS, THE RESTRICTIONS SHALL NOT PROHIBIT HIM FROM COOPERATING WITH LEWIS COUNTY MENTAL HEALTH OFFICIALS OR ANY OTHER SUBSEQUENT TREATING PHYSICIANS THROUGH CONSULTING WITH AND MAKING PATIENT RECORDS AVAILABLE; WITHIN 30 DAYS SHALL UNDERGO AN INPATIENT PSYCHIATRIC EVALUATION AND BOARD APPROVED TREATMENT IF NECESSARY; HIS PRIVILEGE TO PRESCRIBE CONTROLLED SUBSTANCES IS SUSPENDED AND SHALL SURRENDER HIS CURRENT CONTROLLED SUBSTANCE REGISTRATION. UPON SUCCESSFUL COMPLETION OF ANY REQUIRED PSYCHIATRIC TREATMENT, MAY PETITION THE BOARD FOR REINSTATEMENT.

MCNICOL, STANLEY P DO, DATE OF BIRTH JANUARY 23, 1947, LICENSE NUMBER 0006735, OF 5 PAVILLION COURT, SACRAMENTO, CA, WAS DISCIPLINED BY MICHIGAN ON NOVEMBER 8, 1993.
DISCIPLINARY ACTION: 12-MONTH LICENSE SUSPENSION
OFFENSE: PHYSICAL OR MENTAL ILLNESS INHIBITING THE ABILITY TO PRACTICE WITH SKILL AND SAFETY

MCNICOL, STANLEY P DO, LICENSE NUMBER 20A4531, OF RANCHO CORDOVA, CA, WAS DISCIPLINED BY CALIFORNIA ON JANUARY 5, 1996.
DISCIPLINARY ACTION: 3-MONTH LICENSE SUSPENSION; 180-MONTH PROBATION
OFFENSE: FAILURE TO COMPLY WITH A PREVIOUS BOARD ORDER
NOTES: VIOLATION OF PROBATION. MENTAL CONDITION REQUIRING TREATMENT.

MCNICOL, STANLEY PAGE DO OF 2451 NE KRESKY ROAD SUITE F, CHEHALIS, WA, WAS DISCIPLINED BY DEA ON OCTOBER 25, 1991.
DISCIPLINARY ACTION: SURRENDER OF CONTROLLED SUBSTANCE LICENSE
OFFENSE: DISCIPLINARY ACTION BY ANOTHER STATE OR AGENCY
NOTES: REVOCATION OF MEDICAL LICENSE.

MERLEY, ROBERT W MD WAS DISCIPLINED BY WASHINGTON ON JANUARY 20, 1989.
DISCIPLINARY ACTION: SURRENDER OF LICENSE
NOTES: ACKNOWLEDGES THAT HE IS UNDER INVESTIGATION BY THE BOARD CONCERNING HIS ABILITY TO PRACTICE MEDICINE WITH REASONABLE SKILL AND SAFETY TO PATIENTS. PERMANENTLY RETIRED FROM MEDICAL PRACTICE SINCE 3/21/89 AND HAS NO PLANS TO RESUME PRACTICE; MAY ONLY RESUME PRACTICE WITH PRIOR BOARD APPROVAL.

MESSNER, ROBERT C MD, LICENSE NUMBER 0009334, OF RICHLAND, WA, WAS DISCIPLINED BY WASHINGTON ON MARCH 15, 1991.
OFFENSE: SUBSTANCE ABUSE
NOTES: ON 7/9/85 HIS LICENSE WAS SUSPENDED BASED UPON A FINDING OF IMPAIRED PRACTICE AS A RESULT OF EXCESSIVE OR INAPPROPRIATE USE OF ALCOHOL. SUSPENSION STAYED ON 9/20/85; HAS BEEN IN COMPLIANCE WITH BOARD'S ORDERS AND HAS TAKEN ACTIVE ROLE IN HIS RECOVERY SINCE THEN. LICENSE REINSTATED IN FULL.

MEYERS, GEORGE C MD, LICENSE NUMBER 0C36092, OF BELLEVUE, WA, WAS DISCIPLINED BY CALIFORNIA ON JULY 18, 1994.
DISCIPLINARY ACTION: LICENSE REVOCATION
OFFENSE: DISCIPLINARY ACTION BY ANOTHER STATE OR AGENCY
NOTES: ACTION BY WASHINGTON STATE BOARD RELATED TO CHARGES OF IMPAIRED PHYSICAL AND COGNITIVE FUNCTIONING TO THE EXTENT THAT SAFE PRACTICE CANNOT BE RENDERED. DEFAULT DECISION.

MEYERS, RONALD A MD, LICENSE NUMBER 0G70050, OF PORT ANGELES, WA, WAS DISCIPLINED BY CALIFORNIA ON AUGUST 17, 1994.
DISCIPLINARY ACTION: 60-MONTH PROBATION
OFFENSE: DISCIPLINARY ACTION BY ANOTHER STATE OR AGENCY
NOTES: ACTION BY FLORIDA BOARD ON ALLEGATIONS OF FAILURE TO MAINTAIN PROPER DOCUMENTATION OF REQUIRED CONTINUING MEDICAL EDUCATION CREDITS AND FRAUDULENT MISREPRESENTATION OF COMPLIANCE WITH CONTINUING MEDICAL EDUCATION REQUIREMENTS. REVOCATION STAYED.

MINIELLY, RICHARD W MD, LICENSE NUMBER 0030525, OF ATHENS, PA, WAS DISCIPLINED BY WASHINGTON ON OCTOBER 6, 1995.
NOTES: AGREED NOT TO PRACTICE SURGERY IN WASHINGTON UNTIL HE APPEARS BEFORE THE BOARD AND SUBMITS TO AN EVALUATION OF HIS SURGICAL SKILLS.

MINIELLY, RICHARD WESLEY MD, LICENSE NUMBER 0152508, OF 3523 COUNTRY CLUB ROAD, ENDWELL, NY, WAS DISCIPLINED BY NEW YORK ON APRIL 28, 1994.
DISCIPLINARY ACTION: 3-MONTH LICENSE SUSPENSION; 21-MONTH PROBATION
OFFENSE: SUBSTANDARD CARE, INCOMPETENCE, OR NEGLIGENCE
NOTES: GUILTY OF GROSS NEGLIGENCE AND GROSS INCOMPETENCE. REMAINDER OF 2 YEAR SUSPENSION STAYED; SHALL NOT PERFORM LASER SURGERY.

MINIELLY, RICHARD WESLEY MD, DATE OF BIRTH MARCH 27, 1943, LICENSE NUMBER 1040198, OF 117 PROFESSIONAL RD, ROANOKE RAPIDS, NC, WAS DISCIPLINED BY MICHIGAN ON AUGUST 21, 1995.
DISCIPLINARY ACTION: 6-MONTH LICENSE SUSPENSION; FINE
OFFENSE: DISCIPLINARY ACTION BY ANOTHER STATE OR AGENCY
NOTES: FAILURE TO REPORT/COMPLY. $2,000 FINE.

MINIELLY, RICHARD WESLEY MD, DATE OF BIRTH MARCH 27, 1943, LICENSE NUMBER 022570E, OF PO BOX 1122, 117 PROF. ROAD, ROANOKE RAPIDS, NC, WAS DISCIPLINED BY PENNSYLVANIA ON OCTOBER 2, 1995.
DISCIPLINARY ACTION: PROBATION
OFFENSE: DISCIPLINARY ACTION BY ANOTHER STATE OR AGENCY
NOTES: RECIPROCAL ACTION IN NEW YORK. LICENSE SUSPENDED; STAYED IN FAVOR OF PROBATION WITH TERMS AND CONDITIONS. PROBATION CONCURRENT WITH PROBATION IN NEW YORK. PROBATION TERMINATED ON 12/30/96.

MITCHELL, WILLIAM B MD OF COLUMBIA, SC, WAS DISCIPLINED BY

- WASHINGTON -

SOUTH CAROLINA ON FEBRUARY 11, 1988.
DISCIPLINARY ACTION: DENIAL OF NEW LICENSE
OFFENSE: SUBSTANCE ABUSE
NOTES: DENIAL OF APPLICATION DUE TO LACK OF DOCUMENTED COMMITMENT TO SOBRIETY

MITCHELL, WILLIAM B MD, LICENSE NUMBER 0009317, OF CLAREMORE, OK, WAS DISCIPLINED BY WASHINGTON ON JUNE 19, 1992.
DISCIPLINARY ACTION: PROBATION
NOTES: ALLEGATIONS OF ACTION TAKEN IN ANOTHER STATE. ON 5/11/95 HIS REQUEST TO TERMINATE THIS PROBATION GRANTED.

MOFFETT, CHARLES MD WAS DISCIPLINED BY WASHINGTON ON MARCH 19, 1993.
DISCIPLINARY ACTION: SURRENDER OF LICENSE
OFFENSE: OVERPRESCRIBING OR MISPRESCRIBING DRUGS
NOTES: UNDER INVESTIGATION BY THE BOARD FOR PRESCRIBING CONTROLLED SUBSTANCE WITHOUT KEEPING MEDICAL RECORDS. VOLUNTARY RETIREMENT EFFECTIVE 6/18/93: HAS NO PLANS TO RESUME PRACTICE SUBSEQUENT TO THE DATE OF RETIREMENT; HIS RETIREMENT SHALL BE PERMANENT; MAY RESUME PRACTICE ONLY WITH PRIOR BOARD APPROVAL; WILL NOTIFY THE BOARD IF HE PLANS TO RESUME PRACTICE IN THIS OR ANY OTHER JURISDICTION. THE BOARD MAY RELEASE ANY INFORMATION RELATING TO THE CURRENT INVESTIGATION TO THE PROPER AUTHORITIES IN ANY JURISDICTION IN WHICH HE PLANS TO PRACTICE; THE BOARD MAY TAKE ACTION UPON FAILURE TO COMPLY. THE INVESTIGATION WAS TERMINATED.

MONTOJO, PEDRO M MD, LICENSE NUMBER 0016153, OF SPARTA, TN, WAS DISCIPLINED BY WASHINGTON ON DECEMBER 18, 1992.
DISCIPLINARY ACTION: SURRENDER OF LICENSE
OFFENSE: SUBSTANDARD CARE, INCOMPETENCE, OR NEGLIGENCE
NOTES: NEGLIGENCE.

MONTOJO, PEDRO M MD, LICENSE NUMBER 0C38665, OF SPARTA, TN, WAS DISCIPLINED BY CALIFORNIA ON SEPTEMBER 5, 1994.
DISCIPLINARY ACTION: 60-MONTH PROBATION
OFFENSE: DISCIPLINARY ACTION BY ANOTHER STATE OR AGENCY
NOTES: DISCIPLINED BY WASHINGTON STATE BOARD FOR FAILURE TO EXERCISE PROPER JUDGMENT IN THE CARE OF FIVE PATIENTS IN THE HOSPITAL EMERGENCY ROOM BY A NON-ER PHYSICIAN. REVOCATION STAYED.

MONTOJO, PEDRO M MD, LICENSE NUMBER 0016153, OF SPARTA, TN, WAS DISCIPLINED BY WASHINGTON ON JUNE 30, 1995.
DISCIPLINARY ACTION: DENIAL OF LICENSE REINSTATEMENT
NOTES: THE BOARD DENIED HIS REQUEST TO RESCIND THE RETIRED STATUS AGREEMENT OF 12/18/92.

MONTOJO, PEDRO M MD WAS DISCIPLINED BY TENNESSEE ON OCTOBER 17, 1995.
DISCIPLINARY ACTION: 60-MONTH PROBATION
OFFENSE: DISCIPLINARY ACTION BY ANOTHER STATE OR AGENCY
NOTES: DISCIPLINARY ACTION IN WASHINGTON FOR UNPROFESSIONAL CONDUCT.

MOORE, CLOISE BARTON MD, LICENSE NUMBER 0019654, OF SEQUIM, WA, WAS DISCIPLINED BY WASHINGTON ON JULY 10, 1991.
DISCIPLINARY ACTION: 120-MONTH PROBATION; FINE
OFFENSE: SEXUAL ABUSE OF OR SEXUAL MISCONDUCT WITH A PATIENT
NOTES: UNPROFESSIONAL CONDUCT WITH THREE PATIENTS, INCLUDING SEXUAL MISCONDUCT WITH ONE PATIENT WHOM HE VISITED AT HOME, INJECTED WITH DEMEROL, AND THEN HAD SEXUAL INTERCOURSE WITH. HE INJECTED THIS PATIENT WITH DEMEROL ON HOME VISITS AT LEAST 50 TIMES BETWEEN 11/4/82 AND 6/16/83. TEN YEAR SUSPENSION STAYED TO BECOME PROBATION. CONDITIONS OF PROBATION INCLUDE: SHALL NOT ENGAGE IN ANY UNCHAPERONED PRIVATE CONTACT WITH FEMALE PATIENTS OR STAFF UNDER HIS SUPERVISION; SHALL HAVE A LICENSED PERSON IN THE ROOM WHEN HE SEES ANY FEMALE PATIENT OR A FEMALE RELATIVE OF SUCH PATIENTS; SHALL PROVIDE IMMEDIATE WRITTEN NOTICE TO ALL OF HIS PRESENT FEMALE STAFF THAT HE IS UNDER DISCIPLINARY RESTRICTIONS IMPOSED BY THE BOARD AND THAT A MONITOR MUST BE PRESENT AS DESCRIBED ABOVE; SHALL NOT DIAGNOSE OR TREAT ANY FEMALE WITH WHOM HE HAS OR HAS HAD A PRIVATE OR SEXUAL RELATIONSHIP, OR THEIR FAMILY MEMBERS, EXCEPT FOR EMERGENCIES AND WHEN ON-CALL COVERING FOR ANOTHER PHYSICIAN; PRACTICE SHALL BE MONITORED BY A BOARD APPROVED PHYSICIAN, WHO SHALL SUBMIT QUARTERLY REPORTS TO THE BOARD; SHALL PROVIDE EACH HOSPITAL AND OTHER MEDICAL FACILITY IN WHICH HE HAS PRIVILEGES WITH A COPY OF THE FINAL ORDER; SHALL BE EVALUATED SIX MONTHS FROM EFFECTIVE DATE OF THIS ORDER AND THEREAFTER EVALUATED YEARLY; SHALL ENTER TREATMENT WITH A PHYSICIAN OR OTHER PSYCHIATRIC HEALTH CARE PROVIDER APPROVED BY BOARD; SHALL PERMIT A REPRESENTATIVE OF THE DEPARTMENT OF HEALTH TO MAKE ANNOUNCED VISITS TO INSPECT RECORDS, INTERVIEW STAFF, AND OTHERWISE REVIEW HIS PRACTICE; SHALL MEET WITH THE BOARD FOR COMPLIANCE HEARINGS EVERY SIX MONTHS; SHALL STOP ALL HOUSE CALLS EXCEPT THAT HE MAY MAKE HOME VISITS WHEN ACCOMPANIED BY A PERSON LICENSED OR REGISTERED TO DO SO; SHALL STOP ALL AFTER HOURS TREATMENT, CONSULTATION, EVALUATION, OR OTHER CONTACT WITH FEMALE PATIENTS; SHALL STOP ALL NONTHERAPEUTIC TOUCHING OF FEMALE PATIENTS, THEIR FAMILY, AND STAFF MEMBERS; SHALL WRITE TRIPLICATE PRESCRIPTIONS FOR ALL PRESCRIPTIONS FOR CATEGORY I-V SCHEDULED DRUGS; SHALL SUCCESSFULLY COMPLETE 75 HOURS AT CATEGORY I WITH AT LEAST 25 HOURS IN PAIN MANAGEMENT AND THE REMAINING HOURS TO BE IN THE AREA OF ADDICTIONOLOGY, WITH CREDIT FOR A PAIN SEMINAR COURSE TAKEN IN 10/89, AND SHALL COMPLETE THIS REQUIREMENT WITHIN TWO YEARS OF THE DATE OF THIS ORDER; $1000 FINE; MUST INFORM THE BOARD IF HE LEAVES THE STATE; MAY NOT REQUEST MODIFICATION OF ORDER FOR FIVE YEARS. ON 2/22/94 HIS REQUEST FOR MODIFICATIONS GRANTED PERMITTING HIM TO SEE FEMALE PATIENTS IN A HOSPITAL OR NURSING HOME UNCHAPERONED. ON 1/20/95 THE BOARD DENIED HIS REQUEST FOR ELIMINATION OF A REQUIREMENT REQUIRING HIM TO USE TRIPLICATE PRESCRIPTION PADS. ON 2/12/96 HIS REQUEST FOR RELEASE FROM THE BOARD'S JURISDICTION GRANTED AND LICENSE IS UNCONDITIONAL AND NO LONGER SUBJECT TO RESTRICTION EFFECTIVE 2/15/96.

MOORE, GEORGE A JR MD, DATE OF BIRTH JANUARY 29, 1928, LICENSE NUMBER 0011794, WAS DISCIPLINED BY KENTUCKY ON MAY 22, 1987.
DISCIPLINARY ACTION: SURRENDER OF LICENSE
OFFENSE: DISCIPLINARY ACTION BY ANOTHER STATE OR AGENCY
NOTES: MOORE SUBSEQUENTLY WITHDREW HIS SURRENDER AND REQUESTED A HEARING. MOORE WAS CONVICTED ON 5/15/79 IN CALIFORNIA SUPERIOR COURT OF 2 FELONY COUNTS, UNLAWFUL POSSESSION AND PRESCRIBING OF CONTROLLED SUBSTANCES, FOR WHICH HE WAS PLACED ON 3 YEARS PROBATION AND FINED $635. THE CALIFORNIA MEDICAL BOARD HAD

PLACED HIM ON 4 YEARS PROBATION WITH REVOCATION STAYED ON 8/27/75. HE AGREED ON 5/23/78 TO SURRENDER HIS CALIFORNIA LICENSE EFFECTIVE 12/6/79. NEW YORK REVOKED HIS LICENSE ON 3/12/86

MOORE, GEORGE A JR MD, DATE OF BIRTH JANUARY 29, 1928, LICENSE NUMBER 0011794, WAS DISCIPLINED BY KENTUCKY ON APRIL 25, 1989.
DISCIPLINARY ACTION: LICENSE REVOCATION
NOTES: BASED ON FAILURE TO APPEAR AT HEARING

MOORE, GEORGE A JR MD, DATE OF BIRTH JANUARY 29, 1928, OF 2522 SHORELAND DR SOUTH, SEATTLE, WA, WAS DISCIPLINED BY MEDICARE ON AUGUST 10, 1990.
DISCIPLINARY ACTION: EXCLUSION FROM THE MEDICARE AND/OR MEDICAID PROGRAMS
OFFENSE: DISCIPLINARY ACTION BY ANOTHER STATE OR AGENCY
NOTES: LICENSE REVOCATION OR SUSPENSION.

MORRISON, KENNETH J MD WAS DISCIPLINED BY WASHINGTON ON MAY 18, 1989.
DISCIPLINARY ACTION: 60-MONTH PROBATION; RESTRICTION PLACED ON CONTROLLED SUBSTANCE LICENSE
OFFENSE: SUBSTANCE ABUSE
NOTES: UNABLE TO PRACTICE WITH REASONABLE SKILL AND SAFETY BECAUSE OF ABUSE OF ALCOHOL AND PRESCRIPTION MEDICATION; ON 12/19/88 USED AND/OR SELF-PRESCRIBED DARVON FOR HIMSELF WHILE A RESIDENT IN AN INPATIENT DRUG AND ALCOHOL TREATMENT PROGRAM. FIVE YEAR SUSPENSION, STAYED TO PROBATION UNDER THE FOLLOWING TERMS AND CONDITIONS: SHALL NOT PRESCRIBE CONTROLLED SUBSTANCES FOR HIS OWN USE OR FOR ANY MEMBER OF HIS FAMILY; SHALL NOT POSSESS OR USE CONTROLLED SUBSTANCES, INCLUDING ALCOHOL, FOR HIS OWN USE, UNLESS PRESCRIBED BY ANOTHER PHYSICIAN FOR LEGITIMATE THERAPEUTIC PURPOSES; SHALL COMPLY WITH THE REQUIREMENTS OF A BOARD APPROVED TREATMENT PROGRAM, AND WILL MAINTAIN SATISFACTORY STATUS IN THE PROGRAM; SHALL SUBMIT TRIPLICATE PRESCRIPTIONS ON ALL CONTROLLED SUBSTANCES, SCHEDULE II THROUGH V, TO THE BOARD ON A QUARTERLY BASIS; SHALL NOT PRESCRIBE SCHEDULE II DRUGS FOR ANY PATIENT FOR MORE THAN THREE CONSECUTIVE DAYS IN ANY 90 DAY PERIOD EXCEPT FOR TERMINALLY ILL CANCER PATIENTS; SHALL NOT PRESCRIBE SCHEDULE III-V DRUGS FOR MORE THAN THREE WEEKS WITHOUT A CONCURRING CONSULTATION; SHALL ATTEND A CONTINUING MEDICAL EDUCATION SEMINAR ON THE MANAGEMENT OF CHRONIC PAIN WITHIN SIX MONTHS; SHALL APPEAR BEFORE THE BOARD EVERY 12 MONTHS OR UPON BOARD REQUEST; MAY REQUEST A CHANGE IN ANY OF THE CONDITIONS OF THIS ORDER IN NO SOONER THAN ONE YEAR; MUST NOTIFY THE BOARD IN WRITING IF HE LEAVES WASHINGTON.

MORTON, KAREN A MD, LICENSE NUMBER 0027156, OF TACOMA, PIERCE COUNTY, WA, WAS DISCIPLINED BY WASHINGTON ON AUGUST 5, 1992.
DISCIPLINARY ACTION: EMERGENCY SUSPENSION
OFFENSE: PROVIDING FALSE INFORMATION TO THE BOARD
NOTES: CHARGES OF MISREPRESENTATION OR CONCEALMENT OF A MATERIAL FACT IN OBTAINING A LICENSE, AND INABILITY TO PRACTICE WITH REASONABLE SKILL AND SAFETY.

MORTON, KAREN ANN MD WAS DISCIPLINED BY WASHINGTON ON JUNE 18, 1993.
DISCIPLINARY ACTION: LICENSE SUSPENSION
OFFENSE: PHYSICAL OR MENTAL ILLNESS INHIBITING THE ABILITY TO PRACTICE WITH SKILL AND SAFETY
NOTES: UNABLE TO PRACTICE WITH REASONABLE SKILL AND SAFETY TO THE PUBLIC BY REASON OF A MENTAL CONDITION. ON 11/24/89 HAD NOT BEEN TRUTHFUL ABOUT HER PAST MENTAL HEALTH TREATMENT WHEN SHE APPLIED FOR LICENSURE; RECEIVED INPATIENT AND OUTPATIENT TREATMENT FOR MENTAL ILLNESS ON SEVERAL OCCASIONS FROM 1987 THROUGH 1991; DISCHARGED FROM HER POSITION IN 7/91 FOR POOR CLINICAL PERFORMANCE; AN EVALUATION IN 7/92 FOUND THAT SHE HAD A MENTAL ILLNESS AND COGNITIVE DEFICITS. HER LICENSE TO PRACTICE MEDICINE INDEFINITELY SUSPENDED; SHALL PETITION THE BOARD IN WRITING FOR AUTHORIZATION TO APPLY FOR LICENSURE; AGREES TO COMPLY WITH ANY REQUIREMENTS IMPOSED UPON HER BY THE BOARD IN ORDER TO ASSESS HER ABILITY TO PRACTICE MEDICINE WITH REASONABLE SKILL AND SAFETY TO CONSUMERS; SHALL INFORM THE BOARD IN WRITING OF CHANGES IN HER PRACTICE AND RESIDENCE ADDRESS; MAY PETITION THE BOARD IN WRITING FOR A CHANGE IN THE TERMS/CONDITIONS IN NO SOONER THAN SIX MONTHS.

MORTON, KAREN ANN MD, LICENSE NUMBER 0G64852, OF TACOMA, WA, WAS DISCIPLINED BY CALIFORNIA ON FEBRUARY 6, 1995.
DISCIPLINARY ACTION: LICENSE REVOCATION
OFFENSE: DISCIPLINARY ACTION BY ANOTHER STATE OR AGENCY
NOTES: DISCIPLINE BY WASHINGTON STATE BOARD FOR FALSE INFORMATION IN LICENSE APPLICATION. DEFAULT DECISION.

MOSS, NORMAN W MD, LICENSE NUMBER 0008347, OF YAKIMA, WA, WAS DISCIPLINED BY WASHINGTON ON JANUARY 16, 1987.
DISCIPLINARY ACTION: REPRIMAND; REQUIRED TO TAKE ADDITIONAL MEDICAL EDUCATION
OFFENSE: OVERPRESCRIBING OR MISPRESCRIBING DRUGS
NOTES: DURING 1983, 1984 AND 1985 EXCESSIVELY PRESCRIBED STADOL FOR A PATIENT IN SUCH A MANNER AS TO CREATE AND MAINTAIN A STATE OF ADDICTION IN THAT PATIENT; DIDN'T TAKE A DETAILED MEDICAL HISTORY; SHALL OBTAIN CONTINUING MEDICAL EDUCATION ON MANAGEMENT OF CHRONIC PAIN PATIENTS WITHIN 6 MONTHS; SHALL NOT PRESCRIBE CONTROLLED SUBSTANCES TO THIS PATIENT; SHALL SUBMIT TO BOARD WITHIN 60 DAYS LIST OF CHRONIC PAIN PATIENTS FOR WHOM HE IS PRESCRIBING CONTROLLED SUBSTANCES OR NON-NARCOTIC ANALGESICS; SHALL APPEAR BEFORE THE BOARD IN 6 MONTHS. ON 12/17/93 HE WAS FOUND IN COMPLIANCE WITH THIS ORDER AND RESTRICTIONS AND LIMITATIONS ON HIS LICENSE WERE TERMINATED.

MULDER, HAROLD H MD, LICENSE NUMBER FE11046, OF ESCONDIDO, CA, WAS DISCIPLINED BY CALIFORNIA ON JUNE 30, 1995.
DISCIPLINARY ACTION: SURRENDER OF LICENSE
NOTES: WHILE CHARGES PENDING.

MULDER, HAROLD H MD, LICENSE NUMBER 0016936, OF ESCONDIDO, CA, WAS DISCIPLINED BY WASHINGTON ON DECEMBER 13, 1996.
DISCIPLINARY ACTION: SURRENDER OF LICENSE
NOTES: AGREEMENT TO RETIRE.

MUMFORD, D CURTIS MD, LICENSE NUMBER 0029419, OF PORTLAND, OR, WAS DISCIPLINED BY WASHINGTON ON MAY 31, 1996.
DISCIPLINARY ACTION: SURRENDER OF LICENSE
NOTES: AGREED TO RETIRE IN CONSIDERATION OF TERMINATING A PENDING INVESTIGATION.

MURIBY, NUJUD R MD, LICENSE NUMBER 0012516, WAS DISCIPLINED BY WASHINGTON ON JUNE 7, 1990.

- WASHINGTON -

DISCIPLINARY ACTION: LICENSE SUSPENSION; FINE
OFFENSE: PROFESSIONAL MISCONDUCT
NOTES: SHALL NOTIFY THE BOARD IN WRITING IF HE INTENDS TO RETURN TO WASHINGTON TO PRACTICE MEDICINE. UPON NOTICE OF RETURN TO WASHINGTON, SUSPENSION WILL BE STAYED UPON COMPLIANCE WITH THE FOLLOWING CONDITIONS: SHALL SUBMIT TO A PHYSICAL EXAM ASSESSING HIS PHYSICAL AND MANUAL DEXTERITY FOR SURGERY; SHALL HAVE A REVIEW OF HIS MEDICAL PRACTICE AND YEARLY COMPLIANCE HEARINGS AND PRACTICE REVIEWS; SHALL COMPLETE 50 HOURS OF CONTINUING MEDICAL EDUCATION IN MEDICAL ETHICS AND BREAST SURGERY; SHALL HAVE BOARD APPROVED PLASTIC SURGEON REVIEW HIS FIRST FIVE BREAST SURGERIES IN WASHINGTON; $2,000 FINE.

MURIBY, NUJUD R MD, LICENSE NUMBER 0012516, OF BELLINGHAM, WA, WAS DISCIPLINED BY WASHINGTON ON MAY 20, 1991.
DISCIPLINARY ACTION: RESTRICTION PLACED ON LICENSE; REQUIRED TO TAKE ADDITIONAL MEDICAL EDUCATION
OFFENSE: PROFESSIONAL MISCONDUCT
NOTES: DEMONSTRATED UNPROFESSIONAL CONDUCT IN HIS TREATMENT OF A PATIENT RESULTING IN A LICENSE SUSPENSION 6/7/90; HAS COMPLIED WITH THE CONDITIONS NECESSARY FOR THE STAY OF THE SUSPENSION. BECAUSE LICENSEE DOES NOT INTEND TO PERFORM BREAST SURGERIES OR ANY SURGERIES EXCEPT MINOR SURGERIES IN HIS OFFICE, GROUNDS EXIST TO MODIFY THE 6/7/90 ORDER AS FOLLOWS: MUST TAKE 25 HOURS OF BOARD APPROVED CONTINUING MEDICAL EDUCATION IN THE AREA OF MEDICAL ETHICS, WHICH SHALL BE COMPLETED WITHIN THREE YEARS OF THE SUSPENSION PERIOD; SHALL NOT PERFORM ANY SURGERY, INCLUDING REVISION OF SCARS, EXCEPT MINOR SURGERY, WHICH IS DEFINED AS SURGERY NOT DEEPER THAN THE SUBCUTANEOUS TISSUES AND WHICH REQUIRE ONLY LIMITED LOCAL ANESTHESIA; REMAINDER OF PREVIOUS ORDER STILL IN EFFECT. ON 1/17/92 REQUEST TO DELETE REQUIRED EDUCATION AND SET ASIDE 6/7/90 ORDER DENIED. ON 11/17/93 FURTHER ORDERED: THE SIX HOURS OF CONTINUING MEDICAL EDUCATION COMPLETED ON 11/20/90 WILL BE COUNTED AS PARTIAL FULFILLMENT OF HIS 15 CREDIT HOUR REQUIREMENT; THE NINE REMAINING HOURS OF CONTINUING MEDICAL EDUCATION IN MEDICAL ETHICS SHALL BE PRE-APPROVED BY THE BOARD AND COMPLETED BY 5/20/94. ON 3/4/94 MOTION TO EXTEND THE CONTINUING MEDICAL EDUCATION REQUIREMENT IS DENIED. ON 9/30/94 HIS REQUEST TO RESUME PERFORMING PLASTIC SURGERY PROCEDURES (EXCLUDING BREAST SURGERY OR RECONSTRUCTION) WAS GRANTED. MUST COMPLY WITH TERMS AND CONDITIONS OF A NEW ORDER. ON 4/14/95 AND 5/2/95 REQUEST TO STAY, RECONSIDER OR MODIFY THE ORDER DENIED. ON 10/10/96 HIS REQUEST TO ELIMINATE THE REQUIREMENT OF FUTURE COMPETENCE APPEARANCES DENIED. ON 2/25/97 BOARD GRANTED HIS REQUEST TO TERMINATE THIS ORDER AND LICENSE IS UNRESTRICTED.

MYERS, GEORGE CHRISTOPHER MD, LICENSE NUMBER 0012711, OF BELLEVUE, WA, WAS DISCIPLINED BY WASHINGTON ON APRIL 26, 1991.
DISCIPLINARY ACTION: EMERGENCY SUSPENSION
OFFENSE: PHYSICAL OR MENTAL ILLNESS INHIBITING THE ABILITY TO PRACTICE WITH SKILL AND SAFETY
NOTES: ALLEGATIONS OF HEAD INJURY AND BRAIN SURGERIES RESULTING IN NEUROLOGICAL IMPAIRMENT SUCH THAT HE CANNOT PROVIDE MEDICAL SERVICES FOR THE PUBLIC WITH SKILL AND SAFETY.

MYERS, GEORGE CHRISTOPHER MD, LICENSE NUMBER 0012711, OF BELLEVUE, WA, WAS DISCIPLINED BY WASHINGTON ON JULY 16, 1991.
DISCIPLINARY ACTION: SURRENDER OF LICENSE
NOTES: PERMANENT RETIREMENT EFFECTIVE 5/1/91.

MYERS, RONALD A MD, LICENSE NUMBER 0043456, OF PORT ANGELES, WA, WAS DISCIPLINED BY FLORIDA ON FEBRUARY 12, 1992.
DISCIPLINARY ACTION: SURRENDER OF LICENSE
NOTES: AGREES NEVER AGAIN TO APPLY FOR LICENSURE AS A PHYSICIAN IN FLORIDA.

MYERS, RONALD A MD, LICENSE NUMBER 0019234, WAS DISCIPLINED BY ARIZONA ON OCTOBER 22, 1994.
DISCIPLINARY ACTION: REQUIRED TO ENTER AN IMPAIRED PHYSICIAN PROGRAM OR DRUG OR ALCOHOL TREATMENT; MONITORING OF PHYSICIAN
NOTES: MUST IMMEDIATELY PARTICIPATE IN A BOARD-APPROVED MONITORED AFTERCARE TREATMENT PROGRAM, THE ONE SPONSORED BY ARIZONA BOARD IF HE IS IN ARIZONA OR, IF HE RESIDES IN ANOTHER STATE, A BOARD AFFILIATED PROGRAM IN THAT STATE; MUST PARTICIPATE IN A 12-STEP RECOVERY PROGRAM AND ATTEND AT LEAST THREE WEEKLY MEETINGS; SHALL OBTAIN A BOARD-APPROVED TREATING PHYSICIAN; SHALL ABSTAIN COMPLETELY FROM THE CONSUMPTION OF ALCOHOLIC BEVERAGES AND DRUGS EXCEPT WHEN PRESCRIBED BY HIS TREATING PHYSICIAN; MUST SUBMIT TO WITNESSED RANDOM BIOLOGICAL FLUID COLLECTION; KEEP A LOG OF ANY AND ALL MEDICATIONS PRESCRIBED FOR HIM; SHALL SUBMIT TO ANY EXAMINATIONS OR THERAPY ORDERED BY BOARD; SHALL APPEAR BEFORE BOARD FOR INTERVIEWS UPON REQUEST; SHALL INFORM BOARD OF CHANGE OF ADDRESS OR IF AWAY FOR MORE THAN FIVE DAYS.

MYERS, RONALD A MD WAS DISCIPLINED BY NEVADA ON MAY 5, 1995.
DISCIPLINARY ACTION: SURRENDER OF LICENSE
OFFENSE: DISCIPLINARY ACTION BY ANOTHER STATE OR AGENCY
NOTES: CHARGED WITH DISCIPLINARY ACTION AGAINST HIS LICENSES IN FLORIDA AND CALIFORNIA; RENEWING AND ATTEMPTING TO RENEW A LICENSE BY FRAUD OR MISREPRESENTATION OR BY A FALSE, MISLEADING, INACCURATE OR INCOMPLETE STATEMENT; ENGAGING IN CONDUCT WHICH IS INTENDED TO DECEIVE; FAILING TO NOTIFY THE NEVADA BOARD OF THE DISCIPLINARY ACTIONS TAKEN AGAINST HIS LICENSE IN FLORIDA AND CALIFORNIA. VOLUNTARY SURRENDER OF LICENSE WHILE HE IS UNDER INVESTIGATION.

MYERS, RONALD A MD, LICENSE NUMBER 0019234, WAS DISCIPLINED BY ARIZONA ON AUGUST 5, 1996.
DISCIPLINARY ACTION: REPRIMAND
OFFENSE: DISCIPLINARY ACTION BY ANOTHER STATE OR AGENCY
NOTES: IN 12/91, HE VOLUNTARILY RELINQUISHED HIS FLORIDA LICENSE AND AGREED NEVER AGAIN TO APPLY FOR LICENSURE IN FLORIDA IN ORDER TO AVOID ADMINISTRATIVE PROSECUTION FOR FAILING TO MAINTAIN AND SUBMIT DOCUMENTATION VERIFYING THE REQUIRED HOURS OF CONTINUING MEDICAL EDUCATION CREDITS FROM 1/1/88 THROUGH 12/31/89; HE RENEWED HIS FLORIDA LICENSE BY FRAUDULENT MISREPRESENTATION BY CERTIFYING HE HAD COMPLETED THESE CONTINUING MEDICAL EDUCATION REQUIREMENTS.

NADLER, IRA R MD, LICENSE NUMBER 0023496, OF MEDICAL LAKE, SPOKANE, WA, WAS DISCIPLINED BY WASHINGTON ON MARCH 5, 1992.

- WASHINGTON -

DISCIPLINARY ACTION: EMERGENCY SUSPENSION
NOTES: ALLEGATIONS OF IMPAIRMENT.

NADLER, IRA R MD, LICENSE NUMBER 0023496, OF MEDICAL LAKE, WA, WAS DISCIPLINED BY WASHINGTON ON AUGUST 19, 1994.
DISCIPLINARY ACTION: PROBATION; RESTRICTION PLACED ON LICENSE
OFFENSE: PHYSICAL OR MENTAL ILLNESS INHIBITING THE ABILITY TO PRACTICE WITH SKILL AND SAFETY
NOTES: SHALL ABIDE BY PRACTICE RESTRICTIONS ORDERED BY THE COMMISSION, COMPLY WITH THE TERMS OF HER CONTRACT WITH WASHINGTON PHYSICIANS HEALTH PROGRAM AND CONTINUE ONGOING PSYCHIATRIC CARE WITH REPORTS SUBMITTED TO THE COMMISSION. SHALL APPEAR BEFORE THE COMMISSION IN SIX MONTHS. ON 10/7/96 HIS REQUEST TO TERMINATE THIS ORDER GRANTED AND LICENSE UNRESTRICTED.

NADLER, IRA RAMINS MD, LICENSE NUMBER 0093010, OF 104 N. GRANT NO B, MEDICAL LAKE, WA, WAS DISCIPLINED BY NEW YORK ON JUNE 9, 1994.
DISCIPLINARY ACTION: LICENSE REVOCATION
OFFENSE: DISCIPLINARY ACTION BY ANOTHER STATE OR AGENCY
NOTES: WASHINGTON BOARD SUMMARILY SUSPENDED HIS LICENSE.

NAKATA, KENNETH M MD, LICENSE NUMBER 0022688, OF SEATTLE, WA, WAS DISCIPLINED BY WASHINGTON ON OCTOBER 16, 1992.
DISCIPLINARY ACTION: LICENSE SUSPENSION
OFFENSE: SEXUAL ABUSE OF OR SEXUAL MISCONDUCT WITH A PATIENT
NOTES: SEXUAL CONTACT WITH A PATIENT. LICENSE SUSPENDED FOR A MINIMUM OF TWO YEARS. ON 6/12/95 ORDER MODIFIED REQUIRING SEMI-ANNUAL RATHER THAN QUARTERLY REPORTS FROM HIS TREATING PSYCHOLOGIST TO THE BOARD. ON 9/18/95, BOARD AGREED THAT ALTHOUGH LICENSE SHALL REMAIN SUSPENDED, HE MAY RENEW HIS LICENSE BY 10/16/95 BY SUBMITTING REQUIRED FORMS; SHALL HAVE UNTIL 4/16/97 TO SUBMIT PROOF OF REQUIRED CONTINUING MEDICAL EDUCATION CREDITS.

NASH, ROBERT A MD, LICENSE NUMBER 005065A, WAS DISCIPLINED BY WYOMING ON DECEMBER 29, 1993.
DISCIPLINARY ACTION: RESTRICTION PLACED ON LICENSE; REQUIRED TO TAKE ADDITIONAL MEDICAL EDUCATION
NOTES: PERMANENTLY ENJOINED FROM PROVIDING OR PERFORMING ANY COUNSELING OR TREATMENT TO ANY FEMALE PATIENTS UNLESS AN ATTENDANT IS PHYSICALLY PRESENT IN THE EXAMINING OR COUNSELING ROOM OR AREA AT ALL TIMES; SHALL PROVIDE TO THE BOARD WITHIN 6 MONTHS WRITTEN CERTIFICATION OF ATTENDANCE AND SUCCESSFUL COMPLETION OF THE "PATIENT-THERAPIST RELATIONSHIPS: CRITICAL ISSUES OF THE 90S" SEMINAR; SHALL APPEAR BEFORE THE INFORMAL INTERVIEWERS IN 10/94 TO DISCUSS HIS MEDICAL PRACTICE; SHALL NOT SEEK MODIFICATION OR TERMINATION OF THE TERMS AND RESTRICTIONS OF THIS DECREE FOR TWO YEARS.

NASH, ROBERT A MD, LICENSE NUMBER 0005955, WAS DISCIPLINED BY ARIZONA ON MARCH 27, 1995.
DISCIPLINARY ACTION: RESTRICTION PLACED ON LICENSE
NOTES: PERMANENTLY ENJOINED FROM PROVIDING OR PERFORMING ANY COUNSELING OR TREATMENT TO ANY FEMALE PATIENT UNLESS PHYSICIAN, NURSE OR SOCIAL WORKER IS PHYSICALLY PRESENT IN THE EXAMINING OR COUNSELING ROOM; SHALL COMPLY WITH ALL TERMS OF THE WYOMING CONSENT DECREE OF 12/29/93 AND 1/23/94 ENFORCEMENT ORDER; SHALL APPEAR BEFORE THE BOARD UPON REQUEST; SHALL NOT SEEK TO MODIFY OR TERMINATE THIS ORDER FOR TWO YEARS.

NASH, ROBERT A MD, LICENSE NUMBER 0028684, OF EVANSTON, WY, WAS DISCIPLINED BY WASHINGTON ON OCTOBER 6, 1995.
DISCIPLINARY ACTION: RESTRICTION PLACED ON LICENSE
NOTES: CANNOT PROVIDE COUNSELING OR TREATMENT TO ANY FEMALE PATIENT UNLESS AN ATTENDANT IS PHYSICALLY PRESENT IN THE ROOM AT ALL TIMES.

NEACE, LEWIS C MD WAS DISCIPLINED BY WASHINGTON ON FEBRUARY 6, 1990.
DISCIPLINARY ACTION: SURRENDER OF LICENSE
NOTES: ADVISED THAT HE IS UNDER INVESTIGATION BY THE MEDICAL DISCIPLINARY BOARD CONCERNING HIS ABILITY TO PRACTICE MEDICINE WITH REASONABLE SKILL AND SAFETY TO PATIENTS; RETIREMENT; RETROACTIVE TO 1/22/90 AND HAS NO PLANS TO RESUME PRACTICE SUBSEQUENT TO THAT DATE; AGREED THAT HIS RETIREMENT SHALL BE PERMANENT AND THAT HE MAY ONLY RESUME PRACTICE IN WASHINGTON WITH PRIOR APPROVAL FROM THE BOARD; SHALL NOTIFY THE BOARD IF HE PLANS TO RESUME PRACTICE IN THIS OR ANY OTHER JURISDICTION. INVESTIGATION WAS TERMINATED.

NEACE, LEWIS C MD WAS DISCIPLINED BY WASHINGTON ON FEBRUARY 6, 1990.
DISCIPLINARY ACTION: SURRENDER OF LICENSE
NOTES: PERMANENTLY RETIRING FROM MEDICAL PRACTICE EFFECTIVE 2/1/90 WITH NO PLANS TO RESUME PRACTICE SUBSEQUENT TO THAT DATE.

NEWTON, DOUGLAS MD, LICENSE NUMBER 0G35807, OF KENNEWICK, WA, WAS DISCIPLINED BY CALIFORNIA ON SEPTEMBER 9, 1994.
DISCIPLINARY ACTION: SURRENDER OF LICENSE
NOTES: VOLUNTARY SURRENDER OF LICENSE WHILE CHARGES PENDING.

NEWTON, DOUGLAS E MD, LICENSE NUMBER 0017963, WAS DISCIPLINED BY WASHINGTON ON MAY 21, 1993.
DISCIPLINARY ACTION: PROBATION; FINE
OFFENSE: SEXUAL ABUSE OF OR SEXUAL MISCONDUCT WITH A PATIENT
NOTES: PROVIDED TREATMENT OUTSIDE HIS AREA OF COMPETENCE WHICH CONSISTED OF GENERAL AND RELIGIOUS COUNSELING FOR A PATIENT COMPLAINING OF ANOREXIA AND OTHER EMOTIONAL PROBLEMS; HE AGREES THAT HE LACKED THE EDUCATION AND/OR EXPERIENCE TO PROVIDE ADEQUATE TREATMENT FOR THESE CONDITIONS; ENGAGED IN SEXUAL CONDUCT WITH THE PATIENT. LICENSE SUSPENSION, STAYED AS PROBATION UNDER THE FOLLOWING TERMS AND CONDITIONS: SHALL ENTER INTO TREATMENT WITH A BOARD APPROVED HEALTH CARE PROFESSIONAL EXPERIENCED IN WORKING WITH HEALTH CARE PROVIDERS WITH PRACTICE PROBLEMS, INCLUDING SEXUAL IMPROPRIETY, PERSONALITY DEFICITS, AND GENERAL LIFE PROBLEMS; SHALL FOLLOW THE RECOMMENDATIONS OF HIS TREATMENT PROVIDER AND HAVE THEM REPORT TO THE BOARD WITHIN SIX MONTHS AND YEARLY THEREAFTER; SHALL UNDERGO AN INDEPENDENT EVALUATION TO ASSESS HIS PROGRESS IN TREATMENT AND HIS ABILITY TO PRACTICE SAFELY BY A BOARD APPROVED HEALTH CARE PROFESSIONAL WITHIN SIX MONTHS AND YEARLY THEREAFTER; SHALL RESTRICT HIS PRACTICE TO WORKING IN A HOSPITAL EMERGENCY DEPARTMENT AND SEE NO OTHER PATIENTS WITHOUT PRIOR APPROVAL OF THE BOARD; SHALL HAVE A CHAPERONE PRESENT WHEN EXAMINING AND TREATING FEMALE PATIENTS; ALL COUNSELING ACTIVITIES OF ANY NATURE SHALL BE CONDUCTED IN

AN ENVIRONMENT THAT IS ENTIRELY VOLUNTARY, NON-INTRUSIVE, AND UNPRESSURED; SHALL PROVIDE A COPY OF THIS ORDER TO HIS PRESENT AND FUTURE COLLEAGUES IN THE HOSPITAL EMERGENCY DEPARTMENT AND THE HOSPITAL CHIEF OF STAFF; SHALL ENSURE THAT ANY INDIVIDUAL ACTING AS HIS CHAPERONE WHEN EXAMINING OR TREATING FEMALE PATIENTS IS FULLY AWARE OF THE REQUIREMENTS OF THE BOARD ORDER; SHALL APPEAR BEFORE THE BOARD IN SIX MONTHS AND SHALL CONTINUE TO MAKE SUCH COMPLIANCE APPEARANCES ANNUALLY; THE BOARD SHALL MAKE ANNOUNCED VISITS SEMI-ANNUALLY INITIALLY AND ANNUALLY THEREAFTER, TO INSPECT HOSPITAL AND/OR OFFICE AND MEDICAL RECORDS, INTERVIEW STAFF OR SUPERVISORS, REVIEW OTHER ASPECTS OF HIS PRACTICE; MAY PETITION THE BOARD FOR A CHANGE IN THE TERMS/CONDITIONS IN NO SOONER THAN TWO YEARS; SHALL INFORM THE BOARD IN WRITING OF CHANGES IN HIS PRACTICE AND RESIDENCE ADDRESS; MUST NOTIFY THE BOARD IN WRITING IF HE LEAVES WASHINGTON; THE PERIOD OF PROBATION/SUSPENSION SHALL BE TOLLED FOR ANY TIME PERIOD WHICH HE RESIDES AND/OR PRACTICES OUTSIDE OF WASHINGTON; SHALL PAY A $500 FINE. ON 3/6/95, THE COMMISSION DENIED HIS REQUEST FOR CLARIFICATION OR RECONSIDERATION OF THIS ORDER. ON 5/20/95 THE COMMISSION DENIED HIS REQUEST TO CLARIFY AND/OR MODIFY THIS ORDER. ON 6/25/97 BOARD GRANTED HIS REQUEST TO TERMINATE THIS ORDER AND LICENSE IS UNRESTRICTED.

NGHIEM, THIEU L MD, LICENSE NUMBER 0C40993, OF OLYMPIA, WA, WAS DISCIPLINED BY CALIFORNIA ON APRIL 4, 1992.
DISCIPLINARY ACTION: LICENSE REVOCATION
OFFENSE: DISCIPLINARY ACTION BY ANOTHER STATE OR AGENCY
NOTES: DISCIPLINED BY WASHINGTON BOARD FOR SEXUAL MISCONDUCT WITH FEMALE PATIENTS.

NGHIEM, THIEU LENH MD WAS DISCIPLINED BY WASHINGTON ON OCTOBER 26, 1989.
DISCIPLINARY ACTION: EMERGENCY SUSPENSION

NGHIEM, THIEU LENH MD, LICENSE NUMBER 0016066, WAS DISCIPLINED BY WASHINGTON ON FEBRUARY 28, 1990.
DISCIPLINARY ACTION: LICENSE REVOCATION
OFFENSE: SEXUAL ABUSE OF OR SEXUAL MISCONDUCT WITH A PATIENT
NOTES: DURING 1988 HAD INAPPROPRIATE SEXUAL CONTACT, INCLUDING INAPPROPRIATE EXAMINATIONS AND INAPPROPRIATELY POSING QUESTIONS OF A SEXUAL NATURE, TO 3 PATIENTS. NO PETITION FOR REINSTATEMENT WILL BE CONSIDERED FOR 10 YEARS.

NGHIEM, THIEU LENH MD, DATE OF BIRTH JULY 16, 1924, OF 1330 WILSON NE, OLYMPIA, WA, WAS DISCIPLINED BY MEDICARE ON MARCH 5, 1991.
DISCIPLINARY ACTION: EXCLUSION FROM THE MEDICARE AND/OR MEDICAID PROGRAMS
OFFENSE: DISCIPLINARY ACTION BY ANOTHER STATE OR AGENCY
NOTES: LICENSE REVOCATION OR SUSPENSION.

NGUYEN, BANG DUY MD WAS DISCIPLINED BY WASHINGTON ON APRIL 22, 1989.
DISCIPLINARY ACTION: PROBATION; REQUIRED TO TAKE ADDITIONAL MEDICAL EDUCATION
OFFENSE: SUBSTANDARD CARE, INCOMPETENCE, OR NEGLIGENCE
NOTES: HIS OFFICE HAS NOT BEEN MAINTAINED IN A STATE OF CLEANLINESS AND STERILITY THAT IS ADEQUATE TO MEET ACCEPTABLE STANDARDS OF MEDICAL PRACTICE; INSTRUMENTS HAVE NOT BEEN PROPERLY STERILIZED, EXAMINING AND COMMON AREAS HAVE NOT BEEN MAINTAINED PROPERLY, AND THERE HAS BEEN INADEQUATE AND INSUFFICIENT SUPPLY OF EQUIPMENT NECESSARY FOR THE CONDUCT OF ROUTINE OFFICE PROCEDURES; PROVIDED CARE TO PATIENTS WHICH FALLS BELOW THE ACCEPTABLE STANDARDS OF MEDICAL CARE IN THE AREAS OF CHARTING, DIAGNOSIS, AND TREATMENT, REFERRAL, AND PRESCRIPTION AND ADMINISTRATION OF MEDICATION. INDEFINITE SUSPENSION STAYED AS PROBATION UNDER THE FOLLOWING TERMS AND CONDITIONS: SHALL ENSURE THAT HIS OFFICE AND THE PROCEDURES HE PERFORMS FALL WITHIN ACCEPTABLE STANDARDS OF CLEANLINESS AND STERILITY FOR PHYSICIANS; SHALL BE SUPERVISED BY SPECIFIED PHYSICIAN UNDER THE TERMS OF A WRITTEN PRECEPTORSHIP AGREEMENT; BOARD APPROVED PHYSICIAN SHALL REVIEW 30 PATIENT CHARTS PER QUARTER, WHICH HAVE BEEN SELECTED AT RANDOM BY THE BOARD FROM HIS PATIENTS' RECORDS AND SUBMIT QUARTERLY REPORTS; SHALL CONTRACT WITH A MEDICAL SUPPLY COMPANY TO PROVIDE ALL THE STERILE PACKS AND CLEAN SPECULUMS FOR HIS PRACTICE AND UPON BOARD REQUEST SHALL SUBMIT EVIDENCE OF THE CONTRACTUAL AGREEMENT AND INVOICES FOR EQUIPMENT PROVIDED; SHALL KEEP A LOG OF ALL SURGICAL PROCEDURES HE PERFORMS; SHALL PERMIT THE BOARD TO MAKE UNANNOUNCED VISITS TO INSPECT RECORDS, INTERVIEW STAFF, AND REVIEW HIS PRACTICE TO MONITOR COMPLIANCE WITH THIS ORDER; BY 12/31 OF EACH YEAR OF THIS ORDER SHALL SUBMIT VERIFICATION OF ATTENDANCE AT A WEEK LONG REVIEW OF FAMILY PRACTICE; SHALL ENSURE THAT HE PROPERLY DISPOSES OF ALL OUTDATED MEDICINES AND ALL MEDICINES PRESCRIBED TO PATIENTS WHICH COME INTO HIS POSSESSION; SHALL MAKE A COMPLIANCE APPEARANCE BEFORE THE BOARD ONCE A YEAR OR MORE FREQUENTLY AT THE REQUEST OF THE BOARD; MAY REQUEST CHANGE IN ANY OF THE CONDITIONS OF THIS ORDER NO SOONER THAN ONE YEAR; IF HE LEAVES WASHINGTON HE MUST NOTIFY THE BOARD IN WRITING; MAY REQUEST REINSTATEMENT OF HIS LICENSE IN NO SOONER THAN FIVE YEARS.

NGUYEN, BANG DUY MD, LICENSE NUMBER 0021157, OF SEATTLE, WA, WAS DISCIPLINED BY WASHINGTON ON DECEMBER 14, 1995.
NOTES: AGREED ORDER WITH TERMS AND CONDITIONS INCLUDING TO BE EVALUATED AT THE COLORADO PERSONALIZED EDUCATION FOR PHYSICIAN PROGRAM.

NICOLAS, ARCADIO F MD, LICENSE NUMBER 0012366, WAS DISCIPLINED BY WASHINGTON ON JUNE 16, 1989.
DISCIPLINARY ACTION: 60-MONTH PROBATION; REQUIRED TO TAKE ADDITIONAL MEDICAL EDUCATION
OFFENSE: LOSS OR RESTRICTION OF HOSPITAL PRIVILEGES
NOTES: IN 4/87 HOSPITAL PRIVILEGES RESTRICTED AFTER A REVIEW OF HIS RECORDS OF 1986. HE ADMITTED THAT MANY OF THE HISTORY AND PHYSICALS HE PERFORMED WERE NOT DICTATED IMMEDIATELY AFTER ADMISSION; MANY OF THE PROGRESS NOTES AND HISTORIES WERE BRIEF AND ABBREVIATED AND MAY HAVE BEEN OF LIMITED USEFULNESS TO OTHER PHYSICIANS INTERPRETING SUCH NOTES; OFFICE DOCUMENTATION REGARDING MANAGEMENT OF DIABETIC PATIENTS INADEQUATE; ADMITS TO DEFICIENCIES OF HIS MANAGEMENT OF PATIENTS WITH DIABETES MELITIS AND THAT CURRENT MEDICAL PRACTICE REQUIRES MORE AGGRESSIVE MANAGEMENT WITH TIGHTER CONTROL OF BLOOD SUGAR. HOSPITAL PRIVILEGES WERE PLACED UNDER THE FOLLOWING TERMS AND CONDITIONS: FOR ALL HOSPITAL PATIENTS INCLUDING THOSE AT THE HOSPITAL FOR OBSERVATION, MUST CONTACT FOR CONSULTATION A BOARD CERTIFIED PRIMARY CARE CONSULTANT, EITHER MEDICINE OR

FAMILY PRACTICE, AT THE TIME OF ADMISSION AND ALL ADMITTING ORDERS SHOULD DOCUMENT THIS; SHALL NOT BE INCLUDED IN THE ROTATION FOR ASSIGNMENT OF ATTENDING PHYSICIANS TO PATIENTS WITHOUT A REGULAR PHYSICIAN; TERMS AND CONDITIONS OF BOARD PROBATION: SHALL COMPLETE A BOARD APPROVED ONE WEEK UPDATE TRAINING COURSE IN FAMILY PRACTICE AND 25 HOURS OF CONTINUING MEDICAL EDUCATION RELATED TO THE AREAS OF SUBSTANCE ABUSE, DETOXIFICATION, AND PRESCRIPTION OF NARCOTICS WITHIN ONE YEAR; IF HE SEEKS STAFF PRIVILEGES AT ANY OTHER HOSPITAL, SHALL NOTIFY THE BOARD AND NOTIFY THE HOSPITAL OF THIS ORDER; SHALL PERMIT A REPRESENTATIVE OF THE BOARD TO MAKE PERIODIC VISITS TO INSPECT AND REVIEW RECORDS AND TO MONITOR COMPLIANCE WITH THIS ORDER AT LEAST ONCE A YEAR; SHALL APPEAR BEFORE THE BOARD FOR COMPLIANCE APPEARANCES EVERY SIX MONTHS OR UPON BOARD REQUEST; SHALL NOTIFY THE BOARD IN WRITING IF HE LEAVES WASHINGTON AND PERIODS OF TIME OUTSIDE OF WASHINGTON WILL NOT APPLY TO THE LIMITATION PERIOD; MAY PETITION NO EARLIER THAN THREE YEARS TO HAVE THE BOARD REVIEW WHETHER THE FIVE YEAR TERM SHOULD BE SHORTENED. SHALL ASSUME ALL COSTS.

NICOLAS, ARCADIO F MD, LICENSE NUMBER 0012366, OF PORT ANGELES, WA, WAS DISCIPLINED BY WASHINGTON ON DECEMBER 20, 1990.
DISCIPLINARY ACTION: 60-MONTH PROBATION; 60-MONTH RESTRICTION PLACED ON CONTROLLED SUBSTANCE LICENSE
OFFENSE: FAILURE TO COMPLY WITH A PREVIOUS BOARD ORDER
NOTES: AN ORDER OF PROBATION OF 6/16/89 STEMMED FROM ALLEGATIONS OF MISPRESCRIBING MEDICATIONS; LICENSE SUMMARILY SUSPENDED 11/16/90 FOR CONTINUING THESE PRESCRIBING PRACTICES AND FOR FAILURE TO COMPLY WITH THE REQUIREMENTS FOR ADDITIONAL TRAINING AND EDUCATION CONTAINED IN THE 6/16/89 ORDER. CONDITIONS OF PROBATION INCLUDE: COMPLETION OF COURSE OFFERED BY THE SOCIETY OF ADDICTION MEDICINE AND ONE IN FAMILY PRACTICE REVIEW WITHIN ONE YEAR; MUST ATTAIN CERTIFICATION IN CARDIAC ADVANCED LIFE SUPPORT AND DISCONTINUE PERFORMING TREADMILL STRESS TESTS UNTIL CERTIFIED; MUST USE TRIPLICATE PRESCRIPTION FORMS; SHALL NOT STOCK NOR HAVE SAMPLES OF CONTROLLED SUBSTANCES IN OFFICE; SHALL PERMIT PHYSICIAN SELECTED BY BOARD TO REVIEW PATIENT CHARTS QUARTERLY FOR THE FIRST YEAR AND ANNUALLY THEREAFTER; SHALL NOTIFY THE BOARD OF PERIODS HE LIVES OR WORKS OUTSIDE WASHINGTON; MUST APPEAR BEFORE THE BOARD EVERY SIX MONTHS FOR ONE YEAR AND ANNUALLY THEREAFTER TO DEMONSTRATE COMPLIANCE.

NICOLAS, ARCADIO F MD, LICENSE NUMBER 0012366, OF PORT ANGELES, WA, WAS DISCIPLINED BY WASHINGTON ON SEPTEMBER 10, 1991.
DISCIPLINARY ACTION: SURRENDER OF LICENSE
NOTES: BOARD ENTERED A FINDINGS OF FACT, CONCLUSIONS OF LAW, AND ORDER IN THIS ACTION ON 12/20/90, AND ENTERED A FINDINGS OF FACT, CONCLUSIONS OF LAW, AND ORDER ON STIPULATED MOTION IN THIS ACTION ON 2/15/91. AGREES TO PERMANENTLY RETIRE FROM PRACTICE OF MEDICINE. BOARD WAIVES CONDITIONS PLACED ON LICENSE BY 12/20/90 ORDER.

NICOLAS, ARCADIO F MD, LICENSE NUMBER 0012366, OF PORT ANGELES, WA, WAS DISCIPLINED BY WASHINGTON ON MARCH 4, 1994.
DISCIPLINARY ACTION: LICENSE REINSTATEMENT; 51-MONTH PROBATION
NOTES: LICENSE PUT ON PROBATION SUBJECT TO CONDITIONS.

NICOLAS, ARCADIO F MD, LICENSE NUMBER 0012366, OF PORT ANGELES, WA, WAS DISCIPLINED BY WASHINGTON ON JULY 14, 1995.
DISCIPLINARY ACTION: SURRENDER OF LICENSE
NOTES: AGREED TO RETIRE.

NORMAN, CINDY RAE MD, LICENSE NUMBER 0025479, OF SPOKANE, WA, WAS DISCIPLINED BY WASHINGTON ON FEBRUARY 14, 1991.
DISCIPLINARY ACTION: EMERGENCY SUSPENSION
OFFENSE: SUBSTANCE ABUSE
NOTES: ALLEGATIONS OF PERSONAL USE OF CONTROLLED SUBSTANCES IN 1989 AND 1990, AND FAILED ATTEMPT AT TREATMENT FOR HER ADDICTION.

NORMAN, CINDY RAE MD, LICENSE NUMBER 0025479, OF SPOKANE, WA, WAS DISCIPLINED BY WASHINGTON ON SEPTEMBER 13, 1991.
DISCIPLINARY ACTION: PROBATION; FINE
OFFENSE: SUBSTANCE ABUSE
NOTES: USED HER POSITION AS A PHYSICIAN TO OBTAIN SUBSTANTIAL QUANTITIES OF CONTROLLED SUBSTANCES FOR HER OWN USE BY ISSUING PRESCRIPTIONS WRITTEN FOR FICTITIOUS PERSON; DURING 1989 AND 1990 PERSONALLY USED CONTROLLED SUBSTANCES FOR NON-THERAPEUTIC PURPOSES, INCLUDING THE USE OF MIND-ALTERING CONTROLLED SUBSTANCES; TREATED FOR CHEMICAL DEPENDENCY IN OREGON IN 1990 AND SUBSEQUENTLY SIGNED A FIVE-YEAR CONTRACT WITH THE WASHINGTON MONITORED TREATMENT PROGRAM ON 6/22/90; URINE SPECIMEN PROVIDED BY HER ON 12/7/90 TESTED POSITIVE FOR CODEINE; RETURNED TO OREGON ON 12/19/90 FOR EXTENDED CARE; WAS DISMISSED FROM A RESIDENCY PROGRAM OF INTERNAL MEDICINE AT DEACONESS/SACRED HEART MEDICAL CENTERS IN SPOKANE, WASHINGTON, BECAUSE OF THE POSITIVE URINALYSIS, EFFECTIVE 12/20/90. REVOCATION STAYED; PROBATION GRANTED UNDER FOLLOWING CONDITIONS: SHALL NOT CONSUME ANY ALCOHOL, CONTROLLED SUBSTANCES, OR LEGEND DRUGS, EXCEPT WHEN PRESCRIBED BY A LICENSED PHYSICIAN; SHALL CONTINUE TO UNDERGO ONGOING MONITORING OF HER PSYCHIATRIC MEDICATION AND THERAPY BY HER PSYCHIATRIST; SHALL HAVE HER URINE MONITORED ON A RANDOM BASIS FOR DRUGS AND ALCOHOL AT LEAST FOUR TIMES PER MONTH; MUST ATTEND A MINIMUM OF TWO AA MEETINGS PER WEEK; SHALL NOT PRACTICE MEDICINE MORE THAN 24 HOURS PER WEEK UNLESS APPROVED IN WRITING BY THE WASHINGTON MONITORED TREATMENT PROGRAM; SHALL PROVIDE A COPY OF A LETTER STATING SHE IS CURRENTLY INVOLVED IN RECOVERY FROM ALCOHOL AND SUBSTANCE DEPENDENCE TO ANY EMPLOYER; SHALL MEET WITH THE BOARD EVERY SIX MONTHS AND ANNUALLY THEREAFTER TO PROVE HER COMPLIANCE WITH ORDER; MUST HAVE HER PSYCHIATRIST AND EMPLOYER SUBMIT REPORTS TO THE BOARD; SHALL INFORM THE BOARD IF SHE CHANGES HER ADDRESS OR LEAVES THE STATE; DURATION OF PROBATION NOT COUNTED IF SHE IS OUT OF STATE; MUST PAY A $500 FINE; MAY NOT REQUEST TERMINATION OF THESE RESTRICTIONS FOR FIVE YEARS. ON 4/15/93 ORDER MODIFIED TO REMOVE LIMITATION UPON THE NUMBER OF HOURS SHE MAY PRACTICE MEDICINE AND SHALL APPEAR BEFORE THE BOARD FOR A COMPLIANCE APPEARANCE IN 3/94. ON 6/20/94 HER REQUEST GRANTED TO ALLOW SEMI-ANNUAL RATHER THAN QUARTERLY THERAPIST'S REPORTS; SHALL CONTINUE TO COMPLY WITH THIS ORDER AS MODIFIED.

- WASHINGTON -

NORMAN, CINDY RAE MD, LICENSE NUMBER 0025479, OF SPOKANE, WA, WAS DISCIPLINED BY WASHINGTON ON JUNE 10, 1994.
DISCIPLINARY ACTION: EMERGENCY SUSPENSION
OFFENSE: FAILURE TO COMPLY WITH A PREVIOUS BOARD ORDER
NOTES: FAILED TO COMPLY WITH 09/13/91 ORDER BY USING CONTROLLED SUBSTANCES DURING THE FIRST PART OF JUNE 1994.

NORMAN, CINDY RAE MD, LICENSE NUMBER 00M5498, WAS DISCIPLINED BY IDAHO ON JUNE 10, 1994.
DISCIPLINARY ACTION: EMERGENCY SUSPENSION
OFFENSE: DISCIPLINARY ACTION BY ANOTHER STATE OR AGENCY
NOTES: ON 6/10/94 WASHINGTON PLACED HER LICENSE ON EMERGENCY SUSPENSION. THE IDAHO BOARD ADOPTS THIS RECIPROCAL DISCIPLINE INCORPORATING THE TERMS AND CONDITIONS OF THE WASHINGTON ORDER AND ORDERING HER TO FULLY COMPLY WITH THESE.

NORMAN, CINDY RAE MD, LICENSE NUMBER 0025479, OF SPOKANE, WA, WAS DISCIPLINED BY WASHINGTON ON NOVEMBER 4, 1994.
DISCIPLINARY ACTION: LICENSE SUSPENSION; FINE
OFFENSE: PHYSICAL OR MENTAL ILLNESS INHIBITING THE ABILITY TO PRACTICE WITH SKILL AND SAFETY
NOTES: SHALL PAY A $500 FINE.

NORMAN, CINDY RAE MD, LICENSE NUMBER 00M5498, WAS DISCIPLINED BY IDAHO ON FEBRUARY 13, 1995.
DISCIPLINARY ACTION: LICENSE SUSPENSION; FINE
OFFENSE: DISCIPLINARY ACTION BY ANOTHER STATE OR AGENCY
NOTES: IN 11/94 WASHINGTON SUSPENDED HER LICENSE BASED ON DRUG USE AND NONCOMPLIANCE WITH A PREVIOUS ORDER. THE IDAHO BOARD FOR THE PURPOSE OF RECIPROCAL DISCIPLINE INCORPORATES THE TERMS AND CONDITIONS OF THIS ORDER AND ORDERS HER TO FULLY COMPLY WITH THEM.

NOVAK, FREDDIE P MD, LICENSE NUMBER 0G61059, OF PORTLAND, OR, WAS DISCIPLINED BY CALIFORNIA ON MAY 26, 1994.
DISCIPLINARY ACTION: 60-MONTH PROBATION
OFFENSE: DISCIPLINARY ACTION BY ANOTHER STATE OR AGENCY
NOTES: DISCIPLINE BY OREGON BOARD FOR IMPAIRMENT DUE TO EXCESSIVE USE OF CONTROLLED DRUGS. REVOCATION STAYED.

NOVAK, FREDDIE PATRICK MD, LICENSE NUMBER 0028055, OF 1848 N WINCHELL ST, PORTLAND, OR, WAS DISCIPLINED BY GEORGIA ON JULY 1, 1992.
DISCIPLINARY ACTION: NONRENEWAL OF LICENSE
OFFENSE: DISCIPLINARY ACTION BY ANOTHER STATE OR AGENCY
NOTES: LICENSE SUSPENDED IN OREGON 1/9/92. REVOKED FOR NONRENEWAL.

NOVAK, FREDDIE PATRICK MD, LICENSE NUMBER 0025150, OF OR, WAS DISCIPLINED BY WASHINGTON ON DECEMBER 17, 1992.
DISCIPLINARY ACTION: EMERGENCY SUSPENSION
OFFENSE: DISCIPLINARY ACTION BY ANOTHER STATE OR AGENCY
NOTES: SUSPENSION/REVOCATION AND OR RESTRICTION OF HIS LICENSE TO PRACTICE IN ANOTHER JURISDICTION AND BEING UNABLE TO PRACTICE WITH REASONABLE SKILL AND SAFETY.

NOVAK, FREDDIE PATRICK MD, LICENSE NUMBER 0025150, WAS DISCIPLINED BY WASHINGTON ON MARCH 19, 1993.
DISCIPLINARY ACTION: PROBATION; FINE
OFFENSE: DISCIPLINARY ACTION BY ANOTHER STATE OR AGENCY
NOTES: ON 8/23/91 OREGON LICENSE SUSPENDED BASED ON EXCESSIVE USE OF CONTROLLED SUBSTANCES; URINE SAMPLE TESTED POSITIVE FOR COCAINE ON 11/29/91; SURRENDERED OREGON LICENSE IN LIEU OF FURTHER PROCEEDINGS IN 1/92. PROBATION SUBJECT TO TERMS AND CONDITIONS AS FOLLOWS: SHALL NOT PRACTICE MEDICINE IN WASHINGTON UNTIL HE UNDERGOES A PSYCHOLOGICAL AND PHYSICAL EXAMINATION; SHALL APPEAR BEFORE THE BOARD AND BE REQUIRED TO PRESENT EVIDENCE OF HIS RECOVERY FROM HIS ADDICTION TO DRUGS AND ALCOHOL, INCLUDING THE RESULTS OF THE PSYCHOLOGICAL AND PHYSICAL EXAMINATION; SHALL INFORM THE BOARD IN WRITING OF CHANGES IN PRACTICE AND/OR RESIDENCE ADDRESS; SHALL PAY A $250 FINE. ON 3/23/95 HIS REQUEST FOR MODIFICATION OF THIS ORDER WAS DENIED.

NOVAK, FREDDIE PATRICK MD WAS DISCIPLINED BY NEVADA ON JUNE 30, 1993.
DISCIPLINARY ACTION: LICENSE REVOCATION
OFFENSE: DISCIPLINARY ACTION BY ANOTHER STATE OR AGENCY
NOTES: ON 03/05/93 CHARGED WITH FAILING TO REPORT WITHIN 30 DAYS, AND CONTINUAL FAILURE TO REPORT TO THE BOARD, THE SUSPENSION AND SURRENDER OF HIS OREGON LICENSE TO PRACTICE MEDICINE.

O'CONNOR, EDMUND MD, LICENSE NUMBER 0094667, OF 20624 WEST RICHMOND ROAD, BOTHELL, WA, WAS DISCIPLINED BY NEW YORK ON MARCH 30, 1995.
DISCIPLINARY ACTION: SURRENDER OF LICENSE
OFFENSE: DISCIPLINARY ACTION BY ANOTHER STATE OR AGENCY
NOTES: ACTION BY THE WASHINGTON QUALITY ASSURANCE COMMISSION FOR FAILING TO MAINTAIN AN ACCURATE PATIENT RECORD. ADMITTED THAT A HANDWRITTEN NOTATION OF 6/87 REGARDING NOTIFYING A PATIENT OF ABNORMAL TEST RESULTS WAS WRITTEN ON 1/25/89.

O'CONNOR, EDMUND J MD, LICENSE NUMBER 0011628, OF KIRKLAND, WA, WAS DISCIPLINED BY WASHINGTON ON AUGUST 19, 1994.
DISCIPLINARY ACTION: 36-MONTH PROBATION; FINE
OFFENSE: FALSIFYING OR ALTERING PATIENT RECORDS
NOTES: ALTERED AND/OR FALSIFIED THE MEDICAL RECORDS OF A PATIENT. MUST IMPLEMENT A SYSTEM TO PROVIDE WRITTEN NOTICE OF LAB RESULTS WITHIN FIVE WORKING DAYS OF RECEIPT OF THOSE RESULTS. SHALL APPEAR BEFORE THE COMMISSION IN SIX MONTHS, ALLOW SEMI-ANNUAL COMPLIANCE AUDITS OF HIS PRACTICE AND PAY A $2500 FINE WITHIN 90 DAYS. ON 9/25/96 HIS REQUEST TO TERMINATE THIS ORDER GRANTED AND LICENSE UNRESTRICTED.

OGUNMOLA, OLUFEMI MD, LICENSE NUMBER A026320, OF RANCH0 PALOS VERDES, CA, WAS DISCIPLINED BY CALIFORNIA ON JULY 3, 1987.
DISCIPLINARY ACTION: LICENSE REVOCATION
OFFENSE: SEXUAL ABUSE OF OR SEXUAL MISCONDUCT WITH A PATIENT
NOTES: SEXUAL MISCONDUCT WITH PATIENTS DURING PELVIC EXAMS

OGUNMOLA, OLUFEMI MD OF CA, WAS DISCIPLINED BY WASHINGTON ON MAY 27, 1993.
DISCIPLINARY ACTION: DENIAL OF NEW LICENSE
OFFENSE: DISCIPLINARY ACTION BY ANOTHER STATE OR AGENCY
NOTES: SEVERAL CONVICTIONS OF RAPE, MORAL TURPITUDE, AND REVOCATION OF HIS LICENSE TO PRACTICE IN ANOTHER STATE.

OH, GEORGE DUCKJOO MD, LICENSE NUMBER 0011523, OF TACOMA, WA, WAS DISCIPLINED BY WASHINGTON ON DECEMBER 16, 1994.
DISCIPLINARY ACTION: 60-MONTH PROBATION; FINE
OFFENSE: PROFESSIONAL MISCONDUCT
NOTES: ALLEGATIONS OF FRAUDULENT BILLING. MUST UTILIZE THE "SOAP" CHARTING FORMAT, COMPLETE 10 HOURS OF CATEGORY I CONTINUING MEDICAL EDUCATION IN MEDICAL ETHICS AND PAY A $15,000 FINE.

- WASHINGTON -

OH, GEORGE DUCKJOO MD, LICENSE NUMBER 0011523, OF TACOMA, WA, WAS DISCIPLINED BY WASHINGTON ON DECEMBER 15, 1995.
DISCIPLINARY ACTION: MONITORING OF PHYSICIAN
NOTES: AGREED TO SEVERAL TERMS AND CONDITIONS, INCLUDING HAVING A MENTOR REVIEW HIS PATIENT RECORDS.

OH, GEORGE DUCKJOO MD, LICENSE NUMBER 0011523, WAS DISCIPLINED BY WASHINGTON ON APRIL 19, 1996.
DISCIPLINARY ACTION: SURRENDER OF LICENSE
NOTES: PREVIOUS ORDER OF 12/15/95 PLACED CERTAIN RESTRICTIONS AND CONDITIONS ON HIS LICENSE AND PRACTICE OF MEDICINE. ORDER CONCLUDED WITH VOLUNTARY RETIREMENT EFFECTIVE 6/30/96; SHALL NOTIFY THE BOARD IF HE PLANS TO RESUME HIS PRACTICE OF MEDICINE IN WASHINGTON AND MAY RESUME PRACTICE ONLY UPON PRIOR BOARD APPROVAL.

OLLEE, HENRY P MD, LICENSE NUMBER 0014551, OF FEDERAL WAY, WA, WAS DISCIPLINED BY WASHINGTON ON JANUARY 18, 1991.
DISCIPLINARY ACTION: 60-MONTH PROBATION; FINE
OFFENSE: SUBSTANDARD CARE, INCOMPETENCE, OR NEGLIGENCE
NOTES: CHARGED WITH NEGLIGENCE IN PRACTICE OF MEDICINE AND SURGERY RESULTING IN SERIOUS HARM TO PATIENT. FAILED TO TIMELY DIAGNOSE PATIENT'S INFILTRATING MODERATELY WELL-DIFFERENTIATED ADENOCARCINOMA IN COLON. PATIENT DIED ON 10/7/86 FROM COMPLICATIONS CAUSED BY THE CANCER. CONDITIONS OF PROBATION: SHALL RECOMMEND APPROPRIATE SCREENING, PER AMERICAN CANCER SOCIETY PROTOCOL, TO ALL HIS REGULAR PATIENTS WHO FALL WITHIN THEIR GUIDELINES FOR SCREENING FOR COLON CANCER; SHALL APPEAR BEFORE THE BOARD IN ONE YEAR TO PROVE COMPLIANCE; SHALL ALLOW INSPECTION OF PRACTICE BY A BOARD REPRESENTATIVE; SHALL INFORM THE BOARD IN WRITING IF HE CHANGES HIS ADDRESS OR MOVES OUT OF STATE; TIME SPENT OUT OF STATE DOESN'T COUNT TOWARDS PROBATION TIME; SHALL COMPLETE SEVEN HOURS OF CONTINUING MEDICAL EDUCATION IN THE AREA OF CANCER-RELATED GASTROINTESTINAL DISORDERS WITHIN ONE YEAR; SHALL SUBMIT A REPORT WITHIN SIX MONTHS ON THE APPROACH TOWARD AND DIAGNOSIS OF SPECIFIC GASTROINTESTINAL DISEASES; $500 FINE. ON 1/15/93 HE WAS FOUND IN COMPLIANCE AND PROBATION TERMINATED.

OLMSTEAD, STEPHEN F MD WAS DISCIPLINED BY WASHINGTON ON OCTOBER 30, 1989.
DISCIPLINARY ACTION: MONITORING OF PHYSICIAN
OFFENSE: FAILURE TO COMPLY WITH A PREVIOUS BOARD ORDER
NOTES: NONCOMPLIANCE WITH THE STIPULATION AND ASSURANCE OF DISCONTINUANCE OF FEBRUARY 1988 BY FAILING TO COMPLY WITH THE REQUIREMENTS OF THE WASHINGTON MONITORED TREATMENT PROGRAM AND DID NOT MAINTAIN SATISFACTORY STATUS IN THAT PROGRAM IN THAT HE MISSED THREE GROUP THERAPY SESSIONS AND DID NOT CALL PROGRAM 24 HOURS IN ADVANCE TO LET THEM KNOW HE WOULD NOT BE ATTENDING. ADDICTED TO NARCOTICS AND SUFFERS FROM THE DISEASE OF CHEMICAL DEPENDENCE. TEN YEAR SUSPENSION, STAYED UNDER THE FOLLOWING TERMS AND CONDITIONS: SHALL PARTICIPATE IN, COOPERATE FULLY WITH, AND MAINTAIN SATISFACTORY STATUS WITH THE PROVISIONS OF THE LAWYER ASSISTANCE PROGRAM WITH REPORTS OF HIS PROGRESS AND COMPLIANCE ON A QUARTERLY BASIS TO THE BOARD; SHALL ATTEND MEETINGS OF NARCOTICS ANONYMOUS OR AA TWICE WEEKLY; SHALL CONTINUE TO SEE HIS PSYCHIATRIST ONCE A WEEK WHO SHALL REPORT TO THE BOARD EVERY SIX MONTHS FOR ONE YEAR AND ONCE EVERY YEAR THEREAFTER; SHALL APPEAR BEFORE THE BOARD EVERY SIX MONTHS FOR COMPLIANCE REVIEWS AND TO REPORT ON HIS RECOVERY; MAY PETITION FOR MODIFICATION OF THIS ORDER AFTER ONE YEAR.

OOI, JAMES PENG GWEN MD, LICENSE NUMBER 0033746, OF SAN DIEGO, CA, WAS DISCIPLINED BY WASHINGTON ON OCTOBER 6, 1995.
DISCIPLINARY ACTION: DENIAL OF NEW LICENSE
NOTES: WOULD NOT CONSIDER ANOTHER APPLICATION UNTIL HE COMPLETED A TERM OF PROBATION IN CALIFORNIA, PASSED THE AMERICAN BOARD OF CERTIFICATION OF FAMILY PRACTICE AND PROVIDED UPDATED APPLICATION DOCUMENTATION. ON 5/15/96 THE BOARD TERMINATED ITS JURISIDICTION AND HE WAS LICENSED IN WASHINGTON.

OPPENHEIM, ELLIOTT B MD, LICENSE NUMBER 0013915, OF BELLEVUE, WA, WAS DISCIPLINED BY WASHINGTON ON JUNE 21, 1990.
DISCIPLINARY ACTION: FINE; RESTRICTION PLACED ON LICENSE
OFFENSE: SUBSTANDARD CARE, INCOMPETENCE, OR NEGLIGENCE
NOTES: ADMITTED THAT HE DID NOT CORRECTLY AND/OR APPROPRIATELY TREAT A PATIENT WITH EMOTIONAL/MENTAL PROBLEMS, RESULTING IN HER HOSPITALIZATION; DID NOT CORRECTLY AND/OR APPROPRIATELY TREAT A MALE PATIENT BY INCORRECTLY PLACING AN ENDOTRACHEAL TUBE WHILE THE PATIENT WAS UNCONSCIOUS; THE PATIENT DIED SHORTLY THEREAFTER. SUSPENSION STAYED WITH CONDITIONS: MUST NOT APPLY FOR EMERGENCY ROOM PRIVILEGES; MUST ENGAGE IN PSYCHOTHERAPY AND AN ANNUAL INDEPENDENT PSYCHOLOGICAL/PSYCHIATRIC EVALUATION; PRACTICE MONITORED BY BOARD APPROVED SUPERVISOR; MUST NOT DISCUSS HIS PERSONAL LIFE WITH PATIENTS; MUST NOT ENGAGE IN MENTAL HEALTH COUNSELING OR PSYCHOTHERAPY; MUST HAVE A FEMALE LICENSED STAFF PERSON PRESENT WHEN HE IS WITH A FEMALE PATIENT OR FEMALE RELATIVES OF A PATIENT; MUST SUBMIT TO ANNOUNCED OR UNANNOUNCED PRACTICE REVIEWS; $2000 FINE; MUST MAINTAIN CURRENT ACLS CERTIFICATION; MUST OBTAIN 50 ADDITIONAL CONTINUING MEDICAL EDUCATION HOURS IN EMERGENCY CARE; MUST APPEAR BEFORE THE BOARD ANNUALLY FOR A COMPLIANCE REVIEW. MAY NOT PETITION FOR MODIFICATION FOR TWO YEARS; MUST INFORM BOARD OF CHANGE IN ADDRESS, HOSPITAL, OR IF HE LEAVES THE STATE.

OPPENHEIM, ELLIOTT B MD, LICENSE NUMBER 0013915, WAS DISCIPLINED BY WASHINGTON ON MAY 14, 1991.
DISCIPLINARY ACTION: EMERGENCY SUSPENSION
OFFENSE: SUBSTANDARD CARE, INCOMPETENCE, OR NEGLIGENCE
NOTES: ALLEGED TO HAVE PROVIDED CARE TO TWO PATIENTS THAT RESULTED IN INJURY TO THE PATIENTS OR CREATED AN UNREASONABLE RISK THAT THE PATIENTS WOULD BE HARMED, INCLUDING DEATH OF ONE PATIENT.

OPPENHEIM, ELLIOTT B MD, LICENSE NUMBER 0013915, OF BELLEVIEW, KINGS COUNTY, WA, WAS DISCIPLINED BY WASHINGTON ON JUNE 21, 1991.
DISCIPLINARY ACTION: FINE; RESTRICTION PLACED ON LICENSE
NOTES: SUSPENSION STAYED ON CONDITIONS: MUST NOT ACCEPT EMERGENCY ROOM PRIVILEGES; MUST ENGAGE IN PSYCHOTHERAPY AND AN ANNUAL INDEPENDENT PSYCHOLOGICAL/PSYCHIATRIC EVALUATION; PRACTICE MONITORED BY BOARD-APPROVED CONSULTANT; MUST NOT DISCUSS HIS PERSONAL LIFE WITH PATIENTS; MUST

NOT ENGAGE IN MENTAL HEALTH COUNSELLING OR PSYCHOTHERAPY; MUST HAVE A FEMALE LICENSED STAFF PERSON PRESENT WHEN HE IS WITH A FEMALE PATIENT OR HER FEMALE RELATIVES; MUST SUBMIT TO UNANNOUNCED PRACTICE REVIEWS; $2000 FINE; MUST MAINTAIN CURRENT EMERGENCY ROOM CERTIFICATION; MUST OBTAIN 50 HOURS ADDITIONAL CONTINUING MEDICAL EDUCATION IN EMERGENCY CARE; MUST APPEAR BEFORE BOARD ANNUALLY. MAY NOT PETITION FOR MODIFICATION FOR TWO YEARS.

OPPENHEIM, ELLIOTT B MD, LICENSE NUMBER 0013915, OF KIRKLAND, WA, WAS DISCIPLINED BY WASHINGTON ON FEBRUARY 18, 1993.
DISCIPLINARY ACTION: LICENSE REVOCATION; FINE
OFFENSE: FAILURE TO COMPLY WITH A PREVIOUS BOARD ORDER
NOTES: IN SPRING 1989 WHEN RESPONDING TO QUESTIONS CONCERNING HIS BACKGROUND IN ORDER TO BE AN EXPERT WITNESS, HE LIED AND SAID THERE WAS NOTHING TO AFFECT HIS CREDIBILITY; LATER ADMITTED THAT HE HAD ACTUALLY BEEN PREVIOUSLY CONVICTED OF POSSESSING AND DISTRIBUTING COCAINE, HAD WRITTEN A LOT OF PHONY PRESCRIPTIONS FOR THE DRUG AND HAD LOST HIS LICENSES IN BOTH WASHINGTON AND CALIFORNIA; ON 6/5/91 TESTIFIED WASHINGTON LICENSE HAD BEEN REINSTATED FROM 5/91 EMERGENCY SUSPENSION WHEN IN FACT IT HADN'T BEEN UNTIL 6/21/91; THIS INFORMATION RENDERED HIS EXPERT WITNESS SERVICES OF NO VALUE ALTHOUGH HE CHARGED $5,000; FAILED TO REVEAL THE TRUE STATUS OF HIS BACKGROUND TO AT LEAST TWO OTHER LAWYERS EMPLOYING HIS SERVICES. LICENSE REVOKED FOR A MINIMUM OF 20 YEARS. HE SHALL REFUND ALL THE FEES COLLECTED IN PREVIOUS CASES AND PROVIDE AN ACCOUNTING TO THE BOARD OF HOW HE CALCULATED THE AMOUNT TO BE RETURNED; HE SHALL PAY A FINE OF $43,000 WITHIN 120 DAYS. ON 9/17/93 ORDER MODIFIED DICTATING TERMS OF A PAYMENT SCHEDULE AND LOWERING THE TOTAL AMOUNT DUE UPON DISMISSAL OF HIS APPEAL.

ORAVETZ, JAN MD WAS DISCIPLINED BY WASHINGTON ON MAY 15, 1987.
DISCIPLINARY ACTION: RESTRICTION PLACED ON LICENSE
OFFENSE: SUBSTANDARD CARE, INCOMPETENCE, OR NEGLIGENCE
NOTES: IN 1984 AND 1985 ENGAGED IN INCOMPETENT AND/OR NEGLIGENT TREATMENT BEFORE AND DURING ADMINISTRATION OF GENERAL ANESTHESIA DURING FOUR SURGICAL PROCEDURES AT HUMANA HOSPITAL, TACOMA; IN ONE CASE APPLIED A BLOOD PRESSURE CUFF TO THE AFFECTED SIDE OF A POST MASTECTOMY PATIENT WHICH IS AGAINST ACCEPTED STANDARD OF CARE; ATTEMPTED SEVERAL TIMES WITHOUT SUCCESS TO PERFORM SPINAL ANESTHESIA IN ANOTHER PATIENT WHICH PREVIOUS ATTEMPTS PROVED UNSUCCESSFUL DUE TO BONY OVERGROWTH OF THE LUMBAR SPINE; FAILED TO DOCUMENT UNSUCCESSFUL ATTEMPTS; NEGLIGENT PRACTICE LED TO CARDIAC ARREST AND ULTIMATE DEATH OF A THIRD PATIENT; HAS VOLUNTARILY CEASED PRACTICE OF SURGICAL ANESTHESIA IN 5/85; PRACTICE LIMITED TO SPECIALTY OF PAIN MEDICINE; BEFORE PRACTICING SURGICAL ANESTHESIA AGAIN WILL SUBMIT A RETRAINING PROGRAM FOR BOARD APPROVAL

PALMASON, EDWARD P MD WAS DISCIPLINED BY WASHINGTON ON MARCH 8, 1996.
DISCIPLINARY ACTION: SURRENDER OF LICENSE
OFFENSE: FAILURE TO COMPLY WITH A PREVIOUS BOARD ORDER
NOTES: UNDER INVESTIGATION CONCERNING NONCOMPLIANCE WITH A PRIOR ORDER. VOLUNTARY RETIREMENT EFFECTIVE 6/01/94: HAS NO PLANS TO RESUME PRACTICE; HIS RETIREMENT SHALL BE PERMANENT; MAY RESUME PRACTICE ONLY WITH PRIOR BOARD APPROVAL; WILL NOTIFY THE BOARD IF HE PLANS TO RESUME PRACTICE IN THIS OR ANY OTHER JURISDICTION. THE CURRENT INVESTIGATION WAS TERMINATED.

PARK, JAMES F MD, LICENSE NUMBER 0004606, OF VANCOUVER, WA, WAS DISCIPLINED BY WASHINGTON ON DECEMBER 31, 1993.
DISCIPLINARY ACTION: SURRENDER OF LICENSE
OFFENSE: SEXUAL ABUSE OF OR SEXUAL MISCONDUCT WITH A PATIENT
NOTES: ALLEGATIONS THAT HE HAD SEXUAL CONTACT WITH TWO PATIENTS MORE THAN 18 YEARS AGO. IN LIEU OF TERMINATION OF INVESTIGATION RETIREMENT SHALL BE PERMANENT; MAY RESUME PRACTICE ONLY WITH THE PRIOR APPROVAL OF THE BOARD; HE WILL NOTIFY THE BOARD IF HE PLANS TO RESUME PRACTICE IN THIS OR ANY OTHER JURISDICTION.

PARK, JOHN C MD, LICENSE NUMBER 0022518, OF TACOMA, WA, WAS DISCIPLINED BY WASHINGTON ON OCTOBER 16, 1992.
DISCIPLINARY ACTION: PROBATION; REQUIRED TO TAKE ADDITIONAL MEDICAL EDUCATION
OFFENSE: SUBSTANDARD CARE, INCOMPETENCE, OR NEGLIGENCE
NOTES: BETWEEN 6/86 AND 5/90 HE POSSESSED, USED, PRESCRIBED OR DISTRIBUTED CONTROLLED SUBSTANCES OR LEGEND DRUGS OTHER THAN FOR LEGITIMATE OR THERAPEUTIC PURPOSES IN SEVERAL CASES INCLUDING INJECTIONS OF GENTAMYCIN, STEROIDS OR ESTROGEN IN NUMEROUS CASES; ALSO ENGAGED IN INCOMPETENT, NEGLIGENT OR MALPRACTICE CAUSING UNREASONABLE RISK TO THE PATIENT IN THAT HE PRESCRIBED NSAIDS FOR PATIENTS WITH KIDNEY OR GASTROINTESTINAL DIFFICULTIES; FAILED TO PERFORM AND/OR RECORD APPROPRIATE EXAMS OR EVALUATIONS; FAILED TO EVALUATE THE CAUSE OF ANEMIA IN SIX PATIENTS. CONDITIONS OF PROBATION ARE AS FOLLOWS: SHALL BE SUPERVISED BY A BOARD APPROVED PHYSICIAN WHO WILL SUBMIT A QUARTERLY REPORT OF HIS ACTIVITIES AND PROGRESS TO THE BOARD; SHALL ATTEND AND PARTICIPATE IN FAMILY PRACTICE TRAINING AS DESIGNATED BY THE BOARD; SHALL READ CURRENT MEDICAL JOURNALS AND/OR TEXTBOOKS RECOMMENDED BY HIS MONITOR; A BOARD APPROVED PHYSICIAN WILL EVALUATE AT LEAST 30 PATIENT CHARTS PER QUARTER AND PROVIDE A WRITTEN REPORT TO THE BOARD; SHALL, BEFORE THE END OF 1993, TAKE A CLINICAL EXAMINATION AND/OR THE SPEX EXAMINATION; SHALL APPEAR BEFORE THE BOARD IN ONE YEAR; THE BOARD MAY MAKE UNANNOUNCED VISITS ANNUALLY TO HIS PRACTICE; SHALL PAY $3,000; SHALL INFORM THE BOARD OR CHANGES IN HIS PRACTICE AND RESIDENCE ADDRESS AND MOST NOTIFY THEM IF HE LEAVES WASHINGTON TO RESIDE OR PRACTICE OUTSIDE THE STATE; PERIOD OF PROBATION SHALL BE TOLLED FOR ANY TIME PERIOD DURING WHICH HE RESIDES AND/OR PRACTICES OUTSIDE WASHINGTON. AS OF 12/17/93 HAD NOT YET COMPLIED WITH CONDITIONS BUT WAS GRANTED A ONE MONTH EXTENSION.

PARK, JOHN C MD, LICENSE NUMBER 0022518, OF TACOMA, WA, WAS DISCIPLINED BY WASHINGTON ON JULY 14, 1995.
DISCIPLINARY ACTION: 36-MONTH PROBATION; REQUIRED TO TAKE ADDITIONAL MEDICAL EDUCATION
OFFENSE: SUBSTANDARD CARE, INCOMPETENCE, OR NEGLIGENCE
NOTES: COMMITTED UNPROFESSIONAL CONDUCT BY PROVIDING SUBSTANDARD CARE TO A NUMBER OF PATIENTS AND FAILING TO COMPLY WITH A COMMISSION ORDER. SHALL PRACTICE UNDER SUPERVISION; SHALL ATTEND A PHYSICIAN REFRESHER COURSE; SHALL PARTICIPATE IN

A ONE-WEEK FAMILY PRACTICE UPDATE, SHALL PERMIT THE DEPARTMENT OF HEALTH TO REVIEW HIS RECORDS.

PATEL, BHAGWAT MD, LICENSE NUMBER 0022628, OF GAITHERSBURG, MD, WAS DISCIPLINED BY WASHINGTON ON OCTOBER 15, 1992.
OFFENSE: OVERPRESCRIBING OR MISPRESCRIBING DRUGS
NOTES: INAPPROPRIATE PRESCRIBING. LICENSE CONDITIONED UPON HIS COMPLIANCE WITH TERMS AND CONDITIONS STATED IN ORDER FOR A MINIMUM OF FIVE YEARS. ON 5/27/94 LICENSE REINSTATED IN FULL.

PATEL, GIRISH U MD WAS DISCIPLINED BY WASHINGTON ON MAY 3, 1993.
DISCIPLINARY ACTION: LICENSE SUSPENSION
OFFENSE: DISCIPLINARY ACTION BY ANOTHER STATE OR AGENCY
NOTES: LICENSE REVOCATION IN COLORADO DUE TO FINDING THAT HE COMMITTED GROSSLY NEGLIGENT MEDICAL PRACTICE BY REASON OF HIS TREATMENT OF PATIENTS WHILE AFFECTED BY ALCOHOL. HIS LICENSE IS INDEFINITELY SUSPENDED IN WASHINGTON WHICH SHALL ONLY BE STAYED BY A WRITTEN MOTION AND OF HIS PERSONAL APPEARANCE BEFORE THE BOARD AND A FINDING THAT HE HAS SUBMITTED AN EVALUATION BY THE COLORADO PERSONALIZED EDUCATION FOR PHYSICIAN PROGRAM AND ALL PSYCHIATRIC/ADDICTION EVALUATIONS; PARTICIPATION IN THE WASHINGTON PHYSICIAN'S HEALTH PROGRAM; AGREES TO ABIDE BY ANY COMPLIANCE REQUIREMENTS IN ANY FUTURE ORDER GRANTING A STAY OF SUSPENSION; SHALL INFORM THE BOARD IN WRITING OF CHANGES IN HIS PRACTICE AND RESIDENCE ADDRESS.

PATEL, HARSHAD M MD, LICENSE NUMBER 0052109, OF 48 SHORT STREET, TAUNTON, MA, WAS DISCIPLINED BY MASSACHUSETTS ON SEPTEMBER 9, 1992.
DISCIPLINARY ACTION: LICENSE REVOCATION
OFFENSE: PROFESSIONAL MISCONDUCT
NOTES: SEXUAL MISCONDUCT.

PATEL, HARSHAD M MD, LICENSE NUMBER 0052109, OF 48 SHORT STREET, TAUNTON, MA, WAS DISCIPLINED BY MASSACHUSETTS ON DECEMBER 29, 1993.
DISCIPLINARY ACTION: 60-MONTH PROBATION
NOTES: STAYED SUSPENSION.

PATEL, HARSHAD M MD, LICENSE NUMBER 0022663, OF TAUNTON, MA, WAS DISCIPLINED BY WASHINGTON ON APRIL 21, 1995.
NOTES: AGREED TO APPEAR BEFORE THE BOARD BEFORE BEGINNING OR RESUMING THE PRACTICE OF MEDICINE IN WASHINGTON.

PERKINS, CAROL L MD OF 17000-140TH ST. N.E. SUITE 204, WOODINVILLE, WA, WAS DISCIPLINED BY DEA ON NOVEMBER 21, 1995.
DISCIPLINARY ACTION: SURRENDER OF CONTROLLED SUBSTANCE LICENSE
NOTES: IN LIEU OF ORDER TO SHOW CAUSE.

PERKINS, HAROLD DOYLE MD, LICENSE NUMBER 0012142, OF SEATTLE, WA, WAS DISCIPLINED BY WASHINGTON ON MARCH 10, 1995.
DISCIPLINARY ACTION: PROBATION; FINE
NOTES: PROBATION UNDER THE FOLLOWING TERMS AND CONDITIONS: SHALL COMPLY WITH CERTAIN RESTRICTIONS ON HIS PRESCRIBING; SHALL COMPLETE 25 HOURS OF CONTINUED MEDICAL EDUCATION IN PRESCRIBING. $5,000 FINE. ON 6/25/97 BOARD GRANTED HIS REQUEST TO TERMINATE THIS ORDER AND LICENSE IS UNRESTRICTED.

PETROSKE, JAMES L MD OF 2250 NW FLANDERS, #103, PORTLAND, OR, WAS DISCIPLINED BY DEA ON APRIL 27, 1989.
DISCIPLINARY ACTION: SURRENDER OF CONTROLLED SUBSTANCE LICENSE
OFFENSE: OVERPRESCRIBING OR MISPRESCRIBING DRUGS
NOTES: PRESCRIBED EXCESSIVE AMOUNTS OF METHYLPHENIDATE. SURRENDERED LICENSE TO PRACTICE MEDICINE IN OREGON FOLLOWED BY VOLUNTARY SURRENDER OF CONTROLLED SUBSTANCE REGISTRATION.

PETROSKE, JAMES L MD WAS DISCIPLINED BY WASHINGTON ON MARCH 15, 1990.
DISCIPLINARY ACTION: EMERGENCY SUSPENSION

PETROSKE, JAMES L MD WAS DISCIPLINED BY WASHINGTON ON JUNE 22, 1990.
DISCIPLINARY ACTION: LICENSE REVOCATION
OFFENSE: DISCIPLINARY ACTION BY ANOTHER STATE OR AGENCY
NOTES: OREGON BOARD RESTRICTED LICENSE 7/13/88 AND ON 1/25/89 ACCEPTED SURRENDER OF LICENSE IN LIEU OF PROCEEDING TO A CONTESTED HEARING ON POSSIBLE REVOCATION OF HIS LICENSE. MAY PETITION FOR REINSTATEMENT AT ANY TIME.

PETROSKE, JAMES LAWRENCE MD, DATE OF BIRTH MAY 11, 1933, LICENSE NUMBER 0015511, OF PO BOX 2908, PORTLAND, OR, WAS DISCIPLINED BY MINNESOTA ON JANUARY 28, 1991.
DISCIPLINARY ACTION: LICENSE REVOCATION
OFFENSE: DISCIPLINARY ACTION BY ANOTHER STATE OR AGENCY
NOTES: VIOLATING FEDERAL LAW RELATING TO THE PRACTICE OF MEDICINE; ENGAGING IN UNETHICAL AND UNPROFESSIONAL CONDUCT; INABILITY TO PRACTICE MEDICINE WITH REASONABLE SKILL AND SAFETY BY REASON OF CHEMICALS; BECOMING HABITUATED TO INTOXICANTS; PRESCRIBING DRUGS FOR OTHER THAN MEDICALLY ACCEPTED THERAPEUTIC PURPOSES; ENGAGING IN CONDUCT WITH PATIENTS WHICH IS SEXUAL.

PETROSKE, JAMES LAWRENCE MD, DATE OF BIRTH MAY 11, 1933, OF 2250 N W FLANDERS, PORTLAND, OR, WAS DISCIPLINED BY MEDICARE ON JULY 24, 1991.
DISCIPLINARY ACTION: EXCLUSION FROM THE MEDICARE AND/OR MEDICAID PROGRAMS
OFFENSE: DISCIPLINARY ACTION BY ANOTHER STATE OR AGENCY
NOTES: LICENSE REVOCATION OR SUSPENSION.

PHELPS, JANICE K MD WAS DISCIPLINED BY WASHINGTON ON MARCH 17, 1989.
DISCIPLINARY ACTION: RESTRICTION PLACED ON CONTROLLED SUBSTANCE LICENSE; REQUIRED TO TAKE ADDITIONAL MEDICAL EDUCATION
OFFENSE: OVERPRESCRIBING OR MISPRESCRIBING DRUGS
NOTES: ABOUT 4/09/85 SHE INDISCRIMINATELY PRESCRIBED A DANGEROUS COMBINATION OF DRUGS TO HER PATIENT, EVEN AFTER DISCUSSION WITH THE PATIENT ABOUT THE HEMLOCK SOCIETY ABOUT 3/28/85 WHEN SHE WAS OR SHOULD HAVE BEEN OTHERWISE AWARE THAT THIS PATIENT POSED A SERIOUS SUICIDAL RISK. IN THE COURSE OF HER TREATMENT OF THIS PATIENT SHE NEGLIGENTLY AIDED AND ASSISTED THE PATIENT TO FORMULATE AND CARRY OUT A PLAN TO COMMIT SUICIDE BY THE INGESTION OF DRUGS. PATIENT SUFFERED HARM AFTER INGESTING THESE DRUGS RESULTING IN HOSPITALIZATION AND FURTHER EXTENSIVE TREATMENT. COMMITTED ACTS OF DISHONESTY BY OBLITERATING HER MEDICAL RECORDS ON THIS PATIENT APPROXIMATELY ONE YEAR AFTER THE ENTRY ON OR ABOUT 5/03/85 AND THEN ADDING THE PHRASE "WRONG PATIENT" AND TWO LATER ENTRIES DATED 5/3/85 AND 5/6/85 SHE COMMITTED ACTS OF

- WASHINGTON -

DISHONESTY. 10 YEAR SUSPENSION, STAYED UNDER THE FOLLOWING TERMS AND CONDITIONS: SHALL PARTICIPATE IN AND SUCCESSFULLY COMPLETE AN INDIVIDUALIZED BOARD APPROVED RESIDENCY-TYPE PROGRAM IN THE TREATMENT OF DEPRESSION AND SHALL SUBMIT TO THE BOARD DETAILED INFORMATION ABOUT THIS PROGRAM IN NO LATER THAN 90 DAYS; IN NO LATER THAN 30 DAYS, SHALL COMMENCE USING TRIPLICATE PRESCRIPTION FORMS FOR ALL PRESCRIBING OF LEGEND DRUGS IN HER PRACTICE; HER PRACTICE SHALL BE SUBJECT TO RANDOM, UNSCHEDULED PRACTICE REVIEWS BY THE BOARD AT A MINIMUM OF TWICE A YEAR AND SHE SHALL COOPERATE IN FULL WITH THE REVIEW WHICH SHALL INCLUDE BUT NOT BE LIMITED TO HER PRESCRIBING PRACTICES AND RECORD KEEPING WHICH SHALL BE MAINTAINED IN A SOAP FORMAT, DOCUMENTATION OF BETTER COMMUNICATION WITH PATIENTS' PRIMARY PHYSICIANS, DOCUMENTATION OF IMPROVED NETWORKING WITH SUICIDAL PATIENTS AND THEIR SUPPORT SYSTEM, AND DOCUMENTATION OF INSTRUCTING PATIENTS TO RETURN UNUSED MEDICATIONS PRIOR TO OBTAINING NEW PRESCRIPTIONS; WITHIN 90 DAYS, SHALL SUBMIT TO THE BOARD A PHARMACOLOGY UPDATE COURSE FOR APPROVAL AND SHALL SUCCESSFULLY COMPLETE THE COURSE; SHALL APPEAR FOR ANNUAL COMPLIANCE APPEARANCES BEFORE THE BOARD; BEFORE PRESCRIBING FOR ANY CONDITION OTHER THAN FOR TREATMENT OF PATIENTS' ADDICTION OR DEPRESSION, SHALL CONSULT AND DOCUMENT SUCH CONSULTATION WITH THE PATIENTS' PRIMARY PHYSICIAN OR, IF THE PATIENT DOES NOT HAVE A PRIMARY PHYSICIAN, THEN WITH AN APPROPRIATE CONSULTANT AND IN THE CONSULTATION, SHALL AT A MINIMUM ADVISE THE PRIMARY PHYSICIAN OR APPROPRIATE CONSULTANT ABOUT THE DRUGS SHE INTENDS TO PRESCRIBE AND THE MEDICAL INDICATIONS THEREFORE; UPON SATISFACTORY COMPLIANCE WITH THE TERMS OF THIS ORDER, MAY PETITION FOR MODIFICATION IN FIVE YEARS; MUST NOTIFY THE BOARD IN WRITING IF SHE LEAVES TO RESIDE OR PRACTICE OUTSIDE THE STATE AND TIME SPENT OUTSIDE WASHINGTON SHALL NOT APPLY TO THE REDUCTION OF THE PERIOD OF SUSPENSION UNLESS REQUIRED BY AND IS PART OF THE INDIVIDUALIZED RESIDENCY-TYPE PROGRAM.

PHELPS, JANICE K MD WAS DISCIPLINED BY WASHINGTON ON AUGUST 14, 1989.
DISCIPLINARY ACTION: SURRENDER OF LICENSE
NOTES: VOLUNTARY SURRENDER AND SHE SHALL DISMISS THE APPEAL NOW PENDING IN THE KING COUNTY SUPERIOR COURT OF THE BOARD'S 3/17/89 ORDER WHICH SHALL REMAIN ON THE RECORD IN THE FILES MAINTAINED BY THE BOARD.

PILLOW, RANDOLPH MD WAS DISCIPLINED BY WASHINGTON ON FEBRUARY 16, 1990.
DISCIPLINARY ACTION: SURRENDER OF LICENSE
NOTES: STATEMENT OF CHARGES HAD BEEN ISSUED BY BOARD. ADVISED BOARD HE HAD RETIRED 1/31/86 WITH NO PLANS TO RESUME PRACTICE. IN CONSIDERATION OF WITHDRAWAL OF STATEMENT OF CHARGES, RETIREMENT SHALL BE PERMANENT.

PLASTINO, JOHN P MD WAS DISCIPLINED BY WASHINGTON ON APRIL 11, 1989.
DISCIPLINARY ACTION: RESTRICTION PLACED ON CONTROLLED SUBSTANCE LICENSE; MONITORING OF PHYSICIAN
OFFENSE: OVERPRESCRIBING OR MISPRESCRIBING DRUGS
NOTES: PRESCRIBED LARGE AMOUNTS OF MORPHINE SULFATE IN A NONTHERAPEUTIC MANNER TO HIS PATIENT RESULTING IN THE PATIENT'S CONTINUED ADDICTION TO MORPHINE SULFATE. HIS PRESCRIBING PRACTICES HAVE BEEN THE SUBJECT OF TWO PRIOR BOARD ACTIONS. HIS LICENSE TO PRACTICE MEDICINE AND SURGERY IN WASHINGTON SHALL BE CONDITIONED ON HIS COMPLIANCE WITH THE FOLLOWING TERMS AND CONDITIONS: SHALL SUBMIT TRIPLICATE PRESCRIPTIONS ON ALL CONTROLLED SUBSTANCES, SCHEDULE II THROUGH V; SHALL NOT PRESCRIBE SCHEDULE II DRUGS FOR MORE THAN THREE DAYS EXCEPT FOR TERMINALLY ILL CANCER PATIENTS; SHALL NOT PRESCRIBE SCHEDULE III-V DRUGS FOR MORE THAN THREE WEEKS; SHALL PERMIT A COMPREHENSIVE PRACTICE REVIEW BY THE BOARD AS DEEMED NECESSARY; AFTER SEVEN YEARS SHALL APPEAR BEFORE THE BOARD TO SHOW COMPLIANCE AND TO APPLY FOR A LIFTING OF THE RESTRICTIONS ON HIS LICENSE TO PRACTICE.

PLAYER, GLENN S MD, LICENSE NUMBER 0002406, OF VANCOUVER, WA, WAS DISCIPLINED BY WASHINGTON ON NOVEMBER 18, 1993.
DISCIPLINARY ACTION: SURRENDER OF LICENSE
OFFENSE: OVERPRESCRIBING OR MISPRESCRIBING DRUGS
NOTES: ALLEGATIONS OF NON-THERAPEUTIC PRESCRIBING OF MEDICATIONS FOR LONG-TERM WEIGHT CONTROL. HIS RETIREMENT IS PERMANENT AND RETROACTIVE TO 06/01/93 AND HE WILL NOTIFY THE BOARD IF HE PLANS TO RESUME PRACTICE IN WASHINGTON.

POKORNY, KAREL MD OF 6122 BAYVIEW DRIVE NORTH EAST, TACOMA, WA, WAS DISCIPLINED BY DEA ON SEPTEMBER 29, 1995.
DISCIPLINARY ACTION: SURRENDER OF CONTROLLED SUBSTANCE LICENSE
NOTES: IN LIEU OF PUBLIC INTEREST REVOCATION.

POLO, GUILLERMO MD, LICENSE NUMBER 0008454, OF LONGVIEW, WA, WAS DISCIPLINED BY WASHINGTON ON APRIL 27, 1990.
DISCIPLINARY ACTION: PROBATION; REQUIRED TO TAKE ADDITIONAL MEDICAL EDUCATION
OFFENSE: PROFESSIONAL MISCONDUCT
NOTES: BETWEEN 1 AND 5/88 FAILED TO PROVIDE ADEQUATE SUPERVISION OF PHYSICIAN ASSISTANT BY FAILING TO DETECT AND TERMINATE OVERPRESCRIBING OF CERTAIN CONTROLLED SUBSTANCES AND DID NOT APPROVE A PRESCRIPTION FOR VALIUM AS REQUIRED BY THE UTILIZATION PLAN. PROBATION TO LAST AT LEAST ONE YEAR, WITH THE FOLLOWING CONDITIONS: SHALL COMPLY WITH TERMS SPECIFIED IN UTILIZATION PLAN FOR EACH PHYSICIAN ASSISTANT, INCLUDING PROVIDING DIRECT SUPERVISION AND REVIEWING AND COUNTERSIGNING PATIENT CHARTS; MUST WRITE ALL ORDERS AND PRESCRIPTIONS OF CONTROLLED SUBSTANCES; PHYSICIAN ASSISTANT SHALL WRITE PRESCRIPTIONS FOR SCHEDULE III NARCOTICS ONLY ON AN EMERGENCY BASIS, IN QUANTITIES NOT TO EXCEED 8 PILLS OR 2 FLUID OUNCES; SHALL ALLOW UNANNOUNCED PRACTICE REVIEWS; SHALL ATTEND CONTINUING MEDICAL EDUCATION COURSE ON CHRONIC PAIN MANAGEMENT WITHIN ONE YEAR; MAY PETITION FOR TERMINATION OF PROBATION AFTER ONE YEAR. ON 1/17/92 PROBATION TERMINATED.

POLO, GUILLERMO MD, LICENSE NUMBER 0008454, OF LONGVIEW, WA, WAS DISCIPLINED BY WASHINGTON ON DECEMBER 13, 1996.
DISCIPLINARY ACTION: SURRENDER OF LICENSE
NOTES: AGREEMENT TO RETIRE.

QUINN, JOHN R MD WAS DISCIPLINED BY WASHINGTON ON NOVEMBER 20, 1987.
DISCIPLINARY ACTION: LICENSE REINSTATEMENT; 60-MONTH PROBATION
NOTES: SHALL SUBMIT ANNUAL CPA AUDITS.

- WASHINGTON -

RAMOS, MANUEL F MD OF 833 171ST PLACE NE, BELLEVUE, WA, WAS DISCIPLINED BY MEDICARE ON MARCH 23, 1989.
DISCIPLINARY ACTION: 36-MONTH EXCLUSION FROM THE MEDICARE AND/OR MEDICAID PROGRAMS
OFFENSE: SUBSTANDARD CARE, INCOMPETENCE, OR NEGLIGENCE
NOTES: VIOLATIONS OCCURRED IN GETTYSBURG, SOUTH DAKOTA. SUBSTANDARD CARE OF 12 PATIENTS. MEDICARE EXCLUSION WOULD TERMINATE RAMOS' EMPLOYMENT WITH THE INDIAN HEALTH SERVICE

RAMOS, MANUEL F MD, DATE OF BIRTH DECEMBER 31, 1938, OF 17108 NE 35TH STREET, BELLEVUE, WA, WAS DISCIPLINED BY MEDICARE ON AUGUST 9, 1990.
DISCIPLINARY ACTION: 36-MONTH EXCLUSION FROM THE MEDICARE AND/OR MEDICAID PROGRAMS
NOTES: PEER REVIEW ORGANIZATION RECOMMENDATION.

RAY, DEBABRATA MD OF 3638 KATHLEEN ANN DR, ST. LOUIS, MO, WAS DISCIPLINED BY ILLINOIS ON SEPTEMBER 1, 1989.
DISCIPLINARY ACTION: 36-MONTH PROBATION
OFFENSE: PRACTICING WITHOUT A VALID LICENSE
NOTES: PRACTICED AS A PHYSICIAN ASSISTANT PRIOR TO LICENSURE

RAY, DEBABRATA MD OF ST LOUIS, MO, WAS DISCIPLINED BY MISSOURI ON AUGUST 1, 1991.
DISCIPLINARY ACTION: 13-MONTH PROBATION
OFFENSE: DISCIPLINARY ACTION BY ANOTHER STATE OR AGENCY
NOTES: PRIOR TO LICENSURE IN ILLINOIS, ENGAGED IN THE UNAUTHORIZED PRACTICE OF MEDICINE; ILLINOIS BOARD ISSUED DR. RAY A LICENSE UNDER THREE YEAR PROBATION. MISSOURI LICENSE ISSUED UNDER PROBATIONARY TERMS AND CONDITIONS UNTIL 9/23/92.

RAY, DEBABRATA MD, LICENSE NUMBER 0023160, OF CHESTERFIELD, MO, WAS DISCIPLINED BY WASHINGTON ON JUNE 19, 1992.
OFFENSE: DISCIPLINARY ACTION BY ANOTHER STATE OR AGENCY
NOTES: SUSPENSION OR RESTRICTION OF A LICENSE IN ANOTHER STATE. ORDERED TO COMPLY WITH THE TERMS IMPOSED ON HIS LICENSE BY ILLINOIS. ON 2/28/94 ALL RESTRICTIONS FROM LICENSE WERE REMOVED.

RAY, LANCE I MD, DATE OF BIRTH MAY 15, 1944, LICENSE NUMBER 0012094, WAS DISCIPLINED BY WASHINGTON ON NOVEMBER 14, 1990.
DISCIPLINARY ACTION: EMERGENCY SUSPENSION
NOTES: ALLEGATIONS INCLUDE UNPROFESSIONAL CONDUCT AND INABILITY TO PRACTICE WITH REASONABLE SKILL AND SAFETY TO CONSUMERS.

RAY, LANCE I MD, DATE OF BIRTH MAY 15, 1944, LICENSE NUMBER 0012094, OF SEATTLE, WA, WAS DISCIPLINED BY WASHINGTON ON MARCH 25, 1991.
DISCIPLINARY ACTION: LICENSE REVOCATION
OFFENSE: SUBSTANCE ABUSE
NOTES: LICENSE SUMMARILY SUSPENDED ON 11/14/90. DIVERTED RITALIN, A CONTROLLED SUBSTANCE, FOR HIS OWN NON-THERAPEUTIC USE; BETWEEN 4-6/90 PRESCRIBED FIORINAL WITH CODEINE FOR PATIENT IN NONTHERAPEUTIC AMOUNTS, PATIENT HAD BEEN HOSPITALIZED IN 3/90 AND WITHDRAWN FROM FIORINAL; BETWEEN 4-6/90 OBTAINED $12,635 FROM A PATIENT BUT PRESENTED NO BILLS FOR MEDICAL SERVICES TO THE PATIENT; WAS ALSO PAID $1,354.23 BY MEDICARE FOR HIS TREATMENT OF THE PATIENT FROM 3/30/90 TO 5/17/90; BEGAN TREATMENT FOR MAJOR DEPRESSION IN 7/88; ALLOWED TO VOLUNTARILY RESIGN HIS PRIVILEGES AT PROVIDENCE MEDICAL CENTER IN SEATTLE ON 9/24/90 FOR ADMINISTRATIVE REASONS, INCLUDING INABILITY TO PROVIDE CERTIFICATION OF MALPRACTICE INSURANCE; ON 9/8/90 PERFORMED SURGERY AT PROVIDENCE MEDICAL CENTER WITHOUT QUALIFIED SURGICAL ASSISTANT AS REQUIRED; ON 3/12 AND 3/14/91 WROTE PRESCRIPTIONS FOR PATIENTS WHILE LICENSE WAS SUSPENDED. NO RIGHT TO REAPPLY FOR ONE YEAR; SHALL SUBMIT TO AN IN-PATIENT PSYCHIATRIC AND CHEMICAL DEPENDENCY EVALUATION WITHIN 20 DAYS; SHALL APPEAR WITHIN 60 DAYS FOR DETERMINATION OF ADDITIONAL CONDITIONS, AND SHALL DEVISE A PLAN FOR FINANCIAL RESTITUTION TO THE ESTATE OF THE PATIENT; SHALL CONTINUE CONTINUING MEDICAL EDUCATION AS IF HIS LICENSE WERE ACTIVE.

RAY, LANCE I MD, DATE OF BIRTH MAY 15, 1944, LICENSE NUMBER 0025565, OF 18666 NORTH 72ND AVENUE, GLENDALE, AZ, WAS DISCIPLINED BY NEW JERSEY ON JUNE 7, 1994.
DISCIPLINARY ACTION: LICENSE REVOCATION; FINE
OFFENSE: DISCIPLINARY ACTION BY ANOTHER STATE OR AGENCY
NOTES: DISCIPLINARY ACTION TAKEN IN WASHINGTON FOR INAPPROPRIATE DISTRIBUTION OF CONTROLLED DANGEROUS SUBSTANCES FOR OTHER THAN LEGITIMATE MEDICAL PURPOSES. ASSESSED A $1,000 PENALTY. LICENSE REINSTATED ON 3/14/96: SHALL NOT PRACTICE UNTIL HE HAS APPEARED BEFORE THE BOARD TO DEMONSTRATE TO ITS SATISFACTION THAT HIS PRACTICE WOULD NOT ENDANGER THE HEALTH AND WELFARE OF THE PUBLIC.

RAY, LANCE I MD, DATE OF BIRTH MAY 15, 1944, LICENSE NUMBER 0024076, WAS DISCIPLINED BY ARIZONA ON APRIL 20, 1996.
DISCIPLINARY ACTION: 60-MONTH PROBATION; REQUIRED TO TAKE ADDITIONAL MEDICAL EDUCATION
OFFENSE: DISCIPLINARY ACTION BY ANOTHER STATE OR AGENCY
NOTES: DISCIPLINARY ACTION TAKEN BY WASHINGTON AND NEW JERSEY; WASHINGTON REVOKED HIS LICENSE IN 3/91; IN 3/95, PASSED SPECIAL PURPOSE EXAMINATION; IN 6/95, WASHINGTON BOARD WITHDREW REVOCATION; SINCE THE SUMMER OF 1995, HAS NOT BEEN IN COMPLIANCE WITH PAYMENT PLAN SET BY WASHINGTON BOARD IN 6/92 TO REPAY $41,500 TO THE ESTATE OF A PATIENT; IN 6/94 NEW JERSEY REVOKED HIS LICENSE BASED ON THE WASHINGTON ORDER; IN 3/96, NEW JERSEY BOARD REINSTATED HIS LICENSE AND ORDERED THAT HE NOT PRACTICE SURGERY UNTIL HE HAD MET WITH THE BOARD AND DEMONSTRATED THAT HIS PRACTICE WOULD NOT ENDANGER THE HEALTH OF THE PUBLIC. EXCEPT FOR RESTITUTION TO PATIENT'S ESTATE, ARIZONA BOARD FINDS HIS CONDUCT HAS BEEN CORRECTED, MONITORED AND RESOLVED. PROBATION WITH TERMS: SHALL REMAIN IN PSYCHIATRIC TREATMENT WITH A BOARD-APPROVED TREATING PSYCHIATRIST WHO SHALL SUBMIT QUARTERLY REPORTS; SHALL CONTINUE MAKING FULL RESTITUTION TO ESTATE OF PATIENT IN WASHINGTON; IN THE EVENT THAT HE IS NOT ACCEPTED INTO HIS INTENDED FELLOWSHIP PROGRAM, SHALL COMPLETE A 30-DAY MINI-RESIDENCY IN SURGERY.

REICHMANN, FRANK J MD, LICENSE NUMBER 0013545, OF EVERETT, SNOHOMISH COUNTY, WA, WAS DISCIPLINED BY WASHINGTON ON JULY 7, 1992.
DISCIPLINARY ACTION: EMERGENCY SUSPENSION
NOTES: ALLEGATIONS OF IMPAIRMENT.

REICHMANN, FRANK J MD WAS DISCIPLINED BY WASHINGTON ON SEPTEMBER 7, 1993.
DISCIPLINARY ACTION: LICENSE REVOCATION
OFFENSE: SUBSTANCE ABUSE
NOTES: FAILURE TO FOLLOW THROUGH WITH APPROPRIATE TREATMENT FOR HIS ALCOHOL/CHEMICAL DEPENDENCY IN THAT HE DID NOT RETURN TO INPATIENT TREATMENT OR PARTICIPATION WITH THE WASHINGTON MONITORED

TREATMENT PROGRAM. MAY NOT REAPPLY FOR LICENSURE FOR 10 YEARS.

REITER, JACK M MD, LICENSE NUMBER 0010990, OF SEATTLE, WA, WAS DISCIPLINED BY WASHINGTON ON DECEMBER 23, 1996.
DISCIPLINARY ACTION: RESTRICTION PLACED ON LICENSE
OFFENSE: SUBSTANDARD CARE, INCOMPETENCE, OR NEGLIGENCE
NOTES: COMMITTED ACTS OF NEGLIGENCE. RESTRICTIONS ON LICENSE FOR AT LEAST TWO YEARS.

RENDELL, HEIDI S MD, LICENSE NUMBER 0019337, OF MUKILTEO, WA, WAS DISCIPLINED BY WASHINGTON ON JULY 2, 1990.
DISCIPLINARY ACTION: FINE; RESTRICTION PLACED ON CONTROLLED SUBSTANCE LICENSE
OFFENSE: OVERPRESCRIBING OR MISPRESCRIBING DRUGS
NOTES: CHARGED WITH PRESCRIBING ROXICODONE, DALMANE, RESTORIL, AND HALCION TO ONE PATIENT FOR OTHER THAN LEGITIMATE MEDICAL PURPOSES. CONDITIONS OF ORDER: SHALL SUBMIT CONSECUTIVELY NUMBERED TRIPLICATE PRESCRIPTIONS ON ALL CONTROLLED SUBSTANCES SCHEDULE II THROUGH V; SHALL NOT PRESCRIBE SCHEDULE II DRUGS FOR MORE THAN THREE DAYS, EXCEPT FOR TERMINALLY ILL CANCER OR AIDS PATIENTS; SHALL NOT PRESCRIBE SCHEDULE III DRUGS FOR MORE THAN THREE WEEKS AND SCHEDULE IV AND V DRUGS FOR MORE THAN FOUR WEEKS; SHALL PERMIT PRACTICE REVIEW BY THE BOARD; SHALL COMPLETE CONTINUING MEDICAL EDUCATION IN THE AREA OF DRUG ADDICTION AND CHRONIC PAIN MANAGEMENT WITHIN TWO YEARS; SHALL APPEAR IN TWO YEARS TO SHOW COMPLIANCE; $350 FINE. ON 10/15/92 BOARD FOUND HER IN FULL COMPLIANCE WITH THIS ORDER AND REINSTATED HER LICENSE IN FULL.

RESOL, JUAN H MD OF P O BOX 160, MEADE, KS, WAS DISCIPLINED BY WASHINGTON ON APRIL 19, 1990.
DISCIPLINARY ACTION: 60-MONTH PROBATION; REPRIMAND
OFFENSE: SUBSTANDARD CARE, INCOMPETENCE, OR NEGLIGENCE
NOTES: IN 12/84 FAILED TO PROPERLY DIAGNOSE AND TREAT A PATIENT WITH GASTRO-DUODENAL PERFORATION, WHICH RESULTED IN SERIOUS HARM TO THE PATIENT. PATIENT DEVELOPED PERITONITIS AND DIED. 5/19/89 SUSPENSION STAYED PENDING COMPLETION OF THE FOLLOWING CONDITIONS OF PROBATION: SHALL COMPLETE TEN HOURS OF CONTINUING MEDICAL EDUCATION ON MANAGEMENT OF ACUTE ABDOMEN; MUST APPEAR BEFORE THE BOARD BEFORE PRACTICING IN WASHINGTON; MUST SUBMIT TO RANDOM RECORD REVIEWS; MAY NOT REQUEST TERMINATION OF PROBATION FOR THREE YEARS.

RICE, JAMES W MD, LICENSE NUMBER 0015479, OF SEATTLE, WA, WAS DISCIPLINED BY WASHINGTON ON NOVEMBER 20, 1992.
DISCIPLINARY ACTION: PROBATION
OFFENSE: OVERPRESCRIBING OR MISPRESCRIBING DRUGS
NOTES: INAPPROPRIATE PRESCRIBING OF MEDICATION. MUST FOLLOW TERMS AND CONDITIONS AS STATED IN ORDER FOR A MINIMUM OF THREE YEARS. ON 12/15/94 WAS IN COMPLIANCE; REQUEST FOR RELEASE FROM PROBATIONARY TERMS WAS DENIED. ON 12/11/95 HIS REQUEST TO TERMINATE THIS ORDER WAS GRANTED AND LICENSE IS UNRESTRICTED.

RILEY, ROBERT J DO WAS DISCIPLINED BY WASHINGTON ON APRIL 20, 1989.
DISCIPLINARY ACTION: PROBATION; RESTRICTION PLACED ON LICENSE
NOTES: REINSTATEMENT FROM 5/12/86 SUSPENSION. INDEFINITE PROBATION UNDER CONDITIONS: SHALL NOT TREAT ANY PATIENT UNDER THE AGE OF 18, EXCEPT FOR RENDERING EMERGENCY CARE FOR LIFE-THREATENING CONDITIONS, UNTIL REGULAR SUBSTITUTE MEDICAL CARE CAN BE PROVIDED; HIS PRACTICE RECORDS SHALL BE SUBJECT TO AUDIT ON A RANDOM BASIS; AND SHALL CONTINUE TO RECEIVE PSYCHIATRIC TREATMENT FOR AT LEAST ONE YEAR WHO SHALL REPORT TO THE BOARD ON A SEMI-ANNUAL BASIS. ORDER MODIFIED ON 11/30/90 SUCH THAT HE SHALL BE RELIEVED OF THE REQUIREMENT OF ON-GOING PSYCHIATRIC CARE; ALL OTHER CONDITIONS REMAIN IN EFFECT. MAY PETITION THE BOARD FOR REINSTATEMENT AFTER THREE YEARS.

ROBERTON, JAMES W MD, LICENSE NUMBER 0019584, OF FEDERAL WAY, WA, WAS DISCIPLINED BY WASHINGTON ON NOVEMBER 22, 1996.
NOTES: AGREED NOT TO RENEW HIS LICENSE UPON ITS EXPIRATION ON 12/29/96.

ROBERTS, WILLIAM V MD WAS DISCIPLINED BY NEBRASKA ON OCTOBER 5, 1987.
DISCIPLINARY ACTION: PROBATION

ROBERTS, WILLIAM V MD WAS DISCIPLINED BY WASHINGTON ON NOVEMBER 16, 1990.
OFFENSE: DISCIPLINARY ACTION BY ANOTHER STATE OR AGENCY
NOTES: MISSOURI LICENSE SURRENDERED AND IMMEDIATELY REINSTATED AND PLACED ON PROBATION FOR 3 YEARS ON 8/25/89 WITH THE FOLLOWING CONDITIONS: SHALL APPEAR BEFORE BOARD AT VARIOUS INTERVALS AND ACCEPT UNANNOUNCED VISITS FROM BOARD REPRESENTATIVES; SHALL NOT ACCEPT CONTROLLED SUBSTANCE AUTHORITY; SHALL NOT PRACTICE WITHOUT WRITTEN CONSENT OF THE BOARD. LICENSE IN NEBRASKA PLACED ON PROBATION 10/5/87 BECAUSE, IN FILING FOR LICENSE, INDICATED HE HAD NEVER HAD A LICENSE DENIED, REVOKED, SUSPENDED OR LIMITED WHEN STATES HAD TAKEN SUCH ACTIONS. WASHINGTON BOARD ORDERED THAT HE COMPLY WITH THESE TWO ORDERS, THAT HE NOT PRACTICE IN WASHINGTON WITHOUT BOARD CONSENT, AND THAT HE ADVISE THE BOARD OF ANY CHANGE OF ADDRESS.

ROBINSON, RALPH R MD, DATE OF BIRTH JULY 7, 1913, LICENSE NUMBER 0011914, WAS DISCIPLINED BY KENTUCKY ON MARCH 24, 1988.
DISCIPLINARY ACTION: 60-MONTH PROBATION; FINE
NOTES: NO SCHEDULE II, IIN, III OR IIIN CONTROLLED SUBSTANCE PRIVILEGES DURING PROBATION; 15 HOURS OF CONTINUING MEDICAL EDUCATION IN AREA OF PHARMACOLOGY PER YEAR FOR 2 YEARS; FINED $1,000

ROBINSON, RALPH R MD OF MIDDLESBORO, KY, WAS DISCIPLINED BY OHIO ON JANUARY 11, 1989.
DISCIPLINARY ACTION: LICENSE SUSPENSION
NOTES: INDEFINITE SUSPENSION

ROBINSON, RALPH R MD, DATE OF BIRTH JULY 7, 1913, LICENSE NUMBER 0006617, WAS DISCIPLINED BY OKLAHOMA ON FEBRUARY 3, 1989.
DISCIPLINARY ACTION: 60-MONTH PROBATION; RESTRICTION PLACED ON CONTROLLED SUBSTANCE LICENSE
OFFENSE: DISCIPLINARY ACTION BY ANOTHER STATE OR AGENCY
NOTES: ACTION IN KENTUCKY ON OR ABOUT 3/24/88 WHERE HE VOLUNTARILY ENTERED INTO AN AGREED ORDER OF PROBATION FOR FIVE YEARS FOR PRESCRIBING, DISPENSING, OR ADMINISTERING OF CONTROLLED SUBSTANCES OR NARCOTIC DRUGS IN INDISCRIMINATE OR EXCESSIVE AMOUNT CONSIDERED GOOD MEDICAL PRACTICE OR WITHOUT MEDICAL NEED. PROBATION UNDER THE FOLLOWING TERMS AND CONDITIONS: SHALL NOT PRESCRIBE, ADMINISTER, OR DISPENSE ANY SCHEDULE II OR SCHEDULE III CONTROLLED DANGEROUS SUBSTANCES OR NARCOTIC DRUGS; MAY

PRESCRIBE SCHEDULE IV AND SCHEDULE V CONTROLLED DANGEROUS SUBSTANCES ONLY ON SERIALLY-NUMBERED, DUPLICATE PRESCRIPTION PADS AND SHALL MAKE THE COPIES AVAILABLE TO THE BOARD; SHALL SUBMIT TO THE BOARD ADDRESS/CHANGE OF ADDRESS; SHALL APPEAR BEFORE THE BOARD UPON REQUEST AND SHALL SUBMIT ANY REQUIRED REPORTS; SHALL PAY COSTS; MUST APPEAR BEFORE BOARD PRIOR TO RESUMING PRACTICE; PROBATION HELD IN ABEYANCE UNTIL HE RETURNS TO OKLAHOMA.

ROBINSON, RALPH R MD OF MIDDLESBORO, KY, WAS DISCIPLINED BY OHIO ON MAY 13, 1989.
DISCIPLINARY ACTION: SURRENDER OF LICENSE

ROBINSON, RALPH R MD, LICENSE NUMBER 0008135, OF MIDDLESBORO, KY, WAS DISCIPLINED BY SOUTH CAROLINA ON JULY 14, 1989.
DISCIPLINARY ACTION: SURRENDER OF LICENSE
NOTES: NOT ELIGIBLE FOR REINSTATEMENT

ROBINSON, RALPH R MD OF MIDDLESBORO, KY, WAS DISCIPLINED BY MISSOURI ON SEPTEMBER 15, 1989.
DISCIPLINARY ACTION: 120-MONTH PROBATION
OFFENSE: DISCIPLINARY ACTION BY ANOTHER STATE OR AGENCY
NOTES: LIMITATION OF CONTROLLED SUBSTANCE PRESCRIBING AUTHORITY BY ANOTHER STATE OR AGENCY.

ROBINSON, RALPH R MD WAS DISCIPLINED BY WASHINGTON ON FEBRUARY 16, 1990.
DISCIPLINARY ACTION: PROBATION; RESTRICTION PLACED ON CONTROLLED SUBSTANCE LICENSE
OFFENSE: DISCIPLINARY ACTION BY ANOTHER STATE OR AGENCY
NOTES: ON 12/6/89 BOARD ISSUED A STATEMENT OF CHARGES REGARDING FREQUENTLY PRESCRIBING, DISPENSING OR ADMINISTERING CONTROLLED SUBSTANCES FOR UNDIAGNOSED PAIN, FOR PROLONGED PERIODS OF TIME AND IN INAPPROPRIATE COMBINATIONS; HIS LICENSE HAS BEEN RESTRICTED IN KENTUCKY, ALABAMA, OKLAHOMA AND NORTH CAROLINA. THE FOLLOWING PROVISIONS OF THE KENTUCKY ORDER ARE ADOPTED BY WASHINGTON: UNABLE TO PRESCRIBE, ADMINISTER, OR DISPENSE SCHEDULE II, IIN, III, OR IIIN CONTROLLED DANGEROUS SUBSTANCES DURING PROBATION; MUST OBTAIN 15 HOURS PER YEAR OF CONTINUING MEDICAL EDUCATION IN PHARMACOLOGY FOR THE FIRST 2 YEARS OF PROBATION. WHEN HIS PRESCRIBING PRIVILEGES ARE REINSTATED IN COMMONWEALTH OF KENTUCKY, MAY APPLY FOR REINSTATEMENT IN WASHINGTON.

ROBINSON, RALPH R MD OF MIDDLESBORO, KY, WAS DISCIPLINED BY TENNESSEE ON MAY 14, 1990.
DISCIPLINARY ACTION: 60-MONTH PROBATION; RESTRICTION PLACED ON CONTROLLED SUBSTANCE LICENSE
OFFENSE: DISCIPLINARY ACTION BY ANOTHER STATE OR AGENCY
NOTES: MAY NOT PRESCRIBE SCHEDULE II OR III DRUGS DURING PROBATION, HOWEVER, PHYSICIAN MAY REAPPLY FOR FULL DEA PRIVILEGES AFTER TWO YEARS. MUST COMPLETE CONTINUING MEDICAL EDUCATION COURSE IN PHARMACOLOGY

ROBINSON, RALPH R MD WAS DISCIPLINED BY WASHINGTON, D.C. ON SEPTEMBER 5, 1990.
DISCIPLINARY ACTION: PROBATION
OFFENSE: DISCIPLINARY ACTION BY ANOTHER STATE OR AGENCY
NOTES: DISCIPLINED BY KENTUCKY FOR CONDUCT THAT WOULD BE GROUNDS FOR DISCIPLINARY ACTION IN THE DISTRICT OF COLUMBIA; FILED WITH THE BOARD A DOCUMENT HE KNEW OR SHOULD HAVE KNOWN WAS FALSE OR MISLEADING.

ROBINSON, RALPH R MD, LICENSE NUMBER C019518, OF MIDDLESBORO, KY, WAS DISCIPLINED BY CALIFORNIA ON JANUARY 10, 1991.
DISCIPLINARY ACTION: SURRENDER OF LICENSE
NOTES: VOLUNTARY SURRENDER WHILE CHARGES PENDING.

ROBINSON, RALPH R MD OF MIDDLESBORO, KY, WAS DISCIPLINED BY VIRGINIA ON APRIL 9, 1991.
DISCIPLINARY ACTION: PROBATION
OFFENSE: DISCIPLINARY ACTION BY ANOTHER STATE OR AGENCY
NOTES: DISCIPLINARY ACTION IN OTHER STATES.

ROBINSON, RALPH R MD, DATE OF BIRTH JULY 7, 1913, LICENSE NUMBER 0011914, OF BELL COUNTY, KY, WAS DISCIPLINED BY KENTUCKY ON MARCH 4, 1993.
DISCIPLINARY ACTION: SURRENDER OF LICENSE
NOTES: IN LIEU OF INQUIRY CONCERNING MEDICAL PRACTICE.

ROBINSON, RALPH R MD, DATE OF BIRTH JULY 7, 1913, LICENSE NUMBER 0016797, OF MIDDLESBORO, KY, WAS DISCIPLINED BY VIRGINIA ON FEBRUARY 17, 1994.
OFFENSE: DISCIPLINARY ACTION BY ANOTHER STATE OR AGENCY
NOTES: ON 2/18/93 KENTUCKY BOARD ACCEPTED HIS RETIREMENT FROM THE ACTIVE PRACTICE OF MEDICINE IN THAT JURISDICTION AND AGREED TO TERMINATE INQUIRY INTO HIS PRESCRIBING OF CONTROLLED SUBSTANCES UNTIL HE REACTIVATES HIS KENTUCKY LICENSE. SURRENDER OF PRIVILEGE TO RENEW VIRGINIA LICENSE IN LIEU OF FURTHER ADMINISTRATIVE PROCEEDINGS.

ROBINSON, RALPH R MD OF 1032 18TH STREET SOUTH, BIRMINGHAM, AL, WAS DISCIPLINED BY DEA ON APRIL 7, 1995.
DISCIPLINARY ACTION: RESTRICTION PLACED ON CONTROLLED SUBSTANCE LICENSE
OFFENSE: PROFESSIONAL MISCONDUCT
NOTES: ALLEGED CONTROLLED SUBSTANCE VIOLATIONS.

ROBINSON, RALPH ROLLIN MD OF KY, WAS DISCIPLINED BY NORTH CAROLINA ON JANUARY 31, 1989.
DISCIPLINARY ACTION: 60-MONTH PROBATION

ROBINSON, RALPH ROLLIN MD, LICENSE NUMBER 00E7253, OF MIDDLESBORO, KY, WAS DISCIPLINED BY TEXAS ON DECEMBER 1, 1990.
DISCIPLINARY ACTION: LICENSE REVOCATION
NOTES: PHYSICIAN, UNDER BOARD DISCIPLINARY ORDER, REQUESTED CANCELLATION OF LICENSE. IF HE REAPPLIES, BOARD DISCIPLINARY ORDER WILL BE REACTIVATED.

ROBINSON, WENDELL E MD, LICENSE NUMBER 00M2970, WAS DISCIPLINED BY IDAHO ON JANUARY 24, 1993.
DISCIPLINARY ACTION: 60-MONTH PROBATION; FINE
OFFENSE: DISCIPLINARY ACTION BY ANOTHER STATE OR AGENCY
NOTES: ON 10/16/92 HE ENTERED INTO A CONSENT AGREEMENT WITH WASHINGTON BOARD WHICH WAS INVESTIGATING ALLEGATIONS THAT HE HAD SEXUALLY HARASSED A NURSE AND INTERFERED WITH AN INVESTIGATION OF THESE ALLEGATIONS. CONDITIONS OF WASHINGTON ORDER WHICH IDAHO HAS ADOPTED: SHALL OBTAIN COUNSELING FROM A BOARD-APPROVED THERAPIST WHO SHALL SUBMIT REPORTS TO THE BOARD; SHALL PROVIDE A COPY OF THE ORDER ANY WHERE THAT HE HAS PRIVILEGES; SHALL COMPLETE 10 HOURS OF CONTINUING MEDICAL EDUCATION IN MEDICAL ETHICS; SHALL APPEAR BEFORE THE BOARD IN ONE YEAR TO VERIFY COMPLIANCE; REPRESENTATIVE OF BOARD MAY MAKE UNANNOUNCED VISITS TO HIS PRACTICE; SHALL INFORM THE BOARD OF CHANGE OF ADDRESS OR IF HE LEAVES THE STATE; SHALL PAY A $1,000 FINE WITHIN 90 DAYS.

- WASHINGTON -

ROBINSON, WENDELL E MD, LICENSE NUMBER 0011542, OF RICHLAND, WA, WAS DISCIPLINED BY WASHINGTON ON MAY 3, 1994.
DISCIPLINARY ACTION: 36-MONTH PROBATION; FINE
NOTES: SHALL COMPLY WITH ALL CONDITIONS AND RESTRICTIONS PERTAINING TO CORONARY ANGIOGRAPHICS AND CONDITIONS CONCERNING CONTINUING MEDICAL EDUCATION. MUST PAY A $1000 FINE WITHIN 90 DAYS AND APPEAR BEFORE BOARD WHEN DIRECTED.

ROBINSON, WENDELL E MD, LICENSE NUMBER 00M2970, WAS DISCIPLINED BY IDAHO ON JULY 11, 1994.
DISCIPLINARY ACTION: 36-MONTH PROBATION; FINE
OFFENSE: DISCIPLINARY ACTION BY ANOTHER STATE OR AGENCY
NOTES: ON 5/22/94 WASHINGTON PLACED LICENSE ON PROBATION BASED ON ALLEGATIONS OF UNPROFESSIONAL CONDUCT WITH REGARD TO PERFORMING A CAROTID ANGIOGRAPHY ON A PATIENT THAT WAS OTHERWISE IN STABLE CONDITION. CONDITIONS OF WASHINGTON PROBATION WHICH IDAHO HAS ADOPTED ARE AS FOLLOWS: SHALL ONLY PERFORM CORONARY ANGIOGRAPHY STUDIES CONSISTENT WITH SPECIFIED CRITERIA; HE MUST CONSULT WITH A CARDIOLOGIST-MONITOR APPROVED BY THE BOARD OR ITS DESIGNEE PRIOR TO EVERY NON-EMERGENT CORONARY ANGIOGRAPHY; ON A QUARTERLY BASIS, HE SHALL FORWARD TO THE BOARD A COPY OF ALL OFFICE PATIENT CHARTS AND HIS WRITTEN REQUEST TO HAVE ALL HOSPITAL RECORDS FORWARDED FOR THOSE PATIENTS HE HAS PERFORMED ON OR PROPOSED ANGIOGRAPHY STUDIES; SHALL COMPLETE 24 HOURS OF CONTINUING MEDICAL EDUCATION IN CARDIOLOGY WITHIN 18 MONTHS; HIS COMPLIANCE WITH THE ABOVE WILL BE MONITORED QUARTERLY FOR THE FIRST YEAR AND SEMI-ANNUALLY EVERY YEAR THEREAFTER; SHALL PAY A $1,000 FINE WITHIN 90 DAYS.

ROBINSON, WENDELL E MD, LICENSE NUMBER 0A24617, OF RICHLAND, WA, WAS DISCIPLINED BY CALIFORNIA ON APRIL 23, 1995.
DISCIPLINARY ACTION: 60-MONTH PROBATION
OFFENSE: DISCIPLINARY ACTION BY ANOTHER STATE OR AGENCY
NOTES: DISCIPLINE BY WASHINGTON STATE MEDICAL BOARD AS A RESULT OF CHARGES OF SEXUAL HARASSMENT AT KADLEC HOSPITAL. REVOCATION STAYED.

ROCK, HERMAN H MD, LICENSE NUMBER G005460, OF CITRUS HEIGHTS, CA, WAS DISCIPLINED BY CALIFORNIA ON JULY 5, 1990.
DISCIPLINARY ACTION: LICENSE REVOCATION
OFFENSE: DISCIPLINARY ACTION BY ANOTHER STATE OR AGENCY
NOTES: DISCIPLINARY ACTIONS BY NEVADA BOARD AND NEW MEXICO BOARD.

ROCK, HERMAN H MD, LICENSE NUMBER 0014843, OF RENO, NV, WAS DISCIPLINED BY WASHINGTON ON OCTOBER 18, 1991.
NOTES: PERMANENTLY RETIRES FROM MEDICAL PRACTICE; STATEMENT OF CHARGES ISSUED AS RESULT OF BOARD INVESTIGATION WITHDRAWN. EFFECTIVE DATE OF RETIREMENT IS 10/28/91 OR UPON SERVICE TO THE PHYSICIAN, WHICHEVER IS SOONER.

ROCK, HERMAN HENRY MD WAS DISCIPLINED BY NEVADA ON DECEMBER 1, 1987.
DISCIPLINARY ACTION: LICENSE SUSPENSION
OFFENSE: SUBSTANDARD CARE, INCOMPETENCE, OR NEGLIGENCE
NOTES: INDEFINITE SUSPENSION; BASED ON ISSUE OF MEDICAL COMPETENCE

ROCK, HERMAN HENRY MD WAS DISCIPLINED BY NEVADA ON MARCH 10, 1988.
DISCIPLINARY ACTION: SURRENDER OF LICENSE
OFFENSE: FAILURE TO COMPLY WITH A PROFESSIONAL RULE
NOTES: FAILURE TO PASS COMPETENCY EXAM RESULTED IN LICENSE SUSPENSION PER STIPULATED AGREEMENT. SUBSEQUENT FAILURE TO PASS FLEX II REQUIRED REVOCATION PER STIPULATED AGREEMENT.

ROCK, LEWIS B MD, LICENSE NUMBER 0020657, OF SEATTLE, WA, WAS DISCIPLINED BY VIRGINIA ON DECEMBER 18, 1996.
DISCIPLINARY ACTION: LICENSE SUSPENSION
OFFENSE: DISCIPLINARY ACTION BY ANOTHER STATE OR AGENCY
NOTES: REVOCATION IN CALIFORNIA BASED ON PROBATION IN WASHINGTON. HE HAS REQUESTED REINSTATEMENT. HEARING TENTATIVELY SCHEDULED FOR 4/97.

ROCK, LEWIS BURNHAM MD, LICENSE NUMBER 0027081, OF SEATTLE, WA, WAS DISCIPLINED BY WASHINGTON ON SEPTEMBER 29, 1994.
DISCIPLINARY ACTION: FINE; RESTRICTION PLACED ON LICENSE
NOTES: STAYED SUSPENSION ON FOLLOWING TERMS AND CONDITIONS: MAY TREAT MALE PATIENTS ONLY, IS PROHIBITED FROM ENGAGING IN SOLO PRACTICE, SHALL OBTAIN TREATMENT AND ONGOING THERAPY AND SHALL PAY A $1,000 FINE. ON 5/5/95, FOUND IN COMPLIANCE WITH THIS ORDER BUT HIS REQUEST TO MODIFY THIS ORDER DENIED IN SEVERAL RESPECTS, EXCEPT HE IS PERMITTED TO ENGAGE IN A SOLO PRACTICE WITH MALE PATIENTS ONLY. ON 5/1/96 ORDER AMENDED TO PERMIT HIM TO TREAT ADULT MALE PATIENTS WITHOUT MONITORING AND TREAT FEMALE PATIENTS UP TO 12 YEARS OF AGE AND MALE PATIENTS UP TO 17 YEARS OF AGE WITH A CHAPERONE PRESENT. ON 12/20/96 HIS REQUEST TO MODIFY ORDER GRANTED AND HE IS ABLE TO TREAT ADULT MALE PATIENTS WITHOUT RESTRICTION AND TREAT FEMALE PATIENTS OF ANY AGE AND MINOR PATIENTS WITH A CHAPERONE PRESENT. ON 1/23/97 BOARD GRANTED HIS REQUEST TO TERMINATE THIS ORDER AND LICENSE IS UNRESTRICTED.

ROCK, LEWIS BURNHAM III MD, LICENSE NUMBER 0C41108, OF SEATTLE, WA, WAS DISCIPLINED BY CALIFORNIA ON MAY 10, 1996.
DISCIPLINARY ACTION: LICENSE REVOCATION
OFFENSE: DISCIPLINARY ACTION BY ANOTHER STATE OR AGENCY
NOTES: DISCIPLINARY ACTION IN WASHINGTON FOR SEXUAL MISCONDUCT. DEFAULT ACTION.

RODRIGUEZ, BENJAMIN MD, LICENSE NUMBER 0025062, OF WALLA WALLA, WA, WAS DISCIPLINED BY WASHINGTON ON MARCH 17, 1989.
DISCIPLINARY ACTION: MONITORING OF PHYSICIAN
OFFENSE: PROFESSIONAL MISCONDUCT
NOTES: ON OR ABOUT 1/20/88 APPROVAL WAS GRANTED BY THE BOARD AUTHORIZING HIM TO ACT AS A SUPERVISING PHYSICIAN FOR A PHYSICIAN ASSISTANT. BETWEEN JANUARY AND MARCH 1988 HE FAILED TO ENSURE THAT ALL PERTINENT NOTES AND ORDERS CONCERNING PATIENT CARE PROVIDED BY THE PHYSICIAN ASSISTANT WERE COUNTERSIGNED AS REQUIRED BY THE UTILIZATION PLAN. HE SHALL COMPLY WITH THE FOLLOWING CONDITIONS: SHALL COMPLY WITH THE TERMS SPECIFIED IN THE UTILIZATION PLAN FOR EACH PHYSICIAN ASSISTANT WHICH SHALL INCLUDE BUT NOT BE LIMITED TO REVIEWING AND COUNTERSIGNING PATIENT CHARTS; SHALL ENSURE COMPLIANCE WITH REGULATION WHICH PROHIBITS ADVERTISING BY A PHYSICIAN'S ASSISTANT; DURING PERIODS WHEN HE IS UTILIZING A PHYSICIAN ASSISTANT, SHALL UNDERGO A PERIODIC PRACTICE REVIEW BY THE BOARD WHICH SHALL INCLUDE REVIEW OF PATIENT RECORDS OF AT LEAST ONE TIME EVERY SIX MONTHS FOR A PERIOD OF THREE YEARS BEGINNING FROM THE DATE OF ACCEPTANCE OF THE NEXT PHYSICIAN ASSISTANT

- WASHINGTON -

REGISTRATION WITH HIM AS THE PRIMARY PHYSICIAN SPONSOR; SHALL BEAR THE COSTS ASSOCIATED WITH THIS ORDER. ON 10/18/96 BOARD GRANTED HIS REQUEST TO TERMINATE THE TERMS AND CONDITIONS OF THIS ORDER AND GRANTED HIM AN UNRESTRICTED LICENSE.

ROHRSSEN, MERLIN MD, LICENSE NUMBER 0008787, OF SEATTLE, WA, WAS DISCIPLINED BY WASHINGTON ON NOVEMBER 4, 1994.
DISCIPLINARY ACTION: SURRENDER OF LICENSE

ROLLER, FRANKLIN D MD, LICENSE NUMBER C026350, OF YERINGTON, NV, WAS DISCIPLINED BY CALIFORNIA ON JUNE 8, 1987.
DISCIPLINARY ACTION: 60-MONTH PROBATION
OFFENSE: DISCIPLINARY ACTION BY ANOTHER STATE OR AGENCY
NOTES: REVOCATION STAYED; DISCIPLINED BY THE NEVADA MEDICAL BOARD

ROLLER, FRANKLIN D MD, LICENSE NUMBER C026350, OF YERINGTON, NV, WAS DISCIPLINED BY CALIFORNIA ON DECEMBER 12, 1988.
DISCIPLINARY ACTION: LICENSE REVOCATION
OFFENSE: DISCIPLINARY ACTION BY ANOTHER STATE OR AGENCY
NOTES: DEFAULT DECISION; NEVADA LICENSE DISCIPLINED BY THAT STATE.

ROLLER, FRANKLIN D MD OF 111 GOLDFIELD AVENUE, YERINGTON, NV, WAS DISCIPLINED BY ILLINOIS ON MARCH 1, 1989.
DISCIPLINARY ACTION: LICENSE SUSPENSION
OFFENSE: DISCIPLINARY ACTION BY ANOTHER STATE OR AGENCY
NOTES: INDEFINITELY SUSPENDED AFTER HIS NEVADA LICENSE WAS DISCIPLINED

ROLLER, FRANKLIN D MD OF 207 GOLDFIELD AVENUE, YERINGTON, NV, WAS DISCIPLINED BY DEA ON JANUARY 3, 1996.
DISCIPLINARY ACTION: SURRENDER OF CONTROLLED SUBSTANCE LICENSE
OFFENSE: DISCIPLINARY ACTION BY ANOTHER STATE OR AGENCY
NOTES: STATE BOARD.

ROLLER, FRANKLIN DELANO MD WAS DISCIPLINED BY WASHINGTON ON DECEMBER 14, 1990.
DISCIPLINARY ACTION: PROBATION; MONITORING OF PHYSICIAN
OFFENSE: DISCIPLINARY ACTION BY ANOTHER STATE OR AGENCY
NOTES: NEVADA BOARD STAYED A REVOCATION AND PLACED HIS LICENSE ON PROBATION 4/3/87; CALIFORNIA BOARD STAYED A REVOCATION AND PLACED LICENSE ON PROBATION 6/8/87, AND THEN REVOKED LICENSE 12/12/88. WASHINGTON REVOCATION STAYED WITH THE FOLLOWING CONDITIONS OF PROBATION: SHALL COMPLY WITH ALL CONDITIONS OF NEVADA ORDER, AND WASHINGTON BOARD SHALL HAVE THE RIGHT TO MONITOR PRACTICE AS SET FORTH IN THE NEVADA ORDER; SHALL ALLOW BOARD TO OBTAIN INVESTIGATORY FILES FROM NEVADA; MAY PETITION FOR CHANGE IN TERMS OF ORDER ONLY AFTER NEVADA REINSTATES HIS LICENSE; SHALL INFORM BOARD IF HE MOVES OR LEAVES THE STATE.

ROSENBERG, MARK JEFFREY MD, LICENSE NUMBER 0020570, OF BAINBRIDGE ISLAND, WA, WAS DISCIPLINED BY WASHINGTON ON FEBRUARY 15, 1991.
DISCIPLINARY ACTION: RESTRICTION PLACED ON LICENSE; MONITORING OF PHYSICIAN
OFFENSE: FAILURE TO COMPLY WITH A PROFESSIONAL RULE
NOTES: BOARD ENTERED INTO STIPULATION AND ASSURANCE OF DISCONTINUANCE ON 4/27/90 BASED ON HIS HAVING A PERSONAL RELATIONSHIP AND SEXUAL CONTACT WITH A PATIENT BETWEEN 1985 AND 1988, WHICH RESULTED IN EMOTIONAL HARM TO THE PATIENT. ONE PROVISION OF THE ORDER WAS THAT HE SHOULD INFORM ALL CURRENT FEMALE PATIENTS OF THIS INVOLVEMENT, WITH THIS VERIFIED BY HAVING A STAFF PERSON PRESENT; HE DID NOT COMPLY WITH THIS REQUIREMENT. SUSPENSION MAY BE STAYED SUBJECT TO COMPLIANCE WITH FOLLOWING CONDITIONS: PRIOR TO ANY EVALUATION, MEDICATION REVIEW, TREATMENT, OR OTHER PROFESSIONAL SERVICE, MUST INFORM ALL CURRENT AND FUTURE PATIENTS THAT HE IS UNDER BOARD ORDER AS A RESULT OF SEXUAL MISCONDUCT WITH A PATIENT; WHENEVER HE PROVIDES ANY OF THE ABOVE SERVICES, THERE MUST BE ANOTHER LICENSED HEALTH CARE PROFESSIONAL PRESENT, APPROVED BY THE BOARD'S STAFF; ALL STAFF MEMBERS SHALL BE PROVIDED WITH A COPY OF THIS ORDER; SHALL ENGAGE IN NO PHYSICAL CONTACT IN OR OUT OF THE OFFICE SETTING WITH ANY PERSON WITH WHOM HE HAS A DOCTOR/PATIENT RELATIONSHIP; SHALL LIMIT PHYSICAL EXAMINATIONS TO TAKING BLOOD PRESSURE AND PULSE OF CLOTHED PATIENTS; SHALL NOT ESTABLISH OR MAINTAIN A PERSONAL RELATIONSHIP WITH ANY PRESENT OR PRIOR PATIENT; SHALL UNDERGO TREATMENT WITH A PROFESSIONAL APPROVED BY THE BOARD UNTIL THE BOARD APPROVES DISCONTINUANCE OF TREATMENT; SHALL BE EVALUATED YEARLY BY A BOARD APPROVED SPECIALIST; SHALL DOCUMENT ALL PROFESSIONAL CONTACT WITH PATIENTS; HIS RECORDS SHALL BE PERIODICALLY AUDITED BY THE BOARD; SHALL APPEAR BEFORE THE BOARD EVERY SIX MONTHS; SHALL PERMIT A REPRESENTATIVE OF THE BOARD TO MAKE UNANNOUNCED VISITS TO INSPECT GROUNDS, INTERVIEW STAFF AND CO-THERAPISTS, AND REVIEW PRACTICE; MAY NOT PETITION FOR MODIFICATION FOR TWO YEARS; SHALL INFORM BOARD IF HE LEAVES THE STATE. ON 6/18/92 ORDER MODIFIED SUCH THAT COMPLIANCE APPEARANCES BEFORE THE BOARD WERE REDUCED TO ONCE EVERY 12 MONTHS RATHER THAN ONCE EVERY SIX MONTHS AND UNANNOUNCED VISITS TO REVIEW PRACTICE WERE REDUCED TO ONCE A YEAR. ON 9/6/94 A SUSPENSION OF THE REPORTING, COMPLIANCE AND THERAPY REQUIREMENTS GRANTED EFFECTIVE 9/1/94 AS HE WAS CLOSING HIS WASHINGTON PRACTICE AND TRAVELING OUT OF THE COUNTRY. THE TERMS OF THE ORIGINAL ORDER, AS AMENDED AND SUPPLEMENTED, WERE REVIVED AND ARE IN FULL FORCE AND EFFECT AS OF 12/9/96 WHEN HE RETURNED TO WASHINGTON. ON 12/9/96 HIS REQUEST TO ELIMINATE THE RESTRICTIONS OF HIS LICENSE WAS DENIED, AND HE WAS ORDERED TO SUBMIT A LETTER FROM A THERAPIST REGARDING HIS ABILITY TO PRACTICE IN A SAFE MANNER.

ROYS, DAVID S MD, LICENSE NUMBER 0010221, OF SEATTLE, WA, WAS DISCIPLINED BY WASHINGTON ON APRIL 19, 1996.
DISCIPLINARY ACTION: PROBATION; REQUIRED TO TAKE ADDITIONAL MEDICAL EDUCATION
NOTES: PROBATION FOR ONE YEAR OR UPON SATISFACTORY COMPLETION OF COURSES IN THE PRESCRIBING OF CONTROLLED SUBSTANCES, WHICH EVER PERIOD IS LONGER. ON 5/21/97 BOARD GRANTED HIS REQUEST TO TERMINATE THIS ORDER AND LICENSE IS UNRESTRICTED.

RUE, GEORGE H JR MD, LICENSE NUMBER 0004440, OF PORTLAND, OR, WAS DISCIPLINED BY OREGON ON APRIL 12, 1990.
DISCIPLINARY ACTION: LICENSE SUSPENSION

RUE, GEORGE H JR MD OF TAYLORS, SC, WAS DISCIPLINED BY WASHINGTON ON OCTOBER 7, 1991.
DISCIPLINARY ACTION: SURRENDER OF LICENSE
OFFENSE: DISCIPLINARY ACTION BY ANOTHER STATE OR AGENCY
NOTES: UNDER INVESTIGATION BY BOARD CONCERNING

ALLEGATIONS OF UNPROFESSIONAL CONDUCT RELATING TO ACTIONS TAKEN AGAINST LICENSE BY OTHER STATE, AND FURTHER ALLEGATIONS OF PHYSICAL AND MENTAL IMPAIRMENT. RETIREMENT FROM PRACTICE EFFECTIVE IMMEDIATELY.

SAID, MOHAMMAD H MD, LICENSE NUMBER 0018311, OF EPHRATA, WA, WAS DISCIPLINED BY WASHINGTON ON APRIL 15, 1994.
DISCIPLINARY ACTION: RESTRICTION PLACED ON LICENSE; RESTRICTION PLACED ON CONTROLLED SUBSTANCE LICENSE
OFFENSE: OVERPRESCRIBING OR MISPRESCRIBING DRUGS
NOTES: UNPROFESSIONAL CONDUCT IN HIS PRESCRIBING OF CONTROLLED SUBSTANCES AND SUPERVISION OF A PHYSICIAN ASSISTANT. SHALL COMPLY WITH RESTRICTIONS ON HIS PRESCRIBING PRACTICES; SHALL NOT UTILIZE PHYSICIAN ASSISTANTS IN HIS PRACTICE AND SHALL NOT BE A SPONSORING OR ALTERNATE SPONSORING PHYSICIAN FOR A PHYSICIAN ASSISTANT; SHALL KEEP APPROPRIATE RECORDS; SHALL APPEAR BEFORE THE COMMISSION IN SIX MONTHS; SHALL COMPLETE 25 HOURS OF CONTINUING MEDICAL EDUCATION IN THE AREA OF UTILIZATION OF PHYSICIAN ASSISTANTS, PHARMACOLOGY, PAIN MANAGEMENT OR ADDICTION AND SHALL PAY $750 IN COSTS. ON 2/24/95 HIS REQUEST FOR TERMINATION OF THE ORDER WAS DENIED. ON 7/3/95 HIS REQUEST WAS GRANTED TO SUPERVISE AND DIRECT THE ACTIONS OF PHYSICIAN ASSISTANTS AT COLUMBIA BASIN HOSPITAL BUT ONLY TO THE EXTENT REQUIRED BY THE HOSPITAL BY-LAWS OF A SPONSORING PHYSICIAN WITH STAFF PRIVILEGES; HIS REQUEST TO TERMINATE ORDER WAS DENIED. ON 6/16/96 HIS REQUEST TO TERMINATE ORDER DENIED BUT ORDER MODIFIED BY ELIMINATING RESTRICTIONS ON HIS ABILITY TO PRESCRIBE MEDICATIONS AND UTILIZE AND SPONSOR PHYSICIAN ASSISTANTS IN HIS OFFICE PRACTICE. ON 7/23/97 BOARD GRANTED HIS REQUEST TO TERMINATE THIS ORDER AND LICENSE IS UNRESTRICTED.

SAID, MOHAMMAD H MD, DATE OF BIRTH OCTOBER 22, 1938, WAS DISCIPLINED BY NORTH DAKOTA ON NOVEMBER 17, 1995.
DISCIPLINARY ACTION: RESTRICTION PLACED ON LICENSE; RESTRICTION PLACED ON CONTROLLED SUBSTANCE LICENSE
OFFENSE: DISCIPLINARY ACTION BY ANOTHER STATE OR AGENCY
NOTES: DISCIPLINARY ACTION TAKEN IN WASHINGTON. RESTRICTIONS BECOME EFFECTIVE IN EVENT HE RESUMES PRACTICING IN NORTH DAKOTA AND INCLUDE: SHALL WRITE ALL PRESCRIPTIONS FOR ANALGESIC MEDICATIONS SCHEDULE II, III AND IV AND BENZODIAZEPINES ON TRIPLICATE SEQUENTIALLY NUMBERED PRESCRIPTION PADS; SHALL NOT PRESCRIBE ANALGESIC MEDICATION (SCHEDULE II, III AND IV) TO A PATIENT WHO HE KNOWS OR SHOULD KNOW TO BE A PRESENT OR PREVIOUS DRUG ADDICT OR DRUG ABUSER OR SEEKER EXCEPT IN TRAUMA OR WHERE JUSTIFIED BY BONA FIDE MEDICAL CIRCUMSTANCES; SHALL NOT PRESCRIBE NARCOTIC ANALGESICS FOR CHRONIC PAIN/SUBJECTIVE PAIN SYNDROMES IN THE ABSENCE OF SUFFICIENT EVIDENCE OF ACUTE EXACERBATIONS OF SUCH AFFLICTIONS; SHALL NOT UTILIZE PHYSICIAN ASSISTANTS IN HIS PRACTICE OR SERVE AS A SPONSORING PHYSICIAN OR AN ALTERNATE SPONSORING PHYSICIAN FOR A PHYSICIAN ASSISTANT; SHALL ENSURE THAT HIS RECORD KEEPING SHALL INCLUDE SUFFICIENT DESCRIPTION OF SUBJECTIVE COMPLAINTS AND OBJECTIVE FINDINGS TO REFLECT INDICATIONS FOR DIAGNOSIS AND TREATMENT AND TO DOCUMENT PROPER USE OF CONTROLLED SUBSTANCES.

SANDERSON, JOHN D MD, LICENSE NUMBER 0031399, OF MERCER ISLAND, WA, WAS DISCIPLINED BY WASHINGTON ON SEPTEMBER 24, 1993.
DISCIPLINARY ACTION: RESTRICTION PLACED ON LICENSE; MONITORING OF PHYSICIAN
OFFENSE: PROVIDING FALSE INFORMATION TO THE BOARD
NOTES: ALLEGATIONS OF SEXUAL CONTACT WITH PATIENTS AND MISREPRESENTATION IN HIS LICENSE APPLICATION OF PREVIOUS RESTRICTIONS PLACED ON HIS HOSPITAL PRIVILEGES IN ANOTHER STATE. LICENSE TO PRACTICE IS CONDITIONED UPON HIS COMPLIANCE WITH TERMS AND CONDITIONS FOR A MINIMUM OF FIVE YEARS: SHALL BE SUBJECT TO PERIODIC PRACTICE REVIEWS AND ANNUAL REVIEW BY THE BOARD; IF HE ENGAGES IN CLINICAL PRACTICE SHALL HAVE A MONITOR PRESENT FOR ALL FEMALE PATIENTS; SHALL OBTAIN COUNSELING FROM A BOARD APPROVED HEALTH CARE PROFESSIONAL WHO SHALL PROVIDE REPORTS TO THE BOARD.

SANDERSON, JOHN D MD, LICENSE NUMBER 0G42246, OF BAINBRIDGE ISLAND, WA, WAS DISCIPLINED BY CALIFORNIA ON MAY 26, 1995.
DISCIPLINARY ACTION: SURRENDER OF LICENSE
NOTES: WHILE CHARGES PENDING.

SARGENT, PAUL R DO WAS DISCIPLINED BY WASHINGTON ON SEPTEMBER 28, 1990.
OFFENSE: PHYSICAL OR MENTAL ILLNESS INHIBITING THE ABILITY TO PRACTICE WITH SKILL AND SAFETY
NOTES: AS A RESULT OF A CLOSED HEAD INJURY RECEIVED IN A MOTORCYCLE ACCIDENT HE IS UNABLE TO PRACTICE OSTEOPATHIC MEDICINE AND SURGERY AND THEREFORE IS PLACED ON INACTIVE STATUS; SO HE CANNOT ENGAGE IN THE PRACTICE OF OSTEOPATHIC MEDICINE AND SURGERY IN WASHINGTON. AT REASONABLE INTERVALS HE WILL BE GIVEN THE OPPORTUNITY TO DEMONSTRATE THAT HE CAN RESUME COMPETENT PRACTICE.

SARGENT, PAUL R MD, LICENSE NUMBER 0009651, OF TAYLORS, SC, WAS DISCIPLINED BY WASHINGTON ON JULY 12, 1991.
DISCIPLINARY ACTION: SURRENDER OF LICENSE
OFFENSE: PHYSICAL OR MENTAL ILLNESS INHIBITING THE ABILITY TO PRACTICE WITH SKILL AND SAFETY
NOTES: A 4/28/89 MOTORCYCLE ACCIDENT HAS RENDERED HIM UNABLE TO PRACTICE MEDICINE WITH REASONABLE SKILL AND SAFETY TO CONSUMERS. RETIREMENT SHALL BE PERMANENT. ONLY ALLOWED TO PRACTICE IN WASHINGTON WITH PRIOR WRITTEN BOARD APPROVAL; MAY PETITION THE MEDICAL BOARD IN WRITING AT ANYTIME TO REINSTATE HIS LICENSE, PROVIDED THAT THE MEDICAL BOARD IS PROVIDED WITH PHYSICAL EXAMINATION REPORTS FROM A BOARD CERTIFIED NEUROLOGIST, AND MENTAL EXAMINATION REPORTS FROM LICENSED OR CERTIFIED HEALTH PROFESSIONALS.

SATO, KENNETH K MD, LICENSE NUMBER 0005404, OF PULLMAN, WA, WAS DISCIPLINED BY WASHINGTON ON JUNE 13, 1994.
DISCIPLINARY ACTION: 60-MONTH PROBATION; FINE
OFFENSE: OVERPRESCRIBING OR MISPRESCRIBING DRUGS
NOTES: ALLEGATIONS OF NON-THERAPEUTIC PRESCRIBING PRACTICES. SHALL COMPLETE 25 HOURS OF CONTINUING MEDICAL EDUCATION IN THE AREAS OF PRESCRIBING CONTROLLED SUBSTANCES, ADDICTION OR SUBSTANCE ABUSE; MUST ALSO USE TRIPLICATE PRESCRIPTION BLANKS WHEN PRESCRIBING CONTROLLED SUBSTANCES; OBEY RESTRICTIONS PLACED ON HIS PRESCRIBING PRACTICES; APPEAR ANNUALLY BEFORE THE BOARD AND ALLOW SEMI-ANNUAL OFFICE INSPECTIONS; MUST PAY A $1000 FINE.

- WASHINGTON -

SATO, KENNETH K MD, LICENSE NUMBER 0005404, OF PULLMAN, WA, WAS DISCIPLINED BY WASHINGTON ON OCTOBER 6, 1995.
DISCIPLINARY ACTION: RESTRICTION PLACED ON CONTROLLED SUBSTANCE LICENSE
NOTES: PROHIBITED FROM PRESCRIBING OR DISPENSING CONTROLLED SUBSTANCES. 12/09/96 GRANTED PERMISSION TO PRESCRIBE SCHEDULE V COUGH SYRUPS, PROVIDED THAT ALL SUCH PRESCRIPTIONS ARE WRITTEN ON TRIPLICATE PRESCRIPTION PADS.

SATO, KENNETH K MD OF NORTH 1045 GRAND, PULLMAN, WA, WAS DISCIPLINED BY DEA ON JANUARY 23, 1996.
DISCIPLINARY ACTION: SURRENDER OF CONTROLLED SUBSTANCE LICENSE
OFFENSE: DISCIPLINARY ACTION BY ANOTHER STATE OR AGENCY
NOTES: STATE BOARD.

SAYRE, MICHAEL MD, LICENSE NUMBER 0030636, OF WALLA WALLA, WA, WAS DISCIPLINED BY CONNECTICUT ON MAY 17, 1994.
DISCIPLINARY ACTION: 24-MONTH PROBATION; MONITORING OF PHYSICIAN
OFFENSE: DISCIPLINARY ACTION BY ANOTHER STATE OR AGENCY
NOTES: BASED ON WASHINGTON STATE'S DISCIPLINE; INCOMPETENCE/NEGLIGENCE. PROBATION BEGINNING WHEN HE BEGINS PRACTICE IN CONNECTICUT. TERMS OF PROBATION AS FOLLOWS: SUPERVISION WITH PERIODIC REPORTS.

SAYRE, MICHAEL C MD, LICENSE NUMBER 0029156, OF WALLA WALLA, WA, WAS DISCIPLINED BY WASHINGTON ON MARCH 19, 1993.
DISCIPLINARY ACTION: REQUIRED TO TAKE ADDITIONAL MEDICAL EDUCATION
OFFENSE: SUBSTANDARD CARE, INCOMPETENCE, OR NEGLIGENCE
NOTES: PRIOR TO SURGERY IN WHICH HE WAS THE ATTENDING ANESTHESIOLOGIST FAILED TO ENSURE THAT THE VENTILATOR WAS ON THEREBY DEPRIVING THE PATIENT OF OXYGEN DURING SURGERY; FAILED TO RECOGNIZE AND/OR REACT TO THIS CAUSING THE PATIENT TO SUFFER ANOXIC ENCEPHALOPATHY AND DIE 20 DAYS LATER. SHALL COMPLETE 25 HOURS OF CONTINUING MEDICAL EDUCATION IN THE AREA OF ANESTHESIOLOGY BY 6/1/94; SHALL SUCCESSFULLY COMPLETE A SPECIFIED PROCTORING PLAN; SHALL PAY A $500 FINE.

SAYRE, MICHAEL C MD, DATE OF BIRTH NOVEMBER 29, 1946, LICENSE NUMBER 0D39621, WAS DISCIPLINED BY MARYLAND ON APRIL 5, 1994.
OFFENSE: DISCIPLINARY ACTION BY ANOTHER STATE OR AGENCY
NOTES: ON 3/16/93 HE ENTERED INTO AN AGREED ORDER WITH THE WASHINGTON BOARD IN WHICH HE ADMITS THAT, PRIOR TO A SURGERY IN WHICH HE WAS THE ATTENDING ANESTHESIOLOGIST, HE FAILED TO ENSURE THAT THE VENTILATOR WAS ON THEREBY DEPRIVING THE PATIENT OF OXYGEN DURING SURGERY AND FAILED TO RECOGNIZE AND/OR REACT TO THE FALLING OXYGEN SATURATION RATE; AS A RESULT THE PATIENT SUFFERED ANOXIC ENCEPHALOPATHY, WAS PLACED ON LIFE SUPPORT AND DIED 20 DAYS LATER AFTER THE FAMILY DECIDED TO REMOVE HIM FROM LIFE SUPPORT; CONDITIONS OF WASHINGTON ORDER INCLUDED CONTINUING MEDICAL EDUCATION AND A FINE; ON 9/2/93 WASHINGTON ORDER WAS TERMINATED. CONDITION OF MARYLAND ORDER: SHALL NOT PRACTICE IN THE STATE UNTIL HE APPEARS BEFORE AND OBTAINS APPROVAL OF THE BOARD.

SAYRE, MICHAEL C MD, DATE OF BIRTH NOVEMBER 29, 1946, LICENSE NUMBER 0030053, WAS DISCIPLINED BY COLORADO ON JULY 8, 1996.
DISCIPLINARY ACTION: REPRIMAND

SAYRE, MICHAEL C MD, LICENSE NUMBER 0006962, OF 330 LILLIAN LANE, WATERLOO, IA, WAS DISCIPLINED BY HAWAII ON DECEMBER 20, 1996.
DISCIPLINARY ACTION: FINE
OFFENSE: DISCIPLINARY ACTION BY ANOTHER STATE OR AGENCY
NOTES: ACTION IN VERMONT AND DOCUMENTS RECEIVED FROM WASHINGTON, CONNECTICUT, AND IOWA BOARDS. FAILED TO REPORT DISCIPLINARY DECISION IN ANOTHER JURISDICTION. $500 ADMINISTRATIVE FINE. LICENSE EXPIRED ON 1/31/96.

SCEATS, DONALD J MD, DATE OF BIRTH MARCH 16, 1922, LICENSE NUMBER 0002648, OF 507 W. 14TH STREET, PUEBLO, CO, WAS DISCIPLINED BY MONTANA ON MAY 17, 1989.
DISCIPLINARY ACTION: RESTRICTION PLACED ON LICENSE; REPRIMAND
OFFENSE: DISCIPLINARY ACTION BY ANOTHER STATE OR AGENCY
NOTES: FOR FAILING TO DISCLOSE DISCIPLINARY ACTION IN ANOTHER STATE IN RENEWING LICENSE; RESTRICTIONS PER COLORADO ORDER

SCEATS, DONALD J MD, DATE OF BIRTH MARCH 16, 1922, LICENSE NUMBER C017014, OF PUEBLO, CO, WAS DISCIPLINED BY CALIFORNIA ON JULY 26, 1989.
DISCIPLINARY ACTION: SURRENDER OF LICENSE

SCEATS, DONALD J MD, DATE OF BIRTH MARCH 16, 1922, LICENSE NUMBER 0002648, OF 507 W. 14TH STREET, PUEBLO, CO, WAS DISCIPLINED BY MONTANA ON NOVEMBER 27, 1989.
DISCIPLINARY ACTION: SURRENDER OF LICENSE

SCEATS, DONALD J MD, LICENSE NUMBER 0013031, OF PUEBLO, CO, WAS DISCIPLINED BY COLORADO ON FEBRUARY 15, 1991.
OFFENSE: SUBSTANDARD CARE, INCOMPETENCE, OR NEGLIGENCE
NOTES: MAY NOT NOW OR IN THE FUTURE PRACTICE MEDICINE IN COLORADO WITHOUT MAKING APPLICATION AND RECEIVING BOARD'S APPROVAL.

SCEATS, DONALD J MD, DATE OF BIRTH MARCH 16, 1922, LICENSE NUMBER 0004683, OF PUEBLO, CO, WAS DISCIPLINED BY WASHINGTON ON MAY 18, 1991.
DISCIPLINARY ACTION: SURRENDER OF LICENSE
OFFENSE: DISCIPLINARY ACTION BY ANOTHER STATE OR AGENCY
NOTES: ON 8/14/87 COLORADO RESTRICTED HIS LICENSE BY PROHIBITING CARE OF LEVEL II OR III INFANTS AND FURTHER RESTRICTED HIS NEONATAL PRACTICE; ON 2/27/88, WHILE APPLYING FOR RENEWAL OF MONTANA LICENSE, STATED HE HAD NOT HAD ANY DISCIPLINARY ACTIONS TAKEN AGAINST HIM; MONTANA ENTERED INTO ORDER ON 5/17/89 REQUIRING HIM TO REPORT ANY DISCIPLINARY PROCEEDINGS OR VOLUNTARY LICENSE SURRENDERS WITHIN 30 DAYS; ACCEPTED THE SURRENDER OF HIS LICENSE ON 11/27/89 IN LIEU OF PROCEEDING TO HEARING ON CHARGES THAT HE HAD FAILED TO REPORT SURRENDERING HIS CALIFORNIA LICENSE WITHIN 30 DAYS; HE SURRENDERED CALIFORNIA LICENSE ON 6/7/89. AGREES NOT TO APPLY FOR REINSTATEMENT FOR AT LEAST ONE YEAR; MUST CONCLUDE ALL MEDICAL BUSINESS AND FORMALLY CLOSE PRACTICE WITHIN 90 DAYS.

SCHWISOW, DON MD OF 7600 WEST 13TH STREET AVENUE, KENNEWICK, WA, WAS DISCIPLINED BY DEA ON APRIL 18, 1994.
DISCIPLINARY ACTION: RESTRICTION PLACED ON CONTROLLED SUBSTANCE LICENSE
OFFENSE: OVERPRESCRIBING OR MISPRESCRIBING DRUGS
NOTES: EXCESSIVE PRESCRIBING.

SCHWISOW, DONOVON MD OF KENNEWICK, BENTON COUNTY, WA, WAS DISCIPLINED BY WASHINGTON ON FEBRUARY 12, 1992.
DISCIPLINARY ACTION: RESTRICTION PLACED ON LICENSE
NOTES: CONDITIONAL LICENSE ISSUED WITH SPECIFIC TERMS

- WASHINGTON -

AND CONDITIONS.

SCONZERT, ALAN CARL MD, LICENSE NUMBER 0029514, OF PASCO, WA, WAS DISCIPLINED BY WASHINGTON ON MAY 31, 1996.
DISCIPLINARY ACTION: REPRIMAND
NOTES: REQUIRED TO UNDERGO ANGER-MANAGEMENT THERAPY AND OTHER TERMS AND CONDITIONS.

SEVERSON, JEWELL A MD, LICENSE NUMBER 0004972, OF BREMERTON, WA, WAS DISCIPLINED BY WASHINGTON ON JUNE 1, 1993.
DISCIPLINARY ACTION: SURRENDER OF LICENSE
OFFENSE: SUBSTANDARD CARE, INCOMPETENCE, OR NEGLIGENCE
NOTES: ALLEGATIONS OF NONTHERAPEUTIC PRESCRIBING AND SUBSTANDARD CARE. IN LIEU OF FURTHER PROCEEDINGS AGREES TO RETIREMENT AND HAS NO PLANS TO RESUME PRACTICE IN WASHINGTON; AND HE WILL NOTIFY THE BOARD IF HE PLANS TO RESUME PRACTICE IN WASHINGTON OR ANY OTHER JURISDICTION.

SHEPARD, PHILLIP B MD OF HELENA, MT, WAS DISCIPLINED BY VIRGINIA ON OCTOBER 1, 1987.
DISCIPLINARY ACTION: LICENSE REVOCATION

SHEPARD, PHILLIP B MD, LICENSE NUMBER 0028735, WAS DISCIPLINED BY MICHIGAN ON OCTOBER 19, 1988.
DISCIPLINARY ACTION: LICENSE REVOCATION

SHEPARD, PHILLIP B MD, DATE OF BIRTH NOVEMBER 14, 1943, LICENSE NUMBER 0004524, OF 1206 EAST PIKE #505, SEATTLE, WA, WAS DISCIPLINED BY MONTANA ON SEPTEMBER 3, 1990.
DISCIPLINARY ACTION: LICENSE REINSTATEMENT; RESTRICTION PLACED ON LICENSE
OFFENSE: PROFESSIONAL MISCONDUCT
NOTES: VOLUNTARY SURRENDER ON 3/25/86 DUE TO BOARD'S INVESTIGATION INTO PRACTICE FOR DEVIATE SEXUAL CONDUCT. REINSTATEMENT WITH CONDITIONS: PATIENT CARE SHALL BE ONLY FOR ADULTS OR EMERGENCY ROOM/URGENT CARE; MAY DO AIDS COUNSELING OR RESEARCH; ALL PATIENT CONTACT SHALL HAVE THE PRESENCE OF A THIRD PARTY AT ALL TIMES; SHALL UNDERGO CONTINUAL PSYCHOTHERAPY WITH THERAPIST PROVIDING QUARTERLY REPORTS; SHALL ENTER INTO A PERMANENT CONTRACT WITH THE MONTANA PROFESSIONAL ASSISTANCE PROGRAM; SHALL INFORM ANY FACILITY WHERE HE PROVIDES SERVICES OF THE ORDER. MODIFICATION OF CONDITIONS ON 3/23/92 TO PROVIDE CLARIFICATION.

SHERMAN, JOSEPH W MD, LICENSE NUMBER 0024877, OF COLBERT, WA, WAS DISCIPLINED BY WASHINGTON ON DECEMBER 22, 1995.
NOTES: REMOVED HIS SUSPENSION, BUT IMPOSED TERMS AND CONDITIONS WHICH INCLUDE REQUIRING HIM TO REIMBURSE COSTS AND COOPERATE WITH AN INVESTIGATION. ON 9/24/96 HE WAS RELEASED FROM STAYED SUSPENSION AND LICENSE IS NOW UNRESTRICTED.

SHERWIN, DUANE O MD WAS DISCIPLINED BY WASHINGTON ON JULY 26, 1989.
DISCIPLINARY ACTION: SURRENDER OF LICENSE
NOTES: IN ACKNOWLEDGMENT OF A STATEMENT OF CHARGES CONCERNING HIS ABILITY TO PRACTICE MEDICINE WITH REASONABLE SKILL AND SAFETY, ADVISED THE BOARD THAT HE SHALL RETIRE FROM MEDICAL PRACTICE EFFECTIVE 10/01/89 AND THAT HE WAS NO PLANS TO RESUME PRACTICE SUBSEQUENT TO THAT DATE; AGREES THAT HIS RETIREMENT SHALL BE PERMANENT AND THAT HE MAY RESUME PRACTICE ONLY WITH PRIOR BOARD APPROVAL; WILL NOTIFY THE BOARD IF HE PLANS TO RESUME PRACTICE IN ANY OTHER JURISIDICTION. INVESTIGATION WAS TERMINATED.

SHINKOSKEY, ALMON C DO, LICENSE NUMBER 0OPO783, WAS DISCIPLINED BY WASHINGTON ON MAY 3, 1996.
DISCIPLINARY ACTION: FINE; RESTRICTION PLACED ON CONTROLLED SUBSTANCE LICENSE
OFFENSE: SUBSTANDARD CARE, INCOMPETENCE, OR NEGLIGENCE
NOTES: CONDUCT IN TREATING THREE PATIENTS DEMONSTRATED INCOMPETENCE; HIS CHART NOTES FAILED TO REVEAL ANY TREATMENT PLAN, REFERRAL OR RECOMMENDATION FOR OTHER THERAPY AS ALTERNATIVE TO DRUG THERAPY; CONDUCT EITHER RESULTED IN AN INJURY OR PLACED THE PATIENTS AT UNREASONABLE RISK; HIS PRESCRIPTION OF LEGEND DRUGS WITH CONTROLLED SUBSTANCE INGREDIENTS DOES NOT SUPPORT THERAPEUTIC PURPOSES IN THREE PATIENTS HE TREATED BETWEEN 7/86 AND 4/94 WITH NO MONITORING OF THE PROTRACTED USE OF THE PRESCRIBED DRUGS; AND UNPROFESSIONAL CONDUCT PROMOTING PERSONAL GAIN FROM ANY UNNECESSARY OR INEFFICACIOUS DRUG OR TREATMENT IN THAT HE BILLED FOR SERVICES NOT RENDERED IN THESE THREE CASES. THREE YEAR SUSPENSION, STAYED UNDER CONDITIONS: UNANNOUNCED PRACTICE REVIEWS FROM THE BOARD REGARDING COMPLIANCE; SHALL SUBMIT TO THE BOARD QUARTERLY DECLARATIONS OF COMPLIANCE; SHALL KEEP PATIENT RECORDS IN A SPECIFIED MANNER; SHALL ATTEND 24 HOURS OF COURSE WORK EMPHASIZING PAIN MANAGEMENT OF PATIENTS, FOUR HOURS OF COURSE WORK IN MEDICAL RECORD KEEPING, AND FOUR HOURS OF COURSE WORK IN CPT BILLING AND CODING TO BE COMPLETED BY 6/09/98; AND SHALL USE TRIPLICATE PRESCRIPTION FORMAT AND PROTOCOL FOR ALL PRESCRIPTIONS OF LEGEND DRUGS, INCLUDING THOSE WITH CONTROLLED SUBSTANCES INGREDIENTS WHICH SHALL BE SUBMITTED TO THE BOARD MONTHLY. $9,000 FINE.

SHOCK, PETER MD WAS DISCIPLINED BY WASHINGTON ON JULY 2, 1990.
DISCIPLINARY ACTION: RESTRICTION PLACED ON LICENSE
NOTES: IS IN COMPLIANCE WITH BOARD ORDERS OF 4/18/86, 12/12/86, 7/26/87, 3/18/88, 11/28/88, AND 6/15/89. MEDICAL LICENSE REINSTATED WITH THE FOLLOWING CONDITIONS: HE SHALL HAVE AN ADULT CHAPERONE PRESENT AT ALL TIMES WHEN EXAMINING, TREATING, OR CONSULTING A FEMALE PATIENT AND IS NOT LIMITED TO BREAST AND PELVIC EXAMINATIONS, TREATMENTS, OR CONSULTATIONS, EXCEPT WHEN TREATING PATIENTS ON AN INPATIENT BASIS IN A HOSPITAL SETTING. HE SHALL INSURE THAT ALL EMERGENCY OR AFTER-HOURS FEMALE PATIENT CARE IS ATTENDED BY AN ADULT CHAPERONE AS WELL.

SHULL, FREDERICK W MD, LICENSE NUMBER 0042853, OF BELLINGHAM, WA, WAS DISCIPLINED BY NEW YORK ON JANUARY 21, 1987.
DISCIPLINARY ACTION: LICENSE REVOCATION

SHULL, THOMAS E MD, LICENSE NUMBER 0020297, OF TACOMA, PIERCE COUNTY, WA, WAS DISCIPLINED BY WASHINGTON ON MARCH 5, 1992.
DISCIPLINARY ACTION: EMERGENCY SUSPENSION
NOTES: ALLEGATIONS OF IMPAIRMENT.

SHULL, THOMAS E MD, LICENSE NUMBER 0020297, OF GOSHEN, IN, WAS DISCIPLINED BY WASHINGTON ON OCTOBER 22, 1992.
DISCIPLINARY ACTION: LICENSE SUSPENSION
OFFENSE: SUBSTANCE ABUSE
NOTES: MORAL TURPITUDE, CURRENT MISUSE OF ALCOHOL, AND ABUSE OF A CLIENT.

- WASHINGTON -

SHULL, THOMAS EARL MD, DATE OF BIRTH APRIL 26, 1929, LICENSE NUMBER 1037255, OF 1741 B COLLEGE MANOR DR, GOSHEN, IN, WAS DISCIPLINED BY INDIANA ON DECEMBER 17, 1992.
DISCIPLINARY ACTION: 3-MONTH EMERGENCY SUSPENSION
OFFENSE: DISCIPLINARY ACTION BY ANOTHER STATE OR AGENCY
NOTES: WHILE EMPLOYED AT A CLINIC IN WASHINGTON IN LATE 1991 HE EXHIBITED ERRATIC, ABERRANT AND HOSTILE BEHAVIOR TOWARDS PATIENTS AND FELLOW EMPLOYEES. ALCOHOL WAS REPEATEDLY SMELLED ON HIS BREATH. AFTER BEING FIRED FROM THE CLINIC HE MADE THREATS AGAINST FORMER EMPLOYERS. ALSO WROTE BAD CHECKS. WASHINGTON LICENSE SUMMARILY SUSPENDED 3/5/92, AND INDEFINITELY SUSPENDED 10/22/92. ORDERED TO UNDERGO PSYCHOLOGICAL AND SUBSTANCE ABUSE EVALUATION, WHICH HE HAD NOT DONE AS OF 12/17/92. AS OF 1/29/93 THE SUMMARY SUSPENSION IS CONTINUED IN FULL EFFECT WITH FOLLOWING CONDITIONS: HE MUST UNDERGO A PSYCHIATRIC AND SUBSTANCE ABUSE EVALUATION TO BE PERFORMED BY A BOARD APPROVED PSYCHIATRIST OR CERTIFIED ADDICTIONOLOGIST. THE BOARD WILL RECEIVE A REPORT, CONTAINING A HISTORY, EVALUATION, DIAGNOSIS, PROGNOSIS AND COURSE OF TREATMENT, IF ANY, FROM THE EXAMINING PHYSICIAN; SHALL ENTER INTO AN AGREEMENT WITH THE INDIANA STATE MEDICAL ASSOCIATION'S IMPAIRED PHYSICIAN PROGRAM AND ADHERE TO IT; A COPY OF THIS ORDER IS TO BE SENT TO THE MEDICAL LICENSING BOARDS OF OREGON, MONTANA, WASHINGTON, AND CALIFORNIA. EFFECTIVE 2/25/93, THE EMERGENCY SUSPENSION CONTINUES AS DOES CONDITION THAT HE SHALL ENTER INTO AN AGREEMENT WITH THE INDIANA STATE MEDICAL ASSOCIATION'S IMPAIRED PHYSICIAN PROGRAM AND ADHERE TO IT; EFFECTIVE 5/4/93, 6/10/93 AND 6/24/93 THE EMERGENCY SUSPENSION WAS CONTINUED FOR A PERIOD NOT TO EXCEED 90 DAYS.

SHULL, THOMAS EARL MD, DATE OF BIRTH APRIL 26, 1929, LICENSE NUMBER 0002894, OF 1741B COLLEGE MANOR DRIVE, GOSHEN, IN, WAS DISCIPLINED BY MONTANA ON FEBRUARY 10, 1993.
DISCIPLINARY ACTION: LICENSE REVOCATION
OFFENSE: DISCIPLINARY ACTION BY ANOTHER STATE OR AGENCY
NOTES: RECIPROCAL TO WASHINGTON'S ACTION.

SHULL, THOMAS EARL MD, DATE OF BIRTH APRIL 26, 1929, LICENSE NUMBER 1037255, OF 1741 B COLLEGE MANOR DRIVE, GOSHEN, IN, WAS DISCIPLINED BY INDIANA ON FEBRUARY 24, 1994.
DISCIPLINARY ACTION: LICENSE SUSPENSION; 120-MONTH PROBATION
OFFENSE: DISCIPLINARY ACTION BY ANOTHER STATE OR AGENCY
NOTES: AS OF 1/27/94 HE HAD NOT OBTAINED A STAY OF THE SUSPENSION ON HIS WASHINGTON LICENSE ALTHOUGH HE HAS INFORMED THE WASHINGTON BOARD OF HIS TREATMENT FOR ALCOHOL DEPENDENCE AND BIPOLAR DISORDER AND THAT HE WISHES TO REMAIN IN INDIANA; ON 2/10/93 IN A DEFAULT DECISION MONTANA LICENSE WAS REVOKED BASED ON THE WASHINGTON ACTION; ON 2/17/93 PLED GUILTY TO OPERATING A MOTOR VEHICLE WITH .10% OR MORE BLOOD ALCOHOL LEVEL; 60 DAY JAIL SENTENCE SUSPENDED WITH CONDITIONS; LETTERS FROM PHYSICIAN INDICATE HE HAS SUCCESSFULLY COMPLETED TREATMENT AND HE CONTINUES TO ACTIVELY PARTICIPATE IN RECOVERY ACTIVITIES INCLUDING AA MEETINGS AND A CONTRACT WITH MEDICAL ASSOCIATION. SUSPENSION INDEFINITE PENDING SUCCESSFUL COMPLETION OF SPEX EXAM. CONDITIONS OF PROBATION: SHALL ONLY WORK UNDER THE ON-SITE SUPERVISION OF A LICENSED PHYSICIAN; MAY ONLY WORK 30 HOURS PER WEEK; SHALL HAVE SUPERVISOR SUBMIT MONTHLY REPORTS TO THE BOARD; MAY NOT POSSESS DEA OR CONTROLLED SUBSTANCES REGISTRATION; SHALL ATTEND AT LEAST 3 AA/NARCOTICS ANONYMOUS OR CADUCEUS MEETINGS PER WEEK WITH QUARTERLY REPORTS TO THE BOARD; SHALL MAINTAIN AND COMPLY WITH HIS PHYSICIAN ASSISTANCE CONTRACT WITH MONTHLY REPORTS TO THE BOARD; SHALL HAVE PSYCHIATRIST SUBMIT MONTHLY REPORTS; SHALL NOTIFY THE BOARD OF A CHANGE IN TREATING PHYSICIANS; SHALL APPEAR BEFORE THE BOARD QUARTERLY. LICENSE AUTOMATICALLY REINSTATED ON PROBATION ON 9/8/94 AFTER HE PASSED THE SPEX EXAM. ORDER MODIFIED ON 2/15/95: THE REQUIREMENT TO WORK ONLY UNDER THE ON-SITE SUPERVISION OF A LICENSED PHYSICIAN IS DELETED; MAY WORK ONLY 40 HOURS PER WEEK; ALL OTHER TERMS AND CONDITIONS REMAIN IN FULL FORCE AND EFFECT.

SIEGEL, RICHARD B MD OF NEW YORK, NY, WAS DISCIPLINED BY WASHINGTON ON NOVEMBER 23, 1991.
DISCIPLINARY ACTION: DENIAL OF NEW LICENSE

SINGER, MICHAEL MD, LICENSE NUMBER 0024557, OF BLOOMFIELD HILLS, MI, WAS DISCIPLINED BY WASHINGTON ON JANUARY 17, 1991.
DISCIPLINARY ACTION: REPRIMAND
OFFENSE: PROVIDING FALSE INFORMATION TO THE BOARD
NOTES: ON APPLICATION FOR LICENSE OF 10/22/86 HE ANSWERED THAT HE HAD NOT USED ANY LEGEND DRUG OR CONTROLLED SUBSTANCE FOR OTHER THAN THERAPEUTIC PURPOSES OR BEEN ADDICTED TO, OR TREATED FOR ADDICTION TO OR ABUSE OF, ANY CONTROLLED SUBSTANCE, DRUG OR CHEMICAL. ADMITS HE USED FENTANYL FROM EARLY 1984 TO 7/87 AND THAT IN 7/87 HE ENTERED AN INPATIENT SUBSTANCE ABUSE PROGRAM AND CONTINUED IN THE WASHINGTON MONITORED TREATMENT PROGRAM UNTIL 4/89; IN 5/89 HE MOVED TO MICHIGAN AND BEGAN PARTICIPATING IN THEIR IMPAIRED PHYSICIAN PROGRAM; HAS BEEN IN RECOVERY FOR APPROXIMATELY 3 ½ YEARS. BEFORE RETURNING TO PRACTICE IN WASHINGTON, SHALL APPEAR BEFORE THE BOARD WITH EVIDENCE OF CONTINUING RECOVERY AND ABSTINENCE.

SKOPEC, HOWARD M MD, LICENSE NUMBER 0G20237, OF ESCONDIDO, CA, WAS DISCIPLINED BY CALIFORNIA ON NOVEMBER 23, 1991.
DISCIPLINARY ACTION: 4-MONTH LICENSE SUSPENSION; 80-MONTH PROBATION
OFFENSE: SEXUAL ABUSE OF OR SEXUAL MISCONDUCT WITH A PATIENT
NOTES: SEXUAL RELATIONS WITH A FEMALE PATIENT, GROSS NEGLIGENCE, INCOMPETENCE IN PSYCHOTHERAPY PRACTICE, REVEALED CONFIDENTIAL PATIENT SECRET. REVOCATION STAYED.

SKOPEC, HOWARD MICHAEL MD, LICENSE NUMBER 0002050, OF ESCONDIDO, CA, WAS DISCIPLINED BY WASHINGTON ON FEBRUARY 19, 1993.
DISCIPLINARY ACTION: FINE
OFFENSE: DISCIPLINARY ACTION BY ANOTHER STATE OR AGENCY
NOTES: LICENSE PLACED ON PROBATION IN CALIFORNIA FOR GROSS NEGLIGENCE AND INCOMPETENCE AND SEXUAL MISCONDUCT. SUSPENSION STAYED PROVIDED HE COMPLY WITH THE FOLLOWING TERMS AND CONDITIONS: IN ORDER TO LIFT SUSPENSION, MUST APPEAR BEFORE THE BOARD AND BRING THE MOST CURRENT WRITTEN EVALUATION OF HIS MENTAL STATUS BY HIS PSYCHOTHERAPIST OR HIS MOST RECENT THERAPIST, A COMPREHENSIVE ASSESSMENT OF HIS PRACTICE SKILLS BY HIS MONITOR, A SIGNED RELEASE OF HIS RECORDS FOR ANY MENTAL HEALTH TREATMENT WHILE HE WAS ON PROBATION IN

- WASHINGTON -

CALIFORNIA; DOCUMENTATION OF THE CURRENT STATUS OF HIS CALIFORNIA MEDICAL LICENSE; SHALL INFORM THE BOARD OF ANY CHANGES IN HIS PRACTICE AND RESIDENCE ADDRESS; SHALL PAY A $500 FINE.

SKOPEC, HOWARD MICHAEL MD WAS DISCIPLINED BY NEW HAMPSHIRE ON JUNE 8, 1993.
DISCIPLINARY ACTION: LICENSE REVOCATION

SMALL, DELBERT F MD OF SOUTH 5012 ST ANDREWS LN, SPOKANE, WA, WAS DISCIPLINED BY DEA ON AUGUST 2, 1989.
DISCIPLINARY ACTION: SURRENDER OF CONTROLLED SUBSTANCE LICENSE
OFFENSE: OVERPRESCRIBING OR MISPRESCRIBING DRUGS
NOTES: ORDERED 500 UNITS DEXTROAMPHETAMINE DESPITE RETIREMENT FROM ACTIVE MEDICAL PRACTICE; USED AND DISPENSED TO FAMILY MEMBERS ILLEGALLY; VOLUNTARILY SURRENDERED DEA REGISTRATION AND 474 UNITS DEXTROAMPHETAMINE ON 06/26/89.

SMITH, DIANA J MD, LICENSE NUMBER 0015141, WAS DISCIPLINED BY ARIZONA ON OCTOBER 15, 1993.
DISCIPLINARY ACTION: LICENSE REVOCATION
OFFENSE: OVERPRESCRIBING OR MISPRESCRIBING DRUGS
NOTES: HAS A MEDICAL CONDITION WHICH PREVENTS HER FROM SAFELY ENGAGING IN THE PRACTICE OF MEDICINE AT THIS TIME; PRESCRIBED DEMEROL ON 05/08/93 AND 12/3/91 FOR HER HUSBAND; REFUSED TO PRODUCE PATIENT RECORDS FOR INSPECTION BY THE BOARD ON ANY PATIENT FOR WHOM SHE CLAIMED TO HAVE PRESCRIBED OR DISPENSED CONTROLLED SUBSTANCES; HAD LARGE QUANTITIES OF CONTROLLED SUBSTANCES DELIVERED TO HER RESIDENCE, INCLUDING A PACKAGE DELIVERED 07/07/93 CONTAINING 4 500-UNIT DOSE CONTAINERS OF HYDROCODONE WITH APAP AND ONE VIAL DIAZEPAM AND OTHER ASSORTED PHARMACEUTICALS WHICH WERE NOT PROPERLY STORED OR CONTROLLED; SHALL NOT BE ALLOWED TO APPLY FOR A LICENSE TO PRACTICE MEDICINE IN ARIZONA FOR ONE YEAR FROM THE EFFECTIVE DATE OF THIS ORDER; IN ADDITION TO THE ONE-YEAR PERIOD SET FORTH ABOVE, PRIOR TO APPLYING FOR LICENSURE IN ARIZONA, SHE MUST FIRST DEMONSTRATE TO THE SATISFACTION OF THE BOARD THAT SHE IS PHYSICALLY, MENTALLY AND MEDICALLY COMPETENT TO SAFELY ENGAGE IN THE PRACTICE OF MEDICINE, AND PROVIDE PROOF THAT SHE HAS NOT MISUSED ALCOHOL AND/OR LICIT OR ILLICIT DRUGS OR SUBSTANCES OR HAS SUCCESSFULLY COMPLETED LONG-TERM TREATMENT FOR SUBSTANCE ABUSE AND HAS AT LEAST 18 MONTHS DOCUMENTED SOBRIETY FOLLOWING TREATMENT.

SMITH, DIANA J MD OF WA, WAS DISCIPLINED BY DEA ON AUGUST 12, 1994.
DISCIPLINARY ACTION: REVOCATION OF CONTROLLED SUBSTANCE LICENSE
OFFENSE: DISCIPLINARY ACTION BY ANOTHER STATE OR AGENCY
NOTES: ON 10/14/93 VOLUNTARILY RELINQUISHED HER LICENSE IN ARIZONA.

SMITH, THOMAS J MD, LICENSE NUMBER 0016322, OF SEATTLE, WA, WAS DISCIPLINED BY WASHINGTON ON NOVEMBER 16, 1990.
DISCIPLINARY ACTION: PROBATION; FINE
OFFENSE: FAILURE TO COMPLY WITH A PREVIOUS BOARD ORDER
NOTES: BOARD ENTERED ORDER 8/21/87 STATING FOLLOWING RESTRICTIONS: SHALL ONLY PRESCRIBE CLASS II OR III DRUGS FOR LEGITIMATE THERAPEUTIC PURPOSES; MAY NOT PRESCRIBE ANY SCHEDULE II OR III DRUGS FOR CHRONIC NON-MALIGNANT PAIN; MUST WRITE PRESCRIPTIONS FOR SCHEDULE II, III AND IV DRUGS ON TRIPLICATE SEQUENTIALLY NUMBERED PADS AND KEEP ONE COPY AS A LOG OF ALL PRESCRIPTIONS; AGREES TO MAKE PRESCRIPTION RECORDS AND MEDICAL RECORDS AVAILABLE FOR PRACTICE REVIEW. HE VIOLATED THIS ORDER IN SEVERAL INSTANCES AS FOLLOWS: FROM THE TIME OF THE ORDER THROUGH 11/89 PRESCRIBED CONTROLLED SUBSTANCES TO THREE PATIENTS ENGAGED IN DRUG SEEKING BEHAVIOR, FOR CHRONIC NON-MALIGNANT PAIN, AND DID NOT NOTE PRESCRIPTIONS IN HIS RECORDS OR USE TRIPLICATE PRESCRIPTION FORMS; PRESCRIBED TO ANOTHER PATIENT FOR CHRONIC NON-MALIGNANT PAIN WITHOUT NOTING PRESCRIPTIONS IN HIS RECORDS AND WITHOUT USING TRIPLICATE PRESCRIPTIONS. SUSPENSION STAYED TO PROBATION WITH FOLLOWING CONDITIONS: $3,000 FINE; MAY PRESCRIBE SCHEDULE II-IV SUBSTANCES TO INPATIENTS; MAY NOT PRESCRIBE AFTER THEY LEAVE HOSPITAL; FOR 90 DAYS AFTER HE SHALL WRITE TRIPLICATE PRESCRIPTIONS FOR ALL SCHEDULED DRUGS; MAY ONLY PRESCRIBE WITHIN THE WRITTEN CRITERIA ESTABLISHED BY BOARD; SHALL OBTAIN A BOARD APPROVED PROCTOR TO REVIEW PRACTICE WEEKLY, WITH MONTHLY REPORTS TO THE BOARD; BOARD MEMBER MAY MAKE UNANNOUNCED INSPECTIONS OF PRACTICE; SHALL COMPLETE 25 HOURS OF CATEGORY I CONTINUING MEDICAL EDUCATION IN AREA OF CONTROLLED SUBSTANCES AND CHEMICAL DEPENDENCY OR CHRONIC PAIN MANAGEMENT PER YEAR; SHALL APPEAR BEFORE THE BOARD TO VERIFY COMPLIANCE; SHALL INFORM THE BOARD OF A CHANGE OF ADDRESS OR IF HE LEAVES THE STATE; TIME OUT OF STATE NOT TAKEN OFF PROBATION TIME; MAY PETITION FOR MODIFICATION IN 7/91, BUT PROBATION SHALL LAST AT LEAST TWO YEARS. ON 11/18/93 HE WAS FOUND TO BE IN COMPLIANCE WITH THIS ORDER AND ORDER WAS TERMINATED.

SOSSONG, NORMAN MD, LICENSE NUMBER 0G39936, OF LAKEPORT, CA, WAS DISCIPLINED BY CALIFORNIA ON MARCH 18, 1991.
DISCIPLINARY ACTION: 3-MONTH LICENSE SUSPENSION; 81-MONTH PROBATION
OFFENSE: SEXUAL ABUSE OF OR SEXUAL MISCONDUCT WITH A PATIENT
NOTES: ACTION BASED ON SEXUAL MISCONDUCT WITH FEMALE PATIENTS. REVOCATION STAYED.

SOSSONG, NORMAN MD OF MIDDLETOWN, CA, WAS DISCIPLINED BY WASHINGTON ON FEBRUARY 18, 1992.
DISCIPLINARY ACTION: DENIAL OF NEW LICENSE
NOTES: MAY NOT REAPPLY FOR A LICENSE UNTIL THE RESTRICTIONS ON HIS CALIFORNIA LICENSE ARE RESOLVED.

SOUDA, ROBERT M MD, LICENSE NUMBER 00D1497, OF DALLAS, TX, WAS DISCIPLINED BY TEXAS ON NOVEMBER 30, 1994.
DISCIPLINARY ACTION: SURRENDER OF LICENSE
NOTES: DENIES ALLEGATIONS CONCERNING POSSIBLE VIOLATIONS OF THE MEDICAL PRACTICE ACT BUT SURRENDERS LICENSE IN LIEU OF FURTHER INVESTIGATION. SHALL NOT PETITION FOR REINSTATEMENT OF LICENSE.

SOUDA, ROBERT M MD, LICENSE NUMBER 0011338, OF DALLAS, TX, WAS DISCIPLINED BY WASHINGTON ON MARCH 8, 1996.
DISCIPLINARY ACTION: SURRENDER OF LICENSE
OFFENSE: DISCIPLINARY ACTION BY ANOTHER STATE OR AGENCY
NOTES: ACTION IN TEXAS. AGREED TO RETIRE.

SPRINGEL, RONALD D MD, LICENSE NUMBER 0024392, OF SPOKANE, WA, WAS DISCIPLINED BY WASHINGTON ON MARCH 4, 1988.
DISCIPLINARY ACTION: EMERGENCY SUSPENSION
OFFENSE: FAILURE TO COMPLY WITH A PREVIOUS BOARD ORDER
NOTES: FAILED TO COMPLY WITH TERMS OF PROBATIONARY

- WASHINGTON -

LICENSE, SUFFERED RELAPSE IN DRUG ADDICTION AND DIVERTED METHADONE FROM HIS EMPLOYER FOR PERSONAL USE.

SPRINGEL, RONALD D MD, LICENSE NUMBER 0024392, OF SPOKANE, WA, WAS DISCIPLINED BY WASHINGTON ON JULY 22, 1988.
DISCIPLINARY ACTION: 60-MONTH LICENSE REVOCATION; REQUIRED TO ENTER AN IMPAIRED PHYSICIAN PROGRAM OR DRUG OR ALCOHOL TREATMENT
OFFENSE: CRIMINAL CONVICTION OR PLEA OF GUILTY, NOLO CONTENDERE, OR NO CONTEST TO A CRIME
NOTES: FAILED TO COMPLY WITH CONDITIONS OF PREVIOUS BOARD ORDER; SUFFERED A RELAPSE IN DRUG ADDICTION TREATMENT AND DIVERTED METHADONE FROM HIS EMPLOYER FOR HIS OWN PERSONAL USE; CONVICTED ON A PLEA OF GUILTY TO FEDERAL FELONY CHARGES OF UNLAWFUL ACQUISITION OF CONTROLLED SUBSTANCES FOR WHICH HE WILL BE SENTENCED 8/26/88; CANNOT APPLY FOR REINSTATEMENT FOR 3 YEARS AND WHEN HE HAS COMPLETED AN IN-PATIENT SUBSTANCE ABUSE TREATMENT PROGRAM; THAT HE HAS REMAINED DRUG AND ALCOHOL FREE FOR 12 MONTHS. ON 11/4/94 BOARD GRANTED HIS REQUEST TO HAVE AN UNRESTRICTED LICENSE.

SPRINGEL, RONALD D MD, LICENSE NUMBER 022426E, OF YAKIMA, WA, WAS DISCIPLINED BY PENNSYLVANIA ON SEPTEMBER 27, 1988.
DISCIPLINARY ACTION: LICENSE SUSPENSION
OFFENSE: CRIMINAL CONVICTION OR PLEA OF GUILTY, NOLO CONTENDERE, OR NO CONTEST TO A CRIME
NOTES: PLED GUILTY TO ONE COUNT OF VIOLATING USE OF METHADONE, WHICH VIOLATED HIS MEDICAL PROBATION IN ALASKA; SENTENCED TO ONE-YEAR IMPRISONMENT ALASKA'S PROBATION WAS REVOKED AND HE WAS SENTENCED TO AN ADDITIONAL YEAR AND TO FOUR CONCURRENT THREE YEAR TERMS OF IMPRISONMENT

STANK, THOMAS MARK MD WAS DISCIPLINED BY WASHINGTON ON MAY 21, 1993.
DISCIPLINARY ACTION: REQUIRED TO TAKE ADDITIONAL MEDICAL EDUCATION; MONITORING OF PHYSICIAN
OFFENSE: SEXUAL ABUSE OF OR SEXUAL MISCONDUCT WITH A PATIENT
NOTES: ENGAGED IN A SEXUAL RELATIONSHIP WITH A FEMALE WHO AT A POINT IN TIME WAS HIS PATIENT FOR THE TREATMENT OF IRITIS BUT WAS NOT AND IS NOT A CONTINUING PATIENT FOR ANY OTHER MATTER. SHE HAS MADE NO COMPLAINT TO THE BOARD AND HER EYE PROBLEM WAS SUCCESSFULLY TREATED. SHALL NOT PRACTICE IN THIS STATE WITHOUT PRIOR BOARD APPROVAL; SHALL HAVE COMPLETED 25 HOURS OF BOARD APPROVED CONTINUING MEDICAL EDUCATION IN THE AREAS OF MEDICAL ETHICS, SEXUAL HARASSMENT, AND/OR BOUNDARY PROBLEMS IN THE PHYSICIAN/PATIENT RELATIONSHIP WITHIN THREE YEARS; SHALL NOT HAVE ANY SEXUAL CONTACT OR SEXUALLY ORIENTED CONTACT WITH ANY PATIENT OR IMMEDIATE MEMBER OF A PATIENT'S FAMILY; SHALL PROVIDE A COPY OF THIS ORDER TO HIS CURRENT EMPLOYER AND TO ALL SUBSEQUENT EMPLOYERS WITHIN THREE YEARS; FOR A PERIOD OF THREE YEARS, SHALL ASK HIS EMPLOYER TO PROVIDE A YEARLY STATEMENT DOCUMENTING THE EMPLOYER'S KNOWLEDGE OF THIS ORDER AND A STATEMENT REGARDING HIS/HER UNDERSTANDING OF DRDOSTANK'S COMPLIANCE; MAY PETITION THE BOARD FOR A CHANGE IN THE TERMS/CONDITIONS OF THE ORDER IN NO SOONER THAN TWO YEARS; SHALL INFORM THE BOARD IN WRITING OF CHANGES IN HIS PRACTICE AND RESIDENCE ADDRESS; SHALL PAY $1,000 COSTS.

STANLEY, JOHN L MD, LICENSE NUMBER 0004293, OF BREMERTON, WA, WAS DISCIPLINED BY WASHINGTON ON JANUARY 24, 1994.
DISCIPLINARY ACTION: SURRENDER OF LICENSE
OFFENSE: SEXUAL ABUSE OF OR SEXUAL MISCONDUCT WITH A PATIENT
NOTES: ALLEGATIONS OF HAVING SEXUAL CONTACT WITH FEMALE PATIENTS.

STANLEY, JOHN L MD, LICENSE NUMBER 0004293, OF BREMERTON, WA, WAS DISCIPLINED BY WASHINGTON ON DECEMBER 16, 1994.
DISCIPLINARY ACTION: DENIAL OF LICENSE REINSTATEMENT

STANSFIELD, STEPHEN J MD, LICENSE NUMBER 0017540, OF QUINCY, WA, WAS DISCIPLINED BY WASHINGTON ON MARCH 4, 1994.
DISCIPLINARY ACTION: 18-MONTH PROBATION
OFFENSE: SUBSTANDARD CARE, INCOMPETENCE, OR NEGLIGENCE
NOTES: ALLEGATIONS OF NEGLIGENCE.

STANTON, FRANK A MD, LICENSE NUMBER 0G13030, OF POULSBO, WA, WAS DISCIPLINED BY CALIFORNIA ON JUNE 14, 1995.
DISCIPLINARY ACTION: 60-MONTH PROBATION
OFFENSE: PROFESSIONAL MISCONDUCT
NOTES: UNPROFESSIONAL CONDUCT FOR A PSYCHIATRIST TO LIE ON THE BED WITH A FEMALE PATIENT EVEN THOUGH NOTHING OF A SEXUAL NATURE OCCURRED. REVOCATION STAYED.

STAUDINGER, SUZANNE MD WAS DISCIPLINED BY WASHINGTON ON DECEMBER 15, 1989.
DISCIPLINARY ACTION: FINE; RESTRICTION PLACED ON LICENSE
OFFENSE: SUBSTANDARD CARE, INCOMPETENCE, OR NEGLIGENCE
NOTES: ON 6/29/87 MADE A NEGLIGENT CHOICE OF PROCEDURE FOR REMOVAL OF THE PRODUCTS OF CONCEPTION AT A GESTATIONAL AGE OF 16 WEEKS AFTER FETAL DEMISE WAS CONFIRMED; FAILED TO REALIZE THAT SHE HAD NOT REMOVED THE PRODUCTS OF CONCEPTION OR THAT SHE HAD PERFORATED THE PATIENT'S UTERUS; TWO WEEKS LATER A LAPAROTOMY WAS PERFORMED IN WHICH A FETUS WAS REMOVED FROM THE PATIENT'S CAVITY. HER PRACTICE SHALL BE RESTRICTED SO AS TO PROHIBIT HER FROM CONDUCTING INTRAUTERINE OPERATIONS UNTIL SHE COMPLETES THE FOLLOWING REQUIREMENTS: SHALL COMPLETE 50 HOURS OF CONTINUING MEDICAL EDUCATION CREDITS IN OBSTETRICS/GYNECOLOGY WHICH SHALL HAVE SOME EMPHASIS ON INTRAUTERINE OPERATIONS AND INDICATIONS FOR SAID OPERATIONS; SHALL ENTER INTO A BOARD APPROVED PART TIME PRECEPTORSHIP TO INCLUDE PRACTICAL AND DIDACTIC TRAINING; THE PRECEPTOR SHALL REPORT TO THE BOARD WHEN HE/SHE BELIEVES THAT SHE HAS HAD SUFFICIENT INTRAUTERINE TRAINING; SHALL PERSONALLY APPEAR BEFORE THE BOARD AND OBTAINS WRITTEN PERMISSION FROM THE BOARD BEFORE RESTRICTION IS LIFTED; $500 FINE.

STAVIG, DARRELL MD, LICENSE NUMBER 0005318, OF REDMOND, WA, WAS DISCIPLINED BY WASHINGTON ON NOVEMBER 20, 1992.
DISCIPLINARY ACTION: SURRENDER OF LICENSE

STEFANAC, VERA MD OF 3216 NE 45TH PL SUITE 212, SEATTLE, WA, WAS DISCIPLINED BY DEA ON FEBRUARY 22, 1996.
DISCIPLINARY ACTION: SURRENDER OF CONTROLLED SUBSTANCE LICENSE
OFFENSE: DISCIPLINARY ACTION BY ANOTHER STATE OR AGENCY
NOTES: STATE BOARD.

STEFANAC, VERA M MD, LICENSE NUMBER 0023387, OF SEATTLE, WA, WAS DISCIPLINED BY WASHINGTON ON AUGUST 25, 1995.
DISCIPLINARY ACTION: SURRENDER OF LICENSE
NOTES: AGREED TO RETIRE.

- WASHINGTON -

STEWART, JAMES M MD OF TACOMA, PIERCE COUNTY, WA, WAS DISCIPLINED BY WASHINGTON ON MAY 21, 1992.
DISCIPLINARY ACTION: DENIAL OF NEW LICENSE
NOTES: MAY NOT REAPPLY FOR A LICENSE UNTIL SPECIFIC TERMS AND CONDITIONS HAVE BEEN MET.

STIER, ROBERT A MD, LICENSE NUMBER 0002814, OF SPOKANE, WA, WAS DISCIPLINED BY WASHINGTON ON SEPTEMBER 13, 1991.
NOTES: IN ORDER OF 9/18/87 HE AGREED TO CERTAIN PRESCRIPTION PRACTICES AND A 3 YEAR PERIOD OF SUPERVISION; ON 10/21/88 SUPERVISION WAS TERMINATED AND HE WAS ORDERED TO CONTINUE COMPLIANCE WITH ALL OTHER TERMS OF THE 9/18/87 ORDER. DUE TO HIS COMPLIANCE, BOARD'S JURISDICTION OVER THIS MATTER IS NOW TERMINATED; ALL REMAINING CONDITIONS ON LICENSE REMOVED.

STILES, RICHARD A MD, LICENSE NUMBER 0004626, OF YAKIMA, WA, WAS DISCIPLINED BY WASHINGTON ON MARCH 8, 1996.
DISCIPLINARY ACTION: SURRENDER OF LICENSE
NOTES: AGREED TO RETIRE.

STOWENS, DANIEL W MD, LICENSE NUMBER 0029365, OF SEATTLE, WA, WAS DISCIPLINED BY WASHINGTON ON NOVEMBER 15, 1996.
DISCIPLINARY ACTION: RESTRICTION PLACED ON CONTROLLED SUBSTANCE LICENSE
OFFENSE: SUBSTANDARD CARE, INCOMPETENCE, OR NEGLIGENCE
NOTES: ALLEGED NEGLIGENCE AND NON-THERAPEUTIC PRESCRIBING. RESTRICTED HIS PRESCRIBING OF PSYCHOTROPIC MEDICATIONS.

STRAIT, GAIL B MD, LICENSE NUMBER 0010088, OF TACOMA, WA, WAS DISCIPLINED BY WASHINGTON ON JUNE 2, 1995.
DISCIPLINARY ACTION: 1-MONTH PROBATION; RESTRICTION PLACED ON CONTROLLED SUBSTANCE LICENSE
NOTES: SHALL SPEAK PERSONALLY WITH A PHARMACIST OR OTHER MEDICAL PROFESSIONAL WHO CALLS CONCERNING A PATIENT'S MEDICATION AND SHALL MAKE A CHART ENTRY CONCERNING THAT CONVERSATION; SHALL USE TRIPLICATE PRESCRIPTION FORMS FOR LEGEND DRUGS FOR THREE MONTHS. RELEASED FROM JURISIDICTION WITH AN UNRESTRICTED LICENSE ON 4/04/96.

STRANGE, MEL K MD, LICENSE NUMBER 0019211, OF HOQUIAM, WA, WAS DISCIPLINED BY WASHINGTON ON APRIL 15, 1994.
DISCIPLINARY ACTION: PROBATION; FINE
OFFENSE: SEXUAL ABUSE OF OR SEXUAL MISCONDUCT WITH A PATIENT
NOTES: ALLEGATIONS THAT HE HAD A SEXUAL RELATIONSHIP WITH A PATIENT. THREE YEAR SUSPENSION STAYED. CONDITIONS OF PROBATION: SHALL HAVE A CHAPERONE PRESENT WHEN TREATING FEMALE PATIENTS OR WHEN FEMALE RELATIVES OF PATIENTS ARE PRESENT; SHALL DISSEMINATE A LETTER TO ALL FEMALE PATIENTS OUTLINING THIS REQUIREMENT; SHALL DISSEMINATE THE ORDER TO ANY FACILITY WHERE HE HAS PRIVILEGES AND TO HIS OFFICE STAFF; SHALL UNDERGO TREATMENT BY A BOARD APPROVED THERAPIST WHO SHALL SUBMIT QUARTERLY REPORTS; $2,000 FINE. ON 2/1/95 HIS REQUEST WAS GRANTED AND FINE REDUCED TO $1,000. ON 7/24/95 PROVISION REQUIRING THERAPY WAS TERMINATED SUBJECT TO HIS THERAPIST PROVIDING A FINAL, COMPREHENSIVE REPORT. ON 9/24/96 HIS REQUEST TO TERMINATE THIS ORDER DENIED. ON 3/22/97 BOARD GRANTED HIS REQUEST TO TERMINATE THIS ORDER AND LICENSE IS UNRESTRICTED.

STRAWN, DALE A MD, DATE OF BIRTH FEBRUARY 20, 1912, LICENSE NUMBER 0011219, OF LYNDEN, WA, WAS DISCIPLINED BY KENTUCKY ON MARCH 27, 1991.
DISCIPLINARY ACTION: SURRENDER OF LICENSE
NOTES: DISCIPLINED BY BLANCHFIELD ARMY COMMUNITY HOSPITAL.

STRAWN, DALE A MD, LICENSE NUMBER 0A11316, OF CANADA, WAS DISCIPLINED BY CALIFORNIA ON OCTOBER 17, 1991.
DISCIPLINARY ACTION: LICENSE REVOCATION
OFFENSE: DISCIPLINARY ACTION BY ANOTHER STATE OR AGENCY
NOTES: DISCIPLINED BY THE ARMY MEDICAL SERVICES CORP IN KENTUCKY. DEFAULT DECISION.

STROLE, JANERIK MD OF SOUTH BEND, PACIFIC COUNTY, WA, WAS DISCIPLINED BY WASHINGTON ON MAY 4, 1992.
DISCIPLINARY ACTION: RESTRICTION PLACED ON LICENSE
NOTES: CONDITIONAL LICENSE ISSUED WITH SPECIFIC CONDITIONS.

SUNWOO, HYUNG B MD, LICENSE NUMBER 0027167, OF MERCER ISLAND KING COUNTY, WA, WAS DISCIPLINED BY WASHINGTON ON FEBRUARY 14, 1992.
DISCIPLINARY ACTION: EMERGENCY SUSPENSION
NOTES: ALLEGATIONS OF IMPAIRED PRACTICE.

SUNWOO, HYUNG B MD, LICENSE NUMBER 0027167, OF MERCER ISLAND, WA, WAS DISCIPLINED BY WASHINGTON ON OCTOBER 6, 1995.
DISCIPLINARY ACTION: LICENSE SUSPENSION
NOTES: INDEFINITE SUSPENSION UNTIL HE PRESENTS EVIDENCE THAT HE CAN PRACTICE MEDICINE SAFELY.

SUNWOO, HYUNG BO MD WAS DISCIPLINED BY MAINE ON JANUARY 11, 1994.
DISCIPLINARY ACTION: LICENSE SUSPENSION
OFFENSE: DISCIPLINARY ACTION BY ANOTHER STATE OR AGENCY
NOTES: ACTION TAKEN BY WASHINGTON. MENTAL HEALTH IMPAIRMENT. INDEFINITE SUSPENSION.

SUNWOO, HYUNG-BO MD, LICENSE NUMBER 0131624, OF 3500 90TH AVE. S.W. APT. 261, MERCER ISLAND, WA, WAS DISCIPLINED BY NEW YORK ON JUNE 11, 1996.
DISCIPLINARY ACTION: LICENSE REVOCATION
OFFENSE: DISCIPLINARY ACTION BY ANOTHER STATE OR AGENCY
NOTES: ACTION IN WASHINGTON FOR NOT BEING CAPABLE OF PRACTICING MEDICINE WITH REASONABLE SKILL AND SAFETY.

SUTHERLAND, ELEANOR I MD, LICENSE NUMBER 0017018, OF FEDERAL WAY, WA, WAS DISCIPLINED BY WASHINGTON ON JULY 20, 1990.
DISCIPLINARY ACTION: REQUIRED TO TAKE ADDITIONAL MEDICAL EDUCATION; MONITORING OF PHYSICIAN
OFFENSE: OVERPRESCRIBING OR MISPRESCRIBING DRUGS
NOTES: SHE PRESCRIBED ADDICTIVE MEDICATIONS INCLUDING VALIUM, VICODIN, BENZODIAZEPINES, AND OPIATES FOR A PATIENT OVER FIVE YEAR PERIOD; KNEW OR SHOULD HAVE KNOWN THAT PATIENT WAS OR BECAME DEPENDENT ON MEDICATIONS; THE COURSE OF DRUG THERAPY DID NOT PROVIDE LONG TERM RELIEF FOR THE CHRONIC PAIN, NAUSEA AND VOMITING EXPERIENCED BY THE PATIENT; FAILED TO IDENTIFY PATIENT'S FAMILY HISTORY OF SUBSTANCE ABUSE; FAILED TO TREAT PATIENT'S PSYCHOLOGICAL SYMPTOMS OF SUBSTANCE DEPENDENCY; FAILED TO RECOGNIZE AND SUPPORT PATIENT'S EFFORTS TO DECREASE HER DRUG DEPENDENCY; FAILED TO FOLLOW THE ADVICE OF SPECIALISTS REGARDING THIS PATIENT. STATE FAILED TO ESTABLISH BY A PREPONDERANCE OF THE EVIDENCE SERIOUS HARM TO THE PATIENT. FIVE YEAR SUSPENSION STAYED WITH CONDITIONS: SHE SHALL NOT TREAT PATIENT OR ANY MEMBER OF HER FAMILY; SHALL PERMIT BOARD REPRESENTATIVE TO MAKE UNANNOUNCED OR

ANNOUNCED VISITS; SHE SHALL APPEAR BEFORE BOARD EVERY 12 MONTHS FOR COMPLIANCE HEARINGS; SHALL COMPLETE 50 HOURS OF CONTINUING MEDICAL EDUCATION IN AREAS OF DRUG AND ALCOHOL DEPENDENCY; MAY NOT APPLY FOR MODIFICATION SOONER THAN THREE YEARS. ON 7/23/95 HER REQUEST TO TERMINATE RESTRICTIONS GRANTED AND LICENSE NOW UNRESTRICTED.

SWANS ON, CRAIG E MD, LICENSE NUMBER 0A41844, OF WOFFORD HEIGHTS, CA, WAS DISCIPLINED BY CALIFORNIA ON MARCH 30, 1994.
DISCIPLINARY ACTION: 60-MONTH PROBATION
OFFENSE: SUBSTANDARD CARE, INCOMPETENCE, OR NEGLIGENCE
NOTES: GROSS NEGLIGENCE, INCOMPETENCE, UNPROFESSIONAL CONDUCT IN THE CARE AND TREATMENT OF PATIENTS. REVOCATION STAYED.

SWANS ON, CRAIG E MD, LICENSE NUMBER 0027758, OF WOFFORD HEIGHTS, CA, WAS DISCIPLINED BY WASHINGTON ON APRIL 21, 1995.
OFFENSE: DISCIPLINARY ACTION BY ANOTHER STATE OR AGENCY
NOTES: SUSPENSION STAYED; SHALL COMPLY WITH TERMS OF PROBATION CONTAINED IN CALIFORNIA ORDER. SHALL APPEAR BEFORE THE BOARD BEFORE COMMENCING PRACTICE IN WASHINGTON. ON 8/14/97 BOARD GRANTED HIS REQUEST TO TERMINATE THIS ORDER.

TAIT, ARNOLD C MD WAS DISCIPLINED BY WASHINGTON ON AUGUST 24, 1988.
DISCIPLINARY ACTION: EMERGENCY SUSPENSION
NOTES: MUST IMMEDIATELY SURRENDER HIS LICENSE.

TAIT, ARNOLD C MD WAS DISCIPLINED BY WASHINGTON ON MAY 19, 1989.
DISCIPLINARY ACTION: SURRENDER OF LICENSE
OFFENSE: PROFESSIONAL MISCONDUCT
NOTES: CRIMINAL CHARGES FILED AND THEN RESOLVED BY A DIVERSION AGREEMENT. SHALL RETIRE FROM THE PRACTICE OF MEDICINE AND SHALL SURRENDER HIS LICENSE TO PRACTICE MEDICINE IN WASHINGTON, IN LIEU OF REVOCATION WHICH SHALL BE PERMANENT AND EFFECTIVE IMMEDIATELY UPON ACCEPTANCE OF THIS ORDER. HE AGREES TO NOTIFY THE BOARD IF HE PLANS TO RESUME PRACTICE IN ANY OTHER JURISDICTION AND ABIDE BY TERMS OF DIVERSION AGREEMENT.

TAIT, ARNOLD C MD, LICENSE NUMBER 00G5191, OF SUNNYSIDE, WA, WAS DISCIPLINED BY CALIFORNIA ON APRIL 19, 1990.
DISCIPLINARY ACTION: LICENSE REVOCATION
OFFENSE: DISCIPLINARY ACTION BY ANOTHER STATE OR AGENCY
NOTES: IN WASHINGTON, SUMMARY SUSPENSION FOLLOWED BY SURRENDER OF LICENSE IN LIEU OF REVOCATION IN CONNECTION WITH FEDERAL INDICTMENT FOR DISTRIBUTION OF A CONTROLLED SUBSTANCE.

TASHAKKOR, EZZATOLLAH MD, LICENSE NUMBER 0022603, OF BELLEVUE, WA, WAS DISCIPLINED BY WASHINGTON ON NOVEMBER 15, 1996.
NOTES: AGREED TO CERTAIN UNSPECIFIED TERMS AND CONDITIONS ON HIS LICENSE.

TAYLOR, DARYL MD, LICENSE NUMBER 0018047, OF BREMERTON, WA, WAS DISCIPLINED BY WASHINGTON ON MARCH 4, 1994.
DISCIPLINARY ACTION: LICENSE SUSPENSION
NOTES: UNABLE TO PRACTICE WITH REASONABLE SKILL AND SAFETY. MAY PETITION FOR REINSTATEMENT UPON SATISFACTORY COMPLETION OF AN APPROVED TREATMENT PROGRAM.

TAYLOR, DARYL C MD WAS DISCIPLINED BY WASHINGTON ON JULY 1, 1993.
DISCIPLINARY ACTION: EMERGENCY SUSPENSION
NOTES: ALLEGATIONS WHICH INDICATE THE INABILITY TO PRACTICE WITH REASONABLE SKILL AND SAFETY TO CONSUMERS.

TAYLOR, DARYL C MD, LICENSE NUMBER 0G30743, OF SANTA MARIA, CA, WAS DISCIPLINED BY CALIFORNIA ON MAY 27, 1995.
DISCIPLINARY ACTION: 120-MONTH PROBATION
OFFENSE: DISCIPLINARY ACTION BY ANOTHER STATE OR AGENCY
NOTES: DISCIPLINE BY WASHINGTON STATE BOARD RELATED TO ALCOHOL PROBLEM. REVOCATION STAYED.

THOMAS, GORDON G MD, LICENSE NUMBER 0006092, OF AUBURN, WA, WAS DISCIPLINED BY WASHINGTON ON JULY 15, 1991.
DISCIPLINARY ACTION: FINE; RESTRICTION PLACED ON LICENSE
OFFENSE: SUBSTANDARD CARE, INCOMPETENCE, OR NEGLIGENCE
NOTES: FROM 6/11/88 TO 2/16/89 HE TREATED A PATIENT FOR TIGHTNESS IN THE THROAT, INCLUDING A PRESCRIPTION FOR XANAX; FAILED TO RECORD PRESCRIPTIONS IN CHARTS, FAILED TO OBSERVE, MONITOR, AND RECORD PHYSICAL AND PSYCHOLOGICAL EFFECTS OF THE DRUG, FAILED TO PERFORM CHEMICAL MONITORING, AND FAILED TO FULLY INFORM THE PATIENT OF THE POSSIBILITY OF DRUG DEPENDENCY AND POTENTIAL PROBLEMS ASSOCIATED WITH DISCONTINUANCE; THE PATIENT ATTEMPTED TO WITHDRAW, SUFFERED WITHDRAWAL SYMPTOMS, AND ENTERED AN INPATIENT DRUG TREATMENT PROGRAM. HE PROVIDED MEDICAL TREATMENT TO A SECOND PATIENT FROM APPROXIMATELY 10/85 TO 12/89; AFTER A FEW MONTHS HE DEVELOPED AN ONGOING SOCIAL AND SEXUAL RELATIONSHIP WITH PATIENT; HE ADMITTED THAT IN ORDER TO AVOID HAVING HER REPORT TO THE BOARD THAT HE HAD INFECTED HER WITH GENITAL HERPES, HE PAID HER $125,000 AND PURCHASED A CAR FOR HER WORTH $25,000. ADMITS HE SIGNED AN APPLICATION FOR REAPPOINTMENT AT VALLEY MEDICAL CENTER INDICATING THERE WERE NO CLAIMS AGAINST HIM WHEN THERE WERE PENDING MALPRACTICE CLAIMS. HE IS CURRENTLY UNDER BOARD ORDER OF 1/18/88 RESULTING FROM CONCERNS RELATING TO ELECTIVE FACIAL COSMETIC SURGERIES AND TO HIS BILLING PRACTICE. SUSPENSION STAYED UPON CONDITIONS: SHALL CONTINUE TWICE WEEKLY THERAPY; SHALL SUBMIT TO SEMI-ANNUAL PSYCHOLOGICAL EVALUATIONS; SHALL APPEAR BEFORE THE BOARD FOR A COMPLIANCE REVIEW EVERY SIX MONTHS; SHALL PERMIT REVIEW OF MEDICAL CASES BY A BOARD APPROVED PHYSICIAN; SHALL MAINTAIN MEDICAL CHARTS ON EACH PATIENT FOR WHOM HE WRITES A PRESCRIPTION; SHALL USE TRIPLICATE PRESCRIPTION FORMS; SHALL HAVE NO SOCIAL CONTACT WITH PATIENTS OR THEIR RELATIVES EXCEPT HANDSHAKES; SHALL NOT DATE ANY PATIENT OR RELATIVE OF A PATIENT; SHALL NOT PROVIDE MEDICAL SERVICES TO ANY PERSON HE IS DATING OR THEIR FAMILY MEMBERS; SHALL NOT DISCUSS HIS PERSONAL LIFE WITH ANY PATIENT OR THEIR RELATIVES; SHALL PROVIDE A LETTER TO EACH PATIENT EXPLAINING BOARD ORDER; SHALL HAVE NO FURTHER CONTACT WITH THE TWO PATIENTS MENTIONED; SHALL PROVIDE A COPY OF BOARD ORDER TO EACH MEMBER OF HIS STAFF, CURRENT AND FUTURE; SHALL HAVE A FEMALE STAFF PERSON PRESENT AS A CHAPERONE WHEN HE IS WITH A FEMALE PATIENT OR PATIENT'S FEMALE RELATIVE; SHALL PERMIT ANNOUNCED AND/OR UNANNOUNCED VISITS BY A BOARD REPRESENTATIVE; SHALL COMPLETE 50 UNITS OF CONTINUING MEDICAL EDUCATION IN THE AREA OF PROFESSIONAL ETHICS AND PROFESSIONAL BOUNDARIES WITHIN TWO YEARS; $3,000 FINE; MAY NOT PETITION FOR MODIFICATION OF THIS ORDER FOR TWO

YEARS.

THOMAS, GORDON G MD, LICENSE NUMBER 0006092, WAS DISCIPLINED BY WASHINGTON ON AUGUST 20, 1993.
DISCIPLINARY ACTION: FINE; RESTRICTION PLACED ON LICENSE
OFFENSE: FAILURE TO COMPLY WITH A PREVIOUS BOARD ORDER
NOTES: NONCOMPLIANCE WITH A PREVIOUS BOARD ORDER OF 7/15/91 IN THAT HE DID NOT INCLUDE INFORMATION REGARDING HIS SEXUAL CONTACT WITH A PATIENT IN REQUIRED PATIENT LETTERS; DID NOT HAVE FEMALE STAFF PERSON PRESENT AS CHAPERONE EACH TIME HE WAS WITH A FEMALE PATIENT OR FEMALE RELATIVE OF A PATIENT. LICENSE RESTRICTED UNDER THE FOLLOWING TERMS AND CONDITIONS: SHALL NOT PERFORM SURGERY OF ANY DESCRIPTION OR TYPE, INCLUDING T & A PROCEDURES, OR ANY INVASIVE PROCEDURES OF ANY KIND INCLUDING, BUT NOT LIMITED TO, INSERTION OF EAR TUBES; HIS PRACTICE IS RESTRICTED TO THE MEDICAL ASPECTS OF OTOLARYNGOLOGY; THESE RESTRICTIONS APPLY TO ALL PRACTICE SETTINGS, INCLUDING HOSPITALS, SURGICAL CENTERS AND OFFICE SETTING; SHALL PROVIDE A COPY OF THIS ORDER TO ALL CURRENT AND FUTURE OFFICE STAFF MEMBERS; REQUIRED TO HAVE A BOARD APPROVED PERSON PRESENT IN THE ROOM AT ALL TIMES WHEN HE IS EXAMINING, TREATING, OR CONSULTING FEMALE PATIENTS OR FEMALE RELATIVES OF A PATIENT OF ANY AGE; HIS CHAPERON SHALL INDICATE ON THE PATIENT'S CHART HIS OR HER PRESENCE DURING THE ENTIRE TREATMENT, EXAMINATION, OR CONSULTATION; HIS PRACTICE SHALL BE LIMITED TO ONLY AN OFFICE PRACTICE; AGREES THAT HE SHALL RETIRE FROM MEDICAL PRACTICE IN WASHINGTON EFFECTIVE 1/31/94 AND THAT HE HAS NO PLANS TO RESUME PRACTICE IN WASHINGTON; SHALL SURRENDER HIS WASHINGTON STATE MEDICAL LICENSURE AND CERTIFICATES TO THE BOARD ON 1/31/94; SHALL APPEAR BEFORE THE BOARD IN THREE MONTHS AND PRESENT PROOF THAT HE IS IN COMPLIANCE; THE BOARD MAY MAKE ANNOUNCED OR UNANNOUNCED VISITS TO HIS PRACTICE TO INSPECT OFFICE AND OR MEDICAL RECORDS, INTERVIEW OFFICE STAFF OR SUPERVISORS, AND REVIEW OTHER ASPECTS OF HIS PRACTICE; SHALL PAY A $2,000 FINE.

THOMAS, GORDON GEORGE MD, DATE OF BIRTH FEBRUARY 13, 1931, LICENSE NUMBER 0016007, OF AUBURN, WA, WAS DISCIPLINED BY IOWA ON DECEMBER 4, 1990.
DISCIPLINARY ACTION: LICENSE SUSPENSION
OFFENSE: DISCIPLINARY ACTION BY ANOTHER STATE OR AGENCY
NOTES: INDEFINITE SUSPENSION.

THOMPSON, SHAHNAZ MD, LICENSE NUMBER 0014045, OF ABERDEEN, WA, WAS DISCIPLINED BY WASHINGTON ON FEBRUARY 3, 1994.
DISCIPLINARY ACTION: LICENSE REVOCATION
OFFENSE: SUBSTANDARD CARE, INCOMPETENCE, OR NEGLIGENCE
NOTES: NEGLIGENCE AND NON-THERAPEUTIC PRESCRIBING.

THORNTON, DELL MD, LICENSE NUMBER 0008163, OF REPUBLIC, FERRY COUNTY, WA, WAS DISCIPLINED BY WASHINGTON ON MAY 4, 1992.
DISCIPLINARY ACTION: EMERGENCY SUSPENSION
OFFENSE: SUBSTANDARD CARE, INCOMPETENCE, OR NEGLIGENCE

TOKAR, RONALD LEE MD, LICENSE NUMBER 0017543, OF WALLA WALLA, WA, WAS DISCIPLINED BY OREGON ON OCTOBER 4, 1991.
DISCIPLINARY ACTION: RESTRICTION PLACED ON LICENSE
NOTES: VOLUNTARY LIMITATION.

TRACY, HAROLD L MD, DATE OF BIRTH FEBRUARY 28, 1920, LICENSE NUMBER 0013559, OF MOSES LAKE, WA, WAS DISCIPLINED BY IOWA ON MAY 15, 1990.
DISCIPLINARY ACTION: LICENSE SUSPENSION
NOTES: LICENSE SUSPENDED INDEFINITELY.

TRACY, HAROLD L MD, DATE OF BIRTH FEBRUARY 28, 1920, OF 607 EAST RIVIERA, MOSES LAKE, WA, WAS DISCIPLINED BY MEDICARE ON JANUARY 1, 1991.
DISCIPLINARY ACTION: 84-MONTH EXCLUSION FROM THE MEDICARE AND/OR MEDICAID PROGRAMS
NOTES: PEER REVIEW ORGANIZATION RECOMMENDATION.

TREPP, ROBERT D DO WAS DISCIPLINED BY WASHINGTON ON NOVEMBER 30, 1990.
DISCIPLINARY ACTION: 1-MONTH LICENSE SUSPENSION; 60-MONTH PROBATION
OFFENSE: SUBSTANCE ABUSE
NOTES: SUBSTANCE ABUSE PROBLEM AND UNPROFESSIONAL CONDUCT. REVOCATION, STAYED. SHALL BE REINSTATED ON FIVE YEAR PROBATION PROVIDED THAT HE HAS COMPLIED WITH THE REQUIREMENT FOR A BOARD APPROVED PSYCHIATRIC EXAMINATION AND HAS BEEN FOUND ABLE TO PRACTICE OSTEOPATHIC MEDICINE AND SURGERY WITH REASONABLE SKILL AND SAFETY; SHALL UNDERGO BOARD APPROVED PSYCHIATRIC TREATMENT IF REQUIRED BY EVALUATION; HIS PRIVILEGE TO PRESCRIBE OR DISPENSE SCHEDULE II CONTROLLED SUBSTANCES IS SUSPENDED; HIS PRIVILEGES TO PRESCRIBE OR DISPENSE SCHEDULES III, IV, AND V CONTROLLED SUBSTANCES IS SUBJECT TO TRIPLICATE PRESCRIPTION FORM PROGRAM; AT THE END OF SIX MONTHS MAY PETITION THE BOARD TO REINSTATE HIS SCHEDULE II CONTROLLED SUBSTANCE PRIVILEGES, SUBJECT TO THE TRIPLICATE PRESCRIPTION FORM PROGRAM; SHALL CONTINUE TO PARTICIPATE IN THE WASHINGTON MONITORED TREATMENT PROGRAM AND PROVIDE REPORTS TO THE BOARD; THE PROGRAM DIRECTOR SHALL REPORT TO THE BOARD EVERY SIX MONTHS; SHALL APPEAR IN PERSON UPON BOARD REQUEST; SHALL REGULARLY ATTEND AA OR NARCOTICS ANONYMOUS AND HIS ATTENDANCE SHALL BE CONFIRMED BY THE MONITORED TREATMENT PROGRAM DIRECTOR; SHALL ABSTAIN COMPLETELY FROM THE PERSONAL USE OR POSSESSION OF CONTROLLED SUBSTANCES OR ANY DRUGS REQUIRING A PRESCRIPTION EXCEPT WHEN LAWFULLY PRESRIBED TO HIM FOR THERAPEUTIC PURPOSES; SHALL IMMEDIATELY SUBMIT TO BIOLOGICAL FLUID TESTING UPON BOARD REQUEST; SHALL SUBMIT QUARTERLY DECLARATIONS UNDER PENALTY OF PERJURY TO THE BOARD REGARDING COMPLIANCE; $2,000 CIVIL PENALTY; MAY PETITION THE BOARD FOR REINSTATEMENT AFTER SUCCESSFUL COMPLETION OF FIVE YEAR PROBATION.

TREPP, ROBERT D DO WAS DISCIPLINED BY WASHINGTON ON MAY 17, 1991.
DISCIPLINARY ACTION: EMERGENCY SUSPENSION

TREPP, ROBERT D DO WAS DISCIPLINED BY WASHINGTON ON OCTOBER 10, 1991.
DISCIPLINARY ACTION: LICENSE SUSPENSION; SUSPENSION OF CONTROLLED SUBSTANCE LICENSE
OFFENSE: FAILURE TO COMPLY WITH A PREVIOUS BOARD ORDER
NOTES: FAILED TO COMPLY WITH THE 11/30/90 ORDER: FAILED TO CONTINUE PARTICIPATION IN THE WASHINGTON MONITORED TREATMENT PROGRAM; LEFT THE STATE WITHOUT FIRST NOTIFYING THE PROGRAM; DID NOT SEEK PERMISSION TO MISS A SCHEDULED GROUP MEETING AND NOT AVAILABLE FOR URINE MONITORING. SHALL CONTINUE WITH PSYCHIATRIC TREATMENT UNTIL FURTHER BOARD NOTICE; THE TREATING PSYCHIATRIST SHALL PROVIDE THE BOARD WITH QUARTERLY

- WASHINGTON -

REPORTS; SHALL RE-ENTER THE WASHINGTON MONITORED TREATMENT PROGRAM; THE PROGRAM DIRECTOR OF THE WMTP SHALL REPORT TO THE BOARD IN WRITING EVERY SIX MONTHS; SHALL SUBMIT QUARTERLY DECLARATIONS UNDER PENALTY OF PERJURY REGARDING COMPLIANCE.

TREPP, ROBERT D DO WAS DISCIPLINED BY WASHINGTON ON MARCH 27, 1992.
DISCIPLINARY ACTION: LICENSE REVOCATION
OFFENSE: FAILURE TO COMPLY WITH A PREVIOUS BOARD ORDER
NOTES: ON 10/22/91 USED COCAINE FOR NON-THERAPEUTIC PURPOSES AND WITHOUT A PRESCRIPTION; SHALL NOT APPLY FOR LICENSURE FOR FIVE YEARS. DEFAULT ACTION.

TREPP, ROBERT D DO, LICENSE NUMBER 20A4042, OF SAN DIEGO, CA, WAS DISCIPLINED BY CALIFORNIA ON AUGUST 13, 1993.
DISCIPLINARY ACTION: LICENSE REVOCATION
OFFENSE: DISCIPLINARY ACTION BY ANOTHER STATE OR AGENCY
NOTES: ACTION TAKEN BY ANOTHER STATE FOR SUBSTANCE ABUSE; SEXUALLY ASSAULTING A PATIENT. DISPENSING COCAINE TO A PATIENT FOR NON-MEDICAL PURPOSE.

TREW, GEORGE MD, LICENSE NUMBER MD10301, OF MEDFORD, OR, WAS DISCIPLINED BY OREGON ON JANUARY 4, 1990.
DISCIPLINARY ACTION: EMERGENCY SUSPENSION

TREW, GEORGE DO WAS DISCIPLINED BY OREGON ON APRIL 15, 1991.
DISCIPLINARY ACTION: SURRENDER OF LICENSE
OFFENSE: FAILURE TO COMPLY WITH A PREVIOUS BOARD ORDER
NOTES: ALLEGED VIOLATION PROBATION/VOLUNTARY LIMITATION.

TREW, GEORGE MD, LICENSE NUMBER 0024024, OF MEDFORD, OR, WAS DISCIPLINED BY WASHINGTON ON APRIL 22, 1991.
DISCIPLINARY ACTION: EMERGENCY SUSPENSION
OFFENSE: DISCIPLINARY ACTION BY ANOTHER STATE OR AGENCY
NOTES: ON 8/9/90 OREGON MEDICAL LICENSE WAS REVOKED, REVOCATION STAYED, AND HE WAS PLACED ON 10 YEARS PROBATION WHEN HE WAS FOUND TO HAVE ENGAGED IN THE HABITUAL USE OF ALCOHOL. ON 1/8/90 HE ENTERED AN INPATIENT TREATMENT PROGRAM FOR ALCOHOL ABUSE; WAS DISCHARGED FROM THE PROGRAM ON 2/12/90.

TREW, GEORGE MD, LICENSE NUMBER 0024024, OF MEDFORD, OR, WAS DISCIPLINED BY WASHINGTON ON OCTOBER 2, 1991.
DISCIPLINARY ACTION: LICENSE REVOCATION
OFFENSE: DISCIPLINARY ACTION BY ANOTHER STATE OR AGENCY
NOTES: ON 4/10/91 OREGON ACCEPTED THE SURRENDER OF HIS LICENSE IN LIEU OF FURTHER DISCIPLINARY ACTION FOR VIOLATION OF THE PROVISION OF PREVIOUS BOARD ORDER REQUIRING THAT HE COMPLETELY REFRAIN FROM THE USE OF ALCOHOLIC BEVERAGES.

TREW, GEORGE MD OF LOS ALAMOS, NM, WAS DISCIPLINED BY NEW MEXICO ON DECEMBER 15, 1993.
DISCIPLINARY ACTION: DENIAL OF NEW LICENSE
OFFENSE: PROFESSIONAL MISCONDUCT

TRUSCHEL, TIMOTHY L MD WAS DISCIPLINED BY WASHINGTON ON APRIL 16, 1993.
DISCIPLINARY ACTION: 60-MONTH PROBATION; FINE
OFFENSE: SEXUAL ABUSE OF OR SEXUAL MISCONDUCT WITH A PATIENT
NOTES: HE COMMENCED A SEXUAL RELATIONSHIP WITH A PATIENT DIAGNOSED WITH BIPOLAR DISORDER AND DEPRESSION WITHIN TWO WEEKS OF THEIR LAST THERAPY SESSION. HE IS NOW MARRIED TO THIS WOMAN. FIVE YEAR PROBATION UNDER THE FOLLOWING TERMS AND CONDITIONS: SHALL HAVE NO PERSONAL OR INTIMATE CONTACT WITH ANY PAST, CURRENT, OR FUTURE FEMALE PATIENTS, OTHER THAN HIS WIFE; SHALL NOTIFY ALL CASE MANAGERS, THERAPISTS, AND OTHER MENTAL HEALTH PROFESSIONALS INVOLVED IN REFERRING PATIENTS TO HIM THAT HE IS UNDER DISCIPLINARY ACTION; FOR ALL OF HIS CURRENT AND FUTURE FEMALE PATIENTS HE SHALL TAKE ONE OF THE FOLLOWING STEPS: SHALL PROVIDE WRITTEN NOTICE, THAT HE IS UNDER DISCIPLINARY RESTRICTIONS, SHALL ENSURE THAT THE FEMALE PATIENT READS AND SIGNS THE NOTIFICATION, AND SHALL PLACE THE SIGNED NOTIFICATION IN THE PATIENT'S CHART; SHALL HAVE A CASE MANAGER, THERAPIST, OR OTHER MENTAL HEALTH PROFESSIONAL PRESENT AT ALL TIMES WHEN HE SEES THE PATIENT AND SHALL HAVE THAT PERSON SIGN THE PATIENT'S CHART FOR EACH PATIENT; IF THE FIRST TWO OPTIONS ARE NOT POSSIBLE HE SHALL PLACE AN EXPLANATION IN THE PATIENT'S CHARTS AND HAVE THAT EXPLANATION COUNTERSIGNED BY ANOTHER MENTAL HEALTH PROFESSIONAL SHALL APPEAR BEFORE THE BOARD IN ONE YEAR AND PRESENT PROOF THAT HE IS IN COMPLIANCE; SHALL CONTINUE TO MAKE COMPLIANCE APPEARANCES ANNUALLY UNTIL THE PROBATION IS LIFTED; THE BOARD SHALL MAKE ANNOUNCED ANNUAL VISITS TO HIS PRACTICE TO INSPECT OFFICE AND OR MEDICAL RECORDS, INTERVIEW STAFF OR SUPERVISORS, AND REVIEW OTHER ASPECTS OF HIS PRACTICE; SHALL INFORM THE BOARD IN WRITING OF CHANGES IN HIS PRACTICE AND RESIDENCE ADDRESS; MUST NOTIFY THE BOARD IF HE LEAVES TO RESIDE OR PRACTICE OUTSIDE OF WASHINGTON; THE PERIOD OF PROBATION SHALL BE TOLLED FOR ANY TIME DURING WHICH HE RESIDES AND/OR PRACTICES OUTSIDE OF THE STATE; SHALL COMPLETE A TOTAL OF 25 COURSE HOURS OF BOARD APPROVED CONTINUING MEDICAL EDUCATION IN THE AREAS OF APPROPRIATE PHYSICIAN-PATIENT RELATIONSHIPS, TRANSFERENCE, AND COUNTER-TRANSFERENCE, AND/OR MEDICAL ETHICS WITHIN TWO YEARS. ; SHALL PAY A $500 FINE; MAY PETITION THE BOARD FOR A CHANGE IN TERMS AND CONDITIONS OF THIS ORDER IN NO SOONER THAN ONE YEAR.

TRUSCHEL, TIMOTHY L MD, LICENSE NUMBER 0041020, OF TUMWATER, WA, WAS DISCIPLINED BY FLORIDA ON AUGUST 17, 1994.
DISCIPLINARY ACTION: SURRENDER OF LICENSE
OFFENSE: DISCIPLINARY ACTION BY ANOTHER STATE OR AGENCY
NOTES: CHARGED WITH HAVING LICENSE ACTED UPON BY ANOTHER JURISDICTION AND FAILING TO NOTIFY THE BOARD OF THIS WITHIN 30 DAYS; FAILED TO NOTIFY BOARD OF ADDRESS CHANGE. VOLUNTARY RELINQUISHMENT OF LICENSE. AGREES NEVER AGAIN TO APPLY FOR LICENSURE AS A PHYSICIAN IN FLORIDA.

TRUSCHEL, TIMOTHY L MD, LICENSE NUMBER 0G60326, OF OLYMPIA, WA, WAS DISCIPLINED BY CALIFORNIA ON OCTOBER 20, 1994.
DISCIPLINARY ACTION: SURRENDER OF LICENSE
NOTES: WHILE CHARGES PENDING.

TUOHY, CEDRIC E M JR MD, LICENSE NUMBER 0004792, OF SNOHOMISH, WA, WAS DISCIPLINED BY WASHINGTON ON DECEMBER 13, 1996.
DISCIPLINARY ACTION: SURRENDER OF LICENSE
NOTES: AGREEMENT TO RETIRE.

TURPIN, JACK T MD, DATE OF BIRTH MAY 8, 1926, OF PO BOX 888, MONROE, WA, WAS DISCIPLINED BY MEDICARE ON FEBRUARY 26,

- WASHINGTON -

1990.
DISCIPLINARY ACTION: EXCLUSION FROM THE MEDICARE AND/OR MEDICAID PROGRAMS
OFFENSE: DISCIPLINARY ACTION BY ANOTHER STATE OR AGENCY
NOTES: LICENSE REVOCATION OR SUSPENSION.

TUURA, JAMES L MD OF 21616 76TH AVENUE W SUITE 200, EDMONDS, WA, WAS DISCIPLINED BY DEA ON NOVEMBER 17, 1993.
DISCIPLINARY ACTION: SURRENDER OF CONTROLLED SUBSTANCE LICENSE
NOTES: DISCIPLINARY BOARD ORDERED RETIREMENT AND SURRENDER OF CONTROLLED SUBSTANCES AND LEGEND DRUG PRESCRIBING PRIVILEGES.

TUURA, JAMES L MD, LICENSE NUMBER 0008643, OF EDMONDS, WA, WAS DISCIPLINED BY WASHINGTON ON MARCH 4, 1994.
DISCIPLINARY ACTION: SURRENDER OF LICENSE
OFFENSE: OVERPRESCRIBING OR MISPRESCRIBING DRUGS
NOTES: IN LIEU OF THE ISSUANCE OF A STATEMENT OF CHARGES FOLLOWING AN INVESTIGATION OF INAPPROPRIATE PRESCRIBING.

UHM, DO SUNG MD WAS DISCIPLINED BY WASHINGTON ON SEPTEMBER 2, 1987.
DISCIPLINARY ACTION: 36-MONTH PROBATION; 36-MONTH RESTRICTION PLACED ON LICENSE
OFFENSE: LOSS OR RESTRICTION OF HOSPITAL PRIVILEGES
NOTES: GAVE SUBSTANDARD CARE TO TWO PATIENTS. IN THE FIRST HE FAILED TO APPROPRIATELY TREAT THE SIGNS OF PRE-ECLAMPSIA INCLUDING ATTENDING THE PATIENT WHOSE BLOOD PRESSURE WAS 220/130; IN THE SECOND HE FAILED TO PROPERLY MONITOR THE PATIENT'S FLUID AND ELECTROLYTE BALANCE, DELAYING A D&C WHILE THE PATIENT CONTINUED TO BLEED; HOSPITAL PRIVILEGES WERE RESTRICTED AT VALLEY MEDICAL CENTER ON 11/21/85; FOR EACH YEAR OF PROBATION WILL OBTAIN 50 HOURS OF CONTINUING MEDICAL EDUCATION IN THE AREA OF DIAGNOSIS AND TREATMENT OF OB/GYN PATIENTS; SHALL OBTAIN A SECOND OPINION ON ANY HIGH RISK CASES; SUPERVISOR WILL REPORT TO THE BOARD ON A QUARTERLY BASIS; SHALL COOPERATE WITH RANDOM REVIEW OF HIS RECORDS.

VAID, VEDBRAT MD, LICENSE NUMBER 0010943, OF SPOKANE, WA, WAS DISCIPLINED BY WASHINGTON ON OCTOBER 19, 1994.
DISCIPLINARY ACTION: 36-MONTH PROBATION; FINE
NOTES: MUST HAVE A CHAPERON PRESENT WHEN TREATING PATENTS; MUST COMPLETE 10 HOURS OF CATEGORY I CONTINUING MEDICAL EDUCATION IN MEDICAL ETHICS; MUST COMPLETE 10 HOURS OF EDUCATION AND TRAINING IN THE AREA OF SEXUAL HARASSMENT, GENDER SENSITIVITY AND/OR ANGER MANAGEMENT AND PAY A $1,000 FINE.

VASQUEZ, FRANCIS A MD, DATE OF BIRTH FEBRUARY 27, 1929, LICENSE NUMBER 0017373, WAS DISCIPLINED BY IOWA ON AUGUST 1, 1989.
DISCIPLINARY ACTION: LICENSE SUSPENSION
NOTES: INDEFINITE SUSPENSION. MAY FILE AN APPLICATION FOR REINSTATEMENT IN ONE YEAR. ON 1/25/91 THE BOARD DENIED HIS REQUEST FOR REINSTATEMENT STATING THAT HE FAILED TO ESTABLISH THAT THE BASIS FOR THE SUSPENSION NO LONGER EXISTS.

VASQUEZ, FRANCIS A MD, DATE OF BIRTH FEBRUARY 27, 1929, OF 513 KNOLLWOOD DRIVE SE, CEDAR RAPIDS, IA, WAS DISCIPLINED BY MEDICARE ON DECEMBER 13, 1989.
DISCIPLINARY ACTION: EXCLUSION FROM THE MEDICARE AND/OR MEDICAID PROGRAMS
OFFENSE: DISCIPLINARY ACTION BY ANOTHER STATE OR AGENCY
NOTES: LICENSE REVOCATION OR SUSPENSION.

VASQUEZ, FRANCIS A MD, LICENSE NUMBER 0005320, WAS DISCIPLINED BY WASHINGTON ON MARCH 19, 1992.
DISCIPLINARY ACTION: LICENSE SUSPENSION
NOTES: INDEFINITE SUSPENSION.

VASQUEZ, FRANCIS A MD, DATE OF BIRTH FEBRUARY 27, 1929, LICENSE NUMBER 0017373, OF 717 A AVENUE NE, CEDAR RAPIDS, IA, WAS DISCIPLINED BY IOWA ON SEPTEMBER 3, 1992.
DISCIPLINARY ACTION: PROBATION; RESTRICTION PLACED ON LICENSE
OFFENSE: SEXUAL ABUSE OF OR SEXUAL MISCONDUCT WITH A PATIENT
NOTES: HAS ADMITTED TO "AFFAIRS" WITH SIX PATIENTS OVER A 20 YEAR PERIOD, AND ADDITIONAL SEXUAL CONTACT WITH FOUR TO FIVE OTHERS; HAS COME TO ACCEPT FULL RESPONSIBILITY FOR HIS ACTIONS AND ACKNOWLEDGES THAT HE INITIATED THE SEXUAL RELATIONSHIPS WITH THE PATIENTS; APPRECIATES THAT PATIENTS WERE SEVERELY HARMED BY HIS ACTIONS. LICENSE REINSTATED ON INDEFINITE PROBATION WITH CERTAIN TERMS AND CONDITIONS: MAY NOT TREAT FEMALE PATIENTS; MUST PRACTICE PSYCHIATRY IN A CLINIC OR INSTITUTIONAL SETTING; IF HE LEAVES IOWA MUST IMMEDIATELY NOTIFY THE BOARD AND SURRENDER HIS LICENSE; SHALL WITHIN 30 DAYS SUBMIT NAMES OF THREE LICENSED PSYCHIATRISTS OR PSYCHOLOGISTS TO OBTAIN BOARD APPROVAL; SHALL CONTINUE COUNSELING WITH QUARTERLY REPORTS; SHALL ATTEND SEXUAL ADDICTS ANONYMOUS ON A WEEKLY BASIS; SHALL NOTIFY THE BOARD IF HE CHANGES ADDRESS; SHALL SUBMIT QUARTERLY REPORTS THAT HE IS IN COMPLIANCE; SHALL MAKE APPEARANCES BEFORE THE BOARD ANNUALLY AND/OR UPON REQUEST; MAY NOT APPLY FOR AN UNRESTRICTED LICENSE FOR FIVE YEARS.

VILLANUEVA, CESAR L MD, LICENSE NUMBER 0012981, OF PRAIRIE VILLAGE, KS, WAS DISCIPLINED BY WASHINGTON ON AUGUST 16, 1991.
DISCIPLINARY ACTION: SURRENDER OF LICENSE
OFFENSE: DISCIPLINARY ACTION BY ANOTHER STATE OR AGENCY
NOTES: HE ENTERED INTO A PROBATION AGREEMENT WITH THE MISSOURI BOARD ON 10/23/87 RESTRICTING HIS LICENSE.

VISKOVITCH, BORKO MD, LICENSE NUMBER 0018932, OF RICHLAND, WA, WAS DISCIPLINED BY WASHINGTON ON JUNE 21, 1994.
DISCIPLINARY ACTION: LICENSE REVOCATION
OFFENSE: SUBSTANDARD CARE, INCOMPETENCE, OR NEGLIGENCE
NOTES: FINDINGS OF NEGLIGENCE.

VO, THUONG MD OF 9081 BOLSA AVENUE, WESTMINSTER, CA, WAS DISCIPLINED BY MEDICARE ON FEBRUARY 9, 1987.
DISCIPLINARY ACTION: 120-MONTH EXCLUSION FROM THE MEDICARE AND/OR MEDICAID PROGRAMS
OFFENSE: CRIMINAL CONVICTION OR PLEA OF GUILTY, NOLO CONTENDERE, OR NO CONTEST TO A CRIME
NOTES: PROGRAM-RELATED CONVICTION.

VO, THUONG MD, LICENSE NUMBER 0A37851, OF SANTA ANA, CA, WAS DISCIPLINED BY CALIFORNIA ON OCTOBER 28, 1991.
DISCIPLINARY ACTION: LICENSE REVOCATION
OFFENSE: CRIMINAL CONVICTION OR PLEA OF GUILTY, NOLO CONTENDERE, OR NO CONTEST TO A CRIME
NOTES: MEDI-CAL FRAUD CONVICTION. JUDICIAL REVIEW FILED, NO STAY ORDER.

VO, THUONG MD, LICENSE NUMBER 0022074, OF 3839 W FIRST ST STE B8, SANTA ANA, CA, WAS DISCIPLINED BY GEORGIA ON MARCH 27, 1992.
DISCIPLINARY ACTION: NONRENEWAL OF LICENSE
OFFENSE: DISCIPLINARY ACTION BY ANOTHER STATE OR AGENCY

NOTES: DISCIPLINARY ACTION IN CALIFORNIA. ADMINISTRATIVE REVOCATION FOR FAILURE TO RENEW.

VO, THUONG MD WAS DISCIPLINED BY WASHINGTON ON APRIL 16, 1993.
DISCIPLINARY ACTION: LICENSE REVOCATION
OFFENSE: DISCIPLINARY ACTION BY ANOTHER STATE OR AGENCY
NOTES: PLED GUILTY IN CALIFORNIA TO GRAND THEFT, CONSPIRACY AND FALSE CLAIMS, CONVICTED ON 12/05/86, SENTENCED TO ONE YEAR IN ORANGE COUNTY JAIL, PLACED ON FIVE YEARS PROBATION, AND ORDERED TO PAY $25,000 IN RESTITUTION. THE CONVICTION WAS BASED UPON DEFRAUDING THE MEDI-CAL SYSTEM AND FELONIOUSLY TAKING MONEY FROM THE STATE OF CALIFORNIA AND COMPUTER SCIENCES CORPORATION. CALIFORNIA REVOKED HIS LICENSE ON 10/28/91. SHALL CEASE CARE AND TREATMENT OF PATIENTS IN WASHINGTON; SHALL CONCLUDE ALL BUSINESS AND FORMALLY CLOSE HIS PRACTICE IN NO LATER THAN 90 DAYS; SHALL PETITION THE BOARD IN WRITING FOR AUTHORIZATION TO APPLY FOR LICENSURE IF HE WISHES TO REAPPLY, BUT IN NO SOONER THAN ONE YEAR.

VO, THUONG MD OF 19932 ROTHERT LANDE, HUNTINGTON BEACH, CA, WAS DISCIPLINED BY DEA ON SEPTEMBER 3, 1993.
DISCIPLINARY ACTION: REVOCATION OF CONTROLLED SUBSTANCE LICENSE
OFFENSE: DISCIPLINARY ACTION BY ANOTHER STATE OR AGENCY
NOTES: ON 9/19/91 MEDICAL BOARD OF CALIFORNIA REVOKED HIS PHYSICIAN AND SURGEON CERTIFICATE; HE IS NOT AUTHORIZED TO HANDLE CONTROLLED SUBSTANCES IN CALIFORNIA.

VO, THUONG MD OF 3839 W FIRST ST, SANTA ANA, CA, WAS DISCIPLINED BY DEA ON SEPTEMBER 17, 1993.
DISCIPLINARY ACTION: REVOCATION OF CONTROLLED SUBSTANCE LICENSE
OFFENSE: DISCIPLINARY ACTION BY ANOTHER STATE OR AGENCY
NOTES: REVOCATION OF CALIFORNIA LICENSE 10/28/91. FILED FALSE MEDI-CAL CLAIMS.

VOEGTLIN, JOSEPH W MD WAS DISCIPLINED BY WASHINGTON ON AUGUST 20, 1993.
DISCIPLINARY ACTION: SURRENDER OF LICENSE
NOTES: UNDER INVESTIGATION CONCERNING HIS ABILITY TO PRACTICE MEDICINE WITH REASONABLE SKILL AND SAFETY TO PATIENTS. VOLUNTARY RETIREMENT EFFECTIVE 7/92 AND HAD NO PLANS TO RESUME HIS MEDICAL PRACTICE: RETIREMENT SHALL BE PERMANENT; MAY RESUME PRACTICE ONLY WITH PRIOR BOARD APPROVAL; WILL NOTIFY THE BOARD IF HE PLANS TO RESUME PRACTICE IN THIS OR ANY OTHER JURISDICTION; INVESTIGATION TERMINATED.

VON REIS VIEK, CHRISTA MD, LICENSE NUMBER 026973L, OF 540 CANTERSHIRE PLACE, BREMERTON, WA, WAS DISCIPLINED BY PENNSYLVANIA ON OCTOBER 25, 1991.
DISCIPLINARY ACTION: LICENSE SUSPENSION
OFFENSE: CRIMINAL CONVICTION OR PLEA OF GUILTY, NOLO CONTENDERE, OR NO CONTEST TO A CRIME
NOTES: ON 5/12/89 SHE WROTE TWO PRESCRIPTIONS, ONE OF WHICH WAS FOR DALMANE, TO A PERSON NOT A PATIENT BUT A MEMBER OF HER SUPPORT GROUP; THE DEA NUMBER USED WAS EXPIRED. ON 5/28/91 SHE PLED GUILTY TO OBTAINING A CONTROLLED SUBSTANCE BY FRAUD, THE CONTROLLED SUBSTANCE BEING DALMANE, A SCHEDULE IV CONTROLLED SUBSTANCE; SHE WAS SENTENCED TO 24 MONTHS COMMUNITY SUPERVISION FOLLOWING RELEASE FROM CONFINEMENT, 20 DAYS CONFINEMENT AND/OR 160 HOURS OF COMMUNITY SERVICE, PLUS FINES AND COST.

VU, DAM MD, LICENSE NUMBER MD12474, OF PORTLAND, OR, WAS DISCIPLINED BY OREGON ON JANUARY 25, 1994.
DISCIPLINARY ACTION: LICENSE REVOCATION

VU, DAM MD, LICENSE NUMBER 0018907, OF BEAVERTON, OR, WAS DISCIPLINED BY WASHINGTON ON DECEMBER 16, 1994.
DISCIPLINARY ACTION: SURRENDER OF LICENSE

VU, DAM MD, DATE OF BIRTH SEPTEMBER 9, 1953, OF 15474 N W WHITE FOX DRIVE, BEAVERTON, OR, WAS DISCIPLINED BY MEDICARE ON AUGUST 3, 1995.
DISCIPLINARY ACTION: 36-MONTH EXCLUSION FROM THE MEDICARE AND/OR MEDICAID PROGRAMS
OFFENSE: CRIMINAL CONVICTION OR PLEA OF GUILTY, NOLO CONTENDERE, OR NO CONTEST TO A CRIME
NOTES: CONVICTED OF A CRIME RELATED TO THE DELIVERY OF HEALTH CARE OR FINANCIAL MISCONDUCT INVOLVING A GOVERNMENT-OPERATED PROGRAM.

WALLACE, JAMES F MD WAS DISCIPLINED BY WASHINGTON ON DECEMBER 11, 1987.
DISCIPLINARY ACTION: REQUIRED TO TAKE ADDITIONAL MEDICAL EDUCATION; CEASE AND DESIST ORDER
OFFENSE: OVERPRESCRIBING OR MISPRESCRIBING DRUGS
NOTES: TREATED A PATIENT FOR CHRONIC ANXIETY; IN RENDERING SUCH TREATMENT HE ALLEGEDLY USED DRUGS IN INAPPROPRIATE AND NEGLIGENT MANNER, RESULTING IN SERIOUS HARM TO THE PATIENT; AGREES TO DESIST FROM ALLEGED ACTIONS AND PROVIDE PROOF HE HAS ATTENDED CONFERENCE ON MANAGEMENT OF CHRONIC PAIN OR COMPARABLE PROGRAM APPROVED BY BOARD

WALLS, DAVID MD WAS DISCIPLINED BY WASHINGTON ON MAY 21, 1990.
DISCIPLINARY ACTION: SURRENDER OF LICENSE
OFFENSE: SUBSTANCE ABUSE
NOTES: SUFFERS FROM CHEMICAL DEPENDENCY; CONTINUES TO CONSUME ALCOHOL AND BE UNABLE TO ATTEND TO HIS MEDICAL PRACTICE AS A RESULT OF THIS CONSUMPTION. HE RETIRED FROM MEDICAL PRACTICE EFFECTIVE 01/31/90; RETIREMENT IS PERMANENT.

WARNER, GLENN A MD, LICENSE NUMBER 0003877, OF SEATTLE, WA, WAS DISCIPLINED BY WASHINGTON ON JULY 14, 1995.
DISCIPLINARY ACTION: LICENSE REVOCATION
OFFENSE: SUBSTANDARD CARE, INCOMPETENCE, OR NEGLIGENCE
NOTES: PROVIDED SUBSTANDARD CARE TO SEVERAL PATIENTS. REVOCATION STAYED BY SUPERIOR COURT AND HE WAS PERMITTED TO PRACTICE PENDING THE APPEAL OF THE COMMISSION ORDER UNDER THE FOLLOWING CONDITIONS: SHALL NOT PRACTICE RADIATION ONCOLOGY; SHALL PERMIT ALL PATIENT CHARTS TO BE REVIEWED BY A BOARD DESIGNATED PHYSICIAN; SHALL PROVIDE ONCOLOGICAL CARE CONSISTENT WITH THE STANDARD OF CARE IN THE MEDICAL COMMUNITY; SHALL OBTAIN WRITTEN INFORMED CONSENT BEFORE USING NON-TRADITIONAL METHODS OF DIAGNOSIS AND TREATMENT.

WATTS, ARTHUR B MD OF BELLINGHAM, WA, WAS DISCIPLINED BY WASHINGTON ON SEPTEMBER 18, 1987.
DISCIPLINARY ACTION: RESTRICTION PLACED ON LICENSE
OFFENSE: SUBSTANDARD CARE, INCOMPETENCE, OR NEGLIGENCE
NOTES: ALLEGEDLY HAS BEEN INCOMPETENT OR NEGLIGENT IN THE PRACTICE OF MEDICINE RESULTING IN SERIOUS HARM TO 4 PATIENTS IN JULY 1978; RESTRICTIONS: SHALL NOT BE THE PRIMARY PHYSICIAN IN ANY OBSTETRICAL OR SURGICAL SETTING; WHEN PATIENTS ARE ADMITTED TO HOSPITAL HE SHALL SEEK APPROPRIATE CONSULTATION WITH PHYSICIAN OF APPROPRIATE SPECIALITY WITHIN 12 HOURS OF

ADMISSION; SHALL COMPLY WITH ALL PRIOR DIRECTIVES REGARDING LIMITATIONS ON PRACTICE IN HOSPITALS; SHALL INFORM ANY HOSPITAL WHERE HE PRACTICES OF THESE RESTRICTIONS;

WENBERG, KENNETH F MD, LICENSE NUMBER 0025365, OF CAMANO, WA, WAS DISCIPLINED BY WASHINGTON ON JANUARY 18, 1994.
OFFENSE: DISCIPLINARY ACTION BY ANOTHER STATE OR AGENCY
NOTES: VOLUNTARY LIMITATION IMPOSED ON HIS LICENSE BY OREGON. MUST COMPLY WITH ALL TERMS AND CONDITIONS IMPOSED BY THE STATE OF OREGON.

WENBERG, KENNETH FRED MD, LICENSE NUMBER MD14131, OF STANWOOD, OR, WAS DISCIPLINED BY OREGON ON JANUARY 18, 1989.
DISCIPLINARY ACTION: RESTRICTION PLACED ON LICENSE

WENBERG, KENNETH FRED MD, LICENSE NUMBER MD14131, OF HEPPNER, OR, WAS DISCIPLINED BY OREGON ON FEBRUARY 8, 1989.
DISCIPLINARY ACTION: RESTRICTION PLACED ON LICENSE
NOTES: NO OBSTETRICS PRACTICE. NO LONGER RESTRICTED AS OF 1/28/92.

WHITE, JEFFREY RICHARD MD, DATE OF BIRTH JULY 9, 1956, OF NORTH 27108 BEAR LAKE ROAD, CHATTAROY, WA, WAS DISCIPLINED BY MEDICARE ON MAY 4, 1995.
DISCIPLINARY ACTION: EXCLUSION FROM THE MEDICARE AND/OR MEDICAID PROGRAMS
OFFENSE: FAILURE TO COMPLY WITH A PROFESSIONAL RULE
NOTES: DEFAULTED ON PUBLIC HEALTH SERVICE EDUCATION LOAN. REINSTATED ON 6/27/95.

WHITE, MANUEL MD, DATE OF BIRTH JUNE 2, 1916, OF PO BOX 5058, HELENA, MT, WAS DISCIPLINED BY MONTANA ON SEPTEMBER 8, 1992.
DISCIPLINARY ACTION: DENIAL OF NEW LICENSE
OFFENSE: PROVIDING FALSE INFORMATION TO THE BOARD
NOTES: FRAUD ON APPLICATION, NEGLIGENCE, FALSIFICATION OF PATIENT RECORDS, MENTAL INABILITY TO SAFELY ENGAGE IN PRACTICE OF MEDICINE, LACK OF GOOD MORAL CHARACTER.

WHITE, MANUEL MD, LICENSE NUMBER 0004393, WAS DISCIPLINED BY WASHINGTON ON MARCH 19, 1993.
DISCIPLINARY ACTION: SURRENDER OF LICENSE
OFFENSE: SUBSTANDARD CARE, INCOMPETENCE, OR NEGLIGENCE
NOTES: BETWEEN 1986 AND 1991 HE FAILED TO CONFORM HIS CONDUCT TO GENERALLY ACCEPTED STANDARDS OF CLINICAL PROFESSIONAL PRACTICE IN THAT HE EXHIBITED IMPAIRED SURGICAL JUDGEMENT AND DIAGNOSTIC SKILLS, INAPPROPRIATE OR UNTIMELY WORK-UP OF PATIENTS, MEDICATION ERROR AND NON-STERILE TECHNIQUES AND COMMUNICATION PROBLEMS AFFECTING PATIENT CARE. RETIREMENT FROM PRACTICE IN WASHINGTON HAS ALREADY OCCURRED AND HE HAS NO PLANS TO RESUME PRACTICE; HE AGREES TO NOTIFY THE BOARD IF HE PLANS TO RESUME PRACTICE IN WASHINGTON.

WILLIAMS, DAVID V MD OF 208 W. LOCUST, CENTRALIA, WA, WAS DISCIPLINED BY MEDICARE ON FEBRUARY 27, 1987.
DISCIPLINARY ACTION: FINE
OFFENSE: SUBSTANDARD CARE, INCOMPETENCE, OR NEGLIGENCE
NOTES: FINED $2,773.98; INADEQUATE TREATMENT OF ONE PATIENT'S HYPOKALEMIA, CONGESTIVE HEART FAILURE, SEPSIS AND RENAL DYSFUNCTION; PATIENT DIED

WILLIAMS, JOYCE L MD OF NORTH BEND, KING COUNTY, WA, WAS DISCIPLINED BY WASHINGTON ON JANUARY 27, 1992.
DISCIPLINARY ACTION: LICENSE SUSPENSION

WILLIAMS, JOYCE L MD WAS DISCIPLINED BY WASHINGTON ON JULY 24, 1992.
DISCIPLINARY ACTION: RESTRICTION PLACED ON LICENSE
NOTES: REQUIRED TO MEET SPECIFIC TERMS AND CONDITIONS IN ORDER TO RECEIVE CONDITIONAL LICENSE. MODIFICATIONS TO THE ORDER MAY BE PETITIONED TO THE BOARD NO LESS THAN SIX MONTHS FROM THE DATE OF ORDER.

WILLIAMS, JOYCE LAREE MD, DATE OF BIRTH MAY 30, 1955, LICENSE NUMBER 0007542, OF 181-12TH STREET, SW, SIDNEY, MT, WAS DISCIPLINED BY MONTANA ON OCTOBER 6, 1993.
DISCIPLINARY ACTION: RESTRICTION PLACED ON LICENSE
OFFENSE: DISCIPLINARY ACTION BY ANOTHER STATE OR AGENCY
NOTES: ON 06/07/94, AFTER COMPLIANCE WITH ORIGINAL AGREEMENT, AMENDMENT ADDED TO ALLOW DR. WILLIAMS TO TAKE TEN INSTEAD OF SIX DELIVERIES A MONTH. ON 11/31/94 AMENDMENT REMOVED ALL RESTRICTIONS.

WILLIAMS, VIRGINIA MD, LICENSE NUMBER 0014808, OF EDMONDS, WA, WAS DISCIPLINED BY WASHINGTON ON APRIL 30, 1991.
DISCIPLINARY ACTION: EMERGENCY SUSPENSION
OFFENSE: SUBSTANCE ABUSE
NOTES: WAS TREATED FOR CHEMICAL DEPENDENCY IN 7/87 AND SIGNED A CONTRACT WITH THE WASHINGTON MONITORED TREATMENT PROGRAM ON 7/1/87; WAS SUBSEQUENTLY TREATED FOR CHEMICAL DEPENDENCY IN 4/88; ON 1/9/91 SHE APPEARED FOR WORK IN RESPONSE TO A SURGICAL BACK-UP CALL FOR AN ANESTHESIOLOGIST; WAS OBSERVED TO HAVE SLURRED SPEECH AND ALCOHOL ON HER BREATH; SUBMITTED TO A BLOOD ALCOHOL TEST WHICH REVEALED A LEVEL OF .032%. PRIVILEGES WERE SUSPENDED AT GENERAL HOSPITAL AND PROVIDENCE HOSPITAL ON 1/14/91; ENTERED FURTHER TREATMENT ON 1/16/91.

WILLIAMS, VIRGINIA MD, LICENSE NUMBER 0014808, WAS DISCIPLINED BY WASHINGTON ON APRIL 16, 1993.
DISCIPLINARY ACTION: PROBATION; RESTRICTION PLACED ON LICENSE
OFFENSE: SUBSTANCE ABUSE
NOTES: TREATED FOR CHEMICAL DEPENDENCY AND RELAPSED ON A FEW OCCASIONS BETWEEN 7/87 AND 2/92; ON 1/14/91 HER HOSPITAL PRIVILEGES WERE SUSPENDED FOR HAVING RESPONDED TO A SURGICAL BACK-UP CALL AND SUBSEQUENTLY TESTING positive FOR ALCOHOL. HAS MAINTAINED SOBRIETY SINCE 2/12/92. INDEFINITE SUSPENSION, STAYED AS PROBATION UNDER THE FOLLOWING TERMS AND CONDITIONS: SHALL COMPLETELY ABSTAIN FROM THE POSSESSION OR USE OF ALCOHOL BEVERAGES AND CONROLLED SUBSTANCES UNLESS PRESCRIBED BY ANOTHER PHYSICIAN CERTIFIED IN ADDICTION MEDICINE FOR LEGITIMATE THERAPEUTIC PURPOSE; HER PRACTICE SHALL BE IN A GROUP SETTING ONLY; AGREES TO FOLLOW THE RECOMMENDATIONS OF HER TREATING PSYCHIATRIST REGARDING PSYCHOTHERAPEUTIC MEDICATIONS; SHALL NOT PRESCRIBE LEGEND OR CONTROLLED SUBSTANCES FOR HER OWN USE, FOR ANY MEMBER OF HER FAMILY OR FOR FRIENDS; SHALL GIVE A COPY OF THIS ORDER TO ALL OF HER TREATING PHYSICIANS/ AND OR DENTISTS PRIOR TO TREATMENT, ALL MEMBERS OF ANY ANESTHESIOLOGY GROUP WITH WHICH SHE IS PRACTICING, ALL HOSPITAL ADMINISTRATORS, CHIEFS OF STAFF, ANESTHESIOLOGY, SURGERY, AND OPERATING ROOM SUPERVISORS AT ANY INSTITUTION AT WHICH SHE HAS PRIVILEGES; SHALL EXECUTE A CONTRACT AND MAINTAIN SATISFACTORY STATUS WITH THE WASHINGTON PHYSICIAN HEALTH PROGRAM (WPHP) AND SHALL

COMPLY WITH ALL OF THE REQUIREMENTS OF THAT PROGRAM, AS WELL AS COMPLYING WITH THE REQUIREMENTS OF ANY EMPLOYER CONTRACT/AGREEMENT ENTERED INTO WITH AN EMPLOYER; SHALL SUBMIT TO RANDOM URINALYSIS OR BLOOD TESTS AS REQUIRED TO DO SO BY THE WPHP CONTRACT AND/OR UPON BOARD REQUEST; AGREES THAT BOTH ORAL AND WRITTEN COMMUNICATION REGARDING HER COMPLIANCE WITH THE WPHP CONTRACT AND HER WORK PERFORMANCE MAY BE SHARED WITH ANY HOSPITAL(S) OR OTHER HEALTH CARE FACILITIES OR ORGANIZATIONS AT WHICH SHE HAS PRIVILEGES OR PROVIDES MEDICAL SERVICES; AGREES SHE WILL NOTIFY THE BOARD OF HER EMPLOYMENT AND/OR PRACTICE ARRANGEMENT AND WILL FURTHER NOTIFY THE BOARD OF ANY CHANGE IN THE LOCATION OR NATURE OF HER PRACTICE; SHALL HAVE THE CHIEF OF STAFF AND WPHP SUBMIT REPORTS EVERY SIX MONTHS FOR TWO YEARS; SHALL CONTINUE WITH ONGOING MONTHLY PSYCHOTHERAPY WITH BOARD APPROVED PSYCHOTHERAPIST AND ONGOING WEEKLY THERAPY WITH BOARD APPROVED THERAPIST/HEALTH CARE COUNSELOR WHO WILL SUPPLY REGULAR REPORTS; SHALL ATTEND, WITHIN ONE YEAR A BOARD APPROVED ANESTHESIOLOGY REVIEW/REFRESHER COURSE OF 25-50 CONTINUING MEDICAL EDUCATION CREDITS; MAY PETITION FOR A CHANGE IN THE TERMS/CONDITIONS IN NO SOONER THAN ONE YEAR; SHALL APPEAR BEFORE THE BOARD IN SIX MONTHS AND PRESENT PROOF THAT SHE IS IN COMPLIANCE; SHALL INFORM THE BOARD IN WRITING IF SHE LEAVES WASHINGTON. ON 3/4/94 BOARD GRANTED HER PETITION TO MODIFY THIS ORDER AND ALLOW HER TO PRACTICE IN THE AREA OF PEDIATRICS. ALL OTHER CONDITIONS OF THIS ORDER REMAIN IN EFFECT. ON 6/12/95 THE COMMISSION GRANTED HER REQUEST TO MODIFY THIS ORDER TO PERMIT HER TO BE EMPLOYED AT THE CHEK CLINIC IN LYNWOOD WASHINGTON. ON 3/8/96 THE COMMISSION GRANTED HER REQUEST TO MODIFY THIS ORDER TO PERMIT HER TO SEEK EMPLOYMENT AT ANY CHEC CLINIC. ON 9/11/97 BOARD GRANTED HER REQUEST TO TERMINATE THIS ORDER.

WILSON, DAVID Q MD, LICENSE NUMBER 0015722, OF SEATTLE, WA, WAS DISCIPLINED BY WASHINGTON ON NOVEMBER 6, 1992.
DISCIPLINARY ACTION: RESTRICTION PLACED ON LICENSE
OFFENSE: PROFESSIONAL MISCONDUCT
NOTES: ALLEGATIONS OF MORAL TURPITUDE AND ABUSE OF A CLIENT. LICENSE LIMITED PENDING FURTHER DISCIPLINARY PROCEEDINGS: SHALL HAVE NO CONTACT WITH PATIENTS; SHALL NOT PRESCRIBE MEDICATION FOR, NOR CONSULT WITH OTHER PHYSICIANS ABOUT ANY PATIENT; PRACTICE SHALL BE LIMITED TO REVIEWING MEDICAL RECORDS AND PROVIDING CONSULTATION BASED ON HIS REVIEW OF RECORDS FOR THE SOCIAL SECURITY ADMINISTRATION.

WILSON, DAVID Q MD, LICENSE NUMBER 0015722, OF SEATTLE, WA, WAS DISCIPLINED BY WASHINGTON ON FEBRUARY 19, 1993.
DISCIPLINARY ACTION: RESTRICTION PLACED ON LICENSE
OFFENSE: CRIMINAL CONVICTION OR PLEA OF GUILTY, NOLO CONTENDERE, OR NO CONTEST TO A CRIME
NOTES: SEXUALLY MOLESTED A CHILD BETWEEN 1985 AND 1991 TO WHOM HE HAD PROVIDED MEDICAL TREATMENT; PLED GUILTY TO THREE COUNTS OF CHILD MOLESTATION. CONDITIONS ON LICENSE AS FOLLOWS: SHALL HAVE NO CONTACT WITH PATIENTS; SHALL NOT PRESCRIBE MEDICATION FOR, PROVIDE DIRECT SERVICE TO NOR CONSULT WITH OTHER PHYSICIANS ABOUT ANY PATIENT EXCEPT IN AN EMERGENCY SITUATION; SHALL BE LIMITED TO REVIEWING MEDICAL RECORDS AND PROVIDING CONSULTATION BASED ON HIS REVIEW OF RECORDS FOR THE SOCIAL SECURITY ADMINISTRATION; SHALL COMPLY WITH ANY COUNT ORDER ISSUED WHICH ADDRESSES RESTITUTION FOR HIS VICTIM; SHALL RECEIVE OUTPATIENT SEX OFFENDER TREATMENT; SHALL INFORM THE BOARD IF HE CHANGES HIS RESIDENCE ADDRESS; SHALL PAY A $2,000 FINE.

WIMBERGER, HERBERT C MD, LICENSE NUMBER 0008293, OF SEATTLE, WA, WAS DISCIPLINED BY WASHINGTON ON DECEMBER 16, 1994.
DISCIPLINARY ACTION: FINE; RESTRICTION PLACED ON LICENSE
OFFENSE: SEXUAL ABUSE OF OR SEXUAL MISCONDUCT WITH A PATIENT
NOTES: ALLEGATIONS OF SEXUAL CONTACT WITH TWO PATIENTS BETWEEN 1967 AND 1973. MUST PROVIDE THERAPY TO MALES AND COUPLES ONLY, UNDERGO THERAPY BY A THERAPIST APPROVED BY THE COMMISSION AND PAY A $2,000 FINE. ON 3/31/97 BOARD GRANTED HIS REQUEST TO TERMINATE THIS ORDER AND LICENSE IS UNRESTRICTED.

WOLNER-HANSSEN, PAL MD, LICENSE NUMBER 0021388, OF SWEDEN, WAS DISCIPLINED BY WASHINGTON ON FEBRUARY 19, 1993.
OFFENSE: SUBSTANDARD CARE, INCOMPETENCE, OR NEGLIGENCE
NOTES: HAD A SEXUAL RELATIONSHIP WITH HIS RESEARCH ASSISTANT FROM 1986 TO 1990; PROVIDED MEDICAL TREATMENT TO HER AT THIS TIME IN THAT HE PRESCRIBED FLUOXETINE FOR THIS ASSISTANT DESPITE THE FACT THAT BIRTH CONTROL PILLS WERE CONTRAINDICATED BECAUSE OF HER HISTORY OF MIGRAINES, PRESCRIBED OTHER MEDICATIONS, INSERTED AN IUD AND DREW BLOOD; REQUESTED THAT THE ASSISTANT GIVE HIM SOME OF THE MEDICATION FOR HIS OWN USE; AGREES NOT TO RENEW HIS LICENSE TO PRACTICE IN THE STATE WITHOUT FIRST PETITIONING THE BOARD.

WORTH, LAWRENCE W MD, LICENSE NUMBER 0014016, OF SPOKANE, WA, WAS DISCIPLINED BY WASHINGTON ON MARCH 8, 1996.
DISCIPLINARY ACTION: PROBATION
NOTES: PROBATION UNDER SEVERAL TERMS AND CONDITIONS.

WRIGHT, VIRGIL G MD, LICENSE NUMBER 0015338, OF HAMILTON, BERMUDA, WAS DISCIPLINED BY WASHINGTON ON APRIL 15, 1994.
OFFENSE: SUBSTANDARD CARE, INCOMPETENCE, OR NEGLIGENCE
NOTES: ALLEGATIONS OF NEGLIGENCE. MAY NOT PRACTICE IN WASHINGTON UNTIL HE UNDERGOES A PSYCHOLOGICAL AND PHYSICAL EVALUATION AND APPEARS PERSONALLY BEFORE THE BOARD.

WRIGHT, WILLIAM H MD, LICENSE NUMBER 0009272, OF TACOMA, WA, WAS DISCIPLINED BY WASHINGTON ON MARCH 8, 1996.
DISCIPLINARY ACTION: SURRENDER OF LICENSE
NOTES: AGREED TO RETIRE.

YARNALL, STEPHEN MD, LICENSE NUMBER 0008510, OF EDMONDS, WA, WAS DISCIPLINED BY WASHINGTON ON MAY 27, 1994.
DISCIPLINARY ACTION: 36-MONTH PROBATION; FINE
OFFENSE: PROFESSIONAL MISCONDUCT
NOTES: ENGAGED IN SOCIAL AND/OR SEXUAL CONTACT WITH THREE PATIENTS. HIS THERAPIST SHALL SUBMIT SEMI-ANNUAL REPORTS TO THE BOARD; MUST HAVE A CHAPERONE PRESENT WHEN HE IS ALONE WITH A FEMALE PATIENT OR ANY FEMALE RELATIVE OF A PATIENT AND SHALL BE RE-EVALUATED BY A BOARD APPROVED EVALUATOR; SHALL ALLOW SEMI-ANNUAL OFFICE AND RECORDS INSPECTIONS; COMPLETE 25 HOURS OF CONTINUING MEDICAL EDUCATION IN THE AREA OF MEDICAL ETHICS AND PAY A $2000 FINE. ON

- WASHINGTON -

3/4/97 HIS REQUEST TO TERMINATE REQUIRED THERAPY GRANTED.

YEW, HASEONG E MD, LICENSE NUMBER 0026225, OF EDMONDS, WA, WAS DISCIPLINED BY WASHINGTON ON MARCH 5, 1992.
NOTES: CHARGES OF IMPAIRMENT. SUSPENSION STAYED ON CONDITION THAT DR. YEW COMPLY WITH TERMS AND CONDITIONS OF THE ORDER. ORDER MODIFIED ON 10/22/92. ON 5/26/94 BOARD GRANTED HIS REQUEST TO TERMINATE THIS ORDER AND LICENSE REINSTATED IN FULL.

YOUNG, TIMOTHY G MD, LICENSE NUMBER 0007046, OF POULSBO, WA, WAS DISCIPLINED BY WASHINGTON ON MARCH 25, 1991.
DISCIPLINARY ACTION: LICENSE REVOCATION
OFFENSE: OVERPRESCRIBING OR MISPRESCRIBING DRUGS
NOTES: IN 2/87 STARTED TREATING PATIENT WHO PRESENTED AS CHEMICALLY DEPENDENT; PROVIDED HER WITH PERCODAN, RITALIN, DEMEROL, DOLOPHINE, VALIUM, KLONOPIN AND GLUTETHIMIDE; PRESCRIPTIONS WERE NOT APPROPRIATELY DOCUMENTED; LARGE AMOUNTS OF DRUGS PRESCRIBED SUGGESTED DIVERSION OF AT LEAST SOME OF THE MEDICATIONS, WHICH RESPONDENT KNEW OR SHOULD HAVE KNOWN; KNEW PATIENT HAS BEEN IN A DRUG TREATMENT PROGRAM, AND YET BEGAN PRESCRIBING CONTROLLED SUBSTANCES TO PATIENT ON SECOND OR THIRD VISIT, AND CONTINUED PRESCRIBING VARIOUS CONTROLLED SUBSTANCES AT FREQUENT INTERVALS; PRESCRIBED MEDICATIONS WITHOUT PERFORMING ADEQUATE EVALUATION TO CONFIRM PATIENT'S SELF-REPORT OF MEDICAL INDICATIONS; PRESCRIBING LARGE AMOUNTS OF CONTROLLED SUBSTANCES OVER A LONG PERIOD OF TIME TO A KNOWN DRUG ADDICT WAS HARMFUL TO THE PATIENT; PAID RENT ON PATIENT'S APARTMENT, WAS CO-OWNER OF PATIENT'S MOTOR VEHICLE, TOOK PATIENT ON 10 DAY BOAT TRIP ON HIS BOAT, PURPORTEDLY FOR A NARCOTIC MEDICATION WITHDRAWAL PROJECT, SHARED LIVING QUARTERS WITH PATIENT, AND OCCASIONALLY SPENT NIGHT WITH PATIENT, ALTHOUGH DENIES SEXUAL CONTACT TOOK PLACE; PRESCRIBED NON-PSYCHIATRIC MEDICATIONS WITHOUT MONITORING PATIENT'S COURSE. ADVISED SECOND PATIENT, AN ADMITTED ALCOHOLIC WHO HAD COMPLETED AN ALCOHOL TREATMENT PROGRAM, THAT SHE COULD DRINK ALCOHOL IN MINIMAL AMOUNTS; PATIENT FOLLOWED ADVICE AND SOMETIMES EVEN CONSUMED EXCESSIVE AMOUNTS OF ALCOHOL; AND WHILE HE DENIES ADVISING PATIENT TO SECRETLY INTRODUCE XANAX AND DEXEDRINE INTO SPOUSE'S BEVERAGES TO FACILITATE RESPONSIVENESS, SPOUSE AND SUBSEQUENT TREATING PHYSICIAN CORROBORATED PATIENT'S TESTIMONY. MAY NOT REAPPLY FOR LICENSURE FOR ONE YEAR; MUST OBTAIN A PSYCHIATRIC AND CHEMICAL DEPENDENCY EVALUATION WITHIN 30 DAYS, APPEAR BEFORE THE BOARD IN FOUR MONTHS, AND OBTAIN 40 HOURS OF ADDITIONAL MEDICAL EDUCATION IN THE AREAS OF ADDICTION, CHEMICAL DEPENDENCY, AND CODEPENDENCY WITH ONE YEAR. ON 07/01/91 MEDICAL BOARD'S DECISION TO REVOKE HIS LICENSE FOR ONE YEAR WAS REVERSED AND REMANDED TO KITSAP COUNTY SUPERIOR COURT. THE COURT DIRECTED THE BOARD TO HOLD A HEARING ON ALLEGATIONS, UNLESS THE MATTER IS SETTLED EARLIER. HE MAY PRACTICE MEDICINE UNDER THE FOLLOWING CONDITIONS SET BY THE COURT: MAY PRESCRIBE ONLY IF BOARD DESIGNATED PHYSICIAN CO-SIGNS FORMS; PRESCRIPTION RECORDS SHALL BE IN TRIPLICATE AND OPEN TO THE BOARD; SHALL NOT ENGAGE IN SOCIAL CONTACT WITH PATIENTS; SHALL PERMIT A BOARD REPRESENTATIVE TO MAKE ANNOUNCE VISITS TO INSPECT AND REVIEW PRACTICE; SHALL NOT DIAGNOSE OR TREAT ANY FEMALE HE HAS A PERSONAL RELATIONSHIP WITH; SHALL NOT TREAT ANY PATIENT FOR DRUG DEPENDENCE OR ADDICTIONS; SHALL NOT TREAT OUTSIDE THE AREA OF PSYCHIATRY.

YOUNG, TIMOTHY G MD, LICENSE NUMBER 0007046, OF BREMERTON, KITSAP COUNTY, WA, WAS DISCIPLINED BY WASHINGTON ON MAY 26, 1992.
DISCIPLINARY ACTION: LICENSE REVOCATION
OFFENSE: SUBSTANDARD CARE, INCOMPETENCE, OR NEGLIGENCE
NOTES: MAY NOT APPLY FOR RE-LICENSURE FOR A MINIMUM OF THREE YEARS.

ZEILENGA, DONALD W MD OF LONGVIEW, WA, WAS DISCIPLINED BY WASHINGTON ON OCTOBER 29, 1990.
DISCIPLINARY ACTION: EMERGENCY SUSPENSION

ZEILENGA, DONALD W MD, LICENSE NUMBER 0015270, OF LONGVIEW, WA, WAS DISCIPLINED BY WASHINGTON ON DECEMBER 14, 1990.
DISCIPLINARY ACTION: PROBATION; FINE
OFFENSE: SEXUAL ABUSE OF OR SEXUAL MISCONDUCT WITH A PATIENT
NOTES: ENGAGED IN INAPPROPRIATE SEXUAL CONDUCT WITH ONE PATIENT FROM ABOUT 5/22/86 THROUGH 11/87. HE CONTACTED THIS PATIENT BY PHONE ON 3 OCCASIONS WHILE UNDER BOARD INVESTIGATION IN RELATION TO HIS SEXUAL RELATIONSHIP WITH HER, QUESTIONING HER INVOLVEMENT AND WARNING THAT HER IDENTITY WOULD BE EXPOSED IN NEWSPAPERS IF SHE COOPERATED WITH THE INVESTIGATION. ENGAGED IN INAPPROPRIATE SEXUAL CONDUCT WITH A SECOND PATIENT DURING THE FALL OF 1981. IN BOTH CASES HE USED HIS POSITION AS A PHYSICIAN TO TAKE ADVANTAGE OF PATIENTS' VULNERABILITY BY ENGAGING IN PERSONAL AND SEXUAL RELATIONSHIPS WITH PATIENTS. SUSPENSION STAYED; CONDITIONS OF PROBATION: SHALL NOT ENGAGE IN ANY SOCIAL OR SEXUAL CONTACT WITH PATIENTS, STAFF UNDER HIS SUPERVISION, OR FORMER PATIENTS; SHALL HAVE LICENSED PERSON IN THE ROOM WHEN TREATING OR CONSULTING WITH A FEMALE PATIENT OR FEMALE RELATIVES OF A PATIENT; SHALL PROVIDE WRITTEN NOTICE OF THESE RESTRICTIONS TO PATIENTS, STAFF, AND ANY FACILITY WHERE HE PRACTICES; SHALL NOT TREAT ANY FEMALE WITH WHOM HE HAD A PERSONAL RELATIONSHIP, NOR SHALL HE TREAT MEMBERS OF HER FAMILY; SHALL HAVE A BOARD APPROVED SUPERVISOR MONITOR PRACTICE WITH QUARTERLY REPORTS TO THE BOARD; SHALL CONTINUE IN WEEKLY THERAPY WITH QUARTERLY REPORTS TO THE BOARD; SHALL UNDERGO TWO POLYGRAPH TESTS; SHALL APPEAR BEFORE THE BOARD TWICE A YEAR; SHALL ALLOW BOARD REPRESENTATIVE TO MAKE UNANNOUNCED VISITS TO REVIEW AND INSPECT PRACTICE; $1,000 FINE; MUST INFORM BOARD IF HE LEAVES THE STATE; MAY NOT REQUEST A CHANGE IN STIPULATIONS FOR FIVE YEARS. ON 1/17/91, ORDER ON REQUEST FOR CLARIFICATION REGARDING NOTIFICATION TO PATIENTS OF THE CHARGES BROUGHT AGAINST THE PHYSICIAN BY THE BOARD WAS SIGNED. ON 1/14/93 ORDER MODIFIED TO PROVIDE FOR CHANGES IN THE FREQUENCY OF TREATMENT TO ONCE EVERY TWO WEEKS UPON WRITTEN INDICATION BY THERAPIST THAT THIS IS APPROPRIATE. ON 7/3/95 HIS REQUEST TO TERMINATE ORDER GRANTED AND LICENSE NOW UNRESTRICTED.

ZEILENGA, DONALD W MD, LICENSE NUMBER 0G20408, OF LONGVIEW, WA, WAS DISCIPLINED BY CALIFORNIA ON JANUARY 29, 1994.
DISCIPLINARY ACTION: SURRENDER OF LICENSE

- WASHINGTON -

NOTES: VOLUNTARY SURRENDER OF LICENSE WHILE CHARGES PENDING.

ZEILENGA, DONALD WILLIAM MD OF LONGVIEW, WA, WAS DISCIPLINED BY ILLINOIS ON SEPTEMBER 1, 1992.
DISCIPLINARY ACTION: PROBATION
OFFENSE: DISCIPLINARY ACTION BY ANOTHER STATE OR AGENCY
NOTES: DISCIPLINED BY WASHINGTON FOR UNPROFESSIONAL CONDUCT. INDEFINITE PROBATION.

ZUCKER, NORMAN MD, LICENSE NUMBER G036394, OF LOS ANGELES, CA, WAS DISCIPLINED BY CALIFORNIA ON FEBRUARY 4, 1991.
DISCIPLINARY ACTION: LICENSE REVOCATION
OFFENSE: DISCIPLINARY ACTION BY ANOTHER STATE OR AGENCY
NOTES: DISCIPLINED BY STATE OF WASHINGTON BOARD FOR INCOMPETENT AND UNSAFE PRACTICE IN SEVERAL CASES. DEFAULT DECISION.

ZUCKER, NORMAN MD WAS DISCIPLINED BY WASHINGTON ON JULY 18, 1991.
DISCIPLINARY ACTION: CEASE AND DESIST ORDER
OFFENSE: PRACTICING WITHOUT A VALID LICENSE
NOTES: ON 11/20/89 HIS LICENSE WAS REVOKED AND HE WAS NOT TO REAPPLY FOR 10 YEARS; A MOTION TO STAY THIS REVOCATION WAS DENIED BY THE SUPERIOR COURT. BETWEEN 12/7/89 AND 1/27/90, ACTING THROUGH HIS RECEPTIONIST, HE AUTHORIZED SEVEN REFILLS OF PRESCRIPTIONS; HE ALSO APPROVED REFILLS SUBSEQUENT TO 11/29/90; HE LISTED HIMSELF AS M.D. IN HIS NEWSLETTERS IN THE FIRST SIX MONTHS OF 1990, STATING IN ONE HE WOULD "CONTINUE TO RENDER HEALTH CARE WITHOUT A LICENSE IF NEED BE."

ZUCKER, NORMAN MD, DATE OF BIRTH FEBRUARY 14, 1947, OF 700 SOUTH 320TH ST, FEDERAL WAY, WA, WAS DISCIPLINED BY MEDICARE ON MAY 8, 1992.
DISCIPLINARY ACTION: EXCLUSION FROM THE MEDICARE AND/OR MEDICAID PROGRAMS
OFFENSE: DISCIPLINARY ACTION BY ANOTHER STATE OR AGENCY
NOTES: LICENSE REVOCATION OR SUSPENSION.

WYOMING
1996 serious action rate: 3.59/1000
1994 ranking: 31st

The Wyoming Board of Medical Examiners sent copies of 1989 disciplinary orders, as well as orders from June 1993 through December 1996, that include the physician's name, address, the date and type of action taken, and the reason for the action. The Board also sent us a list of disciplinary actions taken from February 1990 through December 1994 that include the physician's name, degree, and the date and type of action taken.

The information provided covers disciplinary actions taken against allopathic physicians (MDs) and osteopathic physicians (DOs).

Besides disciplinary actions taken by the State Medical Board, this listing also includes actions taken by the Medicare/Medicaid programs, the FDA, and the DEA against physicians located in this state. Disciplinary actions taken by other states against physicians located in Wyoming or that match a physician disciplined by Wyoming (see Appendix 2 for an explanation of the matching protocol) are also included.

> Although we have made every effort to match physicians' names correctly, some materials we received did not include complete information on middle names, license numbers, birth dates or addresses. Therefore, consumers should remember that non-disciplined physicians and physicians with different disciplinary actions may have similar names to those disciplined physicians listed in this state. Consumers should also remember that if they want the most current information on the status on a physician's license, they should contact the medical board of the state in which the physician practices or had practiced.

According to the Federation of State Medical Boards, Wyoming took 3 serious disciplinary actions against MDs in 1996. Compared to the 836 MDs licensed in the state, Wyoming had a serious disciplinary action rate of 3.59 serious actions per 1,000 MDs and a ranking of 31st on that list (see Table A, Findings, pg. 14).

The tables below summarize the data Public Citizen received from Wyoming.

Table 1. Disciplinary Actions Against MDs and DOs 1989 through 1996*

Action	Number	Percent**
Revocation	4	10.0%
Surrender	3	7.5%
Suspension	4	10.0%
Probation	1	2.5%
Practice Restriction	5	12.5%
Action Taken Against Controlled Substance License	0	0.0%
Other Actions	23	57.5%
Total Actions	**40**	**100.0%**

* This table lists only the two most serious disciplinary actions taken against a physician.
** Percentages may not total 100% due to rounding.

Table 2. Offenses for which MDs and DOs were Disciplined 1989 through 1996*

Offense	Number	Percent
Criminal Conviction	1	5.6%
Sexual Abuse of or Sexual Misconduct with a Patient	1	5.6%
Substandard Care, Incompetence or Negligence	0	0.0%
Misprescribing or Overprescribing Drugs	2	11.1%
Substance Abuse	3	16.7%
Disciplinary Action Taken Against License by Another State or Agency	1	5.6%
Other Offenses	10	55.6%
Total Records With Offense Listed	**18**	**100.0%**

* Includes only those actions for which an offense was listed and for which we had a corresponding term in our database.

If you feel that your doctor has not given you proper medical care or has mistreated you in any way--whether or not he or she is listed in this report--it is important that you let your state medical board know. Even if they do not immediately act on your complaint, it is important that the information be recorded in their files because it is possible that other people may have filed or will file complaints about the same doctor. Send a brief written description of what occurred to the addresses below or call the phone numbers listed for more information on how to file a complaint.

Address
Wyoming Board of Medicine
Carole Shotwell, JD, Executive Secretary
Colony Building, 2nd Floor
211 W. 19th Street
Cheyenne, WY 82002
(307) 778-7053

Listing of Doctors Sanctioned by Offense

Sexual Abuse of or Sexual Misconduct with a Patient
CLIMACO, JESUS L

Criminal Conviction or Plea of Guilty, Nolo Contendere, or No Contest to a Crime
TAYLOR, JACK E

Overprescribing or Misprescribing Drugs
FOWLER, ROBERT W
TESORO, AUGUSTO

Substance Abuse
OGLESBY, RICHARD J
REES, JOSEPH RICHARD
SRIDHARAN, PALUR V

Caution: This list is designed to be used only in conjunction with the rest of this book which includes additional information on each physician such as license number, date of action and more complete descriptions of the offenses.

DISCIPLINARY ACTIONS

AARON, JOHN MD WAS DISCIPLINED BY IOWA ON DECEMBER 17, 1987.
DISCIPLINARY ACTION: DENIAL OF NEW LICENSE

AARON, JOHN MD, DATE OF BIRTH MAY 11, 1954, OF 5401 SHIRE COURT, FAIR OAKS, CA, WAS DISCIPLINED BY MONTANA ON JANUARY 13, 1989.
DISCIPLINARY ACTION: DENIAL OF NEW LICENSE
OFFENSE: PROVIDING FALSE INFORMATION TO THE BOARD
NOTES: FALSIFIED APPLICATION

AARON, JOHN MD WAS DISCIPLINED BY ALASKA ON JULY 13, 1990.
DISCIPLINARY ACTION: DENIAL OF NEW LICENSE
OFFENSE: DISCIPLINARY ACTION BY ANOTHER STATE OR AGENCY
NOTES: FALSIFIED APPLICATION; DISCIPLINARY ACTION IN NEVADA.

AARON, JOHN MD WAS DISCIPLINED BY WYOMING ON JULY 5, 1991.
DISCIPLINARY ACTION: DENIAL OF NEW LICENSE

AARON, JOHN MD, LICENSE NUMBER 045839L, OF 11618 FAIR OAKS BLVD, FAIR OAKS, CA, WAS DISCIPLINED BY PENNSYLVANIA ON OCTOBER 23, 1991.
DISCIPLINARY ACTION: FINE; REPRIMAND
OFFENSE: PROVIDING FALSE INFORMATION TO THE BOARD
NOTES: ON HIS LICENSE APPLICATION FOR PENNSYLVANIA, FAILED TO PROVIDE A COMPLETE DISCLOSURE OF MEDICAL SCHOOLS HE ATTENDED; FAILED TO INDICATE HE HAD A MEDICAL LICENSE IN NEVADA AND THAT DISCIPLINARY ACTION AGAINST HIS MEDICAL LICENSE HAD BEEN TAKEN BY NEVADA; SUBMITTED A NOTARIZED COPY OF HIS STANDARD ECFMG CERTIFICATE WHICH HAD BEEN REVOKED IN 11/85; ON 7/13/90 THE ALASKA MEDICAL BOARD DENIED HIS APPLICATION FOR LICENSURE FOR NOT PROVIDING FULL DISCLOSURE OF INFORMATION ON THE APPLICATION. ISSUED UNRESTRICTED LICENSE TO PRACTICE; MUST PAY $700 CIVIL PENALTY.

BLOUNT, JAMES J MD, LICENSE NUMBER 003044A, OF 192 UINTA DRIVE, GREEN RIVER, WY, WAS DISCIPLINED BY WYOMING ON JANUARY 3, 1994.
DISCIPLINARY ACTION: LICENSE REVOCATION
OFFENSE: FAILURE TO COMPLY WITH A PROFESSIONAL RULE
NOTES: DURING 5/93 AND 6/93 BOARD RECEIVED INFORMATION THAT HE MAY HAVE APPROVED PRESCRIPTIONS FOR MEDICATIONS WHICH HAD PREVIOUSLY BEEN ACQUIRED BY A NON-PHYSICIAN EMPLOYEE WHO WAS NOT QUALIFIED BY LICENSURE OR OTHERWISE TO PRESCRIBE MEDICATIONS AND WHO MAY HAVE BEEN ACQUIRING SUCH PRESCRIPTIONS FOR KNOWN ADDICTS OR DRUG ABUSERS; HE MAY HAVE ALLOWED THIS PERSON TO PRESCRIBE FOR PERSONS WHOM HAD NOT BEEN EXAMINED BY DR. BLOUNT FOR PURPOSE OF DETERMINING WHETHER SUCH MEDICATION THERAPY WAS MEDICALLY JUSTIFIED; HE HAS FAILED OR REFUSED TO PROVIDE REQUESTED INFORMATION, APPEAR AT THE INFORMAL INTERVIEW, AND PROVIDE WRITTEN NOTICE OF INTENT TO APPEAR AT THE CASE HEARING; NUMEROUS ATTEMPTS OF THE BOARD TO CORRESPOND WITH HIM HAVE BEEN RETURNED OR UNANSWERED; HE WILL BE ASSESSED COSTS ASSOCIATED WITH PROCEEDING. DEFAULT DECISION.

BLOUNT, JAMES J MD, DATE OF BIRTH AUGUST 20, 1937, OF PO BOX 11135, SAN BERNARDINO, CA, WAS DISCIPLINED BY MEDICARE ON NOVEMBER 9, 1994.
DISCIPLINARY ACTION: EXCLUSION FROM THE MEDICARE AND/OR MEDICAID PROGRAMS
OFFENSE: DISCIPLINARY ACTION BY ANOTHER STATE OR AGENCY
NOTES: LICENSE REVOKED FOR REASONS BEARING ON PROFESSIONAL PERFORMANCE.

CLIMACO, JESUS L MD, LICENSE NUMBER 002251A, OF 1204 HILLTOP DRIVE #109, ROCK SPRINGS, WY, WAS DISCIPLINED BY WYOMING ON SEPTEMBER 4, 1992.
DISCIPLINARY ACTION: EMERGENCY SUSPENSION

CLIMACO, JESUS L MD, LICENSE NUMBER 002251A, OF 1204 HILLTOP DRIVE #109, ROCK SPRINGS, WY, WAS DISCIPLINED BY WYOMING ON DECEMBER 4, 1992.
DISCIPLINARY ACTION: SURRENDER OF LICENSE
OFFENSE: SEXUAL ABUSE OF OR SEXUAL MISCONDUCT WITH A PATIENT
NOTES: COMPLAINT RECEIVED ON 09/03/92 THAT HE HAD ENGAGED IN SEXUAL EXPLOITATION OF A MINOR PATIENT AND A CRIMINAL COMPLAINT FILED AGAINST HIM BASED ON THE SAME SET OF FACTS; SURRENDER IN LIEU OF FURTHER PROCEEDINGS BUT DOES NOT CONSTITUTE ADMISSION OF THE ALLEGATIONS.

CLIMACO, JESUS L MD, DATE OF BIRTH SEPTEMBER 20, 1937, OF 533 GOBEL STREET, ROCK SPRINGS, WY, WAS DISCIPLINED BY MEDICARE ON OCTOBER 11, 1993.
DISCIPLINARY ACTION: 60-MONTH EXCLUSION FROM THE MEDICARE AND/OR MEDICAID PROGRAMS
OFFENSE: CRIMINAL CONVICTION OR PLEA OF GUILTY, NOLO CONTENDERE, OR NO CONTEST TO A CRIME
NOTES: CONVICTED OF PATIENT ABUSE.

DEVOUS, A SCOTT MD WAS DISCIPLINED BY WYOMING ON JUNE 8, 1990.
DISCIPLINARY ACTION: LICENSE REVOCATION

DEVOUS, A SCOTT MD WAS DISCIPLINED BY WYOMING ON APRIL 22, 1991.
DISCIPLINARY ACTION: LICENSE SUSPENSION
OFFENSE: PROFESSIONAL MISCONDUCT
NOTES: UNPROFESSIONAL CONDUCT AND FAILURE TO PROPERLY SUPERVISE NONPHYSICIANS. ON 8/19/91 RESTORATION/REINSTATEMENT.

DICKERSON, ROBERT MD OF POWELL, WY, WAS DISCIPLINED BY KANSAS ON SEPTEMBER 10, 1991.
NOTES: STIPULATION AND ENFORCEMENT ORDER.

DUFFY, JOHN L DR, LICENSE NUMBER 0018508, WAS DISCIPLINED BY MINNESOTA ON JANUARY 11, 1992.
DISCIPLINARY ACTION: LICENSE SUSPENSION
NOTES: INDEFINITE SUSPENSION.

DUFFY, JOHN L MD, DATE OF BIRTH JANUARY 20, 1933, LICENSE NUMBER 0017137, OF 1111 ALDRICH, BOONE, IA, WAS DISCIPLINED BY IOWA ON OCTOBER 11, 1993.
DISCIPLINARY ACTION: PROBATION; RESTRICTION PLACED ON LICENSE
OFFENSE: DISCIPLINARY ACTION BY ANOTHER STATE OR AGENCY
NOTES: SETTLEMENT TO CHARGES OF AN ACTION TAKEN IN WISCONSIN. PRACTICE RESTRICTED TO CARE FOR MALES ONLY. INDEFINITE PROBATION.

DUFFY, JOHN L MD, LICENSE NUMBER 004408A, OF 1111 ALDRICH, BOONE, IA, WAS DISCIPLINED BY WYOMING ON JANUARY 7, 1994.
DISCIPLINARY ACTION: LICENSE REVOCATION
OFFENSE: DISCIPLINARY ACTION BY ANOTHER STATE OR AGENCY
NOTES: DISCIPLINED BY MINNESOTA AND WISCONSIN BOARDS BASED UPON IMPAIRMENT AND PSYCHIATRIC PROBLEMS. HE FAILED OR REFUSED TO PROVIDE A WRITTEN NOTICE OF INTENT TO APPEAR AT THE CASE HEARING. HE WILL BE ASSESSED COSTS OF

- WYOMING -

PROCEEDING. DEFAULT DECISION.

DUFFY, JOHN L MD, DATE OF BIRTH JANUARY 20, 1933, OF 1315 MAPLEWOOD DR NE, CEDAR RAPIDS, IA, WAS DISCIPLINED BY MEDICARE ON NOVEMBER 9, 1994.
DISCIPLINARY ACTION: EXCLUSION FROM THE MEDICARE AND/OR MEDICAID PROGRAMS
OFFENSE: DISCIPLINARY ACTION BY ANOTHER STATE OR AGENCY
NOTES: LICENSE REVOKED FOR REASONS BEARING ON PROFESSIONAL PERFORMANCE.

DUFFY, JOHN LOUIS MD, LICENSE NUMBER 0017494, OF 1111 ALDRICH AVENUE, BOONE, IA, WAS DISCIPLINED BY WISCONSIN ON SEPTEMBER 24, 1992.
DISCIPLINARY ACTION: SURRENDER OF LICENSE
OFFENSE: PHYSICAL OR MENTAL ILLNESS INHIBITING THE ABILITY TO PRACTICE WITH SKILL AND SAFETY
NOTES: LICENSE SUMMARILY SUSPENDED ON 6/25/92 BASED ON A COMPLAINT WHICH ALLEGED THAT HIS LICENSE IN MINNESOTA HAD BEEN SUSPENDED, THAT HE WAS UNABLE TO PRACTICE WITH SKILL AND SAFETY, AND THAT HE HAD COMMITTED UNPROFESSIONAL CONDUCT. HE IS PRESENTLY UNABLE TO UNDERGO THE TREATMENT RECOMMENDED BY HIS PHYSICIANS, AND AGREES THAT HE IS PRESENTLY UNABLE, BY REASON OF MEDICAL CONDITION, TO PRACTICE MEDICINE WITH SKILL AND SAFETY TO PATIENTS, AND DESIRES TO SURRENDER HIS LICENSE AND REGISTRATION UNTIL SUCH TIME AS HE CAN DEMONSTRATE RECOVERY.

DUFFY, JOHN LOUIS MD OF RR 1 BOX 289, FOREST CITY, IA, WAS DISCIPLINED BY DEA ON MAY 13, 1996.
DISCIPLINARY ACTION: SURRENDER OF CONTROLLED SUBSTANCE LICENSE
NOTES: IN LIEU OF ORDER TO SHOW CAUSE.

FANCHER, JOHN H MD WAS DISCIPLINED BY WYOMING ON APRIL 2, 1995.
DISCIPLINARY ACTION: DENIAL OF NEW LICENSE

FOWLER, ROBERT W MD, LICENSE NUMBER 001657A, OF 1133 GRANADA, CASPER, WY, WAS DISCIPLINED BY WYOMING ON JULY 20, 1992.
DISCIPLINARY ACTION: SURRENDER OF LICENSE
OFFENSE: OVERPRESCRIBING OR MISPRESCRIBING DRUGS
NOTES: BOARD INVESTIGATION OF PRESCRIBING PRACTICES.

GARRISON, RICHARD L MD, LICENSE NUMBER 004180A, WAS DISCIPLINED BY WYOMING ON JUNE 6, 1989.
DISCIPLINARY ACTION: REPRIMAND
OFFENSE: LOSS OR RESTRICTION OF HOSPITAL PRIVILEGES
NOTES: REPRIMANDED FOR ATTEMPTING TO OBTAIN A LICENSE BY MISREPRESENTATION; RESPONDED NO TO QUESTION WHETHER ADVERSE CHARGES HAD BEEN MADE AGAINST HIM; BUT CHARGES HAD BEEN MADE AT HERBERT J. THOMAS MEMORIAL HOSPITAL. ON 9/16/85 HOSPITAL SUMMARILY SUSPENDED OBSTETRICAL PRIVILEGES; AFTER REVIEW OF OBSTETRICAL CHARTS FOUND INSTANCES OF MISMANAGEMENT, FAILURE TO FOLLOW COMMON OBSTETRICAL STANDARDS AND FAILURE TO OBTAIN CONSULTATIONS IN 17 OF 28 CASES; CREDENTIALS COMMITTEE RECOMMENDED HE COULD PRACTICE WITH MONITORING RESTRICTIONS; RECOMMENDATION REJECTED; 12/6/85 ADMINISTRATOR AGREED TO DISMISS SUSPENSION PROCEEDINGS; 12/13/85 HE RESIGNED; WYOMING LICENSE GRANTED, HAD BEEN PRACTICING WITH TEMPORARY LICENSE. ALTHOUGH WYOMING WAS TECHNICALLY CORRECT IN CLAIMING THAT GARRISON HAD LOST SOME HOSPITAL PRIVILEGES, HIS SUSPENSION WAS LATER OVERTURNED BY THE HOSPITAL AND THE WEST VIRGINIA BOARD TOOK NO ACTION AGAINST HIM. THUS, HE WAS ESSENTIALLY CLEARED BY ALL WEST VIRGINIA AUTHORITIES AND FELT HE WAS RESPONDING HONESTLY TO THE QUESTION ON WYOMING'S APPLICATION.

GURON, AZAD S MD OF 26 GILLIS DRIVE #218, NEWFOUNDLAND CANADA, WAS DISCIPLINED BY WYOMING ON SEPTEMBER 28, 1992.
DISCIPLINARY ACTION: RESTRICTION PLACED ON LICENSE
NOTES: PRACTICE RESTRICTED TO ANESTHESIOLOGY ONLY AND SHALL NOT BE PERMITTED TO PRACTICE IN ANY OTHER AREA OF MEDICINE.

HOLTZ, ALBERT I MD, LICENSE NUMBER 003022A, WAS DISCIPLINED BY WYOMING ON FEBRUARY 16, 1990.
DISCIPLINARY ACTION: NONRENEWAL OF LICENSE
OFFENSE: PROFESSIONAL MISCONDUCT
NOTES: ON 2/2/87 APPEARED AT INTERVIEW BEFORE BOARD TO RESPOND TO ALLEGATIONS HE HAD ABANDONED PATIENT IN ADVANCED STAGES OF PREGNANCY; DENIED ALLEGATIONS BUT AGREED TO REQUEST IN WRITING A RESTRICTION PROHIBITING FURTHER PROVISION OF PRENATAL CARE; FAILED AND REFUSED TO DO THIS ALLOWING LICENSE TO LAPSE ON JULY 1, 1987

HOUSTON, ROBERT E MD WAS DISCIPLINED BY WYOMING ON JUNE 15, 1993.
DISCIPLINARY ACTION: MONITORING OF PHYSICIAN
NOTES: REVEALED IN HIS APPLICATION FOR LICENSURE THAT HE HAS HAD PRIOR MENTAL (BIPOLAR) DISORDER DIAGNOSIS AND TREATMENT AND IS PRESENTLY IN TREATMENT. CONDITIONS PLACED ON HIS LICENSE AS FOLLOWS: MUST CONTINUE HIS TREATMENT BY HIS PRESENT TREATING PSYCHIATRIST AND PSYCHOLOGIST FOR SUCH TIME AS THEY RECOMMEND; SHALL SUBMIT OR CAUSE TO BE SUBMITTED TO THE BOARD ON A QUARTERLY BASIS, STARTING WITH THE THIRD QUARTER OF 1993, REPORTS FROM HIS TREATING PSYCHIATRIST AND PSYCHOLOGIST AS LONG AS HIS TREATMENT CONTINUES.

HOUSTON, ROBERT E MD, LICENSE NUMBER 0010347, OF 4012 AVON, CASPER, WY, WAS DISCIPLINED BY SOUTH CAROLINA ON JULY 27, 1994.
NOTES: LICENSE SHALL BE PLACED ON INACTIVE STATUS EFFECTIVE IMMEDIATELY; PRIOR TO REACTIVATION WILL APPEAR BEFORE THE BOARD AND PRESENT DOCUMENTATION TO DEMONSTRATE HIS ABILITY AND CLINICAL COMPETENCY TO PRACTICE.

KLEPPINGER, KENT M MD WAS DISCIPLINED BY WYOMING ON SEPTEMBER 28, 1994.
DISCIPLINARY ACTION: 60-MONTH PROBATION; REQUIRED TO TAKE ADDITIONAL MEDICAL EDUCATION
NOTES: SHALL MEET WITH THE BOARD WITHIN ONE YEAR AND EACH YEAR THEREAFTER FOR FIVE YEARS TO REVIEW HIS QUALIFICATION TO CONTINUE THE PRACTICE OF MEDICINE; SHALL COMPLETE 15 HOURS OF CONTINUING MEDICAL EDUCATION REPENTANCE THE NEXT THREE YEARS DEALING WITH MEDICAL OR PROFESSIONAL ETHICS OR SEXUAL MISCONDUCT.

LANDRETH, KNUTE JR MD WAS DISCIPLINED BY WYOMING ON JUNE 20, 1990.
NOTES: LETTER OF CENSURE.

LANDRETH, KNUTE JR MD, DATE OF BIRTH AUGUST 15, 1945, LICENSE NUMBER 0022198, OF SHERIDAN, WY, WAS DISCIPLINED BY COLORADO ON APRIL 14, 1993.
DISCIPLINARY ACTION: LICENSE SUSPENSION
OFFENSE: FAILURE TO COMPLY WITH A PREVIOUS BOARD ORDER
NOTES: FAILURE TO SUBMIT TO MENTAL OR PHYSICAL EXAMINATION. LICENSE SUSPENDED UNTIL HE SUBMITS TO EXAMINATION.

- WYOMING -

LEVENSON, ALVIN J MD WAS DISCIPLINED BY WYOMING ON NOVEMBER 8, 1995.
DISCIPLINARY ACTION: DENIAL OF NEW LICENSE
NOTES: DURING HIS PERSONAL INTERVIEW WITH THE BOARD WHEN DISCUSSING HIS PRESENT MEDICAL, PERSONAL, AND PROFESSIONAL CIRCUMSTANCES, HE FREQUENTLY EXHIBITED INAPPROPRIATE ANGER, HOSTILITY, AND VERBAL COMBATIVENESS AND AN INABILITY TO THINK AND EXPRESS HIMSELF IN A RATIONAL AND COHERENT MANNER. THIS DEMONSTRATION FURTHER CORROBORATED THE CONCERNS EXPRESSED IN A REFERENCE LETTER THAT HE HAS DIFFICULTY IN INTERPERSONAL RELATIONSHIPS WHICH, COULD BE REASONABLY VIEWED AS POSING A DANGER TO THE HEALTH AND SAFETY OF THE PATIENTS AT THE WYOMING STATE HOSPITAL.

MACKAY, CALVIN R MD WAS DISCIPLINED BY WYOMING ON JUNE 8, 1990.
DISCIPLINARY ACTION: LICENSE REVOCATION

MACKAY, CALVIN R MD, DATE OF BIRTH JULY 20, 1923, OF 7677 BARRINGTON, CUCAMONGA, CA, WAS DISCIPLINED BY MEDICARE ON JUNE 26, 1991.
DISCIPLINARY ACTION: EXCLUSION FROM THE MEDICARE AND/OR MEDICAID PROGRAMS
OFFENSE: DISCIPLINARY ACTION BY ANOTHER STATE OR AGENCY
NOTES: LICENSE REVOCATION OR SUSPENSION. REINSTATED ON 5/26/93.

MACKAY, CALVIN R MD WAS DISCIPLINED BY WYOMING ON JULY 3, 1991.
DISCIPLINARY ACTION: DENIAL OF LICENSE REINSTATEMENT

MACKAY, CALVIN R MD, LICENSE NUMBER 0000549, OF 7677 BARRINGTON, CUCAMONGA, CA, WAS DISCIPLINED BY HAWAII ON MARCH 19, 1992.
DISCIPLINARY ACTION: 24-MONTH LICENSE REVOCATION
OFFENSE: PROVIDING FALSE INFORMATION TO THE BOARD
NOTES: MISREPRESENTED A NUMBER OF MALPRACTICE SUITS IN WYOMING AND CALIFORNIA. AFTER WYOMING REVOKED HIS MEDICAL LICENSE, HE FAILED TO REPORT SAID DISCIPLINARY ACTION TO THE HAWAII BOARD OF MEDICAL EXAMINERS. REVOCATION FOR TWO YEARS. ANY REAPPLICATION FOR LICENSURE MUST BE ACCOMPANIED BY ADEQUATE DOCUMENTATION THAT HE WOULD PRACTICE IN FULL ACCORDANCE WITH THE LAW.

MACKAY, CALVIN R MD, LICENSE NUMBER 0C13096, OF RANCHO CUCAMONGA, CA, WAS DISCIPLINED BY CALIFORNIA ON MARCH 13, 1993.
DISCIPLINARY ACTION: REPRIMAND

MACKAY, CALVIN REYNOLD MD, LICENSE NUMBER 003924A, OF 7677 BARRINGTON, RANCHO CUCAMONGA, CA, WAS DISCIPLINED BY WYOMING ON FEBRUARY 6, 1993.
DISCIPLINARY ACTION: LICENSE REINSTATEMENT; RESTRICTION PLACED ON LICENSE
OFFENSE: PROVIDING FALSE INFORMATION TO THE BOARD
NOTES: IN RESPONDING TO QUESTIONS IN THE APPLICATION FOR LICENSE TO PRACTICE MEDICINE, AS WELL AS THE TWO RENEWAL QUESTIONNAIRES, HE PROVIDED INCORRECT AND UNTRUE ANSWERS TO QUESTIONS RELATING TO THE NUMBER OF MALPRACTICE ACTIONS WHICH HAD BEEN FILED AGAINST HIM. LICENSE REINSTATED BUT RESTRICTED AGAINST THE PRACTICE OF GENERAL OR ORTHOPEDIC SURGERY. SHALL PROVIDE THE WYOMING STATE BOARD OF MEDICINE WITH WRITTEN NOTICE OF HIS INTENTION TO RETURN TO WYOMING 45 DAYS PRIOR TO RESUMING PRACTICE IN THE STATE AND MUST SUBMIT TO A PERSONAL INTERVIEW BEFORE THE BOARD. ALSO KNOWN AS C. REYNOLDS MACKAY.

MAHAFFEY, GENE DO WAS DISCIPLINED BY WYOMING ON NOVEMBER 13, 1991.
DISCIPLINARY ACTION: DENIAL OF NEW LICENSE

MARLER, MARY E MD, LICENSE NUMBER 003221A, WAS DISCIPLINED BY WYOMING ON JANUARY 27, 1994.
DISCIPLINARY ACTION: LICENSE SUSPENSION
OFFENSE: PROVIDING FALSE INFORMATION TO THE BOARD
NOTES: ALLEGATIONS OF INCAPACITY AND/OR INCOMPETENCE TO PRACTICE MEDICINE; MENTAL OR PHYSICAL DISABILITY RENDERING MEDICAL PRACTICE UNSAFE; ATTEMPTING TO RENEW OR OBTAIN LICENSE BY MISREPRESENTATION.

MARLER, MARY E MD, DATE OF BIRTH MARCH 7, 1945, OF 8204 STATE HIGHWAY 789, LANDER, WY, WAS DISCIPLINED BY MEDICARE ON NOVEMBER 9, 1994.
DISCIPLINARY ACTION: EXCLUSION FROM THE MEDICARE AND/OR MEDICAID PROGRAMS
OFFENSE: DISCIPLINARY ACTION BY ANOTHER STATE OR AGENCY
NOTES: LICENSE SURRENDERED FOR REASONS BEARING ON PROFESSIONAL COMPETENCE.

MARLER, MARY E MD OF LOCKPORT, IL, WAS DISCIPLINED BY ILLINOIS ON AUGUST 1, 1996.
DISCIPLINARY ACTION: LICENSE SUSPENSION
OFFENSE: DISCIPLINARY ACTION BY ANOTHER STATE OR AGENCY
NOTES: ACTION IN WYOMING. INDEFINITE SUSPENSION.

NARAMORE, LLOYD S MD WAS DISCIPLINED BY ALASKA ON DECEMBER 9, 1994.
DISCIPLINARY ACTION: DENIAL OF NEW LICENSE
OFFENSE: DISCIPLINARY ACTION BY ANOTHER STATE OR AGENCY
NOTES: ACTION IN ANOTHER STATE.

NARAMORE, LLOYD S JR DO, DATE OF BIRTH MARCH 2, 1945, LICENSE NUMBER 1006969, OF 225 N COURT AVE, COLBY, KS, WAS DISCIPLINED BY MICHIGAN ON DECEMBER 1, 1995.
DISCIPLINARY ACTION: LICENSE REVOCATION
OFFENSE: DISCIPLINARY ACTION BY ANOTHER STATE OR AGENCY
NOTES: FAILURE TO REPORT/COMPLY.

NARAMORE, LLOYD S DO, DATE OF BIRTH MARCH 2, 1945, LICENSE NUMBER 0002235, OF COLBY, KS, WAS DISCIPLINED BY KENTUCKY ON MAY 28, 1996.
DISCIPLINARY ACTION: LICENSE REVOCATION
OFFENSE: DISCIPLINARY ACTION BY ANOTHER STATE OR AGENCY
NOTES: DISCIPLINARY ACTION TAKEN BY OTHER STATE BOARDS.

NARAMORE, LLOYD STAN DO WAS DISCIPLINED BY WYOMING ON FEBRUARY 18, 1995.
DISCIPLINARY ACTION: SURRENDER OF LICENSE
NOTES: VOLUNTARY SURRENDER.

NARAMORE, LLOYD STAN DO, LICENSE NUMBER 2001095, WAS DISCIPLINED BY INDIANA ON DECEMBER 7, 1995.
DISCIPLINARY ACTION: SURRENDER OF LICENSE
OFFENSE: DISCIPLINARY ACTION BY ANOTHER STATE OR AGENCY
NOTES: SURRENDER IN LIEU OF FURTHER DISCIPLINARY PROCEEDINGS. PENDING MURDER AND ATTEMPTED MURDER CHARGES, ON 5/2/95 KANSAS REVOKED HIS LICENSE. ON 2/18/95 VOLUNTARILY RELINQUISHED LICENSE TO WISCONSIN FOR NOT ANSWERING TRUTHFULLY THAT HE WAS UNDER INVESTIGATION BY ANOTHER LICENSING BOARD. SHALL PAY COSTS OF $318.52.

NARAMORE, LLOYD STANLEY DO, DATE OF BIRTH MARCH 2, 1945, LICENSE NUMBER 0030724, WAS DISCIPLINED BY COLORADO ON

- WYOMING -

JUNE 15, 1995.
DISCIPLINARY ACTION: SURRENDER OF LICENSE

NARAMORE, LLOYD STANLEY JR DO, LICENSE NUMBER 0002518, OF LOVELL, WY, WAS DISCIPLINED BY OHIO ON JANUARY 26, 1996.
DISCIPLINARY ACTION: EMERGENCY SUSPENSION
OFFENSE: CRIMINAL CONVICTION OR PLEA OF GUILTY, NOLO CONTENDERE, OR NO CONTEST TO A CRIME
NOTES: FOUND GUILTY IN DISTRICT COURT OF CHEYENNE COUNTY, KANSAS, OF SECOND DEGREE MURDER, A FELONY. OTHER ADDRESS: TOPEKA, KANSAS.

NASH, ROBERT MD OF PO BOX 177, EVANSTON, WY, WAS DISCIPLINED BY NEW MEXICO ON MAY 20, 1994.
OFFENSE: DISCIPLINARY ACTION BY ANOTHER STATE OR AGENCY
NOTES: LICENCE PLACED UNDER UNSPECIFIED CONDITIONS.

NASH, ROBERT A MD, LICENSE NUMBER 005065A, WAS DISCIPLINED BY WYOMING ON DECEMBER 29, 1993.
DISCIPLINARY ACTION: RESTRICTION PLACED ON LICENSE; REQUIRED TO TAKE ADDITIONAL MEDICAL EDUCATION
NOTES: PERMANENTLY ENJOINED FROM PROVIDING OR PERFORMING ANY COUNSELING OR TREATMENT TO ANY FEMALE PATIENTS UNLESS AN ATTENDANT IS PHYSICALLY PRESENT IN THE EXAMINING OR COUNSELING ROOM OR AREA AT ALL TIMES; SHALL PROVIDE TO THE BOARD WITHIN 6 MONTHS WRITTEN CERTIFICATION OF ATTENDANCE AND SUCCESSFUL COMPLETION OF THE "PATIENT-THERAPIST RELATIONSHIPS: CRITICAL ISSUES OF THE 90S" SEMINAR; SHALL APPEAR BEFORE THE INFORMAL INTERVIEWERS IN 10/94 TO DISCUSS HIS MEDICAL PRACTICE; SHALL NOT SEEK MODIFICATION OR TERMINATION OF THE TERMS AND RESTRICTIONS OF THIS DECREE FOR TWO YEARS.

NASH, ROBERT A MD, LICENSE NUMBER 0005955, WAS DISCIPLINED BY ARIZONA ON MARCH 27, 1995.
DISCIPLINARY ACTION: RESTRICTION PLACED ON LICENSE
NOTES: PERMANENTLY ENJOINED FROM PROVIDING OR PERFORMING ANY COUNSELING OR TREATMENT TO ANY FEMALE PATIENT UNLESS PHYSICIAN, NURSE OR SOCIAL WORKER IS PHYSICALLY PRESENT IN THE EXAMINING OR COUNSELING ROOM; SHALL COMPLY WITH ALL TERMS OF THE WYOMING CONSENT DECREE OF 12/29/93 AND 1/23/94 ENFORCEMENT ORDER; SHALL APPEAR BEFORE THE BOARD UPON REQUEST; SHALL NOT SEEK TO MODIFY OR TERMINATE THIS ORDER FOR TWO YEARS.

NASH, ROBERT A MD, LICENSE NUMBER 0028684, OF EVANSTON, WY, WAS DISCIPLINED BY WASHINGTON ON OCTOBER 6, 1995.
DISCIPLINARY ACTION: RESTRICTION PLACED ON LICENSE
NOTES: CANNOT PROVIDE COUNSELING OR TREATMENT TO ANY FEMALE PATIENT UNLESS AN ATTENDANT IS PHYSICALLY PRESENT IN THE ROOM AT ALL TIMES.

OGLESBY, RICHARD J MD, LICENSE NUMBER 003712A, WAS DISCIPLINED BY WYOMING ON JUNE 24, 1992.
DISCIPLINARY ACTION: REQUIRED TO ENTER AN IMPAIRED PHYSICIAN PROGRAM OR DRUG OR ALCOHOL TREATMENT; MONITORING OF PHYSICIAN
OFFENSE: SUBSTANCE ABUSE
NOTES: ALLEGED THAT HE HAS ENGAGED IN REPEATED USE OF DRUGS AND/OR INTOXICANTS TO SUCH A DEGREE AS TO RENDER HIM UNABLE TO PRACTICE MEDICINE WITH REASONABLE SKILL AND SAFETY TO PATIENTS. CONDITIONS OF CONSENT ORDER ARE AS FOLLOWS: SHALL START AND CONTINUE REGULAR INVOLVEMENT IN A SUBSTANCE ABUSE AFTERCARE AND COUNSELING PROGRAM; SHALL SUBMIT TO RANDOM URINALYSIS UNDER SPECIFIED CONDITIONS WITH FAILURE CONSTITUTING GROUNDS FOR DISCIPLINE; SHALL APPEAR BEFORE THE BOARD FOR A PERSONAL INTERVIEW ON 6/93 TO DETERMINE WHETHER CONDITIONS SHOULD BE CONTINUED, MODIFIED OR TERMINATED. ON 6/15/93 NUMBER OF URINALYSIS SCREENS WERE REDUCED.

OGLESBY, RICHARD JAMES MD OF RAWLINS, WY, WAS DISCIPLINED BY UTAH ON JULY 3, 1995.
OFFENSE: DISCIPLINARY ACTION BY ANOTHER STATE OR AGENCY
NOTES: DISCIPLINARY ACTION BY WYOMING FOR AN ACCUSATION OF ALCOHOL ABUSE; HOSPITAL STAFF PRIVILEGES JEOPARDIZED ON ALLEGATIONS OF SEXUAL HARASSMENT AND PRACTICING BELOW STANDARD OF CARE. LICENSE ISSUED SUBJECT TO CERTAIN TERMS AND CONDITIONS WHICH SHALL BE IN EFFECT UNTIL JUNE 1997. ON 6/19/97 LICENSE REINSTATED WITH FULL PRIVILEGES.

RAINEY, DEBRA K MD, LICENSE NUMBER 004477A, WAS DISCIPLINED BY WYOMING ON DECEMBER 16, 1993.
DISCIPLINARY ACTION: LICENSE SUSPENSION
OFFENSE: PROVIDING FALSE INFORMATION TO THE BOARD
NOTES: ALLEGATIONS CONCERNING RENEWAL OF LICENSE BY MISREPRESENTATION, PRESCRIBING OR SUPPLYING NARCOTICS OR ADDICTING SUBSTANCES TO AN ADDICT OR ABUSER AND/OR TO SELF AND/OR FAMILY MEMBERS. INAPPROPRIATE/UNNECESSARY MEDICAL SERVICES. PHYSICAL AND/OR MENTAL DISABILITY, REPEATED USE OF DRUG OR INTOXICANTS TO A DEGREE RENDERING HER UNABLE TO SAFELY PRACTICE, NEGLIGENCE OR MALPRACTICE, UNPROFESSIONAL AND/OR DISHONORABLE CONDUCT CONTRARY TO RECOGNIZED STANDARDS OF ETHICS.

RAINEY, DEBRA K MD, DATE OF BIRTH JUNE 15, 1956, OF 30 FISH CREEK ROAD, WHEATLAND, WY, WAS DISCIPLINED BY MEDICARE ON NOVEMBER 9, 1994.
DISCIPLINARY ACTION: EXCLUSION FROM THE MEDICARE AND/OR MEDICAID PROGRAMS
OFFENSE: DISCIPLINARY ACTION BY ANOTHER STATE OR AGENCY
NOTES: LICENSE SUSPENDED FOR REASONS BEARING ON PROFESSIONAL COMPETENCE. REINSTATED ON 3/27/95.

RAINEY, DEBRA K MD, LICENSE NUMBER 0012879, WAS DISCIPLINED BY MAINE ON MARCH 14, 1995.
OFFENSE: DISCIPLINARY ACTION BY ANOTHER STATE OR AGENCY
NOTES: PIGGYBACK ON ACTION TAKEN BY WYOMING. LICENSE MODIFIED WITH CONDITIONS BY CONSENT AGREEMENT.

RAINEY, DEBRA K MD, LICENSE NUMBER 004477A, WAS DISCIPLINED BY WYOMING ON MARCH 15, 1995.
DISCIPLINARY ACTION: MONITORING OF PHYSICIAN
NOTES: REINSTATED FROM SUSPENSION WITH THE FOLLOWING CONDITIONS: SHALL ONLY ENGAGE IN THE PRACTICE OF MEDICINE WHILE UNDER THE SUPERVISION OF A BOARD LICENSED PHYSICIAN; SHALL NOTIFY THE BOARD IN WRITING OF ANY AND ALL CHANGES TO THE APPROVED PRACTICE ARRANGEMENT; SHALL PROVIDE TO THE BOARD A RELEASE SIGNED BY HER GRANTING TO THE BOARD THE AUTHORITY TO DISCUSS HER PERFORMANCE AND COMPLIANCE WITH HER SUPERVISING PHYSICIAN; SHALL CONTINUE HER TREATMENT BY HER PRESENT TREATING THERAPIST, PSYCHIATRIST, OR PSYCHOLOGIST, WITH QUARTERLY REPORTS; TREATMENT SHALL CONTINUE UNTIL FURTHER NOTICE FROM THE BOARD; SHALL SUBMIT TO THE BOARD STARTING ON 6/30/95 SEMI-ANNUAL REPORTS IN WRITING DESCRIBING HER PRACTICE, HER PROGRESS IN THERAPY, AND HER PERSONAL SITUATION; SHALL CONSENT TO AND COOPERATE WITH ANY RANDOM REVIEW OF HER OFFICE CHARTS AND RECORDS BY THE BOARD UPON REQUEST; SHALL MEET

- WYOMING -

WITH THE BOARD; MAY SEEK REMOVAL OR MODIFICATION OF THE CONDITIONS UPON HER LICENSE AFTER TWO YEARS; ON 6/2/95 ORDER MODIFIED SUCH THAT SHE MAY SEEK MODIFICATIONS IN ONE YEAR.

RAINEY, DEBRA K MD, LICENSE NUMBER 0027315, OF CHEROKEE, IA, WAS DISCIPLINED BY IOWA ON MAY 1, 1995.
DISCIPLINARY ACTION: PROBATION; MONITORING OF PHYSICIAN
OFFENSE: DISCIPLINARY ACTION BY ANOTHER STATE OR AGENCY
NOTES: ACTION TAKEN BY THE WYOMING MEDICAL LICENSING AUTHORITIES. PROBATION TERMS REQUIRE COMPLIANCE WITH THE WYOMING PROBATION, TREATMENT WITH A BOARD APPROVED PSYCHIATRIST, AND REQUIREMENT THAT HER IOWA PRACTICE BE SUPERVISED BY A BOARD APPROVED PHYSICIAN. INDEFINITE PROBATION.

REES, JOSEPH RICHARD MD OF OGDEN, UT, WAS DISCIPLINED BY UTAH ON NOVEMBER 25, 1991.
DISCIPLINARY ACTION: 60-MONTH PROBATION; 60-MONTH CONTROLLED SUBSTANCE LICENSE PLACED ON PROBATION
OFFENSE: FAILURE TO COMPLY WITH A PROFESSIONAL RULE
NOTES: SELF-ADMINISTRATION OF CONTROLLED SUBSTANCES WITHOUT AUTHORIZATION; FAILURE TO MAINTAIN REQUIRED RECORDS OF CONTROLLED SUBSTANCES PURCHASED AND ADMINISTERED. CONTROLLED SUBSTANCES LICENSE REVOCATION STAYED, AS WAS SUSPENSION ON MEDICAL LICENSE. ON 12/2/96 PROBATIONS ON LICENSES TO PRACTICE MEDICINE AND TO PRESCRIBE AND ADMINISTER CONTROLLED SUBSTANCES WERE TERMINATED AND LICENSES WERE REINSTATED WITH FULL PRIVILEGES.

REES, JOSEPH RICHARD MD OF 924 24TH STREET #4, OGDEN, UT, WAS DISCIPLINED BY WYOMING ON JUNE 23, 1993.
DISCIPLINARY ACTION: 36-MONTH MONITORING OF PHYSICIAN
OFFENSE: SUBSTANCE ABUSE
NOTES: REVEALED IN HIS APPLICATION FOR LICENSURE THAT HE HAD A PRIOR HISTORY OF ALCOHOL DEPENDENCY. LICENSE ISSUED ON FOLLOWING CONDITIONS: SHALL PARTICIPATE IN A SUBSTANCE ABUSE AFTERCARE PROGRAM; SHALL SUBMIT SEMIANNUAL REPORTS OF HIS PARTICIPATION IN COUNSELING AND MEDICATION MONITORING; IF HE INTENDS TO PRACTICE IN WYOMING HE WILL INFORM THE BOARD 30 DAYS IN ADVANCE AND SHALL SUBMIT COPIES OF URINE SCREENS RECEIVED IN COMPLIANCE WITH AGREEMENT WITH UTAH. FOLLOWING COMPLIANCE WITH TERMS AND CONDITIONS OF THIS ORDER, ON 6/16/96 CONDITIONS EXPIRED AND LICENSE WAS UNRESTRICTED AND WITHOUT CONDITIONS.

REES, JOSEPH RICHARD MD, LICENSE NUMBER 0G15150, OF OGDEN, UT, WAS DISCIPLINED BY CALIFORNIA ON SEPTEMBER 25, 1995.
DISCIPLINARY ACTION: 60-MONTH PROBATION
OFFENSE: DISCIPLINARY ACTION BY ANOTHER STATE OR AGENCY
NOTES: DISCIPLINARY ACTION IN UTAH ON 11/25/91 FOR SELF-USE OF DRUGS. ACTION IN WYOMING ON 6/23/93 FOR ALCOHOL ABUSE. ACTION BY THE U.S. AIR FORCE ON 1/29/93 FOR MEDICAL MISMANAGEMENT AND INADEQUATE DOCUMENTATION. REVOCATION, STAYED.

REES, JOSEPH RICHARD MD OF OGDEN, UT, WAS DISCIPLINED BY UTAH ON NOVEMBER 9, 1995.
DISCIPLINARY ACTION: RESTRICTION PLACED ON CONTROLLED SUBSTANCE LICENSE
OFFENSE: FAILURE TO COMPLY WITH A PREVIOUS BOARD ORDER
NOTES: PRESCRIBED HYDROCODONE OR OTHER MEDICATIONS CONTAINING THAT CONTROLLED SUBSTANCE CONTRARY TO CURRENT RESTRICTIONS ON HIS LICENSE. HE MUST SUBMIT A COMPREHENSIVE LIST TO THE DIVISION WHICH SETS FORTH THE GENERIC NAMES OF ALL CONTROLLED SUBSTANCES HE BELIEVES ARE NECESSARY TO MAINTAIN HIS SURGICAL PRACTICE. THIS LIST IS TO BE REVIEWED AND APPROVED BY THE PHYSICIANS LICENSING BOARD. HE SHALL NOT PRESCRIBE OR ADMINISTER ANY CONTROLLED SUBSTANCES NOT SPECIFICALLY IDENTIFIED ON THIS LIST. ON 1/29/96 RESTRICTIONS TO PRESCRIBE AND ADMINISTER CONTROLLED SUBSTANCES SCHEDULES II-V WERE TERMINATED. ON 12/2/96 PROBATION ON HIS LICENSE TO PRACTICE MEDICINE AND TO PRESCRIBED AND ADMINISTER CONTROLLED SUBSTANCES WAS TERMINATED AND SAID LICENSES WERE REINSTATED WITH FULL PRIVILEGES.

RODRIGUEZ, ENCARNACION MD WAS DISCIPLINED BY WYOMING ON OCTOBER 8, 1995.
DISCIPLINARY ACTION: DENIAL OF NEW LICENSE
OFFENSE: FAILURE TO COMPLY WITH A PREVIOUS BOARD ORDER
NOTES: FAILED TO TAKE THE SPEX ON OR BEFORE 10/03/95 WITHIN ONE YEAR OF THE 10/02/94 BOARD DECISION THAT WAS A REQUIREMENT OF LICENSURE.

RYDER, ROBERT CHARLES MD, LICENSE NUMBER 0A24968, OF CASPER, WY, WAS DISCIPLINED BY CALIFORNIA ON APRIL 14, 1995.
DISCIPLINARY ACTION: LICENSE REVOCATION
OFFENSE: SUBSTANDARD CARE, INCOMPETENCE, OR NEGLIGENCE
NOTES: GROSS NEGLIGENCE, INCOMPETENCE AND REPEATED NEGLIGENT ACTS IN FAILING TO PROPERLY DIAGNOSE AND TREAT SIGNS AND SYMPTOMS OF SEPSIS IN A NEWBORN HE DELIVERED AT HIS BIRTHING CENTER. ALTERED THE INFANT'S RECORDS DISHONESTLY. DEFAULT DECISION.

RYDER, ROBERT CHARLES MD OF 12425 ALLIN STREET, LOS ANGELES, CA, WAS DISCIPLINED BY DEA ON APRIL 18, 1995.
DISCIPLINARY ACTION: SURRENDER OF CONTROLLED SUBSTANCE LICENSE
OFFENSE: DISCIPLINARY ACTION BY ANOTHER STATE OR AGENCY
NOTES: STATE BOARD.

SARANGA, JEAN J MD OF 991 WINTHER WAY, SANTA BARBARA, CA, WAS DISCIPLINED BY WYOMING ON JULY 28, 1992.
DISCIPLINARY ACTION: RESTRICTION PLACED ON LICENSE
NOTES: PRACTICE RESTRICTED TO THAT OF CHILD AND ADOLESCENT PSYCHIATRY ONLY.

SINGER, JONATHAN W DO, LICENSE NUMBER 0003723, OF CHEYENNE, WY, WAS DISCIPLINED BY OHIO ON MARCH 19, 1990.
DISCIPLINARY ACTION: 12-MONTH LICENSE SUSPENSION; 60-MONTH PROBATION
OFFENSE: PROVIDING FALSE INFORMATION TO THE BOARD
NOTES: COMMISSION OF FRAUD, MISREPRESENTATION OR DECEPTION IN APPLYING FOR RENEWAL OF OHIO LICENSE, DISCIPLINARY ACTION AGAINST CLINICAL PRIVILEGES BY THE DEPARTMENT OF THE AIR FORCE; REVOCATION STAYED, INDEFINITE SUSPENSION, MINIMUM ONE YEAR, CONDITIONS FOR REINSTATEMENT. SUSPENSION AFFIRMED BY COURT OF APPEALS. ON 2/26/92 THE OHIO SUPREME COURT REFUSED JURISDICTION OF THE APPEAL OF THIS DECISION. LICENSE REINSTATED ON 1/12/94 SUBJECT TO PROBATIONARY TERMS AND CONDITIONS OF THIS ORDER.

SRIDHARAN, PALUR V MD, LICENSE NUMBER 002923A, WAS DISCIPLINED BY WYOMING ON JUNE 5, 1992.
DISCIPLINARY ACTION: MONITORING OF PHYSICIAN
OFFENSE: SUBSTANCE ABUSE
NOTES: ALLEGED THAT HE HAS ENGAGED IN REPEATED USE OF INTOXICANTS TO SUCH A DEGREE AS TO RENDER HIM UNABLE TO PRACTICE MEDICINE WITH REASONABLE

- WYOMING -

SKILL AND SAFETY TO PATIENTS. IN LIEU OF HEARING, HE AGREES TO THE FOLLOWING TERMS AND CONDITIONS: SHALL SUBMIT TO AN EXAMINATION BY A SPECIFIED PHYSICIAN AND SHALL REPORT TO THE BOARD THE RESULTS OF EXAMINATION AND TREATMENT RECOMMENDATIONS; SHALL SUBMIT TO RANDOM URINALYSIS UNDER SPECIFIED CONDITIONS WITH FAILURE CONSTITUTING GROUNDS FOR BOARD DISCIPLINE; SHALL APPEAR BEFORE THE BOARD AT ITS 6/93 MEETINGS TO DETERMINE WHETHER THE CONDITIONS SHOULD BE CONTINUED, MODIFIED OR TERMINATED. ON 7/12/93 CONSENT ORDER MODIFIED AS FOLLOWS: THE NUMBER OF RANDOM URINALYSIS SCREENS WERE REDUCED; SHOULD HE COMPLY WITH TERMS AND CONDITIONS OF THE CONSENT ORDER AND THIS AMENDMENT ALL SUCH TERMS AND CONDITIONS SHALL EXPIRE ON 6/5/97 AND AT THAT TIME, LICENSE SHALL BE FULL AND UNCONDITIONAL.

SRIDHARAN, PALUR V MD, LICENSE NUMBER 0028717, OF RAWLINS, WY, WAS DISCIPLINED BY FLORIDA ON JUNE 17, 1993.
DISCIPLINARY ACTION: LICENSE SUSPENSION; FINE
OFFENSE: DISCIPLINARY ACTION BY ANOTHER STATE OR AGENCY
NOTES: LICENSE ACTED AGAINST BY LICENSING AUTHORITY OF ANOTHER JURISDICTION. FAILED TO REPORT TO THE BOARD, IN WRITING, WITHIN 30 DAYS IF ACTION TAKEN IN ANOTHER JURISDICTION; FAILED TO NOTIFY BOARD OF NEW ADDRESS. MUST PAY $1,000 FINE; SUSPENSION UNTIL HIS WYOMING LICENSE IS COMPLETELY UNENCUMBERED AND HE APPEARS BEFORE THE BOARD AND DEMONSTRATES HIS ABILITY TO PRACTICE MEDICINE WITH REASONABLE SKILL AND SAFETY; MUST UNDERGO EVALUATION BY PHYSICIAN RECOVERY NETWORK. UPON REINSTATEMENT, LICENSE MAY BE PLACED ON PROBATION FOR A MINIMUM OF FIVE YEARS, WITH TIME FRAME AND TERMS SET AT THAT TIME. SUCH TERMS AND CONDITIONS, SHALL INCLUDE, AT A MINIMUM, COMPLIANCE WITH RECOMMENDATIONS OF THE PHYSICIANS RECOVERY NETWORK.

STEVENSON, GEORGE C MD WAS DISCIPLINED BY WYOMING ON FEBRUARY 7, 1994.
DISCIPLINARY ACTION: DENIAL OF NEW LICENSE
OFFENSE: PHYSICAL OR MENTAL ILLNESS INHIBITING THE ABILITY TO PRACTICE WITH SKILL AND SAFETY
NOTES: PHYSICAL AND MENTAL DISABILITY INCLUDING DETERIORATION DUE TO AGE, RENDERING THE PRACTICE OF MEDICINE UNSAFE. UNPROFESSIONAL AND/OR DISHONORABLE CONDUCT AND FAILURE TO PRODUCE DOCUMENTATION AND OTHER INFORMATION REQUESTED BY THE BOARD.

STOLL, TERRENCE A MD OF 110 EAST ARAPAHOE, THERMOPOLIS, WY, WAS DISCIPLINED BY DEA ON FEBRUARY 10, 1989.
DISCIPLINARY ACTION: RESTRICTION PLACED ON CONTROLLED SUBSTANCE LICENSE
OFFENSE: OVERPRESCRIBING OR MISPRESCRIBING DRUGS
NOTES: WROTE EXCESSIVE PRESCRIPTIONS FOR DILAUDID AND WROTE PRESCRIPTIONS TO KNOWN ADDICTS.

TAYLOR, JACK E MD WAS DISCIPLINED BY WYOMING ON FEBRUARY 6, 1994.
DISCIPLINARY ACTION: DENIAL OF LICENSE REINSTATEMENT
OFFENSE: CRIMINAL CONVICTION OR PLEA OF GUILTY, NOLO CONTENDERE, OR NO CONTEST TO A CRIME
NOTES: SERVED A THREE YEAR TERM IN A FEDERAL PENITENTIARY DUE TO SEVERAL INCIDENTS INVOLVING CONTROLLED SUBSTANCE PRESCRIPTIONS FOR FAMILY MEMBERS AND FRIENDS WITH WHOM HE HAD OR WAS HAVING SEXUAL RELATIONSHIPS AND HIMSELF; DOES NOT POSSESS THE CURRENT AND COMPLETE KNOWLEDGE NEEDED TO PROVIDE APPROPRIATE MEDICAL CARE AND TREATMENT AND HAS NOT PRACTICED SINCE 1986.

TESORO, AUGUSTO MD, LICENSE NUMBER 002280A, WAS DISCIPLINED BY WYOMING ON NOVEMBER 29, 1993.
DISCIPLINARY ACTION: REQUIRED TO TAKE ADDITIONAL MEDICAL EDUCATION
OFFENSE: OVERPRESCRIBING OR MISPRESCRIBING DRUGS
NOTES: WYOMING STATE BOARD OF PHARMACY DISCOVERED NUMEROUS PRESCRIPTIONS FOR WYOMING RESIDENTS WRITTEN BY HIM WHILE HE WAS LIVING IN ALABAMA; HAD NOT EXAMINED PATIENTS PRIOR TO WRITING PRESCRIPTIONS. PERMANENT INJUNCTION FROM PRESCRIBING OR DIAGNOSING BY PHONE, MAIL OR OTHER INDIRECT COMMUNICATION AND FROM PRESCRIBING OR DIAGNOSING OR TREATING WITHOUT PRIOR CONTEMPORANEOUS EXAMINATION OF THE PATIENT. MUST NOTIFY BOARD IN WRITING AT LEAST 30 DAYS PRIOR TO RETURNING TO WYOMING TO PRACTICE AND COMPLETE CONTINUING MEDICAL EDUCATION IN PROPER PRESCRIBING OF CONTROLLED SUBSTANCES WITHIN ONE YEAR.

TESORO, AUGUSTO MD OF MONTGOMERY, AL, WAS DISCIPLINED BY ILLINOIS ON JULY 1, 1995.
DISCIPLINARY ACTION: REPRIMAND
OFFENSE: DISCIPLINARY ACTION BY ANOTHER STATE OR AGENCY
NOTES: DISCIPLINED IN THE STATE OF WYOMING..

TESORO, AUGUSTO TORRIJOS MD, DATE OF BIRTH AUGUST 10, 1940, OF 1912 MORSE LEE ST, EVANSTON, WY, WAS DISCIPLINED BY IOWA ON NOVEMBER 7, 1991.
DISCIPLINARY ACTION: DENIAL OF NEW LICENSE
OFFENSE: PROVIDING FALSE INFORMATION TO THE BOARD
NOTES: ACTION BASED ON FALSE ANSWERS ON APPLICATION.

WINGATE, JAMES MD WAS DISCIPLINED BY WYOMING ON NOVEMBER 13, 1991.
DISCIPLINARY ACTION: DENIAL OF NEW LICENSE

WUCHINICH, JANE M MD, DATE OF BIRTH SEPTEMBER 30, 1945, OF P O BOX 549, LYMAN, WY, WAS DISCIPLINED BY MEDICARE ON OCTOBER 11, 1988.
DISCIPLINARY ACTION: EXCLUSION FROM THE MEDICARE AND/OR MEDICAID PROGRAMS
OFFENSE: DISCIPLINARY ACTION BY ANOTHER STATE OR AGENCY
NOTES: LICENSE REVOCATION OR SUSPENSION. NO LONGER LISTED AS EXCLUDED AS OF 9/30/92.

YOUNG, JAMES R MD, DATE OF BIRTH JANUARY 9, 1941, LICENSE NUMBER 004257A, OF P.O. BOX 549, LYMAN, WY, WAS DISCIPLINED BY WISCONSIN ON JUNE 5, 1989.
DISCIPLINARY ACTION: EMERGENCY SUSPENSION
OFFENSE: PHYSICAL OR MENTAL ILLNESS INHIBITING THE ABILITY TO PRACTICE WITH SKILL AND SAFETY
NOTES: REQUIRED TO UNDERGO PSYCHIATRIC EVALUATION

YOUNG, JAMES R MD, DATE OF BIRTH JANUARY 9, 1941, LICENSE NUMBER 004257A, OF PO BOX 549, LYMON, WY, WAS DISCIPLINED BY WYOMING ON OCTOBER 10, 1989.
DISCIPLINARY ACTION: LICENSE SUSPENSION
OFFENSE: FAILURE TO COMPLY WITH A PREVIOUS BOARD ORDER
NOTES: IN AUGUST 1989 BOARD ENTERED ORDER REINSTATING HIS PREVIOUSLY-SUSPENDED LICENSE UPON FULFILLMENT OF CONDITIONS ONE OF WHICH IS TREATMENT OF DISORDER UNDER THE CARE OF BOARD CERTIFIED PSYCHIATRIST; DETERMINED AFTER RECEIVING REPORT THAT HE WAS IN SUBSTANTIAL COMPLIANCE ON 9/29/89; NOW SAYS HE WILL NOT COMPLY WITH PORTION OF BOARD ORDER REFERENCING 'AFOREMENTIONED DISORDER'; SUSPENSION UNTIL SUCH TIME AS LICENSEE MAY

- WYOMING -

CLARIFY INTENTION TO ABIDE BY TERMS AND
CONDITIONS OF AUGUST ORDER; PETITION FOR
JUDICIAL REVIEW OF INITIAL ORDER FILED IN DISTRICT
COURT FOR LARAMIE COUNTY 9/29/89. CASE PENDING AS
OF MAY 1990

YOUNG, JAMES R MD, LICENSE NUMBER 004257A, WAS DISCIPLINED
BY WYOMING ON JULY 9, 1991.
DISCIPLINARY ACTION: RESTRICTION PLACED ON LICENSE
NOTES: LICENSE REINSTATED. MUST LIMIT PRACTICE TO
          CERTAIN AREAS OR INSTITUTIONS.

Public Citizen is an acclaimed nonprofit membership advocacy organization that has been at the forefront of consumer issues for nearly 30 years.

Since its founding by Ralph Nader in 1971, Public Citizen has fought for consumer rights in the marketplace, for safe and secure health care, for fair trade, for clean and safe energy sources and for corporate and government accountability.

Based in Washington, D.C., Public Citizen is dedicated to advancing consumer rights through lobbying, litigation, research, publications and information services.

Public Citizen accepts no corporate or government funds.

If you would like to join Public Citizen or purchase a publication, please complete the form at right and mail it with your check or money order made out to Public Citizen to:

**Public Citizen
1600 20th Street N.W.
Washington, D.C. 20009**

Combination Membership includes the bi-monthly *Public Citizen News* and the monthly *Health Letter*; **Basic Membership** includes *Public Citizen News*. See following page for information on the *Health Letter*.

Publications Orders

Qty	Item #	Title	Price	Total
	FQ8__	*Questionable Doctors*, region __	$20.00	
	F8018	*Delivering a Better Childbirth....*	$15.00	
	F8565	*Medical Records: Getting Yours*	$10.00	
	F8603	*Physicians Disciplined for.....*	$15.00	
		Public Citizen Members: Deduct 20% *		
		Publications Subtotal		
		Shipping and handling (see chart)		

Public Citizen Membership/Newsletter Subscriptions

Qty	Item	Price	Total
	Combination Membership**	$35.00	
	Basic Membership***	$20.00	
	Health Letter Subscription	$18.00	
	Worst Pills Best Pills News Subscription	$20.00	
	Membership/Subscription Subtotal		
	Publications/Shipping Subtotal		
	PUBLICATIONS/MEMBERSHIP/SUBSCRIPTIONS TOTAL		

QDB98

☐ **Gift from**   ☐ **Ordered by**

Name (please print)

Mailing address

City/State/Zip

Phone number

☐ **Gift to**   ☐ **Send to**

Name (please print)

Mailing address

City/State/Zip

Payment (all orders *must* be prepaid):

☐ Charge to credit card

☐ VISA ☐ MC ☐ AMEX   Expiration Date: _____

Credit Card Number

Signature (as it appears on card)

☐ Payment enclosed (make check or money order payable to *Public Citizen*)

Please allow 4 to 6 weeks for delivery of publications; 6 to 8 weeks for your first issue of subscriptions.

***20 percent member discount applies to publication orders only.** Discounts have already been applied to membership and newsletters.

Shipping and Handling

Publications Subtotal	S & H charge
$1.00—$5.99	add $1.00
$6.00—$11.99	add $2.50
$12.00—$24.99	add $3.50
$25.00—$99.99	add $5.00
$100.00—$150.00	add $7.50

****Combination Membership** includes membership, *Public Citizen News*, 12 issues of the *Health Letter*, and discounts on other Public Citizen publications.

*****Basic Membership** includes membership, *Public Citizen News*, and discounts on other Public Citizen publications.

These titles represent only a portion of our current publications. For a complete brochure, to order publications by phone, get information on overnight delivery orders outside the continental U.S., or for information on membership/subscriptions call (800) 289-3787 or (202) 588-1000, M-F 9am—5pm EST. Call for any bulk orders.

What you can do to protect yourself and your loved ones from dangerous pharmaceuticals.

Worst Pills Best Pills News

Every year, more and more drugs come onto the market. What can you do to stay informed? *Worst Pills Best Pills News* is Dr. Sidney Wolfe's monthly report updating lifesaving information about drugs taken by people of any age.

Find out how to prevent adverse drug reactions and which drugs should not be taken together—and which drugs should not be taken at all.

Get answers to your questions about the medical advice and care you receive—and how to ask your doctor important questions about the drugs prescribed for you.

Protect your health. Stay Informed.
Subscribe to *Worst Pills Best Pills News* Today.

$20 for one full year.*

Vital information about important health care issues.

Health Letter

This award-winning, monthly publication brings you crucial information about what's new on a wide range of health issues.

Find out the latest developments in the quality of health care, your health insurance, which doctors and hospitals are questionable, and the most recent problems with managed care.

Keep yourself informed about the recall of drugs, medical devices and consumer products.

Arm yourself with the essential information you need to make better health care decision. Subscribe to our *Health Letter* today.

Annual subscription is $18 for 12 issues.*

PUBLICATIONS

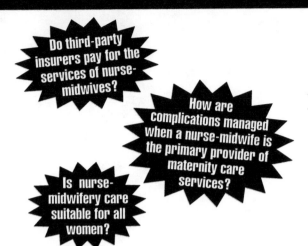

Do third-party insurers pay for the services of nurse-midwives?

How are complications managed when a nurse-midwife is the primary provider of maternity care services?

Is nurse-midwifery care suitable for all women?

Find out the answers to these and more with:

Delivering a Better Childbirth Experience
A Consumers' Guide

Get the answers to the most common questions asked about nurse-midwives with this valuable consumer guide.

This report includes descriptions of 414 nurse-midwifery practices in 47 states that attend in-hospital births and details of 41 freestanding birth center practices.

1995, Item # F8018.
$15.00.*

Medical Records: Getting Yours

If you needed your medical records to check an insurance policy or to check their accuracy, would you know you to go about getting them? Does your state allow full access?

This useful guide for consumers and professionals includes:

Definitions of medical records • Step-by-step guide to getting your medical records • Glossary of terms to help you understand your own records • State-by-state access guide

1995, Item # F8565.
$10.00.*

We name over 500 physicians disciplined for sex-related offenses in this report—

About four in ten are still practicing medicine!

Physicians Disciplined for Sex-Related Offenses

The physicians come from a variety of medical specialities and include a doctor guilty of abusing his teenage psychiatric patients, a physician who drugged a patient unconscious before sexually abusing her, and a pediatrician who repeatedly had sex with her 13-year-old son.

Find out how you can better protect yourself and your loved ones with this important publication.

1997, Item # F8603.
$15.00.*

Questionable Doctors Regional Editions

When ordering *Questionable Doctors* regional editions, please specify the number of the region you are ordering. Regional editions are $20.00 each.*

Region 1 (#FQ801): Arkansas, Louisiana, Mississippi; **Region 2 (#FQ802):** Alaska, Idaho, Montana, Oregon, Washington, Wyoming; **Region 3 (#FQ803):** Arizona, Colorado, Nevada, New Mexico, Utah; **Region 4 (#FQ804):** California, Hawaii; **Region 5 (#FQ805):** Connecticut, Maine, Massachusetts, New Hampshire, Rhode Island, Vermont; **Region 6 (#FQ806):** Delaware, New Jersey; **Region 7 (#FQ807):** District of Columbia, Maryland, Virginia; **Region 8 (#FQ808):** Florida; **Region 9 (#FQ809):** Alabama, Georgia; **Region 10 (#FQ810):** Illinois, Indiana; **Region 11 (#FQ811):** Iowa, Missouri; **Region 12 (#FQ812):** New York; **Region 13 (#FQ813):** Kentucky, North Carolina, South Carolina, Tennessee; **Region 14 (#FQ814):** Kansas, Nebraska, North Dakota, South Dakota; **Region 15 (#FQ815):** Oklahoma, Texas; **Region 16 (#FQ816):** Minnesota, Wisconsin; **Region 17 (#FQ817):** Michigan, Ohio; **Region 18 (#FQ818):** Pennsylvania, West Virginia.

---

*See order form on previous page.